Heinrich Heine: Self Portrait

AND OTHER PROSE WRITINGS

Heinrich Heine: Self Portrait

AND OTHER PROSE WRITINGS

SELECTED, EDITED, AND TRANSLATED BY
FREDERIC EWEN

THE CITADEL PRESS
SECAUCUS, N.J.

TO THE MEMORY OF TWO SOLDIERS

David McKelvy White
Lieut. Leonard E. Kurz

CONTENTS

SELF-EXILE [1831–1848]

LAZARUS [1848–1856]

The Story Teller

Religion, Art and Life

Israel

Germany

The Citizen of the World

Heinrich Heine

HUMANITY'S SOLDIER

HEINRICH HEINE

ॐ *Humanity's Soldier*

BY FREDERIC EWEN

HEINRICH HEINE WAS BORN IN DÜSSELDORF on December 13, 1797, and died in Paris, on February 17, 1856. His life-span thus embraces one of the most exciting periods of modern European history—Napoleon, the Congress of Vienna, the Revolutions of 1830 and 1848. Since he was no indifferent onlooker on world events, his works reflect and interpret them sensitively. He was a Jew, and a German. He was brought up in the Rhineland, which was the first of the German states to feel the impact of the French Revolution and the advent of Napoleon. Wherever the French armies advanced, the walls of medievalism fell. The six and thirty kings who had ruled the German states with the sleepy security of feudal sovereigns and had been supported by a privileged landed aristocracy, a complaisant clergy, and a submissive, predominantly agrarian population, were powerless to oppose the tide of new ideas brought by irresistible armies. They fell—as the medieval fortresses of their ancestors before newly discovered gun-powder. The new revolutionary laws which were promulgated broke the power of the landed aristocracy and the clergy, effected the redistribution of the land, abolished serfdom and the payment of tithes, established legal and religious equality.

By 1809, Austria and Prussia were completely humbled, and the German states were replaced by three political units: the Rhine Confederation, the Kingdom of Prussia, and the Austrian Empire. All were under the sway of Napoleon. Strange phenomenon! Not all of the victories of Prussia combined had done as much for Germany as this foreign domination! In the words of the German historian, Franz Mehring, "It introduced Germany into the orbit of the modern civilized nations."

To the Jews it appeared as if Messiah had come. They achieved the status of citizens. Ghetto walls were broken down. For the first time since the fifteenth century, Jews were permitted to enter the city of Cologne, where the French commissioner said to them: "All traces of slavery are now abolished . . . You shall account to God alone for your religious beliefs, and as to your civil status, all men stand equal before the law." What humiliations they had hitherto been exposed to! Let Ludwig Börne describe them for us as he saw them in Frankfurt before the Emancipation:

"On Sundays, they were not allowed to leave their street, lest they be beaten by drunkards. Before their twenty-fifth year they were not allowed to marry, so that their offspring might be strong and healthy. On holidays they could not take a walk outside of the gate before six o'clock in the afternoon, for fear that the excessive heat of the sun might harm them. They were prevented from using public sidewalks and were forced to betake themselves through the fields, so that their agricultural talent might be stimulated. If a Jew crossed a street and a Christian called out: '*Mach mores, Jud!*', the former had to take off his hat and through his courtesy cement more closely the love between the two religious groups."

Not to mention the special taxes, the restriction of occupations, and other such unpleasantnesses. Now and then an exceptional Jew had achieved the status of *Schutzjude*, of a "protected" or "privileged" Jew. Such had been the case of Moses Mendelssohn. But for the other Jews, their faith was, in Heine's impish words, not a religion, "but a calamity."

It is not at all likely that young Harry Heine, as he was then called, understood much of what was happening. By the time he had reached the age of understanding, many things in the Rhineland had changed

—and not for the better. But during the twenty years the French administered that region, the middle classes and peasantry achieved a degree of freedom they had never known before, and the Jews a sense of self-respect along with their title of citizens. The Rhineland was close to France. It was never to be completely free of French influences and ideas, and being industrially and economically more advanced, it remained one of the most liberal centers of Germany.

HEINE'S CHILDHOOD WAS A HAPPY ONE. His father, Samson Heine—the family name had originally been Bückeburg—was not the romantic figure his son was later to describe, but he was a kindly, soft, somewhat weak man who loved the pleasures of life much more than the drudgeries of his dry-goods business. He was not affluent when he came to Düsseldorf, but Peira van Geldern fell in love with him, and despite the opposition of her parents and the local rabbinical authorities, she married him. They settled in the Bolkerstrasse, which their first-born son was destined to make immortal.

Peira (or Betty) Heine was the strong member of the family. She may not have been as intellectual as her son pretended. But she was none the less a daughter of the Enlightenment, read Rousseau, and took a prominent—her son sometimes thought a too prominent and decisive—interest in the education of her children. Her temper was eminently practical. She despised poetry as so much romantic nonsense, and planned distinguished worldly careers for her son Harry—which she altered from time to time to suit historical necessities. They ranged all the way from a brilliant ambassadorial post to the more commonplace, though no less powerful, position of a banker, à la Rothschild. That these dreams were all doomed to frustration was not the mother's fault.

Heine was alert, eager, and bright. After a preliminary tutoring at the hands of a Frau Hindermans and a Jewish *melamed* in a private Hebrew school, he entered the local lyceum at the age of seven. The latter was housed in a Franciscan convent. The course of studies, though in the main directed and conducted by priests, was modeled on the French curriculum and was astonishingly liberal. Heine was never to forget the excellent impression made on him by Rector Schallmeyer, who combined the best qualities of the French Enlightenment with the thoroughness of a Catholic priest, and who set the young boy an example of tolerance he was later to repay by a noble literary tribute.

Harry studied Greek, French, and Hebrew, as well as many other subjects, and proved to be so promising a pupil that the Rector—and his mother, too—were convinced Harry would go very far if he ever took holy orders.

Under his very eyes, historical events succeeded one another with lightning speed. When he was nine, he witnessed Joachim Murat's entry into Düsseldorf as Napoleon's vice-regent. When he was fourteen, he saw Napoleon riding down the lime-tree avenue of the royal gardens. Not long thereafter came the frightful debacle of the Russian campaign and the retreat from Moscow. Then Leipzig, Elba, the Congress of Vienna, Waterloo, and the inglorious finale on St. Helena . . .

1815. IT SEEMED AS IF THE CLOCK OF HISTORY had been turned back half a century. "Legitimacy" was in the saddle again, and the Congress of Vienna began to undo all the work of the French Revolution and Napoleon. The victors set about to divide the spoils and they consecrated their piracy with the aura of holiness. England, Russia, Prussia and Austria were now the dominant powers. The Holy Alliance, that unholy partnership of Russia, Austria and Prussia, proclaimed the gospel of obedience and adjured all subject peoples "to abide by the solemn truths taught by the religion of God, our Saviour." It was not the first time, nor was it to be the last, that the name of the Crucified One was invoked to sanctify the enslavement of nations. Europe was now to be tranquillized—if necessary, at the point of the bayonet. In Vienna sat Prince Metternich, the brain of the Holy Alliance, the satanic physician who meant to cure Europe of her infernal malady—freedom.

The watch-dogs of reaction were set loose. The great crusade against all liberal ideas began. Wherever men rose up to free themselves—in Italy, or Portugal, or Spain,—there the Holy Alliance sent its armies to crush them.

The patriotic zeal of the Germans, who had rallied to expel the French invaders and to crush Napoleon, was to be rewarded in a peculiar manner. When he was in sore need, crushed and humiliated, Frederick William III of Prussia had promised his people a constitution and a parliament. As a matter of fact, between 1810 and 1820, he gave them five such solemn promises, only to break each of them with equal solemnity. Now that the battle was won, he ordered even the name of the "War for Freedom"—*Freiheitskrieg*—changed to "War of Liberation"—*Befreiungskrieg*. The very word Freedom was suspect. The Congress of Vienna had decreed and brought into being a "German Confederation" of thirty-eight states. Prussia, now swollen by the absorption of one half of Saxony, Pomerania, and the Rhine provinces, stood at their head. With indefatigable efficiency and thoroughness all the achievements of the revolutionary and Napoleonic eras were abrogated. The universities, which had been the centers of the patriotic revival, were placed under special surveillance. Student organizations were spied on—and subsequently dissolved. University professors were investigated, and those found "unreliable" were either dismissed or imprisoned. The Carlsbad Resolutions of 1819 reestablished a general censorship and victimized such eminent scholars as Arndt, Schleiermacher, Humboldt, and the Welckers.

As always in times of repression, the Jews suffered most. The economic crisis which followed the "Wars of Liberation" made it particularly easy to turn the discontent of the people against them. The Jews had already lost most of the economic and political rights they had achieved during the Emancipation. In many towns, they were forced to return to their ghettoes. They were expelled from Lübeck and Bremen. In Frankfurt, where they had bought civic rights with a payment of 450,000 gulden, they were told after the Restoration that the agreement was void. But no effort was made to repay the gold. Once more they were locked up in the Judengasse.

Anti-Semitic pogroms took place all over Germany. University professors and scholars provided the learned ammunition against the Jews. The great philosopher J. G. Fichte saw in them an inimical state within a state, and urged that they be packed off to the Promised Land. Hartwig Hundt (sic!) counselled that they be sold to the English as slaves. The chorus of Jew-baiting and anti-Semitism mounted in a terrifying degree. It seemed as if the Middle Ages had returned.

BARRED FROM PRACTICALLY ALL OCCUPATIONS except trading and money-lending, a number of Jews had profited from the economic upsurge brought about by the Napoleonic wars, when their business sense was greatly in demand. It was during this period that a number of prominent Jewish banking dynasties were established—notably those of the Rothschilds and the Foulds. The rigid caste system which prevailed in most of the German states had barred the aristocracy from commerce and money-lending. With the collapse of the feudal restrictions during the Napoleonic era, the way was opened to the Jews as well as to many others to participate in the economic and political life of their country. In 1807, thirty out of fifty-two banks of Berlin were in Jewish hands. It was this fact that the Jew-baiters kept constantly in mind, altogether oblivious of the fact that in Prussia alone ninety-two percent of the Jewish population consisted of petty retail traders, peddlers, and beggars.

Among the most successful of Hamburg Jews was Heine's uncle, Solomon Heine—Samson's brother. He had begun life with practically nothing, but by 1816 he was governor of a bank, and one of the wealthiest men in town. True, as a Jew, he was ineligible to become a citizen of the free city of Hamburg. But he consoled himself for that disqualification when town councillors and even better men doffed their hats to him in the street, and were royally entertained at the luxurious villas he owned.

Betty Heine, whose dreams of a diplomatic and clerical career for Harry had gone down in ruins, now planned to make him a great banker. He was dispatched to a business school, and shortly thereafter he was apprenticed to a banking firm in Frankfurt. What a future his parents foresaw for a nephew of the great Solomon Heine! Hamburg became the magnet of their hopes and prayers. When the uncle beckoned, the nephew came to him, and was installed in a banking house, and not long thereafter provided with his own establishment, "Harry Heine & Co.", dealers in British manufactured goods. The firm did not prosper, and was liquidated in 1819. It became obvious that Heine was not suited for a business career. Perhaps he would be more successful at law. Uncle Solomon was willing to help, and in the summer of that year, Heine left Hamburg for the University of Bonn.

Emotionally he was never to leave Hamburg, no matter how far he was to move from that city. It was to remain forever the "castle of affronts," which held him in its grasp. The proud, dominating uncle, whom he admired, revered, hated, and feared, and against whose rock-ribbed strength of mind and fortune he was pitting his own more sensitive poetic genius and intellect, became almost symbolic of the world the poet wanted to conquer and dominate. Heine wished to be accepted in his own right—but instead, he was merely the needy son of an unsuccessful brother—and a would-be poet, to boot. Like all solid and substantial Philistines of Hamburg, Solomon

Heine too looked down on all artists as impractical dreamers for, like Philistines all over the world, he measured success by the gold standard. Solomon Heine was never able to understand why anyone who was capable of doing other things should ever trouble to write verses.

Solomon Heine had an eighteen-year-old daughter, a proud, spoiled, good-looking girl. Heine fell in love with her, with a violence that was to remain one of the major fixed points—and fixations—of his entire life. Like her father, Amalie was contemptuous of poetry, insensible to the arts, and indifferent to her poor but brilliant cousin, of whom great things might be expected once he settled down to a respectable career. In his eyes, she was the most desirable object in the world—she possessed beauty, wealth, and station—and he was henceforth to love and hate her, as he loved and hated his uncle. Neither father nor daughter accepted him at his own worth, and rejection by them became one of the most crucial psychological factors in his mental history. The bitter injury he suffered at the hands of Amalie he kept carefully concealed from even his best friends. Very rarely did he refer to it in his conversation or letters. He communicated it only in his poetry.

GERMAN UNIVERSITY LIFE AFTER THE NAPOLEONIC WARS was not in a flourishing state. At one time centers of nationalist revival, the universities were, after 1815, special objects of governmental suspicion. Student associations, the so-called Burschenschaften, were animated by strong anti-French and anti-Semitic feelings, and their gaze was fixed on the past, on the one-time "greatness of Germany" which they dreamt of resurrecting once more. Caste distinctions were finely drawn, and duelling and student rowdyism were the fashion.

However, the university at Bonn had preserved some of its earlier distinction. It had a brilliant faculty, especially in the fields in which Heine was interested, philosophy, literature, and history. Here A. W. von Schlegel, who with his brother, Friedrich, was one of the dioscuri of the Romantic movement in Germany, held court. Young Heine was impressed by him. For August Wilhelm Schlegel was not only the prophet of the "religion of art," as the Romantics conceived it, but he was also one of its ablest interpreters. Though no very original poet or dramatist in his own right, he was one of those indispensable stimuli to other poets—a penetrating critic of younger men's efforts and a formidable translator and interpreter of foreign literature. His version of Shakespeare was then already a classic. In addition, he had brought to the Germans a very sympathetic understanding of Italian, Spanish, and Oriental literature. Heine relished the older man's enthusiasms and interests. Schlegel was drawn to the lively and budding talents of the youth. He encouraged his early poetical efforts, called his attention to Byron's works, urged him to translate them, and impressed upon him the importance of form.

But Heine was not happy at Bonn—nor, was he, for that matter, ever to be happy in any of the other universities he attended. He was a Jew, he had little interest in the mystical Pan-Germanism of the fraternities, their offensive snobbery and their loud boastfulness which only concealed their inner poverty of thought and their frustrations. In addition, he was unwell, very much in love, and far from the girl he adored.

From Bonn he went on to Göttingen, and liked it there even less. He found the intellectual life of the university completely arid, the professors mediocre, and the aristocratic students insufferable. What was most depressing was the total absence of interest in German history and letters. In a student body of 1300, there were only nine who possessed sufficient interest to attend courses on the history of the German language. "Oh, Germany," he wrote at that time, "land of oaks and stupidity!" Yet he managed to write a number of poems, and began preparing them for publication. "The sausages and university professors" who, as he was to write later, made Göttingen famous, had not dampened his poetic ambitions. But his days at the university were numbered. He became involved in a silly duel with one of his fellow students, and though the affair was settled amicably, the university authorities, acting in this instance even more stupidly than university authorities have a right to, gave him a *consilium abeundi*— in student slang, his "walking papers."

His NEXT STOP WAS BERLIN. Before transferring there, he revisited his family. With them matters had been going from bad to worse. Samson Heine's business affairs had fallen on evil days as a result of the economic crisis following the wars, and the whole family had moved closer to Hamburg and the benefactions of Solomon Heine. The disgraced student found the home atmosphere depressing. "My father is in a bad mood, my mother suffers from a migraine, my sister has a cold, and both my brothers write bad poetry," he wrote in one of his letters. The poet was in none too happy a state himself. There were matters he could not divulge to his family. For example, the shock he had experienced on learning that his cousin Amalie was betrothed to Johann Friedländer. The wound rankled and festered. "The moment I came near Hamburg," he wrote to one of his friends, "it was as if all that I had thought and felt during the intervening years had vanished." He visited the house in which his beloved lived—like Almansor, a character in a play he was composing—and stood under her window. Concerning the other cause of his sorrow he could be even less communicative. It is only too likely that during his stay at Göttingen he had contracted a venereal disease and was already beginning to suffer those tortures which, at a much later date, were to bring him to his "mattress grave."

He was glad to leave. Berlin represented a pleasant change from Hamburg. Though the city itself was unattractive and without character, it was intellectually alive. Hegel was holding forth brilliantly at the university. In the Berlin salons, presided over by witty and charming ladies, mostly Jewish, one could meet the cream of Berlin's literary and artistic life. Mendelssohn's daughter, Henriette Herz, Sarah Levy, Elise von Hohenhausen, translator of Byron, and Rahel Varnhagen von Ense each ruled an intellectual domain. Rahel was then already in her fifties, a brilliant though not good-looking woman. A Jewess by birth, she had, like so many of her contemporaries, become thoroughly assimilated, had married a Christian, and with magnificent gusto and tact had gathered around her men like Alexander von Humboldt, the greatest of contemporary naturalists, Hegel, the mighty architect of philosophical systems, Ranke, the historian, and the poets Chamisso and Fouqué. Heine, already known for his poetry, was drawn into the magic circle, and fell under the sway of the charming *salonnière*.

Until her death she was to remain his guardian angel—an intellectual mother who guided, reproved, corrected, and encouraged the erratic young genius. Perhaps she understood him better than most of the other people he came in contact with. She, in turn, was attracted by this Byronic, wayward, slight and pale poet, dressed like a dandy, blond-haired, retiring, melancholy, and ironical. He was a Jew—already racked by "Judenschmerz"—seeking to understand his relation to his own people. She was a convert to Protestantism who had lost complete touch with Jews. He found the ghetto all around him. She innocently believed—she was to learn better toward the end of her life—that she had broken down the walls of the ghetto by entering the capacious bosom of the German Protestant church. She was not alone in that belief. In the first decade of the nineteenth century no less than one tenth of the German Jewish population had been converted either to Protestantism or to Catholicism—if not converted, at least baptized.

Among the unconverted Jews of Berlin, the desire to bring their coreligionists into the orbit of German culture and thought had produced the Society for Jewish Culture and Science. Founded two years before Heine's arrival in that city, it included the most brilliant of Berlin's Jewish intellectuals—Leopold Zunz, great Jewish historian and savant, Eduard Gans, distinguished legal philosopher and ardent Hegelian, Moses Moser, Ludwig Marcus, and many others. The Society was established to carry forward the liberating work of Moses Mendelssohn, to break down the walls of the ghetto, to raise the intellectual level of the Jewish community, to effect a marriage between traditional Judaism and modern scientific and philosophical systems—to modernize the Jew and to enlighten the Christian concerning the Jew. Its magic wand was the new historical method, which it applied to a reinterpretation of Jewish history and culture. Its goal was the emancipation of a disfranchised minority. It was a movement of intellectuals, with a profound faith in the power of the word. In the hothouses of their quixotic intellectualism they already saw blooming the full flower of the emancipation.

Heine, who was in search of some sort of group identification, joined the Society in 1822, and became its secretary as well as an instructor in its school. Keen as he was, it did not take him long to see the futility of the venture. He observed its isolation from the masses of the Jewish people—he saw how narrow and abstruse were its efforts to approach them. In Berlin, the Society could boast of only fifty members; in Hamburg, of no more than twenty. Rich Jews saw no need to support it—poor Jews knew nothing about it, and even if they could have read the learned dissertations which appeared in its short-lived magazine, they would not have understood them. Having failed to uncover the social and economic roots of discrimination (although the pogroms of 1819 were still vividly before all German Jews), the Society was doomed to failure. The remarkable scholarly achievements of his fellow-members, especially those of Zunz, Heine knew how to honor. But he was under no illusions about the spurious tolerance which seemed to prevail in the literary salons.

Given the proper occasion, that too would evaporate—along with the pipe-dreams of Jewish romantics.

Heine was a very keen observer. In Berlin he saw how the salons, the theaters, and the opera—not to mention the doings at the royal court—served as safety valves for popular feelings and unrest. While Hegel was electrifying crowded university halls with his oratory, and unfolding before astonished eyes the whole panorama of the Progress of Reason—which culminated in the absolutism of the Prussian state—the Berlin police were suppressing political discussions, persecuting Polish students for their anti-Russian agitation, taking careful note of Schleiermacher's lectures, and prohibiting the performance of Goethe's *Egmont* and Schiller's *William Tell*, and the ubiquitous censor was red-pencilling even the most innocent political remarks.

Heine was no orthodox believer. His early education, his eighteenth century reading and the lectures of Hegel had long given his religious faith its *coup de grâce*. But he was not one to accept that spurious substitute and fashionable affectation which then went under the name of "reform" Judaism. At one time a movement of enlightenment and emancipation, it now was nothing but veiled effort on the part of a well-to-do section of the Jewish population—the Jewish bourgeoisie—to merge with bourgeois Christianity through gradual obliteration of differences, such as those of religious service (substitution of German for the Hebrew prayers, introduction of organ-music, etc.), customs and dress. On a brief visit to Prussian Poland, Heine had had the occasion to observe the wretched conditions of both Poles and Jews in the Posen region. But he came away with a healthy respect for both of these national groups because they appeared to have preserved an inner dignity and strength of conviction he found lacking in their German counterparts. He published an essay on Poland which aroused dismay, because he dared to portray Germans faithfully, and because he "raised the Jews to the *tiers état* of Poland." Speaking of middle-class Jews of Berlin and Hamburg he knew so well, he was forced to admit: "We no longer have the strength to wear beards, to fast, to hate, and to suffer hatred."

Yet his contact with the Society for Jewish Culture and Science had very positive consequences for Heine. It deepened and broadened his understanding of Jewish problems and awakened in him a strong desire to become more thoroughly acquainted with Jewish history. It was to be the starting point for that literary preoccupation with Jewish subjects which was soon to find expression in *The Rabbi of Bacherach*. He had discovered that the greatest portion of the Jews were poor, disinherited, and humble. He had once tended to identify the rich Hamburg Jews with all Jews, and had failed to see that the characteristics they manifested were those of the social class to which they had risen—that the new finance aristocracy was the same the world over, that the new Philistinism was international.

THE FIRST PUBLISHED BOOK of Heine's poetry, *Poems by H. Heine*, appeared in Berlin in December 1821. It was a slim volume, containing a number of poems which had already appeared in magazines. It was unquestionably the work of a young man of talent; but certain small sections of it were unmistakably the work of a new genius.

Unknowingly, he was ushering in a new era in literature. Many years later, when he came to evaluate his own place in German letters, he wrote: "With me the old school of lyrical poetry comes to an end; with me the modern German lyric begins."

He was right. For he was, at one and the same time, the last of the great Romantics, and the first of the great moderns.

Romanticism in literature is a protean thing. It varies from place to place, and from time to time. There have been hundreds of attempts to define its character, and they have all failed simply because they regarded it as a single movement and tried to fix its nature outside the context of geography and history. The Romantic Movement in literature is the expression of the bourgeois revolutions of the eighteenth and the nineteenth centuries. It is the translation into the vivid language of poetry, music, and the pictorial arts of the struggle of the modern world for the emancipation of the middle classes, and is the artistic and fervent counterpart of the Declaration of Independence and the Declaration of the Rights of Man. It speaks in the name of humanity—because the liberating class is allied with and assisted by the more inarticulate lower classes and rallies them for the overthrow of feudal and absolutist prerogatives. But the bourgeois revolutions did not break out in all European countries at the same time. England led the way. Then France followed. Germany was far behind.

The character of literary and artistic movements is determined by their historical conditions. Hence it follows that the so-called "Romantic" schools—much as they may have in common—betray marked differences. In England, where the revolutions had already taken place and the bourgeoisie had already come into power, Romanticism was saturated with the spirit of freedom. Burns chanted "A man's a man for a' that," while young Wordsworth spoke of the bliss of being alive in the day of the French Revolution. Young Coleridge, William Hazlitt, and William Blake were similarly inspired. In France, which did not deliver its crushing blows to feudal absolutism until 1789—the struggle between the old and the new schools is much sharper, and the victory of the new school comes at a later date. But the latter, likewise, is filled with the great ideals of liberty and equality though it has its own plentiful crop of dreamers, nostalgics, and restless geniuses. The new voices in France are those of Victor Hugo, Lamartine, Gautier, Vigny, and George Sand. But once the bourgeoisie has triumphed, and through its victories more clearly reveals and even enlarges the fissures and cleavages in society, once the old hopes of "liberty, equality, and fraternity" for all of mankind fall very short of fulfillment, Romanticism enters upon an era of disenchantment and disintegration.

But where was Germany in the era of revolutions? Politically and economically backward, a conglomeration of rival states, feudal or semi-feudal in character, still suffering from the devastations of the Thirty Years' War—Germany was not to experience her bourgeois revolution for years to come. Her middle classes were only beginning to emerge on the historical scene. The fervor which the French Revolution inspired in her writers and thinkers, in men like Friedrich Schiller and the youthful Goethe, was quickly extinguished. The brilliant young men and women—and there were many of them—who sought to find expression in literature and art were hemmed in on all sides by the triviality and pettiness of provincial life; the oppressive hand of the monarchs and the nobility was felt everywhere; the six and thirty ruling fathers supervised all thoughts and activities of their subjects—but left them one great realm of freedom—that of the imagination. In fantasy, in the dream world of unreality, in sickliness, and in death many of the German Romantics found a free field in which to roam. The pathetic strivings and careers of such great talents as Novalis, Hölderlin, and Kleist (German Romanticism is full of early deaths, suicides, and insanity) are clear symptoms of the intensity of frustrations which prevailed. Revolt, instead of turning against the outside world, consumed itself within—and almost always died of passiveness and inertia. Is it an accident that the dream-world of the German Romantics often became the companion of darkness and obscurantism and medieval reaction, or that so many of them eventually became the pillars of either the religious or political *status quo*—like the brothers Schlegel, for example? Is it any wonder that those who advocated action and sought to change the world around them generally found their way into prison or exile?

The German Romantics made their finest contributions to literature in the lyric, the ballad, and the short story. The magnificent ballad collections of Herder and of Arnim and Brentano brought together the greatest treasures of popular poetry. Goethe himself had written simple ballads and lyrics—and men like Eichendorff, Uhland, and Wilhelm Müller followed in his steps.

Heine's first book of poems echoed many traditional strains. Dreams, death, the grave, the supernatural, all the faded paraphernalia of a dying romanticism, are to be found in it. Side by side with these, one suddenly comes upon such miracles as "The Two Grenadiers" and "Belshazzar," and the wonderful quatrains—sharp and gem-like —in which the poet's unhappy love finds an outlet. These are anticipations of the quintessential Heine in their revelation of poetic economy, dramatic and narrative gift, simple and vivid realism, and exquisite music.

The book was well received. Heine's royalties consisted of forty copies, a number of which he dispatched to other poets. Goethe never troubled to acknowledge the receipt of the volume.

By the time his second book appeared, in April 1823, Heine's poetical genius had grown considerably. *Tragedies, and a Lyrical Intermezzo* contains, in addition to two immature poetic plays, *Almansor* and *William Ratcliff*, his first perfect group of lyrics. These reveal the consummate artist. *Lyrical Intermezzo* is a cycle of love poems—a tiny novel in verse—which begins with the ecstatic and laconic "In May, the magic month of May," continues the story through longing and heartbreak—"On wings of song" and "A pine tree towers lonely"—in which dream and waking disenchantment alternate, and concludes with the fervent vow to end this sorrow and to bury "the evil old songs."

Great composers have set these poems to music on innumerable occasions. The world has taken them to its heart, and ever since they have become the folksongs of the people. For in them Heine uttered what many people felt and could understand easily, spoke in their speech, and what he transmuted into music and images became their music and their images. Gone is the ancient panoply of a dreary romanticism. This is the new poetry of lyrical realism, shaped to a perfection that conceals its artistry—the meticulous metrical structure, the fine chiselling of each line and stanza, the rounded completeness of the word. Here and there one experiences that "ironic shock"—the sudden transition from one emotional state to another, the twist which brings one up with a start, as if the poet were mocking his own sorrows, as if he were distrustful of his own feelings . . .

HEINE WAS NOW ALMOST TWENTY-SIX. He had produced a great work of art. He should have felt very happy. Instead, he was depressed, sick in heart and body, and at a loss as to what to do next. The idea of practising law seemed more distasteful than ever. He was haunted by the thought of leaving Germany and going to Paris.

Instead, he went back to Lüneburg, near Hamburg, where his family now lived. He was received without fanfare. "My mother," Heine wrote to his friend Moser, "read my tragedies and songs, but did not like them over-much, my sister can barely stand them, my brothers do not understand them, and my father hasn't even read them." Lüneburg was excruciatingly dull, and in July he went off to Hamburg, irresistibly drawn by the "lovely cradle of his sorrows." Amalie Heine was no longer there. She was married and lived on her husband's estate in Prussia. But the old woe burned afresh. "Hamburg, my Elysium and Tartarus—all in one!" he complained. "Place that I detest and love most of all, where horrible feelings torment me, and yet where I long to stay, and where I shall certainly often return in the future . . ."

He had a special gift for creating Elysium—as well as the less fortunate one of creating Tartarus. Amalie was gone. But Amalie's younger sister, Therese, had blossomed into a beautiful girl. She was now sixteen. It cannot have been merely her remarkable resemblance to her older sister that stirred the sick poet. With that fatal gift of unhappy repetition which is the lot of the sickly, Heine proceeded to "fall in love" once more. This "homecoming" was indeed a thing of bitterness and dread! Was he again to be doomed to love unhappily? Hamburg seemed no better than Lüneburg. The same tasteless humdrum pursuit of gold, the same contempt for the poet. Heine found scant consolation in returning contempt for contempt. He was still dependent on his rich uncle, who had agreed to finance the poet's studies for another period, but had not taken the trouble to conceal his feelings and who pointed to Heine's own fellows, now already successful businessmen, while he was still a mere student.

But neither uncle, nor Hamburg, nor a glum family, nor even a new love-affair kept him from his literary work. His play, *Almansor*, which had been produced in Brunswick, was hissed off the boards in a demonstration provoked by a drunken Jew-baiter. In January 1824, he was back at Göttingen. He immersed himself in the study of Roman law, but he was patently bored, and sought solace in the reading of Jewish history, and writing a story about the Rabbi of Bacherach. He was glad of any chance to break the monotony of his existence, and in the fall he set off on a trip to the Harz mountains. On the way, he stopped at Weimar and paid his respects to Goethe. For days, he had been preparing himself for the great moment, but when he was face to face with the Olympian, he lost his voice, and stammered sheer inanities.

On June 28, 1825 he formally went over to the Protestant faith, and the following month he received his degree. In August he returned to Hamburg with a doctor's diploma, a baptismal certificate, and a very heavy heart. The diploma and the certificate gave him the right to practise law. His heavy heart reproached him for his betrayal of his finest feelings. He despised converts—and himself not least of all. There was some measure of consolation in the knowledge that he had brought back from Göttingen precious manuscripts containing two prose works, *The Journey to the Harz* and the first section of *The Rabbi of Bacherach*, as well as a considerable number of new poems.

Though he was inwardly at war with himself, revolted by his own renegacy which he was reluctant to rationalize, his genius matured and his creativeness expanded. Hamburg was no better than before. "I am now hated by both Christians and Jews," he wrote ironically. "I have become a true Christian—I now sponge on rich Jews." "I often get up at night and stand before a mirror and call myself all sorts of names." The greater the hostility of the outside world, the more intensely he felt the need to fulfill himself as an artist.

The publishing firm of Hoffmann and Campe of Hamburg was a most enterprising one. Julius Campe, its head, was a shrewd man who had made it his business to publish the works of authors who were either suspect or banned in the German states and hence in great demand. Among his writers he numbered Ludwig Börne, Gutzkow,

Dingelstedt, and Hoffmann von Fallersleben. To this list he was now to add Heine, in what was destined to be a life-long association. It was under the imprint of Hoffmann and Campe that Heine's next book—the first volume of the *Travel Pictures*—appeared in May 1826. In addition to his first major prose work, *The Journey to the Harz*, it contained two new series of poems, *The Homecoming* (*Die Heimkehr*) and the first cycle of the *North Sea Poems*. Rarely had a publisher been so well favored by fortune. The book proved immediately successful.

With *The Journey to the Harz*, Heine established himself as a great German prose writer. Prose gave him an opportunity to be discursive, to write by association—to leap from one emotion to another, to be sentimental, reflective, impudent, and satirical at the same time, to combine simplicity with complexity—in short, to ramble mentally, as he was doing physically through the Harz region, and to give free rein to his rich fancy. Heine was thoroughly German—and what German did not relish wandering on foot through the country-side, sadly jubilant, awake and dreaming at the same time, idling in body here and there, while his soul roved freely all through the world? But Heine's was no mere sentimental travel diary. His was a poet's book, thumbing its nose shamelessly at the pedants of Göttingen, at the stupidities and pretentiousness of university life, at Philistinism, at the rowdy student fraternities, and the little youngsters who were already aping the pedantries of their elders. His was a poet's book which looked to the mountains and pastures for inspiration—and to shepherds, miners, and country-folk for companionship. Prose alternates with verse—just as one mood follows another: seriousness and triviality; impudence and humility. But throughout—as in all great humor—there is the undertone of earnestness, for Heine was already, as in the lovely *Mountain Idyll*, proclaiming himself the "Knight of the Holy Ghost" who was battling for the equality and happiness of mankind.

So much for *The Journey to the Harz*. To poetry also, Heine was bringing fresh poetic materials. He had read about the ocean in Byron's works, but he had not fully appreciated its grandeur and power until he came upon the North Sea himself. "The sea is my true element," he wrote to Varnhagen von Ense. He felt like those Greek legionnaires of whom Xenophon tells, who in their retreat from Persia came once more upon the friendly Greek waters, and cried, "Thalatta, thalatta!" To give voice to his exultation, he devised a new poetic form, an unrhymed free verse, which could render the surge and thunder of the ocean and express the riot of his own heart, its laughter, doubts and fear.

In the traditional quatrains of *The Homecoming* he was more subdued, singing again of love's sorrow—was it Therese he was mourning now?—modulating and varying the theme with exquisite mastery. For his sister Charlotte he wrote the delightful reminiscence of their childhood; for his friend Count Breza the jovial poem, "I dreamed: I am the dear Lord God"; for himself and his love, "Beside the fisherman's cottage," and "You lovely fishermaiden"; for an unknown girl, "You're lovely as a flower"; and for the whole world, the most famous of all his poems, "The Loreley."

This was to be a sort of last testament to a lost love. From now on, he proposed to turn to new themes and from his restored heart he promised to write songs glorifying a new spring.

"I HEAR THAT MY *Travel Pictures* ARE THE TALK OF GERMANY," he wrote to one of his friends shortly after the appearance of the book. Spurred on by its enthusiastic reception, he set to work on a sequel, which, he predicted, would be "something remarkable, not because of its idle gossip, but because it treats of world-affairs. . . . Napoleon and the French Revolution are in it—in life size."

Heine was as good as his word. The new book of travel sketches was not a tame replica of *The Journey to the Harz*, as many hoped it would be. No, the new book was to be a challenge to the German people. Poor, dreamy-eyed Germany was to be roused from her sweet slumber, that contented, quiet slumber, which was only disturbed from time to time by the rattling of prisoners' chains, the suppressed rumblings of discontent, and the clatter of the censor's shears. For Heine was about to sing a paean of praise to an idea—a great idea—the very greatest idea, it seemed to him, the world had seen—the idea of Napoleon. He was to embody that idea in the person of a little French drummer, Le Grand. Hence the title of his book, *Ideas—Book Le Grand*. In a day of humiliation and depression, it was to glorify *"les jours de gloire!"*—the heroic glory of France. It was a bold thing to do—to try to rouse anti-French Germans from their dreams of the past into reality by evoking pictures of French heroism. We Germans, Heine says in effect, compose heroic epics; the French live them. We possess a fervent imagination, and the French very little of one. "That is perhaps the reason the good Lord has helped them out in another fashion; all they need to do is to recount faithfully what they have seen and done in the last thirty years and they have a literature of experience such as no other nation and no other age has produced."

In extolling Napoleon, Heine was merely reflecting the general feeling of hundreds of writers of the period. He himself was later to revise and moderate his judgment—always honoring the genius of the man of action, though he was to deplore the despotism of the world-conqueror—but at this time he saw in Napoleon the man who had swung himself aloft by his genius, and through the mighty concurrence of a historical epoch and his own personality had become the conqueror of kings, ruler of half the world, and destroyer of the rotting bastions of a feudal Middle Age.

But there was much more in these new travel pictures than hosannas to Napoleon. There were charming stories of Heine's childhood and youth, his first sight of the French and of Napoleon, and the remarkable French drummer. There were reflections on literature and people, thrown together helter-skelter—an intellectual and sentimental journey in the manner of Sterne, with political and philosophical reflections which would have startled that Englishman. This was a book which would not pass unnoticed. As if in anticipation of the storm he expected would break, Heine sailed for England on the eve of its publication.

His uncle Solomon had generously provided him with a draft for four hundred pounds, part of it for expenses; the whole amount, however, was intended as a letter of introduction for the nephew of the great banker. That nephew proceeded to live like a banker, and in the course of a few months ran through more than half of the money. In addition to taking advantage of the amenities of the land, Heine observed it very closely. He disliked England, he disliked London— he was repelled by the fever of activity, the mercantile spirit which seemed to prevail, the misery and poverty he saw all around him. Here were the fruits of England's commercial and industrial triumphs. He observed the rigorous caste system, which was kept alive there, though without the ostentation and brashness of the continental nobility. And he saw Wellington, the little man who had vanquished Napoleon the Great.

He returned to Hamburg in September 1827. His uncle fumed at his extravagance. His second volume of *Travel Pictures* was a *succès de scandale.* Immediately on its appearance it had been prohibited in the Rhineland, Austria, and Hanover. He saw Amalie once more. He learned that Therese was about to be engaged to a Dr. Halle. "The world is stupid and insipid and disagreeable," he wrote to Varnhagen, "and reeks of faded violets." Not even the publication of his collected poems, *The Book of Songs,* could raise his spirits.

He was eager to be gone, and when the publisher Cotta offered him the joint-editorship of the *Political Annals,* which was appearing in Munich, Heine eagerly accepted. Soon, however, he grew weary of his job, the climate of Munich did not agree with him, and the high expectations he had nurtured of obtaining court appointment or a university post had failed to materialize. He had not been too squeamish about the methods he employed. He flattered and com-promised—he, the sworn foe of the aristocracy—and in turn, he was plagued by a cabal of "enemies and intriguing priests." He was happy to report that the government thought him "not so bad." But he got nowhere. In the summer of 1828 he left for Italy. Like hundreds of other pilgrims, he set foot on Italian soil with reverence. He visited Milan, Genoa, Florence, Verona, and, of course, Marengo, and he spent considerable time in Lucca. His mind was touched and saddened by the ruins of ancient greatness—they appealed to him because he felt that he too was a ruin. But living people interested him much more, and it was about them that he was to write in his next *Travel Pictures.*

While he was in Venice he received news of his father's grave ill-ness. He hastened home. In Würzburg he learned that Samson Heine had died on December 2.

He was thirty-one years old—and still a bird of passage. The rest-less wanderer longed for rest—yet he was incapable of achieving it, at least in Germany. He seemed to be a barometer not only of his own internal pressures but of those of Europe as well. He was at work on the third volume of the *Travel Pictures* and looked back with nostalgia on his Italian trip. "Alas," he wrote to Friederike Robert, "I am sick and wretched, and as if in self-mockery, I am now writing about one of the most splendid periods of my life, of a time when, drunk with pride and happy love, I exulted on the mountain-tops of the Apennines and dreamed of wild, great deeds which would re-sound in every corner of the earth, even to the farthest isles, where the sailor would speak of me in the evening by the fireside. Now you see how tame I've become since my father's death. All I desire now is to be like a little kitten on some far-off island, to sit by a warm hearth and listen to stories of great deeds."

His tensions found release in work. Into his books of Italian and English travel sketches he was writing his political testament—his last words on German soil. They were to be his summing up. He had charted his course, and uncertain and haphazard as it might seem to other eyes, it began to show direction and goal. His understanding of his times had matured profoundly. He was now ready to appraise the European situation with self-assurance. He had stood on the battle-field of Marengo, but he no longer saw Napoleon with the eyes of his youth. Awe-inspiring as the figure might seem, it was that of a despot, the last of world conquerors. History was entering upon a new order of upheavals, and these were the consequences not of national ambitions but of new alignments—of "parties." Two vast armies were massing in Europe—cutting across national lines—those of the old order and of the new. "Every age has its own task," he wrote in the *English Fragments*. "And what is the great task of our day? It is emancipation. Not simply the emancipation of the Irish, the Greeks, the Frankfurt Jews, the West Indian blacks, and all such oppressed peoples, but the emancipation of the whole world, and especially of Europe, which has now come of age and is tearing herself loose from the apron-strings of the privileged classes, the aristocracy." Feudalism had made its valuable contributions to history, he admitted; but today it was an anachronism, "an obstacle which revolts all civilized minds." With unparalleled imaginative sweep he traced the movements of emancipation in the history of the world. Those revolutions for the equality of mankind were begun by Christ—continued during the Reformation by the Peasants' Revolts, and proudly advanced by the glorious French in the eighteenth century That revolution was still incomplete.

"Freedom," he proclaimed, "is a new religion, the religion of our age. If Christ is no longer the God of this religion, he is, at least, one of its high priests; and his name sheds comforting beams into the hearts of his young disciples. The French are the chosen people of this new religion. In their language are written its first gospels and dogmas. Paris is the New Jerusalem, and the Rhine is the Jordan which divides the land of freedom from the country of the Philistines."

As a farewell, he was also settling accounts with his personal enemies—especially the poet, Count Platen. He had never intended to insert an attack on him in the *Travel Pictures*, where it now seems altogether out of place, but the provocations were such as his self-respect could no longer ignore. Count Platen was a poet of the Munich circle—a man of talent with a penchant for verses modelled on pseudo-Oriental and pseudo-Greek themes. He inclined—to put it mildly—toward paganism, especially in his worship of beautiful boys. In the first volume of the *Travel Pictures* Heine had included some verses by Karl Immermann which poked fun at Platen's Orientalism. Platen savagely retorted in a play, *The Romantic Oedipus*, in which he set himself the task of chastising both Heine and Immermann. Platen's satirical comedy was a vulgar attack on Heine's Jewish ancestry, his baptism, and his "garlic smell." Platen had underestimated his adversary. Heine was provoked, and with all the weapons of invective at his command—and they were devastating weapons—he struck back and annihilated his foolhardy opponent, along with all his Munich coadjutors. Heine's German readers were appalled at this vehemence directed against an aristocrat and a poet of standing. It is hard today to agree with them. Platen had touched Heine where he was most sensitive. He had attacked him as a Jew.

In June 1830 he was in Heligoland on the North Sea. He was tired and listless, torn by the conflicts within him, by hope and despair, love and hatred, longing for rest and need for action. Where was he to go? Italy lay prostrate under the Austrian heel. England was a huge market-place of traders and hagglers. America was an equalitarian Tartarus, in which, however, millions of Negroes were branded with the mark of Cain. France was languishing under a restored Bourbon tyranny. As if to remove himself from the ugly present, he immersed himself in the history of the French Revolution and in the Bible.

Then suddenly came the glad tidings. In July the people of Paris had risen up against Charles X and driven him from the throne. Heine knew little of the details of the revolution, nor of the events which followed. All he heard was that the citizens of Paris had erected barricades and had fought the Bourbon monarchy and overthrown it. The revolution he had longed for had at last come! Even in far-off Heligoland it seemed as if a new day had dawned. A local fisherman said, "The poor have won." And the poet exclaimed, "Lafayette, the tricolor, the Marseillaise!" Gone was the torpor which had numbed his faculties. Gone was all despair. He knew what to do. "I am the son of the Revolution and I take up the charmed weapons upon which my mother has breathed her magic blessing." He thought that all people in Europe would understand the meaning of the July days. Perhaps the Germans, too, would turn their oak-trees into barricades for the liberation of the human spirit! Perhaps he himself was no Don Quixote, dreaming idle dreams. "The Gallic cock has crowed for a second time," he cried to his countrymen. It seemed to him as if Germans were beginning to rouse themselves from their metaphysical dreams. Perhaps their philosophical cycle was now completed, and they were ready to embark on their political revolution?

Anxiously he waited. Europe was on fire. In the winter of 1830 the Poles rose up against Czar Nicholas I. Belgium proclaimed her independence of Holland. There were rumblings in Aix, in Cologne. Charles of Brunswick was driven from the throne. In many localities the uprising took curious and disturbing forms. Thus, for example, in Hamburg, the rage of the populace was directed against the Jews.

Paralyzed for a moment, the forces of reaction began bestirring themselves very soon. The Polish uprising was crushed in 1831. The sporadic upsurges in the German states were quickly quelled.

The liberals were again in retreat. Heine could now read the writing on the wall, but he did what he was to do so often in times of great crisis—he wrote a new call to arms. This took the form of a preface to a pamphlet, "Kahldorf on the Nobility." He knew what he was about and what risks he was running. "I am full of evil omens," he confessed to Varnhagen. His days in his homeland were numbered. In April 1831 he left Germany. On the first of May he crossed the Rhine.

"HE WAS A FINE MAN OF THIRTY-FIVE OR THIRTY-SIX YEARS, with every appearance of robust health; one would have said a German Apollo, to see his high white forehead, pure as a marble table, which was shadowed with great masses of brown hair. His blue eyes sparkled with light and inspiration; his round, full cheeks, graceful in contour, were not of the tottering romantic lividness so fashionable at that date . . . A slight pagan *embonpoint*, which was expiated later on by a truly Christian emaciation, rounded the lines of his form. He wore neither beard, nor moustache, nor whiskers; he did not smoke nor drink beer, and, like Goethe, even had a horror of these things."

That was the way Heine appeared to the poet Théophile Gautier shortly after his arrival in Paris.

The "German Apollo" loved Paris. For Paris was not a city—it was a civilization. It was the nerve center of Europe—the great electric power-house which sent out political and intellectual currents throughout the world. Heine wandered through the streets as if under constant enchantment. "Paris, the singing, the springing," seemed like a new life after the slow death of Hamburg and Lüneburg, and the dry, sand-like pedantry and hair-splitting of Berlin. In its streets had been fought the great political and cultural battles of the world. Every nook and alley was replete with history. But Paris was not a monument to a dead past—Paris was a living, pulsing city, and Parisians were alive, gay, witty,—and so very polite! Paris was one great salon where one could meet the great writers and thinkers of France— Victor Hugo, Alfred de Vigny, Gautier, George Sand, Honoré de Balzac, Alfred de Musset, Daumier, Berlioz and Meyerbeer.

Paris was the political workshop of Europe. In its smithies had been wrought the great liberating words and deeds of revolution. Only recently the French had driven out a Bourbon who had sought to throttle them with a regime of resurrected émigrés and priests, and had tried to stifle all opposition by suppression of the press and a severe modification of the electoral laws. Charles X went, and Louis Philippe of the house of Orléans came in. In place of nobility and clergy, the financial bourgeoisie was now in power, and its symbol, Louis Philippe, the "citizen king", paraded the streets with his citizen hat and umbrella, and shook hands with all other citizens of Paris. The great new day of glory, it was true, had not yet been ushered in; as a matter of fact, the workers of France who had fought and shed their blood in the revolution were not yet allowed to vote, and out of a total French population of thirty millions, only about 200,000 could go to the polls.

The great heart of the French Revolution which was named Paris found a place for many exiles from less fortunate lands, especially Germany, and Heine was welcomed with open arms. Like Ulysses, he became a "part of all that he met." He was caught up in the whirl of Parisian life. He was not merely a German man of letters. He was in Paris precisely because he was also a political thinker. And what better place than Paris to explore all the various manifestations of political thought?

While he was still in Hamburg, meditating departure, he had come across the program of the Saint-Simonians and had been greatly attracted by it. In fact, he had already then fancied himself a prospective member of the cult. Here in Paris, in the Salle Taitbout, he had occasion to participate in the fiery discussions of that group. The master and founder of the new religion, Claude Henri de Rouvroy, Count de Saint-Simon, had been dead for six years. A legendary figure, such as not even the most imaginative novelist could have invented, Saint-Simon had been in turn heir to a princely fortune, pauper, salesman, merchant, adventurer, engineer, scholar, soldier in the American Revolutionary armies—and builder of new worlds. Like his famous contemporaries, Charles Fourier and the English manufacturer, Robert Owen, he was deeply moved by the lot of "the most numerous and poorest class in society"—"*la classe la plus nombreuse et la plus pauvre*"—whose hopes for a better world appeared to have miscarried when the triumphant property-owning middle classes shattered a decaying feudal regime. Those lower classes of society were too weak and too poorly organized to challenge the dominance of the new masters, for capitalist production was still very immature. Undaunted by neglect and poverty, Saint-Simon set about providing correctives for the injustices he saw about him, and produced plan after plan for the amelioration of society. He wished to found what he called a "physico-political science." He identified the moral and physical well-being of man. He combined the passionate faith of the eighteenth century encyclopedists with what was for his time a penetrating understanding of the structure of society. In his eyes, the French Revolution was not merely a struggle that involved the nobility and the bourgeoisie, but the propertyless lower classes as well. The victory of the propertied classes had produced a society in which men were now divided into workers and idlers. "All men should work," Saint-Simon proclaimed. Among the workers he included not only artisans and proletarians, but manufacturers, merchants, and bankers. Science and industry could provide the solution for the distresses of mankind, and leadership should be placed in the hands of scholars, manufacturers, and bankers. Politics was merely the science of production. The "golden age" of mankind was not to be sought in the past but in the future. That future "belongs to us." Religion had the function of helping man to achieve happiness through work and well-being here on earth. The watchwords of the new century were to be the trinity of Love, Wisdom, and Power, or Religion, Science, and Industry.

With that in view, Saint-Simon addressed fervent words to the ruling princes of Europe. "Princes: Harken to the voice of God who speaks to you through me. Be good Christians once more. Cease thinking that your hired armies, your nobles, your heretical clergy and your corrupt judges are your mainstays. United in the name of Christianity, learn to fulfill all the duties which she imposes on the powerful. Recall that she commands you to use all your energies to increase as quickly as possible the social well-being of the poor."

The notion that the princes and rulers of the world—including those newly anointed ones, the manufacturers and bankers—would unite to achieve the well-being of mankind and once and for all remove poverty from the face of the earth was touching. That somehow the benefactions of the dominant powers would rain down on those below was the naive faith of many of the Utopian socialists. Saint-Simon did not live long enough to see the class which was most numerous and most dispossessed of worldly goods grow to sufficient strength to wrest some measure of happiness and well-being through its own efforts.

Inspired by the doctrines of the new religion which proclaimed the unity of flesh and spirit, challenged the despotism of the aristocracy and the clergy, and wished to assure the benefits of work to all mankind, Heine attended the meetings of the Saint-Simonians frequently, and no doubt was struck by the contrast between the ideals debated there—already the mantle of the first prophet was being fought over by his succession—and the world outside. While the Saint-Simonians argued and the Fourierists fulminated—the princes of the stock-exchange who had brought Louis Philippe into power speculated and enriched themselves, at the expense of a poorly industrialized country, consisting in the main of small manufacturers, artisans, shop-keepers and farmers. Louis Philippe steered the ship of state carefully, trimming the sails whenever necessary. *"Jamais une position nette,"* Metternich said of him. He was an opportunist, the king of the middle course, of the so-called *"juste-milieu."* (Heine said that he was also the king of the "juste-millionaires.") And his two leading statesmen, Adolphe Thiers and François Guizot, two sides of the same coin—one a "constitutional monarchist," the other a "legitimist"—were both minions of the *status quo*, and kept a watchful eye on the people below. Louis Philippe was certainly worth the eighteen million francs he received each year, not only to the French financiers, but to all the ruling houses of Europe.

These matters did not escape Heine's observant eyes. He rendered a vivid account of them to his German readers in Cotta's *Allgemeine Zeitung*. Prudence and a rigid censorship made for some discreet omissions or toning down—for Metternich's agents were active in Paris and not without influence there. By turns Heine was attracted and repelled by Louis Philippe. He saw in the king a tight-rope walker. He watched with keen interest the manipulations on the stock-exchanges, he noted the peculiar responses of their quotations to internal and external affairs, and began to understand where the true masters of France and her King resided. He sensed the rumblings that went on underneath the surface of the *juste-milieu*, which seemed so calm, so tranquil. He attended the meetings not only of the Saint-Simonians, but also of other socialist societies, and he listened very carefully. He met many of their most prominent leaders, men like Blanqui—whose oratory and sincerity impressed him,—Pierre Leroux, Louis Blanc. He was on intimate footing with Prosper Enfantin and Michel Chevalier, leading Saint-Simonians. He described the ominous little upsurges—occasioned now by the cholera, now by the funeral of some important political figure—which were symptomatic of the unrest of the Paris population.

He attended concerts, art exhibitions, and the theatre. He strolled on the boulevards, and observed men and women, especially the latter. He was a welcome visitor in the literary salons, particularly that of the Princess Belgioioso—that attractive and fabulous blue-stocking in whose life the sublime and the ridiculous merged fantastically. A generous patroness, herself an exile from Italy, she interceded with Thiers, and obtained for Heine a government stipend of 4800 francs a year, a fact which came to light only in 1848, not without unpleasant consequences for the poet.

HE NEVER LOST TOUCH WITH GERMANY. He could not have, even if he had wanted to, for there were at that time almost 80,000 Germans in Paris, a great number of them political exiles. Among these were ardent republicans. The most consistently militant of these was Ludwig Börne, who was considerably older than Heine, and like him, a converted Jew and a political rebel. The Germans in exile naturally looked to Heine for support, but he, who rarely failed to compromise himself in his writings, was loath to attach himself to parties. Though he was in sympathy with the Saint-Simonians, he never became one of them. As for the republicans, Heine thought them too radical, prosaic, and impractical. They, on their side, naturally resented what appeared to them to be equivocation. Heine was forever opening himself to this sort of attack. His insights were frequently profounder than his actions—and his actions sometimes lagged behind his thoughts. He was a declared enemy of the *status quo,* in disfavor with the political authorities of the German states, a Saint-Simonian at heart; yet he preferred to adhere to a romantic conception of monarchism. Inconsistencies such as this pervaded his whole life. They gave occasion for gossip, some of it very unsavory, and most of it unjustified. How unjustified, Heine was to prove when the occasion demanded.

The censorship had been harrying him and his publisher, Campe, for a long time. Not even the formidable Cotta was immune from it. In response to a courteous but firm warning from Gentz, a henchman of Metternich's, Heine's journalistic contributions to the *Allgemeine Zeitung* were terminated.

On May 27, 1832, 25,000 men and women gathered at Hambach to celebrate the anniversary of the winning of the Bavarian constitution. The speeches were fiery, though the demands raised were moderate: "one Germany," political reforms, support of Polish independence. Side by side with the black, red and gold, fluttered the banners of France and Poland. Heine and Börne had been invited to participate, but only the latter was present. Fearful of another July revolution, the Federal Diet immediately struck back. On June 18, it announced that in every case its authority superseded that of the individual state members. It imposed an even more rigid censorship, arrested Dr. Wirth and Siebenpfeiffer, who had participated in the Hambach festival, and suppressed their journals.

Though he had openly expressed his opposition to the German republicans, Heine did not leave them in the lurch. His own correspondence had been mutilated by the censorship, and he decided now on publishing an ungarbled version of his preface to the volume of *French Affairs,* in both French and German. It was his "*J'accuse,*" launched against Austria, and even more forcefully against Prussia. His pen dipped in the most corrosive acid of brilliant invective and irony, he laid bare the hypocrisy of Prussia and her King, Frederick William III, who had so often perjured himself before the very subjects who had rescued him from Napoleon and whom he was now generously requiting with the heavy Prussian bludgeon. He excoriated the equanimity of the Germans, who like the "great fool" were only too willing to cringe and cower. "I took no part in their follies," he said, speaking of the republicans, "but I shall always share their misfortunes." He made an irrevocable vow: "I will not go back to my native land so long as a single one of these noble fugitives, who could not listen to reason because enthusiasm carried them away, languishes miserably in a foreign land." Beware, he warns the monarch, beware of the great "German fool." Some day he may rise and crush you. . . .

That was his answer to the autocrats, Junkers, and ignoble kings. That was his answer to critics who had called him a time-server. He urged Campe to publish the preface in its entirety, without mutilations: "Just because the cause of liberalism is in such a bad way these days, everything possible must be done for its sake. I know that the doors of Germany will be closed to me so long as I live, should my preface appear. But it *must* appear."

That was to be the pattern of his life henceforth. Whenever he thought he could "quietly slip back into the realm of poetry," something horrible would occur to rouse him and lash him right back into the arena of conflict and controversy. Now it was the sight of German emigrants on their way to Algeria—good, solid Suabian peasants who had never harmed anyone and yet had been driven from their land by the unsupportable oppressions at home—now it was another story of persecution in Germany.

A group of writers, called "Young Germany," whose program, if program it may be called, professed a mild kind of Saint-Simonianism and an aesthetic which asked for a closer tie between literature and the problems of the day, soon fell foul of the authorities. The leaders of the school were Ludolf Wienbarg, Theodore Mundt, Heinrich Laube, and Karl Gutzkow. Their radicalism was of a very vague kind, more emotional than political. A spiteful enemy of theirs, the critic Wolfgang Menzel—once a friend of theirs and Heine's—launched a vicious attack on them, charging them with being pro-French, pro-Jewish, immoral and indecent. On December 10, 1833, the Federal Diet promulgated its now infamous decree "against the wicked, anti-Christian, blasphemous literature that wantonly treads all morality, modesty, and decency under foot." It explicitly banned the works of the "Young Germans", both past and future, and forbade their publication and their circulation. Heine was included in the proscription. Börne, whose name had been omitted through an oversight, was later added to the list. The authors who were then in Germany were prosecuted; some fled, some were imprisoned, some recanted.

From Paris, Heine wrote a defense of his literary colleagues. In *The Informer*, which he aimed at Menzel, he defended the patriotism and morality of "Young Germany," and contrasted these unfavorably with Menzel's. He himself had been called anti-German and Francophile. The cry had been raised again when he published two of his most important critical prose works, *The Romantic School* and *Religion and Philosophy in Germany*. The edict of the Diet was unquestionably intended to cut him off completely from his German readers. In his own equivocal fashion—perhaps with tongue in cheek —he addressed a humble plea to the Federal Diet, protesting his patriotism and morality.

The Romantic School AND *Religion and Philosophy in Germany* appeared originally in French and were designed to acquaint Frenchmen with the intellectual life of Germany. But the books had an even higher purpose—to recapitulate the achievements of German literature and philosophy and to formulate a program for the future.

Though written in a sprightly vein, they are serious works nonetheless. Read today, in the light of recent historical events, they strike one as amazingly keen appraisals of men and ideas. For Heine was studying these not with the abstracted air of some *Privatdozent*, who writes of literature and philosophy as if they existed in worlds apart from our own, but as manifestations of life within the framework of history, and as reflections of "social" meaning.

His own standpoint was that of Saint-Simon, a believer in progress. "I believe in progress. I believe that mankind is destined for happiness, and I have a better opinion of the deity than those pious souls who imagine that He created man only for suffering. Yes, here on earth I would establish by means of the blessings of free political and industrial institutions that beatific state which according to the opinions of the pious will be realized only on the Day of Judgment— and in Heaven."

He pleads for a "rehabilitation of the material"—not as something opposed to spirituality, but as the greatest manifestation of spirituality. The schism brought into the world by the Judaeo-Christian ideal— the schism of flesh and spirit—was now to be healed by a third testament, which he calls "the new pantheism." Hence he attacks the glorification of the Middle Ages—Catholic feudalism, with its chivalry, its hierarchies, and its corporations—as a futile attempt to revive a dead corpse. He does not deny the historical contributions of feudalism in its own day. But today, we must "vindicate the delights of this world, this beautiful garden of the Lord—our inalienable patrimony." "Bread," he wrote, paraphrasing a saying of St. Just's, "is the divine right of man." The German Romantic School was saturated with the spirit of medievalism—the "Christian-Pan-German" outlook. Brilliantly Heine exhibits the historical conditions which made the soil for such views favorable. The country was in the profoundest depths of humiliation. Its kings lay humbled at the feet of Napoleon. The present was ugly. But the past appeared beautiful. Especially the past that revealed a united Germany—a Holy Roman Empire—powerful and whole. That German past was a useful magic formula with which to rouse Germans from their slumber and inspire them to throw off the yoke of the French conqueror. Once that had taken place, the leaders of the Romantic School became the upholders of the restoration, the apostles of reaction, clothing it in the garb of medieval romance, giving the dead corpse the appearance of life. One by one they found their way into the receptive arms of obscurantism. The heaven-stormers who had so vehemently proclaimed the freedom of the heart now spoke the language of submissiveness. Such was the history of Tieck, Werner, Adam Müller, the Schlegels, Arnim, Brentano. Those who did not follow them, men like Jean Paul or Uhland, were silent or in exile. Thus had the Romantic worship of sickness, death, medievalism, and anarchic love run its full cycle.

But the "poetry of life is greater than the poetry of death," Heine insisted. Hence even Goethe, whom the Romantics rejected because of his paganism and his lack of national feeling, is censured because of his Olympian aloofness. Poetry which does not lead to action is sterile.

No different was the course of German philosophy as Heine traces it. That too had run its full gamut—from the time of Luther, through Spinoza, Mendelssohn, and Lessing, "the continuer of Luther," culminating in the Robespierre of philosophy, Immanuel Kant. It spoke the language of freedom and was the ally of reason. But now the great philosophers too had gone over to the camp of reaction. In Berlin Hegel was justifying the Prussian state, in Munich Schelling was preaching the glories of medievalism.

German philosophy was no longer that finely spun web of abstract, aerial arguments which honestly sought to test the basis of knowledge and experience. German philosophy was a serious thing—something for Frenchmen to treat with gravity. Heine warns the French not to minimize its implications, not to rest content with the traditional picture of Germans as idle dreamers who never act. In words pregnant with prophecy he sketches the future, when those indefatigable weavers of philosophical systems would turn from revolutions in thought to revolutions in life, and begin translating ideas into deeds. "Remain on your guard," he adjures the French. "Always be armed!"

"Despite your present Romanticism, you are really classicists at heart, and you know Olympus well. Among the naked gods and goddesses who there rejoice over nectar and ambrosia, you may see one immortal who even amidst all this festive gaiety always wears a coat of mail and bears a helmet on her head and a spear in hand. It is the Goddess of Wisdom."

IN 1834, HEINE MET MATHILDE. Her real name was Crescentia Eugénie Mirat. She was nineteen, and he thirty-seven. She had come from the country to work in her aunt's glove and shoe shop in the Passage Choiseul. Bright, gay, light-hearted, temperamental, still excited by the wonders of Paris, she caught the fancy and heart of the world-famous poet, who was at home in the most fashionable and intellectual salons, who associated with the great men and women of politics, literature and finance—the strange German poet, who for some reason had been seeking out his loves in the streets of Paris. She had never heard of Henri Heine, of whom thousands of people spoke with respect and admiration. In her eyes he was a charming young man who wanted her. To him she was the pretty Parisian child, delightful to love and fondle.

"Have you ever seen a real Parisian grisette?" he wrote to a friend. "Frank, sprightly, always cheerful, faithful and true? You must not read your German ideas into my picture, otherwise you will soil it. Mathilde is not a passionate creature; but neither is she sentimental. She is really a good girl. Not an innamorata in the lyrical style, but such a friend as only a Frenchwoman can be."

Gossips of the academic and non-academic variety have made much of this relationship between Germany's greatest lyric poet and an ignorant Paris girl, and their estimates of Mathilde have not always been flattering. They have tended to forget that the marriage—for a marriage it was, though it was not formalized until seven years later—lasted through more than twenty years, until the poet's death—that it survived the trials of temperamental and intellectual differences, the inconstancies of the poet, and the ordeal of the "mattress grave."

He loved her not as one loves a mature woman—completely—but as a child-wife. His emotional insecurities—which could not be totally satisfied by the cursory amours of the Paris boulevards, the real or imagined Hortenses, Clarissas, Kittys and Katharinas—required that he *possess*, but even his possession of Mathilde was incomplete. He was always unsure of her, because he was always unsure of himself. He was still the rejected lover of Amalie, of Therese, perhaps even of the Princess Belgioioso—he was always in dread of being rejected.

She gave him as much as she received. She bore with his moods, his jealousies, his waywardness—he bore with her extravagance and flightiness. In the physical relation they found partial satisfaction for emotional incompleteness. She was his "song of songs"—his "wife and child"—and as she chattered, sang, or scolded, and she did all of these with gusto, he listened with delight and amazement. She lived for the day and the pleasures thereof, and made the most of an imperfect world. She did not read his poems, and she probably did not understand what he meant when he referred to her as the body, and to himself as the soul. If he was the soul, he was always fleeing and returning to the physical frame. Like his own Tannhäuser, he was always the thrall of Venus.

Ludwig Börne died in 1837.

It is sad to reflect that the staunchest champion of German republicanism, and Heine, the most brilliant of German literary radicals, rarely saw eye to eye on political matters. Together, they would have constituted a formidable expression of German liberal opinion abroad. As it was, their open and concealed feuds constitute an unpleasant chapter in the history of German liberalism. In his relations with Börne, Heine revealed himself as less generous than might have been expected of a professed foe of autocracy.

Three years after Börne's death, Heine published a little book on him which roused a storm of resentment, culminating in a slightly ridiculous affair of honor.

The immediate cause of Heine's bitter attack was the unfavorable reference to him which Börne had made in his *Letters from Paris*. Ludwig Börne's career had paralleled that of Heine in many respects. He was a Jew, who had lived in Frankfurt, and he had gone through all the vicissitudes of the Jews during the period of the Emancipation and the reaction. He had lost a small government post, his pension had been reduced, and he had finally turned Protestant. He was one of the most valiant and clear-sighted of dramatic critics, at a time when neither the theater nor theatrical criticism was held in great esteem. He brought to his judgments a keen social conscience, and one of his most famous reviews had attacked anti-Semitism on the German stage. He fell in love with Jeannette Wohl, a very gifted woman who was then separated from her husband. Under the pressure of reaction at home, and subsequent to the Carlsbad Resolutions, he grew more and more pronouncedly militant, and his visits to France strengthened his liberal convictions. He had been fighting all along for a moderate program of reform—popular representation through annual parliaments, freedom to engage in occupations, equality before the law— all to be achieved within the framework of a constitutional monarchy. The July Revolution made a republican of him, made him, in fact, the most articulate of German republicans abroad. Like Heine, he came to understand the social and economic implications of the struggles which were being waged—that the world was entering upon a war between the rich and the poor—and in his *Letters from Paris*, which, along with Heine's *French Affairs*, constitutes the keenest analysis of the political events of the day by Germans (aside from that of Marx and Engels), he carried on unremitting warfare against the monarchy.

What it was that Heine actually resented in Börne it is hard to tell. Börne was, in Heine's eyes, a "Nazarene," a puritan; Heine was a hedonist, a pagan. Börne was a circumscribed person, narrow and single-minded in the pursuit of his objectives; but he was incorruptible and inflexible. He would take Heine to task for his political indifference, his running after Parisian women, and his preoccupation with "aesthetic" subjects. He called Heine the "Jesuit of liberalism," in whom no one could have faith, because he "had no faith in himself. . . . Now he defies absolutism; now Jacobinism." Heine had expressed himself in no dubious tones about the futile character of German republicanism. Heine regarded political institutions as secondary; the essence was the economic struggle of the lower classes for well-being. But Heine had opened himself, in one way or another, to many of the charges contained in Börne's criticism. Was Heine's avowed monarchism any less futile than Börne's republicanism? And more defensible? It may have been the implication of venality which rankled most bitterly, though even on that score Heine could boast that his hands were clean and that his actions spoke for him.

Whatever our opinion as to the differences between Heine and

Börne, there can be doubt that in making uncomplimentary references to the relationship between Börne and Frau Wohl (now Frau Strauss) Heine's conduct was most reprehensible. Herr Strauss challenged Heine to a duel, in which the latter was slightly wounded. Thus the affair was terminated. Heine himself later expressed genuine regret for his slighting remarks about Jeannette Wohl. But the stain on Heine's reputation could not so easily be erased.

IT WAS AMAZING THAT IN THE MIDST OF ALL THESE TROUBLES he could go on creating. For in addition to the Börne scandal, he was suffering from nearly total blindness. For some time now, he had been writing mostly prose. Now suddenly he returned to poetry. In the next four years he was to compose two of his longest and most important single poems, *Atta Troll* and *Germany—A Winter's Tale*.

He was vacationing in the French Pyrenees during the summer of 1841 when he conceived the idea of writing a strange phantasy, a "swan song" of Romanticism, whose thousand years' reign was now coming to an end. What better setting than the rugged mountains near Cauterets? In the market-place of the town he had watched with interest the performance of dancing bears. That was to be his subject— bears! His imagination took fire. Men have always passed judgment on bears—now let the bears judge man. Atta Troll, princely bear, and his wife Mumma, entertain the populace by dancing. Suddenly, Atta Troll breaks loose and escapes into his mountain cave, where he rejoins his brood. Here he gives himself over to moral reflections. To his son he says: Do not trust men, not even Germans. Once they were good, but now they are all atheists. What a sad lot they are! Just as they once brutally sacrificed their own kind to their ancient gods, they now sacrifice them to the modern god of gold. They speak of the sacredness of property, by which they mean the right to steal,—as if Nature had brought us into the world equipped with pockets! We bears will bring equality into the world—for all—except that we will forbid the Jews to dance. Such are Atta Troll's homilies. In the meantime, his master, Laskaro, has begun the chase, accompanied by the poet. With the aid of Laskaro's mother, a witch, Atta Troll is lured back and killed. Mumma ends up in a Paris zoo, where she is being wooed by a polar bear. And Atta's pelt now graces the bedroom of the poet's little friend, Juliette. Fittingly, the poem is dedicated to Varnhagen von Ense—"my chosen comrade-in-arms, who helped to bury the old times, and was midwife to the new."

FOR MANY YEARS HE HAD DREAMT OF RETURNING TO HAMBURG for a brief stay. He longed to see his mother and his sister, Charlotte, his uncle Solomon, and his publisher Campe. In the fall of 1843 he was in Hamburg again after an absence of twelve years. But he soon returned to Paris, in December, because he had gone without his Mathilde, and could not bear to stay away from her. He was to make another trip the following year—this time accompanied by Mathilde—to see his mother for the last time.

Not long after his return from his first trip, when the idea of writing a long poem on Germany had already taken shape, he met a young man of twenty-six, like himself an exile from Germany. The brilliant journalist had been the editor of a liberal magazine, *Die Rheinische Zeitung*, but after its suppression in the spring of 1843, he came to Paris to continue his studies. Now he was collaborating with Arnold Ruge on a new venture, the *Deutsch-Französische Jahrbücher*, and was about to participate in the publication of a German newspaper in Paris, *Vorwärts*. Naturally he had sought out the most brilliant and witty of German poets in Paris in order to win him for his publications. The young man's name was Karl Marx. The two became fast friends. Marx had been an admirer of Heine's for years, and knew most of his poems by heart. Heine was attracted by the brilliant intellect of the German revolutionary, and the charm and wit of his wife, Jenny von Westphalen.

Marx's sharp analytic mind, his profound knowledge, and clarity of vision stimulated the poet. Heine's poems took on incisive political tones. Under Marx's influence he wrote for the *Jahrbücher* and *Vorwärts* those amazing and devastating satires in which he exposed to ridicule the rulers of Germany, the impotent new King of Prussia, Frederick William IV, and King Ludwig of Bavaria. It was in the *Vorwärts* that Heine read of the uprising of the Silesian weavers in June 1844. Deeply moved, he wrote Germany's greatest social lyric, "The Silesian Weavers." It was in the *Vorwärts* that a portion of his most provocative satirical poem, *Germany*, was published.

For the shorter *Poems for the Times* were merely preliminary skirmishes. Heine was drawing his long-bow for a master-shot. The complete poem, *Germany—A Winter's Tale*, appeared in the fall of 1844.

Heine knew what to expect. In his preface, he anticipates the obloquy and denigration which his new work would encounter. Of course, he would be called "a contemner of his fatherland," and "a friend of the French." It was the same old story. Yes, he contends, "I am a friend of the French, as I am the friend of all men who are sensible and good. . . . Do not fear. I will not yield the Rhine to the French for the simple reason that the Rhine belongs to me. Yes, it is mine by the inalienable right of birth. I am the free Rhine's even freer son; my cradle is on its banks. When we complete the work left unfinished by the French, when we destroy slavishness in its very last hiding place, i.e., heaven, when we liberate from abasement God who dwells in human beings on earth, when we become the saviours of God, when we restore dignity to the poor people who are deprived of happiness, and to genius condemned to scorn and to desecrated beauty . . . , then we will inherit not only Alsace and Lorraine, but all of France, and thereafter all of Europe; yes, all the world will become German."

This was not a Pan-German speaking. It was the citizen of the world who wished to erase national boundaries and who saw all of humanity united in a brotherhood of equals.

Then the poem begins. The poet is in Germany once more. When he touches German soil he feels young again. The foolish customs officer examines his bags, overlooking the more dangerous contraband to be found in the poet's head. The gloomy reality of German life contrasts with the vision of a Germany that might be.

> A new song and a better song
> Oh, friends I'll sing for you,
> Here on earth we mean to make
> Our paradise come true.
>
> We mean to be happy here on earth,
> Our days of want are done,
> No more shall the lazy belly waste
> What toiling hands have won.

Legend and contemporary history are fused in the magic of the poet's call for German liberation. The new Aristophanes who could scourge with scorpions could also be tender and loving. The coming of revolution is anticipated in the magnificent figure of the axe-man who accompanies the poet and materializes the latter's thought. I have become no sheep, Heine tells his fellow-Germans. I am still unvanquished. The figure of Barbarossa is invoked, with humor as well as passion, to come and shatter the bastions of stupidity and tyranny.

That is the dream. But what Heine actually sees in Hamburg, when the goddess Hammonia vouchsafes him a vision of the future, is too horrible to tell. The anti-climactic conclusion is perhaps the sole weakness of the poem. After the incomparable preparation, one expects a call to arms—not a warning to the King to respect poets, because their vengeance is mightier than that of Jove. Even Heine must have known that poets do not have that much power!

HE WAS DECIDEDLY UNWELL. He was losing his eyesight. Sometimes he was totally blind. A gradual paralysis of his face was an omen the meaning of which neither he nor his physicians fully understood. He still moved about, was gay and as witty as ever.

In December 1844 Solomon Heine died. He had been assisting his nephew with an annual allowance of 4800 francs which, together with his income as a writer and a grant from the French government, assured him of a comfortable, though by no means luxurious, life. He had expected his uncle would continue to provide for him in his will. What was his shock when he was informed by Solomon's heir, Karl Heine, that the will provided for a legacy of 8000 francs—and no more! Heine was beside himself with rage and disappointment. He had known all along that the Hamburg cabal had been conspiring against him; he knew that his cousin, Karl, hated him; but he had never suspected that his uncle would be so completely influenced by the gossip. Karl Heine offered to continue the annual payments provided Heine agreed to a censorship of all his writings in which the family was mentioned. The squabble which followed the publication of the will, the charges, countercharges, threats, and counterthreats do not make for pleasant reading. It was a mean vengeance on the part of the uncle, a millionaire; and an even meaner one on the part of his heir. After all, Heine was a world-famous poet, and he was a sick man. When reports of his approaching death began to multiply, Karl Heine became alarmed, and in February 1847 settled on him an annual payment to be continued during Mathilde's life.

The poet's health was rapidly deteriorating. His face was now completely paralyzed. He could not eat. He suffered frequent fainting spells. His body had shrunk. "I know I am past saving," he wrote to Campe.

IN 1848 A STORM SWEPT OVER EUROPE. It arose in France, and then blew across the Rhine, into Austria, and beyond. There had been signs and portents which the discerning eye could not fail to understand. An economic crisis had broken out in England. In France, the peasants and workers of Tours rose in protest against the rise in food prices. The social structure of France had changed considerably within twenty years; heavy industry had made notable advances, and the number of workers had increased correspondingly. Industrial capitalism now began to challenge the rule of the financial aristocracy, a corrupt, irresponsible, and venal group which had speculated itself into fortunes on the stock-exchanges of Europe. The economic crisis of 1847 brought matters to a head. Almost two-thirds of the working population of Paris were thrown out of work. Tradesmen and artisans went bankrupt. Despite the iron rule which Louis Philippe and his masters imposed on the country, despite the banning of all meetings, the people of Paris rose up.

On February 22, the workers and artisans of Paris came out into the streets. The next day barricades were erected. Then the National Guard went over to the insurgents. On the 24th, Louis Philippe abdicated, and the cry of "Long live the Republic!" resounded through the streets. A middle-class provisional government was proclaimed, a ten-hour work day was announced, universal suffrage was established, and the first election was set for April 23.

The hearts of the ruling monarchs of Europe were sick with dread. Leopold of Belgium wrote to Frederick William IV of Prussia: "The terrible misfortune in Paris represents a most serious danger not only to European monarchs, but to the very existence of society. . . . Property, family, religion, even our treasured freedom and security are at stake."

On March 13, the people of Vienna rose and drove Metternich from the country. On March 18, the citizens of Berlin forced the surrender of their king. In almost every major city of Europe uprisings took place. In London, the Chartists marched on Parliament bearing a petition with six million signatures.

Unfortunately, once they were in power, the leaders of the Revolution, mostly middle-class representatives, became uncertain of their aims, suspicious of one another and fearful of their working-class allies. Soon they leagued against them with their enemies. Such was the history of the French uprising, where men like Louis Blanc, Lamartine, and Barbès turned against the workers. The Hungarian and Polish revolts were soon crushed through Russian intervention. In Germany, Frederick William IV showed his contempt for his people by scornfully rejecting the imperial crown offered him by the Frankfurt Assembly on May 18, 1848. "Against democrats our only remedy is the army."

The counter-revolution marched swiftly and ruthlessly. The workers of Paris were provoked into an uprising in June 1848, and massacred by an army led by General Cavaignac. Louis Napoleon was elected President of the Second French Republic. By the *coup d'état* of 1852 he succeeded in having himself proclaimed Emperor of France.

There were few men in Europe who fully understood the meaning of the events which had taken place. Thousands of exiles poured through Paris and London. Among the very few of them who looked at the historical struggles with clear and critical eyes were Marx and Engels. They pointed to a new and astonishing phenomenon that had taken place in this revolution—an independent force had emerged which was destined to make history. It was the working class. On the basis of their analysis they had already—on the eve of the Revolution—written the most important political document of the century, the *Communist Manifesto*.

THE STREETS WERE FILLED WITH THE SOUND OF GUNS and shouting, when Heine went out for the last time in May 1848. Thereafter he was confined to the "mattress grave" for eight long years. The German Apollo whom Gautier had greeted seventeen years before, was now a bearded, emaciated skeleton, powerless to move from his couch in the Rue d'Amsterdam. He had to be carried like an infant.

But his mind remained impenetrable to the ravages of sickness. It burned clearly and intensely, and illumined the darkness around him. His wit was no less sharp than before. The visitors who came to see him, sometimes impelled by kindness, often by curiosity, were not always aware of the agonies he was suffering. He was almost completely blind. To see them, he would raise one eyelid with his hand. A quip or jest was always at the tip of his tongue. From the next room would come the chatter or laughter of Mathilde, and Heine would stop, listen, and smile. She tended him faithfully, brought him coffee with rich cream. He jestingly observed that she was growing stout.

His interest in the world outside never abated. Books and newspapers were read to him, and the gossip of the town was brought to him. He who had loved life so much—and who still loved it passionately—was now confined to living it vicariously. For eight years he wrestled with Death. His mother never knew the gravity of his illness.

He was done with politics. Yet the publication by the *Revue Rétrospective* of Louis Philippe's list of pensioners, with Heine's name among them, and the subsequent accusation that he had been a hireling of Guizot's and of France, forced from him a proud self-vindication. The new Napoleon failed to inspire him. "The beautiful ideals of political morality, legality, civic virtue, freedom and equality, the roseate morning dreams of the eighteenth century, for the sake of which our fathers met their death so bravely, and which we, no less eager for the martyr's crown, dreamt together with them—now lie at our feet, broken, scattered potsherds. . . ." He had foreseen and forewarned.

But his poetic genius grew in richness and maturity. It was during those mattress-grave years that he attained the peak of his poetical powers. In *Romancero*, which was published in 1851, and in the 1854 collection of his poems—the last to appear in his lifetime—he stands revealed as one of the great European poets.

His fancy roved far and wide. At night he composed his poems, and in the morning he dictated them to his secretary. In those nocturnal wanderings, as sane and vigorous as those on which any poet ever ventured, he ranged through history and all the lands of the world. *Romancero* is the gem of Heine's balladry, the equal of that composed anywhere. His ballad characters are for the most part historical figures, Charles I of England, Marie Antoinette, King David, the Persian poet Firdusi, the troubadour Geoffrey Rudel, Cortez the Conquistador. Into them he concentrated all of his great dramatic genius —the genius he possessed of simplifying, objectifying and compressing. Where shall we find the equal of "The Battlefield of Hastings," "The Asra," or "Woodland Solitude"? They are modern creations with the subtle psychological overtones which only a great modern poet could give them. This is not the work of a dying poet, but of one who has reached the fullness of poetical vitality. Here too is to be found *Lazarus*, a great litany of suffering—also objectified and transmuted—that litany which is defiance of death and victory over it— ironic, grim, touching, chiding. Was he not Lazarus himself of whom it is written that he "was a certain beggar . . . which was laid at the gate of the rich man, full of sores, and desiring to be fed with the crumbs which fell from the rich man's table. Moreover the dogs came and licked his wounds." The lot of the poet in the world is not a happy one, whether he be the God Apollo or Firdusi.

Here too are *The Hebrew Melodies*, the flower of his Jewish poems, including the magnificent hymn to Princess Sabbath, the symbol and the glory of all ceremonials through which the immortality of a people speaks—and his unforgettable reconstruction of Jehuda Halevy, the epitome of the woeful and heroic history of Israel.

He was the pilgrim of sorrow who had left the Greek Parnassus or Mount Olympus, and reluctantly had returned to the altar of a personal Jehovah. He now told himself and the world that he had foresworn the freethinking of an earlier day, the roseate Hellenism of the German Apollo, and the god of Hegel, and had come back to a personal God, to whom he would now confide his most secret midnight thoughts as well as his personal affairs, whom he could chide and reprove and with whom he could argue.

How hard it was to tear himself from those lovely deities of ancient Greece! Even as late as 1851 he confessed:

"I have abjured nothing, not even my old heathen gods, from whom I did indeed turn away, but the parting was affectionate and friendly. It happened in May 1848, on the day on which I left my house for the last time, that I took leave of those glorious idols whom I had adored in the days of my good fortune. Painfully I dragged myself to the Louvre, and I was near collapse when I entered the lofty hall where the blessed goddess of beauty, Our Lady of Milo, stands on her pedestal. I lay at her feet for a long time, and I wept violently. And the goddess looked down upon me compassionately, and at the same time so disconsolately, as if to say, 'Can you not see that I am without arms and powerless to help you?' "

Upon its publication, *Romancero* at once went into four editions. Julius Campe, who had for over three years refrained from even writing the sick poet, must have been overjoyed.

THE LAST YEARS OF HIS LIFE were spent in the Rue Matignon, close to the Champs Elysées. From near and far friends and relatives came to see him—perhaps for the last time. Therese Heine, a very unhappy woman, and Charlotte; his brothers Gustav and Maximilian, both successful men; the poets Béranger, Gérard de Nerval (who predeceased Heine), Heinrich Laube, and his old friend, Elise von Hohenhausen.

Gautier saw him for the last time in January 1856. "Illness had attenuated, emaciated, dissected him at will, and with the unwearied patience of an artist of the Middle Ages; from the statue of a Greek god it had shaped a Christ gaunt as a skeleton, in which the nerves, the tendons, and the veins were revealed. Thus ravaged, he was still beautiful. When he raised his heavy eyelid a flash shot from his half-blinded pupil. Genius resuscitated this dead face. Lazarus came forth from his grave for a few minutes."

He fell in love again—this time with a mysterious girl who came to him one day in July 1855, and visited him frequently till the day of his death. She had a past—checkered and obscure. She had been the mistress of Heine's friend Meissner before she came to know the poet. After Heine's death, she became the mistress of Taine, and wrote under the name of Camille Selden. Whoever she was, "la Mouche" (the "Fly"), as he called her, lightened his last days. To her he wrote his saddest and most amusing letters; for her he wrote some of his loveliest verses. Both are grotesquely marked by paroxysms of frustration which overcame the poet now condemned to platonic amours.

Catherine Bourlois, his nurse, was the last person to see him alive. On February 17, 1856, four o'clock in the morning, he died. He had asked for and was given the simplest of funerals. Neither a Catholic nor a Protestant clergyman officiated. A hundred people accompanied his last remains to the cemetery in the Montmartre district. Mignet, Dumas and Gautier were among those who paid him a last tribute, and Gautier wrote: "There was neither a long procession, nor lugubrious music, nor muffled drums, nor black cloth starred with orders, nor emphatic discourse, nor tripods crowned with green flames." But the mourners knew that they "were assisting at the funeral of a king of the mind."

THE BATTLE OVER HEINE which was carried on even during his lifetime, continued with unabated fury after his death. During the last years of his life, he had been writing his autobiography and confessions. Soon after his death, the Heine family succeeded in laying its hands on a good portion of his literary remains and probably destroyed them. The "Castle of Affronts" haunted him even in his grave.

Mathilde survived him until 1883. He had provided for her—and she remained faithful to his memory, though, if legend is to be credited, not to his whimsical wishes. He is alleged to have asked her to marry again, so that at least one person might regret his death!

His German fatherland, which found room for innumerable monuments to innumerable German mediocrities, did not deem him worthy of such a memorial, and the column designed by the sculptor Herter finally found a haven in New York. The Nazis officially consecrated the obloquy by consigning him to oblivion and by removing his name from his most famous poems. No greater tribute could have been paid any poet. He had become part of the living poetry of the people, and his poems had become folksongs. The work of desecration still continues, and the legend of a heartless, insincere, Francophile, traitorous Heine persists in many academic halls and is trumpeted abroad by "scholars" who have never ventured beyond the confines of their libraries and many of whom had by their complacency or worse paved the way for the coming of the Third Reich.

"Not marble nor the gilded monuments of princes shall outlive his powerful rhyme." Nor, one might add, the jabbering of geese. He had many faults—he was inconsistent, often frivolous, cynical, if you will, weak and wayward. The gold of his genius was not unalloyed. But he stands revealed today, for all that, as a great poet and humanitarian. He is a modern whose eye pierced the future. What he foresaw has since come to pass.

Within himself he shadowed the conflicts of his times, the struggle between the old and the new. Within him the "Nazarene"—the Judaeo-Christian ideal of renunciation and poverty—struggled with the "Hellene," the life-affirming, the cheerful, the realistic. He had once thought to cut himself loose from the Jewish people. He became the German Apollo with a baptismal certificate. But he only found the terms of the struggle changed—not the struggle itself. For what did such titles as "Nazarene" and "Hellene" mean in a world of ineluctable conflicts for bread and decency?

He came to see history not as a disjointed mass of incoherent facts, but as a process which revealed the struggles of mankind for freedom. All great martyrs of freedom joined hands in that indivisible work. Christ was such a liberator. And Moses too. Martin Luther, and in a greater measure, Thomas Münzer, the peasant leader. And the heroic men of the French Revolution. Heine was not the least—nor the last—of them.

In his day he saw the struggle assuming new forms. Armies of the dispossessed were challenging the divine rights of the possessors. Wherever he looked, he witnessed preparations for war. Was he not among the very few Germans who had correctly appraised the role of the Chartists—that first organized political movement of the working-class in England? Had he not time and again drawn attention to the neglected but potentially mighty forces of socialism in France?

Had he not confidently proclaimed the great task of the nineteenth century to be the liberation not of this or that oppressed minority, but of all oppressed peoples? He had incessantly warred on Junkers, aristocrats, autocrats, political clergy. He hated the moneyed aristocracy with all the virulence of a Balzac—but unlike the latter he looked to the future and not to the past for liberation from them.

"We have measured the earth, weighed the forces of Nature, reckoned the resources of industry, and behold!—we have found that the earth is spacious and wide enough for everyone to build his hut of happiness on it—that the earth can feed us all decently, if only every one of us works, and no one lives at another's expense—that it is no longer necessary to preach the blessedness of heaven to the large masses of the poor."

He wrote that he might be read. He never separated the word from the deed, and the deed from its social consequences. He had consecrated himself to the task of making "the great portion of mankind understand our own times," so they would no longer "allow themselves to be provoked by the hireling scribblers of the aristocracy into hatred and war." He foresaw a "great confederation of peoples—the Holy Alliance of Nations," when "we shall not longer need to sustain standing armies of many hundreds of thousands of murderers because of mutual distrust. We shall use our swords and horses to plow with, and we shall win peace, prosperity and freedom."

Though he was a true citizen of the world—rather, *because* he was a true citizen of the world—he loved his own land, not the land of dreamy-eyed sluggards, of phantasts, of arrogant rulers, but the country of good, simple people, the miners of the Harz, the fisherfolk of Nordeney. He honored all great Germans who had contributed to the emancipation of the human mind—Luther, Lessing, Kant, Goethe and Schiller. He was proud of being a German poet. He wished to bring Germany into the mainstream of European history and culture.

That he did not succeed in doing so is the tragedy of Germany and of the world.

DACHAU, BELSEN, MAJDANEK—are they not objectified fulfillment of Heine's predictions? The nation of professors, *Privatdozenten*, doctors of philosophy, musicians and poets—had it not become one vast army of destruction, such as Heine described in his book on *Religion and Philosophy in Germany?* Have not the invokers of the old pagan gods, the worshippers of Aryanism, the unrelenting hordes of Pan-Germans fulfilled the worst of Heine's fears?

As he had assigned to the Germans the role of liberators of the world, provided they allied themselves with the great forces of freedom and equality, so he came to see the liberation of the Jews as a phase of world freedom. His identification with the Jews—like his identification with Germans—was the fruit of a wisdom which taught him that all wars and warriors for freedom have a common fatherland, that battles of humanity merge into one another, that to fight as a Jew and to fight as a German meant to fight against oppression and tyranny and exploitation.

So he sought in the history and martyrdom of the Jews for a clue to an understanding of them. He who had once thought of them as symbolized by the hagglers and money-changers of Hamburg came to honor them as men, "mighty and unyielding . . . despite eighteen centuries of persecution and misery." He reappraised the Bible, their "portable fatherland" and its giant hero Moses, in whom he saw one of the great emancipators of mankind, a hater of slavery at a time when Hellenes and the whole world surrounding the little land of Palestine was still slave-ridden. *The Rabbi of Bacherach* had reaffirmed Israel's heroism in the character of Sarah, whose words, addressed to a cynical renegade, were written in Heine's own blood: "My noble Lord," she says, "if you would be my knight, you must fight whole nations, and in that battle there are scant thanks to be won, and even less honor. And if you would wear my colors, then you must sew yellow rings on your cloak, or bind a blue-striped scarf around you. For such are the colors, the colors of my house, the House of Israel, the house of misery, which is despised and scorned in the streets by the children of good fortune."

In 1840, the Turks revived in the blood-libel of Damascus the gruesome, ancient accusation that Jews used Christian blood for their Passover ritual. Heine was roused to indignation. He saw more clearly than before the political and social roots of anti-Semitism. He was shocked by the indifference of the rich Jews of France to the plight of their coreligionists; he lashed out at the hypocrisy of French political leaders, who along with the reactionary cliques of French society were using the libel to advance their own political interests in the Near East.

Heine's great essay on Shakespeare's *Merchant of Venice* marks the apex of his understanding of the nature of anti-Semitism. Aside from the fact that it is one of the more remarkable examples of Shakespeare criticism, it is a brilliant analysis of the role of Shylock, the Jew, who is contrasted with his "Christian" victims. Heine's most pregnant words are devoted to the social role of the Jews. They are so far ahead of the general thinking of his day—and even of our own—that they deserve repeated quotation:

"The common people hated in the Jews only the possessors of money; it was always the heaped-up metal which drew the lightning of their wrath down on the Jews. They were glad if religion allowed them to give full sway to this hatred." Today, anti-Semitism "no longer wears the gloomy, fanatical monk's mien, but the flabby, 'enlightened' features of a shopkeeper, who is afraid of being outdone in his business dealings by Jewish business sense." Why did the Jews engage so predominantly in commerce and trade? "The whole world compelled them to be rich" by barring them from all other enterprises, and then "hated them for their riches."

It was natural that Heine should draw the conclusion that Jews would only achieve emancipation when "the emancipation of the Christians was fully won and secured." Hence the Messiah who came to liberate mankind would free not only Israel, "but all of suffering humanity."

YET HIS MIND RECOILED AT ACCEPTING the inexorable consequences of his own thoughts. He who had spoken powerful words on world emancipation was content to remain a professed monarchist! The destroyer of romantic fictions held on to the romantic fiction of a beneficent king who would reconcile the conflicts of society, check and neutralize a parasitic money-aristocracy, and an equally parasitic nobility and clergy, and win bread and happiness for the common man.

He was too honest not to perceive the character of the coming struggles, of what he called the "great duel" between the possessors and the dispossessed. Often he had said, "Bread is the divine right of man." But the romantic poet within him trembled for the future of poetry once the people had set about vindicating the divine right to bread. In the coming revolution, would the world of dreams and poetry and music go down in ruins, and his own *Book of Songs* serve to wrap groceries? Perhaps his faith in man was not so strong as he had claimed. Perhaps his prophetic vision was blurred. His *Book of Songs* was eventually mutilated not by people fighting for equality and happiness, but by a nation bent on domination, fed and abetted by the very moneyed aristocracy he had himself castigated.

But the die was cast, and so he concludes with sorrow:

"A terrible syllogism holds me in its grip, and if I am unable to refute the premise, 'that every man has the right to eat,' then I am forced to submit to all its consequences. From much thinking about it I am on the verge of losing my reason. I see all the demons of truth dancing triumphantly around me, and at length the generosity of despair takes possession of my heart and I cry: 'For long this old society has been judged and condemned. Let justice be done! Let this old world be smashed in which innocence is long since dead, where egoism prospers, and man battens on man! Let these whited sepulchres be destroyed from top to bottom, these caverns of falsehood and iniquity. And blessed be the grocer who shall one day use the pages of my poems as paper bags for the coffee and snuff of poor old women, who in this present world of injustice too often have to go without that solace. *Fiat justitia, pereat mundus!*' "

BUT THE WORLD DOES NOT PERISH WHERE JUSTICE IS DONE. When the world achieves complete justice, of the kind of which Heine wrote, his books will not serve as wrapping paper for grocers. For grocers, along with millions of others, will read Heine and preserve his works and the works of all great masters. It is after all the people who have kept his memory alive; they have sung and recited his poems for generations. They will honor in him not only the poet of love but also the poet of freedom, the greatest wit of the century, the satirist whose place is beside Aristophanes, Cervantes, Rabelais, Swift, Molière, and Anatole France. They will honor in him the great critic and social thinker.

They will echo his own imperishable epitaph:

I have never laid great store by poetic glory, and whether my songs are praised or blamed matters little to me. But lay a sword on my bier, for I have been a good soldier in the wars of human liberation.

Self Portrait

IN GERMANY [1797–1830]

ઠ Prologue

THE NIGHT IS STILL. Only outside the rain splashes against the roofs and the melancholy autumn wind moans.

My wretched sick room is at this moment almost luxuriously comfortable, and I sit in my arm-chair, and my pains have ceased.

Suddenly, you, fair vision, enter, without even moving the latch on my door, and you sit down on the cushion at my feet. Lay your lovely head on my knee and listen—but do not look up at me.

For I will tell you the fairy tale of my life.

If now and then large drops fall on your tresses, pay no attention to them. It is not the raindrops oozing through the roof. Do not weep. Only press my hand, and do not speak.

AROUND MY CRADLE PLAYED THE LAST MOONBEAMS of the eighteenth and the first dawn of the nineteenth century.

MY MOTHER TELLS ME THAT, DURING HER PREGNANCY, she saw an apple hanging in someone else's garden, but refrained from taking it, lest her child become a thief. As a result, all my life long, I have had a secret longing for fine apples, along with a respect for another's property—and a horror of stealing.

♔ *Düsseldorf*

THE TOWN OF DÜSSELDORF IS VERY BEAUTIFUL, and if you think of it when you are far away and happen to have been born there, you are strangely affected. I was born there, and I feel as if I had to go home at once. When I say *home*, I mean the Bolkerstrasse, and the house where I was born. The house will some day be famous, and I have told the old woman who now owns it under no circumstances to sell it. The whole house would now hardly fetch as much as the tips which elegant green-veiled English ladies will give the maid when she shows them the room where I first saw the light of day, and the henhouse where my father used to lock me up for stealing grapes, and the brown door on which my mother taught me to write letters with chalk. Heavens, Madame, if ever I turn out to be a famous writer, it will have cost my poor mother trouble enough to make me one.

But at present my fame is still sleeping in the marble quarries of Carrara. The paper laurel wreath with which they have crowned my brow has not yet spread its fragrance throughout the world, and when elegant green-veiled English ladies come to Düsseldorf, they do not so much as look at the famous house, but go straight to the market place to inspect the colossal, black equestrian statue standing in the middle of it. It is said that this statue represents the Prince Elector Jan Wilhelm. He wears black armor, and has a long flowing wig. As a boy I was told that the artist, while casting this statue, observed with horror that there was not metal enough, and so all the citizens came running with their silver spoons to help him complete the casting. And I used to stand for hours before the statue, racking my brains with the question: How many silver spoons can be contained within it; and how many apple-tarts can be bought with all that silver? For apple-tarts were then my passion.—Now it is love, truth, freedom, and cray-fish soup. Indeed, close to the Elector's statue at the corner of the theater there generally stood a comical-looking, bow-legged fellow, with a white apron and a basket of piping hot apple-tarts which he hawked in an irresistible falsetto: "Apple-tarts, fresh from the oven! Sweet smelling apple-tarts!" As a matter of fact, when the Tempter tried to seduce me in my riper years, he spoke with the very same alluring falsetto, and I should never have stayed at Signora Julietta's for twelve full hours, if she had not used that sweet, savory apple-tart voice on me. To tell the truth, apple-tarts would never have attracted me so much, had not bandy-legged Herman covered them so mysteriously with his white apron—and it was this white apron—but I am digressing. I was speaking of the equestrian statue, with so many silver spoons inside it, and not a spoon-full of soup—the statue which represents the Elector Jan Wilhelm.

They say he was a decent sort of fellow, a great lover of art, and even very talented. He founded the art-gallery at Düsseldorf, and in the observatory there you can still see an extraordinary and ingenious collapsible goblet made of wood, which he carved in his leisure hours—of which he had twenty-four every day.

In those days princes were not so care-ridden as they are now. Their crowns grew firmly on their heads, and at night they pulled night-caps over them, and slept peacefully. And the people slept peacefully at their feet, and on awaking each morning they said: "Good morning, father!" And the prince replied: "Good morning, my dear children!"

But suddenly all this changed. One morning, when we awoke at Düsseldorf and were about to say, "Good morning, father!", our father was gone. The whole town was in a state of numb bewilderment and in a funereal mood; and the people stole silently to the market-place and read the long announcement on the door of the town-hall. The weather was dreary, and yet Kilian, the emaciated tailor, was standing in his nankeen jacket, which he generally wore in the house, and his blue woollen stockings hung down so that his bare little legs looked out mournfully, and his thin lips quivered while he muttered to himself the words of the proclamation. An old pensioned soldier of the Palatinate read in a somewhat louder voice, and now and then a bright tear dropped on his honest, grizzled moustache. I stood beside him and wept too, and asked him why we were weeping. He replied: "The Elector wishes to thank you." Then he began reading again, and when he came to the words, "for your proved loyalty," and "we release you from your allegiance," he wept even more bitterly. It is odd to see an old man in a faded uniform and with a scarred soldier's face bursting into tears. While we were reading, the electoral coat-of-arms was taken down from the town-hall; and everything assumed as bleak an aspect as if people were awaiting an eclipse of the sun. The town-councillors went about with a languid, discharged sort of gait, and even the all-powerful bailiff looked as if he no longer had orders to give and stood so calm and indifferent, although crazy Aloysius was again standing on one leg and rattling out the names of the French generals, grimacing idiotically, while the drunken cripple Gumpertz rolled in the gutter and sang, "*Ça ira, ça ira!*" [1]

But I went home sobbing, "The Elector wishes to thank you." My mother could do nothing; I knew what I knew, and refused to be comforted. I went to bed weeping, and that night I dreamt that the world had come to an end. The beautiful flower-gardens and green meadows there were rolled up and put away like rugs; the town bailiff climbed up a high ladder and took down the sun; tailor Kilian stood by and said to himself, "I must go home and put on my best clothes, for I am dead and I'm going to be buried this very day." And it grew darker and darker. A few stars glimmered fitfully, and even these fell down like yellow leaves in autumn. Gradually everyone disappeared, and I, poor child, wandered about disconsolately, till at last I stood by a row of willows on a desolate farm, and saw a man who was turning up the earth with a spade, and by his side stood a hideous, malicious woman, with something in her apron that resembled a severed head. It was the moon! She laid it with anxious care into the open grave; and behind me stood the old pensioned soldier of the Palatine who sobbed and spelled out the words, "The Elector wishes to thank you."

When I awoke, the sun was shining through my window as usual. In the streets, drums were beaten, and when I entered our parlor and bade my father "Good morning" (he was in his white dressing-gown), I heard the nimble-footed barber telling my father in all details, while he was doing his hair, that today the new Archduke Joachim would be crowned in the town-hall,[2] that he belonged to a very good family, that he was married to Emperor Napoleon's sister, and was himself a man of address, wore his beautiful black hair in curls, and was shortly to make his entry and could not fail to please all the ladies. Meanwhile the drumming continued in the streets. I went to the door and saw the French troops marching in—that glorious, gay nation, which has marched through the world with song and triumph,—the cheerfully serious faces of the grenadiers, the bear-skin caps, the tricolor cockades, the gleaming bayonets, the *voltigeurs*, jubilant and full of *point d'honneur*, and the all-powerful, silver-laced drum-major, who could throw his gold-knobbed baton as high as the second story, and his glances as far as the third—where pretty girls sat at the windows. I was overjoyed at the prospect of having soldiers quartered with us—my mother was not—and I hurried to the market place. There everything was changed, as if the whole world had been freshly painted. There was a new coat of arms on the town-hall; the iron railings of the balcony were hung with embroidered velvet; French grenadiers stood guard; the old councillors had put on fresh faces and wore their Sunday best and looked at one another in French and said, "*bon jour*". Ladies were peering from every window, curious citizens and smart soldiers filled the square, and we boys clambered up the huge horse of the Elector and looked down on the motley crowds in the market place.

Our neighbor's boy Pitter and lanky Kurz nearly broke their necks on this occasion; though this would have proved no misfortune, for Pitter afterward ran away from home, enlisted, deserted, and was shot dead in Mayence; Kurz, on the other hand, later began making geographical explorations into other people's pockets, was chosen an active member of a public treadmill, broke the iron ties which bound him to that institution and to his country, crossed the waters in safety, and died in London from wearing too tight a necktie which knotted of itself when an official of the crown pulled away the plank on which he happened to be standing.

Lanky Kurz told us that there was no school today on account of the coronation. We waited a long while for things to start. At last the balcony of the town-hall was filled with gaily dressed gentlemen, flags and trumpets, and the Burgomaster, in his famous red coat, made a speech, somewhat extenuated like India rubber or a knitted nightcap into which a stone has been thrown—not, however, the philosopher's stone. A few of the phrases I could catch distinctly, for example, that they meant to make us all happy; and when he finished, the trumpets blew, the flags fluttered, the drums were beaten, and there were shouts of "*Vivat!*" and I also shouted "*Vivat!*", at the same time holding on fast to the old Elector. And I had need of a firm hold, for I was getting quite dizzy and began to think that people were standing on their heads, because the world was turning; and the Elector with his wig seemed to nod and whisper, "Hold tight!" And it was only the sound of the cannon being fired on the ramparts that brought me to my senses, and I slowly dismounted from the Elector's horse.

On my way home, I again saw crazy Aloysius dancing on one leg, while he rattled out the names of the French generals; and the cripple Gumpertz wallowing drunk in the gutter, roaring, "*Ça ira, ça ira.*" And I said to my mother, "They want to make us all happy; that is why there is no school today."

ࣧ *The French Drummer*

THE NEXT DAY THE WORLD WAS ITSELF AGAIN. There was school once more, as before, and learning by heart, as before. Roman kings, dates, nouns in *-im*, irregular verbs, Greek, Hebrew, geography, German, mental arithmetic—Lord! the very thought makes my head whirl— all had to be learned by heart. And much of it served me afterward in good stead. Thus if I had not known the Roman kings by heart, it would not have mattered a bit to me later whether Niebuhr [3] had or had not proved their non-existence. And if I had not learned dates, how could I later have found my way around Berlin, where the houses are exactly alike, like drops of water, or like grenadiers, and where it is impossible to find your best friend unless you remember the numbers of his house? I used to connect every one of my acquaintances with a historical event the date of which corresponded to the number of his house; and I would always recall a historical event when an acquaintance appeared. Thus, for example, on meeting my tailor, I thought at once of the Battle of Marathon; on seeing the immaculate banker Christian Gumpel, I thought at once of the destruction of Jerusalem; on seeing one of my debt-ridden Portuguese friends, I thought instantly of Mohammed's flight; on seeing the university proctor, whose rigorous integrity was well known, I instantly thought of Haman; the moment I cast eyes on Waldzeck,[4] I thought of Cleopatra. Alas, the poor beast is dead, and those tear-ducts are now dry, and we may say with Hamlet, "Take her for all in all, she was an old wench; we oft shall look upon her like again!" I repeat, dates are indispensable. I know certain persons who had nothing in their heads but a few dates, and knew how to find the right houses in Berlin, and are now full professors. But at school these endless numbers were the death of me. Arithmetic was even worse. I understood subtraction best: for here we have an excellent rule of thumb: "Four from three, no go; you've got to borrow one." Only I would advise you, while you're at it, to borrow a few extra pennies—for you never can tell. As for Latin, Madame, you have no idea how complicated that is. The Romans would surely never have found time to conquer the world if they had had to learn Latin first. These fortunate creatures already knew in their cradles which nouns formed the accusative in -*im*. But I had to learn it in the sweat of my brow. But it is good that I know it. For had I on the 20th of July, 1825,—in the university hall of Göttingen, where I publicly defended my Latin thesis—Madame, it would have been worth your while to have been there—had I then said *sinapem* instead of *sinapim*, it is likely that some freshman would have noticed it, and I would have been eternally disgraced. *Vis, buris, sitis, tussis, cucumis, amussis, cannabis, sinapis*—these words have made such a stir in the world because though they belong to a definite class,—they're still exceptional. That is why I respect them so highly, and the knowledge that I have them at hand if ever I should need them, gives me inward peace and comfort during many a dark hour. However, Madame, the *verba irregularia*—they differ from the *verba regularia* in that they entail more floggings—are frightfully difficult. In the dank cloisters of the Franciscan convent which was close to my schoolroom, there hung a large crucifix of grey wood, a grim piece of carving, which even today haunts my dreams, staring at me with blood-shot eyes. Before this image I would often stand and pray: "Oh, thou poor god, tortured like me—if it is possible, grant that I may keep the *verba irregularia* in my head."

Of Greek I do not even trust myself to speak. The medieval monks were not altogether wrong when they asserted that Greek was the invention of the devil. God knows the suffering it caused me! With Hebrew I fared better, for I have always had a strong predilection for the Jews, although to this hour they crucify my good name. But I could never advance in Hebrew as far as my watch, which was on intimate terms with pawnbrokers and had thus acquired many Jewish habits. For example, it would not go on Saturday. And it learned the sacred tongue and later on even acquired the grammar. How often, as I lay sleepless, was I amazed to hear it ticking persistently to itself: *katal, katalta, katalti; kittal, kittalta, kittalti—pokat, pokadeti, pikat—pik—pik—.*[5]

However, I grasped much more of the German language—and that is no child's play. For we poor Germans, who are already sufficiently plagued by the quartering of soldiers upon us, military service, the poll tax and a thousand other taxes, we have in addition saddled ourselves with Adelung,[6] and torture one another with the accusative and the dative. A good deal of my German I learned from old Rector Schallmeyer, a good priest, who took an interest in me from my earliest childhood. But I also learned something about it from Professor Schramm, who had written a book on perpetual peace, and in whose classroom my schoolmates always did the most fighting.

But I got on best of all in Abbé d'Aulnoi's French class. The Abbé was a French émigré, who had written a number of grammars, wore a red wig, and capered about when he was holding forth on his *Art poétique* or his *Histoire allemande*. He was the only one in the *gymnasium* who taught German history. But even French has its difficulties, and before you can master it, you must have plenty of soldiers quartered on you, plenty of drumming, plenty of *apprendre par coeur*,[7] and above all, you must not be a *bête allemande*. Yes, there were many bitter words. I remember, as if it were yesterday, the trouble I got into over *la religion*. Six times at least I was asked, "Henri, what is the French for *der Glaube?*" And six times, each time more tearfully, I answered, "It is *le crédit.*" And the seventh time, the examiner, purple with rage, shouted, "It is *la religion!*" And a rain of blows descended and all my school-mates laughed. Madame, since that day I never hear the word *religion* without feeling a cold shiver running down my back, and my cheeks reddening with shame. And to be candid, I have found *le crédit* more useful to me through life than *la religion*. At this moment I remember that I still owe the landlord of the "Lion" at Bologna five thalers, and on my honor I pledge myself to owe him another five on condition that I will never again hear that miserable word, *la religion*.

Parbleu, Madame! I have attained considerable proficiency in French. I understand not only *patois*, but even aristocratic governess French. Not long ago, at a fashionable party, I understood nearly half the discourse of two German countesses, each of whom could number more than sixty-four years, and as many ancestors. Indeed, at the Café Royal in Berlin I once heard Monsieur Hans Michel Martens [8] parley in French, and caught the sense of every word, although there was no sense in it. One must know the genius of a language, and that can best be learned from drumming. *Parbleu!* how much do I not owe the French drummer who was so long billeted on us, who looked like the devil, and yet was as kind as an angel and such an excellent drummer!

He had a small, agile figure; a fierce, black moustache, beneath which the red lips curled defiantly, while his fierce eyes darted here and there. Small boy that I was, I clung to him like a burr, and helped him to polish his buttons till they shone like mirrors, and whiten his vest with chalk, for Monsieur Le Grand liked to look well.—I followed him when he was on guard, to the roll-call, on parade—here everything was a brilliant gleam of arms and festive joy—*les jours de fête sont passés!* Monsieur Le Grand knew only a little broken German, only the necessary phrases, such as bread, kiss, honor—but he could make himself perfectly understood on the drum. For instance, when I did not know the meaning of *liberté*, he would drum the *Marseillaise*—and I understood him. If I did not know the meaning of *égalité*, he beat the march, *Ça ira, ça ira—les aristocrates à la lanterne!* And I understood. If I did not know the meaning of *bêtise*, he beat out the Dessauer March, which Germans drummed in the Champagne, as Goethe also reports—and I understood him. Once he wanted to explain to me the word *l'Allemagne*, and he drummed that very primitive and all too simple melody which is often played at fairs for dogs to dance to, *dumb, dumb, dumb,*—I was angry, but still, I understood him.

In the same way, he taught me modern history. I did not understand a word of what he said, but since he constantly accompanied himself on the drum while he spoke, I knew what he meant. This is, after all, the best method of teaching. The storming of the Bastille, of the Tuileries, etc., are easily grasped when you know what drum-beat they were taken to. In our school texts we merely read: "Their Excellencies the barons and counts and their most noble consorts were beheaded. Their Highnesses the dukes and princes and their very noble consorts were beheaded. His Majesty the King and his most noble Consort were beheaded."—But not until you hear the drums beating the bloody guillotine march, do you begin to understand the whys and wherefores. Madame, that is truly a wonderful march! When I first heard it, it thrilled me to the very marrow of my bones, and I was glad when I forgot it. One does forget such things when one grows older. A young man nowadays has so much else to remember— whist, boston, genealogies, acts of parliament, dramaturgy, liturgy, carving at the table.—As a matter of fact, I have for some years past been unable to recall that mighty tune, though I racked my brain.

But strange to say, Madame, not so long ago I was dining with a whole menagerie of counts, princes, princesses, chamberlains, ladies-in-waiting, court butlers, mistresses of the robe, keepers of the plate, mistresses of the chase, and the Lord knows how many other titled lackeys,—and their underlackeys were waiting obsequiously behind their chairs, shoving piled-up plates under their noses—while I sat there, unheeded and neglected, with nothing to occupy my jaws; so I made little bread pellets, and began tapping on the table,—and to my horror I was suddenly drumming the bloody, long-forgotten guillotine march.

"And what happened?"

Madame, these people never allow themselves to be disturbed while they eat, and do not understand that other people, when they have nothing to eat, suddenly take to drumming, and drum very strange marches, supposedly long forgotten.

ᵇ⋙ *What Is God?*

IF I NOW ASK, "WHAT IS GOD? WHAT IS HIS NATURE?"—even as a small child I asked, "What is God like? What does He look like?" At that time I could spend all day looking up at the sky, and in the evening I was quite disconsolate because I had not even caught a glimpse of the most holy countenance of God,—only the grey, silly grimaces of the clouds. I was utterly confused by the bits of astronomical information which, in that period of enlightenment, not even the smallest child was spared. I could not get over wondering at the fact that all these thousands of millions of stars were great and beautiful globes, like our own, and that one single God ruled over all these radiant myriads of worlds. Once in a dream, I remember, I saw God, in the farthest distance of high heaven. He was gazing contentedly out of a little window of heaven, with his pious old face with its little Jewish beard, and he was scattering handfuls of seeds, which, as they fell from heaven, opened up in endless space, and grew to tremendous size, until they finally turned into radiant, flourishing, inhabited worlds, each one as large as our own. I have never been able to forget this face. I often saw this cheerful old man in my dreams, scattering the seeds of worlds from his tiny window in heaven. Once I even saw him cluck with his tongue, just as our maid used to do when she gave the hens barley. I could only see the falling seed always expanding into vast, shining globes; but I could never see the great hens, which were probably lying in wait somewhere with wide-open beaks, ready to be fed with these scattered world-spheres.

ᙖ My Name Is Harry

HEINRICH, HARRY, HENRY—all these names sound sweet when sweet lips speak them. Best of all, surely, is Signor Enrico. So I was called in those clear blue summer nights, spangled with great silver stars, in that noble and unhappy land, which is the homeland of beauty, and which has brought forth Raphael Sanzio of Urbino, Joachimo Rossini—and Princess Christina Belgioioso.

Since my present physical condition deprives me of all hope of ever mingling again in society—which, as a matter of fact, no longer exists for me—I have stripped myself of all the fetters of personal vanity, which bind all who associate with others in the so-called world of fashion.

I can therefore speak without reserve about a mishap which is bound up with my name, "Harry," and which poisoned and embittered the fairest springtime of my life.

The facts are these: In my native town there was a man called the "Scavenger," because every morning he drove through the streets with his cart, drawn by a donkey, and stopped at every house, where he took up the refuse which the maids had collected in orderly heaps, and carted it out to the dump. The man looked like his occupation, and the donkey, who looked like his master, stood motionless before the houses, or moved according to the tone of voice in which the scavenger called out: "Haarüh!"

Was that his real name, or only a call? I don't know. But I am sure that I suffered an inordinate amount of persecution at the hands of my school-mates and the children of our neighbors, because my name "Harry" resembled that call so closely. To provoke me they would pronounce it exactly as the scavenger did, and when I grew angry, the rascals would look innocent and ask me how my name and the donkey's were to be pronounced, so that they might not be confused. But they seemed intentionally thick-headed, and insisted that the scavenger always dragged out the first syllable, while he cut the second short, and that at other times his call sounded exactly like my name. The scoundrels practised the most ridiculous variations, mixing up the donkey with myself, and vice-versa, and played all kinds of silly pranks which amused everyone else, but brought me to tears.

When I complained to my mother, she said that I must study hard and be clever, and then no one would take me for an ass.

But the similarity of my name and that of shabby long-ears continued to be my bugbear. The big boys would pass me on the street and greet me with "Haarüh," and so would the smaller boys—but from a distance. In school the same theme was turned to account, but with refined cruelty, whenever a donkey cropped up in our lessons. They then squinted at me, and I would always blush. It is unbelievable how adept schoolboys are in inventing or calling attention to personal weaknesses.

For example, someone would inquire: "What is the difference between a zebra and the ass of Balaam, the son of Beor?" And the reply would be, "One speaks zebraic, and the other Hebraic." Then came the question, "What is the difference between the scavenger's donkey and his namesake?" And the impudent reply was, "We don't know." Then I wanted to fight them, but I was held back, and my friend, Dietrich, who could draw such beautiful pictures of saints, and later became a famous painter, would comfort me on such occasions by promising me one of his pictures. He painted Saint Michael for me— but the wretch was making fun of me. The archangel had the features of the scavenger, and his steed looked much like the donkey, and instead of a dragon, his lance had pierced the carcass of a dead cat.

Even fair-haired, gentle, girlish Franz, whom I loved so dearly, betrayed me once. He took me in his arms, laid his cheek tenderly against mine, pressed me to his breast—and then suddenly whispered a mocking, "Haarüh"—and ran away, but kept intoning the hated name, so that it rang through all the cloisters of the monastery.

❧ Time and Place

THE CAUSES OF SUBSEQUENT PHENOMENA are to be sought in the faintest beginnings. It is surely important that when I was only thirteen years old, I knew all systems of free thought—which I learned from no one else but a venerable clergyman, who did not, however, in the least neglect his spiritual duties; so that from my earliest years I saw how religion and doubt can live together side by side without giving rise to hypocrisy. And this produced within me not only unbelief, but also the most tolerant sort of indifference.

Time and place are also of importance. I was born at the end of the sceptical eighteenth century, in a town which, during my childhood, was governed not only by French men, but also by the French spirit. . . .

౭❧ *My Mother*

MY MOTHER HAD IN MIND GREAT, AMBITIOUS PROJECTS FOR ME, and her whole plan of education was directed to that end. She played the principal role in the history of my development. She mapped out the program of all my studies; and even before I was born, she had begun her educational plans. I followed her express wishes obediently; but I must confess that she was to blame for the unfruitful nature of most of my endeavors and efforts in public life, for that never accorded with my temper. It was the latter, far more than material conditions, which determined my future.

Within us are to be found the stars of our fortune.

At first it was the glory of the Empire that dazzled my mother. The daughter of an iron monger of our neighborhood, who was on intimate terms with my mother, had become a duchess and told my mother that her husband had won many battles and was about to be promoted to a kingship. Alas! Henceforth, my mother dreamed of golden epaulets for my shoulders, and the most elaborately embroidered office of honor at the court of the Emperor, to whose service she was planning to dedicate me. Hence, I had to pursue a course of studies which would promote such a career. And though I had been taught enough mathematics at the Lyceum, and had been sufficiently stuffed by my dear old Professor Brewer with geometry, statics, hydrostatics, hydraulics, and what not—until it seemed that I was swimming in an ocean of logarithms and algebra—I had in addition to take private lessons in such subjects as would enable me to become a great strategist, or if need be, the administrator of some conquered provinces.

But with the fall of the Empire, my mother was forced to renounce the splendid career which she had dreamed for me. The studies which had been pursued with that end in view were discontinued, and strange to tell, never even left a trace in my mind—so utterly foreign were they to me. They were merely a mechanical accomplishment, which I threw off as so much useless rubbish.

Now my mother began to dream of a brilliant future for me in another field.

The house of Rothschild, to whose head my father was related, had already at that time entered upon its legendary prosperity. Other princes of banking and industry had grown up around us; and my mother declared that the hour had arrived when a man with brains might achieve the most unbelievable success in business, and could rise to the loftiest pinnacle of temporal power. She resolved, therefore, that I too should become a financial magnate. Now I was forced to study foreign languages, especially English, geography, book-keeping; in short, to acquire all the knowledge relating to trade and commerce, by land and sea.

So that I might learn something of banking and the export trade, I had later to pay visits to the offices of one of my father's bankers and the warehouse of a wholesale grocer—the first lasted at the most three weeks and the latter four. But I did learn how to draw up a bill of exchange, and to recognize a nutmeg.

A famous merchant, with whom it was intended that I become an *apprenti millionaire*, was of the opinion that I had no talent for business; and I laughingly agreed that he might be right.

Soon, however, a great commercial crisis arose, and many of our friends, my father as well, lost their fortunes. The commercial soap-bubble burst even more quickly and lamentably than the imperial one, and my mother had to dream up another career for me.

She came upon the idea that I must by all means study law. For she had observed that for generations in England, and even in France and constitutional Germany, the legal profession had been all-powerful; that lawyers, in particular, because they were in the habit of speaking publicly, managed through their chattering to play important roles and rise to the highest public offices. My mother's observation was quite accurate. Since the new university of Bonn had just been established, and its law faculty was composed of the most celebrated professors, she forthwith sent me to Bonn, where I sat at the feet of Mackeldey and Welker, and fed on the manna of their learning.

Of the seven years which I spent at German universities, I squandered three beautiful, blooming years in the study of Roman casuistry,—of jurisprudence—that most illiberal of sciences! What a horrible book is the Corpus Juris, that bible of egoism! Like the Romans who wrote it, their Codex Juris has always been an object of aversion to me. Those robbers wished to secure their robberies, and what they conquered with the sword, they sought to protect with their laws. Hence the Roman was at once soldier and lawyer—a most revolting combination. Indeed, it is to these Roman thieves that we owe the theory of private property, which had hitherto existed only in fact. Roman Law—so highly lauded—represents the development of this doctrine to its most vicious consequences, and is at the basis of all modern legislation, yes, of all modern state institutions, although it stands in the sharpest contrast to religion, morality, humanity, and reason.

I completed those execrable studies, but I could never bring myself to make use of my achievement—perhaps it was because I also felt that others might easily excel me as advocates and pettifoggers. So I put away my law degree.

My mother looked graver than ever. But I was now a grown-up man, and I had reached the age when I could dispense with her motherly supervision.

The good woman had likewise grown older, and though she surrendered the supreme command of my life after these numerous fiascos, she always regretted that I had not dedicated myself to an intellectual calling.

She is now a matron of eighty-seven. Her mind has not dimmed with age. She never assumed to herself the right to direct my own thoughts. Toward me she has always been considerateness and love personified.

Her religion was a strict deism, which was completely in keeping with her ever present good sense. She was a disciple of Rousseau.[9] She had read his *Émile*, suckled her children herself, and education was her hobby. She had had a good education, and had studied together with one of her brothers, who became a distinguished physician, but who died at an early age. Even when she was a young girl, she had to read Latin dissertations and other learned works to her father, and often amazed the old man with her questions.

Her reason and sensibility were the very embodiments of sanity. It was not from her that I inherited my disposition for the fantastic and the romantic. As I mentioned before, she lived in constant dread of poetry. She tore all novels from my hands, and never allowed me to attend the theater, forbade me to take part in the customary games, and kept a strict eye on my companions. She scolded the maids for telling ghost stories in my presence. In short, she did everything in her power to safeguard me from superstition and poetry.

She was frugal, but only toward herself. When it came to giving pleasure to others, she could be extravagant. Since she did not care for money, though she appreciated its value, she gave with a free hand and often astonished me by her open-handed generosity.

What sacrifices she was forced to make for her son's sake, during those hard years when she not only arranged his program of studies, but gave him the means of realizing it! When I entered the university, my father's affairs were in a very sad state. My mother sold her jewels, her precious necklace and earrings, to insure my subsistence during the first four years at the university.

ৈ My Uncle, Simon de Geldern

NEXT TO MY MOTHER, IT WAS MY UNCLE, Simon de Geldern, who was most concerned with my education. He died twenty years ago. He was a queer duck, of unprepossessing—even somewhat foolish—appearance. He had a small stoutish figure, with a pale, stern face, and a nose that was as straight as a Greek's, but at least one third longer. In his youth, we were told, his nose had been of ordinary length, but had been thus inordinately elongated by his bad habit of constantly tugging at it. When we children asked our uncle if this was true, we were always warmly rebuked for such disrespectful speech—and then our uncle would pull at his nose once more.

He wore clothes of an older style—short breeches, white silk stockings, buckled shoes, and in accordance with the ancient fashion, a longish pigtail, which used to bob from one shoulder to the other, cut all kinds of capers, and appeared to laugh at its master behind his back as the little fellow tripped through the streets.

Often when my good uncle sat lost in thought, or reading a newspaper, I was overcome by the sinful desire to steal up and take hold of his pigtail and tug at it as on a bell-rope; whereupon my uncle would grow very angry, and wring his hands in grief over the younger generation, which respected nothing and was restrained by neither human nor divine authority, and would surely end by profaning the Holy of Holies.

However, if the man's exterior was not calculated to inspire respect, the inner man, the soul of him, was all the more worthy of regard. He had the most honest and generous heart I have ever met upon this earth. The honesty of this man recalled the stern sense of honor to be found in the old Spanish drama—and his loyalty was like that of its heroes. He never had occasion to be the "physician of his honor"— and yet he was a "resolute prince," with the greatness of a knight, although he did not declaim in four-foot trochees, did not aspire to the palm of death, and wore a dull coat with tails instead of the splendid cloak of the knight.

He was by no means an ascetic enemy of the senses. He loved fairs, and the wine-shop of Rasia, the hostess, where he liked to eat fieldfares and juniper berries. But he would gladly and firmly sacrifice all the fieldfares in the world, with all the world's pleasures, when an idea was at stake which he knew to be true and good. And he would do so without pretense—yes, even shamefacedly, so that no one ever saw that beneath that droll exterior was hidden the soul of a martyr.

Judged by worldly standards, his life was a failure. Simon de Geldern had pursued the so-called humanistic studies, the *humaniora*, at the college of the Jesuits. When the death of his parents gave him the freedom to choose a career, he refused to do so, and renounced all practical studies at foreign universities, and chose instead to stay at home, in Düsseldorf, in "Noah's Ark"—as the little house which was left to him by his father was called—with its prettily carved and gaily painted representation of Noah's ark above the door.

A man of untiring industry, he gave himself up to all his learned hobbies and crotchets, to his bibliomania, and particularly to his passion of writing for political newspapers and obscure magazines. Parenthetically be it said that not only his writing but also his thinking cost him much effort.

This passion for authorship may have arisen from a desire to be of some public use. He took part in all the questions of the day, and became addicted to reading newspapers and pamphlets. His neighbors called him "Doctor," certainly not because he was learned, but because his father and brother had been physicians. The old women could not be dissuaded from believing that the son of the old doctor, who had so often cured them, had inherited his father's remedies; for when they were ill, they came running to him with vials of urine, and implored him to look at it and tell them what ailed them. When my poor uncle was thus disturbed in his studies, he grew angry, and cursed the old hags and sent them packing.

This uncle had great influence on my mental growth, and for this I can never be sufficiently grateful. No matter how different our points of view—however wretched his literary efforts may have been—they may have done much to arouse in me a desire to write.

My uncle wrote in a stiff, formal style, such as is taught in the Jesuit schools, where Latin is the principal subject of study. He could never warm to my way of expressing myself—which seemed to him too light, frivolous, and irreverent. But the zeal with which he recommended ways of improving my mind was of greatest benefit to me.

When I was yet a boy, he presented me with the finest and most costly works. He placed at my disposal his own library, which was rich in the classics and the most important tracts of the times, and he even allowed me to rummage in the trunks which were in the attic of Noah's ark, and which contained the old books and manuscripts of my late grandfather.

What secret joy leaped up in the boy's heart as he passed whole days in that attic—which was in fact only a huge garret! It was certainly no charming haunt; its sole inhabitant was an old Angora cat, which did not believe too strictly in cleanliness, and only rarely swept with her tail some of the dust and cobwebs from the ancient rubbish that was piled up there.

But my heart was young and in bloom—and the sun shone so brightly through the little dormer window, that everything seemed as if suffused by the light of fantasy, and even the old cat was transformed into an enchanted princess, freed once more from her brute form, and she could now reveal herself in her former beauty and glory, while the attic would certainly change into a magnificent palace—as always happens in fairy tales.

But the good old fairy tale times are gone. Cats remain cats; and the garret in "Noah's Ark" remained a dusty store-room, a hospital for incurable household goods, an almshouse for old furniture, in its last stages of decrepitude, and kept only for sentimental reasons and out of regard for the pious memories which are bound up with them.

੪୬ Simon de Geldern, the "Oriental"

THE BEST AND MOST PRECIOUS DISCOVERY in those dusty old chests was a notebook in the handwriting of my grandfather's brother, who was known as the "Chevalier," or the "Oriental," and about whom my old aunts used to tell many tales. This great-uncle, whose name was likewise Simon de Geldern, must have been a singular saint. He was nicknamed the "Oriental" because he had travelled widely in the East and always wore oriental clothes when he came back. He appears to have sojourned longest in the coastal towns of Morocco, where he acquired the armorer's craft from a Portuguese and did well by it. He made a pilgrimage to Jerusalem, where he was visited by an ecstatic vision while praying on Mount Moria. What did he see? He never told.

An independent tribe of Bedouins, who did not adhere to Islam but to some form of Mosaic faith, and had their quarters in one of the unknown oases of the North African desert chose him as their leader or sheik. This warlike little tribe feuded with all its neighbors and was the terror of all caravans. To speak plain European, my late great-uncle, the devout visionary of sacred Mount Moria, became a robber chieftain. In these beautiful surroundings he also came by that knowledge of horse-breeding and riding which aroused so much astonishment when he returned to the West.

At various courts where he stayed for some time, he shone as much by his personal beauty and dignity as by the splendor of his eastern dress, which cast a spell over all—especially the ladies. He impressed people most by his pretended secrets, and no one dared disparage the mighty necromancer to his exalted patrons. The spirits of intrigue feared the spirits of the Cabbala. Only his own arrogance could bring ruin upon him; and my old aunts used to shake their heads strangely and mysteriously when they muttered something about the "Oriental's" gallantry toward a very exalted lady—the discovery of which made it necessary for him to quit the court and the land in haste. He escaped death only through flight, after leaving behind all his belongings—and he owed his deliverance to his expert horsemanship.

After this adventure, he appears to have found a more secure, though also a more straitened, existence in England. So much I gather from a pamphlet of my uncle's which was printed in London, and which I came upon by chance when I climbed to the loftiest shelf in the library at Düsseldorf. It was a declamation in French verse entitled, "Moses on Horeb," and may have had something to do with the vision I mentioned above. But the preface was in English and bore a London date. The verse, like all French verse, was lukewarm rhymed gruel; but his English prose betrayed the dispirited, proud man who finds himself in distress. From this notebook I could not obtain much definite information; owing perhaps to his cautiousness, it was filled with Arabic, Syriac, and Coptic letters, among them an unusually large number of French quotations—and particularly this verse:

Où l'innocence périt, c'est un crime de vivre.[10]

HE WAS A DIFFICULT PUZZLE—THIS GREAT-UNCLE OF MINE. He lived one of those strange lives which were possible only at the beginning or in the middle of the eighteenth century. He was part visionary, and propagandized for cosmopolitan Utopias, which were designed to bring happiness to this world; part soldier of fortune, who is aware of his powers, and breaks down or vaults the barriers of a decaying social system. But all in all, he was a complete man.

His charlatanism cannot be denied—but it was of no common order. He was none of your ordinary impostors who draw peasants' teeth in the market-place—no, he forced open the doors of the palaces belonging to the great of the earth, and plucked out their strongest molars, as once Sir Huon of Bordeaux did to the Sultan of Babylon.

And what man of any consequence is not something of a charlatan? Worst of all are the charlatans of modesty, with their conceit of always doing things humbly! Whoever wishes to affect the crowd, must use some quackery. But the end justifies the means. Did not God himself, when proclaiming the Law on Mount Sinai, avail himself of lightning and thunder, although the Law itself was so perfect, so divine and good, that it could have dispensed with all addenda of resin and kettle-drums? But the Lord knew his audience, who stood openmouthed with their oxen and sheep at the foot of the mountain, and who were sure to be more forcibly impressed by physical sleight of hand than by all the miracles of eternal thought.

However that may be, this great-uncle occupied the boy's imagination to an extraordinary extent. Everything I heard about him impressed itself indelibly on my young mind, and I was so deeply preoccupied with his wanderings and his fortunes, that very often, in the middle of the day, I was overcome by an uncanny feeling, and it seemed to me that I myself was my deceased great-uncle and merely continuing an existence that had long since ceased.

At night my dreams were haunted by the same thought. My life at that time resembled a great newspaper, the upper half of which contained the events of the day—news and debates; while the lower half fantastically recorded the romantic past in a succession of dreams, like a series of *feuilletons*. In these dreams I identified myself completely with my great-uncle. It was horrible to feel that I was someone else and belonged to another age. There were regions I had never visited, and experiences I had never suspected—yet I wandered among them sure-footed and self-possessed.

Here I met men in strange, garishly colored dress—men with wild adventurous features, and I pressed their hands as if I had known them for a long time. I understood their strange, unfamiliar speech—I answered them, to my own amazement, in their own tongue—I gesticulated with a vehemence which was not mine, and said things utterly at odds with my customary thoughts.

This singular state of affairs lasted about a year.

❧ *My Paternal Grandfather*

MY FATHER WAS A VERY MONOSYLLABIC CHARACTER. He spoke very little. Once when I was a small boy—it was at the time when I spent my week-days at the Franciscan school and the Sabbath at home—I took the occasion to ask him about my grandfather. Half-laughing, half-vexed he said, "Your grandfather was a little Jew with a long beard."

The following day, when I came to class, where my schoolmates were already assembled, I hastened to announce the great news that my grandfather was a little Jew with a long beard.

Scarcely had I conveyed this piece of information, than it began flying from mouth to mouth, was repeated with all sorts of intonations, and accompanied by all sorts of animal noises. The boys jumped on desks and benches; tore down the multiplication tables from the wall, so that they clattered to the floor along with the ink-stands. What a laughing, bleating, grunting, barking and crowing pandemonium broke loose! And the constant refrain was that my grandfather was a little Jew with a long beard.

Our teacher heard the uproar, came rushing back in a fury, and asked who had started the turmoil. As invariably happens, everyone tried to excuse himself—but at the end of the interrogation it was proved that poor me had caused all the uproar, and I received a good thrashing for my offense.

These were the first blows I received on this earth. And on that occasion I reflected philosophically that the good Lord who created canings also made certain in his kind wisdom that he who administered them eventually grew tired—otherwise they could never be borne.

The cane with which I was thrashed was a yellow one; but the welts it left on my back were black and blue. I have never forgotten them.

Nor have I forgotten the name of the master who beat me so unmercifully. It was Father Dickerscheit. He was not long thereafter dismissed from the school, for reasons which I know, but will not tell.

ALONG WITH THE NAME OF THE MAN who administered my first beating, I always remembered the cause of it—the unhappy bit of genealogical information. And the after-effect of those early impressions has been so strong that whenever I hear of little Jews with long beards, a weird chill of recollection creeps up and down my spine. "A burned cat dreads the fire," says the proverb. It is obvious that I have not since then been inclined to inquire more closely about my suspect grandfather, or his pedigree, or to inform the big public about him—as I once did the little one.

ಶ್ My Father

I HAVE ALREADY TOLD YOU that my father's beauty had something effeminate about it. I do not mean to imply by this that he was something less than a man. That he was virile he proved in his youth—and I am the living witness thereof. I intend no slur. I have in mind only his physical appearance, which was not rigid and firm, but soft, round and tender. The contours of his face lacked decisiveness; they were somewhat indefinite. In his later years, he became stout; but even when he was young, he was not thin.

In this conjecture I am confirmed by a portrait which was lost in a fire in my mother's house, representing my father as a young man of eighteen or nineteen, in a red uniform, his hair powdered and provided with a bag-wig.

THE RED UNIFORM in which my father is represented in the portrait betokens his official capacity in Hanover. My father was in the retinue of Prince Ernest of Cumberland at the outbreak of the French Revolution, and accompanied him on his campaigns in Flanders and Brabant, in the capacity of quartermaster or commissary—or, as the French have it—*officier de bouche*.[11] The Prussians call it a "mealworm."

The young man's real office was that of favorite to the Prince, a Brummel *au petit pied*, but without the striped cravat—and in the end he suffered the fate of all such playthings of princely favor. To the very last my father was firmly convinced that the Prince, who later became King of Hanover, had not forgotten him; but he was hard put to it to explain how it was that the Prince never sent for him, or asked about him, especially since he could not be sure that his former favorite might not be living in reduced circumstances.

Of that campaign were begotten many of my father's dubious proclivities, from which my mother was only gradually able to wean him. For instance, he could be very easily induced to gamble for high stakes; and he was a patron of the dramatic arts or rather, of their priestesses; and he was passionately devoted to dogs and horses. When he came to Düsseldorf, where out of love for my mother he was setting up as a merchant, he brought with him twelve of the most beautiful horses. But at the express wish of his bride, he disposed of them; for she protested that such four-legged capital consumed too much fodder and brought in no profit at all.

It was harder for my mother to effect the dismissal of the stable-boy, a thick-set fellow, who was always lounging in the company of some stray scamp or other, and playing cards in the stable. He finally departed of his own free will with a gold repeater belonging to my father and a few other precious jewels.

When she was finally rid of this good-for-nothing, my mother also gave my father's hunting dogs their freedom—with the exception of one dog, called "Joli," though he was hideous to behold. He found favor in her eyes because he had nothing of the hunting-dog about him, but was a faithful and respectable bourgeois house-dog. He lived in my father's old coach in the empty stable, and when my father and he met they would always exchange significant looks. "Yes, Joli," my father would sigh; and Joli would wag his tail sadly.

I am sure the dog was a hypocrite. Once, when my father was in a bad mood, and his favorite protested with too much whining against some kicks, he admitted that the wretch was shamming. In the end, Joli became very mangy; and when he turned into a perambulating flea-barracks, he was drowned, and my father did not object. Man sacrifices his four-footed favorites as indifferently as princes sacrifice their two-footed ones.

From his days of campaigning also arose my father's boundless love of the military—or rather, his love of playing soldiers, and his delight in that gay, idle life, in which gold spangles and scarlet caps conceal the inner emptiness, and tipsy conceit struts about posing as valor.

BOUNDLESS LOVE OF LIFE was his dominant trait. He was pleasure-loving, gay, and full-blooded. His mind was a perpetual carnival. The dance music was never too noisy, and the violins were always in tune. Within him always dwelt the cheerfulness of the blue sky and fanfares of lightheartedness. He was carefree—always forgetful of the day that was gone and never giving a thought to the day that was to come.

This disposition was in strange contrast to the gravity of his stern and tranquil face, of his mien and every movement of his body. One who did not know him, and saw for the first time this serious, powdered head and the imposing mien, might well have taken him for one of the Seven Wise Men of ancient Greece. But closer acquaintance with him disclosed that he was neither a Thales, nor a Lampsacus,[12] deeply immersed in cosmogonic problems. True, his gravity was not something borrowed, but it did call to mind those old bas-reliefs in which a merry boy is depicted holding a tragic mask before his face.

Indeed, he was a great child, with a child-like naiveté, which dull virtuosos of the mind might easily take for simplicity, but which often betrayed, through some profound expression, an extraordinary intuition.

He would sense, with his mental feelers, what it took wise men a great deal of time to understand by reflection. He thought not so much with his head as with his heart, and he had the most lovable heart you can imagine. His smile, which often played around his lips, contrasted queerly but charmingly with this gravity, and was the sweet reflection of his good nature.

His voice, too, though masculine and resonant, had a child-like quality, I might almost say, a wood-note quality, like the call of the red-breast. When he spoke, it went straight to the heart, as if it did not need ears to be heard.

IN ALL THE WORLD there was no one I loved as much as him. He has been dead for over twenty-five years. I never thought that I would lose him; and even now I can scarcely believe that he is gone. It is so hard to convince oneself that people we love very much are really dead. But they are not dead; they live on within us and in our souls. There has scarcely been a night when I did not think of my father. When I wake up in the morning, it often seems to me as if I were hearing the sound of his voice, like the echo of a dream. And then I have the feeling that I must dress quickly, and hurry down to him where he is sitting in his large room—just as I used to do when I was a boy.

He was in the habit of rising very early, and applying himself to his affairs—winter and summer—and I would usually find him sitting at his writing table. Without looking up, he would reach out his hand to me to be kissed. Such a beautiful, sculptured, distinguished hand, which he would always wash in almond powder. I can still see it in front of me: every blue vein, criss-crossing this dazzling white, marble hand.—I seem to breathe the fragrance of the almonds—and my eyes fill with tears.

Sometimes there was even more than kissing of the hand. My father would take me between his knees and kiss my forehead. One morning he embraced me with unusual tenderness and said: "I dreamed fine things about you last night, and I am very well satisfied with you, my dear Harry." As he spoke these naive words, a smile played about his lips, as if to say: "No matter how naughty Harry may actually be, I shall always dream nice things about him, so that I may love him undisturbed."

ஃ I Saw Napoleon

WHEN I THINK OF THE GREAT EMPEROR, my memory grows green as summer and as golden. A long avenue of lime-trees in blossom rises up before me. On the leafy branches nightingales are singing. The waterfall ripples. In their round flower-beds the flowers dreamily wave their fair heads.

Between me and the flowers there was ever a strange communion. The painted tulips bowed to me with the condescending pride of a beggar; the sickly lilies nodded to me with melancholy tenderness; the wine-flushed roses laughed a welcome to me from afar; the night-violets sighed. I was not then acquainted with the myrtle and the laurel, for they had no lustrous blossoms with which to attract me. But I was most intimate with the mignonette (with whom I am no longer on good terms). I am speaking of the palace gardens at Düsseldorf, where I used often to lie on the grass and reverently listen to Monsieur Le Grand as he recounted the heroic exploits of the great Emperor, at the same time beating out the marches to which those deeds were performed, so that it seemed as if I myself were present there. I saw the march across the Simplon—the Emperor at the head and the grave grenadiers clambering up behind him, while the startled birds screamed and the glaciers thundered in the distance. I saw the Emperor on the bridge of Lodi, clasping the standard. I saw the Emperor in his gray cloak at Marengo. I saw the Emperor on horse-back at the battle of the Pyramids—nothing but powder-smoke and Mamelukes. I saw the Emperor at the battle of Austerlitz—whee! how the bullets whistled above the smooth ice! I saw, I heard the battle of Jena—dumb—dumb—dumb—I saw, I heard the battles of Eylau, Wagram— No! I could hardly stand it! Monsieur Le Grand beat the drum till my ear-drums almost burst.

BUT WHAT WERE MY FEELINGS when I saw him at last with my own eyes—with my own blessed eyes, the Emperor himself!—Hosannah! It was in the avenue of the same palace gardens at Düsseldorf. As I shouldered my way through the gaping crowd, I thought of battles and deeds which Monsieur Le Grand had been beating for me on the drum. My heart beat the grand march, and yet I thought at the same time of the police regulations which imposed a fine of five thalers on anyone who dared ride through the avenue. And the Emperor and his retinue rode right through the avenue; the shuddering trees bowed when he passed; the rays of the sun trembled fearfully as they peered through the green foliage; and in the blue sky above a golden star sailed into view. The Emperor wore his simple green uniform, and the little, history-making hat. He rode a white palfrey, which moved so calmly, so proudly, so surely, so magnificently!—Had I been the

Crown Prince of Prussia I would have envied that pony. Carelessly, loose in his saddle, the Emperor sat, one hand holding up the reins, and the other patting the horse's neck good-naturedly. It was a hand like sunlit-marble, a powerful hand, one of those two hands which had tamed the many-headed hydra of anarchy and had quelled the feuds of nations—and that very hand was now good-naturedly stroking the horse's neck. The face was also the same hue as we see in marble busts of the Greeks and Romans. The features were nobly proportioned as those of the ancients, and on the face was inscribed: "Thou shalt have no gods before me." A smile which warmed and calmed all hearts hovered about his lips, and yet everyone knew that those lips had only to whistle—*et la Prusse n'existait plus* [13]—those lips had but to whistle, and the tocsin of clericalism was sounded; those lips had but to whistle, and the whole Holy Roman Empire would dance. And those lips smiled and the eyes smiled, too. Eyes as clear as the heavens; eyes which could read men's hearts, which at a glance embraced everything in the world—while we see things only one by one, and only as painted shadows. The brow was not so clear; the genii of future battles were already brooding there; and at times a frown passed across it. These frowns were his creative thoughts— those great, seven-league-boot thoughts, with which the Emperor's mind invisibly bestrode the world—and I believe that each of these thoughts would have furnished a German writer with enough material to last him a lifetime.

The Emperor rode calmly down the avenue. No policeman barred his way. Behind him, on snorting chargers, ornate in gold and jewels, proudly rode his retinue. The drums were beaten; the trumpets sounded. Near me crazy Aloysius whirled round and round and cackled out the names of his generals. Close by, drunken Gumpertz bellowed, and the people shouted with a thousand voices, "Long live the Emperor!"

The Emperor is dead. On a desolate island in the Indian Ocean is his lonely grave, and he, for whom the earth was too narrow, rests peacefully beneath a hillock where five weeping willows droop their green tresses in sorrow and a pious rivulet ripples by with sad lament. There is no inscription on his tombstone. But Clio, with the unerring chisel of history, has written invisible words on it, which will re- sound through the centuries like spirit voices.

Britannia! Yours is the sea! But the sea has not water enough to wash away the stain bequeathed you on his death-bed by the dying giant. Not that windbag son of yours, Sir Hudson [14]—no, you yourself were the Sicilian desperado hired by perjured kings to avenge secretly on the man of the people what the people had once openly done to one of them. And he was your guest, and had seated himself by your hearth.—

To the end of time the French boys will sing and tell of the brutal hospitality of the "Bellerophon," and when these songs of scorn and tears are heard across the Channel, the cheeks of all honorable Britons will burn with shame. But a day will come when this song will be wafted across—and Britain will be no more! The proud nation will be humbled in the dust; the tombs in Westminster Abbey will lie in ruins, the royal dust which they enclose will be forgotten. And St. Helena will be the holy sepulchre to which the nations of the East and the West will make their pilgrimage in gaily decked caravels, and they will fortify their hearts with great memories of the deeds of their worldly savior, who suffered at the hand of Hudson Lowe, as is written in the gospels according to Las Casas, O'Meara, and Antommarchi.[15]

Strange! The three greatest adversaries of the Emperor have already met their horrible fate: Londonderry cut his own throat; Louis XVIII rotted away on the throne; and Professor Saalfeld—is still professor at Göttingen.

ૐ Josepha the Pale

INDEED, IT WAS NOT WITCHCRAFT which sometimes drove me to the woman from Goch. I kept up her acquaintance, and I may have been about sixteen when I began coming to her house more frequently than ever—drawn by a spell more potent than all her bombastic Latin philtres. She had a niece, also barely sixteen but looking somewhat older, because she had shot up so suddenly into a tall, slender young woman. As a result, she was very thin. She had that kind of narrow waist we note among the quadroons of the West Indies, and since she wore neither corset nor a dozen petticoats, her clothes clung to her body like the moist drapery of a statue. But no marble statue could vie with her in beauty. She was life itself, and revealed in every movement the rhythm of her body,—so to speak, the very music of her soul.

None of the daughters of Niobe had a face so nobly sculptured.[16] Its color, like that of her skin, was a changeable white. Her great, deep, dark eyes always looked as if they were propounding a riddle and calmly awaited the answer; while her mouth, with its narrow, high-arching lips and chalk-white, rather long teeth seemed to say, "You are too stupid. You'll never guess it."

Her hair was red, quite blood-red, and hung down in long tresses over her shoulders, so that she could bind it under her chin. Then it seemed to me as if her throat had been cut, and the blood was gushing in red streams.

Josepha—or Red "Sefchen," as the Goch woman's beautiful niece was called—had a voice which was not especially melodious; sometimes her vocal chords seemed muffled to the point of being voiceless; but suddenly, when overcome by passion, so resonant a tone broke forth, that I was profoundly moved, particularly because her voice was so much like mine.

At times, when I heard her speak, I was frightened, because I thought it was I who was speaking. Her songs reminded me of dreams in which I used to hear myself singing in the same fashion.

She knew many old folksongs, and may have awakened in me a taste for them. But there can be no doubt that she had a very great influence on the budding poet, so that my first poems in *Dream Pictures*, which I wrote not long after, have a grim and gloomy coloring—like the relationship which then cast its bloody shadow on my young life and thoughts.

Among the songs which Josepha sang to me, there was one she had learned from Zippel, who had often sung it to me when I was a child. I remember two stanzas and will give them here, particularly since I cannot find this poem in any of the existing collections of folksong.

Wicked Tragig is speaking:

> "Ottilie mine, Ottilie dear,
> You will not be the last, I fear,
> Speak, will you hang from yon high tree?
> Or will you swim in yon blue sea?
> Or will you kiss the naked sword,
> That has been given by the Lord?"

And Ottilie replies:

"I will not hang from yon high tree,
I will not swim in yon blue sea.
But I will kiss the naked sword,
That has been given by the Lord."

Once Red Sefchen sang the song to me, and when she came to the
end of this stanza, and I saw how deeply moved she was, I too was
overcome, so that I burst into tears and we fell into each other's arms,
and sobbed, and neither of us spoke for over an hour, while our tears
ran down, and we looked at each other as through a veil.

I begged Sefchen to write down the words for me, and she did—
not in ink, but in her own blood. I have lost that crimson autograph,
but the verses remained indelibly impressed in my memory.

Sefchen's father was the brother of the Goch woman's husband,
and also an executioner. When he died, though he was quite young,
the Goch woman took the infant to live with her. But when her husband died not long thereafter and she moved to Düsseldorf, she
transferred the child to her grandfather, who lived in Westphalia, and
was also an executioner. There in the "Freehouse"—as the executioner's dwelling was called—Sefchen stayed till she was fourteen, when
her grandfather died, and she was taken back by the Goch woman.

Because of her dishonorable descent, Sefchen lived a solitary life
until she grew to be a young woman. Even in her grandfather's house
she was cut off from all associations. Hence her shyness, the very
sensitive recoil at any strange contact, her mysterious reveries, combined with the most stubborn defiance, the most saucy wilfulness
and wildness. Strange! Even in her dreams—as she once admitted to
me—she lived not with human beings, but with animals. In the solitude of the executioner's home she busied herself only with the old
books belonging to her grandfather, who had taught her to read and
write. He was extremely taciturn. Sometimes he would be away for
several days with his assistants, and then the child was all alone in the
"Freehouse," which was close to the gallows, in a densely wooded
but deserted spot. At home there were only three old women, who
always wagged their old grey heads, and constantly kept the spinning wheels whirring, while they coughed, squabbled, and drank a
great deal of brandy.

Particularly on winter nights, when the wind shook the old oaks,
and the great fire in the hearth howled eerily, poor Sefchen ex-

perienced a weird feeling in that lonely house; for she was afraid
of thieves—not live but dead ones—those who had been executed,
but who had wrenched themselves free of the gallows and came
knocking at the low windows, begging to be allowed in to warm themselves. They had such pitiful, frozen faces! One could only frighten
them away by fetching the sword from the armory and threatening
them with it. Then they would vanish away like the whirlwind.

Sometimes they were lured not only by the fire in the hearth, but
by the desire to regain the fingers of which the executioner had robbed
them. If the door was not locked securely, they would even steal
the linen from the cupboards and the beds, for even in death they had
not lost their old thieving urge. One of the old crones, who came upon
one of these dead thieves in time, ran after him, seized a corner of the
sheet he was carrying off as it fluttered in the air, and wrenched his
loot from him at the very moment he reached the gallows and was
making his escape up the gallow-tree.

Only on such days as the grandfather was preparing for a grand
execution did his colleagues from neighboring parts come to visit him.
Then there was much cooking, roasting, carousing, and feasting, but
little talking, and no singing at all. They drank from silver goblets,
instead of the tankards with wooden lids which were served to the dishonorable "Freemaster" and his assistants at the inns they frequented,
while the other guests would drink from tankards with pewter lids.
(In many places it is the custom to smash the cup which the executioner's lips have touched. No one speaks to him. Everyone shuns
him. This ignominy extends even to his family—which is the reason
for intermarriage in executioners' families.)

One fine autumn day, Sefchen told me, when she was eight years
old, an unusual number of visitors came to her grandfather's house,
although no execution or other painful official duty was in sight.
There were more than a dozen visitors, almost all of them very ancient
little men, with iron-grey or bald little heads, and swords under their
long, red cloaks. They were wearing their most old-fashioned, Sunday clothes. They came—so they said—to a "meeting"—and the best
that kitchen and cellar could provide was placed before them at their
noonday meal.

These were the oldest executioners from the most remote regions,
and they had not seen one another for a long time. They shook hands
incessantly, spoke little, mostly in a mysterious sign language, and
amused themselves in their own fashion—*"moult tristement"* [17]—as

Froissart said of the banquet held by the English after the battle of Poitiers.

At nightfall the master of the house sent his helpers away, and bade the old housekeeper bring three dozen bottles of the best Rhine wine from the cellar, and put them on the stone table under the huge oaks which stood in a semicircle outside the house. He also commanded that the iron candlesticks be set up there for the pine torches, and finally, on some pretext or other, he sent the old woman and her two cronies out of the house. Even the openings between the boards of the dog-kennel were stopped up with a horse-blanket, and the dog was securely chained.

Red Sefchen was left alone in the house by her grandfather. She was ordered to wash the great silver goblet carved with figures of sea-gods and dolphins and shell-trumpets, and to place it on the stone table. And then with some constraint he told her to retire at once to her little chamber.

Sefchen washed the Neptune goblet obediently and put it on the stone table, along with the winebottles. But she did not go to bed. Driven by curiosity, she hid behind a bush close to the oaks, where she could hear little, but could observe clearly all that took place.

The strange men came walking solemnly, two by two—her grandfather at the head—and then sat down on high wooden blocks that formed a semi-circle around the stone table. The tapers were lit, and gruesomely lighted up their severe, stone-like faces. For some time they sat without uttering a word—or rather, only murmuring to themselves, perhaps praying. Then the grandfather filled the goblet with wine, and every man emptied it and passed it, after refilling, to his neighbor. After each draught, they shook hands gravely.

Finally Sefchen's grandfather rose to speak. She could hear little of what he said, and understood nothing; but he appeared to be dealing with very sad matters, for big teardrops fell from the old man's eyes, and the others too began to weep bitterly—which was a dreadful sight, for on other occasions the men looked as harsh and weather-beaten as the grey stone figures at church portals, and now tears flowed from their fixed, stony eyes, and they sobbed like children.

And the moon looked down sadly from its misty veil in the starless sky—so that the little eavesdropper's heart almost melted with sorrow. She was especially moved by the grief of one of the little old men, who wept more violently than the others, and cried so loudly that she could hear a few of the words quite distinctly: "Oh, God!

Oh, God! Our sorrow has lasted so long, that no human soul can bear it. Oh, God, You are unjust, yes, unjust!" His companions could calm him only with difficulty.

Finally the company rose from their seats, threw off their red cloaks, and with swords under their arms, marched, two by two, till they came to a tree, by which an iron spade stood ready. With it they quickly dug a deep pit. Sefchen's grandfather now stepped forward. He had not taken off his red cloak like the others, and from under it he produced a white package which was wrapped in a sheet, very narrow and somewhat longer than a Flemish ell. This he carefully placed in the open grave, and then he hastily filled it again.

Poor Sefchen could bear it no longer in her hiding place. At the sight of the secret burial, her hair stood on end. Mental anguish drove her from the spot. She rushed up to her chamber and hid under the bed-clothes, and fell asleep.

The next morning it all seemed like a dream. But when she saw the freshly turned-up earth behind the tree, she knew that what she had seen had actually taken place. For a long time she puzzled her head as to what had been buried in that spot: a child? an animal? a treasure? But she told no one of the nocturnal episode, and as the years passed, it gradually slipped from her mind. Not until five years later, when her grandfather had died and the Goch woman came to fetch her to Düsseldorf, did she open her heart to her aunt. But the latter was far from frightened or amazed by the strange story—on the contrary, she seemed highly pleased. She told Sefchen that it was neither child nor cat nor secret treasure that had been buried in that grave, but the old executioner's sword belonging to her grandfather, which had cut off the heads of hundreds of poor sinners. For it was the custom of executioners not to keep or use a sword, which had struck off a hundred heads—since it no longer resembled other swords, but in time acquired a mysterious consciousness and finally, like a human being, cried for the peace of the grave.

Furthermore, it is believed by many that such swords become cruel from having shed so much blood, and begin to thirst for more. Often, at midnight, one can hear them distinctly, rattling and rumbling violently in the closet. Indeed, some of them even become as knavish and malicious as any of us, and will deceive the unfortunate fellow who has them in his hand into wounding his own best friends. Thus, in the family of the Goch woman, one man had once struck down his own brother with such a sword.

However, the Goch woman admitted that the most extraordinary feats of magic could be performed with such a sword that had executed a hundred. And that very night she hastened to dig up the buried sword from under the designated tree and kept it forever after in her attic among the other magic inplements.

Once, when the Goch woman was away, I begged Sefchen to show me this strange curiosity. I did not have to press her; she went up to the attic and returned with a monstrous weapon, which despite her frail arms, she swung with energy, at the same time reciting this roguish threat:

> "Wilt thou kiss the naked sword,
> That has been given by the Lord?"

To which I replied in the same key: "I will not kiss the naked sword—I will kiss Red Sefchen!" Since she could not very well resist me for fear of wounding me with the fatal steel, she let me clasp her fine hips with ardor and kiss her stubborn lips. Yes, in spite of the executioner's sword, by which a hundred poor rascals had lost their heads, and in spite of the infamy of coming in contact with that dishonored brood, I kissed the executioner's beautiful daughter.

I kissed her not only from tender affection but also to spite society and all its dark prejudices. And at that moment there flared up in me the first of the two flames to which my life was forever after to be devoted: love of beautiful women and love of the French Revolution, that modern *furor francese*, which takes hold of me whenever I battle the mercenaries of the Middle Ages.

I will say no more of my love for Josepha. But this much: It was only a prelude to the great tragedies of my riper years. Thus Romeo mooned over Rosalind before he saw Juliet. In love, as in Roman Catholicism, there is a provisional purgatory, in which one gets used to being roasted before one goes to the real, eternal hell.

᎒ᴥ *Twenty Years Ago . . .*

TWENTY YEARS AGO, I WAS A YOUNG BOY. With what overflowing enthusiasm I would then have extolled the admirable Uhland![18] In those days I felt his excellence more keenly than today. He was closer to me in feeling and thinking. But so much has taken place since! What I then considered so magnificent—those chivalrous and Catholic themes, those knights who hacked and stabbed at one another in noble tourneys, those gentle squires and chaste ladies, those Northland heroes and minnesingers, those monks and nuns, those ancestral vaults with ominous horrors, those wan feelings of renunciation, with knells of tolling bells, and endless wailing—how deeply repugnant all this became to me later! Yes, once everything was different. How often in those days did I sit amid the ruins of the old castle of Düsseldorf on the Rhine, declaiming the loveliest of Uhland's songs,

> "Once the handsome shepherd lad went
> Close to the royal palace gate;
> The maid looked from the battlement,
> And her longing was great.

> "She called to him with gentle word,
> 'Oh, could I but come down to thee,
> How white the lambkins in your herd,
> How red the flowers I see.'

> "The youth called up to her and said:
> 'Oh, couldst thou but come down to me,
> Thy cheeks like full-blown roses red
> Thy arms so white to see.'

> "And every morning passing by
> With silent pain and secret fear,
> He saw far on the castle high
> His dearest love appear.

> "And up to her he gently sang,
> 'Good morning princess fair:'
> Her gentle voice in answer rang,
> 'Many thanks, my shepherd dear.'

> "The winter fled, spring came at last,
> Bright flowers bloomed as before,
> The shepherd by the castle passed,
> But she was seen no more.

> "With mournful voice aloud he cried,
> 'Good morning, princess fair.'

A ghost-like voice from far replied:
'Farewell, my shepherd dear.' "

When I sat among the ruins of that old castle and declaimed this ballad, I sometimes heard the nixens in the Rhine, which runs by at that point, mocking my words, and I heard a sighing and moaning from the waters, mingled with comic pathos:

"A ghost-like voice from far replied:
'Farewell, my shepherd dear.' "

I did not allow these railleries of the water-nymphs to disturb me, even when they tittered ironically at the most beautiful passages in Uhland's poems. I modestly thought they were giggling at me, especially in the twilight, and I declaimed with a somewhat raised voice, to drown out the mysterious terror which the ancient ruins of the castle inspired in me. For there is a legend that at nightfall a headless lady haunts the spot. Often I thought I heard the rustling of her silken train, and my heart beat faster. . . . That was the time and place that I was inspired by the *Poems of Ludwig Uhland*.

Now I have the same volume in my hands once more; but twenty years have since flown by, and in that time I have heard and seen much—very much, indeed,—and I no longer believe in headless beings, and the old ghosts move me no more. The house in which I now sit and read is in the Boulevard Montmartre, and here the wildest storms of the times rage; and the loudest voices of modern history roar. There is laughter, and growling, and beating of the drum. The National Guard sweeps by in double-time, and everyone speaks French.

Is this the place in which to read Uhland's poems? Three times I have recited the conclusion of the above poem, but I no longer feel that nameless woe which once took hold of me when the king's daughter died, and the handsome shepherd lad cried up to her so mournfully:

"Good morning, princess fair.
A ghost-like voice from far replied:
'Farewell, my shepherd dear!' "

Perhaps I have grown cold to these poems ever since I discovered the existence of a love much more painful than that which is suffered for a beloved never possessed, or lost by death. In fact, there is much greater anguish when the beloved reposes continuously in our arms, yet ruins our days and nights by incessant bickering and silly caprice, so that we drive from our heart what we love most, and accompany the accursed-beloved to the stage coach, to see her off:

"Farewell, my princess fair."

Yes, more painful than losing someone at the hands of death is losing someone at the hands of life. For instance, when the adored one turns away from us in some mad access of frivolity, when she insists on going to a ball to which no decent man can take her, and at which, dressed shamelessly, and with hair done up, she throws herself into the arms of the first blackguard who comes along, and turns her back on us. . . .

"Farewell, my shepherd dear."

Perhaps Uhland had no better luck than we. His mood too must have changed since that time. With a few trifling exceptions, he has brought no new poems to the market. I cannot believe that this admirable poetic talent was so scantily endowed by nature as to show only one spring-tide. No. I explain Uhland's silence by the contradiction between the inclinations of his muse and the exigencies of his political position. The elegiac poet, who knew how to sing of the Catholic-feudal past in such beautiful ballads and romances, this Ossian [19] of the Middle Ages, subsequently became a zealous protagonist of popular rights and freedom of thought in the Württemberg Chamber of Deputies. That this democratic and Protestant sentiment of his is genuine, Uhland has proved by the great personal sacrifices he has made for its sake. And as he once won the poet's laurel, so now he has gained the oak wreath of civic virtue. It is because he has been so honorable toward the present, that he can no longer sing the songs of the past with his old-time inspiration. For his Pegasus was a knightly charger, who gladly trotted back into the past; but became unmanageable when turned in the direction of the present. Honest Uhland smiled, dismounted, calmly unsaddled him, and led the wayward horse back into the stable. There he is, to this day, and like his comrade, the horse Bayard,[20] he has all possible virtues, and only one defect—he is dead.

ৡ To Christian Sethe

Hamburg, October 27, 1816

To Studioso Christian Sethe in Düsseldorf.[21] She loves me *not.* You must utter that *last* word softly, very softly. In the first of these little words there is eternal heaven, but in the last only eternal hell. If you could only see your friend's face, so pale and distraught and mad, your justifiable anger at my long silence would soon vanish. It would be best if you could look into my inner soul—then you would come to love me once more. In fact, be sure, dear Christian, that every one of my thoughts is actually a letter addressed to you, at least in the end it turns into one; only recently I scrawled a yard-long, boring letter, in which amid sighs, I unfolded my inner self. from Leda's egg to the destruction of Troy. But I wisely destroyed it since it might fall into strange hands and ruin me. You can't help me anyway.

Let me tell you a little story. You know, Christian, that from the first moment I saw you, I was irresistibly drawn to you, and without being able to account for it myself, you became infinitely dear and precious to me. I think I spoke to you about this some time ago. How often I observed something in your features and particularly in your eyes that incomprehensibly drew me and repelled me at the same time, so that I seemed at once to see in them the most affectionate kindness as well as bitter cold and revolting disdain. And behold, this very enigmatic something I also found in Mollie's look. And this confuses me. For even though I have incontrovertible proof that I am no less dear to her—proof which even Rector Schallmeyer would accept as thoroughly logical and worthy of being placed at the very head of his system—yet my poor loving heart refuses to be convinced—and is always saying: "What do I care about your old logic? I have my own." . . .

I have seen her again.

> "My soul may belong to the devil,
> And my body to the hangman,
> But only I will choose
> My lady fair."

Ah, do you not shudder, Christian? Shudder, for I too am shudder-ing. Burn this letter. May God be gracious to my poor soul! It is not I who wrote these words. It is a pale, wan man who sat in a chair and wrote them. And merely because it was midnight. My God! Madness cannot be guilty of sins. And you, don't you blow too hard, for I have just built me a beautiful house of cards, and right on the very top, I stand and hold her, *her* in my arms. See Christian, only *your* friend would have dared raise his eyes to the all highest (by this token you know him); and of course, it seems that this will also prove his undoing. But you can scarcely imagine how wonderful and de-lightful my undoing seems to me. My motto was ever: *"Aut Caesar, aut nihil."* All, or nothing.

I am a mad chess player. Even with my first move, I've lost the queen, and yet I play and play—for the queen. Shall I go on playing?

> *"Quand on a tout perdu et qu'on n'a plus d'espoir*
> *La vie est un opprobre et la mort un devoir."* [22]

Silence, accursed, blasphemous Frenchman, with your refined des-pair! Do you not know German love? It stands firm and bold upon two unshakable pillars—manly dignity and faith. Only keep me, dear God, under Thy protecting wing from the overwhelming dark power of the moment. To be far from her, for years to suffer burning long-ing—that is hellish agony, and makes me cry out in infernal pain. But to be near her, and yet to languish for weeks fruitlessly for one of her blessed glances—that, oh that, Christian, can tempt even the purest and most devout heart into wild, insane godlessness. . . .

It hurts to think how she spurned my beautiful songs, how she scorned and despised them, even though they were written for her. All in all, her behavior toward me was quite shameful. For all that, believe me, the Muse is dearer to me than ever before. She has be-come my friend and comforter, so mysteriously sweet, and dearly beloved. How well I now understand Goethe's word in *Tasso:*

> "Now all is gone!—But one thing still remains
> Tears, scalding tears, kind Nature has bestowed,
> The cry of anguish, when a man at length
> Can bear no more—Yes, and to me besides
>   She leaves in sorrow melody and speech
> To utter forth the feelings of my woe;

> Though in their mortal anguish men are dumb,
> To me a god has given to tell my grief."

I write much, for I have plenty of time, and the vast commercial speculations don't take up many of my hours. I don't know whether the poems I write now are better than those which I used to write. Only I am sure that they are much gentler and sweeter, like sorrow dipped in honey. I am planning to publish them soon, though it may take a few months. But there is one drawback: they are mostly lovesongs. And since I am a business man, they may do me much harm. You can hardly imagine the atmosphere that exists here. But I can be frank with you.

Aside from the fact that in this hucksters' town there isn't even the slightest feeling for poetry—of course, there are wedding, funeral, and baptismal *carmina*, specially commissioned and paid for in cash—there is also very great tension between the "baptized" and the "unbaptized" Jews. (I call all citizens of Hamburg Jews, and those I wish to differentiate from the circumcised and whom I call "baptized," are commonly known as Christians.) Under these circumstances you can readily foresee that Christian love will not leave the lovesongs of a Jew unmolested. Good advice, which I badly need, comes very dear. Furthermore, I don't know how one goes about preparing a book for publication. That's where you, Christian, can be very helpful, because you understand such matters much better than I.

I live here all alone, as you can gather from these remarks. My uncle lives in the country. There everything is pretty, decked-out, and lick-spittle; and the free and uninhibited deportment of a poet frequently jars upon their sense of etiquette. Diplomatic cocks-of-the-walk, millionaires, sage senators, etc., etc., are not my sort of people. The god-like, magnificent, and Homeric Blücher was here not long ago, and I had the good fortune of dining with him at my uncle's. A chap like him makes it all worth while.

The nephew of the great (??) Heine is everywhere popular and well received. Pretty girls ogle him, their bosom-kerchiefs rise and fall, and their mothers calculate. . . . But don't be alarmed. There is no one here for me, but myself. And who this strange fellow may be, Christian knows better than I . . .

As regards religious matter, I'll have remarkable things to tell you soon. Has Heine gone mad? you will exclaim. But I *must* have a Madonna. Will the heavenly one replace the earthly? I wish to drown my senses. Only in the infinite depths of the mystical can I rid myself of my interminable pain. How pitiful mere knowledge now seems to me in her beggars' weeds! What once seemed crystal clear is empty and void. "Be ye like unto children." For a long time I thought I understood this statement, fool that I was! *Children believe.*

➢ *I Meet August Wilhelm Schlegel* [23]

How DELIGHTED AND ASTONISHED I WAS, when as a very young man, in the year 1819, I studied at the University of Bonn, and there had the honor of seeing that poetic genius, August Wilhelm Schlegel, face to face. He was, with the exception of Napoleon, the first great man it had been my fortune to behold, and I shall never forget that sublime sight. To this very day I feel the sacred tremor which shook my soul when I stood before his desk and heard him speak. In those days I wore the coarse white student coat, the scarlet cap, long blond hair, but no gloves. But Herr A. W. Schlegel wore kid gloves, and was dressed in the latest Paris fashion. He exhaled the scent of fashionable society and *eau de mille fleurs*—he was neatness and elegance personified, and when he spoke of the Lord Chancellor of England, he always added "my friend." At his side stood his valet, dressed in the most complete baronial livery of the house of Schlegel, and trimmed the tapers in the silver candelabra which stood alongside a glass of sugar-water on the lectern in front of this wondrous man. Footmen in livery! Wax tapers! Silver candelabra! "My friend," the Lord Chancellor of England! Kid gloves! Sugar-water! What unheard-of things in the lecture room of a German professor! This magnificence dazzled all of us young people not a little—and especially me—and I composed three odes in honor of Herr Schlegel, all beginning,

"Oh, thou—who—," etc.

But only in verse would I have presumed to address the distinguished man in so familiar a style. His external appearance was not unimposing. A few silver hairs shone on his small head, and his figure was so slender, wasted, and transparent, that he seemed to be all spirit—and almost a symbol of spiritualism.

২ৎ *To F. A. Brockhaus*

[Göttingen, November 7, 1820]

ENCLOSED YOU WILL FIND A MANUSCRIPT, entitled *Dreams and Songs* —which I am submitting for publication. I know that at this moment poetry is not in great public demand, and for that reason not much sought after by publishers. Hence, I turn to you, Herr Brockhaus, because I am aware that as a publisher you are interested in poetry for its own sake, and you have sought to further what is good and unpretentious in our literature, as well as to deflate swaggering conceit— to the joy of the whole world.

Following the example of several of my friends, I know I can leave the matter of remuneration to a man like you. I would only add that I am much less concerned about this, than about the quality of paper and type, for which your publications have always been noted.

I would like to ask you personally to read the manuscript. Knowing your fine feeling for poetry, I am sure that you will find the first portion of my book decidedly original, which is something these days, and what even the most severe critics allow me, especially my Master A. W. von Schlegel. He took my poems apart last winter and summer in Bonn, read them through several times, criticized them, pruned them, set off to better advantage some of their beauties, and, thank God! on the whole praised them.

Since unfortunate circumstances force me to suppress every poem which may be susceptible of political interpretation and to restrict myself only to the amatory pieces, the volume is obviously modest. With the exception of six poems, which were published four years ago in the Hamburg *Wächter*, all the rest are new, and they will afford sufficient evidence of my views on the new poetry, which I have compressed in the enclosed essay.

Please let me know as soon as you can whether you intend using this manuscript. If not, please return it to me by post at the enclosed address.

Respectfully,
H. Heine

My address is, Candidate of Law, H. Heine, c/o Dr. Wyneker, Göttingen.

៛ To Goethe

[Berlin, December 29, 1821]

THERE ARE A HUNDRED REASONS why I should send Your Excellency my poems. I will name only one: I love you. That is reason enough. My versifying, I know, as yet has little merit. Only here and there it shows that I may be able to do something in the future. I was long perplexed as to the nature of poetry. People told me: "Ask Schlegel." He said, "Read Goethe." That I have done faithfully, and if I ever amount to something, I know whom I owe it to.

I kiss your sacred hand, which has shown me and the whole German people the way to heaven, and remain

Your Excellency's
Most obedient and humble
H. Heine
Law Student

៛ To Christian Sethe

Berlin, April 14, 1822

DEAR CHRISTIAN: . . . I am now in a very peculiar mood, and this may explain all. Everything that is German is odious to me. And you unfortunately are German. Everything German affects me like an emetic. German speech splits my eardrums. At times my own poems nauseate me, when I see that they are written in German. Even the writing of these notes makes me retch, because German script irritates my nerves. *Je n'aurais jamais cru que ces bêtes qu'on nomme allemands, soient une race si ennuyante et malicieuse en même temps. Aussitôt que ma santé sera rétablie, je quitterai l'Allemagne, je passerai en Arabie, j'y mènerai une vie pastorale, je serai homme dans toute l'étendue du terme, je vivrai parmi des chameaux qui ne sont pas étudiants, je ferai des vers arabes, beaux comme le Morlaccat, enfin je serai assis sur le rocher sacré, où Mödschuun a soupiré après Leila.*[24]

Oh, Christian, if you only knew how my soul yearns for peace, and yet is torn day after day. I no longer sleep at night. In my dreams I see my so-called friends, hissing into each others' ears their little tales and gossip, which trickle into my brain like molten lead. During the day I am pursued by constant distrust; everywhere I hear my name, followed by derisive laughter. If you wish to poison me, then show me at this moment the faces of Klein, Simons, Bölling, Stucker, Plücker, and my fellow-students and compatriots of Bonn. This miserable rabble has done its share in poisoning the air of Berlin for me. And you, too, Christian, I owe plenty. Christian, oh, Christian! But do not think that I am angry with you, or that some particular incident accounts for the tone of this note. . . .

Berlin, January 21, 1823

DEAR CHRISTIAN: Actually I should not be writing you at all, for I should have to write you everything. Aside from that, you know pretty well how I live and in what mood I find myself. You are no longer here. That is the main theme; all else is gloss.

Sick, alone, persecuted, unable to enjoy life—that's how I live here. Nowadays I write practically nothing. I require shower-baths. I have almost no friends. A pack of scoundrels have been trying in all possible ways to destroy me, and have allied themselves with all my old would-be friends, etc. My plays will certainly appear within six to eight weeks. Dümler will probably publish them. By the next mail, I shall send you my essay on Poland, which I wrote for Breza, while under the waters of the shower. Professor Gubitz with his would-be wit has most disgracefully altered it, and the censor has thoroughly maltreated it. This essay has made me odious to the Barons and the Dukes. Even in higher places my name has already been besmirched. . . .

ह To Moritz Embden

Berlin, February 2, 1823

DEAR EMBDEN: Your letter of the 23rd last made me very happy. I congratulate you on your engagement to my sister. Although the news moved me very deeply, certainly much more deeply than people believe, it did not seem to me a "strange trick of fortune." It appeared rather as something that I had known for a long time—for many years—but had gradually forgotten amid the internal and external tempests of my life.

I hope that you and my sister will make a very happy pair, since Lottchen is capable of appreciating your character, and you hers, while you do not, like our perverted *beau monde*, set undue value upon some outstanding merit in woman, such as intelligence or feeling or appearance, but understand instead that true culture consists in the harmonious balance of all mental powers, and true amiability in the harmony of soul and body. My Lottchen is all music, rhythm and harmony. A brother may be pardoned such expressions in the presence of the bridegroom.

The political portion of your letter pleased me greatly. It is good to know that the future husband of my sister is no revolutionary. I always find it quite natural that the man who lives in comfort and is a happy bridegroom should not desire to overthrow the *status quo*, and should be greatly concerned for his own and Europe's tranquillity. In my case, things are different. I experience a strange sort of feeling when I chance to read in the newspapers that people freeze to death in the streets of London, and that others are starving in the streets of Naples. Although I am a radical in England, and a Carbonari in Italy, I do not belong with the demagogues in Germany, for the simple reason that in the event of their victory a couple of thousand Jewish heads—and those the very best—would roll.

Though our views concerning the events of the day differ so sharply or are even opposed, I am nevertheless sure that this will in no way affect our friendship now that we are related by marriage, a friendship which even at this distance (for a profound discontent will always keep me far from Hamburg) will often cheer, instruct and calm me by its warm sympathy, understanding, instruction, and affectionate encouragement toward one who lives in despondency, error, and in a state of war.

H. Heine

Address: H. H. Stud. Juris from Düsseldorf, in Berlin.

২৺ *To Immanuel Wohlwill*

Berlin, April 7, 1823

To WOLF, NAMED WOHLWILL: [25] . . . Perhaps I am doing the good city of Hamburg an injustice. The mood which came over me when I lived there for a time was not inspired to make me an impartial judge. My inner life was nothing but brooding and immersion in the gloomy pits of a dream world, only occasionally lighted up by fantastic lightning flashes. My outward life was mad, dissipated, cynical, repulsive. In short, I made the latter as different as possible from my life within, lest I be overwhelmed and destroyed by it. Yes, *amice*, it was a stroke of good luck that I emerged from the halls of philosophy into the arena of worldly action, and could begin building my own life philosophically and looking at it objectively, even though I lacked that loftier calm and discretion which are required for a clear view of life's drama. I don't know if you understand me. But should you some day read my memoirs and find in them a description of a crowd of Hamburg citizens, of whom I love a few, hate more, and despise most, you will understand me better.

Suffice it now if I answer a few of your questions and tell you why I cannot come to Hamburg this spring, as you ask, although I am only a few miles away. In four weeks' time I shall be leaving for Lüneburg, where my family lives. I shall stay there for six weeks, and then go to the Rhine, and if possible, to Paris. My uncle has enabled me to study for two more years, so that it won't be necessary for me to seek a professorship in Sarmatia, as I once planned. I imagine things will have changed so much, that I'll have no difficulties in establishing myself in the Rhineland. If not, I'll settle in France. I write French, and I'll embark upon a diplomatic career. The important thing is to restore my health—without which all plans are silly. May God grant me health! The rest I'll take care of myself. My physician is hopeful that a trip, particularly one on foot, will restore me. . . .

I've stopped the shower-baths, since they didn't help much and were terribly expensive. In addition, I must refrain from mental exertions. This winter all I've done is study the non-Semitic portions of Asia and read portions of Schelling and Hegel, rummage through chronicles, and regale myself with the pure beauty breathed by the Greek spirit. Old Wolf calls the latter the *"sempiterna solatia generis humani."* [26] I was not fit to mingle in society. I wrote little. My historical studies were worth even less; and least of all my *History of Medieval German Public Law*. The latter was almost ready for the press last summer, but the many ideas which I derived from my study of Asia, as well as the manner in which Gans treats the right of succession, and above all, the philosophical hints I received from Moser induced me to throw the greater part of my book into the fire, and to postpone the whole until I get to Paris where I'll write all of it in

French. It is very generous of you to tell me how much you liked my essay on Poland. From all sides I have received great praise for my keen understanding of Poland, but I myself cannot agree with it. Last winter I was too miserable—and I still am—to be able to produce something worth while. This essay has stirred up the entire Grand Duchy of Posen, and the comments—i. e., the abuse—in the Posen newspapers run to three times the length of my essay, and come particularly from the Germans there who cannot forgive me for depicting them so faithfully or for having raised the Jews to Poland's third estate. . . .

My poems are still causing a stir in Westphalia and in the Rhineland, and I hear many nice things about them. But how could you dignify the smear in the *Leipziger Literaturzeitung* by even mentioning it? It's the most shallow and insignificant thing that's been said about me. In a few days, I'll send you my *Tragedies.* I've dedicated them to my uncle Solomon Heine. Have you seen him? He is one of the people I esteem most. He is noble and has innate strength. You know that I value the latter above everything else. Have you seen my sister there? She is a charming girl. Do you associate much with women? Take care. The women of Hamburg are pretty. But that's beside the point. You are a quiet, decent, contented soul; and if you glow—it's for humanity's sake. With me it's different. In addition, you are lucky in being very moral. You reflect and make ethical observations and are contented and honest and good; and because you're such a good fellow, I've written you this very long letter.

৯ *To Moritz Embden*

Berlin, May 3, 1823

DEAR EMBDEN: I have your letter of April 28, and hasten to comply with your wish to see my *Tragedies.* I enclose a copy as a token of my regard. May the book meet with your approval. I trust you will see the ethical principles expressed in it. Here you will read how human beings as well as races go down to their doom that is decreed by a higher necessity and designed by Providence for some great end. The true poet does not provide the history of his time, but of all times. Hence a true poem always reflects all contemporary periods.

I fully agree with what you say about the Jews. I am likewise indifferent in religious matters, and my attachment to Judaism stems solely from my deep antipathy to Christianity. Yes, I am a contemner of all positive religions, and yet I will at some future time probably accept the crassest Rabbinical doctrines, merely because I consider them a time-tested antidote.

In a few days I shall go to Lüneburg. But at this moment I am very *malade*, and I am writing these lines in horrible pain.

᎒ᴥ *To Moses Moser*

Lüneburg, May . . . 1823

DEAR MOSER: [27] I arrived in Lupteen on Tuesday evening, after I had travelled and been shaken up Monday night and all of the following day, and vexed by the boring chatter of my travelling companions. I gave free rein to my fancies, and surrendered myself to a great deal of feeling. And I also thought of you. The last of these topics occupied me most. In fact, almost so much that I became sentimental, angry at myself, and would have said many foolish things to you if I had you there in person. If on Monday and Tuesday you experienced all sorts of queer feelings, then I can ascribe it to nothing but sympathetic *rapport*. The next time I am surprised by good thoughts or am suddenly struck by some Hegelian idea, I shall explain it in the same way.

In Lupteen I took a coach and arrived home on Wednesday afternoon at five. You see, I had slept in Lupteen the previous night, and there I was tormented by the most frightful dreams. I saw a throng of people who jeered at me, even the little ones, and in a rage I ran to you, my good Moser, and you opened your friendly arms and you comforted me, and told me not to pay any attention to them, since I was only an Idea; and to prove it, you seized Hegel's *Logic* and showed me an obscure passage there. And then Gans knocked on the window.[28] But I ran like a madman all around the room, and cried, "I am no Idea. I know nothing of an Idea. I never had an Idea in all my life." It was a horrible dream, as I recall it. Gans yelled even louder. And on his shoulder sat little Marcus,[29] shouting in his queer, husky voice all the citations and smiling in such a frightfully friendly way that I awoke in a panic.

I shall spare you the other horrible dream. How the Tr . . . Doctor

Oppert drove up to my house in his great-coach, and came into my room, decked out in his orders and his white silk hose, and confidentially told me that he was an educated man. I shall skip all this tasteless stuff, and merely tell you that I found my parents in good health. . . .

While I was writing this letter, I received your small trunk and your dear note of May 20. Truly, you are the man in Israel who feels most beautifully! I can describe the beautiful feelings of other people only passably. Your feelings are heavy gold bars; mine are flimsy paper currency. The latter gets its value from the confidence people have in it; but paper is only paper, even though the banker may exchange it; and gold is always gold, even though it lie in some corner as a dull clod.

Have you observed from the above image that I am a Jewish poet? Why should I feel embarrassed? We're among friends, and I love to speak in national figures of speech. When some day Ganstown [80] is built and a happier generation blesses the Lulef [81] on the banks of the Mississippi, and crunches Matzos, and a new Jewish literature blooms, then will our present commercial stock-exchange speech become poetical, and a poetical great-grandson of little Marcus, wrapped in Talles and Tefillim, will chant before the entire Ganstown Kille: "They sat by the waters of the Spree, and they counted their treasury notes. And their enemies came and said: 'Give us London bills—the exchange is high.'"

But enough of this self-mockery. . . .

Lüneburg, June 18, 1823

. . . I LIVE HERE IN COMPLETE SOLITUDE. I see no one, for my parents have withdrawn from all society. The Jews here are, as everywhere else, insufferable usurers and scoundrels. The Christian middle classes are distasteful, and animated by a singular hatred. The upper classes are even worse. Our little dog is sniffed at and abused in a special way by the other dogs in the street. Christian dogs harbor open animus against Jewish dogs. . . .

. . . I am strongly tempted to express the great *Judenschmerz* [82] (as Börne calls it) in my magazine article. I'll do this as soon as my head permits. It is frightfully unkind of our dear Lord to torment me with these pains. In fact, it is even poor diplomacy on the part of the Old Gentleman, since he knows how much I can do for him. Perhaps the old Baron of Mt. Sinai and Autocrat of Judea has also become enlightened, has cast off national sentiment and given up his claims and adherents in favor of some vague cosmopolitanism? I'm afraid the Old Gentleman has lost his head, and the *petit juif d'Amsterdam* may with some reason whisper in his ear: "*Entre nous, Monsieur, vous n'existez pas.*" And we? Do we exist? For heaven's sake, never again say that I am only an Idea. You'll drive me raving mad. So far as I'm concerned you can all turn into Ideas. But leave me alone. Just because old Friedländer and Gans and you have turned into Ideas, you want to seduce me too, and turn me into an Idea. . . .

Lüneburg, September 27, 1823

DEAR MOSER: . . . Meanwhile my domestic and financial affairs are in the worst possible state. You call my conduct toward my Uncle unwise. But you do me an injustice. I don't see why I shouldn't maintain my self-respect before my Uncle, as I do before everyone else. You know that I'm no delicate, tender youth, who blushes whenever he has to borrow money, and stammers when he asks his best friend for help. I'm sure I don't have to tell you this. You yourself have had occasion to learn how thick my skin is. But I am not in the habit of using friends or patrons to intercede for me with my Uncle to extort money from him, though he has many millions, and doesn't readily part with a penny. It was a disagreeable job merely to assert my claim to the sum he promised for 1824, and I am vexed to have to write about it again. I want to thank you for your friendly efforts in this regard. I have come to terms with my Uncle. I shall take from him only 100 *louis d'or* for my studies, from January 1824 to 1825, on which I have counted, and I assured him that so far as I was concerned, I would never again trouble him for more.

For such complaisance, my Uncle, at whose country-home in Hamburg I spent many days, has rewarded me by treating me with respectful attention and graciousness. But in the last analysis, I'm a man who can't act differently, and whom no monetary considerations will move to part with his self-respect. So you see, despite my severe headaches, I am continuing my law studies, which will eventually assure me of bread. As you may well imagine, my baptism plays a part in this. No member of my family is opposed to it except me. And this *Me* is a very head-strong character. From my way of thinking you can gather that baptism is a matter of indifference to me. I do not regard it as symbolically very important, and under the circumstances and in the way in which it is being carried out, it will likewise have little significance for others. However, as for me, it may mean that I shall be able to devote myself more fervently to the defense of the rights of my unfortunate co-religionists. And yet I think it beneath my dignity and honor to be baptized merely to obtain a post in dear old Prussia! I really don't know what to do under these wretched circumstances. From sheer spite I'll turn Catholic, and then I'll hang myself. But enough of this horrible subject. We'll leave further discussion till I see you again in a few months.

We are living in sad times. Scoundrels have become our "best" people; and our best people are forced to become scoundrels. I well understand the words of the Psalmist: "Lord, give us this day our daily bread, lest we blaspheme Thy name . . ."

. . . I live here with my parents and have no expenses. It is an unfortunate thing that my whole person is ruled by the budget. Lack of money or excess of it has not the slightest effect on my principles, but all the more on my actions. Yes, great Moser, H. Heine is very small indeed. In fact, little Marcus is bigger than I. This is no joke, but a most serious, bitter-serious matter. I cannot say this too often, lest you apply the criterion of your own great spirit to my actions. My spirit is as elastic as rubber. Often it stretches to infinity; then again it shrinks to nothing. But I have a soul, none the less. *I am positive I have a soul*, as well as Sterne. Let that suffice. . . .

Lüneburg, November 5 (or 6), 1823

DEAR MOSER: I write practically nothing. Headaches and the study of law occupy me exclusively. I have a small number of poems ready, which won't be printed for some time. . . .

In the "Romance" which I sent you,[38] you must change the second verse in the fifth stanza. Insert, "*Wie er sang die Liebesworte*". There is an Abraham of Saragossa, but I found Israel more expressive. The whole subject of the "Romance" is actually a scene from my own life, except that the zoological garden was transformed into the Garden of the Alcaldes, the baroness into a señora, and I myself into St. George or even Apollo. This is only the first portion of a trilogy, the second of which relates how the hero is spurned by his own son, who does not recognize him; and the third shows how the son, now a Dominican, puts his own brethren to the torture. . . .

I have urgent reasons for asking you not to allow this poem to fall into the hands of Christians. . . .

ટ્ર To Rudolph Christiani

Accursed Nest, Göttingen, March 7, 1824

DEAR CHRISTIANI: . . . The outlook for my health is again poor. It is possible that at night I think too much about the Venus de' Medici and about Councillor Bauer's maid. This summer I shall attend Dr. Bauer's lectures on criminal law, and Meister's on the pandects. I am still plugging away at the law, but curses! I don't get very far! I still know the titles of Scott's novels and the stories of Boccaccio or Tieck much better than the titles and novels in the Corpus Juris. Oh, Saint Justinian, have pity on me! So many a poor drudge has grasped you, and I must despair! Oh, all you Roman Emperors take pity! Oh Gaius, Paulus, Papinianus—you damned heathens—you surely must burn in hell for having made the Law so vast. And what a crabbed Jean-Paul-like, that is to say, difficult Latin! Daily I curse Arminius and the Battle of the Teutoburg Forest. Had the latter not taken place, we should all be Romans today and speak Latin, and the Corpus Juris would be as easy for us and as familiar as Clauren's *Mimili*.[34] . . . You say in your letter that it will be hard for me to divest myself completely of my German character. . . . I know that I am one of the most thoroughly German beasts. I know only too well that German is to me what water is to a fish; that I cannot leave this vital-element and that I would soon turn into a dry cod-fish—to keep the piscine figure of speech—if I were ever to leap from my native German waters. At bottom I really love Germany more than anything else in the world. I delight and rejoice in her. My bosom is a repository of German feelings, just as my two books are repositories of German song. My first book is even outwardly quite German. At that time my love for German things had not yet been dimmed. My second book is only inwardly German; its outside is more foreign. It is possible that because she was displeased with things German, my Muse began cutting her German gown in somewhat outlandish fashion. . . .

Göttingen, May 24, 1824

DEAR CHRISTIANI: When one has much to tell, one generally writes nothing. This is a universal custom; and my long silence needs no special excuse. Actually I did not even feel like writing today. The weather is damp and depressing, and in my head it's even more damp and depressing. But I must resume my correspondence. I beg leave to inform you, therefore, that I am still alive. Nothing more. In my next letter I shall perhaps tell you that I have taken a trip, seen many human beings, beasts, etc. Apropos, I was also in Berlin. This city lies on the Spree, has 150,000 inhabitants and 25 souls. And there is one soul among them that has the power of making me blessed. Oh ye gods, I am not sufficiently mad! In Berlin I paid court, was the recipient of very gracious and radiant downward glances, reenforced old friendships, ate well, drank even better—à la Hafiz, inhaled a sufficient quantity of incense, accepted a few kisses, spent thirty *louis d'or*, listened to interminable and stupid gossip, and enjoyed a few delicious hours. I really am not worth the trouble so many people take to cheer me up and amuse me. I'm an irritable, gloomy, head-achy fellow. I might add that my poor head doesn't allow me to mingle in society; and it wasn't mere stubbornness that led me to refuse love effusions and to flee from so much beauty and goodness. . . . While I am writing this, I hear that my cousin, Lord Byron, is dead at Missolonghi.[35] So that great heart has stopped beating! It was great— and it was a heart, and no mean puny egg-hatchery of feeling. Yes, he was a great man. In the realm of suffering he discovered new worlds. He defied wretched mankind and its still more wretched gods—like Prometheus. His name re-echoed as far as the icy mountains of Thule and the burning desert sands of the East. *He was a man! Take him all in all. I shall not look upon his like again.* I have proclaimed universal mourning. English literature still has two eyes: Scott and Moore. But our own is as blind as a bat.

. . . My "Three and Thirty"[36] have had a most extraordinary fate in Berlin. Now they were praised to the skies as the last word in our literature; now they were bespattered by critical mud-slingers and dubbed uninspired aberrations of our times. Some people complain that fame has turned my head, that I write these trifles quickly and carelessly, and that traces of my haste are evident throughout. This is exactly what my brother writes from Lüneburg. In Hamburg he has heard much that was critical of me; for example, that I don't understand German. The editor of the *Posen Zeitung*, a Pole, has asserted the very same thing in his polemical articles against me.

I hear that my tragedies are widely read in the Rhineland and in Westphalia, but not too well understood or admired. That is why they nibble so smugly at my poems and complain about their crudities.

ℰ➤ *To Moses Moser*

Göttingen, June 25, 1824

DEAR MOSER: . . . I live here in the same old rut; that is, I have head-aches seven days in the week. I get up at half past four in the morning, and consider what to begin with. Meanwhile, nine o'clock comes gliding along, and I hasten with my portfolio to my divine Meister—yes, the chap is really godly. He is ideal in his stodginess. He is the perfect antithesis of all that is poetic, and for that very reason a poetic figure. If the material on which he discourses is particularly dry and wooden, he really becomes inspired. As a matter of fact, I am quite satisfied with Meister, and with his help and God's I shall get through the pandects satisfactorily.

Aside from that, I am assiduously studying the Chronicles, especially *historia judaica*. The latter because of its connection with my *Rabbi* [37] and perhaps because of my own personal need. I am strangely moved when I turn the pages of these annals which contain a full measure of instruction and sorrow. The soul of Jewish history becomes clearer and clearer to me, and these spiritual weapons will some day stand me in good stead. I have completed only one third of the *Rabbi*. I have been interrupted by racking pains, and only God knows if I shall finish it soon. In this connection, I came to the conclusion that I am utterly devoid of narrative talent. Perhaps I am unfair to myself. Perhaps it is the material that's really recalcitrant. I think my description of the Passover feast is successful, and I thank you for your information about the *Haggadah*. Would you also translate literally for me the "Caholach Manga" and the short legend of "Maasse be Rabbi Leser?" . . . Also the passage from the Psalms used in the evening prayers: "Ten thousand armed men stand before Solomon's bed." [38] Perhaps I shall append to the *Rabbi* a few pages of illustrations in the English manner; perhaps some original remarks about the Jews and their history. Benjamin of Tudela,[39] who is at this moment cavorting on my table, sends his warmest regards. He asks that Zunz edit him, with a translation.[40] The translation and edition of the Frenchman, Dr. Witte, which I am using, are bad from every point of view—mere school-boy exercises. On the subject of the Jews of Frankfurt I found Schudt very useful. I thoroughly conned both quarto volumes and didn't know whether to be more exasperated by the Jew-hatred which is spread over every page, or amused by the asinine ways in which it is expressed. How much better we Germans manage these things today!

I still lack some information about the Spanish Jews of the 15th century, and particularly the Spanish Academies of that time. Where can I find it? Rather, fifty years prior to their expulsion. It is interesting to observe that in the year in which they were expelled, the new land of religious freedom, America, was discovered. . . .

৪৵ *To J. W. von Goethe*

Weimar, October 1, 1824

I BEG YOUR EXCELLENCY TO GRANT ME THE GOOD FORTUNE to appear before you for a few moments. I shall not trouble you. I shall merely kiss your hand, and go. My name is H. Heine. I am from the Rhineland, and now reside in Göttingen. Before that, I lived for a few years in Berlin, where I associated with a number of your old acquaintances and admirers (the late Wolf, the Varnhagens, etc.) and grew to love you more and more. I am also a poet. Three years ago, I took the liberty of sending you my *Poems*—and a year and a half ago my *Tragedies*—besides a lyrical *Intermezzo* (*Ratcliff* and *Almansor*). Furthermore, I am ill, and three weeks ago I undertook a tour into the Harz mountains for my health. On the Brocken I was seized by an urge to make a pilgrimage to Weimar and pay homage to Goethe. I have come here truly as a pilgrim, that is, on foot, in weather-stained garments, and I await your answer to my prayers.

With enthusiasm and devotion
H. Heine

৪৵ *A Journey to the Harz*

THE TOWN OF GÖTTINGEN, famous for its sausages and university, belongs to the King of Hanover, and contains 999 habitations, various churches, a lying-in-hospital, an observatory, a student jail, a library and a Rathskeller where the beer is excellent. The stream which flows past the town is called the Leine, and in the summer is used for bathing. Its water is very cold, and in some places so broad that my school-mate Lüder had to take quite a run to clear it. The town itself is beautiful, and most agreeable—when you have turned your back upon it. It must be very old, for I remember when I matriculated there five years ago, and was soon thereafter expelled, it already had the same grey, sage look, and was fully provided with watch-men, poodles, dissertations, *thé-dansants*, laundresses, compendiums, roasted pigeons, Guelfic orders, graduates' carriages, pipe-bowls, court councillors, law councillors, deans' counsellors, old fossils, and other imbeciles. There are those who even assert that the town was founded at the time of the Great Migrations, and that every German tribe had left an unbound copy of its stock behind, from whom all the fraternities like the "Vandals," "Frisians," "Suabians," "Teutons," "Saxons," "Thuringians," etc. are descended, who to this day wander through Weender Street in hordes, distinguished by the color of their caps and pipe tassels, fight incessantly on the bloody battlefields of Rasenmühle, Ritschenkrug, and Bovden, preserving the manners and customs of the barbaric invasions, and are governed partly by their *duces*, called "prize-cocks," and partly by their ancient code, called the "Comment," which well deserves a place among the *leges barbarorum.*

The inhabitants of Göttingen may be roughly divided into stu-dents, professors, Philistines and cattle; but among these four classes there is no sharp distinction. The most important are the cattle. It would lead me too far afield to enumerate all the students and all the regular and irregular professors; besides, I do not at this moment recall the names of all the students; while among the pro-fessors, many as yet have no name. Göttingen Philistines must be as numerous as the sand (or better, as the mud) of the sea. Indeed, when I saw them in the morning, with their dirty faces and white bills, planted before the gates of the academic court, I could hardly conceive how God could ever have created so many scoundrels.

Further details about the town of Göttingen may be conveniently studied in *The Topography of Göttingen* by K. F. H. Marx. Although I am under great obligation to the author, who was my physician and very kind to me, I cannot praise his work without reservations, and I must take him to task for not having emphatically enough con-tradicted the erroneous belief that the ladies of Göttingen have over-sized feet. Indeed, I have been engaged for some time now in a serious refutation of this belief; and with this in view, I took courses in comparative anatomy, made excerpts from the rarest volumes in the library, studied the feet of the passing ladies on Weender Street for hours at a stretch, and in the exhaustive treatise which contains the results of these researches, I discuss (1) feet in general, (2) feet in the ancient world, (3) elephants' feet, (4) the feet of the ladies of Göttingen, (5) I shall collate all that was said about their feet in Ullrich's beer-garden, (6) I shall consider them in their context, and in this connection I shall also enlarge on calves, knees, etc., and finally, (7) if I can get paper of sufficient size, I will add a few copperplate facsimiles of Göttingen ladies' feet.

It was very early morning when I left Göttingen, and the learned Dr. —— doubtless was still in bed, dreaming as usual— that he was strolling in a beautiful garden, and the flower-beds were planted with nothing but slips of paper covered with quotations, which glistened wonderfully in the sun; here and there he plucked a few and carefully transplanted them to a new bed, while the nightingales gladdened his old heart with their sweetest songs.

Before the Weender Gate I met two little native schoolboys, one of whom was saying to the other, "I'll have nothing more to do with Theodore. He's a good-for-nothing. Why, yesterday he didn't even know the genitive of *mensa.*" These words may sound unimportant; still I feel bound to report them here; indeed, I would even have them inscribed as a town-motto on the gate; for the young birds peep as the old ones pipe, and those words perfectly express the narrow, dry pedantry of the most highly erudite Georgia Augusta University.

On the highway the fresh morning air was blowing, and the birds were singing merrily, and I too gradually recovered a hearty and cheerful mood. I was in need of such refreshment. Of late I had not left the pandect stables. Roman casuists had covered my brain as if with grey cob-webs. My heart felt as if it were compressed between the iron paragraphs of selfish legal systems. In my ears I heard a constant ringing of "Tribonian, Justinian, Hermogenian, Asinian," and I even mistook a tender pair of lovers seated under a tree for an edition of the *Corpus Juris* with clasped hands.

IT WAS PITCH-DARK WHEN I REACHED OSTERODE. I had no appetite for food and went right to bed. I was dog-tired, and slept like a god. In my dream I was back in Göttingen—in the library. I was standing in a corner of the Hall of Jurisprudence, ransacking old dissertations, and immersed in reading. When I stopped, I noticed to my surprise that night had fallen and the hall was illumined by crystal chandeliers. The church-bell nearby was just striking twelve when the hall door opened slowly, and in came a proud, gigantic woman, deferentially escorted by members and adherents of the law faculty. Though no longer young, the giantess possessed features of austere beauty; her every glance betrayed the sublime titaness, mighty Themis. She held her sword and scale carelessly in one hand; and a roll of parchment in the other. Two young LL.D.'s carried the train of her faded grey robe. On her right the thin Court Councillor Rusticus, the Lycurgus of Hanover, pranced about airily, reciting from the draft of his new law; on her left, her *cavaliere servente*, Privy Councillor Cujacius, was hobbling gallantly, in a good mood, cracking legal jokes at which he laughed so heartily that even the stern goddess frequently bent toward him with a smile, tapped him on the shoulder with her large parchment roll, and whispered amiably, "You little rascal—cutting the trees down from the top!" Then all the other gentlemen approached her, and each of them had something to remark or to offer with a smile—a newly hatched little system, or a pretty little hypothesis, or a similar little abortion of his own little brain.

Through the open door of the hall more strange gentlemen entered and introduced themselves as the other great lights of the illustrious order, mostly angular, sneaky fellows, who with smug self-satisfaction at once let loose definitions and distinctions, and disputed about every tittle of a title in the pandects. And ever more figures kept coming in, old legal savants in outmoded costumes, with long white wigs and long since forgotten faces, greatly amazed that they, the celebrities of the past century attracted so little attention; and they too joined, in their own way, in the general chatter and shrilling and shouting which raged ever more confused and louder around the goddess like the surge of the sea—until suddenly, losing all patience, she cried in tones of the most terrible giant agony: "Silence! Silence! I hear the voice of dear Prometheus. Mocking strength and silent force are chaining the guiltless one to the rock of martyrdom and all your chattering and squabbling cannot cool his wounds nor break his fetters!"

Thus cried the goddess, and streams of tears poured from her eyes. The whole assembly howled as if in fear of death; the ceiling of the hall crashed; the books tumbled from their shelves. In vain did old Münchhausen step from his frame to command order,—the tumult and din grew ever more furious—and I fled from this infernal bedlam into the Hall of History, and took sanctuary where the sacred figures of Apollo Belvedere and the Medicean Venus stand next to each other. I sank down at the feet of the Goddess of Beauty, and in her presence I forgot all that mad tumult from which I had escaped. My enraptured eyes drank in the symmetry and the immortal loveliness of her blessed form; Greek calm entered my soul, and over my head, like a benediction from heaven, Phoebus Apollo poured the sweetest tones of his lyre.

When I awoke I still heard a pleasant ringing in my ears. The herds were on their way to the pasture, and their bells tinkled. The dear golden sun shone through my window and lit up the pictures on the walls of my room—scenes from the War of Liberation, faithfully depicting what heroes we all were; and also execution scenes from the French Revolution, Louis XVI at the guillotine, and similar decapitations, which you cannot look at without thanking God that you are lying safe in bed, drinking excellent coffee, with your head still on your shoulders.

THE DESCENT INTO THE TWO PRINCIPAL MINES AT KLAUSTHAL—"Dorothea" and "Caroline"—I found extremely interesting, and I must give a full account of them.

About a half hour's trip from the town you reach two large, dark buildings, where you are at once received by the miners. They are dressed in loose jackets, of a dark color, generally steel blue, reaching down to the legs; trousers of the same color, leather aprons fastened in the back, and small green felt hats, without rims, like decapitated cones. The visitor is fitted out in the same attire, without the apron, and is conducted, by a master-miner who has lit his miner's lamp, to a dark opening that looks very much like a chimney. After descending as far as his waist, the guide instructs you how to hold on to the ladder, and then asks you to follow him without fear. There is absolutely no danger in the descent, though people unfamiliar with a mine would scarcely believe so. The mere fact that you have to put on a convict's dark dress produces a peculiar sensation. Then you have to climb down on all fours, and the black hole is so dismally black, and God only knows how far down the ladder may extend. But soon you perceive that it is not one single ladder you are climbing down to some dark eternity, but several ladders, each consisting of fifteen to twenty rungs, leading to a small board on which you can stand and which in turn has an opening in it and a new ladder.

I first entered the Caroline mine—the dirtiest and most unpleasant Caroline I've ever come across. The rungs are slimy, and you descend from ladder to ladder; the guide, who is ahead of you, keeps on telling you that there is no danger; but that you must hold tight to the rungs, and not look at your feet; that you mustn't get dizzy nor by your life step on the side boarding where you can hear the creaking of the ascending bucket, and where, a fortnight ago, a careless visitor fell down and unfortunately broke his neck. Below there is a confused hum and rumble. You are constantly stumbling against beams and ropes which draw up the quarried mineral or the water that has trickled down. At times too you come upon excavated passages, called galleries, where you can see the ore itself in the earth, and where the lonely miner sits the whole day through laboriously hammering the bits of metal from the wall. I did not reach the deepest section, where, as some claim, you can hear people in America shouting, "Hurrah, Lafayette!". Between you and me, the point I did reach seemed deep enough,—a constant rumbling and roaring, sinister groaning of machinery, water trickling down everywhere, thick exhalations, and the miner's lamp flickering ever more feebly in the lonesome night. Indeed, I was stupefied; I found it hard to breathe, and had difficulty in holding on to the slippery rungs. I did not feel any of the customary anxiety; but strangely enough in these depths I remembered how the year before, at about the same time, I had experienced a squall on the North Sea, and now I thought how nice and cozy it would be to feel the vessel pitching and tossing, to hear the winds blowing their little trumpet solos, along with the merry shouts of the sailors, and everything cleansed by God's good, free air. Yes, air! I gasped for air as I once more ascended some dozen ladders, and my guide conducted me through a narrow, very long, rock-hewn passage to the Dorothea mine.

Here it is cooler and more airy, and the ladders are cleaner, though longer and steeper than those in the Caroline. My spirits rose, especially when I once more became aware of signs of life. Down below I could see the shimmer of moving lights. Miners with their lamps gradually rose into view and as they passed us, we exchanged the greetings of "God speed!". Like some calm and friendly, though perplexing and mysterious, memory, I beheld the faces of these young and old miners, solemn, and somewhat pale, strangely lit up by their lamps, as they gazed at me with their clear, thoughtful eyes. All day long they had worked in their dark, lonely shafts, and now they were yearning for the blessed light of day, and the eyes of wife and child.

My cicerone himself was one of those thoroughly honest Germans, faithful as a dog. With genuine pleasure he showed me the gallery in which the Duke of Cambridge had dined with his whole retinue on his visit to the mine, where the long wooden dining-table and the great metal chair on which the duke sat are still preserved. These, my worthy miner related, were kept as a memorial, and with animation he told me of all the festivities that had taken place on that occasion, how the whole passage had been adorned with candles, flowers, and festoons; how one of the miners had sung and played the zither and how the dear, fat duke had been pleased and had drunk no end of healths, and how a great number of the miners, and he himself in particular, were ready to die for the dear fat duke and the whole House of Hanover. I am always deeply touched when I witness the simple, natural way in which this feeling of loyalty finds expression. It is so beautiful a feeling—and so thoroughly German too. Other nations may be more clever, more witty, more amusing, but none is so faithful as the faithful German nation. If I were not aware that loyalty is as old as the world, I would be inclined to believe that a German heart had discovered it! German loyalty! It is no modern rhetorical flourish. In your courts, oh, German princes, should be sung and resung the lay of the true Eckhart and the wicked Burgundian who murdered his henchman's children and yet found him faithful and true. You possess the most devoted people in the world, and you are mistaken in thinking that the sensible, faithful, old dog has suddenly gone mad and is snapping at your consecrated calves.

Like German faithfulness, the tiny miner's lamp had led us, with very little flare, calmly and safely through the labyrinths of shafts and galleries. We emerged out of the murky night of the mine—the sun shone—God speed!

Most of the miners live in Klausthal and Zellerfeld, a small adjoining mining town. I visited several of these honest fellows in their homes, observed their modest households, heard some of their songs, which they accompany quite charmingly on the zither, their favorite instrument, asked them to relate their old fairy tales of the mines, and to repeat the prayers which they offer up in common before descending into the dark shaft, and I joined in many of their good prayers. An old guide actually urged me to remain with them and turn miner; and when I bade them farewell, he gave me a message for his brother, who lives in the neighborhood of Goslar, and many kisses for his dear niece.

Static and unruffled as the life of these people may appear, it is nevertheless a true, lively life. The ancient, palsied grandame who was sitting behind the stove opposite the huge clothes-press, may have been sitting there for a quarter of a century, and her thoughts and feelings are surely intimately fused with every cranny of that stove, and every carving of the press. And press and stove, too, live, for a human being has breathed into them a portion of his soul.

THE NIGHT I PASSED IN GOSLAR something very strange happened to me. I still cannot think of it without horror. I am not nervous by nature, but of ghosts I am almost as mortally afraid as of the *Austrian Observer*.

What is fear? Does it originate in reason or in emotion? This is the question I often discussed with Dr. Saul Ascher whenever we happened to meet in Berlin at the Café Royal, where for a time I used to lunch. He always maintained that we fear something because we recognize it as fearful by a process of reasoning. Only reason is a motive force, not emotion. While I would eat a good dinner, he went on demonstrating the advantages of reason. Toward the end of his demonstration, he used to look at his watch, and invariably close with the sentence: "Reason is the highest principle."

Reason! Even now whenever I hear this word, I see before me Dr. Saul Ascher with his abstract legs, his narrow, transcendental-grey dress-coat, his angular, frozen face that might have served as a diagram for a geometry text-book. He was well over fifty—and a personified straight line. In his zeal for the positive, the poor chap had philosophized away from life all beauty, all sunbeams, all faith, all flowers; and he had nothing left but the cold, positive grave. He had a special grudge against the Apollo Belvedere and against Christianity. Against the latter he had even written a pamphlet proving its irrationality and untenability. Altogether he had written a whole stack of books, in which reason vaunts its own excellence. The poor Doctor was certainly quite in earnest about the whole matter, and for this he deserves our respect. Of course, the big joke lay in the fact that he would make such solemn-silly faces when he failed to understand what every child understands because it is a child. Sometimes I called on the rational Doctor in his house and found him with pretty girls. For reason does not forbid sensuality. Once, when I came to visit him again, his servant told me: "The Doctor has just died." And I felt little more than if he had said, "The Doctor has moved."

But let's return to Goslar. "Reason is the highest principle," I told myself as I got into bed, in an effort to compose myself. However, it was no good. I had just been reading in Varnhagen von Ense's *German Tales*, which I had taken along with me from Klausthal, the horrible story of the son whom his own father is about to murder, and who is warned at night by the spirit of his dead mother. The story is told so graphically that a cold shiver ran through me as I read it. Besides, ghost stories produce a greater feeling of horror when read on a journey, and especially at night, in a town, in a house, in a room where one has never been before. You cannot help thinking how many horrors may have been perpetrated on this very spot where you are now lying! Besides, the moon was now shining into my room so dubiously, all sorts of unbidden shadows were moving on the wall, and when I sat up in bed to take a closer look, I saw—

There is nothing more weird than accidentally seeing your own face in the mirror by moonlight. At the same moment a ponderous, yawning clock struck, so long and so slowly, that after the twelfth stroke I was sure that twelve full hours had passed, and it was bound to begin striking twelve all over again. Between the last and the next-to-the-last stroke, another clock struck very fast, almost shrewishly shrill, as if angry at the slowness of her partner. When both iron tongues had stopped and the whole house was still as death, it seemed as if I suddenly heard a shuffling and hobbling, like the uncertain step of an old man. Finally, my door opened, and the late Dr. Saul Ascher entered slowly.

An icy tremor chilled my spine. I shook like an aspen leaf, and hardly dared to look at the ghost. His appearance was unchanged—the same transcendental-grey dress-coat, the same abstract legs, and the same mathematical face—only it was a shade yellower, and the mouth that used to make two angles of 22½ degrees was pinched and the eye-balls had a longer radius. Swaying and leaning on his Spanish cane as usual, he approached me, and addressed me amiably in his customary lazy drawl:

"Don't be afraid and don't imagine that I am a ghost. It is a trick of your imagination if you take me for a ghost. What is a ghost? Give me a definition. Deduce for me logically all the conditions under which a ghost is possible. What rational connection would there be between such an appearance and reason? Reason I say, reason—"

And now the ghost proceeded to an analysis of reason, quoting Kant's *Critique of Pure Reason*, Part II, Section I, Book II, Chapter III—about the distinction between phenomena and noumena; then he constructed a problematical belief in ghosts, piled syllogism on top of syllogism, and ended with the logical conclusion that there was no such thing as a ghost. All the time cold sweat ran down my back, my teeth chattered like castanets. In my mortal agony I nodded unqualified agreement to each proposition with which the phantom doctor reduced the fear of ghosts to absurdity. He remonstrated with such heat that once, absently, instead of his gold watch, he pulled a handful of worms out of his watch-pocket, and noticing his mistake, nervously and with comical haste thrust them back. "Reason is the highest—" then the clock struck one, and the ghost vanished.

≋ *To Moses Moser*

Göttingen, October 25, 1824

INDEED, IF THERE IS IN THIS GOOD GOD'S WORLD one person who has the right to be angry with me, it is Moses Moser of Lupene! How long is it since I've written you, you, my only friend! I am tempted to be angry with you because you haven't written me two or three letters, one after the other, complaining indignantly of my silence. I am self-tormentor enough to persuade myself that you do not care for me. And I've not written to my only friend—and for such a long time! A man who can act in this way must have suffered much. Such indeed was the case. You were too dear to me to be the recipient of the poisoned vapors of my melancholy this summer. I was too much in love with myself to aggravate my suffering by expressing it. I have spent a very sad summer. Nothing but jurisprudence and headaches. My sole distractions were silly student pranks, duels, and a couple of law-suits which I lost. Since I've turned law-student, I get swindled more often than ever. I torture myself with the law like a desperate man, and only God knows if I'm getting anything out of it. Should Meister decline the deanship at the present time, then I'm a lost man. For then Hugo, the friend of my bitterest enemies, will become dean. You know, of course, that I'm not on too friendly terms here, either. That's in the very nature of things.

I've written practically nothing this summer. A few pages of

Memoirs. No poems. Of the *Rabbi* little, scarcely one third. This will be a sizable piece—a thick volume, which I nurse within me with inexpressible love. For it is an offspring of love and not of ambition. As a matter of fact, if I should hearken to the voice of wisdom, I would never write it at all. I can foresee how much harm I shall be doing, and how much enmity I'll provoke. But because it is the fruit of love, it will be an immortal book, an eternal lamp in God's cathedral, and not a sputtering theater candle. I have erased much that I wrote in this book. Only now and then have I succeeded in really understanding all of it. And I pray that God may grant me hours of health, so that I may be able to complete it in peace. Don't laugh at the premature cackling. And don't laugh at the protracted incubation. An ordinary goose egg is of course hatched sooner (and I'm not referring to Dr. Gans) than the dove's egg of the Holy Ghost. You've forgotten to send me the few bits of information in connection with the *Rabbi* for which I asked in my last letter. I want to thank Dr. Zunz a thousand times for the information about the Spanish Jews. Although it is scanty, Zunz has done more with his single penetrating hint than a number of quartos I ransacked in vain, and he will, unknowingly, have influenced my *Rabbi*.

Since Zunz is not the man to stand on formalities, I can save myself a separate letter by asking you to tell him the following: 1. That I love him. 2. That I esteem him. 3. Would he have the kindness to indicate where I can obtain adequate information about the family of the Abarbanels (also called the Abravanels)? In Basnage I found little. I completed my painful reading of Basnage toward the middle of last month.[41] I didn't find what I was looking for; but I did discover much new material, and was mentally and emotionally stirred. Taken as a whole, the book is magnificent. . . . I don't have to tell you that the verses which I am writing now are worth little and are being made solely for my own pleasure. But consider my situation. I spend the whole day at the university, and hear nothing but talk of *stillicidium*, *testaments*, *emphytheusis*, etc. When I have a free hour, and sail off to Thessaly and climb Parnassus, I meet only Jews who raise vegetables (see Basnage), and I speak to them of the sorrows of Israel. Yet I hope to produce some good poems. In my soul I feel the dawning of many a beautiful poem, among them a Faust. I have already begun working on a sketch. But goodness, I've forgotten to tell you that six weeks ago I undertook a long trip; I've been back only a fortnight—and so I was on the road for four weeks. The trip was very healthful and

I feel much stronger for it. I covered the entire Harz on foot, and for the most part alone. I wandered through beautiful mountains, lovely woods and valleys, and once more breathed freely. I returned by way of Eisleben, Halle, Jena, Weimar, Erfurt, Gotha, Eisenach, and Cassel, always on foot. I have had many marvelous and lovely experiences, and if jurisprudence had not followed me like a specter, I might have found the world very attractive. Even my worries crept after me. The additional year of study allotted me by my uncle is coming to an end, but I'm far from through with the law, and in a quandary. Besides, at this moment I am not regarded with particular enthusiasm. I'm not fool enough to conceal it from myself. I well know the reasons for all this shrugging and head-shaking. In a word, people think that I am mentally bankrupt; and I can't blame an astute businessman if he doesn't trust me. You know what I mean. I could have told you much about my trip to the Harz, but I've already begun to write it down, and will probably send it to you this winter to give to Gubitz. There will also be poems in it which you'll like—beautiful and lofty sentiments, and such-like emotional trash. What is one to do? To oppose the insipid commonplaces of the times is an ungrateful business.

❧ To Moritz Embden

Göttingen, May 11, 1825

. . . WILL I SETTLE DOWN IN HAMBURG? Only the gods who created hunger know the answer. I shall certainly not settle there, unless I am assured a livelihood for a few years. In the meantime, I will do all I can. When I next come to Hamburg, I will be baptized, Doctor Juris, and (I trust) in good health.

❧ To Rudolph Christiani

Göttingen, May 26, 1825

. . . I WAS APPALLED BY GOETHE'S APPEARANCE. His face is yellow and mummy-like. His toothless mouth is always moving nervously. His whole body is a picture of human frailty. Perhaps this is the result of his last sickness. Only his eyes are clear and brilliant. Those eyes are the only remarkable things in Weimar today. I was deeply touched by Goethe's very human concern for my health. The late Wolf had spoken to him about it. In many of his features I recognized the Goethe for whom Life—its adornment and preservation—as well as its practical aspects—represented the highest good. For the first time I thoroughly understood the contrast between Goethe's nature and mine. To me all practical things are abhorrent. Fundamentally I despise life, and would recklessly sacrifice it for an idea. That is indeed the dichotomy within me: My reason is always at war with my inherent inclination for the romantic. Now I know why Goethe's writings always repelled me, though I revered him as a poet, and my usual outlook on life harmonized with his. I am really at war with Goethe and his writings; just as my philosophy of life is at war with my inherent inclinations and my secret emotions. But have no fear, my dear Christiani. These wars will not be revealed publicly. I shall always belong to Goethe's free corps. My writings will be the fruits not of crazy enthusiasm but of artistic discretion. . . .

This winter, my dear Christiani, I suffered a great deal. I was as sick as a dog. To the point of desperation. I lived only on pain and medicine. I'm better now, but I still suffer much. I have been seriously affected by this winter's sickness, and that is why I can't move from this spot just yet.

But don't let my parents know anything of this. Despite the hard times, I've accomplished a great deal, especially in the law, and I ventured to take my examinations on May 3, *under the deanship of Hugo*. It all went off quite splendidly. And now I have one load less on my heart. . . .

🖎 *To Moses Moser*

Göttingen, July 22, 1825

DEAR MOSER: I would have answered your letter of the fifth much sooner, if it hadn't been for the conferring of my doctor's degree which only took place yesterday, after repeated postponements. Today, I want only to acknowledge receipt of the ten *louis d'or* and tell you something about the examination. I defended the fourth and fifth theses, "Oaths and *confarreatio*," like a dray horse.[42] It all went very well, and the Dean (Hugo) poured out the most fulsome praises on this festive occasion, and expressed his amazement that a great poet should also be a great jurist. If these words hadn't made me somewhat sceptical, I would have given way to conceit at being compared to Goethe, and by general agreement considered worthy of having my verses set beside his. This was spoken from the professorial chair and in a long Latin oration. The great Hugo said all this from a full heart. Privately he said many more flattering things to me that day, when we went for a ride and later when he invited me to dinner. I think Gans is wrong when he disparages Hugo. Hugo is one of the greatest men of this age. . . .

৪৯ *To Charlotte Embden*

Göttingen, July 31, 1825

. . . MY BEST REGARDS TO MORITZ; and if you are sure that he won't gossip, you can tell him that I am not only a J.D., but also— [43]

৪৯ *To Moses Moser*

Accursed Hamburg, December 14, 1825

DEAR MOSER, BELOVED, BLESSED MAN: You do me great injustice. I do not ask for long letters; a few lines will suffice. But even these you deny me. At no time have I been in greater need of them than now, when civil war is raging in my soul—all my emotions are up in arms—for me, against me, against the whole world. I tell you it's a poor joke. But never mind that.

Here I sit in ABC street, weary of purposeless roving, feeling, and thinking. Outside it is dark and foggy—a devilish spectacle. Old and young are running to the stalls to buy Christmas gifts. When you come to think of it, it's very nice of Hamburg citizens to plan a half a year ahead how they're going to bestow their Christmas presents. You, Moser, won't have cause to complain of my stinginess. I'm short of money, and I don't want to buy you just an ordinary toy, so I'll give you something very special for Christmas: namely, my promise not to shoot myself. At least, not yet. And if you only knew what's taking place within me, you would see that this promise is really a very precious gift and you wouldn't laugh, the way you're laughing now. No, you'd look as serious as I do at this moment.

Recently I read *Werther*—a very lucky thing for me. Also *Kohlhaas* by Heinrich von Kleist.[44] I am all admiration for this writer, and infinitely regret that he shot himself. And yet I can very well see why he did it.

As for my material existence, it isn't worth discussing. You'll see Cohn one of these days, and he can tell you how I came to Hamburg with the intention of becoming a lawyer—and didn't. Cohn probably can't give you the real reasons. Neither can I. I have other matters on my mind—rather, I should say, in my heart, and I won't torment myself trying to explain my actions. I'll stay here till the spring, busy with my own affairs, and, I think, in preparing for the lectures which I'll deliver at the University of Berlin. . . .

. . . Cohn assures me that Gans is preaching Christianity, and seeking to convert the Children of Israel. If he's doing this from conviction, he's a fool. If from hypocrisy, he's a scoundrel. I will not stop loving Gans; but I assure you that I would much rather have heard that he had been stealing silver spoons.

I cannot believe that you, Moser, should be thinking as Gans does, though Cohn vouches for it, and claims to have your own word. I should be very sorry if my baptism were to meet with your approval. I assure you, if the law permitted the theft of silver spoons, I would not have been converted. I'll tell you more when I see you.

Last Saturday I went to the Temple and had the pleasure of hearing, with my own ears, Dr. Salomon blasting all baptized Jews, and particularly taunting those who, "hopeful of obtaining a position (*ipsissima verba*), allowed themselves to be seduced from the faith of their fathers." I assure you the sermon was good, and I am planning to pay the man a visit one of these days. Cohn is very generous toward me. I eat at his table on the Sabbath. He heaps the most glowing *Kugel* on my head, and contritely I munch that sacred national dish, which has done more to preserve Judaism than all the three issues of the magazine. Of course, it's also had a greater circulation. . . .

᭫ How I Became a Christian

THAT I BECAME A CHRISTIAN is entirely the fault of those Saxons who suddenly changed horses at Leipzig, or of Napoleon who surely did not have to go to Russia; or, of his teacher of geography at Brienne who did not tell him that Moscow winters are very cold.[45]

᭫ To Moses Moser

Hamburg, January 9, 1826

. . . I AM NOW HATED BY BOTH CHRISTIANS AND JEWS. I regret that I've been baptized. I don't see that it's helped me very much. On the contrary, it's brought me nothing but misfortune.

᭫ To Wilhelm Müller [46]

Hamburg, June 7, 1826

I TAKE THIS OCCASION to send you a few cordial words, along with my *Travel Pictures.* I would have written you long ago to thank you for the kind way in which you received my tragedies and songs. But I wanted to wait until the somber fog which surrounded my soul had lifted somewhat. For I was ill for a long time, and very miserable. Now I'm only middling, but here on earth this may perhaps be called a happy state. I am doing much better with my poetry, and I have high hopes for the future. The "North Sea" is one of my last poems, and you will see what new notes I have struck, and on what new roads I am embarking. I am sufficiently generous to admit that the brief metrical line of my *Intermezzo* has more than merely accidental resemblance to your usual metrical style; but it probably owes its most intimate accents to your songs. For the beloved songs of Müller I came to know just as I was writing my *Intermezzo.* I began to feel the influence of the German folksong very early in life. Later when I studied at Bonn, August Schlegel revealed to me many poetic secrets, but I believe that it was not until I came on your songs, that I found the pure accents and the genuine simplicity for which I was looking. How clear are your songs! They are truly folksongs. In my poems, on the other hand, only the form has to a certain extent been cast in a popular mold; the content smacks of conventional society. Yes, I am big enough to say again clearly—and I shall eventually say it publicly—the reading of your seventy-seven poems revealed to me for the first time that new forms can be created from the existing forms of old folksongs, and they may have as popular a character but need not possess the crudity and awkwardness of the old poems. . . .

I myself am in a bad way. As a writer of songs, I am done for—and that you too may sense. Prose is my mistress now, and in the succeeding volumes of the *Travel Pictures* you will read much prosy stuff that is mad, harsh, offensive and angry, and singularly polemical. The times are evil indeed; and he who possesses strength and a free spirit is in duty bound to engage seriously in the battle against evil that struts about so blatantly, and against the commonplace that swaggers insufferably.

I beg you to continue to think favorably of me. Do not mistake me. Let us grow old together in common endeavor. I am vain enough to believe that my name will be spoken in the same breath with yours when we are both no more. Wherefore, while we live, let us be united in love. I will not reread what I have just written. I have let my pen run wild, while thinking of you. I love you too much to weigh too carefully whether I've said too much or too little.

ॐ *To Friedrich Merckel*

Nordeney, August 4, 1826

DEAR MERCKEL: I cannot see the mail go without sending you my greeting. The baths are doing me much good, and that is the most important news I have to convey. I am not so happy here as I was last year, but for this state of affairs my mood is more to blame than the people here. I am often unjust to them. There are times when I fancy that the beautiful lady from Celle is not quite so beautiful as she was in 1825. Even the sea does not seem to be so romantic as it used to be. And yet on its shores I have had the sweetest, loveliest mystical adventures that ever inspired a poet. The moon seemed to want to show me that the world still possessed splendors for me. We spoke never a word. Only one long, deep gaze; and the moon accompanied us with its music; and as she passed me, I seized her hand. I felt its stealthy pressure. My soul trembled and took fire. Afterwards I wept.

But what is the use? Even if I am bold enough to seize happiness, I cannot hold it long enough. I am afraid that suddenly day may come.—Only the dark gives me courage. Her lovely eyes will long live in my heart; and then they will fade away and dissolve into nothing—even as I.

The moon is used to silence. The sea chatters forever, but one can rarely understand its words. But you, the third partner of my secret, you will hold your peace, and so it will remain hidden in its own dark night.

৪৯ *The Tyrol*

THE TYROL IS VERY BEAUTIFUL, but even the most beautiful landscapes cannot charm us if the weather is dreary and the mind is likewise troubled. With me the latter always follows from the first; and since it was raining outside, there was bad weather in my soul too. Only now and then I ventured to thrust my head from the carriage. Then I saw heaven-high mountains that gazed at me solemnly and nodded *bon voyage* with their huge heads and cloud-formed beards. Here and there I noticed a little distant blue mountain, standing as if on tip-toe, and peering curiously over the shoulder of the other mountains, no doubt in order to see me. At the same time the forest streams roared as they dashed down from the heights and gathered in the seething currents of the valley. The inhabitants remained in their neat and pretty cottages, which were dispersed on the steep slopes, and perched on rugged declivities, even up to the very mountain-tops—neat, pretty cottages, usually with a long, balcony-like gallery, adorned with drying clothes, saints' images, flower-pots and maidens' faces. These little houses are also prettily painted, mostly white and green, as if they too were wearing the Tyrolean national costume—green braces over a white shirt. When I saw these cottages standing in the dreary rain, my heart longed to alight and go up to these people, who were surely sitting in them dry and contented. Life up there, I said to myself, must be sweet and snug; the old grandmother is surely telling very familiar tales. While the carriage inexorably drove by, I looked back, again and again, to watch the bluish columns of smoke ascend from the little chimneys. The rain fell more heavily—outside and within me—till the drops almost flowed from my eyes.

But often my heart leaped up, and in spite of the bad weather, it mounted up to those people who live so high up in the mountains and come down perhaps only once in their lives, and know so little of what is happening here below. But they are none the less pious and happy. Of politics they know nothing, except that they have an Emperor who wears a white coat and red breeches. That's what their old uncle told them, and he heard it in Innsbruck with his own ears from Black Sepperl, who had been to Vienna. When the patriots climbed up to them and informed them that now they had a new prince, who wore a blue coat and white breeches, they took their guns, kissed wife and child, and came down from the mountains, and allowed themselves to be killed for the sake of the white coat and the dear old red breeches.

After all, it doesn't matter much what a man dies for, if only he dies for something he loves, for a warm, loyal death is better than a cold, faithless life. The very songs which celebrate such a death, the sweet rhymes and the bright words, warm our hearts when damp mists cling around us and importunate cares oppress us.

Many such songs echoed through my heart as I drove over the mountains of the Tyrol. The familiar fir-trees rustled many a forgotten word of love back into my memory. Especially when the great blue mountain lakes looked at me with their unfathomable yearning, my thoughts turned again to the two children who loved each other so well and died together. It is an old story, and no one believes it today, and I remember only a few scattered lines.

> "There were two royal children
> Who loved each other truly
> They could not come together
> The water was too deep . . ."

These words began to ring in my mind of themselves, when I saw, by the side of one of those blue lakes, a little boy and a little girl

standing on opposite shores, both dressed in the striking and gay national costume, with beribboned green hats on their heads—and they
were sending greetings to each other—

"They could not come together,
The water was too deep . . ."

ᣠ *To Eduard von Schenk* [47]

Leghorn, August 27, 1828

. . . IN TWO OR THREE WEEKS I shall be roaming the land of Dante,
Machiavelli, Leonardo da Vinci, Michael Angelo. There I shall read
your lines. I know you are knee-deep in business. That is why I speak
only of lines. After all, it isn't necessary that people of our sort write
one another long letters. Our books are long letters, intended for
people like us.

Sooner or later you will read in print what I think of Italy. I am
plagued by my ignorance of Italian. I do not understand the people
and cannot talk to them. I see Italy, but do not hear her. Yet I am
not without company. The stones here speak, and I understand their
dumb language. Even they seem to feel deeply what I am thinking. A
broken column of the Roman period, a crumbling Lombard tower,
or a weather-beaten fragment of a Gothic arch understands me well.
For I am myself something of a ruin wandering among ruins. Birds
of a feather. . . . Often it seems to me that the old palaces wish to
whisper some secret to me, and I cannot hear them for the dull noises
of the day. Then I come again at night, and the moon is an excellent
interpreter who understands the language of stones and can translate
it into the dialect of my heart. Yes, at night I can understand Italy
perfectly, for then the young nation with its young, operatic speech
is asleep and the ancients rise from their cool beds and talk to me in
their best Latin. There is something ghostly in coming to a land
where one does not understand the living speech of living people, and
instead knows quite well the language which flourished a thousand
years ago, and is long since dead, and is spoken only by midnight
spirits—a dead tongue.

However, there is one language which can be understood by at
least one half of the human race in all corners of the world, the fairer

half, which is called *par excellence*, the fair sex. This language flour-
ishes especially in Italy. What use are words where the eloquent eyes
cast radiant glances deep into the heart of a poor *Tedesco*, eyes more
eloquent than Demosthenes and Cicero, eyes—I am not lying—which
are as large as stars?

Quand on parle du loup, il est derrière nous.[48] Even at this moment,
my pretty laundress is here, and I must stop washing my own linen.
Adieu, poet of *Belisarius*. I often think of you when I see the laurel,
and the more I think of you, the more I feel compelled to love you.

To Solomon Heine

Lucca, September 15, 1828

THIS LETTER IS BEING SENT FROM THE BATHS OF LUCCA in the Apennines, where I have been taking the waters for the last fortnight.
Nature here is beautiful, and the people are amiable. Breathing this
mountain air, one forgets little cares and sorrows, and the soul expands.

I have been thinking of you so much these days, and I have so often
longed to kiss your hand, that it is quite natural that I should write
to you. If I were to put it off until I came down from the mountains, bitterness and grief would once more enter my heart, and I
should write you something bitter and sorrowful. But that must not
be. I will not think of things I might complain of in you, which are
more considerable than you suspect. So I beg you, leave off some of
your complaints against me, since they all involve money. If they
were reckoned down to the last penny, they would amount to no
more than what a millionaire could quite easily throw away.—But
my complaints against you are incalculable, infinite, for they are of
a spiritual kind, rooted in the depths of offended sensibilities. If by a
single word or a single look I have ever been wanting in respect for
you, or for your house—I have loved you all only too well!—then
you would have the right to be angry. But not now; for if all your
plaints were added up, they would fit comfortably into a purse of no
great dimensions. And even if the grey money bag were too small
to hold all that Solomon Heine complains of in me, and were to
burst—do you think, dear Uncle, that it could equal my heartbreak?
But enough! The sun shines bright; when I look out at the window,

all I see is smiling vine-clad hills. I will not complain. I will only love you, as I have always done, and I will only think of your soul which is more beautiful than all the splendors I have yet seen in Italy. . . .

ᘍᕽ *The Picture Gallery*

I CANNOT REFRAIN FROM MENTIONING the collection of portraits of beautiful Genoese women which are shown in the Palazzo Durazzo. Nothing in the world can touch the soul with such sadness as the sight of portraits of beautiful women who have been dead several hundred years. Melancholy steals over us at the thought that nothing remains of their originals, of all those beauties that were so charming, so coquettish, so witty, so roguish, so capricious. Of all those May-day heads with their April humors, of all that maiden springtime— nothing remains but these multi-colored shadows which a painter, like them long since mouldered away, has painted on a perishable bit of canvas, which is likewise crumbling with age.

And so it is with all of life. The beautiful and the ugly pass away together and leave no trace behind. Death, that fusty pedant, spares the rose as little as the thistle; nor does he forget the solitary blade of grass in the distant wilderness—he destroys relentlessly, ceaselessly. Everywhere he grinds to dust plants and animals, and men and their works. Even those Egyptian pyramids, which seem to defy his destructive rage, are really trophies of his might, memorials of transitoriness, ancient tombs of kings. But even more humiliating than this sense of endless death, than this yawning gulf of annihilation, is the haunting thought that we ourselves die without ever having been originals— but merely copies of long vanished men, who were like us spiritually and physically; that we shall be succeeded by other men, like us in appearance, thought and feeling, and whom Death will likewise destroy,—a dreary, endless repetitious game, in which the fruitful earth is compelled to produce and reproduce more than Death can possibly destroy—so that in her need she must be more concerned about the conservation of the species than the originality of the individual.

The eerie fascination of these thoughts cast a spell over me, as I gazed at the portraits of the beautiful Genoese women in the Durazzo

Palace. One of these produced a gentle storm within me. Even now my eyelids tremble at the remembrance. It was the portrait of my dead Maria!

The custodian of the gallery insisted that the painting represented a Duchess of Genoa, and in the tone of a guide-book, he added, "This portrait was painted by Giorgio Barbarelli of Castelfranco nel Trevigiano, called Giorgione. He was one of the greatest painters of the Venetian school, and was born in the year 1477 and died in 1511."

"Never mind that, Signor Custode. The picture is well executed, although it has been painted a few centuries in advance. But that is no fault. The drawing is correct, the coloring is excellent, and the folds of the draperies are perfect. Pray, have the goodness to take down the picture from the wall, for a few minutes. I want only to blow the dust from those lips and brush away the spider that sits in the corner of the frame. Maria always hated spiders."

"Your Excellency appears to be a connoisseur."

"I was not aware of that, Signor Custode. I have the faculty of being singularly moved by certain pictures, which bring moisture to my eyes. But what do I see? By whom is that portrait of the man in black that hangs over there?"

"It is also by Giorgione,—a masterpiece."

"I beg you, Signor, take that too from the wall for a moment and hold it here beside the mirror, so that I may see whether or not I resemble the picture."

"Your Excellency is not so pale. The picture is a masterpiece by Giorgione; he was the rival of Titian, and was born in the year 1477 and died in 1511."

Dear reader, I much prefer Giorgione to Titian, and I am especially indebted to him for having painted Maria for me. You will at once agree with me that Giorgione painted that picture for me, and not for some old Genoese. And it is a striking resemblance, down to the death-stillness. Not even the expression of pain is absent from the eyes—the kind of pain which is more a matter of dreams than of experience—and very difficult to portray. The whole portrait resembles a sigh breathed onto a canvas. The man in the black cloak is also well portrayed; the spitefully sentimental lips are correctly rendered—almost speech-like,—parted, as though about to tell a story—the story of a knight who wished to kiss his beloved back to life—and when the torch went out—

ᕤᕦ *Count August von Platen and I*

. . . YET SHOULD I SPEAK OUT MY INMOST THOUGHTS, I would confess that I by no means regard Count Platen as the extraordinary fool one would take him to be from his boastfulness and self-adoration. A little folly, it is well known, always accompanies poetry. But it would be frightful if Nature should burden a single man with folly enough for a hundred great poets, and at the same time give him only such a niggling dose of poetry. I have reason to suspect that the Count himself does not believe his own boasts, that poverty-stricken as he is in life as well as in letters, he is compelled by the needs of the moment to act as his own pander; in letters as well as in his life. Hence these phenomena, which have, one might say, more of a psychological than an aesthetic interest; hence the coexistence of a snivelling intellectual paralysis and an affected excess of pride; hence this miserable pooh-poohing of approaching death, and the blustering adoration of immortality; hence the flashes of beggar's pride and the languishings of slavish humility. Hence the constant wailing, "Cotta ⁴⁹ lets me starve! Cotta lets me starve!"—Hence those fits of Catholicism, etc.

I very much question whether the Count is serious about all this Catholicism. Whether he has actually turned Catholic, like certain of his high-born friends, I do not know. That he was on the verge of so doing I heard for the first time from certain journals, which even stated that Count Platen was about to become a monk and retire to a monastery. Evil tongues even said that the vows of poverty and continence—at least so far as women were concerned—would not be difficult for him to observe. As one can well understand, when this news reached Munich, the chimes of piety at once began ringing in the hearts of his friends. In the clerical papers his poems were lauded to the skies with *Kyrie Eleisons* and *Hallelujahs*. Indeed, these holy celibates had cause to rejoice in those poems in which abstinence from carnal contact with women is advocated. Unfortunately, my own poems have the very opposite tendency; and the fact that the priests and choir boys are not pleased by them saddened but hardly surprised me. So that I was not amazed when on the day before my departure, I learned from my friend, Dr. Kolb, that Count Platen entertained unfriendly feelings toward me, and was preparing my complete annihilation in a comedy entitled *King Oedipus*, which had already come into the hands of certain princes and counts at Augsburg—whose names I have forgotten or want to forget. From others I heard that Count Platen hated me and considered me his enemy.

. . . IT WAS IN NORTH GERMANY, where I had suddenly been called by the death of my father, that I first received that monstrous creation which our ostrich of beautiful plumage had finally hatched from the gigantic egg, and which the night-owls of the congregation had long before greeted with their pious croaking, while the noble peacocks beat their wings exultantly. This was to be nothing less than a devouring basilisk. Dear reader, do you know the legend of the basilisk? They say that when a male bird lays an egg—after the fashion of females—a poisonous creature is hatched whose breath pollutes the air, and that it can be destroyed only if a mirror is held up before it, so that it perishes of fright at the sight of its own ugliness.

Sacred grief, which I would not profane, made it possible for me to read *King Oedipus* only two months ago, while I was visiting the watering place in Heligoland. There, inspired by the uninterrupted aspect of the great, bold sea, I immediately perceived the petty mind and the patch-work character of this highborn writer. That masterpiece revealed him at last exactly as he is—in all his blooming decay, his excess of intellectual poverty, his conceit without conception, exactly as he is, forced without force, piqued without being *piquant*, a dried-up water-logged soul, a dismal *fils de joie*. This troubadour of misery, weakened in body and mind, has striven to imitate the most powerful, the most imaginative and the most witty poet of the youthful Grecian world! Nothing is more repulsive than this cramped impotence, which would puff itself into a likeness of power, those painfully culled invectives, encrusted with the mould of aging spite, this stammering, painfully imitated delirium of the soul! As a matter of fact, there is nowhere in this work a trace of that profound world-destructive imagination which underlies every Aristophanic comedy, from which, as from a fantastic, ironic, magic tree, bloom the rich branches of thought, with their nests of singing nightingales and clambering apes. This loftiness of conception, with its death-jubilation and its fireworks of destruction, we cannot, of course, expect from the poor Count. The center, the first and ultimate idea, basis and purpose of his so-called comedy (as well as of his *Fateful Fork*) consists in trivial literary botching—the poor Count was capable of imitating only some of the externals of Aristophanes—only the dainty verses and the coarse expressions. I say "coarse expressions," because I myself have no wish to use more vulgar ones. Like a bickering fish-wife he pours whole potfuls of billingsgate on the heads of the German poets. . . .

. . . FAR WORSE DOES THE "BAPTIZED HEINE" FARE AT HIS HANDS. Yes, yes, dear reader, you are not mistaken. It is I of whom he speaks. In *King Oedipus* you may read that I am a real Jew; that after tossing off some love-songs in a couple of hours, I immediately sit down and circumcise ducats; that on the Sabbath I squat and cower like some long-bearded Jew and chant the Talmud in my nasal sing-song; that on the eve of Passover I slay a Christian child—but that from sheer malice I choose some unhappy writer for that purpose. No, dear reader, do not let me deceive you. You will find no such vivid pictures in *King Oedipus*—and that is the fault I find with it. For Count Platen sometimes has the best themes, but does not know how to handle them. If he had been endowed with a little more imagination, he would at least have pictured me as a secret pawn-broker, and what comic scenes he could have evoked! My soul is pained when I reflect on how many opportunities to be witty the poor Count has missed! How cleverly he could have presented Raupach [50] in the role of a Rothschild of tragedy, from whom royal theatres obtained loans! Oedipus himself, the hero of the play, could have been used to better advantage, if the Count had merely modified the plot of the drama. Instead of having him kill his father Laius, and marry his own mother, Jocasta, he could have managed it so that Oedipus kills the mother and marries his father. The dramatic, p-drastic effect in such a poetical work would have been easy for a Platen to achieve—his own psycho-logical disposition could have been useful; like the nightingale, he had need only to sing the emotions in his own breast, and he could have produced a piece, which, if the gazelle-like Iffland [51] were still alive, would surely have found a place on the boards of our private theatres and been immediately put into rehearsal.

HOWEVER, TRUE MERIT EVER OBTAINS ITS REWARD, and the author of *Oedipus* will surely not escape his, although he has here, as every-where else, completely surrendered to the interests of his noble and spiritual liegemen. Yes, there is an ancient tradition among the peoples of the Orient and the Occident, that every good or evil deed eventually has direct consequences for its doer. And the day will come, when they will arise—be forewarned, dear reader, I am about to indulge in the pathetic and the awesome—the day will come when they will arise from Tartarus, those frightful daughters of Night—the Eumenides! [52] By the Styx!—by this oath the gods have never sworn falsely—the day will come when the dark, primeval sisters of justice will appear, with their serpents' locks and their enraged visages, bearing those serpentine scourges with which they once chastised Orestes, that unnatural malefactor who murdered his mother, Tyndarean Clytemnestra. It may be that even now the Count can hear the hissing of the serpents. I beg you, dear reader, imagine the Wolf's ravine and Samiel's music—perhaps at this very moment the Count is overcome by a secret shudder of the sinner.[53] The heavens grow dark; the birds of night croak; distant thunders roll; lightning flashes. There is a smell of burning resin. Woe! Woe! His illustrious ancestors rise from their graves. "Woe! Woe!" they cry three or four times, over their miserable descendant. They adjure him to don his coat of mail and protect himself against the frightful lashing—for the Eumenides will tear him limb from limb; the scourging serpents will relish his flesh; and like the lecherous King Rodrigo, who was shut in the Tower of Serpents, the poor Count will at last whimper and wail:

> "Alas, they're biting, ah, they're biting
> That with which I sinned." [54]

Do not be alarmed, dear reader. It is all a jest. These horrible Eumenides are nothing but a merry comedy, which I, after a few decades, intend writing under that title; and the tragic verses which just now frightened you so are to be found in the merriest book in the world, *Don Quixote de la Mancha*, where they are recited by a respectable old lady-in-waiting before the entire court. I see that you are smiling again. Let us take leave of each other, laughing and in good cheer. If this last chapter has been somewhat tiresome, that is due to the subject. Besides, it was written to be useful rather than to please, and if I have succeeded in making another fool available to literature, my Fatherland owes me thanks I have ploughed the field, and more gifted writers may sow and reap. The modest knowledge of this merit is my best reward.

To those kings who may be desirous of presenting me, over and above this, with a snuff-box, I say that the book publishing firm of Hoffmann and Campe in Hamburg is authorized to receive anything of that sort on my account.

ટ∾ *Don Quixote*

STRANGE! *The Life and Adventures of the Ingenious Knight Don Quixote de la Mancha, written by Miguel de Cervantes Saavedra,* was the first book which I read after I reached the age of understanding and was to some extent proficient in the art of spelling. I still remember quite distinctly that brief time when I stole away from the house early in the morning to the Palace Garden, in order to read *Don Quixote* undisturbed. It was a beautiful day in May. The budding spring lay half-slumbering in the still morning light, and allowed herself to be praised by the nightingale—her sweet flatterer—who chanted her praises with such caressing tenderness and melting enthusiasm that the most bashful buds burst open, and the lush grass and the fragrant sun-beams kissed more passionately, and the trees and the flowers shuddered from sheer ecstasy. I, however, sat down upon an old moss-covered stone bench, in the so-called Avenue of Sighs, not far from the waterfall, and feasted my little heart on the great adventures of the dauntless knight. In my childish innocence I took everything in dead earnest; no matter how ridiculously the poor hero of the story was treated by fate, I still thought it had to be so and was all a part of heroism, the ridicule as well as the bodily wounds. The former vexed me as deeply as the blows, which I felt in my own soul.

I was a child and did not know the irony with which the Lord has permeated the world, and which the great poets have reflected in their published microcosms. I would shed bitter tears when the noble knight received only blows and ingratitude for his magnanimity, and because I was unskilled in the art of reading, and pronounced every word aloud, all the birds and the streams, the brooks and flowers heard me. Since these guileless creatures know as little of the world's irony as little children, they likewise took everything seriously, and wept with me at the tribulations of the poor knight. In fact, a worn-out old oak sobbed, and the waterfall shook its white beard most vigorously as if inveighing against the wickedness of the world. We felt that the knight's heroism merited no less admiration because the lion turned his back on him, unwilling to do battle; and that his deeds became all the more praiseworthy as his body became ever more wasted and feeble, his protecting armor more worn, and the nag that bore him more pitiful. We despised the low rabble that cudgelled our poor hero so mercilessly, and even more the high-born rabble, who, resplendent in their gay silk cloaks, lofty speech and ducal titles, scorned a man so far superior to them in strength of mind and nobility of soul. Dulcinea's knight rose ever higher in my esteem, and won more of my affection the longer I read in that wonderful book— which happened daily in the same garden; so that by autumn I had already reached the end of the story. And I shall never forget the day on which I read of the sorrowful joust in which the knight had to succumb so ignominiously!

It was a bleak day. Ugly, misty clouds moved along the grey sky. The yellow leaves fell sorrowfully from the trees. Heavy tear-drops hung on the last flowers, which bowed their wilting, dying little heads. The nightingales were long since gone. On all sides I was met by a picture of decay. My heart was ready to break as I read how the noble knight lay on the ground stunned and bruised, and without lifting his visor, spoke to his conqueror in a weak, sick voice, as though from the grave: "Dulcinea is the fairest lady in the world, and I the most luckless knight on earth; but it is not seemly that my weakness belie this truth—therefore, thrust with your lance, Sir Knight!"

Alas! This shining Knight of the Silver Moon, who vanquished the most dauntless and the noblest man on earth, was a disguised barber! . . .

❧ I Am Only a Don Quixote

THAT WAS LONG AGO. Many new springs have bloomed since then, but they always lacked that mighty magic. For alas! I no longer believe the sweet lies of the nightingale—that flatterer of the spring. I know how quickly her glory decays; and when I look at the youngest rosebud, I see her in my mind blooming to a painful crimson, then fading, and blasted by the wind. All around me I see winter in disguise.

But in my breast still glows that flaming love which soars yearningly away from the earth, roves adventurously through the wide, gaping spaces of the heavens, and on high, is repelled by the cold stars, and sinks down again, toward our little earth, and sighing and exulting, acknowledges that in the whole world there is nothing more beautiful or better than the heart of man. That love is enthusiasm—always a god-like thing—whether it act wisely or foolishly. And so the little boy was not squandering the tears he shed at the sorrows of the mad knight—any more than when grown to young manhood, he spent many a night in his study bewailing the death of the saintly heroes of freedom, King Agis of Sparta, Caius and Tiberius Gracchus of Rome, Jesus of Jerusalem, and Robespierre and Saint-Just of Paris.[55] Now that I have donned the *toga virilis* and would be a man, there is no room for tears. I must act like a man, emulate my great predecessors, and please God! some day be wept over by boys and young men.

For on them we can still rely in our cold times. They can still be kindled by the glowing breath wafted to them from old books—and that is why they understand the fiery hearts of today. Youth is self-less in thought and feeling, thinks and feels the truth most profoundly, and never stints of word and deed when it behooves it to take part in struggles. Their elders are petty and self-seeking, are more concerned for the interest on their money than the interests of humanity; they allow their small skiffs to drift smugly down the channels of life, and give little thought to the skipper who is battling the waves on the high seas; or they climb, with inflexible determination, to the heights of a mayoralty or presidency of their club, and shrug their shoulders at the sight of the fallen statues of heroes which the storm has cast down from the pillars of glory. And then how they love to tell us that in their youth they too used to run their heads against stone walls; but later in life, they made their peace with them—for the wall is the absolute, the fixed, that which exists in and of itself—that which is rational because it is real—and he who will not tolerate this most rational, incontrovertibly real, and most rigidly fixed absolutism is *ipso facto* irrational. Alas! even the reprobates who would phi-losophize us into abject slavery are yet more estimable than those miscreants who vindicate despotism not on rational, but on historical, grounds as something sanctified by custom, something that mankind has gradually come to accept, something that is legitimate and legally binding!

Oh, I will not, like Ham, raise the covering from the shame of my

Fatherland! [56] But it is dreadful to see how our Germans have learned to make even slavery talkative, and our German philosophers and historians have racked their brains to justify every form of despotism as rational and lawful—be it ever so doltish and stupid. Silence is the honor of the slave, says Tacitus. These philosophers and historians maintain the contrary, and point to the little ribbons of honor in their lapels.

Perhaps you *are* right—and I am only a Don Quixote, and the reading of all kinds of wonderful books has turned my head, as it did that of the Knight of La Mancha. Jean Jacques Rousseau was my Amadis of Gaul, Mirabeau my Roldan or Agramanth. I have too thoroughly absorbed the heroic deeds of the French Paladins and the Round Table of the National Convention. [57] Naturally, the madness and fixed ideas which I drew from those books are altogether different from those of the Knight of La Mancha. He wished to restore decaying knighthood; I, on the other hand, want utterly to annihilate whatever has survived from that period. And thus we act from diametrically opposite points of view. My colleague mistook windmills for giants; I, on the contrary, see in our giants of today only ranting windmills; he mistook leather wineskins for mighty wizards; I see in our modern wizards only leather wineskins; he mistook every beggar's inn for a castle—every donkey driver for a knight, every stable wench for a lady of the court;—I, on the other hand, look upon our castles as disreputable inns, on our cavaliers as donkey-drivers, on our court-ladies as common stable-wenches. Just as he took a puppet-play to be a noble affair of state, I hold our affairs of state to be wretched puppet plays. But as doughtily as the doughty Knight of La Mancha I fall upon the wooden company.

Alas! Such deeds of heroism often work as much havoc with me as they did with him—and like him I am forced to endure much for the honor of my lady. Were I to abjure her, whether from paltry fear or base greed, I could live comfortably in this real, rational world, and I could lead a lovely Maritorne [58] to the altar,—allow myself to be blessed by bloated magicians, feast with noble donkey-drivers, and beget innocuous stories and other little slaves.

Instead, adorned with the three colors of my lady, I must constantly fight duels, battle my way through untold misery, and I gain no victory which has not cost me something of my heart's blood. Night and day I am sorely beset, for my foes are so insidious that many of them, whom I have dealt a death-blow, still show the semblance of life, and appear in all shapes and molest me day and night. What agonies I already have had to endure from these perfidious ghosts! Wherever love bloomed for me, these crafty specters crept in and nipped the most guileless of buds. Everywhere, where I least expected it, I discovered their slimy silvery tracks—and if I were not careful, I might easily slip, even in the house of my dearest love. You may smile—and think such apprehensions mere figments of the imagination, like Don Quixote's. But imagined sorrow hurts no less; and if a man thinks he has drunk hemlock, he can contract consumption, but he never grows fat on it. That I have grown fat, is sheer calumny.—I assure you I have received no fat sinecure, even though I possess the requisite talents for it. Nor has my blood been enriched by my blood-relatives. I imagine they have done everything in their power to keep me thin. When I was hungry, they fed me adders; when I was thirsty, they gave me gall and wormwood; they poured hell into my heart, so that I wept poison and sighed forth fire; they even crept into my dreams at night—and there I see them—the gruesome larvae, the aristocratic lackey-faces with gnashing teeth, those ominous banker noses, those deadly eyes, staring from their cowls, those spectral hands protruding from sleeves and holding unsheathed knives. . . .

Even the old woman who lives near me—my next-door neighbor—thinks I am crazy and insists that I say the craziest things in my sleep. The other night, she maintains, she heard me cry out distinctly: "Dulcinea is the fairest lady in the world; and I the most luckless knight upon the earth; but it is not seemly that my weakness belie this truth—therefore, thrust with your lance, Sir Knight!"

Ꮽ *To Rahel Varnhagen von Ense*

Berlin, April 1, 1829

FRAU VON VARNHAGEN: "If it is so much trouble for you to come to see me, then you don't have to come at all." This is what you said to me yesterday; if not in so many words—yet that was your meaning. I was still thinking of what you said this morning, and I must confess with regret that for two years I have been badly spoiled by my other fair friends who are always glad to have me with them, no matter on what terms, and how greatly I overestimated my own person. It will take some time before I can be broken of this habit and before I sink as deep in my self-esteem as you would have me do. Until then, you will have to be content with your much-prized fowls who cackle as you would have them, and fit into every cage.

You will probably think me vain. Very well! Time will show that I can easily sacrifice my vanity and all outward show to a noble end. I shall remain as I am—with truth in my heart—Frau von Varnhagen!

ᢒᥬ *To Varnhagen von Ense*

Hamburg, February 4, 1830

TODAY, DEAR FRIENDS, I HAVE SOMETHING OF IMPORTANCE TO TELL YOU— in fact, something of the greatest importance; to wit, I want to thank you for your last letter. Your silence was a source of concern to me, and more painful than all the outcries of my enemies, who have now, by common consent, broken loose against me. But I am not disturbed by them, or by their rage; just as I will not be deceived by the kindness and generosity of my friends. Yes, dear Varnhagen, I feel convinced that if you do not censure me now or condemn my latest book it is from a feeling of generosity. For that I thank you. I'll never forget it.

No one feels more keenly than I that I have done myself incalculable harm with the Platen chapter, that I should have handled the matter differently,—and that I have offended the better section of the public. But I also feel that with all my talents I could not have done better, and that, cost what it may, I had to make an example of him. The national servility and Philistinism of the German people will in this case show itself beautifully. For I doubt whether I have succeeded in divesting the title of Count of its magic.

The question of satisfaction is already on the carpet. You will remember that it was in my mind from the very beginning. And I have deliberately so managed it that it will be of greater moment for the Count to try and obtain satisfaction from me, than for me to obtain it from him. Force of circumstances will in this case take a comic turn. They're complaining that I have done something unheard-of in German literature. As if times never changed! The *Xenien* campaign, carried on by Schiller and Goethe, was only a sham battle. It was an age of art; and art, which is only the semblance of life, was at stake, not life itself. Now the highest interests of life are at stake. Revolution is entering literature, and this war is a much more serious affair.

Perhaps, with the exception of Voss, I am the only representative of that Revolution in our literature; and I believe its manifestation was absolutely essential. I do not believe that here, any more than in my songs, I am likely to find many successors. For the Germans are naturally servile, and people's causes are not very popular here. But one cannot predetermine things; everyone must do what he can. Of course, every individual believes that he is fighting for his own cause, while in fact he is merely representing some general interest. I say this, because in the Platen affair I lay no claims to the honor of people's tribune. I was looking after myself—but my reasons for doing so are to be sought in the general struggles of the times. When the priests of Munich first attacked and flung my Jewishness in my face, I laughed. I thought it was mere stupidity. But when I scented the whole systematic attack, when I saw how the absurd bogey was gradually turning into a menacing vampire, when I saw through the intent of Platen's satire, when I heard from booksellers of the existence of similar productions in manuscript, steeped in the same poison and secretly bandied from hand to hand, then I girded my loins and struck as quickly as possible. Robert, Gans, Michel Beer and others have always suffered these attacks like good Christians, and maintained a prudent silence. I am of another stamp. And that is good. It is good that the evil ones at last find the right man who will fight to vindicate himself and others without fear or pity.

Hamburg, November 19, 1830

DEAR VARNHAGEN: Just as there are birds that have a presentiment of a physical revolution such as storms, floods, etc., so there are men who anticipate the coming of social revolutions, and become mentally paralyzed, stunned or dumbfounded by it. That was my condition this year until the end of July. I was hale and hearty, yet I could do nothing but read the history of the Revolution by day and night. For two months I was by the sea in Heligoland, and when the news of the great week reached me there, it was as if I had known it all along, as though it were merely a sequel to my studies. On the Continent I witnessed the events which took place *here*, and which might well have put a less stout heart out of countenance with the beautiful. Nevertheless, though distraught on all sides, I am undertaking to get out a timely book from old materials. I shall call it "A Supplement to the *Travel Pictures*." I sent it a fortnight ago to Leipzig, where it will be printed for Hoffmann and Campe, and I think you will have it in three weeks. You will not be deceived by my political preface and postscript in which I pretend that the book was written earlier. Two or three sheets of the first half are old matter; and of the second only the concluding essay is new.

The book is deliberately one-sided. I know very well that the Revolution embraces every social interest and that the nobility and the clergy are not its only enemies. But for the sake of clarity, I have represented those as the only allied enemies, so as to consolidate the attack.

I myself hate the aristocratic *bourgeoisie* far more. If my book contributes anything to the emancipation of religious thought in Germany, the land of bigots, I shall be happy, and I shall gladly suffer the painful howling of the zealots. Alas! I am enduring so much that is worse! . . .

࿔ *I Wished to Become an Orator*

HERE, DEAR READER, I WILL MAKE A CONFESSION which you have not expected. You have probably thought that the loftiest ambition of my life has always been to become a great poet, to be crowned on the capitol, as once Messer Francesco Petrarcha was. No. It was the great public orators whom I envied; and I would have given my life to be able to raise my voice in public places, before lively assemblies, to rouse or allay the passions and to produce an immediate effect. Yes, *entre nous*, I will admit that in my inexperienced youth, when we are likely to be seduced by the lure of the stage, I frequently dreamed myself into that kind of part. I desired, by all means, to become a great orator, and like Demosthenes I sometimes declaimed by the sea, when winds and waves howled and raged. Thus one exercises one's lungs, and becomes used to addressing large gatherings even if they are very unruly. Often I spoke in the open field to a great throng of oxen and cows, and I succeeded in out-bellowing the bovine assembly. It was a more difficult job to address a herd of sheep. For no matter what you say, no matter how hard you urge them to liberate themselves, and not to trot like their forebears patiently to the shambles, these mutton-heads always reply, after each sentence, and with the most perfect composure, "Me-e-eh," so that you are beside yourself. In short, I did everything in my power to prepare myself for an appearance as a popular German orator when the hour of the German revolution should strike. But alas! Already on my first attempt I saw that I would never be able to play my favorite tragic role in such a play. And even if Demosthenes, or Cicero, or Mirabeau were alive today, they could never appear as speakers at a German revolution. For, mind you, at a German revolution they smoke! Imagine my horror, when I attended the aforementioned gathering in Paris, and found all the saviors of their Fatherland with pipes in their mouths, and the entire hall so filled with foul tobacco smoke, that my breast was constricted, and it would have been impossible for me to utter a single word. . . .

SELF-EXILE [1831–1848]

ᔕ *The July Revolution*

Heligoland, July 1, 1830

I AM WEARY OF THIS GUERILLA WARFARE and long for peace; at least
for a state of affairs in which I can surrender myself freely to my
natural inclinations, my dreamy way of life, my fantastic reveries
and ruminations. What an irony of fate, that I, who am so fond of
reclining on the soft cushions of sentimental contemplation, should
be marked out to scourge my fellow Germans out of their complacency, and move them to action. I, who most dearly love to pass
my time in watching trailing clouds, in solving metrical word sorcery, in eaves-dropping on the secrets of the elemental spirits, and in
losing myself in the wonder-realms of old tales! . . . I had to edit
"Political Annals," advance the interests of the day, arouse revolutionary action, stir up the passions, and go on pulling the nose of
poor honest Hans, and shake him from his sound sleep of the

giant. . . . Indeed, all I have been able to extract from this giant is a gentle sneeze, and I have been very far from waking him. . . . Even if I snatched the pillow from under his head, he would restore it again with his sleepy hand. . . . Once in despair I was about to set fire to his nightcap, but it was so damp with the sweat of his thought, that it smoked a little. . . . But Hans smiled in his sleep. . . .

I am tired and long for rest. I shall get myself a German nightcap, and draw it over my ears. If only I knew where to lay my head! It is impossible to do so in Germany. Every moment a policeman would come and shake me to find out if I were really asleep, and this very idea robs me of all ease. . . . But in truth, where shall I go? South again? To the land where the citrons and the golden oranges bloom? Alas! Before every citron tree an Austrian sentinel stands and thunders his frightful "Who goes there?" Like the citrons, the golden oranges are now very sour. Or shall I go North? North-east perhaps? Ah! the polar bears are more dangerous than ever, now that they are civilized and wear kid gloves. Or shall I go once more to infernal England, where I would not even wish to hang in effigy, much less live in person! . . .

OR SHALL I GO TO AMERICA, that monstrous prison of freedom, where the invisible chains would oppress me even more heavily than the visible ones at home, and where the most repulsive of all tyrants, the populace, holds vulgar sway! You know well what I think of that accursed land, which I once loved, before I knew it well. . . . And yet I must publicly laud it, merely out of professional duty. . . . You dear German peasants! Go to America! There are no princes or nobles there; all men are equal—equal dolts . . . with the exception, naturally, of a few millions, who have a black or a brown skin, and who are treated like dogs. Actual slavery, which has been abolished in most of the North American states, does not revolt me as much as the brutality with which the free blacks and the mulattoes are treated. Whoever is even in the slightest degree descended from Negroes, and betrays his descent, if not in his color, at least in his features, is forced to suffer the most frightful humiliations, which we in Europe would scarcely believe. At the same time Americans make much of a to-do about their Christianity, and are zealous church-goers. This hypocrisy they have learned from the English, who have bequeathed to them their worst characteristics. Material pursuits are their true religion; money is their God, their only Almighty God.

Of course, there may be many noble souls who in secret deprecate this universal self-seeking and injustice. But if they attack it, they expose themselves to martyrdom, the like of which is inconceivable in Europe. . . .

Heligoland, August 1 [1830]

FEAR AND HOPE ALTERNATE IN MY HEART, and I am very uncertain in my mind.

I have made my peace with the ocean once more (you know relations between us were somewhat strained) and we sit together in the evening and have secret *tête-à-têtes*. Yes, I will shelve politics and philosophy, surrendering myself to the contemplation of nature and art. For all this torment and bother are useless, and although I suffer tortures for the sake of the general good, the latter scarcely profits from it. The world does not move. If it is not fixed and motionless, certainly it revolves in meaningless rotation. Once, when I was young and inexperienced, I thought that great causes ultimately triumph despite the fact that individual soldiers in humanity's wars of liberation go down to defeat. . . .

There is a fresh light today, and despite all the melancholy doubts by which my soul is tormented and assailed, strange presentiments come over me. . . . Something extraordinary is happening in the world. The sea smells of cooking, and the monks in the clouds looked so sad, so troubled last night. . . .

I walked alone by the sea in the twilight. All about me was solemn silence. The high vault of heaven was like a dome of a Gothic cathedral. The stars hung there like countless lamps, but they burned low and flickered. The waves of the sea roared like a hydraulic organ, stormy chorals, full of sorrow and despair, but triumphant withal. Above me was an airy train of white clouds that looked like a procession of melancholy monks, moving along with bowed heads and sorrowful mien. . . . It seemed almost as if they were following a hearse. . . "Who is to be buried? Who is dead?" I said to myself. "Is it the great god Pan?"

Heligoland, August 6 [1830]

WHILE HIS ARMY WAS FIGHTING THE LOMBARDS, the King of the Heruleans sat quietly in his tent playing chess. He threatened with death anyone who should bring him news of defeat. The scout, who was watching the battle from a tree, kept crying, "We are winning!

We are winning!" Until at last he groaned aloud: "Unhappy king! Unhappy Heruleans!" Then the King knew that the battle was lost, but too late. For in that same moment the Lombards rushed into the tent and slew him. . . .

I had just been reading this story in Paul Warnefried,[1] when my thick mail came from the mainland with the news—warm, glowing, hot. There were sunbeams wrapped up in the printed paper; and they kindled my soul to a wild flame. It seemed as if I could set fire to the whole ocean even to the North Pole with the flames of my enthusiasm and the mad exultation which blazed within me. Now I know why all the sea smelled of cooking. The Seine had spread the good news immediately over the whole sea, and in their crystal palaces the lovely water nymphs, who had ever looked with favor on all heroes, had immediately given a *thé-dansant* to celebrate the great event. That is why the whole sea smelled of cake. I ran madly around the house, and kissed my fat land-lady, and her old sea-dog friend. I embraced the Prussian court-magistrate, from whose lips the frosty smile of disbelief had not altogether disappeared. I even clasped the Dutchman to my heart, but his indifferent fat face remained cool and tranquil; and I believe if the July sun had in person tumbled around his neck, Mynheer would merely have fallen into a mild sweat, but under no circumstances would he have begun to smolder. . . .

Heligoland, August 10 [*1830*]

LAFAYETTE, THE TRICOLOR, THE MARSEILLAISE! . . . My longing for peace is gone. I know now what I must do, what I must do. . . . I am the son of the Revolution and I take up the charmed weapons upon which my mother has breathed her magic blessing. . . . Flowers! Flowers! I will crown my head with flowers in this last battle. And my lyre, give me my lyre, that I may sing a battle-hymn. . . . Words like flaming stars that have shot from heaven to burn palaces and illumine hovels! . . . Words like bright javelins, that will go whizzing up to the seventh heaven and smite the pious hypocrites who have crept into the Holy of Holies. I am all joy and song, all sword and flame! . . .

Perhaps I am quite mad. . . . One of those sunbeams wrapped in printed paper has flown into my brain, and all my thoughts are in a white glow. In vain I dip my head in the sea. No water can douse this Greek flame. But it is no different with the rest. The other sea-shore visitors have also been struck by the Parisian sun-stroke, especially the Berliners, who have flocked here in great numbers this year, and cross over from one island to the other, so that one may well say that the whole North Sea has been deluged by them. Even the poor Heligolanders are jubilant, although they understand the events only by instinct. The fisherman who ferried me yesterday to the little island where I bathed, laughed and shouted: "The poor people have won!" Yes, instinctively, the people understand these events much better perhaps than we with all our learning. Thus Frau von Varnhagen once told me a story of how they were waiting for news of the battle of Leipzig, when suddenly the maid rushed into the room, crying with terror, "The nobles have won."

This time, however, the poor have won the battle.

I CANNOT SLEEP ANY LONGER. My overexcited imagination is beset by the most bizarre nocturnal visions. Waking dreams come stumbling one after another and become strangely confused and appear as in a Chinese shadow-play, now dwarf-like, now enormously elongated, so that I am almost driven mad. In this condition it often seems to me that my own limbs have likewise expanded to colossal size, and with giant strides I am running back and forth between Germany and France. Yes, I remember, last night I ran in this fashion through all the German provinces and counties, and knocked on the doors of all my friends and roused them from their sleep. . . . They glared at me with astonished, glassy eyes, so that I was afraid and could not say what I was doing or why I had awakened them. I poked the ribs of many a fat Philistine who snored frightfully, and all he did was yawn and say, "What time is it?"

Dear friends, in Paris the cock has crowed. That is all I know.

On the way to Munich, behind Augsburg, I met a throng of Gothic cathedrals apparently in flight, and they waddled terror-stricken. Tired of so much running around, I took to wings, and flew from star to star. These are not small populated worlds, as some dream, but radiant orbs of stone, desolate and barren. They do not fall down, simply because they do not know where to fall. And so they soar on high, up and down, in great perplexity. I arrived in heaven. All doors were ajar. Long, lofty, echoing halls, with old-fashioned gilding—quite empty. Only here and there in a velvet arm-chair sat an ancient, powdered attendant, in faded scarlet livery, dozing lightly. In some chambers, the doors had been lifted from their hinges; in others they were locked fast and thrice sealed with large, round official seals, like the houses of bankrupts or deceased persons. Finally I came to a room in which an old man sat at a writing desk, rummaging among thick piles of papers. He was dressed in black. His hair was white; his tradesman's face was lined and he asked in a muffled voice, "What do you wish?" In my innocence I took him to be God, and I said quite confidentially, "Ah, dear Lord God, I would like to learn how to thunder. I already know how to strike with lightning. Please, teach me how to thunder!"

"Not so loud," the thin old man replied vehemently, and he turned his back on me and once more rummaged among his papers.

"That is the Keeper of Records," one of the scarlet-liveried servants whispered, as he rose from his reclining chair and rubbed his eyes and yawned. . . .

Pan is dead!

৯৯ *Germany and the July Revolution*

Cuxhaven, August 19 [1830]

YES, EVERYWHERE, IN ALL COUNTRIES men will quickly grasp the meaning of these three July days and recognize in them the victory of their own interests, and celebrate. The great deed of the French speaks so clearly to all the nations and to all minds—the lowest as well as the highest—that even on the steppes the souls of the Bashkirs will be as deeply moved as on the heights of Andalusia. . . .

AND GERMANY? I DO NOT KNOW. Will we at last make good use of our oak forests, that is, build barricades for the liberation of the world? Will we, whom Nature has endowed with so much power, depth, and courage, at last use our godlike gifts and grasp the word of the great Teacher—the doctrine of the rights of man, and proclaim it and bring it to fulfillment?

It is now six years since I wandered through my fatherland on foot, and coming to the Wartburg, visited the cell which housed Dr. Luther. A good man, whom I will allow none to censure. He fulfilled a gigantic task, and we will always kiss his hands in gratitude for it. We will not take it amiss if he did not treat some of our friends too gently when their interpretation of the divine word went beyond his—when they also insisted on equality of man here on earth. Such a proposal, was, of course, untimely then. And Master Hemling, who cut off your head, poor Thomas Münzer,[2] was in some respects perhaps justified, for the sword was in *his* hand and *his* arm was strong! On the Wartburg I visited the armory where hung the old armor, the ancient spiked helmets, round shields, halberds, broadswords, the iron wardrobe of the Middle Ages. I wandered pensively through the halls in company of a university friend, a young aristocratic gentleman, whose father was one of the most powerful quarter-princes in our country and held sway over the whole shivering little slice of territory. His ancestors too had been mighty barons, and the young man revelled in heraldic memories at the sight of all this armor and these weapons, which, as an attached notice indicated, belonged to this or that knight of his family. When he took down an old ancestral longsword from its hook and out of curiosity tried to swing it, he had to admit that it was too heavy for him, and his arm sank weakly. When I saw that—when I saw that the arm of the grandson was too weak to hold his father's sword—I said to myself, "Germany *can* be free."

❧ Pride of Blood

I REMEMBER HOW WHILE STROLLING ON THE TERRACE of a castle one day, I flew into a rage when a dainty little count, my best friend, sought to demonstrate the superior blood of the nobility. In the midst of our argument, his servant committed a small oversight, upon which the noble lord slapped the face of the low-born slave so that the ignoble blood spurted forth. Then the count threw him down the terrace. At that time I was ten years younger, and so I threw the noble count down the terrace. He was my best friend, and he broke a leg. When I saw him again upon his recovery—he was still limping a little—he had not yet been totally cured of his pride of birth and declared anew that the nobility had been installed as the mediator between king and people, after the example of God, who had set the angels between himself and man, and placed them close to his throne, like an aristocracy of heaven.

"Glorious angel," I said, "do take a few steps." Which he did—and even the simile hobbled.

ᢄ Aux Armes Citoyens!

[November 1830]

I DO NOT KNOW WHAT EXTRAORDINARY PIETY prevented me in the least degree from softening a few expressions which appeared somewhat too crude during a subsequent revision of the preceding pages. My manuscript had already turned so yellow with the touch of death, that I shrank from mutilating it. All writing, which has grown old with years, has an inherent right to inviolability, especially these pages, which in a great measure belong to the dark past. For they were written almost a year before the third Bourbon hegira,[3] at a time which was much harsher than the harshest expression—at a time when it seemed that the triumph of freedom would be retarded for a century. It was certainly food for serious thought to see our knights put on self-assured faces, and begin refurbishing their faded escutcheons. How they tourneyed with spear and shield in Munich and Potsdam! How proudly they sat on their chargers, as if they were riding to Quidlinburg and were about to be knighted by Godfrey Bassen![4]

Even more insufferable were the malicious, triumphant little eyes of our little clerics, who knew how to conceal their ears so cunningly under their hoods, that we came to expect the most perfidious trickery. Of course, one could not foresee that these noble knights would shoot so badly and so wide of the mark, and, for the most part, in so cowardly and anonymous a fashion—especially when they took to their heels, facing backward, like fleeing Bashkirs. No more could one foresee how our little clerics would be put to shame.—Alas! it is pitiful to see how maladroitly they used their poisons, how they threw their arsenic in large chunks at our heads, instead of dropping it grain by grain into our soup; how they rummaged in the children's dirty wash for some of the used swaddling clothes and sniffed out foulness; how they even exhumed the fathers of their enemies, to find out whether they were circumcised.

Oh, you fools, who thought that you had discovered that the lion belongs to the cat family; who fussily hiss this wonderful scientific discovery all around you, till the cat confirms on your own flesh his *ex ungue leonem!*[5]

Oh, the dull wights! Who will not see the light until they are hoisted up on lampposts! I would string my lyre with a donkey's guts so that I might worthily chant the praises of these tonsured blockheads!

A mighty fancy takes possession of me. While I sit here, writing, I hear the sound of music under my window, and in the elegiac wrath of the stately tune, I recognize the Marseillaise hymn with which the handsome Barbaroux and his comrades greeted the city of Paris,[6] that *ranz des vaches* of freedom, whose sound awakened home-sickness in the hearts of the Swiss guard in the Tuileries—that triumphant funeral chant of the Gironde—that sweet old cradlesong!

What a song! I tremble with fire and inspiration!—I burn with the star-glow of exultation and the rockets of mockery! Yes, indeed, there must be no lack of those among the great fire-works of Time. Exultant streams of fire-laden song shall pour from the joyous heights of freedom, in bold cascades, even as the Ganges rushes down from the Himalayas! And thou, lovely Satyra, daughter of just Themis and goat-footed Pan, lend me thy aid. For thou art descended, on thy mother's side, from the race of Titans, and like unto me, thou hatest the enemies of thy race, the weakling usurpers of Olympus. Lend me thy mother's sword so that I may judge them, the hateful brood, and give me thy father's pipe so that I may pipe them to death. . . .

Already they hear the fatal piping. They are seized by a panic fear, and they flee, in their animal forms, as once they did when we heaped Pelion upon Ossa—

Aux armes citoyens!

They do us, poor Titans, much injustice in blaming us for the sullen savagery with which, in our rage, we once stormed those heavens. . . . Alas! down below, in Tartarus, it was dark and horrible, and we heard only the howling of Cerberus and the clanging of chains, and we are to be forgiven if we seemed somewhat uncouth by the side of those gods who, refined and well-mannered, *comme il faut*, were revelling in the delights of nectar and the sweet concert of the muses in the gay *salons* of Olympus.

I can write no more. For the music beneath my window intoxicates me as the refrain rises ever more mightily:

Aux armes citoyens!

❧ *To Varnhagen von Ense*

Hamburg, April 1, 1831

DEAR VARNHAGEN: I just want to tell you that I am still alive—if not for pleasure, as Frau von Varnhagen would certainly wish—nevertheless, I am alive. In these hectic times it is more difficult than ever to write letters, unless one has something definite to report, say, ask or offer. Far-reaching world-events are too numerous to be discussed in a letter; and important personal matters seem too trivial by comparison with the great affairs which are taking place daily *without our assistance.* Will things move by themselves without the help of individuals? That is the great question which today I answer in the affirmative, tomorrow in the negative—and the answers I give influence, and in fact dictate, my particular course of action.

When I noticed after last July how many recruits liberalism had suddenly gained, and how the oldest Swiss guard of the ancient regime had suddenly cut up their red coats and made them into Jacobin caps, I was tempted to retire and write art stories. But when the temper became lukewarm, and horrible, though false, news came from Poland, and those who had cried "liberty" hushed their voices, I wrote an introduction to a work on the nobility which you will receive in a fortnight, and in which, moved by the urgencies of the times, I perhaps overshot the mark. You will find there plenty of intentional indiscretions, which you will pardon—as well as the frantically rushed and careless style. In the meantime, I wrote even crazier stuff—which I threw into the fire as soon as things began looking up. And now? Now I think there will be more reaction. I am full of evil omens. Every night I dream that I am packing my bags and going to Paris to breathe the fresh air and give myself up completely to the ecstasies of my new religion, and perhaps to be ordained as its priest. . . .

₴♥ Exile

I HAD WORKED MUCH AND SUFFERED A GREAT DEAL, and when the sun of the July Revolution rose in France, I had gradually become very tired, and I stood in need of some relaxation. Moreover, the air of my native land was daily becoming more unwholesome for me, and I had seriously to contemplate a change of climate. I had visions: the clouds passing up above frightened me; they seemed to be making all kinds of grimaces at me. It sometimes seemed as if the sun were a Prussian cockade. At night I dreamed of an ugly black vulture that preyed on my insides; and I became very melancholy. In addition, I had become acquainted with an old court-councillor of Berlin who had spent many years in the fortress of Spandau, and who told me how unpleasant it was to have to wear iron manacles in winter. I thought it very un-Christian not to warm the irons a little, for if our chains were only warmed somewhat, they would not make so unpleasant an impression, and even cold natures could endure them easily. Care should also be taken to perfume the fetters with the essence of rose and laurel, as is the custom in France. I asked my court-councillor whether oysters were often served at Spandau. He answered, No,—Spandau was too far from the sea. Meat, also, he said, was seldom to be had there, and the only winged creatures obtainable were the flies that fell into one's soup. About the same time I became acquainted with a travelling salesman of a French wine firm, who never tired of praising the gay life in Paris and who told me that the sky was hung with fiddles, and that from morning until night you heard the singing of the *Marseillaise*, and *En avant, marchons*, and *Lafayette aux cheveux blancs*,—that "Liberty, Equality, Fraternity" was inscribed on every street-corner. He likewise recommended the champagne of his firm, and gave me a large number of his business cards, and promised me letters of introduction to the best Parisian restaurants, in case I should ever visit that capital in search of amusement. As I really did need diversion, and Spandau was at too great a distance from the sea for me to procure oysters, and as the fly-soup of Spandau was not especially to my taste, and as, moreover, the Prussian chains are very cold in winter and would not be conducive to my health, I determined to go to Paris, the

fatherland of champagne and the *Marseillaise*, there to drink the former, and to hear the latter, together with *En avant, marchons!* and
Lafayette aux cheveux blancs.

I crossed the Rhine on the first of May, 1831. I did not see the old
river-god, Father Rhine, so I contented myself with dropping my
visiting card into the water. I was told that he was sitting down
below, once more conning Meidinger's French Grammar, for during
the Prussian occupation his French had grown quite rusty, and now
he wished to review it, so as to be prepared for all contingencies. I
thought I heard him conjugate down below: "*J'aime, tu aimes, il aime,
nous aimons. . . .*" But what does he really love? Surely not the
Prussians! I only saw the Cathedral of Strassburg from a distance. He
wagged his head like good old Eckhart when he sees a young blade
wending his way to the Mountain of Venus.

I awoke at St. Denis from a sweet morning sleep, and heard for the
first time the cries of the carters: "Paris! Paris!"—and I heard the
tinkling bells of the licorice-water venders. Here you already breathe
the air of the capital, which is now visible on the horizon. A rascally
guide tried to persuade me to visit the royal tomb, but I had not
come to France to see dead kings. I contented myself with having the
guide tell me the legends connected with the place: how, for example,
the wicked heathen king had St. Denis' head cut off, and how the latter
ran all the way from Paris to Saint Denis, with his head under his arm,
in order to be buried there and have the place named after him.
When you consider the distance, my narrator said, it was a miracle
that anyone could go so far on foot without a head—and he added
with a strange smile, "*Dans des cas pareils, il n'y a que le premier pas
qui coûte.*" That was worth two francs, and I gave them to him
pour l'amour de Voltaire.[7] In twenty minutes I was already in Paris,
entering through the triumphal arch of Boulevard St. Denis, which
was originally erected in honor of Louis XIV, but now served to
grace my entry into Paris. I was truly surprised by the multitudes of
well-dressed people, as tastefully groomed as fashion plates. I was also
impressed by the fact that they all spoke French, which, in Germany,
is the earmark of the fashionable world; but here everyone is as
distinguished as the nobility of my country. The men were all polite,
and the pretty women smiled graciously. If someone accidentally
jostled me, without immediately begging my pardon, I could safely
wager that it was a fellow-countryman; and if a pretty woman looked
somewhat sour, then she had either eaten sauerkraut or could read

Klopstock in the original. I found everything charming; the sky was blue, the air balmy, open-hearted, and the beams of the July sun shimmered playfully. The cheeks of fair Lutetia [8] were still flushed from the flaming kisses of that sun, and the bridal flowers on her bosom were not yet wilted. But here and there on street-corners the words *Liberté, égalité, fraternité* had already been erased. I immediately betook myself to the restaurants to which I had been recommended. The proprietors assured me that they would have made me welcome even without letters of introduction, for I had such an honest and distinguished appearance, which in itself was sufficient recommendation. Never had a German restaurant-keeper addressed me in this fashion, even if he thought so. That kind of churl feels in duty bound to suppress all pleasant remarks, and his German bluntness demands that he say only the most disagreeable things to our face. In the manner and even in the speech of the French there is so much delicious flattery, which costs little and yet is gratifying and refreshing. My poor, sensitive soul, which had so often shrunk back with shyness from the rudeness of my German Fatherland, again expanded in the genial warmth of French urbanity. God has given us tongues so that we may say something pleasant to our fellow-men.

When I arrived, my French was rusty; but after a half hour's conversation with a pretty flower-girl in the Passage de l'Opéra, my speech, which had grown somewhat halting after the battle of Waterloo, became fluent again. I managed to stammer my way into the most gallant conjugations, and explained to my little friend very clearly the Linnean system, in which flowers are classified according to their stamens; but the little one followed a different system, and divided flowers into those that smelled good and those that stank. I believe that she applied a similar classification to men. She was amazed that, despite my youth, I was so learned, and she trumpeted the fame of my erudition through the whole Passage de l'Opéra. I drank in with rapture the delicious aroma of flattery, and had a good time. I walked on flowers, and many a roasted pigeon flew right into my gaping mouth.

❧ *To Varnhagen von Ense*

Paris, June 27, 1831

DEAR FRIENDS: *La force des choses!* The power of things! In truth, it is not I who have carried things to extremes; it is the things which have brought me to extreme points, to the very peak of the world, to Paris—yes, yesterday morning I even stood on the peak of peaks—on the Pantheon. *"Aux grands hommes la patrie reconnaissante."* [9] That I believe is the gold inscription. What mockery! Little men erect these temples to great ones—after their death. They would do better to place such inscriptions over Very's Restaurant and feed the great men well while they are still alive, instead of honoring them when they have died of starvation or other tortures. But Very's is the Pantheon of the little living men; here they sit and eat and drink and invent ironic inscriptions.

Poor La Fontaine has a marble column in Château-Thierry, his birthplace, which cost 40,000 francs. I laughed heartily when I saw it as I drove past. When he was alive, the poor wretch begged for a piece of bread, and after his death they gave him 40,000 francs worth of marble! Jean Jacques Rousseau and men like him, who could scarcely afford a garret in their lifetime, now have entire streets named after them.

Today I shall write you only nonsense; for if I wrote something sensible and the letter fell into the wrong, stupid hands, it might compromise you. For this reason I will write no more. If you have something to tell me, write me in care of Madame Valentin's or Maurice Schlesinger's. Or write in care of Dr. Donndorff à l'Hôtel d'Hollande, Rue Neuve des Bons Enfants à Paris. The last is now my principal address and the safest, if one does not have to fear other indiscretions of the Royal Prussian Post Office.

I am surrounded by Prussian spies. Although I am staying clear of political intrigues, they still fear me most. Naturally, since they are making war on me, they know that I shall strike back—and with all my might. Alas, six months ago I foresaw everything, and would gladly have withdrawn into poetry, and left to others this bloody business, but it could not be. *La force des choses!* We are driven to extremes!

At Frankfurt, where I stayed for a week and talked with several of my co-religionists, I discovered the source of many of my own ills, which I had been unable to explain. My last days in Hamburg were very unpleasant. I did not feel safe. Since the idea of going to Paris had already dawned on me, I was easily swayed when a generous and cautioning hand beckoned to me. However, flight would be easy, if we did not drag the Fatherland along on the soles of our shoes. I am parodying Danton, sorrowfully. It is painful to take a stroll in the Luxembourg, and always to be dragging a piece of Hamburg, Prussia, or Bavaria, on the soles of our shoes.

I shall probably stay here another month, and then I'm going to Boulogne for bathing, then back here—for how long? I can't be worse off here than at home, where I have nothing but strife and trouble, and cannot even sleep peacefully, and all the fountains of life are poisoned to me. Here indeed I am drowning in a whirlpool of occurrences, waves of daily events, in the roar of the Revolution. Into the bargain, I am all sulphur, and while I drown in the human vortex, I am consumed by my own nature.

May Fr. v. V. and you have a good life. Do not forget me. I am oppressed by gloomy forebodings.

Paris, May, 1832

DEAR VARNHAGEN: I have been wanting to write to you for the last two months, but the infernal cholera intervened, and now for a fortnight I have had severe pains in my head. . . .

I need to be sure of your sympathy and that of Frau Varnhagen as much now as at the beginning of my career. For I am as much alone in the world today as then. Only now I have more enemies—always a source of comfort to me, but never an adequate one. You may write me more often now, if you wish, without fear of interception and compromise. I am now on a friendly footing with all the authorities, and if I do not disarm totally, it is merely because of the demagogues, with whom I've had much trouble, and still have. These enemies of moderation would at all cost compel me to resign as people's tribune when I refused to join in their crazy plans. That I did not feel like doing. Now, thank the Lord! the cholera has fortunately rid me of many a tiresome fellow—I mean, of course, fear of the cholera.

It was not from courage that I remained in Paris when the panic broke out. To tell you the truth, I was too lazy. Börne [10] had planned to leave long ago, and it is unjust to ascribe his departure to fear. However, I did not see him for a fortnight before. We are on very bad terms. He has unloosed against me certain Jacobin intrigues, which I did not like at all. I look upon him as crazy.

I shall be very happy to learn that you like my articles in the *Allgemeine Zeitung*. I'm not sure of their value. I wrote them partly to establish myself in this field, partly for mere gain. Do you think it would be worth while to get up a book later of a dozen or so of these articles? This is a form little used nowadays.

I am very much preoccupied with the history of the French Revolution and St. Simonism. I shall write books about both of these. But I must study hard. I have learned to understand much in the past year through my observation of party-agitation and the manifestations of St. Simonism; e. g., the *Moniteur* of 1793, and the Bible. All I require now is good health and a peaceful existence. I did have opportunities of obtaining the latter, but on conditions which could not but be repugnant to me, not as a patriot, but as a man of standing.

I agree with what you have written me about St. Simonism. Michel Chevalier [11] is a very dear friend of mine, one of the noblest men I know. The withdrawal of the St. Simonians will probably be of advantage to their doctrine, which will come into astuter hands—especially its political portions, the doctrine of property, which will be elaborated more thoroughly. As for me, my chief interest is in their religious views, which have merely to be expressed sooner or later to become living realities. Germany will fight most bitterly for her spiritualism. *Mais l'avenir est à nous. . . .*[12]

Paris, March 28, 1833

I AM STILL UNABLE TO WRITE YOU. As soon as I take up my pen to say a word to you my head is in a whirl and my heart is torn apart.[13] And I am ordinarily so calm—self-control itself.

But at this moment things are happening in my life which would move a stone. This morning I received the news of the death of my Uncle van Geldern at Düsseldorf, who died at a time when I must feel his loss more profoundly than ever. Ah, my dear Varnhagen, I now understand the Roman saying: "Life is war." And so I stand in the breach and see my friends falling round about me. Our dear friend has always fought bravely. She has well earned her laurels. Right now I cannot write for weeping. Alas, we poor men, we must fight with tears in our eyes. What a battlefield is this earth!

This morning Heideloff here is publishing a book of mine in German, containing articles on literature which I wrote for *Europe littéraire*. I'll send you both versions. You will find there some lusty sword strokes; for I have faithfully fulfilled my duties as a soldier.

I know that I give you poor comfort, my dear Varnhagen. But no man can give comfort, only Time. Time, sly Saturn, heals all our wounds, only to deal our hearts fresh ones with his scythe.

You understand why I did not write you when Robert passed away, and when his wife followed him soon after that.

Farewell. Write me soon: Rue des Petits-Augustins 4, Hôtel d'-Espagne. I still suffer from a paralyzed hand. Koreff is my physician. I was very ill. Yet I remain active. I will not yield the sword from my hand till I sink to the ground. And till then, I remain your friend, H. Heine.

‹» *To Heinrich Laube* [14]

Paris, July 10, 1833

OLD FRIEND: I have really been treating you as an old friend, for I have postponed answering your letter till now, and yet I felt sure you would not misunderstand me. Be patient with me. I am thoroughly satisfied with you. In these evil times, your support was a most gratifying event for me.

You have no idea of the storm and stress around me. I have on my neck here the *juste milieu*,[15] the party of hypocritical Catholic Carlists and the Prussian spies. For *French Affairs* has appeared in French, with my whole ungarbled preface. Heideloff has also published the latter in German, and it may even now be obtainable in Leipzig, where you will perhaps see it. I would send it to you but for fear of compromising you. Take care. Even here no one is safe. Last Saturday a number of Germans were arrested. I too am afraid of almost momentary arrest.

Perhaps my next letter will be dated from London. I am hinting all this, in order to move you to act with caution and moderation. At this moment you must remain as quiet as possible. Hold our important fortress, the *Elegante Welt*, for the future. Dissimulate. Do not be afraid of being misunderstood. I have never been afraid of that. The publication of my Preface, in the midst of the general anxiety, will teach my public to trust me in the future, even when I pipe somewhat too softly. In due time I shall sound the great trumpet, and I am now engaged in the composition of a few good trumpet-solos.

. I thank you very much for all the nice things you have written and published about me. Rest assured that I understand you, and esteem and honor you truly. You stand far above those others who understand only the externals of the Revolution, but not its more profound questions. These questions concern not forms, nor persons, nor the institution of a republic, nor the limitation of monarchy—no, these concern the material well-being of man. The spiritualistic religion which has been in existence hitherto has been salutary and necessary, as long as the greater portion of mankind lived in misery and had to find solace in a celestial religion. However, since the progress of industry and economy has made it possible to extricate them from their material wretchedness and to make them blessed here on earth—hence—you understand me— And the people will understand us too, when we tell them in due time that henceforth they will eat beef every day instead of potatoes, and work less, and dance more. Believe me, the people are no asses.

I am writing these lines in the bed of my charmingly insistent lady-friend, who would not let me go last night for fear I should be arrested.

8➤ The Emigrants

"I COUNSEL YOU, GOOD FRIEND, let me paint on your sign not a golden angel, but a red lion. I am used to painting red lions, and you will see, that even though I paint a golden angel for you, it will nevertheless look like a red lion."

These words of an honorable fellow-artist stand at the head of the present volume since they meet every possible reproach openly and in advance. Once and for all, let me say that this book—with minor exceptions—was written in the summer and fall of 1831, at a time when I was chiefly occupied with sketches for future red lions. Around me was a great roaring noise and disturbance of all sorts.

Am I not very modest today?

You may depend on it: there is always good reason if people are modest. Of course, the good God has as a general rule made the exercise of modesty and similar virtues very easy for his flock. For instance, it is easy to forgive your enemies, if you don't happen to possess enough wit to harm them, just as it is easy to keep from seducing women, when you are blessed with too unsightly a nose. The sanctimonious of all shades will again sigh deeply over many a poem in this book—but it will no longer do them any good. Another "succeeding generation" has realized that all my words and songs spring from a great, divine and blissfully vernal idea, which if not better than, is at least as respectable as those mournful, mouldy Ash Wednesday ideas which have so sadly deflowered our beautiful Europe and peopled it with specters and Tartuffes. Where I once skirmished, lightly armed—serious, open war is now being waged. And I am no longer in the front ranks.

Thank God! The July Revolution has loosed the tongues that so long remained silent. Yes, when those who suddenly awoke wished to reveal all they had hitherto kept secret, there was much noise, which occasionally deafened my ears disagreeably. At times I was tempted to quit the post of speaker; but that is not so easy as quitting the job of a Privy Councillor, although the latter brings in more than the best public tribunate. People believe that our deeds are the results of some kind of idle choice; that from the stock of new ideas we seize upon one for which we wish to speak or work, fight or suffer, as a philologist would choose a classic on which to comment for the rest of his life. No, we never seize an idea; it is the idea which takes hold of us, enslaves us, lashes us right into the arena, so that we fight for it, gladiators by necessity. So it is with every true tribunate or apostolate. It was a painful confession that Amos made to King Amaziah: "I was no prophet, neither was I a prophet's son, but I was a herdman and a dresser of sycamore trees; and the Lord took me from following the flock and the Lord said unto me: Go, prophesy." It was a painful confession that the poor monk made,[16] when he stood arraigned at Worms, accused by Emperor and Empire for his teaching, and despite his humility of heart, declared he would not recant, and closed with these words: "Here I stand; I cannot do otherwise. God help me. Amen!"

If you knew this sacred compulsion, you would no longer scold us, abuse us, vilify us.—Truly, we are not the masters, but the servants of the word. It was a painful confession that Maximilian Robespierre made: "I am the slave of freedom."

And I too will make confessions now. It was no vain desire of my heart that prompted me to leave everything that was precious and fair and smiling in the Fatherland. Many loved me there; my mother, for instance—but I went, without knowing why. I went because I had to. Afterward I felt weary in spirit, for I had worn the prophet's mantle so long before the July days, that the inner fire had almost consumed me, and my heart had become as faint as a woman's body in the throes of child-birth, because of the mighty words which had surged from it.

I thought: you need me no more. For once, I'll live for myself and write lovely poems, comedies, stories, tender and gay word-comedies stored up in my skull, and I'll quietly slip back into the land of poesy, where I had lived so happily as a boy.

And I could not have chosen a better place to execute this design. It was in a little village close to the sea, near Havre-de-Grâce, in Normandy. A wonderfully beautiful view of the great North Sea—an ever-changing and yet simple vista: today a grim storm; tomorrow a pleasant calm; and above, the white trailing clouds, gigantic, fantastic, as if they were the spectral shades of those Normans who once plied their wild traffic on these waters. Under my window bloomed the loveliest flowers and plants: roses that looked at me amorously; red carnations with shyly pleading scent; and laurel, climbing up the wall toward me and almost growing into my room, like fame which always pursues me. Yes, once I ran panting after Daphne; now she runs after me like a harlot and forces her way into my bed-chamber. What I once desired, has become unpleasant. I wanted peace and I wished that no man would speak of me—least of all, in Germany. And I wanted to write quiet songs, only for myself or at most to read them to some hidden nightingale. And in the beginning it worked. My mind found peace again within the spirit of poetry; familiar noble forms and golden images dawned afresh in my memory. I again became dream-blissful, fable-intoxicated, and as enchanted as of yore, and I had merely to write down with a calm pen what I felt and thought. And I began.

Now everyone knows that in such a mood one does not always keep to one's room, but sometimes runs with beating heart and glowing cheeks into the open fields, without paying heed to the road. And so it happened with me, and without knowing how, I suddenly found myself on the highway leading out of Havre, and in front of me large peasant carts were slowly moving, laden high with all sorts of wretched chests and boxes, old-fashioned furniture, and women and children. The men walked beside them; and great was my surprise when I heard them speak. For they spoke German,—in a Suabian dialect. I realized quickly that these were emigrants. When I looked at them more closely, a sudden feeling rushed over me, such as I had never felt before in all my life. My blood surged suddenly into the chambers of my heart, and beat against my ribs as if it had to get out of my breast, as if it had to get out as quickly as possible, and my breath stuck in my throat. Yes, it was the Fatherland itself, that met me; on those carts sat fair-haired Germany, with her grave blue eyes, her homelike, somewhat too thoughtful face, in the corners of her mouth still that pinched narrowness which had once so bored and angered me; but now it moved me sadly.—For if once, in the full flower of my lusty youth, I berated her native perversities and Philistinism, if I once engaged in some small family squabble with that happy, pompous, burgomasterish, snail's pace Fatherland of mine— as happens in large families—all such memories died in my soul when I saw my Fatherland in distress, in a strange land, in exile. Even her infirmities suddenly grew dear and precious to me; I was even reconciled to her provincial pettiness, and I pressed her hands—I pressed the hands of those emigrants, as if, with this handclasp, I would renew the bonds of love with my Fatherland—and we spoke in German. They too were glad to hear those sounds on a strange highway; the anxious shadows vanished from their faces, and they almost smiled. And the women, some of whom were quite pretty, called down from the carts a pleasant "Griesch di Gott!" and the little boys greeted me, blushingly polite, and the very small ones squealed joyfully with their dear, toothless little mouths.

"And why did you leave Germany?" I asked those poor people. "The land is good, and we would gladly have stayed," they replied, "but we could stand it no longer."

No, I am not one of those demagogues who only seek to rouse the passions; and I will not tell everything that I heard on that country road near Havre, under the free sky, of the mischief done by the high and noble—even the highest—families in the homeland. Besides, the greater indictment lay not in the words themselves, but in the simple and straightforward tone in which they were uttered— or rather, sighed. Nor were these poor people demagogues. The last words of their plaint were always, "What was there to do? Should we have started a revolution?"

I swear by all the gods in heaven and on earth, one tenth part of that which those people had endured in Germany would have produced six-and-thirty revolutions in France, and would have cost six-and-thirty kings their crowns, and their heads as well.

"And yet we could have borne it and would not have left," said an old man of eighty—a Suabian, hence with a double portion of sense: "but we did it for the children's sake. They are not as used to Germany as we are, and perhaps can find happiness abroad. Of course, in Africa they will also have a few things to put up with."

These people were going to Algiers, where they had been promised a tract of land for colonization on favorable terms. "The land is supposed to be good," they said, "but we hear that there are many poisonous snakes there that are very dangerous; and the apes are very troublesome—they filch the crops from the fields, or they even steal the children and drag them off into the woods. That is horrible. But at home the bailiff is ruthless too, if you cannot pay your taxes; the fields are ruined even more by game and hunting; and our children were taken away and put into the army—what should we have done? Should we have started a revolution?"

In honor of mankind I must here mention the sympathy which, according to the testimony of these emigrants, was extended to them on their *via dolorosa* throughout France. The French are not only the wittiest of nations, but also the most compassionate. The very poorest of them sought to show some kindness to these unfortunate strangers, gave them a hand with packing and unloading; lent them their copper kettles for cooking, helped them chop wood, carry water, and wash their clothes. I saw with my own eyes a French beggar-woman give part of her own bread to a poor little Suabian, for which I too thanked her from my heart. It should be remarked, however, that the French know only the material distress of these people. They really cannot understand why these Germans left their Fatherland. For when the French find the oppression of their own rulers insupportable, or even somewhat vexatious, it never occurs to them to take to flight; they give their oppressors the gate—they throw them out of the country, and they themselves remain comfortably at home—in short, they start a revolution.

As for myself, I retained from this meeting a deep sorrow, a black gloom, a leaden despair in my heart, the like of which I cannot describe in words. I, who had been strutting proudly like a conqueror, now walked limply and weakly, like a broken man. It was really not the effect of suddenly aroused patriotism. I felt that it was something

nobler, something better. Besides, I have a mortal distaste for everything that goes by the name of patriotism. Yes, even the thing itself
was somewhat spoiled for me when I saw the mummery of black
fools who had made a regular trade of their patriotism, donning appropriate uniforms and dividing themselves into masters, journeymen and apprentices, and having their guild salutes, which they were
accustomed to use when they roamed and rioted through the land.
I say rioted—but with the most revolting weapon, the knout,—for
fighting with swords was not a part of their trade practices. Father
Jahn, the Hostel-Father Jahn, as is well known, was as cowardly in
war as he was silly.[17] Like their master, most of the journeymen were
merely roughnecks, slimy hypocrites, whose churlishness was not
even genuine. They knew very well that German simple-mindedness
still regards bad manners as a mark of courage and honesty; although
a glance into our jails should make it sufficiently clear that there are
ill-mannered villains and boorish cowards. In France, courage is
courtly and well-bred; and honesty wears gloves and doffs its hat.
In France, too, patriotism consists in love of a native land which is at
the same time the home of civilization and human progress. The
kind of German patriotism I have mentioned, on the other hand,
consisted in hatred of the French, hatred of civilization and of liberalism. Isn't it true, that in praising France so highly, I am no patriot?

It is an odd thing about patriotism—true love of country. A man
can love his country and never know that he loves it, though he lives
to be eighty—but then he has never left home. You do not realize the
meaning of spring until it is winter; and your best songs of May are
written behind the stove. The love of freedom is a prison flower, and
only in captivity can one feel the worth of liberty. Thus love of the
German Fatherland begins at the German frontier, and grows stronger
when one looks at German unhappiness from abroad. In a book
which I just happen to have at hand and which contains the letters
of a departed friend, I was profoundly moved yesterday by the
passage where, in a foreign land, she describes the impression made
on her by the sight of her compatriots in the war of 1813.[18] I will
quote the precious words:

"All morning I wept copious, bitter tears of feeling and mortification. Oh, I never knew that I loved my country so much! I am like
a person who does not know scientifically what blood is worth; yet,
if you take it away from him, he will crumple up just the same."

That is it. Germany—is ourselves. And that is why I suddenly became so faint and sick at the sight of those emigrants, those great streams of blood flowing from the wounds of the Fatherland and losing themselves in the African sands. That is it. It was like a bodily loss, and I felt in my heart an almost physical pain. In vain I tried to console myself with sensible arguments: Africa is also a good country; and the snakes there do not wag their tongues about Christian love; and the apes there are less repulsive than German apes;—and to divert my mind I hummed a song. By chance it was the old song of Schubart's:

> ". . . We must go over the land and the sea
> To torrid Africa . . .

> "At German borders we fill
> Our hands with German earth,
> And kiss it, thanking thus
> For care and guard, for food and drink
> Thee, German Fatherland."

Only these few words of the song, which I heard in childhood, have remained in my memory, and they entered my mind whenever I came to the German frontier. About the author I do not know very much, except that he was a poor German poet, and spent the greater part of his life in prison, and loved freedom. He is dead now, and long since has turned to dust; but his song still lives, for the word cannot be put in prison and left to rot.

I assure you I am no patriot. And if I wept that day, it was because of the little girl. It was already towards evening, and a little German girl whom I had noticed among the emigrants stood alone on the shore, as if lost in thought, and looked out over the wide sea. She may have been eight years old, and wore her hair in two neatly plaited pigtails, and had on a little Suabian skirt of good striped flannel. She had a pale, sickly face, great serious eyes, and in a softly anxious, though at the same time curious, voice she asked me whether that was the ocean.

Far into the night I stood by the sea and wept.

I am not ashamed of those tears. Even Achilles wept by the sea. And his silver-footed mother was compelled to rise from the waves to comfort him. I too heard a voice in the waters—less comforting— but more commanding, rousing, and very wise. For the sea knows all; the stars at night confide to her the most intimate secrets of heaven, and in her depths lie, beside the fabulous sunken empires, the age-old, long-forgotten legends of the earth. At every coast she harkens with her thousand curious billowy ears, and the rivers flowing down toward her bring her all the news they have found in the most distant lands or overheard in the chatter of the little brooks and mountain freshets. But once the sea reveals her secrets to you and whispers the great word of world redemption into your heart—then farewell, peace—farewell, all quiet dreams—farewell, stories and comedies that I began so nicely and which I shall scarcely finish for some time to come!

The golden angel-colors on my palette have almost dried since then, and only a screaming red that looks like blood and is used only for painting red lions has remained soft. Yes, my next book will probably be entirely a red lion, for which my estimable public—after hearing the above confession—will be good enough to forgive me.

H. Heine

Paris, October 17, 1833.

৪৯ *Declaration*

Paris, November 19, 1833

BECAUSE WHEN I WAS A YOUNG MAN I remained unshakably silent in the face of personal attacks directed against me in the public press, it may be assumed that now, in my hardened and more discreet maturity, I have grown fairly indifferent to them, and that only the public interest which I represent would induce me to contradict a number of anonymous falsehoods published in the newspapers. In reference to an article from Paris which appeared in the *Leipziger Zeitung* of November 12, I will therefore say this: I have never sought to obtain a place in the Prussian government; hence my past and my future expressions concerning Prussia cannot be traced to my failure to obtain such a position. I declare further that I have never been so stupid as to say that I would merely have to appear in Germany in order to provoke a revolution there. Furthermore I declare the silly assertion that I have sought or would ever seek the protection of the Prefect of Police, Gisquet, and that of His Excellency Ambassador von Werther against the threats of Prussian officers and nobles to be equally false. I declare that I consider these threats in great part only idle swagger, and that I have only prepared those who are of a like mind with me to obtain in common with myself, adequate satisfaction from such Prussian hot-heads, if necessary. I also declare that I should never have produced a letter which confirmed the existence of such threats, if my opponents had not affirmed it to be a fabrication on my part. Further, I shall in my next book print this letter—an action hardly advisable if the letter were not authentic, and if I did not at the same time possess adequate information concerning its bearer, who looked for me, in my absence from home, at my friends' and finally left the letter with the porter. . . .

ॐ *To Heinrich Laube*

Boulogne-sur-Mer, September 27, 1835

DEAR LAUBE: Thanks, many thanks for the unwearying love which you have shown me! If I have rarely given signs of life, for heaven's sake do not put it down to indifference. You are the only man in Germany who interests me in all respects; I feel that very deeply, therefore I can only seldom write you. I am too profoundly moved when I take up my pen to write to you, and as you certainly must have noticed, I am one of those people who have a horror of anything that unsettles the emotions and avoid it as much as possible. Alas, in spite of the greatest care, an overpowering feeling too often takes hold of us and robs us of that clearness of vision and thought which I would not gladly surrender. As soon as our minds are troubled and our spirits shaken, we are no longer the companions of the gods. This companionship—I may confess it now—I have enjoyed for a long time. I wandered peacefully, in the full light of day; but for the last nine months great storms have swept through my soul, and long, long shadows have beset me on every side. This confession will explain to you my present inactivity. I am still engaged in allaying the storms in my soul, and I am trying, if not to attain the bright light of day, at least to extricate myself from the deep darkness of night.

I received the letter which you sent me by a homeopath, and I was not able to see the bearer, for I was in the country at Saint-Germain, at the chateau of one of the most beautiful, noble and witty women . . . , with whom, however, I am not in love.[19] I am condemned to love only the base and the stupid. . . . Imagine what torture for a man who is clever and proud!

I was not a little concerned about you during your imprisonment. Your letter, though it made me sad, was something of a comfort. I'm sure things will go well with you,—I hope so—though I am afraid you will not escape the fate that pursues all people of our sort. For you too are of those gladiators who die in the arena. . . .

Boulogne-sur-Mer, November 23, 1835

DEAREST LAUBE: Your letter which I hasten to answer, moved me most painfully. I saw from it the unpleasant situation there, and your own alarming troubles. I have not set eyes on a German newspaper since I left Paris three and a half months ago, and except for a few hints in my publisher's letter a month ago, I have heard nothing of the literary horror which has broken out. I charge you by all that you hold dear, even if you do not take sides in the wars which Young Germany is waging, at least maintain a very defensive neutrality, and with never a word attack the young party. Draw a clear line between political and religious questions. In political questions you can make as many concessions as you like, for political forms of states and governments are only instruments; monarchy or republic, democratic or aristocratic institutions are indifferent matters, so long as the battle over the first principles of life, over the very idea of life is still in the balance. Only later does the question arise—how the idea can best be realized in life, whether through monarchy, republic, aristocracy, or even through absolutism—for the last of which I do not feel too great an aversion. By separating these questions one can also allay the scruples of the censor, for discussion of religious principles and morality cannot be suppressed without annulling all freedom of thought and criticism of Protestants. Thus one gains the acquiescence of the Philistines. Understand me, I say "religious principles and morality," although they are like bacon and pork, one and the same. Morality is only religion become custom (i.e. morals); if the religion of the past is decayed, morality too begins to stink. We want a sound religion so that our morals may be made sound, so that they may be more firmly established than at present, when they are founded only upon unbelief and stale hypocrisy.

Perhaps you will have gathered even without these remarks why I have always entrenched myself behind the authority of Protestantism, just as you will easily understand the vulgar subtlety of my opponents who would relegate me to the synagogue, *me*, the born antagonist of Jewish-Mohammedan-Christian deism. You have no idea with what pity I look down on these worms. He who knows the redeeming word of the future has little to fear from these petty hucksters of the present. I know who I am. Lately one of my Saint-Simonian friends in Egypt said something which, though it made me laugh, was seriously intended. He said I was the first Church Father of the Germans.

This Church Father has many things about his ears at present which keep him very busy in France, and make it impossible for him to preach the new gospel in Germany. Should it be necessary, I'll go into harness. It is disgusting to have to deal with Herr Menzel at this time.[20] He is a shabby scoundrel who can easily besmirch you. He is an out and out hypocritical wretch. If words were halters, he'd have hung a long time ago. He is a vulgar, vicious fellow, who should be kicked so that he can never get up again.

That he should attack us now! Now that the opposition has its foot on our necks! Only Menzel could have done that, for he was never seriously on our side. He joined us only after the July Revolution, when he saw some positive advantages for himself in the background.—And so, all boyish thoughts must be put out of mind, now that he is preparing a moral picnic for the anti-liberal party at our expense. Draw on your gauntlets, my dearest friend, and take a good, strong cane, and chastise the dirty wretch as he richly deserves, that is, personally—attack his private life, which offers so many loopholes. That is your business. Get yourself the needed details for a biography from Breslau and Switzerland, where he has been befouling himself. The young men of the university will surely give him the physical drubbing. . . .

I have not the least connection with the rest of Young Germany. I hear they have put my name among the contributors to their new review, but I never gave them permission to do so. Yet these young people will find a strong support in me, and I should be sorry indeed if there were friction between you and them. I beg you to inform them through common friends of your conditional relation to them, so that there may be no fatal misunderstanding. Please do not forget to do this. Under any circumstances you can rely on my sincerest sympathy in all that concerns you personally. I am glad that you have established good relations with some of my Berlin friends. Varnhagen is one of the most extraordinary men—clear and sure. We are so thoroughly of one mind, that we have no need to correspond.

Your question about my returning to Germany made me sad. I confess, though unwillingly, that this self-imposed exile is one of the greatest sacrifices I must make on the altar of Thought. If I returned, I should have to take up a position which would expose me to all possible misinterpretations. I wish to avoid even the semblance of the unseemly. So far as I know, no government can have anything against me. I have kept free from all the agitations of the Jacobins. The famous Preface, which I was wise enough to destroy after it had already been set up at Campe's, was made public later by the Prussian spy Klaproth. The embassy knew this, so that I cannot even be charged with a serious violation of the press regulations. All around me I hear friendly remarks through the diplomats in Paris with whom I am on very good terms. But all these things are reasons for not returning home, rather than for returning.

Add to this the bitterness of the German Jacobins in Paris, who would see in my return home to eat German *Sauerkraut* a proof of my treason to the Fatherland. So far they have only been able to blacken by surmise, for I have given them no factual grist for their slander mills. My trip to Vienna must therefore be postponed for a long time. In a few weeks I shall return to Paris. If you have anything to tell me before then, please write to my present address. Even in case I have left for Paris, your letter will be forwarded. Farewell and be of good cheer.

ࣔ *To the German Diet*

I AM DEEPLY GRIEVED BY THE RESOLUTION which you passed at your thirty-first session of 1835. I confess, Gentlemen, that this sorrow is accompanied by the greatest astonishment at the fact that you have accused me, tried me and sentenced me, without giving me a hearing either orally or in writing, and without having authorized any one to defend me, and without any citation being sent me. Not thus was the Holy Roman Empire accustomed to act in similar circumstances; and the German Diet is its present surrogate. Doctor Martin Luther, of glorious memory, was allowed to appear before the Reichstag armed with a safe conduct, and freely to defend himself in public against all accusations. Far be it from me to presume to compare myself to this esteemed man, who won for us freedom of religious thought. But a disciple may well appeal to the example of the master. If you, Gentlemen, do not wish to grant me a safe conduct to enable me to defend myself before you personally, at least grant me freedom of expression in the German press, and revoke the ban which you have imposed against all my writings.

These words are uttered not in protest, only in petition. If there is something I wish to guard against, it is public opinion which might interpret my enforced silence as an admission of my criminal tendencies or even as a repudiation of my writings. As soon as freedom of expression is granted to me, I hope to show conclusively that my writings are the fruit not of irreligious or immoral caprice, but of a truly religious and moral synthesis, a synthesis long honored not only by a new literary school, called "Young Germany," but also by our most celebrated writers, poets and philosophers. But whatever your decision, you may rest assured that I shall ever obey the laws of my Fatherland. The accident of living outside your jurisdiction will never induce me to utter a contentious word. I honor in you the highest authority of a beloved country. The personal security which residence in a foreign country affords me fortunately permits me, without fear of misinterpretation, to offer you, Gentlemen, my most humble protestations of profoundest reverence.

Paris, Cité Bergère No. 3, January 28, 1836.

ॐ *To August Lewald* [21]

Coudry, May 3, 1836

I HAVE BEEN IN THE COUNTRY SINCE MID-DAY YESTERDAY, enjoying the glorious month of May. . . . As a matter of fact there was a slight snowfall this morning, and my fingers are shaking with cold. My M[athilde] is sitting by my side before the great fireplace and working at my new shirts. The fire seems in no real hurry to burn; it is not at all passionate, and only reveals its presence by a gentle smoke. My recent stay in Paris was very pleasant, and Mathilde brightens my life with the consistent inconsistency of her moods. I think only rarely of poisoning or asphyxiating both of us; we shall probably take our lives in some other way—by reading a book which will bore us to death.

Herr —— said so much to her in praise of my writings that she gave me no peace until I went to Renduel and got the French edition of my *Travel Pictures* for her. But scarcely had she read a page of it, than she grew as pale as death, trembled all over, and begged me for God's sake to shut the book. She had stumbled on a love passage, and being jealous, she cannot suffer that I should have paid homage to any other woman before she entered upon her empire. Indeed, I had to promise her that henceforth I would not address words of tenderness to even imaginary women in my books. . . .

(This very minute I see an old peasant woman coming in order to shave me. I quake at the sight of her blade. I beg you, dear friend, pray for me!)

I am shaved, but how! And what torments! What sufferings a poet has to undergo in this hard world! Especially when he cannot shave himself. But some day I'll learn to do it! In addition, my boots stink horribly. They've smeared them with blubber instead of wax. These rustic pleasures! What a contrast to Paris where the evening before last I heard Giacomo's masterpiece for the tenth time.[22] Levasseur still brays like a wild ass. But what a masterpiece! It is hard for me to praise it adequately. What a masterpiece! . . .

ह≫ *To Julius Campe*

Marseilles, October 7, 1836

DEAREST CAMPE: You may offer up a cock to Aesculapius! I was already at the gates of Death, but as a special favor the immortal gods granted me a stay. When I wrote to you from Amiens, I already felt within me the germs of the sickness which took possession of me the moment I returned to Paris. It was a terrible jaundice, accompanied by the cholera or some such damnable disease. For a whole week I neither ate nor slept—I did nothing but vomit and have cramps. They sent me to Marseilles, and I got here the day before yesterday, feeling pretty well, though my nerves were very much on edge. I find it hard to hold a pen. I'll stay here only a few days. The noise of this haggling seaport has a bad effect on me. Marseilles is French for Hamburg—a thing I can't stand even in the best translation. . . .

೪ To August Lewald

Paris, December 13, 1836

M[ATHILDE] SENDS YOU CORDIAL GREETINGS. While I was away, she spent her widowhood at her mother's. I hear how they are slandering me in Germany. The way this is being done does great honor to the German people. I have never been in doubt about my Fatherland. We are a great nation. We do not prick our enemies with biting epigrams, we bespatter them with real German filth.

೪ To Julius Campe

Paris, January 23, 1837

DEAR CAMPE: . . . I enclose the preface to the third part of the *Salon*. If you read it carefully, you will understand how much trouble it cost me to treat so delicate a subject in a manner which would disarm the ill-will of the governments. I have said everything, without in the least offending. In fact, as a result, the authorities will become more favorably disposed toward me. The most important persons in Prussia are at this moment interested in my return to my Fatherland, but, naturally, I'm not even thinking of that. Yet at all events their intercession will shield me from many future literary annoyances. In Austria, Prince Metternich is well disposed toward me, and disapproves of the persecution to which I have been subjected. Without being servile, I am winning the confidence of statesmen, who see that my revolutionary ardor is not intended to incite the vulgar masses, but to convert those in the highest places. The selflessness which I have displayed in the face of the most alluring offers during the last six years has done more for me than all the flunkeyism of our Germanophiles. . . .

ᛒ *To August Lewald*

Paris, January 25, 1837

. . . You will have received through Herr —— the pretty tapestry which Mathilde made for you. She showed me by this troublesome and boring work that she was very industrious,—hence faithful, while I was away. She must have had as little lack of suitors as blessed Penelope, who gave her husband a far more dubious proof of her fidelity when he returned. Do you really think that Madame Ulysses undid at night the web which she wove during the day? She told this to the old man, when he expressed surprise that there was so little work to show. The wench spent her days and nights with her suitors, but was only spinning intrigues. You will hardly believe with what affectionate care Mathilde worked at your tapestry when she learned that I intended it for you. We live together very happily, that is, I don't have a moment's peace by day or night. I have always been of the opinion that in love one must be *possessive*, and I am one of those who reject the poetry of renunciation. But there is this much of good in Platonic love; it does not prevent a man from dreaming by day and sleeping at night, and anyway, it is inexpensive. . . .

ᛒ *To Julius Campe*

Paris, May 10, 1837

Dearest Campe: . . . I am again on very bad terms with my Uncle Solomon Heine. Last year he insulted me most shamefully, a thing one forgives much less easily when one is mature than when one is young. It is bad enough that this man, as I hear, establishes institutions for the rehabilitation of ruined money-lenders, but lets his nephew and his wife-child starve, and for no fault of theirs. I say my *wife*-child; by the first of these words I mean something nobler than a bride procured through money-lenders and priests. . . .

⁂ *To Maximilian Heine*

Havre-de-Grâce, August 5, 1837 (I think)

DEAR BROTHER MAX: I received Mother's letter a few hours before I left Paris. She told me that you would probably arrange to meet me in London. I went to Boulogne-sur-Mer and left instructions in Paris that my letters be forwarded. But a series of annoyances which beset me the moment I arrived at Boulogne, decided me to come to Havre for the baths which I need so badly. Whether I shall be able to last here a few weeks I do not know, but I can tell you this much, that I cannot go to London this year, and I hasten to tell it to you in case you have already appointed a rendezvous in your letter which has not yet reached me. I am greatly distressed about the matter. I would have loved to see you once more. I say once more, because I have a painful foreboding that I shall leave this world without seeing you with my own eyes. I always see you with the eyes of the spirit, for you are the only member of my family who understands me even though I may not say a word, and to whom I do not have to explain at length that all the troubles of my life have come to me not through my own fault but as a necessary result of my social position and my intellectual endowments. You well know that greatness of character and talent is not forgiven in our time, if their possessor does not purchase pardon of high and low for this crime by a number of petty meannesses!

Please say nothing of this letter to Mother, for she might easily be distressed by its tenor. You see how correct I was not to write you, for I cannot say anything definite to you, and what is indefinite could only cause you anxiety at this great distance. I will not even write you when you're in Russia. I hope you will not believe what is being said about me in Hamburg. I hope that least of all you will believe the vile things which you may hear said of me at Uncle's house. In that house there has always prevailed an *aria cattiva*, which has tainted my good name. Every worm that wished to gnaw at my reputation found there the richest fare. But I've seen to it that my temple of fame should not be built on the Jungfernsteg or Ottensen, with one of Solomon Heine's toadies and protégés installed as High Priest of my fame!

Do not take literally what even Solomon Heine or Karl (who has done me great injury) may say about me. At the time when I was moved to extreme bitterness by sickness (I had the jaundice) and misfortunes that were not my fault, I wrote to Uncle in a tone which should have aroused pity rather than anger. Yet it only aroused anger, and he was guilty of a great injustice toward me, an injustice which has done my honor as well as my material well-being irreparable harm in Paris. That is all he has to complain of me! Surely the few thousand francs I cost him hardly justify all his reproaches—he, the millionaire, the greatest millionaire of Hamburg, whose generosity—I can't go on!

You know that I always loved this man like my own father and now I must—enough! What hurts most is the opinion of the world which cannot explain my uncle's hardness and his refusal to help me otherwise than by some scurvy deed with which I am reproached in my family, but of which nothing is said publicly. Alas, if I would only play some scurvy trick or two, I should stand well with the world and—enough of that!

Good-bye. If you have a free hour write to me. Address your letter c/o General Delivery, Havre-de-Grâce. I am well. Physically I suffer almost no pain, except for my left hand which is crippled up to my elbow. In addition, I am growing very fat. When I sometimes look at myself in the mirror, I become panicky. I look exactly like my late father at the time he was beginning to be no longer handsome. I write much. My most important work is my *Memoirs*, but they will not appear for some time. I should prefer to have them published after my death. But I need the money. Financial need forces me to regale the world with a startling scandal. I've used the knife on some people; on others the *challaf*, or the guillotine.

I've not seen your Counsellor Gretsch in Paris. I hear that he will send articles from Petersburg to the *Journal des Débats* and the *Revue des deux mondes* (favorable ones, of course), which he will pay very well to have published. He is bribing the press on behalf of the Russian government. If he ever came to me with this kind of offer, he would not fare well at my hands. Although the German demagogues have spread the report that I have been bought by the governments, I can swear by the life of my dearest ones, that I have never accepted a penny, even when I was in dire need. And now it is out of the question that I behave so shamefully. Enough! Good-bye, and keep on loving me. Tell me how things are in Hamburg, and particularly about Mother, Lottchen, and Uncle. Is he well? And Henri?

ॐ *To Solomon Heine*

Havre-de-Grâce, September 1, 1837

DEAR UNCLE: I am astonished and deeply grieved to learn from my Brother Max's letter that you are still nursing a grievance against me, and that you still think yourself justified in complaining bitterly about me. Out of affection for you my Brother urges me to write to you in a spirit of love and obedience, and once and for all to remove the misunderstanding which has provided the world with material for so much scandal-mongering. Scandal does not bother me much, and I care little that the world accuses me unjustly of lack of affection or even of ingratitude. My conscience is clear, and, besides, I have taken care that when we all are laid in our graves, my whole life, my whole, unblemished, spotless though unhappy life, shall be known for what it is. But my dear Uncle, I do wish to remove the dislike for me with which your heart is filled, and to win back your former affection. This is what my soul needs most, and I ask you to do me this kindness, I pray and implore you with humility which I have always felt towards you, and the bounds of which I over-stepped only once in my life—and that at a time when unmerited misfortune embittered me deeply, and my dreadful sickness, the jaundice, unbalanced my whole life and inspired me with fears of which you can have no conception. I have never injured you, except with words, and you know that in our family, with our frank and quick-tempered natures, angry words are of little moment, and are immediately regretted if not completely forgotten. Who knows that better than you, dear Uncle, whose words one would have cause to be mortally afraid of, if one didn't know that they came from your heart, and that your heart is full of kindness, love, and generosity? I should not for long feel grieved over your words, no matter how harsh, but it is the incomprehensible, unnatural hardness of your heart that wounds, pains and hurts me most deeply. I say unnatural hardness, for it is contrary to your nature. There must be innumerable insinuations at work, secret influences which, perhaps, neither of us has been aware of, all the more annoying as my suspicions might fall on any one in your circle, even your best friends and relatives, and I cannot be happy about the thing. This misfortune weighs on me more than any other, and you can understand how necessary it is for me to be rid of it. As long as three months ago I wrote you from Granville, begging for forgiveness in case you still nursed some rancor against me. This winter too, when our family was visited by misfortune for a second time, I wrote to Karl, with frankness, and implored him to assure you, dear Uncle, of my unqualified devotion. I don't know whether he has done this. For even Karl may have been touched by the poisonous scandal without knowing it. I would certainly have come to you in Hamburg then, if, on the one hand, my personal safety were not in danger in Germany, and, on the other, my departure from France would not have been misinterpreted.

But I repeat my prayers today, and implore you to open your heart to me generously. I implore you with tears. Misfortune has so bowed me down that I shudder to think of my calamity, if my prayers should go unanswered. You have no idea how unhappy I am at present—unhappy without any fault on my part. Indeed, I owe my troubles to my better qualities, which rend me and are on the verge of undoing me. Every day I must fight against unheard-of persecutions, merely to keep my feet on the ground. You can scarcely imagine the sneaking intrigues which remain after the stormy upheavals of party strife and which poison the sources of life for me. What keeps me upright is my innate intellectual superiority, and the consciousness that there is no man in the world more capable of avenging insults with a few strokes of the pen than I, whether these insults be clandestine or open.

But tell me what is the real reason for the curse which hangs over all men of great genius? Why does the lightning of misfortune strike lofty spirits so often—those towers of humanity,—while it tenderly spares the humble thatched roof of mediocrity? Tell me, why should a man reap sorrow when he sows love? Tell me, why does the man who is so gentle, compassionate, and sympathetic toward strangers, treat his own poor nephew so harshly?

❧ *To Julius Campe*

Paris, September 15, 1837

DEAREST CAMPE: I left Havre a week ago, alarmed by a soreness of the eyes which grew worse by the hour. When I arrived here I could see nothing with my right eye and very little with my left. The best physician here, Sichel, has so far restored me that I am able to go out today, and even to write. But I am not yet able to see the letters distinctly. I am as weak as a fly. I am bled constantly, and I have eaten nothing up to this morning. . . .

❧ *To Johann Hermann Detmold*

Paris, October 3, 1837

DEAREST FRIEND: . . . My eyes are pretty good, and I feel passably well in all other respects. I am now the possessor of two velvet chairs and a good bed of my own. My violent passion for Mathilde grows more chronic every day; she is behaving nicely, and now she plagues me more in my dreams than in reality; but my troubled dreams and gloomy thoughts about the future embitter my days. I enjoy in full the pain of possession. I was lately in the village she comes from and experienced the most incredible, idyllic joy. Her mother gave me Mathilde's first little chemise, and this sad little piece of linen is at present lying in front of me on my writing-table. . . .

❧ *I Am Like the Flying Dutchman*

ALAS, I HAVE LIVED FOR A LONG WHILE IN STRANGE LANDS, and it often seems to me that in my fabulous homesickness I am like the Flying Dutchman and his shipmates who are constantly tossed on the cold waves, and vainly yearn for the peaceful quays, tulips, myfraws, clay pipes, and porcelain cups of Holland. . . . "Amsterdam! Amsterdam! When shall we again see Amsterdam?" they sigh in the storm, while the howling winds hurl them ceaselessly hither and thither, on the accursed waves of their watery hell. I can well understand the pain in the heart of the captain of the bewitched vessel when he said, "If I ever come back to Amsterdam, I'd rather be a stone on one of its street-corners, than leave the town again!" Poor Vanderdecken!

I trust, dear friend, that this letter will find you cheerful and happy, in the full bloom of life—and that the Flying Dutchman's fate will not be mine; to wit, his letters were usually addressed to persons at home who had died long since!

Alas, how many loved ones have gone, while my ship of life was being driven here and there by the worst storms. I feel giddy, and it seems to me as if the stars of heaven were no longer in their appointed places but were moving in wild circles. I close my eyes, and I am overcome by the strangest dreams, that reach out their long arms and drag me to unheard-of places and terrifying horrors. . . . You have no idea, dear friend, how strange and marvelous are the landscapes which I see in my dreams. Frightful sorrows torment me even while I sleep. . . .

Last night I saw myself in a vast cathedral. All was in a dim twilight. Only in the upper regions, through the galleries which rose above the first row of pillars, I saw a procession—flickering lights, red-robed choir-boys bearing immense tapers and standards, brown monks and priests in multi-colored vestments. . . . The procession moved on, strange as a fairy tale, above me, along the dome, and then gradually began to descend, while there below in the nave I fled in haste, up and down, with the unhappy woman on my arm. I do not know what frightened us. We fled, and our hearts beat fiercely, and we sought refuge behind one of the giant columns, but in vain, and we fled on, and the procession came down the winding stairs, and drew ever nearer. . . .

I heard an incomprehensible, melancholy dirge, and what was even stranger, I saw at the head of the procession a tall, pale, somewhat aged woman, whose face still revealed traces of great beauty, and who advanced toward us with measured pace, almost like a dancer at the opera. In her hands she had a wreath of black flowers, which she extended toward us with a theatrical gesture, while sincere and deep sorrow seemed to flow from her large, brilliant eyes. . . .

All at once the scene changed, and we were no longer in a gloomy cathedral, but in a country where the mountains were in motion, and were assuming all sorts of shapes and postures, like human beings; where the trees seemed to burn, together with their leaves, with red flames; and they were burning, indeed. For when the mountains, after crazily moving about, fell flat—as the plain itself—then the trees flared up and turned to dead ashes. . . . At last I was all alone on a vast, arid plain; under my feet there was nothing but yellow sand; above me only a disconsolate, wan sky. I was all alone. My companion had vanished from my side. While I sought her anxiously, I discovered in the sand the statue of a woman, wonderfully beautiful, but with one arm broken off like the Venus de Milo, and in many places the marble was woefully weather-stained. For some time I stood before her, in sorrowful contemplation, till at length someone came riding by. It was a huge bird, an ostrich, riding on a camel—a droll sight; and we spoke for some time about art. "What is art?" I asked him.

"Ask the great stone Sphinx, that crouches in the forecourt of the Museum of Paris," he replied.

My dear friend, do not laugh at my night's adventures. Or have you workaday prejudices against dreams? Tomorrow I leave for Paris. Good-bye.

ह्ऄ *To Varnhagen von Ense*

Paris, February 13, 1838

DEAREST VARNHAGEN: . . . As I have always done since the July Revolution,—with conviction—so I shall henceforth subscribe to the monarchical principle. This I shall do without ambiguous reservations—such as you see among the South German constitutionalists. As you know, dear Varnhagen, I am no friend of the German estates, and I have not spoken out openly against this bit of German buffoonery merely for fear of losing my popularity with the liberal masses, who might think me a servile hireling. . . .

৪৯ *To Julius Campe*

Paris, March 30, 1838

DEAREST CAMPE: At last this desolate, catarrhal, accursed and beastly winter is over! For the last three months I have been depressed and inwardly disturbed as never before. This, and a business which taxes all my energies more than is advisable, is to blame for my not having written to you before. You are mistaken, though, if you think that I am not diligently concerned in your behalf, and although the undertaking which I mentioned has not yet matured, the efforts which I have expended on it are bound to be of the greatest advantage to you. This business was nothing less than the founding of a German paper in Paris, for which I could call on intellectual and material forces beyond anything dreamt of. All that was needed was definite assurance from Prussia that the journal would be permitted circulation in Prussian states. For considering the huge sums of money—other people's money—which were being risked, I had to have some guarantees against the arbitrary caprices of the Prussians, and I had good reason to hope that my honest and reasonable request would be granted. But to my astonishment the old animus against me is not altogether dead yet, and my claims were not met so unconditionally as I had hoped. They will not give me definite permission—and my journalistic plans are surely ruined. But that is another matter.

I would like to tell you that as a result of these transactions, my relations with Prussia have considerably improved—even though they are not yet at their best, I have hopes that the unpleasantness will gradually disappear. In the strictest confidence, Minister Werther in particular is interested in me and has sought to win the others in my behalf. Actually, you have nothing to fear from the Prussian government so far as the complete edition of my works is concerned, even if the old prohibition is not literally revoked. . . .

৪৯ *To Karl Gutzkow* [23]

Granville, August 23, 1838

I WISH TO OFFER YOU MY SINCEREST THANKS for your letter of the sixth. Immediately on its receipt, I wrote to Campe urging him not to send the second volume of *The Book of Songs*, especially the supplement, to press as yet. I shall not publish it until I have sifted its contents again and provided it with an appropriate supplement. You may be right in thinking that certain poems in it might be used by my enemies, for they are as hypocritical as they are cowardly. But so far as I am aware there is among the objectionable poems not a single one that has not already been printed in the first part of the *Salon*. The new supplement, so far as I can recall, is of an inoffensive character. I do not think that I shall have to reject a single poem in later editions and I shall print them with a good conscience, just as I would the *Satyricon* of Petronius, or the *Roman Elegies* of Goethe, had I written those masterpieces. Like the latter, my poems which are under attack are not food for the masses. In this connection you are on the wrong track. Only cultured minds such as can take an intellectual delight in the artistic treatment of questionable and somewhat too natural subjects can find pleasure in these poems. Very few Germans are capable of expressing an independent judgment of these poems since the subject of them, the abnormal amours of the world's madhouse, Paris, is altogether foreign to them. The autonomy of art is here in question, not the moral needs of some respectable married German Philistines in a corner of Germany. My motto is: "Art for art's sake, love for love's sake, and life for life's sake."

What you write about the younger off-shoots of our literature is very interesting. However, I am not afraid of the criticism of these people. If they are intelligent, they will know that I am their strongest pillar, and they must praise me as one of their own in their attack on the ancients. If they are not intelligent—they are certainly not dangerous! I am not nearly so unconcerned as you think. I am trying to fructify my spirit for the future. Not long ago I read the whole of Shakespeare, and now, by the sea, I am reading the Bible. So far as public opinion of my earlier writings is concerned, it depends so much on time and circumstance that I can do little about it here. But I do confess that the great interests of European life are of greater concern to me than my own books—*que Dieu les prenne en sa sainte et digne garde!* . . .

ࣷ *To Giacomo Meyerbeer*

Paris, March 24, 1839

CARISSIMO: If I have failed to write you up to now it is not because I am careless, or, what is worse, indifferent. Alas, since you've left, I miss you wherever I go. For you were the only person to whom I could openly tell my most intimate difficulties. I have since then been extremely busy. Mathilde's illness and the organization of the German newspaper left me no free time. Alas! Both are in a very sad state. Mathilde spits blood, and grows daily worse. And the newspaper got its death warrant from Berlin. In spite of the intercession of important people—Minister von Werther was very much interested in it—the Prussian government will not rescind its unjust and ridiculous proscription of my name. Imagine my vexation! After I had worked at this business all winter and had written close to twenty printed sheets; after I had spent 2500 francs just for current expenses; after I had by superhuman eloquence convinced an ass to risk 150,000 francs on the newspaper; after I had, so far as my honor allowed, humbled myself—and just when I thought myself safe—*l'affaire est tombée dans l'eau!*

Isn't it frightful that a government can unjustly and without any right take my property, by preventing me from deriving full advantage from my reputation, and seeks to ruin my puny finances in such a spiteful way? Last year this act of injustice cost me approximately 60,000 francs, for before the passage by the Diet of the Resolution against Young Germany, and Prussia's total prohibition of my writings, I could have obtained 80,000 francs for a collected edition of my works. But last winter, I was compelled to throw it away on Hoffmann and Campe for a miserable 20,000 francs, merely to be able to buy bread, medicines, and fire-wood!

Varnhagen von Ense can tell you more about this. He too labored on my behalf with zeal. On the whole, I receive testimony of the most touching affection from Germany. I beg you to reassure my friends in Berlin. I am not doing so badly as rumor has it. By the end of this year I will have rid myself of all troubles; I shall not owe a sou; I shall live in modest but honest circumstances. I am saying this to reassure you, lest you misunderstand the complaints I have just made. At this moment I am in no need of money.

I shall spend this summer in Paris, unfortunately away from Mathilde, whom I've sent to her mother's in the country, where she will drink milk and sleep in the cow-barn. This is what the physician insists she must do. I myself will stay in the Chaussée d'Antin, where Dr. Sichel, who can help me the moment my eyes go bad again, is living.

You have no idea how afraid I am of going blind. Only the other day Sichel admitted that I was still in danger and must not write much. But alas, never have I felt the need of reading and writing as this year.

What you say about Uncle Solomon Heine shocked me profoundly. You too seem to have fallen for the legend that I wilfully offended this man, that I behaved coldly toward him, in a word, that I repaid his noblest generosity with blackest ingratitude! Well, the time will come and all mysteries will be solved. However, my dear friend, I shall tell you the whole truth today, all the more eagerly since you are passing through Hamburg and will speak with my uncle. You should be in a position to answer him when he begins his unjust plaints. In this connection I must tell you in confidence that all the stories now current in Germany about Solomon Heine's great generosity toward his nephew, the poet, are sheer romantic nonsense. The sum total of all his generosity, philanthropy, assistance and other forms of magnanimity is so trivial (you will be able to reckon it when you read my *Memoirs*) that you will be more amazed at his actual niggardliness than at those poetic fables which are due, if not to my Uncle's ambiguous statements, to the incredulity of a public which would not but believe that the enormously wealthy millionaire, who spent such vast sums on strangers, must be bounty itself when it came to dealing with his own nephew, the poet! But that is unimportant. I have complained to no other living soul. If I were so minded, I could have levied, like some I know, large tribute on my uncle; and it is perhaps my great error that I did not adopt well-tried methods and, like Moses, strike the rock so that the quenching silver potion might flow. *But I loved that man!* And that was my fault; that is why I came to him only occasionally to ask a few *louis d'or*

I needed for food or to enable me to escape—otherwise I have never pressed him to make any great sacrifices, like the others, who knew how to *smite* the rock. *I loved that man!* And that was my only fault, dear friend. Believe me. I have loved no one more than him. You know how stubborn I am in my feelings. They are buried deep down in my heart, like a steel plate, and no matter how I beat my breast, I can never uproot that infinite reverence for my uncle, that incomprehensible tenderness which I have felt since childhood—and that vexes me and gnaws into me like a worm! How it vexes me! . . .

In the past he used to complain about money. He said I cost him so and so much money. That I was earning nothing. That I was of the same age as Gumpel and Hirsch, who starting with nothing became rich, while I was still poor and in want. These complaints ceased, for, obviously, they were not intended to be taken seriously, for his spirit is noble and lofty, and he respects the poor, needy scholar more than the rich Jewish money-lenders.

Most recently, however, he accused me of two things, one as ridiculous as the other is horrible. He could not stand my saying in a letter that his greatest merit was that he bore my name. Though I do not remember making the remark, I have no doubt that it is true. My uncle never tells a lie. But it is not true that he was grieved, for he is too wise to lay much weight on mere words. He knows too well how I esteem his real worth, his greatness of character, and his remarkable personality. . . .

But the way he interpreted another letter was shocking and horrible—my soul trembles with anger. In it I condoled with him on the death of my poor Aunt.—I assure you on my word of honor there was not a syllable in it to justify his charge that I was brutally heartless. It was a brief, formal letter, wrung from me by the terrible calamity, which I could not have framed otherwise than I did, under the circumstances. Shortly before, I had given my uncle the most sincere assurances that I would never again write him so long as I lived. And now, I had to write him despite all! Actually, only to honor the memory of a woman who stands before me as I saw her in my youth, a kind, smiling fairy, who often shielded me from cruelty and want, who was so beautiful and good. I wrote that letter only to fulfill an obligation toward her. If my Uncle insists in your presence that it was heartless, ask to see the letter I wrote Karl Heine at the same time, and in which my repressed feelings find probably much more violent expression. For I recall after I had finished the letter to Karl Heine, I fainted, and Mathilde had to rub my temples with vinegar and call for help.—I also recall that Detmold's brother saw the letter on my table, read it, and was profoundly affected. This letter must still be in existence, and Karl Heine will show it, if his father insists on seeing it. . . .

৯ To Julius Campe

Paris, September 5, 1841

MY DEAREST CAMPE: Today I should like to inform you of an event which I withheld from you for several days—my marriage with the beautiful and pure creature, who has for years been my helpmate under the name of Mathilde Heine, and has always been honored and regarded as my wife, and whom only a few scandal-mongering Germans of the Frankfurt clique have tried to besmirch with insulting epithets. This vindication of her honor by legal and ecclesiastical authority took place at the same time that I redeemed mine too, which, but slightly jeopardized by the unsubstantiated remarks of a scoundrel, Strauss, was seriously impugned by the infamous testimony of three men.[24] I confess that I was never so disheartened as on the day when I read that shameful declaration, and if I had not succeeded in unmasking and disarming these scoundrels, I should have had recourse to the most terrible and appalling means. Now they are running about like mad dogs trying to provoke me to some open manifestations, so that they can demand satisfaction in place of Strauss. But I am not to be diverted from my true course; I shall meet Strauss in a duel, and although he is trying in all possible ways to escape it, I nevertheless hope to gain my object. A few days ago I was on the point of fighting him, when my second came to me in the night and told me that one of Strauss' seconds could not appear; and that the duel which was to take place in the early morning had again been postponed. Now Strauss declares that the police wish to protect his precious head and that he is being watched; but this is only a respite. He must meet me, even if I have to drag him to the Great Wall of China. If a man wants to fight, he can surmount all obstacles. They want to wear me out—but they will not succeed. Good-bye.

ঌ *To Betty Heine*

Paris, March 8, 1842

MY DEAR, GOOD MOTHER: I hope these words find you in the best of health. I am waiting impatiently to hear how you and Lottchen are, and how things are going with our family. I am feeling much better now. My eyes are quite well again, and all I have to complain of now is paralysis of my face, which is not, however, painful. Unfortunately, my wife has been ill the last ten days; and only today did she venture out of doors once more. In addition, it has been and is now frightfully cold here. I live quietly, prudently, and hopefully. Nothing new is happening—thank God! I am already of those who are happy if nothing changes. I dislike all change and turmoil—so you can see that I have grown old. For the last six months an overpowering mental weariness has come over me, so that I can say with Altfratje, "My *chushem* [25] are failing."

But this is only a passing mood, I am sure—the result of great excitement, of eight years' emotional tension.

My wife (the Lord be praised!) is behaving nicely. She is a thoroughly decent, honest and good creature, without malice or deceit. Unfortunately her temperament is very unstable and her moods unsettled, and she is irritated more often than is good for me. But I am still most deeply devoted to her. She is still my heart's greatest desire—but that too will go the way of all human passions, and I look ahead to this period with trepidation. For then I shall have to endure her moods without the balm of sympathy.

At other times I am plagued by the thought of how helpless and at a loss my wife will be when I die. She is as inexperienced and helpless as a child of three! You see, dear Mother, my troubles are to a great extent due to my hypochondriac brooding. . . .

ᶚ *To Betty Heine and Charlotte Embden*

Paris, May 13, 1842

DEAR, GOOD MOTHER AND DEAR SISTER: Last night I received your letter of the seventh, and so I could at least sleep peacefully. For four and twenty hours I was beside myself, after hearing the news in the papers.[26] I am amazed, dear Lottchen, that you could write so calmly and with so much presence of mind in view of the terrible fire. And I want to thank you with all my heart for reassuring me.

My wife is ill with fright at the terrible news. I hope that the scare and agitation will have no ill effect on any of you. My poor, good Mother! Don't allow yourself to be unduly upset over the material losses. God is a good man. This time, however, he placed altogether too much reliance on the Hamburg fire department.

Good-bye. Regards to my brother-in-law. I hope I'll get some good news today.

ᶚ *To Maximilian Heine*

Paris, April 12, 1843

MY DEAREST BROTHER: If I do not write to you—if for many years I've not written to you—it is for a simple reason. I had so much to say to you, that I did not know where to begin or end. But you are always in my thoughts and almost every day I speak of you to my wife, who would be so glad to see you! In my bitterest troubles I am often fortified by the knowledge that I have a loyal brother who is wholeheartedly devoted to me. And there has been no lack of troubles during the past years.

I am living fairly peacefully at present, for there is a truce between my enemies and myself, though they are still busy agitating in secret, and I must be prepared for all sorts of outbreaks of the deadliest hatred and the most cowardly villainy. All this would count for little, were it not that my worst enemy lives within my own body—that is, in my head; and lately this sickness has entered a very serious phase. Almost all of the left side of my face is paralyzed so far as feeling is concerned. I am still able to move the muscles. Above my left eye-brow, at the root of the nose, I feel a pressure, as of lead, which never ceases; for the last two years it has been there in the same spot. I have felt it less only in moments of great exertion, when I was at work; but thereafter the reaction is all the worse. And as you can imagine, I may not do much work now. What a misfortune! My left eye is very weak and aches, and often doesn't coordinate with the right, so that at times my vision is blurred, and I suffer more than if I were totally blind. For the last two months I have had a seton applied to my neck, but that is only a palliative and I have no faith in any remedy. I am telling you this not because I expect advice, but merely to satisfy your professional curiosity. I have little hope of improvement and contemplate a wretched future.

My wife is a good, frank, cheerful child, almost too much of a child, capricious as only a Frenchwoman can be, and she does not allow me to wallow in melancholy dreams to which I am so predisposed. I have loved her now for more than seven years with a tenderness and passion which are almost incredible. I have enjoyed much happiness in that time, torture and blessedness in an appalling blend, more than my sensitive nature could bear. Shall I now have to taste sobering and bitter dregs? As I said, the thought of the future makes me shudder. Perhaps things will go better than I anticipate in my troubled mind. Stand by me, dearest Brother, and my heart will lean on your brotherly loyalty and unshakable love. . . .

ತಿ To Mathilde Heine

Hamburg, November 19, 1843

MY DEAREST FRIEND: I hope you are well. As for me, my wretched head is still playing tricks on me, and prevents me from concluding my business in Hamburg quickly. I am ill and bored, for I think of you constantly. I am almost mad when my thoughts turn toward Chaillôt. What is my wife, that crazy madcap, doing now? I was crazy not to bring you here with me. For God's sake, do nothing to make me angry when I return. Stay as quietly as possible in your little nest; work, study, suffer virtuous boredom, spin wool like the upright Lucrece, whom you saw at the Odéon. . . .

৪৶ *To Julius Campe*

Paris, April 17, 1844

MY DEAREST CAMPE: It is a month now that I have been free of my eye-ailment. Before that I was almost blind— I could not write, and what was worse, I could not read. You have no idea of the depression which overpowered me. Fortunately my long poem was almost completed.[27] It only wanted the conclusion, and I have supplied that, perhaps very scantily. Since then, I have been busy with copying out this work, and the beautiful, clean manuscript is before me now. I shall go through it again with a magnifying glass, and then I will send it to you direct, via Havre. It is a rhymed poem, which contains four verses to the page and may run to more than ten printed sheets, and it expresses all the ferment in present-day Germany in a most audacious and personal fashion. It is political-romantic, and I hope it will administer a death-blow to the prosaic, bombastic poetry of "tendency." You know that I do not boast, but I am sure that this time I have produced a little work which will create more of a furor than the most popular pamphlets, and will yet have the enduring value of a classic.

At first I intended to add ten to twelve pages of prose and discuss in them the remarkable changes which I had observed in Germany. But while I was blind, I worked out this material more extensively, and now I see that I can make of it one of my most important works, if I fill in the gaps with material collected on a second trip to Germany. The descriptions of my literary friends and acquaintances who have died in the last thirteen years, alone might make a long and interesting book: Hegel, Gans, Cotta, Immermann, M. Beer, Schenk, Arnim, Chamisso, Fouqué, Frau von Varnhagen, the Roberts, Maltiz, and a host of large and small creatures, not to mention Grabbe, the most important,—in brief, a book of personalities who stand out vividly in my mind. . . .

౭⋗ *To Mathilde Heine*

Hamburg, August 20, 1844

MY PRECIOUS LOVE: Since you left, I've done nothing but sigh. I think of you constantly; I suffer from my usual headaches, and these pains are heightened and fed by the unrest in my heart. I will no longer be separated from you! How terrible! I feel more than ever that I must have you with me all the time. You know how agitated I am because I have no news of you yet. Write me, I implore you, as often as you can, at least twice a week, c/o Herren Hoffmann and Campe. The agent will deliver your letters to me personally; he knows where to find me at all times. In two days I shall leave my spacious quarters for a smaller room which will not cost so much, and where I won't be disturbed at night by barking dogs, as I am at present. A whole pack of them has conspired against my sleep; and every night I am driven mad by them.

Write me if you were very sea-sick, if you've been cheated by the customs, or lost something on the way, and most important, if your accommodations at the pension are good. I implore you to tell me the whole truth about these matters, for if you're not comfortable, I'll rush my departure even more than I am doing now. Tell me if your present situation is bearable; if so, I'll be able to conclude my business at greater leisure and in peace. Things here are the same. Everyone asks me how you are, and since I can't tell them, I am all the more disturbed. I hope you can read my scrawl. I have no more ink and the pen is wretched. . . . Stay quietly in your nest, my poor little dove. Don't show yourself in public, so that none of my acquaintances may know that you are in Paris without me.

Your poor dog
Henri Heine

Hamburg, August 27, 1844

MY DEAR NONNOTTE: At last, thank God, at last I have your letter. It came last Sunday, when I could no longer stand the suspense and was overcome by exhaustion such as you can scarcely imagine. Merely at the sight of your letter my heart leaped, I trilled, I danced,

I went to the theater to enjoy the songs and dances. They were performing *The Mute*,[28] and I swallowed four acts of it. I don't know how well the thing was performed; for I was so busy with my own thoughts that I was completely oblivious of the play. I thought only of you, my poor friend, and your dangerous crossing, and the fact that you had been so terribly shaken up by good-for-nothing Neptune, who is certainly not too gallant toward pretty women. That old good-for-nothing heathen god—I'll get even with him by writing a squib! Shameless wretch! Laying violent hands on Nonnotte, my poor lamb! I am also furious at the shameless customs officers, who extorted twenty francs from you for the stockings. Did you not tell them that they were intended to grace the loveliest legs in Chaillôt? However, I believe it is partly my fault, for I should have concealed them near the bottom of the trunk. I am happy that you haven't lost your things, and that no one called out to you, as Odry does, when playing Bilboquet, *"Il n'y a pas de Malle!"* To think I might have lost you in a ship-wreck, or you might have been captured by corsairs! Then, if anyone asked me, "Where is your wife?" I'd have to say, *"Il n'y a pas de Mal!"*

I feel better now that I've heard from you. Write me often, otherwise I'll slip back into my dark moods. Everyone here is well. My uncle played a foolish prank. Despite the fact that he is ill, he travelled to Travemünde for a few days. A thousand compliments to Madame Darte. Regards to Pauline, whose brief letter has made me very happy.

⮞ *To Karl Marx*

Hamburg, September 21, 1844

MY DEAREST MARX: I am again suffering from my deadly eye ailment, and I can scribble these lines only with difficulty. However, the important things I want to tell you I shall be able to say orally, beginning next month, for I am planning to leave. I've been disturbed by a hint from on high and I have no itch to be hunted down and my legs are not trained to wear chains, like Weitling's.[29] He showed me some of the scars. They are attributing to me a greater share in the work of the *Vorwärts* than I can actually boast. To speak quite bluntly, that journal is a master in inciting and compromising people.

Where is that to lead? Even Mäurer has been thrown overboard! I'll tell you more about this when I see you. If only no intrigues are hatched in Paris! My book is off the press, and will not be issued for ten days or two weeks—so that the alarm may not be sounded at once. Today I send you under separate cover the proofs of the political section, which contains my long poem, with a three-fold purpose: First, for your amusement; second, that you immediately do something for it in the German press; and third, if advisable, that you print the best parts of my new poem in the *Vorwärts*. . . .

Good-bye, dear friend, and forgive this confused scrawl. I cannot reread what I've written, but we don't need many signs to understand each other.

ᙠᴗ *To Charlotte Embden*

Paris, December 29, 1844

DEAR, GOOD SISTER: Late last night I received your letter. You can easily imagine what a horrible night I spent.[30] My brain is still dizzy. I cannot think two consecutive thoughts. Although I was prepared for this eventuality, I am more deeply affected than I've been since Father's death. I am amazed that with all this trouble you could get yourself to write me immediately. You are weeping, but I haven't as yet been able to shed tears. That's the advantage you women have, you can weep more easily. My wife is also in tears. Last night she came into my room three times. You are right: Only time can comfort us. How the good child Therese must be suffering! And Karl, poor fellow, how much he must have suffered! I won't write the poor children until I've come to myself and feel much calmer. God, what a calamity!

Our good Uncle Henri—how upset he must be! Give him my love. I have no intention of trying to comfort him. My pen is shaking as I write. My eyes are in a frightful state. If I could only weep! Only yesterday I wrote *him*, although I had forebodings of the calamity! Do give me full details of his last moments. That man has played an important part in my life's history and should be unforgettably portrayed. What a heart! What a head! For a long time now I have been unconcerned about his final arrangements. He himself spoke to me about them, or at least hinted at them pretty clearly. I would have given my last penny to keep him for five or even three years longer. Yes, I would have given half of my remaining years. And how kindly he treated my poor kitten! He said many harsh things to me. He even struck me with his cane this past summer, in a moment of excitement. God! How gladly I'd suffer those strokes again! If I could only weep!

I am anxiously waiting for Mother's sad letter. I know her well. I know that she will not be consoled easily. She will open all her old wounds. . . .

৯ To Johann Hermann Detmold

Paris, January 9, 1845

MY DEAREST DETMOLD: You can always rely on my writing you when I'm in great trouble. Perhaps you have already heard from Hamburg of the great misfortune which has befallen me. I do not mean my uncle's death, but the way in which he has provided for me. From a number of hints I had long suspected that someone had persuaded him that I would squander any large sum or that the governments would confiscate it. My allowance was a settled thing. I must admit in all honesty that I did not expect a considerable legacy, but only that my allowance would be increased. Then, on the 30th, seven days after his death, I received a long letter from Karl Heine, probably written on the day of the funeral, in which my erstwhile good friend tells me bluntly that my uncle has left me only 8000 marks cash in his will, that there is no mention of an allowance, but that he himself will give me 2000 francs annually—on condition that whatever I write about his father would first be submitted in manuscript to him for examination. Yesterday I answered his letter with studied contempt and I told him I would go to court; for as regards the pension, I have evidence to prove my uncle's commitment. . . .

৯ To Julius Campe

Montmorency, July 21, 1845

MY DEAREST FRIEND: I should have answered your last letter at once, if I weren't bed-ridden for a fortnight, and writing with one eye would have made matters worse. I got up today, tired and fagged out, but my first concern is to reassure you as to the state of my health. It is by no means as hopeless as some people in Germany seem to think, to judge from the letters I receive. It is true that in addition to my eye ailment, I suffered paralysis of the upper part of my body, but I hope to get over this soon.

I could not go to a watering-place, and so I went to the country, to Montmorency, where my wife takes good care of me. I have kept up my good spirits, and I am doing much thinking. If my physical condition permits, I'll be delivered this year of a literary offspring and call on your services as mid-wife. But above all, my health must be restored. That is the main thing; all else is secondary, even my financial troubles and the differences with my family, which seem about to be adjusted, though they are not over yet, for I will at no price allow myself to be excited or bothered by abominable disclosures. Therefore, I shall tell you more about my present relations with Karl Heine. He has grievously offended me, but has no idea of the enormity of his crime. . . .

৯৵ *To Varnhagen von Ense*

Paris, January 3, 1846

MY DEAREST VARNHAGEN: This is the first letter I have written in the New Year, and I begin it with my very best wishes. May you be blessed this year with bodily and mental health! I am very sorry to hear that you are weighed down with physical suffering. I should gladly have sent you words of comfort, but Hecuba is a poor comforter. For I have been in a very bad way lately; and my writing constantly reminds me of my physical misfortunes. I can scarcely see my pen writing, for one of my eyes is completely closed, and the other is already closing, and every letter is sheer agony! Hence I gladly take this opportunity of giving you news of myself by mouth of a friend, who, being thoroughly initiated in all my troubles, will be able to tell you in detail how shamefully I've been betrayed by my kith and kin, and what can be done for me in this respect. My friend, Herr Lassalle,[31] the bearer of this letter, is a young man of preëminent intellectual endowments. He is possessed of the soundest learning, the widest knowledge, the keenest acumen I have ever met. He combines a gift of brilliant expression with an enthusiasm for knowledge and an energy of will which are simply astonishing, and if his sympathy for me continues, I expect very real assistance from him. In any case, I have been overjoyed to meet such a combination of knowledge and power, of talent and character, and you too, with your versatility and keenness of insight, will be sure to do him full justice. Herr Lassalle is distinctly a child of his age—of the new day—and refuses to hear of renunciation and modesty with which in our day we dawdled and muddled through life more or less hypocritically. This new generation wishes to enjoy life and fulfill itself in the visible world. We old fellows used to bow down humbly before the invisible, and hunger for phantom kisses and the odors of blue flowers, and renounce and whine, though we may have been happier than those stern gladiators who now meet death so proudly. The thousand-year reign of Romanticism is at an end. I myself was its last fairy king, and I abdicated. If I had not hurled the crown from my head, and donned the smock, I would have been beheaded. Four years ago, before I turned apostate, I still hankered after moonlight gambols with my old dream-comrades—and so I wrote *Atta Troll*, the swan song of the dying age, which I dedicated to you. And that was as should be, for you are my chosen comrade-in-arms, in play and in earnest. Like me, you have helped to bury the old times, and have been mid-wife to the new; yes, we have brought the latter into the world and we are appalled.—We are like the poor hen that hatched duck's eggs, and is horrified to see her young brood plunge into the water and swim at ease!

I am obligated by contract with the bookseller to publish *Atta Troll*,—within the next few months—otherwise I will lose my head in litigations.

You see, my dear friend, how vague and how unsure I am! This weakling mood is to a great extent due to my illness. If the paralysis, which squeezes my chest as with an iron band, goes away, my old energies will once more find release. I am afraid though that it will take a long time. The treachery which was hatched against me in the bosom of my own family, when I was trusting and unarmed, struck me like lightning out of the blue and almost proved the death of me. Whoever considers the circumstances, will agree that it was assassination; slimy mediocrity consumed by bitter envy of genius waited for twenty long years, and at length had its victorious moment. After all, this is an old story, and repeats itself forever.

Yes, I am very sick in body, but my soul has suffered little. A weary flower, it has bent its head somewhat, but it is not withered in the least; it has firm roots in love and truth. And now good-bye, dear Varnhagen. My friend will tell you how much and how constantly I think of you, as you can readily see, when I tell you that I can no longer read, and in the long winter evenings I find cheer only in memories.

✎ To Alexander von Humboldt [32]

Paris, January 11, 1846

DEAR BARON: The good will with which you have honored me for many years gives me the courage to ask you to do me a favor.

I am called to Hamburg this spring by unhappy family affairs, and I would like to avail myself of the opportunity of taking a few days' trip to Berlin, partly to see old friends once more, partly to consult Berlin physicians about a very serious illness.

Since the only aim of such a trip is diversion and the recovery of my health, I cannot be troubled by any *atra cura.* Hence I turn to you, Herr Baron, with the request that you use your great influence to obtain definite assurance from the respective authorities that during my journey through the royal Prussian states I shall not be called upon to answer any accusations involving the past. I know very well that such a request is not in accordance with the administrative routine which prevails in Prussia, but at a time which is itself somewhat exceptional, it should be possible to enrich the old registry with a special rubric for exceptional men of this age.

Please accept my profound thanks in advance, dear Baron, and be good enough to regard my request a token of my respect for you.

✎ To Emma Kann de Albest

Paris, February 1, 1846

MEIN FRÄULEIN: My brother Gustav has informed me of his engagement to you, and while I am sending him my good wishes, I cannot refrain from writing a few friendly words to you. After all the kind and lovely things people have said about you, I look forward to welcoming you as my sister-in-law soon, and knowing you personally. You will probably be making a pleasure trip to Paris, a very simple matter today. Or I may some day stop off in Vienna—on my projected trip to Italy—and then I shall get to know something of the gay Viennese life of which I have heard so much.

In Paris people lead only outwardly happy and carefree lives, but their hearts are sore and weary with daily business. There are plenty of balls, assemblies, concerts; but these too are only a variant of business which one cannot avoid, because the women insist on showing off their finery and the men must make it apparent that they are do-nothings, and merely distinguished men of leisure. You have no idea of how hard people in Paris work, and how serious they really are. I myself seldom take part in these sham public pleasures; I live quite contented within the circle of my small family, that is, my wife and parrot. These two charming creatures are very dear to me—the former more than anything in the world. For eleven years now I have adored her and cared for her constantly. All Heines make good husbands; and in this respect I can cast a favorable augury, dear Fräulein. This is surely an important piece of information. I think you will live a very happy and gay life with my brother.

ও⹀ To Ferdinand Lassalle

Paris, February 11, 1846

MY DEAREST LASSALLE: In your last letter you forgot to inform me of your address, and I hesitate to convey my frank views on a most important matter in your letter through a third hand. However, I want to tell you that everything will be done as you wish. With regard to Mendelssohn—I cannot understand how you can consider the trifling matter of any importance. I shall be glad to comply with your wishes, and henceforth not one bad word will appear against him. I am angry with him for turning Christian. I cannot forgive this man of independent means for putting his great, his prodigious talents at the service of zealots. The more I am impressed by his talents, the more I am outraged by their vile misuse. Had I the fortune to be a grandson of Moses Mendelssohn, I would not use my talents to set to music the Lamb's urine. . . .

ॐ *To Honoré de Balzac*

Paris, February 27, 1846

I BEG YOU TO DINE WITH ME NEXT WEDNESDAY EVENING (March 4) at six. You will find your friends Royer, Gozlan, the Escudiers, Gautier. The last of these claims he knows your address and has undertaken to deliver these lines to you. Reassure me as to their fate by a word or two. Regards from my wife and the other pretty ladies whom you will see on Wednesday.

ॐ *To Julius Campe*

Tarbes, September 1, 1846

MY DEAREST CAMPE: I have put off writing to you for a long while, hoping I should feel better and might have pleasanter things to tell you than I have to say today, but unfortunately my condition, which was growing considerably worse since the end of May, has taken so serious a turn that I am myself alarmed. I recovered somewhat and felt more hopeful during the first weeks I spent at Barèges, but since then I have been advancing at a snail's pace. My organs of speech are so paralyzed that I cannot speak, and I have not been able to eat for four months because I find it hard to chew and swallow and I've completely lost my sense of taste. I am dreadfully thin; my poor paunch has disappeared and I look like a lean, one-eyed Hannibal. Depressing symptoms (constant fainting-spells) have now decided me to hasten back to Paris, so I left Barèges yesterday. I am not at all anxious; on the contrary, I am quite composed, and I bear patiently what cannot be altered, and is, after all, man's fate.

I believe that I am past saving, and that I can only survive in wretchedness and agony for a short while, one or at most two years. But that does not matter; it is the business of the immortal gods who have nothing to reproach me with, for I have always defended their cause on earth with courage and love. The knowledge that I have lived a good life fills my soul with joy even at this grievous time, and I hope will also accompany me in my last hours into the white abyss.

Between ourselves, this is the least to be feared; dying is a horrible thing, not death,—if there is such a thing as death. Perhaps death is our last superstition.

What shall I say about the coincidence that at this moment false reports of my death are being spread in Germany? I am not at all amused. At other times I would have laughed them off. Fortunately I had published at the same time an article in the *Allgemeine Zeitung*, which, I am sure, must have spoiled my enemies' fun, unless they themselves have been spreading the report. . . .

৪৬ *To Betty Heine and Charlotte Embden*

Paris, March 27, 1847

DEAR, GOOD MOTHER: In the last few days the wonderful weather here has been kind to us; but it is still too sultry for my health. Everyone is more or less indisposed; as for me, my eyes are still affected. You can't imagine how unpleasant it is not to be able to read; I am not even able to attend the theater because of the horrible gas lights. I always sit home in the evening, tête-à-tête with my wife, who must now act as substitute for all other amusements. I have rented a beautiful country home in Montmorency—it cost a neat bit of cash,—1000 francs for the season. I shall go out there in May and try to get a complete rest for my nerves. . . .

৪৬ *To Heinrich Laube*

[April 1847]

COME TODAY, FOR TO-MORROW I MAY BE DEAD. The paralysis of my body progresses gradually, and it may take some time before reaching my heart or my brain; and then the whole merry-go-round will be over. . . . But I cannot guarantee against a *salto mortale*, and I want to make my last request of you.

ह्≫ *The Revolution of 1848*

Paris, March 3 [*1848*]

I HAVE NOT AS YET BEEN ABLE to write to you about the events of the
three great days of February, for my head has been in a whirl.—
There's an incessant drumming and shooting going on here, and
always the *Marseillaise!* The last of these—that never-ceasing refrain—almost splits my brain apart, and ah! the most treasonable rabble
of thoughts, which I had kept imprisoned there for years, has broken
loose again. Somewhat to allay the commotion in my soul, I would
hum, ever and anon, some pious old native chant, like *"Heil dir im
Siegerkranz,"* or *"Üb du nur Treu und Redlichkeit"* [33]—but all in
vain! The devilish Gallic song has drowned out all the better tunes in
me. I fear that in the near future these diabolic crazy notes will reach
your ears, and you too will fall prey to their enchantment. So must
the song have sounded which the rat-catcher of Hamlin piped. Does
the Great Author repeat himself? Are His creative powers exhausted?
Did He not once before, some eighteen years ago, here in Paris,
produce the drama, entitled "July Revolution," with which he regaled us this last February? But one can always see a good play twice.
At any rate, this is an improved and enlarged version, and its conclusion is quite new. It was received with thunderous applause. I had
a good seat from which to watch the performance—as a matter of
fact, a reserved seat, for the street in which I found myself by
chance was closed by barricades at either end. It was only with difficulty that they managed to bring me back to my lodgings. I had
full opportunity of admiring the talent of the French in building
barricades. Those lofty bulwarks and fortifications, which it would
take German thoroughness days to complete, were here improvised
in a few moments. They spring as if by magic from the ground; one
would think that the earth-spirits had a hand in the game. The French
are a nimble nation. The heroic deeds which they displayed in those
February days likewise fill us with amazement, but let us not be
staggered by them. Other nations also have courage. Man is by nature
a brave animal. The contempt of death which the French workingman
exhibited while fighting should astonish us only because it does not
spring from a religious consciousness, and has no basis in that touch-

ing faith in a hereafter, where a man is rewarded if he dies for his country here on earth. As great as their courage—and I might say quite as unselfish—was the honesty which distinguished the poor people in blouses and rags. Yes, their honesty was selfless; and in this respect altogether different from that calculating shop-keeper spirit, which tells you that you get more customers and greater profits by being honest than by being a thief—for in the end, there is little advantage in being a thief. Honesty is longer-lived. The wealthy were quite astonished at the fact that the poor starvelings who ruled Paris for three days did not lay hands on other people's property. The rich trembled for their money-chests, and opened their eyes in amazement when they saw that nothing had been stolen. The severity with which the people of Paris treated thieves displeased many—some were quite dismayed to learn that thieves were being shot on the spot. Under this sort of regime, no one could be sure of his life, they thought. Many objects were demolished by the people in their anger—especially in the Palais Royal and the Tuileries—but there was no looting. Only weapons were taken, wherever they could be found—and in the royal palaces the people were allowed to help themselves to provisions. A boy of fifteen who lives in our house and took part in the fighting brought his sick grandmother a jar of preserves which he had taken from the Tuileries. The young hero did not touch any of it, and brought it home unopened. How happy he must have felt when the old lady found the "preserves of Louis Philippe"—as he called them—good to eat! Poor Louis Philippe, to have to take his wanderer's staff once more, and at such an age, and to go to foggy, cold England, where the preserves of exile taste doubly bitter!

LAZARUS [1848–1856]

ह्ल *To Gustav Kolb*

[*March 10, 1848*]

MY DEAR KOLB: I can't see any more, and I can't even walk two steps.
Your poor friend
H. Heine

ह्ल *To Charlotte Embden*

[*Post-marked Passy, June 12, 1848*]

. . . MY WIFE ASKS that I no longer continue to deceive you as to my
true condition,—which I had to do for Mother's sake—so that when
I *peiger*,[1] you will not be shocked. I believe this will not take place
too soon, dear girl; unfortunately I can drag on this way for another
dozen years. The last two weeks I have been so completely paralyzed

that I have to be carried like a child; my legs are as if made of cotton-wool. My eyes are wretched. But my heart is whole, and my brain and stomach are in good condition. I am well taken care of, and have enough to enable me to meet the heavy costs of my sickness. But I whine and complain. My wife is behaving well, and we live here very comfortably. Should I die under the present circumstances, my end will certainly be a better one than that of thousands of others. . . .

৪৯ *To Maximilian Heine*

Paris, December 3, 1848

DEAREST MAX: . . . Two physicians, Dr. Wertheim and Dr. Gruby, are attending me. The first is in charge of my general treatment and visits me several times a day, as a friend as well as a physician. I have hopes that my condition may in time become more tolerable, and that I may soon be able to get out of bed and spend a part of the day in my chair. My eyes too will be better, for they themselves were not affected, only weakened; and because of my cramp, they are some-times shut tight, so that I can see only when I raise my right eyelid with my hand. This actual state of blindness depresses me and to-gether with my illness, produced by my lying in bed, has brought me so low that I weep and sigh—something utterly foreign to my nature and very terrifying and strange to me.

You will not be surprised if one of these days my Muse greets you in the garb of a religious zealot. In my sleepless nights of martyrdom I compose many beautiful prayers, which I do not have written down (all of them are addressed to a very specific God, the God of our Fathers). The old nurse who watches at my bed-side said last night that she knew of a very good prayer against cramps in the knee and I asked her in all seriousness to pray for me, while she was winding up my knee in a heated napkin. The prayer was effectual, and the cramp vanished. But what will they say in heaven about me? Already I can see a number of angels expressing themselves in very scornful terms about me! There, there, look at that unprincipled fellow! When he is sick, he asks old women to pray for him to the same God whom he scorned bitterly when he was well!

Dearest Max, you have no idea of what I have gone through, and how much strength of character—what gigantic strength of character—I have shown in the face of that suffering. If I have not put an end to my agony, it was merely out of regard for my wife— though I should be forgiven, since I've lost all hope of ever enjoying life, and my heart too is dying of many incurable wounds. It seems to me that I could bear any hardship, any sorrow, if only I could go out for a stroll! But to lie continuously on one's back, with a broken heart—to lie on one's injured back—that is insufferable.

My material circumstances have improved somewhat. I have a new apartment which I like more than my old one, but it has only one drawback: it is somewhat small, so that I am forced to be an unwilling participant in the whole household spectacle. At this very moment I am being somewhat distracted by an argument between my wife and my cook. My wife is wonderful, magnificent; and her voice is a musical balm for my sick soul—when she doesn't raise it too high. I love her passionately—and this feeling is strong, stronger even than my sickness, though my body may be limp and helpless.

ɞ A Correction

CERTAIN GERMAN NEWSPAPERS—the Berlin *Haude- und Spenersche Zeitung*—have spread reports concerning the state of my health and finances, which demand correction. I declare that my illness, whether it be called by its rightful name, whether it be a family illness (such as runs in one's family), or one of those private ailments from which Germans suffer who live abroad; whether it be a French *ramollissement de la moelle épinière*, or the German consumption of the spine— whatever it be, it is horrible, racks me night and day, and has seriously undermined not only my nervous system, but my philosophy as well. At certain times, especially when the pain moves agonizingly up and down my spinal chord, I am torn by doubts as to whether man is actually a two-legged god, as the late Professor Hegel assured me in Berlin five and twenty years ago. In the month of May last year I had to take to my bed, and have not gotten up from it since. In the meantime, I admit frankly, a great change has come over me. I am no longer the divine biped. I am no longer the "freest German since Goethe," as Ruge [2] once called me in my sounder days. I am no longer the great Heathen No. 2, who used to be compared to the vine-crowned Dionysus, while colleague No. 1 was granted the title of

Ducal Weimarean Jupiter.[3] I am no longer the joyous and sound Hellene, cheerfully smiling down at the melancholy Nazarene. I am now only a poor Jew, sick unto death, a pallid picture of misery, an unhappy man!

So much for the state of my health—from an authentic source of pain. As for my financial circumstances, they are not, I confess, exactly brilliant; though the reporters in the above-mentioned newspapers overestimate my poverty, and they are altogether in error when they state that my position has been impaired because the allowance given me by my late uncle Solomon Heine had been withdrawn or reduced after his death. I will not bother to trace the genesis of this error, so as to spare myself explanations which may be as distressing to myself as they will be tiresome to others. But I must definitely contradict the error itself, lest my silence make my friends in Germany uneasy and, on the other hand, encourage aspersions upon the most noble sentiments which have always been concealed with silent pride in the human breast. In spite of my aversion to discussing personal affairs, I think it proper to set forth the following facts:

The allowance in question has not been withdrawn or reduced since the death of Solomon Heine, of blessed memory; and it was always paid to the very last penny. In addition, the relative charged with these payments has, since my illness has grown worse, increased the periodical payments with quarterly installments, sufficient almost to double the income. The same relative has also rid me of the bitterest worries of my illness by a generous provision for my dear wife, who loses in me her earthly support. Many inquiries and offers which have come to me from Germany in very affectionate though incorrectly addressed letters will therefore be answered in this confession. For the hearts that are bleeding in my Fatherland—greetings and tears!

Heinrich Heine

Written in Paris (Rue d'Amsterdam, No. 50), April 15, 1849

ࢨ I Reject Hegel [4]

I FIRST LEARNED HOW DIFFICULT IT IS to understand the writings of Hegel—how easy it is to be misled into thinking one understands them, whereas one has merely learned to parrot the dialectical formulas—when, many years later I was engaged in Paris in translating those formulas from the idiom of the abstract school into French, the mother tongue of sound reason and common sense. Here the translator must know exactly what he wishes to say; and the most modest idea is forced to doff its mystical vestments and stand forth naked. I had proposed to write a popular and comprehensible exposition of the whole Hegelian philosophy so as to incorporate it in the new edition of my *De l'Allemagne,* for the sake of completeness. I was busy on that work for two years, and hard put to it to master the recalcitrant material and to present the most abstract portions of it in as popular a form as possible. But when the work was finished at long last, I was overcome by a singular horror, and it seemed as if the manuscript were looking at me with strange, ironic, nay, malevolent eyes. I was in a curious dilemma—the author and his work were no longer in agreement. My mind had at that time already come under the influence of that distaste for atheism of which I have spoken, and since I had to admit that all this godlessness had been most horribly abetted by the philosophy of Hegel, the latter became very unpleasant and distasteful to me.

I had never been over-enthusiastic about Hegel's philosophy—and there was never any question of my being a convinced disciple. I was never an abstract thinker, and I accepted the synthesis of Hegel's doctrines without examination, because its deductions flattered my vanity. I was young and arrogant; it gratified my self-conceit when I was told by Hegel that it was not He who dwelt in heaven, as my grandmother had supposed, but I myself, who dwelt here on earth, who was the Lord God. This foolish pride did not, however, have a pernicious influence on me. On the contrary, it awakened in me a heroic spirit, and I made such a display of generosity and self-sacrifice at that time, that it certainly must have eclipsed the most distinguished and noble deeds of the good Philistines of virtue, who practised virtue merely from a sense of duty and obedience to the laws of morality. Was I not in my own person the living embodiment of moral law, and the fountainhead of all justice and authority? I was primal virtue; I was incapable of sin; I was purity incarnate. The most notorious Magdalens were cleansed by the purifying and expiating power of my love-flames; and they emerged from the embraces of the god as pure as lilies and blushing like chaste roses—virgin once more. I must admit that this rehabilitation of damaged Magdalens sometimes taxed my strength. But I gave without stint, and the cornucopia of my compassion was inexhaustible. I was all love; altogether free of hate. I no longer avenged myself on my enemies—since rightly considered, I had none, or rather acknowledged none. For me there only existed unbelievers who questioned my divinity. Every indignity they offered me was sacrilege; every abuse was blasphemy. Such godlessness, of course, I could not always let pass unpunished; but in those cases it was not human vengeance, but divine judgment that was visited on the sinner. Absorbed in this lofty concern for justice, I would repress at times, with more or less difficulty, all ordinary pity. As I had no enemies, I had no friends—only worshippers who believed in my greatness, adored me, and praised my works, those in verse as well as in prose. Toward this congregation of the truly devout and pious I was especially gracious, particularly toward the young female devotees.

But the expense of playing the role of a god for whom it is unseemly to be dressed in tatters, and who is sparing neither of body or purse, is immense. To play such a role decently, two things are particularly needed: money and robust health. Unfortunately it happened one day—in February, 1848—that both these requisites failed me and my divinity came to an end. Luckily, the highly respected public was at that time occupied with events so grand, so unusual, and so fabulous and dramatic, that it did not observe the change in the affairs of so unimportant a person as myself. Yes, unprecedented and fabulous indeed were the events of those mad February days, when the wisdom of the wisest was disdained, and the elect of folly were raised aloft on the shield. The last became the first; and the lowliest became the highest. Matter, like thought, was turned upside down, and the world was topsy-turvy. In those crazy days, had I been a reasonable man, I should certainly have lost my wits as a consequence of those events. But lunatic as I was then, the very reverse happened; and strange to say, just in the days of universal madness, I regained my senses! Like many other dethroned divinities of that period of upheaval, I too was compelled to abdicate ignominiously, and to return to ordinary life as a private mortal. It was the wisest thing I could do. I returned to the humble fold of God's creatures, and I again bowed in homage to the omnipotence of a Supreme Being, who directs the destinies of this world, and who henceforth should also regulate my earthly affairs. The latter, during the time when I was my own Providence, had drifted into serious confusion, and I was glad to turn them over to a celestial superintendent, who, with his omniscience, really takes better care of them. The belief in the existence of God has since then been to me not only a source of happiness, but it has also relieved me from all those annoying money matters which I detest so greatly. To this belief I also owe considerable economies, for I no longer trouble to provide for myself or for others; and since I am now one of the pious, I contribute almost nothing to the support of the needy. I am too modest to meddle, as formerly, with the management of Divine Providence. I no longer provide relief for the community; I no longer ape Divinity. With pious humility I have informed my erstwhile clients that I am only a miserable creature, a wretched being that has nothing more to do with governing the universe, and that in the future, when in need and affliction, they must turn to the Lord God, who dwells in heaven, and whose budget is as boundless as his loving kindness—whereas I, a poor ex-god, was often compelled, even in my godliest days, to seek the assistance of the devil, when I wished to play the philanthropist.

Tirer le diable par la queue [5]—this is really one of the happiest of French expressions, but the thing itself is very humiliating for a god. Yes, I was very glad to divest myself of my assumed glory, and no philosopher shall ever again convince me that I am a god! I am only a poor human creature, who is not over well—as a matter of fact, very sick. In this condition it is a true comfort for me to know that there is someone in heaven into whose ears I can incessantly pour my litanies of pain, especially after midnight, when Mathilde has sought the rest she so badly needs. Thank God! In such hours I am not alone, and I can pray and whine without hindrance and shame, and I can pour out my whole heart before the Almighty, and confide to Him some things which one is in the habit of keeping even from one's wife.

After the above confession, the kind reader will easily understand why I no longer found pleasure in my work on the Hegelian philosophy. I saw clearly that its publication would benefit neither the public nor the author. I saw that there is more life-giving nourishment for famishing humanity in the thinnest broth from the charity kitchens of Christianity than in the mouldy soup made of the spiderwebs of Hegelian dialectic. Yes, I will confess all. I was seized with a mortal terror of the eternal flames. I know it is sheer superstition, but I was frightened. And so, on a quiet winter's evening, when a glowing fire was burning on my hearth, I availed myself of the occasion, and

I threw the manuscript of Hegelian philosophy into the roaring flames. The burning pages flew up the chimney with a strange hissing and crackling sound.

Thank God! I was rid of it. Alas! would that I could destroy in the same way all that I have ever published concerning German philosophy! But that is impossible; and since I cannot even prevent the republication of books already out of print, as I lately learned to my great regret, no other course remains but to confess publicly that my exposition of German philosophy, especially the first three books of *De l'Allemagne*, contains the most pernicious errors.

ᙡ *To Betty Heine*

Paris, October 24, 1849

DEAR, GOOD MOTHER: I have just received your letter. If you only knew how I hate to write, you would not ask for letters so often. First of all, I have not been able to see well during the last few days. Secondly, I don't have many pleasant things to tell you. May the devil take my eyes! All the quackery helps very little. Only to you, dear Mother, do I write with my own hand. I am unable to dictate, for fear of letting slip some confidence now and then. Congratulations on your Viennese grand-child!

ᙡ *To Heinrich Laube*

Paris, January 25, 1850

DEAREST LAUBE: Only a few days ago I learned that you had become theatrical director in Vienna, and that made me so happy that I could no longer put off writing you at once. The reason I was silent was that I had the painful feeling that I had nothing pleasant to tell you. I was always waiting for a sound hour and for some good news before writing you. But the hours and the news have since become worse. The rumors concerning my state of health are unfortunately more than true. For the last year and three-quarters I have been tortured day and night by the most horrible agonies, confined to my bed, and paralyzed in all my members. Incessant cramps, most insufferable spasms, practically total blindness—a calamity rarely met with in the annals of human suffering—an unheard-of, horrible, insane calamity! I suffer from the most terrible hopelessness and spiritual torments, but I bear these, as I do the physical ones, with a tranquillity I would never have believed I was capable of. My brain has grown weak because I lie constantly on my back and because of overdoses of dulling opiates—but it is not a total ruin, and I hope to preserve some of my clarity to the very end—which, between you and me—is not far off. The stories about my present religious credulity and canting piety are quite nonsensical and even more malicious. There has been no such marked change in my religious feelings. The only internal event which I can report with certainty and self-knowledge is the fact that a February Revolution has broken out in my religious views and thoughts, and that in place of my early principle, which left me fairly indifferent, I have set up a new principle, to which I am attached with no greater fanaticism, and which could not occasion a sudden alteration in my frame of mind. For to come to the point—I have given up the God of Hegel, or rather, the Godlessness of Hegel—and replaced that with the dogma of a real, personal God, external to Nature and the mind of man. This doctrine which can be sustained as effectively as our Hegelian synthesis, had already been profoundly expounded by the ancient Magi, according to the testimony of the Neo-Platonic fragments— and it emerges later in the Mosaic texts with a truth-inspired eloquence not to be found in our modern dialecticians. Hegel has lost much ground with me; and old Moses stands *in floribus*. Oh, if in addition to Moses, I also had his Prophets! It is my great misfortune that even in my present circumstances I cannot rid myself of the daily troubles which unexpectedly come upon me. Although the February Revolution ruined me financially—as it did many others—I have enough left with which comfortably to support a few German poets' families even in my fortune's ruins; but wretched man that I am—I am accustomed to a princely life, and forced to expend unprecedented sums on my illness—and so I do not find what I still have to be enough. I tell you this in confidence, to explain why I am thinking of trying to earn money despite my present condition. Now you know the reason I am sending you my *Faust*, and why I'm asking you to find a place for it. I am now free to do what I want with it. If only I had written a play instead of a ballet, so that you could produce it on the theatrical stage! Now see whether your singing and springing colleagues can do something for the poor writer of pantomimes. I could say with Romeo, Fortune's fool that I am! Now that I am no longer capable of writing a single piece, you turn up with the Burg-theater on your hands. Fifteen years ago I surely would have written one play after another, if offered this opportunity.

I came into the world too soon. That fact, and the false position occasioned by my exile, have been my greatest calamities. I have not heard from Campe for two years; or rather, I have not received replies to my urgent inquiries about the publication of my collected edition. I am too upright and honest to try to explain his silence on grounds of hidden motives. . . .

ह To Julius Campe

Paris, June 1, 1850

DEAREST CAMPE: . . . Since I do not know why you delayed answering my most important inquiries for more than a year, I will not condemn you too severely beforehand. But I do know that your delays have seriously damaged literary interests, and your irresponsibility has perhaps caused me irreparable harm. At a time when the whole world was swept by the greatest revolutions, and when my own mental world underwent most profound convulsions, it would have been advisable to give the public what I had written as quickly as possible, not because it would otherwise have been less valuable to them, but because I can now no longer publish it of my own free will if I am not to be guilty of a sin against the Holy Ghost, and treason against my inner convictions—in other words, if I'm not to be charged with equivocation. I have not turned zealot. But I don't want to play pranks on the Lord. I want to act honorably toward God and man. And so I have boldly torn up everything that sprang from my early blasphemous years—those lovely poison-flowers—and it is possible that in my physical blindness I have also rooted up many an innocent neighboring plant and thrown it into the fire. When I heard the crackling flames, I had a strange feeling. I did not know whether I was a hero or a madman. I felt as if Mephistopheles were standing beside me and was whispering in an ironically comforting voice: "The good Lord will reward you much better than Campe; and you won't have to plague yourself with the printed word; and even before publication, you won't have to haggle with Campe as if over a pair of old trousers."

Ah, dearest Campe, sometimes I wish you did believe in God— if only for a day. Your conscience would then tell you how ungratefully you are treating me at a time when horrible and unheard-of misfortunes have befallen me. Answer me soon, before it is too late. If there is some political reason for your hesitation, or some financial worry, tell it to me outright, so that I may leave appropriate instructions in case I should depart this life before my collected edition goes to press. Don't be afraid of the words "depart this life." I do not use them in any pietistic sense. I don't mean that I would exchange this life for a heavenly one. For though I have come much closer to God, heaven is still some distance away. Don't trust the current rumors that I have become a pious lamb. The religious revolution which has taken place within me is a purely intellectual one—more the product of thought than of beatific sentimentality; and my illness has a small share in it, I am sure.

I have had vast, sublime, awe-inspiring thoughts—but they were thoughts—lightning flashes—not the sulphurous fumes rising from the piss of credulity. I tell you this so that you may not imagine that if I were to undertake the collected edition myself I would expunge slavishly. *Quod scripsi, scripsi.*[6]

೪ *To Betty Heine and Charlotte Embden*

Paris, June 15, 1850

DEAREST MOTHER: Your precious letter with the postscript by Lottchen and Annchen has just reached me, and I would have written sooner if I hadn't had difficulty with my German correspondence, of which I spoke in the last letter. Otherwise nothing new has occurred. As for my illness, it depresses me to have to sing my old laments with all the dreary variations. I repeat: the worst of this illness is that one suffers horribly and it takes a long time to die. You may rely on it that I won't conceal it from you if my condition becomes much worse. If I don't write you, don't worry; it is merely that I lack a trustworthy amanuensis, or that I have no wish to aggravate my depression by giving you unpleasant news. But I think of you constantly, you may be sure. To tell the truth, I want to

survive you to spare you the sorrow of hearing of my death. This is
perhaps my life's chief interest. When I no longer have you, I shall
be able to meet death with a lighter heart. Lottchen has her children
and her husband; and as for my wife, she is so happily constituted
that in the end she will be able to do without me. You see I am
justified in not writing you more frequently—only bitter funereal
letters. I have become a melancholy fool, without a sense of humor. . . .

֍ To Heinrich Laube

October 12, 1850

MY DEAREST LAUBE: . . . My condition has grown worse, for my
spasms are much more severe and more decisive. . . . I lie all
doubled up, in pain day and night, and though I believe in God, I
sometimes do not believe in a good God. The hand of this great
animal baiter lies heavy on me. What a kind and amiable god was I
in my youth, when I soared to such a high state by the grace of
Hegel! I live quite isolated here and see few Germans, except strangers passing through. Meissner was here, and I saw much of him. I
also saw his great compatriot Moritz Hartmann recently. He is very
handsome and all women are in love with him, except the Muses. . . .

I have lost and mourned my friend Balzac.[7] George Sand, the
hussy, has paid no attention to me since I was taken ill; this emancipator has most shabbily maltreated my poor friend Chopin in a
revolting but divinely written novel.

I am losing one friend after the other, and the remaining ones
prove the old saying: Friends in a wreck, go fifty to a peck. But the
saying cuts both ways; it censures not only the accused, but the
accuser as well. For I am to be reproached for being short-sighted
in the choice of my friends, and selecting such light ones. What a mess
of friends I need now to get a bushelful!

Write me soon. My address is Rue d'Amsterdam 50. I forgot to
tell you that as far as my friend Campe is concerned, he has not
written to me for over two years. He is merely content to pay my
semi-annual drafts, which I then draw on, according to contract—
a pittance which would not even suffice to pay my nurse; for in addition to her board, I pay her five francs daily. . . .

ट~ To Betty Heine and Charlotte Embden

Paris, March 12, 1851

DEAR, GOOD MOTHER: I was beside myself with joy when I got your last letter. I had some lines from Lottchen a few days before, but not a syllable from you. At the same time I received a letter from Herr Werth, who began by saying that he had not been able to see you because you were unwell. Any other person would have worried himself to death, but after considerable thought I succeeded in calming myself, for I had to admit that Lottchen would not have written so cheerfully, if you had been in a bad way; and a third person would not have immediately mentioned your indisposition if it had been serious, but would have expressed himself with some hesitation, and in a quite different way. I therefore hope that you are well, dearest Mother. But if anything is seriously wrong, please tell me the truth, because that is never quite so painful as a state of doubt.

I am feeling better—but things move very slowly here. For two years now I have had no need of medicines, or, I should say, my wife does not suffer a vial across the threshold. All physicians have been sent packing to the devil, with the exception of one, whom I sometimes do not see for months at a stretch, and who is so short of stature, that I can almost say I have no physician at all. It is best to choose the least of evils. Nevertheless, I do not think that I shall ever be able to stand up on my feet. I am through with life; and if it weren't for the severe constipation which I suffer here on earth, and if I were sure of a cordial reception up above, I would suffer my fate patiently.

My greatest joy is thinking of you, dear Mother, of Lottchen, my brothers, and the little brood. My wife is behaving in an exemplary way. She lightens my burdens, and cheers my life. Only at times she unwittingly stabs me to the heart with her incurable spendthrift ways. It can't be helped. It is my worst trouble. This spendthrift fever is horrible. And yet I am no miser. I have long since stopped laughing at this matter. . . .

ᑍᕔ *To Gustav Kolb*

Paris, April 21, 1851

MY DEAR KOLB: It is an eternity since I last heard from you; but I always imagined you would one day take the train and some fine morning I would find you standing by my bed. For I am still bedridden; I am constantly on my sick back, which is racked by the most frightful cramps. The stories about my illness which are told in public are nothing in comparison with my actual suffering. All this I can bear with devout patience. I say devout, because I do not entirely dispute the stories about my present piety. In this regard, however, I must assure you that matters are greatly exaggerated, and that I am not to be classed in the least with the so-called zealots. The important thing is that I have for a long time now felt a strong aversion to German atheism and formed much firmer convictions regarding the existence of God; but I waited for a long while before proclaiming it, perhaps in order to surprise God himself. Irresponsible dolts have picked up chance remarks of mine and turned them into the most stupid gossip. I even scented the deliberate intentions of certain people who would gladly have me canonized as a juicy morsel for their heaven. I have taken care that my so-called conversion will cause their table-mates no indigestion.

But how are you, dearest of old friends? Do not fail to visit the Industrial Exposition in London, and go by way of Paris. Here you will find me at Rue d'Amsterdam, No. 50, and you will give me your hand before I enter upon that long journey which no longer requires the use of legs. Thank God, one can dispense with legs there, otherwise, poor lame wretch that I am, I would have to remain down here forever, in this vale of tears. In preparation for this trip, I am setting my papers in order; and here you can do me a service, dearest Kolb, which I ask of you only out of necessity, though I know you are very busy. But I rely on your long and time-tested zeal on my behalf. I need, for a reason which it would take too much time to explain, a collection of all the articles which I published in the *Allgemeine Zeitung,* from the time that Messrs. Thiers and Guizot were ministers, i.e., from March 1, 1840 to the February Revolution. I ask you most urgently, Kolb, to find all the articles of this period without a single exception, and to send them to me either by diligence, or, what will prove less expensive, in a wrapper. How I regret that I did not retain copies of these, so that I am not in a position to restore the changes and omissions made by the editors at that time; also, a good number of these articles, which you never printed, are lost. Should any of these be found, contrary to all expectation, you will render me a particular service by letting me know. What a pity that you did not always give me a free hand in the *Allgemeine*, and especially that you rejected my repeated and emphatic prophecies about Social-ism, to which so little attention was paid then, and which was re-garded as a chimaera or as subtle propaganda. Now it will have to be admitted that I was among the few who foresaw the future clearly. Nothing has surprised me. But much that has happened has disturbed me; and like all prophets I have paid dearly. I really cannot be happy that my most precious convictions have triumphed, since they cost me so much. The same may be the feeling of other honest people, and I believe may be the reason for the general depression which prevails today. Here all is chaos. Everyone has a solution in his pocket—though cash would be better. Long, watered-down parliamentary speeches—but no Spirit of God hovers over the vast abyss! The Chamber and the President fear each other; each falls on his knees in the presence of the other:—like the Moor and Papageno.[8]

I am for the President, body and soul, not only because he is the nephew of the Emperor, but also because he is decent, and the prestige of his great name may serve as an effective bulwark against greater disaster. Like Louis Philippe, Louis Bonaparte is the miracu-lous saviour of the French. Whether he will be able to survive is an-other question. But these men fear nothing, and live only for the hour.

੬❧ To Saint-René Taillandier [9]

Paris, November 3, 1851

DEAR M. TAILLANDIER: . . . My head is too confused for me to be able to dictate fresh notes. I shall confine myself to saying that the date of my birth in my biographical notices is not very accurate. Be-tween you and me the inexactness seems to have arisen from inten-tional errors committed for my sake at the time of the Prussian invasion, in order to save me from the service of His Majesty the King of Prussia. Later, all the family archives were lost in several fires in Hamburg. When I examine my baptismal certificate, I find the 13th of December 1799 as the date of my birth. The most important thing, however, is that I was born—and born on the Rhine, where at the early age of sixteen I composed a poem in honor of Napoleon entitled "The Two Grenadiers," which you will find in my *Book of Songs* and which will show that my whole religion from that time was the Emperor. My ancestors were of the Jewish faith. I have never boasted of this origin, for I felt sufficiently humiliated when I was taken for a member of the human species, while Hegel made me believe that I was a God! I was so proud of my divinity, I believed myself so great, that I could never pass through the gate of Saint Martin or Saint Denis without involuntarily stooping, lest I bump my head against the arch. It was a marvelous time—long since gone, and I cannot think of it without sadness when I compare it with my present state—lying here miserably on my back. My sickness is making horrible inroads!

I have not yet received my *Faust*. As soon as it comes, I'll send it to you under separate cover.

৪৶ *To Georg Weerth*

Paris, November 5, 1851

MY DEAR HERR WEERTH: You may yourself have observed that we more often think of those to whom in our procrastination we owe a reply, than of those to whom we always return the requisite polite letter at once, so as to be rid of them as quickly as possible. And so it happens that you, dear Weerth, are daily more deeply fixed in my memory, while I constantly reproach myself with not having conveyed my thanks to you for your many kind lines, and especially for your last amusing letter. But I was always waiting for a healthy moment, which never came, until today I finally decided,—I do not know why—for I am now more than ever in greater pain, and cross. In the past few weeks my condition has become much worse, and I cannot hope for improvement with my accustomed lightheartedness; and since I am preparing for the worst, I will try at least to meet my epistolary obligations. However, I am conscientiously paying off my other debts too, and I assure you that no poet will go to his grave so respectable a Philistine as I, when the Lord calls me to Himself, to Eternal Life, as the devout would say. I am glad that you liked my preface; unfortunately I was neither in the mood nor at leisure to express what I really wanted to, that is, that I die as a poet, who needs neither religion nor philosophy, and wants nothing with either. The poet very well understands the symbolic language of religion and the abstract rational jargon of philosophy, but neither the religious nor the philosophical gentlemen will ever understand the poet, whose language will always be Greek to them, as Latin is to Herr Massmann.[10] It was this linguistic ignorance which led the gentlemen of both camps to imagine that I had turned bigot. "They can fathom only the creatures of the refuse-heap they resemble," as Goethe, whose divine name I envy, once said.

Speaking of Goethe, some time ago I reread Eckermann's *Conversations with Goethe*, and found in it true satisfaction. Read those two volumes if you do not know them, and if you can dig up the third part of the *Conversations*, which appeared later, try to get it for me. I like to relax my mind with this kind of reading; for the most part, I read travel books now, and for two months I have not left Senegal and Guinea. I think the disgust with which the whites inspire me is responsible for my immersion in the black world, which is really very diverting. I get more fun out of the black Negro kings than out of our own fathers of the people—although they too know little of human rights and regard slavery as something natural.

I hope you will like my *Romancero*, and especially my *Faust*. God knows I do not care much for these books, and they would not have seen the light of day so soon if Campe had not applied the thumbscrews to me. I came by these publications, as a maiden with child—in fact, with two children. Campe can make my meaning clear to you. I am absolutely ignorant of the fate of my books, for once Campe has all he needs I get no more news from him. Perhaps if this letter reaches you in Hamburg, I may learn something from you about it, if you will be good enough to write me.

I am so dulled by opium, which I have taken repeatedly to deaden my pains, that I hardly know what I am dictating. Besides, this morning I had a stupid devil of a compatriot with me who traded ideas with me in a long and boring conversation; from this exchange I may have kept some of his stupid ideas in my head, and may need a few days before I am quite rid of them, and can get some sensible ones.

The man saw everything in a grey light, which was indeed his own color; he said that Germany was standing at the edge of an abyss. Well, I am glad Germany is no fiery charger but a smart long-ears that won't get dizzy and can graze calmly at the very edge of the abyss.

Herr Reinhardt, who is lending me the use of his hand for this letter, asks to be remembered.

Everything is quiet here, except that recently the prefect of police—a second Herod—planned a monstrous Murder of the Innocents against our guiltless countrymen and frightened the poor little ones badly. They all had to report to the prefecture to prove their right to existence—a very hard task for some of them, since they have neither existence nor the means of one. This Herod probably believed that we had a political Saviour among us, and regrettably the denunciation originated with a person not lacking in education, in fact, from a man of letters. These are infernally disgusting and horrible things. When I remember that for years such people could come very close to me, I feel horrified. What a terrible thing is exile! The most revolting aspect of it is that we fall into bad company through it, which we cannot avoid if we do not wish to be exposed to a coalition of all sorts of blackguards. How painfully moving and at the same time embittered is Dante's plaint on the same theme in the *Divine Comedy!*

Good-bye dear friend and keep your cheerful affection for

Your cordially devoted
Heinrich Heine

৯৵ *To Saint-René Taillandier*

Paris, November 21, 1851

DEAR M. TAILLANDIER: . . . My *Romancero* is creating a sensation in Germany; and though my vanity as a poet is thereby little gratified, it is better for my sick state that I am somewhat removed from the scene of my success. Even formerly, when I was well, the enthusiasm of the Germans had something terrifying in it—it did not go well with a certain romantic pride which is a part of my nature.

I would say many flattering things to you, if I had not learned in France to be tactful enough not to say them at a time when you are planning to write an article about me. I hope I've sent you enough material for this piece. I think that you can reproduce my letter to Chasles, although it may be very old and the salient points in it may have little to do with the present. It was written at a time when I was exposed to the persecution of the German Diet, which launched its decrees against Young Germany, of which they proclaimed me the head. At that time, the Gallophobe bulldog, Menzel, howled against us and denounced Young Germany as an infernal conspiracy representing the interests of the Synagogue and betraying Germany to the advantage of France. The self-styled national party incited the multitude against us through equally base and absurd insinuations. We were accused of "Francophilism" and "immorality." I had then good reason to declare that I belonged to the Protestant Church, which, puerile as it may appear today, was of some use in the polemics of that day. The persecutions of the German Diet did me much harm, and fitted in with the hatred of my lesser adversaries. I emerged victorious in an epoch which was one of the most terrible in the history of German authorship. The present generation is luckier; and you, French men of letters, do not properly appreciate your good fortune. . . .

ᘒᕀ *To Julius Campe*

Paris, December 8, 1851

MY DEAR CAMPE: . . . My brother writes me that my proscription by the Austrians is motivated by my poem "Marie Antoinette." I don't believe it; for it appears to me that he is interested in having me spare Austria because of his own position. It really can't be news to the Austrians that Marie Antoinette was guillotined and they have long ago reconciled themselves to this historical fact. It is only natural that you should have had none of your publications prohibited in Austria in the last four years, dear Campe, for these were the fat years of the revolutionary movement, and now the lean ones are beginning once more. . . . At the bookseller Franck's it is being said that the prohibition is directed against you, and not against me; because I am supposed to have been in the pay of the Austrians all the time. In this statement I recognize the voice of the honorable Mr. Vieweg. When I visited the Franck bookstore four years ago, this patron took the occasion of speaking to me—he treated me as an equal, and with his own special brand of insolent familiarity he said to my face that there was a rumor afloat that I was being paid by the Austrians. This bankrupt who had run away from his creditors in Vienna had the insolence to speak about a German poet in this fashion. But I was not excited; in my quiet way I replied, "My dear Vieweg, you are mistaken. I get as little from the Austrians, as the Austrians get from you." His face turned as red as his beard. How fortunate for me that people can think of nothing better to invent, and know so little of my vulnerable side. Surely, I have never given them an opening so far as money is concerned. . . .

৯৶ To Baron James Rothschild

Paris, January 15, 1852

DEAR BARON: The ancient Jews, who were very emotional creatures, were of the opinion that one must never eat a tid-bit in the presence of a child without giving him a taste of it, from fear lest the child "lose a drop of blood," or, as they put it, from *zaar lechayim*, which is more expressive than *rachmones*.[11]

Your noble heart, Baron, seems to have remained true to this generous superstition and whenever your vast financial dealings are blessed by Fortune, you have given a mouthful of it not only to the close friends of your household, but also to the poet, that overgrown child. At this moment, when you are so notably involved in huge undertakings, and will surely emerge more triumphantly millionairish than ever from these revolutionary storms, I take the liberty of informing you that I am not yet dead, although my present condition scarcely deserves the name of living.

A very great and beautiful lady, who has eased my suffering by many a comforting word and is very greatly respected by you, Baroness James Rothschild, will be happy if you show an interest in me sufficiently worthy of you and of me. . . .

Paris, January 19, 1852

MOST HONORED BARON: I have learned with pleasure that you have not forgotten me, and I wish to express my deepest gratitude for the most recent proof of your kindness, by which you have bound me to you. The Lord's blessing is visibly with you, and all contact with you brings luck. I have had this proof for many years; hence your personal good-will toward me has been especially gratifying and comforting. May your generosity always keep it alive. Be convinced that I shall try to prove worthy of it, so far as it is within my power. I often think of you and your noble family. The hours which I had the honor of spending in your presence are a source of joy to me, even in retrospect.

Please be assured of my veneration and humble respect.

ह To Julius Campe

Paris, August 24, 1852

MY DEAREST CAMPE: . . . Just as you once complained about the *Book of Songs*, so you now complain about *Romancero*. For ten years I have patiently heard your whining about the small sales of the *Book of Songs*. *Romancero* is scarcely one year old, so your wails will surely not soon cease. I shall probably die hearing them ring in my ears. . . .

ह To Henri Julia

[End of December 1852?]

DEAR SIR: I have just finished reading your *Friends of Voltaire* and would indeed be happy to talk to you about it. If you have no fear of coming close to a sick man, an unfortunate paralytic, a Job on his bed of sorrows, then do pay me a visit. You will always find me at home. I never go out. This has been the case for the last five years.

Come and we will speak of Voltaire. You love him—and so do I. I love him not only as a philosopher, but also as a man of letters. I may say as a man of letters, and not as a poet. But I also love him for his great love of Freedom. I myself am a worshipper of Freedom, though that is not to say that I have not loved other things in my day. But Freedom fills my entire soul—and as proof thereof see that I am making free to invite you to visit me and to call myself

Your sympathetic reader
Heinrich Heine

ဇာ *To Alexandre Dumas*

Paris, March 28, 1854

MY DEAR DUMAS: . . . Some weeks ago you expressed in your paper the intention of coming to see me soon. That was a good idea. I warn you, however, that if you postpone your visit you may no longer find me in my present apartment, 50 Rue d'Amsterdam, and that I may have moved to another lodging quite unknown to me—and I will not even be able to leave my new address with the porter in case tardy friends like you should ask for me. I have no illusions of my future residence. All I know is that you enter it through a drab and fetid passage, and this entrance displeases me in advance. In addition, my wife weeps whenever I talk of moving.

Madame Heine remembers well all the kindness that you showered on us some twelve years ago.

For six years now I have been bedridden; but at the worst moments of my illness, when I endured the greatest torments, my wife would read your novels to me, and they were the only thing that made me forget the pain.

I devoured them all, and during the reading I would exclaim to myself, "What an ingenious poet is this great fellow, Alexandre Dumas!"

Surely, after Cervantes and Madame Shariar—better known as the Sultana Scheherezade—you are the most amusing story-teller I know What facility! What easy grace! And what a good fellow you are' I find only one fault in you—modesty. You are much too modest.

My God! Those who accuse you of boasting and of rhodomontade, have no idea of the greatness of your talent. They see only vanity Well, I say, that no matter how tall the latter may be, or how high it may leap, it cannot reach up to the knees—what am I saying?—it cannot even reach the calves of your admirable talent. Burn as much incense to yourself as you wish—lavish the most hyperbolic praises on yourself, bask in them to your heart's content—and I defy you to appraise yourself at your true worth for your marvelous works.

Your marvelous works! "*Oui, c'est bien vrai!*" Madame Heine, who is listening as I dictate this letter, cries at this moment; and the parrot she is holding screeches after her: "*Oui, oui, oui, oui!*"

You see, dear friend, that in our house admiration of you is unanimous.

৪৺ *To Julius Campe*

Paris, September 21, 1854

MY DEAR CAMPE: In addition to the first sheets of the second volume of *Lutetia*, and the Dedication, I have also received from the Cassel Buchhandlung the title-page of the book, and I am amazed to see that on the special title-page of *Lutetia* the essential thing is omitted— namely, my name, while that of the publisher appears. If this hadn't been the case, I would have assumed that the special title-page was only an inter-page, which either preceded or followed the special title-page. In any case, I want to tell you how astonished I was.

At this moment I am more than usually sick and also plagued by an extraordinary series of mishaps which arise partly from my change of residence and partly from a succession of deaths. My reader's mother, who died of the cholera, was buried today, and for a week now I have had no one to read to me. By contrast, I am at this moment enjoying a great triumph: for my article in the *Revue des deux Mondes* is arousing wide attention, despite the abridgments. As the editor of the *Revue* said to me yesterday, my article is the sole topic of conversation at this moment, and many people who understand German are impatiently waiting to read the whole of it in the original. My object of achieving enormous publicity has been attained, but it is essential that you rush the book through the press somewhat more rapidly, as I have already told you. The Editor of the *Revue* said that never had an essay aroused so much attention, and that the success of the *Gods in Exile* is not to be compared with it. I cannot help telling you this with some malicious joy, for it is about this very piece that my friend had prognosticated so falsely. . . .

૱ To Joseph Lehmann

Paris, October 5, 1854

MY DEAREST LEHMANN: . . . I have moved my quarters and I now live aux Batignolles, 51, Grand Rue, Paris. However, at the end of the month I will have to leave this new apartment, which I have furnished comfortably, because the prevailing dampness has caused an inflammation of my throat. I am very thankful to you for the information about the *Allgemeine Zeitung*. It is only by accident that I now learn about these things, since I live completely isolated, and see no Germans at all except my two secretaries, who are both too decent to pay heed to German gossip. My book-seller writes to me only of matters involving his interests. Out of regard for me much that happens in Germany is kept from me—which is perfectly ridiculous, for I have long been hardened to all affronts, and I am dead to almost all worldly vanities. My wife has driven most of the Germans from my house; a number of these she has literally thrown out. In the last years many of them have been snatched away by death, some have left, others are confined in insane asylums or prisons, so that as I told you I know nothing of what happens in my Fatherland, especially about matters that it might be needful for me to know in case some outright falsehood is to be contradicted. And in this regard it would be nice of you to keep me better informed. Surely there is nothing that can injure me any more, and there may be much that can still amuse me. Furthermore, as soon as I find some peace, I shall devote myself entirely to the writing of my memoirs and news about the fate and the vicissitudes of my compatriot-friends might be useful. Many of these, who have long been dead, I still imagine to be alive; others I think of as being dead, while they have merely grown stupid or evil.

You have no idea of what a sensational acclaim has been accorded my article in the *Revue des deux Mondes*. In a few weeks it will appear in complete form in my book, *De l'Allemagne*, for which it was written as a concluding chapter. I am publishing my works in French with the firm of Michel Levy Frères, who have been recommended to me as publishers. I had the choice between him and another publisher, a former *bonnetier*, that is, a maker of woollen nightcaps, but I preferred the first, perhaps because he is descended from the tribe of Levi. I believe that he is none the less an honest man and deserving of my trust, and I should most certainly be the last to be guided by my ancient prejudice against the Jews, even if to my great sorrow I should be fatally mistaken. I believe that if they are permitted to make money, they are at least grateful and take less advantage of us than their Christian colleagues. Among them a great civilization of the heart has persisted through two thousand years as an uninterrupted tradition. I think that is the reason they have been able to play so great a part in European culture, because they have had so little to learn in the matter of feeling, and need only acquire learning. . . .

I hardly know what I am dictating. I am sleepy because of an overdose of opium I have taken; and I will close by thanking you once more for your kindness, and I greet you most cordially.

᎒᎒ Self-Vindication

WHEN I WROTE ABOUT THE SO-CALLED CORRUPTION OF GUIZOT, somewhat too objectively, but certainly with a clear conscience and without any hypocritical virtuous indignation, it actually never occurred to me that I myself should be accused, five years later, of participating in such corruption. . . .

How it came about that the otherwise so cautious *Allgemeine Zeitung* fell a victim to such mystification, I will explain later. For the present I content myself with referring to the extra supplement of the Augsburg *Allgemeine Zeitung* of May 23, 1848, in which, in a public declaration, I quite frankly and unequivocally expressed myself on these subtle insinuations. I suppressed all modest feelings of vanity, and in the public pages of the *Allgemeine Zeitung* I made the melancholy confession that poverty, that terrible sickness of exile, had also struck me down at last, and that I too had to have recourse to that "great alms which the French people expend on so many thousands of foreigners who in their zeal for the Revolution had compromised themselves more or less gloriously in their homeland and had sought a hospitable refuge in France."

These were my bare words of explanation. I called things by their most grievous names. Though I might easily have alleged that the pecuniary assistance extended to me as an *allocation annuelle d'une pension de secours,* might well have been considered a worthy acknowledgment of my literary merit, as I had been told with the most delicate courtesy, I still unconditionally attributed this pension to the magnanimity of the nation, and to political brotherly love, which expressed itself here as beautifully and as movingly as it ever did in evangelical compassion. There were men of eminence among my colleagues in exile who called this assistance a subsidy, proud beggar-knights on horseback, who hated all sense of obligation and who called it a loan which would later be repaid with high interest to the French—but I humbled myself in my dire need and called it by its rightful name. In the above-mentioned explanation, I added: "I accepted such pecuniary assistance after the deplorable decree of the Diet had appeared, which sought to ruin me financially as the head of a so-called Young German School, by imposing an anticipatory ban not only on all that I had written, but also on everything that I might subsequently write; and in this way robbed me, without trial or justice, of my possessions and my means of obtaining a livelihood."

Yes, without "trial or justice." I think that in this way I correctly describe the proceedings—unheard-of in the annals of preposterous violence. By a decree of the Government of my native country not only were all my previous writings prohibited, but also everything that I might write in the future. My brain was confiscated; my poor innocent stomach was by this interdict deprived of every means of sustenance. At the same time my name was to be completely erased from the memory of man, and all the censors of my native land received strict injunctions to strike out every passage in the newspapers, pamphlets and books in which I was mentioned—favorably or unfavorably. Short-sighted fools! These decrees and injunctions were powerless against an author whose intellectual interests issued victorious from every persecution, though his finances were brought to utter ruin, so that even now I can feel the effects of their petty malice. But I did not starve, although at the time I was hard pressed by wan care. Living in Paris is so expensive, especially if a man is married and has no children, for these dear little dolls while away the time for the husband—and sometimes for the wife—and there is no need to seek amusement away from home, where it costs so much. Furthermore, I have never learned the art of feeding the hungry with mere words, the more so as nature has endowed me with such a hale exterior that no one would believe my distress. The poverty-stricken, who had before been helped by me, laughed when I told them that in the future I myself would have to starve. Was I not related to all sorts of millionaires? Had not the generalissimo of all millionaires, had not this millionairissimo himself called me his friend—*his friend?* I could never convince my suppliants that the great millionairissimo called me his friend precisely because I did not ask him for money. Had I done so, that would have been the end of our friendship! The days of David and Jonathan, of Orestes and Pylades are gone. My poor, needy blockheads thought that it was quite easy to get things from the rich. They have never seen, as I have, with what fearful iron locks and bars their great money chests are secured. It is only from people who themselves have very little that something can be borrowed, for their chests are not made of iron—and they always want to seem more affluent than they really are.

Indeed, it was no small part of my peculiar misfortune that no one would believe me financially straitened. In the Magna Charta, which, as Cervantes relates, the God Apollo granted poets, the first paragraph declares that the poet is to be believed on his mere word when he assures us that he has no money, and that he is not required to take an oath to that effect. Alas, I appealed in vain to this privilege of my station as poet. So it happened that calumny had an easy task in ascribing the motives which induced me to accept the pension in question to anything but the most natural wants and necessities. I recall that at the time many of my compatriots, among them the most resolute and brilliant of them all, Dr. Marx,[12] came to me and expressed their displeasure at the slanderous article in the *Allgemeine Zeitung*, and advised me not to reply with a single word, since they themselves had already declared in various German journals that I had accepted the pension with a view to more effectively supporting my needy associates. The same was affirmed by the then editor of the *Neue Rheinische Zeitung*, as well as by the friends who comprised his general staff. However, I thanked them for their kind sympathy, and assured them that they had erred; that ordinarily I could use that pension quite well in my own interest, and that I would answer the malicious and anonymous article in the *Allgemeine Zeitung*, not indirectly through my friends, but directly, above my own signature. . . .

TIME, PLACE AND CIRCUMSTANCE did not then permit of any further explanations, but now, that all such considerations no longer exist, I may be allowed to explain even more factually that I could not be bribed by the Guizot Ministry either for what I wrote or for what I did not write. Such retrospective justifications have a peculiar and melancholy charm for men who, like myself, have done with life, and I indulge in them with the indolence of a dreamer. It is as though I were fulfilling a pious obligation to one long dead. At any rate, the following revelations concerning the affairs of France at the time of the Guizot Ministry are in place.

The Ministry of the 29th of November, 1840, should not, as a matter of fact, be called the Guizot Ministry, but the Soult Ministry, since Soult was President of the Council of Ministers. But Soult was only its titular President, much as the reigning King of Hanover has the title of Rector of the University of Georgia-Augusta, while His Magnificence, the temporary Pro-Rector, fulfills the actual duties of the Rector. Despite Soult's absolute authority, there was never much talk of him, except that occasionally the liberal newspapers, when they were satisfied with him, called him the victor of Toulouse, but when displeased, scorned him and declared that he had not won that battle. All the talk was only of Guizot, who for many years continued at the zenith of his popularity with the bourgeoisie, who had been frightened out of their wits by the war-mongering frenzy of his predecessor. It is readily understandable that the successor of Thiers met with even greater sympathy on the other side of the Rhine. We Germans could never forgive Thiers for having drummed us out of our sleep, from our easy, vegetating slumber, and we rubbed our eyes and cried, "Long live Guizot!" Learned men, especially, sang his praises in Pindaric hymns, in which even the ancient prosody, the ancient measures, were imitated, and a German professor of philology, who was passing through Paris, assured me that Guizot was just as great as Thiersch—yes, just as great as my dear, humanitarian friend, Thiersch, the author of the best Greek grammar! Even the German press raved over Guizot, and not only the tame newspapers, but even the wild ones; and this enthusiasm lasted a long time. I recall that not long before the fall of the much lauded favorite of the Germans, I read in the most radical of German journals, in the *Speyerer Zeitung*, an apology for Guizot from the pen of one of those tyrant-eaters whose tomahawk and scalping knife never knew mercy. This enthusiasm for Guizot was especially well represented in the *Allgemeine Zeitung* by my colleague with the sign of Venus, and by my colleague with the Arrow. The first swung the censer with sacerdotal devotion, while the latter maintained sweetness and charm even in his ecstasy. Both held out until the catastrophe.

For my part, ever since I began to take a serious interest in French literature, I recognized and understood Guizot's remarkable qualities, and my writings testify to my early veneration for this world-renowned man. I preferred his rival, Thiers, but only on account of his personality, not because of the temper of his mind, which was narrow and nationalistic, so that he might almost be called a French Pan-German, while Guizot's cosmopolitan outlook was more akin to my own way of thinking. I loved in Thiers many faults which people found in me, while I thought the virtues of Guizot almost repelling. I had often to find fault with Thiers, but always reluctantly; when Guizot compelled my praise, I did so only after a vigorous examination. Indeed I discussed the man who was then the chief subject of conversation only with an independent love of truth, and I always reported faithfully what I heard. It was a point of honor with me to set down unaltered in this book the reports in which the character and ideas of government (not the administrative acts) of the great statesman were most warmly honored, although this resulted in much repetition. The kind reader will observe that these discussions do not extend beyond the end of 1843, when I ceased altogether writing political articles for the *Allgemeine Zeitung*, and confined myself to frequently giving the editor friendly information in our private correspondence; only occasionally did I publish an article on science and the fine arts.

That is indeed the silence, the *not*-writing, of which the *Allgemeine Zeitung* speaks, and which it implies was the sale of my freedom of speech. Is it not more likely that I was wavering in my allegiance to Guizot at that time, and that I had been completely in error regarding him? That was indeed the case; but I could not make such a confession in March 1848. Neither devotion nor decency allowed it. I had therefore, in the aforementioned explanation, to confine myself to answering the perfidious insinuations, which ascribed my sudden silence to bribery, with the bare facts of my relations with the Guizot Ministry. Before the 29th of November, 1840, when M. Guizot assumed the ministry, I never had the honor of seeing him. It was only a month later that I visited him to thank him for having given instructions to the comptroller of his department to pay me my subsidy in monthly installments as before. That visit was the first and last which I ever paid to the illustrious man in my whole life. In the conversation with which he honored me, he spoke warmly and deeply of his high esteem for Germany, and this tribute to my native land, as well as the flattering words he spoke of my own literary productions, were the only coin with which he bribed me. It never occurred to him to ask any service of me. And certainly, it could never have been in the mind of this proud man, who courted unpopularity, to ask of me a paltry blurb in the French press, or the Augsburg *Allgemeine Zeitung*—of me, a stranger, while persons of far greater importance and reliability, such as Baron von Eckstein and the historian Capefigue,[18] both of whom were contributors to the *Allgemeine Zeitung*, had for many years been on a most friendly footing with M. Guizot, and certainly earned his intimate confidence. I never saw M. Guizot again after this interview. I never saw his secretary or anyone else empioyed in his office. I once learned by accident that M. Guizot was often strongly urged by the German embassies to banish me from Paris. I could not help laughing at the thought of the vexation on the faces of those petitioners had they found out that the Minister of whom they were demanding my expulsion was actually supporting me with an annual subsidy. I needed no special hint to understand how little he wanted his noble behavior to be divulged; and my discreet friends, from whom I can conceal nothing, shared my malicious pleasure.

I surely owe a great debt of gratitude to M. Guizot for this pleasure, and for the generosity with which he treated me. Yes, when I was shaken in my faith as to his firmness in resisting royal pretensions, when I saw that he was disastrously dominated by the will of Louis Philippe, and understood the dreadful wrong-headedness of his aristocratic obstinacy and morbid egoism, then the feeling of gratitude would by no means have been able to fetter my pen; I would certainly have pointed out, respectfully but with regret, the mistakes by which the all too submissive Ministry, or rather, the deluded King, were preparing the ruin of the country and of the world. But my pen was silenced by brutal physical hindrances; and I am only now able to make public the real cause of my silence, of my *not*-writing.

Even if I had felt the desire to publish only a word in the *Allgemeine Zeitung* against the unholy system of government of Louis Philippe, it would have been impossible for me for the simple reason that the crafty King had already, before the 29th of November, taken precautions against such a "criminal" attack, or outrage, by a correspondent, by condescending, in His Own Royal Person, to make the then censor of the *Allgemeine Zeitung* at Augsburg not only a "chevalier", but also an Officer of the French Legion of Honor. However, great as was then my predilection for the late King, the Augsburg censors found that I did not love him enough, and struck out every disparaging word, and prevented the publication of many of my articles on the royal policy. But shortly after the February Revolution, when my poor Louis Philippe was driven into exile, it was neither right nor fitting to publish this fact, even if the Augsburg censor had put his *Imprimatur* on it.

There was another and similar confession which the censorship of the heart did not then allow me to make, and which was much more painful than that imposed by the *Allgemeine Zeitung*. No, shortly after the fall of M. Guizot, I dared not openly admit that I had been silent from fear. I had to admit to myself in 1844 that if M. Guizot had learned of my correspondence and had been somewhat displeased with the criticism it contained, this passionate man was capable of supressing his feelings of generosity and acting quite summarily toward his irksome critic. With the expulsion of the correspondent from Paris, the correspondence would likewise have ceased. In truth, His Magnificence had the *fasces* of power in his hands, and could at any time give me the *consilium abeundi*,[14] and then I would immediately have to strap on my knapsack. His beadles with their blue uniforms and their lemon-yellow facings would soon have separated me from my critical studies at Paris, and led me toward those posts— "striped like zebras"—where other beadles with even more distasteful liveries and boorish Germanic manners would have received me—to do me the honors of my Fatherland.

But unhappy poet, were you not a naturalized citizen of France and adequately protected against such ministerial caprice?

Alas! The answer to this question wrings from me the confession which perhaps prudence would bid me smother. But prudence and I have long ago parted company—and I will now recklessly declare that I never became a naturalized Frenchman, and that my naturalization, which is supposed to be a notorious fact, is for all that only a German fable. I do not know what idle or mischievous brain invented it. Several of my fellow compatriots claim that they have sniffed it from some authentic source. They reported it in German newspapers, and I lent support to this error by my silence. My dear literary and political opponents in Germany and many very influential and close enemies in Paris were led astray by it, and believed that

I was protected by French citizenship against the many vexations and machinations by which a foreigner, who is subject to exceptional jurisdiction here, can be so easily persecuted. Through this beneficial mistake I escaped a great deal of malice and plundering at the hands of the commercial people who would have taken advantage of their special privileges in business disagreements. The position of the unnaturalized foreigner in Paris is as difficult as it is, in the long run, expensive. He is harried and cheated, chiefly by naturalized foreigners, who are bent on misusing their recently acquired privileges most disgracefully. Once, as a precaution against these vexations, I complied with the formalities which imply no obligation, while they place one in a position to acquire the rights of citizenship without delay—should that be necessary. Yet I always felt a secret dread of this decisive step. As a result of this cautiousness, and my deep-rooted disinclination to being naturalized, I eventually found myself in a false position, which I must regard as the cause of all my troubles, vexations, and failures during my twenty three years' stay in Paris. The income of a good official position would have adequately covered my large domestic expenses and the requirements of my way of life—which is not so capricious as it is humane and free; but without being naturalized, I found all government posts closed to me. My friends used to hold out to me alluring prospects of high honors and fat sinecures, and there was no lack of examples of foreigners who had mounted the glittering rungs of power and honor in France. I may add that I would have had to fight less with local jealousy than others, for never before had a German won the sympathy of the French to such a degree in the literary, as well as in the social, world, and the most distinguished men sought my company, not as patrons, but as friends. The chivalrous Prince, who was next to the throne, and who was not only a distinguished soldier and statesman, but who also read my *Book of Songs* in the original, would have been only too glad to see me in the service of France, and his influence would have been sufficiently great to advance me in such a career. I shall never forget the kindness with which the great historian of the French Revolution and the Empire, who was then the omnipotent President of the Council, once took my arm in the garden of a princess, who was his friend, and walking with me, urged me at great length and warmly to tell him my heart's desire, and pledged himself to see that it was granted. I can still hear the flattering sound of his voice; and I still smell the scent of the great flowering magnolia which we passed, and which rose with its stately white alabaster flowers into the blue sky, as glorious and proud as the heart of the German poet, in those days of his happiness! Yes; I have uttered the word. It was the foolish arrogance of the German poet which prevented me from becoming a Frenchman, even if only *pro forma*. It was a romantic whim, of which I could not free myself. I have ever been a free-thinker as regards what is usually called patriotism, but I could not rid myself of a certain dread lest I do something which might in the least degree appear a renunciation of my Fatherland. Even in the mind of the most enlightened there always lurks a little mandrake root of superstition, which cannot be torn up. One does not like to speak of it, but it sends its shoots of folly into the most secret crannies of the soul. My marriage with my dear Frau Germania, the blonde bear-skin savage, had never been happy. I can remember lovely moonlit nights when she pressed me tenderly to her large bosom—with its virtuous nipples—these sentimental nights I can count on my fingers; but toward morning dismaying boredom and coldness came upon us, and then began the endless scolding. In the end we lived apart in both bed and board—but it never came to an actual breach. I could never bring myself to renounce my domestic cross. I detest disloyalty of every kind, and I could never renounce a German cat or a German dog, however insupportable their fleas and fidelity might be to me. The smallest suckling-pig of my native land cannot complain of me in this respect. Among the aristocratic and witty swine of Perigord, who nosed up truffles and battened on them, I never denounced the modest grunters who, at home in the forests of Teutoburg, grub the native acorns out of the wooden trough, as once their pious ancestors did when Arminius defeated Varus.[15] I have not lost the bristle of my German nature, not a single bell of my German cap, and I still have the right to fasten to it the black, red and gold cockade. And I still have the right to say to Massmann, "We German donkeys." Had I allowed myself to be naturalized in France, then Massmann would have answered, "I am still a German ass, but not you." And then he would have cut a mocking caper, which would have broken my heart. No, I have never exposed myself to such a disgrace. Naturalization may do for others— a tipsy lawyer in Zweibrücken. A block-head with a brow of iron and a nose of brass may, in order to snap up a schoolmaster's job, give up his Fatherland which knows nothing of him, and wants to know nothing of him—but it is not fitting for a German poet, who has written the most beautiful German poems. It would be a horrible, insane idea for me to have to say that I am a German poet and at the same time a naturalized Frenchman. I should appear to myself like one of those abortions with two heads which are exhibited at fairs. It would cause me untold trouble while writing poetry, if I were to think that one of these heads was beginning to scan the most unnatural Alexandrines in French turkey-cock pathos, while the other was pouring out his feelings in the true, native, natural metres of the German tongue. Alas! I can scarcely put up with their odorless better poets! The verses of the French poets are as repugnant to me as their metres. That perfumed refuse! When I consider the so-called *poésie lyrique* of the French, then I see the full splendor of German poetry and I can plume myself on having won my laurels in that field. We will not yield up a single laurel-leaf; and the stone-cutter who is called upon to adorn our tombstone with an inscription will find no one to protest when he engraves these words: "Here lies a German poet."

ટ્રૅ *To Adolphe Thiers* [16]

Paris, April 14, 1855

Monsieur: You are not in power at the present time, and when you will be, the poor dying man who is penning these lines will have no further need of human protection. Hence I will not be suspected of yielding to mundane impulses if I try today to revive and strengthen the interest with which you have always honored me. Reassured on this score, I should like to confess that the desire to do something to please you played a part—though not exclusively—in the notion which I have had of publishing a collection of letters composing the book, *Lutetia*, which I have the honor of presenting to you. In the present state of mind among my fellow-Germans, this publication will appear somewhat scabrous; and I also doubt whether the French version will meet with much sympathy in France. Perhaps it is appearing at a very unfavorable moment.

That is of little moment. In this book I wished to revive the most brilliant days of that parliamentary epoch symbolized by only three great names: Louis Philippe, Thiers, and Guizot. I do not think I have failed in this purpose. Yes, it is these three names alone that the schoolboys of tomorrow will have to learn by heart. Dame Clio does not have much room in her tablets for heroes of the second order. She loves to epitomize a whole epoch in one great name or in a triumvirate. I have followed the example of the goddess in *Lutetia*, which I beg you to judge as a whole, and not in its details or in its occasionally ill-tempered expressions. If I have been in opposition to the ministry of the first of March (an opposition which was under no circumstance very dangerous), if I have on occasion acted rudely toward you when you were minister, I have never failed to do justice to the man of good will and genius, and to defend him against a crew of my compatriots who spewed forth so many of their mad diatribes and calumnies against him. Time has done justice to these, but during your ministry of 1840 the most absurd lies found credence beyond the Rhine. It was a shameful spectacle to watch that fury mounting by the minute, until at last it burst into a frenzied rage. Certain patriotic asses of my acquaintance gave the signal;—one of these has even been the recipient of benefits from your hand. Other asses in my country answered their cries; a deafening braying broke out on all sides; one could almost say that all Germany had suddenly turned into one ass—braying against M. Thiers.

I would ask you, Monsieur, to pay particular attention to the dates of my letters when you read *Lutetia*, and to recall under what auspices I wrote them. You will no doubt see that at that time I could not decorate my style with servile turns while I spoke of you—when I was living in the very headquarters of German asininity.

Since I am sincerely fond of you, I would be pained if through inadvertence or gaucherie I have said something displeasing to you. In my present condition, I must live on memories, and yours are dear to my heart.

Be assured of my great admiration and my most respectful devotion.

➳ *Reflections*

I DID NOT BECOME A NATURALIZED FRENCHMAN for fear that I would get to love France less well; just as a man cools toward a mistress the moment he is legally wedded to her. I shall continue to live with France without benefit of clergy.

IN FRANCE MY MIND FEELS as if it were in exile, banished into a foreign tongue.

I HAVE THE MOST KINDLY TEMPERAMENT. My wants are modest—a hut, a thatched roof, but a good bed, good food, milk and butter, all very fresh; flowers at my window, a few beautiful trees at my door. And if the good Lord wants to make me quite happy he will give me the pleasure of seeing some six or seven of my enemies strung up on them. With all my heart I shall forgive them, before their death, all the evil they have committed against me while I was alive. Yes, one should always forgive one's enemies—but not until they are hanged.

THE LORD WILL FORGIVE THE FOLLIES which I committed against Him, just as I forgive the follies of my enemies who wrote against me— although they stand as far below me, as I stand below thee, my God!

❧ *I Am a German Poet*

. . . IN THE SPIRITUAL as well as in the worldly hierarchy I have attained neither office nor rank; I have, as they say, really come to nothing in this lovely world. Nothing has become of me—nothing but a poet.

But no, I will not put on a hypocritical humility; I will not disparage that title. It is something to be a poet, especially to be a great lyric poet in Germany, among a people who have surpassed all others in two things—philosophy and poetry. I will not depreciate my fame as a poet with false modesty—the invention of scoundrels. None of my compatriots has won the laurel at so early an age as I; and if my colleague Wolfgang Goethe can complacently sing that "the Chinese with trembling hand paints Werther and Lotte on porcelain," I can, if boasting be in order, match his Chinese fame with one still more legendary—namely, my fame in Japan. . . .

But at this moment I am as indifferent to my fame in Japan as in Finland. Alas! Fame, that once lovely toy, sweet as sugared pineapple and flattery, has for a long time been distasteful to me; it is as bitter to me now as wormwood. With Romeo I can say, "Oh, I am Fortune's fool!" The bowl stands filled before me, but I have no spoon. What does it avail me that at banquets my health is pledged in the choicest wines, and drunk from golden goblets, when I myself am cut off from all that makes life pleasant, and may only moisten my lips with a thin gruel? What does it avail me that enthusiastic youths and maidens crown my marble bust with laurel-wreaths, if at the same time the withered hand of an aged nurse presses cantharides behind my own ears? What does it avail me that all the roses of Shiraz glow so tenderly and exhale their perfume for me—alas! Shiraz is two thousand miles away from the Rue d'Amsterdam, where in the dreary solitude of my sickroom I can smell nothing but the perfume of warmed napkins! Alas, the irony of God weighs heavily upon me. The great Author of the universe, the Aristophanes of heaven, wished to show me—the little, earthly, so-called German Aristophanes—as glaringly as possible what feeble little jests my most bitter sarcasms were in comparison with His own, and how inferior I was to Him in humor and in giant wit.

Yes, the lye of derision which the Master has poured over me is terrible—and His sport is horribly cruel. Humbly do I acknowledge His supremacy, and I prostrate myself in dust before Him. But although I lack His supreme creative powers, my spirit does possess the lightning flash of eternal reason, and I may even summon the wit of God before its tribunal and subject it to respectful criticism. And here I venture to offer the most humble opinion that the horrible game which the Master is playing with his wretched pupil is too protracted. It has already lasted over six years, and is now a little tiresome. Moreover, I should like to take the liberty of observing with due deference that the jest is not new, and that the great Aristophanes of heaven has already used it on a former occasion, and is, therefore, guilty of plagiarizing His own exalted Self. To prove this point, I shall quote a passage from the *Chronicle of Limburg*.[17] This Chronicle is very interesting for those who seek information about the manners and customs of Germany during the Middle Ages. Like a fashion-journal, it describes the wearing apparel of men and women in vogue at each particular period. It also tells of the popular songs which were whistled and sung in that day, and quotes the opening lines of several of them. Thus, it records that during the year 1480 there were whistled and sung throughout all of Germany certain songs which for sweetness and tenderness surpassed any previously heard in German lands. Young and old, and women in particular, were totally bereft of their senses, and they sang them from morn till eve. These songs, so the chronicle continues, were composed by a young priest who was a leper and lived a solitary life, secluded from all the rest of the world. You are surely aware, dear reader, what a horrible disease leprosy was in the Middle Ages, and how the poor wretches who were afflicted with this incurable malady were cast out from all society and from the abodes of men, and were forbidden to come near any human being. Living corpses, they wandered to and fro, muffled from head to foot, a hood drawn over their faces, and carrying in their hands a rattle, a Lazarus rattle as it was called, with which they gave timely warning of their approach, so that every one might get out of their way. The poor priest, of whose fame as a poet the Chronicle spoke so highly, was such a leper, and while all Germany sang and whistled his songs joyfully and jubilantly, he sat dolefully in the desolation of his misery.

Oh, his fame was the old, familiar derision—the horrible jest of God, the same as in my case, although there it appears in the romantic garb of the Middle Ages. The blasé King of Judea said rightly: "There is nothing new under the sun." Perhaps the sun itself, which now shines so imposingly, is itself only an old rehashed jest.

Sometimes in the troubled visions that visit me at night, I seem to see before me the poor priest of the *Limburg Chronicle*, my brother in Apollo, and his sorrowful eyes stare strangely out of his hood; but almost at once he vanishes, and faintly dying away, like the echo of a dream, I hear the jarring notes of his Lazarus rattle.

৪১ *To the Mouche*

3 Avenue Matignon, June 20, 1855

MY VERY GRACIOUS AND CHARMING FRIEND: I am very sorry that I could see you only for a few moments recently. You left an extremely favorable impression, and I am looking forward to seeing you again very soon.

If you can, come tomorrow; in any case, as soon as your time allows. You will announce yourself as you did last time. I am ready to receive you at any hour throughout the day. The best time would be from four till as late as you like. I am writing this with my own hand, despite my eye-trouble, because I do not have a confidential secretary at present. I have much trouble around me, and am still in great pain.

I don't know why your kind sympathy does me so much good. But superstitious man that I am, I imagine that a good fairy is visiting me in my hour of sorrow. It was just the right hour. Perhaps you are a wicked fairy? I must know soon.

Your

Heinrich Heine

DEAREST SOUL: My head is so confused that I no longer know whether I asked you to come today (Thursday) or not until tomorrow (Friday). Today I am indisposed; and to make sure, we'll set your kind visit for Saturday. Then I hope you will certainly come. Come soon!

I am taking this opportunity of sending you the manuscript of the poems, and I ask you to bring it back with you so that we may read it together, and you can note beforehand the changes you would want me to make.

Dear, sweet soul! I am very sick—sick in body and soul. German honor and decency have played me dirty tricks.

I embrace the lotus flower and remain

Your devoted

H.H.

Sunday noon

DEAREST SOUL: My head still aches; but tomorrow I shall be better. I can't stop being angry with you. Imagine! Going out of doors in this bad weather; getting your feet cold—or even wet! And yet stubborn as a mule! and not to listen to reason! You're sure to catch cold! Oh, you naughty lotus flower! She is not to come unless the weather is fine.

Paris, July 20, 1855

SWEETEST LITTLE MOUCHE, or shall I address you not by the emblem in your seal, but by the perfume of your letter? In that case I must call you my most lovely civet-cat. The day before yesterday I received your letter; the little *pattes de mouche* [18] are constantly scratching in my head, and even in my soul. Cordial thanks for your great kindness to me. The poems are very beautiful, and here I repeat what I have already told you.

I too look forward to seeing you soon, *et de poser une empreinte vivante sur les traits suaves et quelques peu souabes*—oh! If I were still a man, this phrase would have less of a Platonic turn! But I am only a spirit—which may be very much to your liking, but not to mine. The French edition of my poems is out and a success. But I will not publish the poems which are still untranslated, for example the *New Spring*, until a few months hence, in one of the last volumes of the French edition. You see, I'm losing no time. Yes, I look forward to seeing you again, *fine mouche de mon âme*, loveliest civet-cat, who is at the same time as gentle as an Angora cat—my favorite species. For a long time I used to like tiger cats—but they are too dangerous and *les empreintes vivantes* which they sometimes left on my face weren't very pleasant. I still feel very ill; constant fits and irritations. I am extremely vexed at my condition—which is hopeless! A corpse languishing for the most lively joys of life! That is horrible. Good-bye. May the baths refresh and invigorate you. Fondest regards.

Your friend
Heinrich Heine

❧ To Betty Heine

Paris, August 10, 1855

DEAREST MOTHER: Since your last letter I have been thinking of nothing but the happy reunion with my dear sister. Everything is arranged—my dear Lottchen will find a place to live in our house when she arrives, and she and one of the nieces (for I would be over-joyed if she would bring Anna or Lehnchen) will be very comfortable here. Yes, it would make me very happy if Lottchen would also bring one of her own children, Annchen or Lehnchen, I don't care which, for I love them both equally, and only age should be a deciding factor in the choice. We have plenty of room now. All our friends who visit us admire the beautiful view and the fresh air we enjoy here, so that we are in the very brilliant center of Paris and at the same time seem to be living in the country. Last week Laube and his wife were here from Vienna, and called on us often. . . .

My wife is cheerful and well. I am still suffering from my old ailment—fits, which are not very painful, but destroy all joy of living, especially my ability to work. . . .

Your faithful son
Harry Heine

ᐓ *To the Mouche*

Paris, August 14 [*1855*]

My dear Friend: You've been in Paris and yet you've delayed coming to see me and pressing my hand. I have a strong desire to smell the sweet perfume of your gloves, to hear the sound of your voice, and to make a vivid impression on your *Schwabengesicht*—your Suabian face. Don't be angry; graceful as you are, there is something in your face of the Suabian oriole. But come soon.

Dearest, sweetest cat! Tomorrow (Wednesday) I won't see you, because the migraine is already announcing its presence in my head. But if it's possible for you to come to me on Friday—that would make up for my having missed you so long. After Friday, any day will suit me equally well. The more often you come the happier I shall be. My dear, lovely *fine mouche!* Flutter around my nose a little with your little wings. I know a song by Mendelssohn with the refrain, "Come soon!" The tune is forever running in my head: "Come soon!"
   I kiss your two dear paws; not all at once; but one after the other—*faute de pouvoir poser une empreinte vivante sur. . . .*

My dearest, lovely Friend: I thank you for your sweet and cordial lines. I am happy that you are well. Unfortunately I am always very ill.—Weak and cross.—Sometimes on the verge of tears by reason of the least prank of Fate. Every invalid is a fool; I don't like being seen in this condition. But I must hear my little Mouche buzzing all the same. Come soon—as soon as it pleases your Grace—as soon as possible, come my dear, little Suabian face. I've scrawled the poem. Sheer, insane Charenton verse. From a madman to a madwoman!

Dearest Soul! I am still very sick, and I won't see you today either. But I hope that you can come tomorrow (Sunday). If you can't come till the day after, send me word.

Your poor Friend
Nebuchadnezzar II.

(For I am as crazy as the Babylonian King, and eat only chopped grass, which my cook calls spinach.)

DEAREST HEART! The weather is bad. So is yours truly. And I am not going to expose my lotus flower to such a spleenish atmosphere. Oh, God, I would so gladly give you a sunny, cheerful Indian day, such as one finds on the banks of the Ganges and—suits lotus flowers.

Come soon—but as I said, not today. I shall expect you on Wednesday afternoon. I think that is convenient for you.

Je pose, etc. etc.

Wednesday, 1 P. M.

DEAREST MOUCHE: I suffer much, and am sick to death. My right eyelid keeps dropping, and I can hardly write any more. But I love you and think of you often, my sweetest. The short story did not bore me at all, and promises well for the future. You are really not as stupid as you look. You are pretty beyond compare, and that delights my senses. Will I see you tomorrow? I don't know as yet; if I don't feel better, the order will be countermanded. A tearful mood has come over me. My heart yawns in spasms and these *bâillements* are insufferable. Would I were dead, or a healthy puppy, who has no more need of ablutions.

Misery thy name is
H.H.

ষ্ট্য *To Julius Campe*

Paris, November 1, 1855

MY DEAR CAMPE: . . . I can hardly see anything today, and my eyes burn. Since I have taken leave of Herr Reinhardt, I have no one to whom I can dictate a German letter. Otherwise I would write you more often. No one now receives letters or replies from me. Much is happening. Three contemptible cliques are attacking me in the crassest way. But I don't care. . . .

ষ্ট্য *To the Mouche*

Wednesday, 3 o'clock

DEAREST SOUL, Am very wretched. Coughed terribly for 24 hours; so I have a headache today—and probably tomorrow. Therefore I beg my sweetest one to come on Friday instead of tomorrow (Thursday). Till then I must languish. My Serinsky was ill and stayed away for the whole week. What a disconcerting bother! I am almost crazy with irritation, pain, and impatience. I will bring charges with the SPCA against dear God for treating me so horridly. I count on your coming this Friday.

Meanwhile, in my thoughts I kiss the little *pattes de mouche*.

Your crazy
H.H.

⮞ To an Unknown Correspondent [Guizot?]

I VERY MUCH REGRET, DEAR SIR, that my fatal infirmity prevents me from paying my respects in person. I would not disguise from you that a very human mental reservation has a share in these regrets. I am at this moment busy on a work in the form of memoirs, in which I undertake to tell the truth—and nothing but the truth—about men and affairs in the society of our day, and I imagine that a chat with you, Monsieur, could give me authentic information about the brilliant and glorious stew in which we are today wallowing. A writer thinks only of the interests of his book; but this egoism is pardonable when you reflect that the publication of this book will in all probability be posthumous.

⮞ To the Mouche

January 1, 1856

DEAREST CHILD: I send you greetings on the New Year, and add a box of chocolates—which at least are *de bon goût*. I know very well that you don't like me to observe these formalities, but we must also pay attention to our surroundings, which might mistake absence of customary attentions for a lack of mutual esteem. I love you so much that personally I don't need to esteem you at all. You are my dear Mouche, and I feel my pains diminish when I think of your loveliness, your charm, and your mind. Unfortunately, I can do nothing for you except send you words like these—mere "coined air." My best wishes for the New Year. I will not utter them. Words! Words!

Tomorrow I may be able to see my Mouche. I'll let her know. In any event she will come the day after tomorrow (Thursday) to her
Nebuchadnezzar II,
Formerly Royal Prussian Atheist,
Now Devout Worshipper of Lotus Flowers

Friday, January 11 [*1856*]

DEAR CHILD: Today I have an attack of migraine, and I'm afraid it will last through tomorrow, or rather break out completely. I hasten to inform you of this, so that you may know in time that there is no school tomorrow, and can make other arrangements to spend your afternoon. I hope that you can definitely come the day after tomorrow (Sunday). If not, let me know, my dear, good child. I will never beat you, even if you should sometimes deserve it, on account of some great silliness. Furthermore, I don't have the strength required for using the rod. I am exhausted, sad, and in pain.

I kiss your *pattes de mouche.*

Sunday morning

No SCHOOL TODAY, *car le mâitre d'école n'est pas encore curé, comme dirait la vieille Liszt.*[19] I shall therefore go without you today. But let me know if you can come tomorrow (Monday). I have a severe headache. It would be selfish to let you come and not be able to say a word to you. I await your reply and remain

The loving Mouche's
Craziest H.H.

Mardi

THE VISIT OF MY DEAR MOUCHE YESTERDAY did me a great deal of good. I have since suffered little pain. I think constantly of the most perfect, most charming, and most lovely little Mouche. But I shall not see her again until the day after tomorrow. What an eternity! In the meantime I could die a hundred times over, and with the greatest of ease. Think of me a little, you silly little goose.

Your most submissive
Hansel

Paris, January 24, 1856

DEAREST MOUCHE: I have passed a miserable, very miserable night, and have almost lost all courage. I count on hearing you buzz around me tomorrow. Also, I've grown as sentimental as a puppy, who is in love for the first time. . . .

₹➤ *Testament*

BEFORE THE UNDERSIGNED NOTARIES OF PARIS, MM. Ferdinand Léon Ducloux and Charles Louis Emile Rousse, and in the presence of

(1) M. Michel Jacot, baker, living at Paris, Rue d'Amsterdam, No. 60, and

(2) M. Eugène Grouchy, grocer, living at Paris, Rue d'Amsterdam, No. 52;

The aforementioned two witnesses meet the prescribed legal requirements as they have severally declared to the undersigned notaries in answer to every question put to them;

And in the bedroom of the hereinafter named Herr Heine, situated on the second story of a house, Rue d'Amsterdam, No. 50; in which bedroom, which is lighted by a window opening on to a courtyard, the aforementioned notaries and witnesses selected by the Testator have gathered together upon his express wish,

Appeared

Herr Heinrich Heine, Writer and Doctor of Laws, residing at Paris, Rue d'Amsterdam, No. 50,

Who, sick of body, but of sound mind, memory and understanding, as appeared to the aforementioned notaries and witnesses in conversation with him—anticipating death, has dictated to the aforesaid M. Ducloux, in the presence of M. Rousse and the witnesses, his will in the following manner:

#1. I appoint Mathilde Crescence Heine, born Mirat, with whom for many years I have spent my good and evil days, and who has nursed me during my long and terrible illness, to be my universal legatee. I bequeath to her all my property whatsoever, and without condition or limitation everything that I possess and may die possessed of, and all my rights in any future possessions.

#2. At a time when I believed that I had an endowed future, I parted with all my literary property on very moderate conditions; unfortunate events subsequently swallowed up the small fortune that I possessed, and my illness made it impossible for me to improve my income in favor of my wife. The allowance which I received from my late uncle Solomon Heine, and which was always the basis of my finances, is only in part assured to my wife. I myself wished it so. I feel at present the greatest regret at not having made better provision for my wife's welfare after my death. The aforesaid allowance from my uncle represented the interest on a capital sum which my benefactor did not wish to place in the hands of such an unbusinesslike poet as myself, so as better to secure for me a lasting enjoyment of it. I counted on this income which had been assured me, when I joined my fate with a person whom my uncle esteemed very highly and to whom he gave many a mark of affectionate regard. Although in his testamentary provisions he did not officially do anything for her, it is none the less to be assumed that such an omission is to be attributed to an unfortunate accident rather than to the feelings of the deceased; he, whose generosity has enriched so many persons who were strangers to his family and to his heart, could not be guilty of such stinginess when it was a question of the fate of the wife of a nephew who had made his name famous. The least hint and word of a man who was generosity itself must be taken as generous. My cousin, Karl Heine, the worthy son of his father, agreed with me in this sentiment and with noble readiness he acceded to my request when I asked him to undertake the formal obligation to pay my wife as a life annuity half the allowance which was provided by his late father. This arrangement was made on the 25th of February, 1847, and I am still touched by the memory of the noble reproaches which my cousin, in spite of our differences, directed against my lack of confidence in his intentions with regard to my wife; when he gave me his hand as a pledge of his promise, I pressed it to my poor blind eyes and moistened it with my tears. Since then my condition has grown worse, and my illness has made many sources of help run dry which I might have left to my wife. These unforeseen chances and changes, and other weighty reasons compel me to turn once more to the sense of decency and justice of my cousin. I urge him most emphatically not to reduce the aforesaid allowance to one half, when he transfers it to my wife after my death, but to pay it to her without curtailment, as I drew it in the lifetime of my uncle. I say expressly, "as I drew it in the lifetime of my uncle," because my cousin, Karl Heine, has for nearly five years, since my illness grew so much worse, more than doubled the amount of my allowance, for which generous consideration I owe him many thanks. It is more than probable that there is no need for this appeal to the liberality of my cousin, for I am convinced that with the first shovelful of earth, which, according to his right as next of kin, he will throw on my grave, if he is in Paris at the time of my demise, he will forget all those painful accusations which I so much regretted and which I have atoned for with my protracted dying; he will then surely remember our former friendship, that relationship and harmony of feeling which united us from our tender youth, and he will accord the widow of his friend a truly fatherly protection; for it is not without some advantage for the peace of the one as of the other, that the living know what the dead demand of them.

#3. I desire that after my decease all my papers and letters should be carefully sealed up and kept for the disposal of my nephew, Ludwig von Embden, to whom I will give further instructions as to the use he is to make of them, without prejudice to the right of property of my universal legatee.

#4. If I die before the collected edition of my works has appeared, and if I have not been able to undertake the supervision of that edition, or even if my death intervene before it is completed, I desire my relative, Herr Dr. Rudolf Christiani, to replace me in the supervision of the publication, and to adhere strictly to the prospectus which I have left with this end in view. If my friend, Herr Campe, the publisher of my works, should desire any alteration in the form in which I have arranged my several writings in the aforesaid prospectus, then I desire that no difficulties be made since I have always submitted to his requirements as a publisher. The main thing is not to include in my writings a single line which I have not expressly intended for publication, or that has been printed without my full signature. An initial is not basis enough upon which to ascribe an article to me which has been published in some journal, for the indication of an author by an initial always depended on the editors, who never departed from the custom of making alterations in the form or content of an article signed only with an initial. I expressly forbid that any writing of any author, no matter how small, be appended to my works on any pretext, unless it be a biographical notice from the pen of one of my old friends whom I have expressly entrusted with such a work. I ask that my will be loyally carried out in this respect, that is, that my books shall not tow along or circulate a piece of writing from another hand.

#5. I forbid that my body shall be submitted to any autopsy after my death; only I think that as my illness often resembled a cataleptic condition, care should be taken to open a vein before I am interred.

#6. If I am in Paris at the time of my decease, and am living not far from Montmartre, I desire to be buried in the churchyard of that name, for I have a preference for that quarter, where I have lived for many years.

#7. I ask that my funeral be as simple as possible, and that the expenses of interment should not exceed the usual amount of those of the humblest citizen. Although I belong to the Lutheran confession by act of baptism, I do not desire that the ministers of that church should be invited to my burial; and I also would forego the services of any other priest at my funeral. This desire does not spring from any sort of free-thinking prejudice. Four years ago I renounced all philosophical pride and I have returned to religious ideas and sentiments. I die in the faith of one God, the eternal creator of the world, whose mercy I beseech for my immortal soul. I regret having sometimes in my writings spoken of sacred things without due reverence, but I was led astray more by the spirit of my times than by my own inclinations. If I have unwittingly offended against good morals and decency, which are the true essence of all monotheistic doctrines of faith, I ask pardon of God and man. I forbid that any speech be made at my grave, either in German or French. At the same time I express a wish that my countrymen, however happily the destinies of our native land should shape themselves, should never bring back my ashes to Germany. I have never cared to devote my person to political mummery. It has been the greatest task of my life to work for a cordial understanding between Germany and France, and to frustrate the plots of the enemies of democracy, who exploit national prejudices and animosities for their own uses. I believe that I have deserved well of my fellow countrymen and of the French, and the claims which I have on their gratitude are no doubt the most valuable legacy which I can bequeath to my universal heirs.

#8. I appoint M. Maxime Joubert, Councillor of the Court of Cassation, to be my executor, and I thank him for the readiness with which he has undertaken this office.

The foregoing will was dictated by Herr Heinrich Heine, and written down by M. Ducloux, one of the undersigned notaries, in his own hand, as the testator dictated, in the presence of the said notaries and witnesses, who have declared in answer to the question, that they are not related to the testator.

And after it was read in the presence of the same persons to the testator, he declared that he abided by it as the exact expression of his will.

Drawn up and completed in the aforesaid bedroom of Herr Heine.

In the year eighteen hundred and fifty one, Thursday, the thirteenth of November, about six o'clock in the evening.

And after a second complete reading, the testator and the witnesses, as well as the notaries, appended their signatures.

❧ *My Place in German Literature*

A WITTY FRENCHMAN—a few years ago this expression would have been considered a pleonasm—once dubbed me an unfrocked Romantic (*romantique défroqué*). I have a weakness for wit—and spiteful as was this appellation, it nevertheless delighted me. For it is apt. Notwithstanding the war of extermination that I waged against Romanticism, I always remained a Romantic at heart—and that in a greater degree than I was myself aware. After I had delivered the most deadly blows to the taste for Romantic poetry in Germany, there stole over me an inexpressible yearning for the blue flower of the romantic dreamland, and I seized my enchanted lyre and sang a song in which I gave free rein to all the lovely extravagances, to all moon-intoxication, to all the blooming, nightingale fancies I once so fondly sang. I knew this was "the last woodland song of Romanticism," and I its last poet. With me the old lyrical school of German poetry comes to an end, and, at the same time, the modern German lyric begins. Writers on German literature will assign this double role to me. It would be unseemly for me to speak at length on this subject, but I may claim with justice that I deserve mention in the history of German Romanticism. For this reason I should have included in my book on Germany an account of my own person, since I sought to give there as complete a history of the Romantic School as possible. My omission in this respect resulted in a gap which I cannot easily fill. The writing of a self-portrait is not merely a very embarrassing, but even an impossible task. I should be a conceited braggart if I brazenly obtruded the good I might be able to say of myself; and I should be a great fool if I exposed to the gaze of the whole world the defects of which I might also be aware. Futhermore, even with the best will in the world, no one can tell the whole truth about onself. No one has as yet succeeded in doing it, neither Saint Augustine, the pious Bishop of Hippo, nor Jean Jacques Rousseau of Geneva—least of all the latter, who, though he proclaimed himself a man of truth and of nature, was at bottom really much more untruthful and unnatural than any of his contemporaries. . . .

৪৯ *Am I a Destroyer of Faith?*

[*1855*]

I HAVE BEEN UPBRAIDED IN MANY QUARTERS for having torn the curtain from the German heaven and revealed the fact that all the gods of the old faith had departed from it, and that only an old spinster with leaden hands and a heart full of sorrow still sits there—Necessity. Alas! I have only forewarned what every man must learn for himself—and what once sounded so strange, is now cried from the housetops on the other side of the Rhine. And in what fanatical tones are these anti-religious sermons often delivered! We now have monks of atheism who would burn M. de Voltaire, because he is an impenitent deist. I must admit that the music does not give me much pleasure—but neither does it frighten me, for I stood behind Maestro Hegel while he was composing it—naturally in very obscure and highly involved symbols, so that not everyone might decipher it. I often used to see him looking around anxiously as if in fear he might be understood. He was very fond of me, for he was sure I would never betray him. As a matter of fact, I then thought that he was very obsequious. Once when I grew impatient with him for saying: "All that is, is rational," he smiled strangely and remarked, "It may also be said that all that is rational must be." Then he looked about him hastily; but he was speedily reassured, for only Heinrich Beer had heard his words. It was not till later that I understood these expressions. Not till later did I understand what he meant when he declared in his *Philosophy of History* that Christianity represents progress because it teaches the doctrine of a God who died; while heathen gods knew nothing of death. What a step forward it would be, if we could declare that God never existed at all!

With the overthrow of the doctrines of faith, ancient morality too was uprooted. But the Germans will long hold on to the latter. They are like certain ladies who remain virtuous till they are forty, and thereafter do not think it worth while to practice the lovely vices, though their morals have become much laxer. The destruction of faith in a heaven has not merely a moral, but also a political significance. The masses will no longer bear their earthly sufferings with Christian resignation. They demand happiness on earth. Communism is the natural consequence of this changed world-outlook— and it is spreading all over Germany. It is quite natural that the proletarians, in their war against the *status quo*, should have as their leaders the most advanced thinkers—the philosophers of the great tradition. These pass from doctrine to action—which is the end of all thought—and they formulate their program. And what is that program? I have long ago dreamed and expressed it as follows: "We do not wish to be sansculottes, or frugal citizens, or economical presidents. We establish a democracy of equally glorious, equally holy, and equally happy gods. You ask for simple dress, austere manners, and unseasoned pleasures. We, on the other hand, demand nectar and ambrosia, purple raiments, costly perfumes, luxury and splendor, dances of laughing nymphs, music and comedy." These words are to be found in my book, *De l'Allemagne*, where I distinctly predicted that the political revolution in Germany would proceed from that philosophy whose system has so often been decried as sheer scholasticism. It was easy for me to prophesy! For I had seen how the dragons' teeth were sowed, from which sprang the armed men of today, who fill the world with the sound of their arms, and who, unfortunately, also destroy one another!

The Story Teller

ટ‍ The Rabbi of Bacherach

In the lower region of the Rhine, where the banks of the river begin to lose their smiling aspect, and mountains and cliffs with their romantic ruined castles seem wilder, and more defiant, and more somberly magnificent, there lies, like a terrifying tale of old, the gloomy ancient town of Bacherach.

Not always were these walls so decayed and broken, with their toothless battlements and their eyeless turrets, in whose crannies the wind whistles and the sparrows make their nests. Not always were these wretched, muddy lanes, which can be seen through the ruined gate, blanketed in a desolate silence, interrupted now and then only by the cries of children, the bickering of women, and the lowing of cattle. These walls were once proud and strong. In these streets there once dwelt a vigorous, free life, power and glory, joy and sorrow, love and hatred. Bacherach was at one time one of those municipalities founded by the Romans during their overlordship of the Rhine. Though the times that followed were troubled and the inhabitants later came under the suzerainty of the Hohenstaufens, and finally of the Wittelsbachs, they managed, after the example of other Rhenish towns, to preserve a tolerably free commonwealth. It consisted of an alliance of several corporations in which the patrician burgesses and the guilds, the latter subdivided according to crafts, strove for supremacy. So that though they were united against the external assaults of the neighboring robber-barons, internally they were constantly torn by their conflicting interests and incessant feuds. There was little social intercourse, great distrust, and even open violence. The Lord Warden sat on the high tower of Sareck, and swooped down like a falcon when he was called—and sometimes even when he was not called. The clergy ruled in darkness, by darkening the minds of the people. By far the most isolated, powerless, and legally disqualified was the small community of Jews, who had first settled in Bacherach in the days of the Romans, and later, during the Great Persecutions, had absorbed large numbers of fugitive coreligionists.

The Great Persecution of the Jews began with the Crusades and raged most furiously around the middle of the fourteenth century, at the end of the Great Plague. The latter, like all public disasters, was attributed to the Jews, for it was held that they had brought down the wrath of God, and with the help of lepers, had poisoned the wells. The enraged populace, and particularly hordes of Flagellants, half-naked men and women who lashed themselves and, chanting mad hymns to the Virgin, swept through the regions of the Rhine and South Germany, murdered many thousands of Jews, tortured them, or violently converted them. Another accusation which cost the Jews rivers of blood and trailed them from the earliest times, through all the Middle Ages and down to the last century, was that stupid and revolting fable, repeated *ad nauseam* in chronicles and legend: that the Jews were in the habit of stealing the consecrated wafer and piercing it with knives till the blood ran; that they slaughtered Christian children for their Passover feast, and used their blood for the evening services. The Jews, already sufficiently hated for their religion, their wealth and their ledgers, became during that festival the ready prey of their enemies, who could encompass their destruction all too easily by spreading rumors of some such child-murder, or even by secretly introducing a child's corpse into the house of an accused Jew and then attacking it at night—while the family was at prayers—murdering, plundering and baptizing. Then great miracles were wrought by the dead child, whose body was discovered and whom the Church finally canonized. Saint Werner [1] is one of these saints, and it was in his honor that the magnificent abbey at Oberwesel was founded, which now forms one of the most beautiful ruins of the Rhine and enchants us with the Gothic splendor of the long ogival windows, lofty pillars and stone carvings, when we pass it on some cheerful, green summer's day—ignorant of its origin. In honor of that saint three other churches were built on the Rhine, and innumerable Jews were tortured or killed. This took place in the year 1287. In Bacherach, too, where one of these Saint Werner churches was built, great suffering was inflicted upon the Jews. However, they survived there for two more centuries after that, and were spared these outbreaks of mob fury, although they were continually subjected to hatred and intimidation.

But the more the Jews of Bacherach were visited by hatred from without, the closer, the more intimate grew their domestic life, the firmer their piety and fear of God. Their Rabbi, named Rabbi Abraham, was a model of godly life. Though still a young man, he was already famed far and wide for his learning. He was born in Bacherach, and his father, who had likewise been Rabbi there, had charged him in his last will to dedicate himself to the same calling and not to leave Bacherach unless his life were in mortal peril. This injunction, and a cabinet full of rare books, was all that his father bequeathed to him, for he had lived in poverty and learning. Yet Rabbi Abraham was a very wealthy man, for he had married the only daughter of his paternal uncle, a jeweler, and had inherited his great wealth. Gossips in the community hinted now and then that the Rabbi had married for money. But the women with one voice denied this and told a different story: how the Rabbi, long before he went to Spain, had been in love with Sara—she was commonly called "Lovely Sara"; how Sara had to wait seven long years till he returned from Spain, for he had wed her against her father's wishes and even against her own inclination by the "betrothal-ring." For every Jew can make a Jewish girl his lawful wife if he succeeds in putting a ring on her finger and saying these words: "I take thee for my wife according to the Laws of Moses and Israel."

At the mention of Spain the sly gossips would smile strangely, and all because of an obscure rumor which claimed that while at the academy at Toledo, Rabbi Abraham had not only zealously studied the Holy Law, but had also adopted Christian customs and become tainted with free thinking—like those Spanish Jews, who at that time attained great cultural heights. In their hearts, however, the gossips put little faith in these reports. For ever since he had returned, the Rabbi's life had been extraordinarily pure and pious and earnest. He practised the least of the religious ceremonials with painstaking scruples; fasted each Monday and Thursday; partook of meat and wine only on the Sabbath and other holidays, and passed his days in prayer and study. By day he expounded the Holy Law in the circle of his students, who were drawn to Bacherach by his fame, and at night he gazed up at the stars in heaven or into the eyes of Lovely Sara. The marriage was childless, yet there was no lack of life or gaiety about him. The great hall of his house, which adjoined the synagogue, was always open to the whole community; people came and went without ceremony, offered brief prayers, traded news, or took counsel when in trouble. Here the children played on the Sabbath morning, while the weekly portion was being read in the synagogue. Here people gathered at weddings and funerals, quarrelled and made peace; here he who was cold found a warm fire and he who was hungry, a well-spread table. In addition, the Rabbi had a host of relatives, brothers and sisters, who with their wives, husbands, and children as well as his and his wife's uncles and aunts and countless others—all of whom regarded the Rabbi as the head of the family— formed a numerous clan and made themselves at home in his house and used to dine there on the high holidays. Such family gatherings assumed a special character on the occasion of the annual Passover celebration, an ancient and wonderful festival, still observed by Jews all over the world on the eve of the fourteenth day of the month of Nissan, in eternal commemoration of their deliverance from the captivity of Egypt.

This is the way it is celebrated: At nightfall, the mistress of the house lights the candles and spreads a table cloth on the table, and places in the middle of it three pieces of the flat, unleavened bread, covers it with a napkin, and on this pile she sets six small dishes, containing the symbolic food: egg, lettuce, horse-radish, a bone of a lamb, and a brown mixture of raisins, cinnamon and nuts. The father of the family sits at this table with all his relatives and friends, and reads to them from a very strange little book, called the Haggadah, the contents of which is a strange admixture of ancestral legends,

wonder-tales of Egypt, curious stories, disputations, prayers and festive songs. Half-way through the service, a grand repast is served,
and even during the recitation, at specified times, portions of the
symbolic food are tasted, as well as a piece of the unleavened bread,
and four cups of wine are drunk. This nocturnal festival is sadly-
merry in character, seriously-playful, and mysterious in its fabled lore.
The traditional sing-song tone in which the head of the house reads
the Haggadah and to which the hearers frequently respond in chorus,
sounds touchingly simple and sincere, and as soothing as a mother's
lullaby, and at the same time so affecting, that even those Jews who
have long since abandoned the faith of their fathers and lusted after
strange joys and honors, are profoundly moved when by chance the
well-known old Passover chants strike their ears.

Once Rabbi Abraham sat in the great hall of his house with his
relatives, disciples, and other guests, and celebrated the eve of the
Passover. In the hall everything was brighter than usual. The table
was hung with a richly embroidered silken cloth, whose golden
fringes touched the floor; the little plates with the symbolic food
glowed with a friendly air, as did the tall wine-filled goblets, embossed with images of holy legends. The men sat in black cloaks and
black, broad-rimmed hats, and white ruffs; the women were dressed
in wonderfully resplendent garments of Lombard stuff, and wore
ornaments of gold and pearls on their necks and heads; and the silver
Sabbath lamp cast its festive light on the devout and happy faces of
old and young. Rabbi Abraham sat reclining on the purple velvet
cushions of a chair raised above the others, as custom enjoins, reading
and singing the Haggadah, and the mixed assembly joined in the
chorus or responded at the designated places. The Rabbi too wore
his black holiday dress. His noble, somewhat austere features seemed
milder than usual. His lips smiled from out of the dark beard, as if
they had something pleasant to relate, and his eyes were filled with
the light of blissful reminiscence as well as anticipation.

Lovely Sara sat by his side, like him raised above the others, and
because she was mistress of the house she wore no jewelry. Only
white linen enclosed her slender body and her pious face. It was a
touchingly beautiful face. The beauty of Jewish women is of a
peculiarly moving kind. A consciousness of the deep misery, the
bitter scorn and the evil fortune to which their relatives and friends
are exposed endows their features with painful tenderness and ap-
prehensive affection, which profoundly touches our hearts. And so,

on this evening, Lovely Sara sat gazing contentedly into her husband's eyes. Now and then she also glanced at the Haggadah which lay before her. The parchment book was bound in gold and velvet, and was an ancient heirloom, showing old wine stains from the time of her grandfather, and with many bold and gaily colored pictures which she had loved to look at as a little girl on Passover eve. They depicted all kinds of biblical stories, such as Abraham breaking his father's stone idols with his hammer; the visit of the angels; Moses slaying the Mizri; Pharaoh sitting in state on his throne, while the frogs gave him no peace even at table; Pharaoh—the Lord be praised!—being drowned, and the Children of Israel crossing the Red Sea cautiously, standing open-mouthed at the foot of Mount Sinai, with their sheep, cows and oxen; pious King David playing the harp; and finally, Jerusalem, with its towers and battlements and temples resplendent in the glory of the sun!

The second cup of wine had already been poured and faces and voices grew ever merrier. The Rabbi took a cake of the unleavened Passover bread and raised it with cheerful greeting, and recited these words of the Haggadah: "Behold! This is the bread of affliction that our fore-fathers ate in the land of Egypt. Let him who is hungry come and taste of it. Let him who is in want come and celebrate the Passover with us. This year we are here; next year we shall be in the Land of Israel! This year we are slaves; next year we shall be free men!"

At this moment, the hall door opened, and two tall, pale men entered, wrapped in broad cloaks, and said: "Peace be with you! We are men of your faith on a journey, and wish to celebrate the Passover with you." And the Rabbi answered quickly and amiably: "Peace be with you! Sit down by me!" The two strangers sat down at the table and the Rabbi continued reading. Sometimes, while the others were saying the responses, he threw tender words to his wife, and playing on the old whimsy that on this evening the head of the Jewish house is regarded as a king, he said to her: "Rejoice, my queen." But she replied, smiling sadly, "We have no prince,"—she meant the son of the house who would, as the Haggadah requires, question his father in the prescribed words about the meaning of the festival. The Rabbi said nothing, but only pointed with his finger to a picture on the open page of the Haggadah, which represented in a quaintly touching manner how three angels came to Abraham to announce that his wife Sara would bear him a son, while she, in the meantime, with feminine wiles, was listening behind the tent-door.

The gentle hint caused a threefold blush to spread over the cheeks of the beautiful woman. She cast down her eyes, and then looked up again lovingly at her husband, who continued chanting the wonderful story of Rabbi Jesua, Rabbi Eleazar, Rabbi Azaria, Rabbi Akiba and Rabbi Tarphon, who sat reclining in Bne-Brak and all night long regaled themselves with the story of the Exodus of the Children of Israel, till their disciples came and told them that day had come and the great morning prayer was already being read in the synagogue.

As Lovely Sara was devoutly listening and gazing steadily at her husband, she observed that his face suddenly froze in an expression of horror, his cheeks and lips grew deathly pale, and his eyes stared like balls of ice. But almost instantly she saw how his features regained their calm and cheerfulness, his lips and cheeks returned to their color, his eyes looked about them merrily; indeed, it seemed as if a peculiar abandon and gaiety had possessed him. Lovely Sara was frightened as never before in her life. A cold dread came over her, less from the momentary sign of horror which she had observed in her husband's face, than from the merriment, which gradually turned to unrestrained exultation. The Rabbi cocked his hat comically first over one ear, then over the other; pulled and twirled at his beard drolly, sang the texts of the Haggadah, as if they were street-catches, and when he came to enumerating the Egyptian plagues,—here it is customary to dip the forefinger in the full wine-cup and cast the adhering drops to the ground—the Rabbi sprinkled the younger girls with the red wine, and there was much wailing over spoiled collars— and ringing laughter. Each moment Sara grew more uneasy at this convulsive and gushing merriment of her husband's, and oppressed by nameless fears, she gazed on the buzzing swarm of resplendent guests who rocked back and forth at ease, nibbled the thin Passover cakes, or sipped wine. gossiped, or sang aloud full of joy and well-being.

Then came the time for supper. All rose to wash, and Lovely Sara brought the great silver basin with richly embossed gold figures, which she held before every guest, while water was poured over his hands. As she was performing this service for the Rabbi, he winked at her significantly, and quietly slipped from the room. Lovely Sara followed him. Hastily he seized her hand, and quickly drew her through the dark alleys of Bacherach—through the town gate, out into the highway which ran along the Rhine toward Bingen.

It was one of those spring nights which, though soft and warm and starry, yet inspire the soul with strange forebodings. The flowers breathed of death; the birds chirped as if maliciously, yet anxiously; the moon cast spiteful streaks of light over the dark, murmuring stream. The lofty cliffs on the banks looked like giants' heads nodding ominously. The watchman on the tower of Castle Strahleck blew a melancholy blast; and at the same time, the funeral bell of Saint Werner's fervently tolled its jarring notes. Lovely Sara still carried the silver basin in her right hand; while her left was held firmly by the Rabbi. She felt his icy fingers and his quivering arm. But she followed her husband in silence, perhaps because she had long been accustomed to obey him blindly and unquestioningly, perhaps because fear sealed her lips.

Below Castle Sonneck, opposite Lorch, close to the spot where the hamlet of Niederheinbach now stands, a flat-topped cliff arches above the bank of the Rhine. The Rabbi ascended it with his wife, looked all about him, and then gazed up into the stars. Trembling and shaken as with death-agony, Lovely Sara stood by his side, and regarded his pale face, which the moon lit up spectrally and over which pain, terror, pity, and rage passed in rapid succession. Suddenly the Rabbi tore the silver basin from her hand and threw it clanking into the Rhine. Then she could no longer bear the agony, and crying out "Merciful Shaddai!" she threw herself at her husband's feet and implored him to reveal the dark secret.

Unable to speak, the Rabbi moved his lips without a sound. At last he cried, "Do you not see the Angel of Death? Down there, he hovers over Bacherach! But we have escaped his sword. Praised be the Lord!" And in a voice still quivering with horror he told her that while he was cheerfully singing the Haggadah, and reclining in comfort, he chanced to glance under the table, and there at his feet he saw the bloody corpse of a little child. "Then I knew," the Rabbi continued, "that our two guests were not of the community of Israel, but of the assembly of the godless, who had plotted to place the corpse in our house by stealth in order to charge us with child-murder, and to stir up the people to plunder and to murder us. I dared not betray that I had seen through that work of darkness; I would simply have hastened my own destruction. Only by craft have I succeeded in saving both of us. Praised be the Lord! Do not grieve, Lovely Sara, our relatives and friends will also be saved. It is only for my blood that these wretches are thirsting. I have escaped them, and they will be content with my silver and gold. Come with me, Lovely Sara, to another land. We will leave our misfortunes behind us, and lest they follow us, I have cast away the last of my possessions, our silver basin, as a peace offering. Come, you are weary. There, below us, Mute William stands by his boat, and he will take us up the Rhine."

Speechless and limp, as if every limb in her body were broken, Lovely Sara sank into the arms of the Rabbi. Slowly he carried her to the river bank. There stood the deaf-mute William, a handsome lad, who, to maintain his old foster mother, a neighbor of the Rabbi's, plied the fishing trade and kept his boat on this spot. It seemed as if he had divined the Rabbi's intention, or had, in fact, been waiting for him. On his lips there was an expression of sweet compassion; his great blue eyes rested with meaning on Lovely Sara, and he lifted her tenderly into the boat.

The mute boy's glance roused Lovely Sara from her lethargy. She suddenly realized that what her husband had told her was no mere dream; and bitter tears flowed down her cheeks, which were now as white as her garments. She sat in the boat, a weeping image of white marble. Beside her sat her husband and Mute William, who was rowing strenuously.

Whether because of the monotonous beat of the oars, or the rocking of the boat, or the vineyard fragrance of the Rhine bank—it always happens that even the saddest person becomes calm when he glides down the clear, beloved Rhine on a spring night. For in truth, kindhearted old Father Rhine cannot bear to see his children weep; he comforts them and rocks them in his trusty arms, and tells them the loveliest tales and promises them his golden treasures, perhaps even the ancient hoard of the Nibelungs, sunk long, long ago. Little by little Lovely Sara's tears subsided; her heaviest woes seemed washed away by the whispering waves. The night lost its dark terrors; and the native hills seemed to bid her a tender farewell. But the gentlest greeting was wafted to her by her favorite mountain, the Kädrich, and in the strange moonlight it seemed as if on its summit stood a lady with anxiously outstretched arms, and the nimble dwarfs swarmed out of their clefts in the rocks, and a horseman came galloping down the mountainside. And Lovely Sara felt like a young girl again; she was sitting once more in the lap of her aunt from Lorch, listening to the pretty story of the bold knight who freed the stolen damsel from the dwarfs, and many other true tales, of the wonderful Whisperdale beyond, where the birds talk as sensibly as men, and of Gingerbread Land, where obedient children go, of enchanted princesses, singing trees, crystal palaces, golden bridges, laughing water-nixies . . .

But in the midst of all these pleasant tales, which seemed to come to life with sound and light, Lovely Sara could hear her father's voice scolding her poor aunt for putting such nonsense into her head. Then it seemed as if she were being placed on a little foot-stool before her father's velvet-covered chair, and he was stroking her long hair with his gentle fingers, looking at her with laughter in his eyes, and rocking comfortably to and fro in his wide, capacious Sabbath gown of blue silk. . . . Yes, it must be the Sabbath, for the flowered spread was on the table. All the silver in the room shone like polished mirrors. The white-bearded sexton of the community sat beside her father, munching raisins and conversing in Hebrew. Little Abraham also came in with a big, impressive book, and respectfully begged leave of his uncle to expound a portion of the Holy Scriptures, so that the latter might be convinced that he had learned a great deal in the past week and deserved much cake and praise. . . . Then the lad put the book on the broad arm of the chair, and expounded the story of Jacob and Rachel; how Jacob lifted up his voice and wept when he first saw his cousin Rachel; how he spoke fondly to her at the well; how he was forced to serve seven years for her; how quickly the years passed, and how he married Rachel and loved her for ever and ever. . . . Suddenly Sara recalled that her father had exclaimed in a merry voice, "How would you like to marry your little cousin Sara?" To which little Abraham had gravely replied, "That I will, and she shall wait seven years." These images stole like twilight through the mind of the beautiful woman; she saw herself and her little cousin, now a man and her husband, playing like children in the leaf-covered tabernacle; how delighted they were with the gay tapestries, flowers, mirrors, and gilded apples! And little Abraham stroked her ever more tenderly; and then he gradually grew bigger and more sullen; and finally quite big and quite sullen. . . . And last of all, she was sitting all alone in her room at home. It was Sabbath eve. The moon poured its light through the window. The door flew open, and cousin Abraham rushed in—in travelling clothes—pale as death, and he seized her hand and placed a golden ring on her finger and said solemnly, "I hereby take you to be my wife, according to the Laws of God and Israel. But now," he added trembling, "I must leave for Spain. Farewell. Seven years you shall wait for me." And he rushed off; and Sara told her father everything, and wept. Her father raged and fumed. "Cut off your hair; for you are a married woman."

And he prepared to ride after Abraham to force him to grant her a letter of divorcement. But Abraham was over the hills; her father returned home silently, and when Lovely Sara was helping him off with his boots, and tried to soothe him by saying that Abraham would be back in seven years, he cursed her and cried: "Seven years long you shall both go begging"—and soon thereafter he died. . . .

Thus the old stories swept through her mind, like a swift shadow-play, with images strangely confused. And among them half-familiar, half-strange bearded faces looked out at her, as well as huge flowers with marvellous broad leaves. It seemed as if the Rhine were murmuring the melodies of the Haggadah; and its pictures rose from the waters, large as life—strangely distorted, crazy pictures. There was forefather Abraham furiously smashing the idols, which hastily reconstituted themselves; Mizri defending himself against the rage of Moses; Mount Sinai encircled by lightning and flame; King Pharaoh adrift in the Red Sea, clutching the jagged golden crown in his teeth; frogs with human faces swimming around; the waves foaming and roaring, and a giant's dark hand, rising threateningly from the deep.

That was Bishop Hatto's Mouse-Tower and the boat was just shooting through the Bingen eddy. Lovely Sara was startled from her dreams, and looked at the hills along the shore, from whose summits castle-lights glimmered, and at whose feet the moonlit mists began to rise. Suddenly it seemed to her that she saw her friends and relatives rushing fearfully past her with corpse-like faces and in white flowing shrouds,—hurrying along the banks of the Rhine. . . .

Everything turned black before her eyes. An icy chill poured through her soul. As if in sleep she could hear the Rabbi repeating the night-prayer, slowly, anxiously, as if at the bed-side of one mortally ill—and as in a dream she stammered the words: "Ten thousand to the right; ten thousand to the left; to shield the king from the dread of the night."

But suddenly the oppressive pall of darkness and terror lifted, the gloomy curtain was snatched from heaven, and above, the holy city of Jerusalem came into view with its towers and gates. The Temple shone in golden splendor; in its forecourt Lovely Sara saw her father, in his yellow Sabbath dressing-gown, smiling cheerfully. From the round windows of the Temple all her friends and relatives greeted her gaily. In the Holy of Holies pious King David kneeled with purple mantle and glittering crown, and his song and harp resounded sweetly. And smiling blissfully, Lovely Sara fell asleep.

WHEN LOVELY SARA OPENED HER EYES, she was almost dazzled by the rays of the sun. The lofty towers of a great city rose before her, and Mute William stood with his boat-hook upright in his boat and guided it through the bustling swarm of many gaily-decked vessels, whose crews were either gazing indolently at the passers-by, or were busy unloading chests, bales and casks, which were brought to shore by lighters. There was a deafening uproar—a constant hallooing of the steersmen, cries of traders from the shore, bickering of the customs officers, who in their red coats, with their white maces and their white faces, were leaping from boat to boat.

"Yes, Lovely Sara," said the Rabbi to his wife, smiling happily, "this is the renowned Free, Imperial and Commercial City of Frankfurt on the Main, and we are now on the river Main itself. Up there, where you see those gay houses, surrounded by green hills, is Sachsenhausen, where the cripple Gumpertz used to get us fine myrrh for the Feast of Tabernacles. Here is the strong Main Bridge, with its thirteen arches. Many, many people, wagons, and horses pass over it safely; and in the center stands a little house about which little Aunt Täubchen used to tell you. In it lives a baptized Jew, who pays to every man who brings him a dead rat six hellers on account of the Jewish community, which is obliged to deliver annually to the City Council five thousand rats' tails as tribute." [2]

At the thought of this war which the Frankfurt Jews were compelled to conduct against rats Sara laughed aloud. The bright sunlight, the gay new world which rose before her had dispelled from her mind the darkness and terror of the past night; and when she was lifted by her husband and Mute William from the boat on to the shore, she was filled with a sense of joyful security. But Mute William gazed long at her with his beautiful, deep-blue eyes—half sorrowfully, half-cheerfully—and then, casting a look full of meaning at the Rabbi, he sprang back into the boat and vanished.

"Mute William closely resembles my dead brother," Lovely Sara remarked. "All angels look alike," the Rabbi replied lightly, and taking his wife by the hand, he led her through the dense crowds on the shore, where there were numerous wooden booths—for this was the time of the Easter Fair. When they had passed the gloomy Main Gate, and entered the city, they found the crowds no less noisy. Here, in a narrow lane one shop stood close by another, every house, as is the custom in Frankfurt, being especially fitted out for trade. On the ground-floor there were no windows, only broad open arched doors, so that one could look inside, and every passer-by could closely examine the goods which were on sale. How amazed was Lovely Sara at the multitude of splendid and precious objects, such as she had never seen before! Here stood Venetians, selling all the luxuries of the Orient and of Italy. Lovely Sara gazed spell-bound at the innumerable tiers of ornaments and jewelry, the gay caps and bodices, the golden spangles and necklaces, and whole store of knick-knacks, which women love to see, and even more to wear. The richly embroidered stuffs of velvet and silk seemed to speak to her, and with their sparkle brought back strange wonders to her mind. And it actually seemed to her that she was once more a little girl, and little aunt Täubchen had really kept her promise and taken her to the Frankfurt Fair; that she was now standing gazing at the beautiful garments about which she had heard so much. With secret joy she considered which articles she would now take back with her to Bacherach. Which of her two little cousins, Blümchen or Vögelchen, would like the blue silken sash better: Would the little green breeches fit little Gottschalk?—And all at once she said to herself: "My God, they are grown up by this time; and yesterday they were all killed!"

She shuddered violently and the fantasies of the night seemed about to rise before her again. But the gold embroidery on the garments glittered once more with a thousand roguish eyes, and teased the dark thoughts from her mind; and when she looked up at her husband's face, she saw that it was unclouded, and wore its habitual expression of gentle seriousness. "Close your eyes, Lovely Sara," said the Rabbi, and led her through the crowds.

What a mad turmoil! Here were mostly tradesmen, loudly vying with one another, or reckoning on their fingers; some were followed by market-porters, who, loaded down with their masters' purchases, trotted behind them to the inns. Others, to judge from their faces, were there merely out of curiosity. The scarlet cloak and the golden chain betrayed the stout town-councillor; while the black, expansive waist-coat suggested the dignified and proud old burgher. The iron-tipped helmet, the yellow leather jerkin and the jingling spurs announced the weighty squire. Hidden underneath the little black velvet cap, peaked above the forehead, was many a rosy girlish face; the young fellows bounded after them, like hunting dogs on the scent, and you could tell that they were dandies by their saucy feather caps, their tinkling, peaked shoes, their silk dress of many colors—the right half was green, and the left red; or the right was streaked like the rainbow, and the left checkered, so that the silly youths looked as if they were cleft in two. Carried along by the crowd, the Rabbi and his wife finally reached the "Roman." This is the great market-place of the town, and is surrounded by high-gabled houses, and takes its name from a huge structure, called "Zum Römer," which had been bought by the town council and dedicated as the town-hall. In this building the German Emperor was elected, and before it tournaments were often held. King Maximilian was a passionate lover of this sport; and since he was then in Frankfurt, a great joust had been arranged in his honor before the "Roman" the previous day. At the wooden lists, which were being removed by carpenters, idlers were still standing and telling how the Duke of Brunswick and the Margrave of Brandenburg had charged one another amid the sound of drums and trumpets, and how Sir Walter the Tramp had unhorsed the Knight of the Bear with such violence that the splinters of the lances flew high in the air; and how tall blond King Max, who was standing on the balcony, surrounded by his court, had rubbed his hands with glee. The cloths of golden stuff were still to be seen on the balustrades of the balconies, and in the Gothic windows of the town-hall. The other houses on the market-place were likewise festively bedecked, and adorned with coats-of-arms; particularly the Limburg House, on the banner of which was painted a maiden who bore a sparrow-hawk in her hand, while a monkey held a mirror before her. On the balcony of the house stood many knights and fair ladies, chatting gaily, while they looked down at the motley crowds below, moving restlessly to and fro, in mad-cap groups, or in processions. What a multitude of idlers and loiterers of every age and class had here crowded together to gratify their curiosity! There was loud laughter, grumbling, thieving, pinching of thighs, cheering—and amid all this, the braying of the trumpet, proclaiming some mountebank quack, who stood with his red cloak, his Merry Andrew, and his monkey on a high scaffold, and cried up his own skill, his tinctures and his marvelous salves, or seriously examined the beaker of urine brought by some old crone, or applied himself to extracting some poor peasant's molar. Two fencing masters, fluttering about in their gay ribbons and brandishing rapiers, met here as if by chance, and fought with mock anger, each declaring after prolonged combat that the other was invincible. Then they took up a collection. And now, with fife and drum, the newly constituted guild of archers marched past; and after them, preceded by a constable with a red pennant, came a rout of vagrant ladies of pleasure from the women's house in Würzburg known as "The Ass." They were on their way to Rosendale, where the honorable municipal authorities had assigned quarters to them during the fair. "Shut your eyes, Lovely Sara," said the Rabbi. For that fantastic, somewhat scantily dressed crew of women, among whom were some very beautiful girls, behaved most indecently. They bared their white bosoms shamelessly; they chaffed passers-by with insolent speech. When they reached St. Catherine's Gate, they swung their long staves, which they rode as if they were hobby-horses, and shrilled the witches' song:

> "Where is the goat? The hellish beast,
> Where is the goat? Oh, bring him quick,
> If there's no goat, at least
> We'll ride upon this stick."

This sing-song could be heard from far, but was soon lost in the long-drawn notes of an approaching church-procession. It was a mournful train of tonsured and bare-footed monks who carried burning wax tapers and banners with images of saints, and large silver crucifixes. At the head marched young boys clad in red and white, bearing smoking censers. In the center of the procession, beneath a magnificent canopy, could be seen priests in white robes trimmed with costly laces or in multi-colored silken stoles. One of them held in his hand a sun-shaped golden vessel, which he raised on high when he reached a shrine near the market-corner; and he half spoke, half sang in Latin. . . . At the same time a little bell was rung, and the multitude suddenly grew silent, fell on their knees, and crossed themselves. The Rabbi spoke to his wife, "Shut your eyes, Lovely Sara!" and quickly drew her after him into an alley and then through a labyrinth of narrow, crooked lanes, and at last across the desolate, empty square which separated the Jewish quarter from the rest of the city.

Before that time the Jews had dwelt between the Cathedral and the bank of the Main—that is, from the bridge to the Lumpenbrunnen, and from the Mehlwage as far as St. Bartholomew's. But the Catholic priests had secured a Papal bull forbidding the Jews to live so near the main church, and the town council had assigned them a place on the

Wollgraben, where they had built their present quarters. This was provided with strong walls, as well as iron chains before the gates to shut them against the mobs. Here they lived in fear and oppression, and with far more vivid memories of previous distress than today. In the year 1240, the unleashed populace perpetrated a great blood-bath among them, which was called the first Jewish massacre, and in 1349, the Flagellants, while passing through the town, set it on fire and accused the Jews of the deed, so that the greater part of them were murdered by an enraged mob or burned alive in their own houses. This was the second Jewish massacre. Later on the Jews were frequently threatened with similar slaughter, and at the time of internal dissensions in Frankfurt, particularly during disputes between the council and the guilds, Christian mobs were often on the point of storming the Jewish quarter. This section had two gates, which were shut from without on Catholic holidays; and from within on Jewish holidays. Before each gate there was a guard-house with municipal guards.

When the Rabbi and his wife reached the gate of the Jewish quarter, the soldiers lay on the benches of their guard-room, as one could see through the open windows, while outside, in the doorway, the drummer sat in the sunlight, improvising on a large drum. He was a powerfully built, heavy-set fellow, wearing a jerkin and hose of fiery yellow cloth, the arms and legs of which were puffed out and richly dotted with small red pads, which looked like innumerable little licking tongues. His chest and his back were cushioned with black cloth, against which hung his drum. On his head he wore a flat round black cap. His face likewise was flat and round, and of an orange-yellow hue, dotted with red pimples, and distorted in a gaping smile. The fellow sat there and drummed the song which the Flagellants had once sung at the massacre of the Jews, and in his hoarse, beery voice he rasped:

> "Our dear Lady
> Walked in the morning dew,
> *Kyrie Eleison*."

"Hans, that's a horrible tune," a voice cried from behind the closed gate of the Jewish quarter. "Hans, and a bad song too. It doesn't go well on the drum—not at all—by my soul, and it's not for the Fair and Easter morning. A bad song, a dangerous song, Hans, little Hans, little drummer—Hänschen, I'm a lonely man, and if you love me, if you love the Star, big Star, tall Nose-Star, then stop it!"

These words were uttered explosively by the invisible speaker, now with quick anxiety, now with a slow sigh, in a voice which alternated between tender softness and raucous loudness, such as one hears among consumptives. The drummer was not moved, and he went on with his song:

> "Then came a little boy
> His beard had run away,
> Hallelujah!"

"Hans!" the voice cried again, "Hans, I am a lonely man, and this is a dangerous song. And I don't like to hear it. I have my reasons. If you love me, sing something else, and tomorrow we shall drink. . . ."

At the mention of "drink," Hans stopped his drumming and his song, and in a gentler tone he said, "The devil take the Jews; but you, dear Nose-Star, are my friend. I protect you. And if we could only drink together often enough, I'd even convert you. I will be your godfather; when you are baptized, you will be happy, and if you have the talent, and you study with me diligently, you may even become a drummer. Yes, Nose-Star, you may even amount to something. I will drum the whole catechism for you, when we drink together tomorrow. But now, open the gate, for here are two strangers who wish to enter."

"Open the gate?" Nose-Star cried, and his voice almost gave out. "Not so fast, dear Hans. One can never tell. One can't tell at all. I am all alone. Veitel Oxhead has the key, and he is now sitting in the corner, mumbling his Eighteen Prayers,[3] and he mustn't be interrupted. And Jakel the Fool is here too, but he is passing water. I'm all alone here."

"The devil take the Jews!" cried Drummerhans, and laughing aloud at his own jest, he trundled to the guard-room and lay down on the bench.

While the Rabbi and his wife stood waiting before the great gate which was shut, they heard behind them a rattling, nasal, somewhat mocking voice. "Starlet, don't drone and groan like that. Take the key from Oxhead's coat pocket, or else stick your nose into the keyhole and open the gate. Those people have been waiting there for a long time."

"People?" cried the frightened Nose-Star. "I thought there was only one. I beg you, Fool—dear Jakel, look out and see who is there."

A small, thickly grated window in the gate was opened, and a yellow cap with two horns, and beneath it the droll, wrinkled jester's face of Jakel the Fool looked out. At once the window was shut again, and an angry voice rasped out, "Open, open the gate. It's only a man and a woman."

"A man and a woman!" Nose-Star groaned. "And when the gate's opened, the woman will take off her gown, and become a man. And then there'll be two men, and we're only three!"

"Don't be a hare," Jakel the Fool replied. "Take heart and be of good courage."

"Courage!" Nose-Star cried, and laughed with angry bitterness. "Hare! Hare! That's a bad comparison. A hare is an unclean beast. Courage! I'm put here not to be courageous, but to be cautious. When there are too many, I'm supposed to call out. By myself I can't hold them back. My arm is weak. I suffer from a boil. I am a lone man. If they shoot at me, I'm a dead man. Then rich Mendel Reiss will sit at his Sabbath meal, wipe the raisin-sauce from his lips, stroke his belly, and perhaps say: 'Tall little Nose-Star was, after all, a very decent chap. If it hadn't been for him, they would have broken through the gate. He let himself be shot dead for us. He was a decent sort. Too bad he's dead—' "

Gradually the tone grew more tender and tearful. But suddenly it rose and became almost bitter. "Courage! So that rich Mendel Reiss may wipe the raisin-sauce from his lips, and pat his belly, and call me a brave fellow. For that I'm to let them shoot me dead? Courage! Be brave! Little Strauss was brave, and yesterday went to see them joust at the 'Roman,' and thought they wouldn't recognize him because of his coat of violet velvet, three florins the yard—magnificent—with its fox-tails, all gold-embroidered. But they belabored his violet coat so long till it lost its color and his back turned violet and no longer looked human. Courage! Leser the cripple was brave. He called our rascal of a magistrate a scoundrel, and they hung him by his feet between two dogs, and Drummerhans beat the drum. Don't be a hare! Where there are many dogs, the hare is done for. I am only one man here, and I'm afraid."

"Swear to that," cried Jakel.

"Yes, I'm really afraid," Nose-Star repeated, sighing. "I know that fear runs in my family. I have it from my mother, may she rest in peace—"

"Yes, yes," Jakel the Fool broke in, "and your mother had it from her father, and he had it from his, and so on, your forefathers had it from one another, all the way back to your first parent, who marched with King Saul against the Philistines and was the first to turn tail. But look, Oxhead is almost through. He has already bowed his head four times. And now he's skipping up and down like a flea at the 'Holy, holy, holy,' and now he's carefully searching in his pocket—"

And in fact, a key rattled, a wing of the gate grated and jarred open, and the Rabbi and his wife entered the deserted Jews' Lane. The man who had opened the gate, a little fellow with a homely, friendly face, nodded absently, like one who does not wish to be disturbed in his thoughts, and after he had again carefully locked the gate, shuffled away to a corner behind it, without saying a word, and went on mumbling his prayers. Jakel the Fool was less reticent, a short fellow, with bandy legs, and a merry, ruddy face and enormous, fleshy hands, which he stretched out in welcome from the wide sleeve of his chequered jacket. Behind him appeared—or rather hid—a tall, lean figure, whose small neck was covered with a feather-like white ruff of fine cambric, and whose thin pale face was adorned with an incredibly long nose, which moved anxiously and inquisitively in every direction.

"God's welcome to a happy holiday!" cried Jakel the Fool. "Do not be amazed that the street is so empty and silent. At this moment, all our people are in the synagogue, and you are just in time to hear the history of the Sacrifice of Isaac. I know it well. It's an interesting story, and if I hadn't heard it before, three and thirty times, I'd listen to it again this year. Mark you, it's an important story, for if Abraham had really killed Isaac, and not the goat—there would have been more goats in the world and fewer Jews." And with a grotesque grimace, Jakel began to sing the song of the Haggadah: "A kid, a kid, which my father bought for two zuzim; a kid, a kid.[4]

"And there came a cat, and devoured the kid, which my father bought for two zuzim; a kid, a kid.

"And there came a dog, and bit the cat which devoured the kid, that my father bought for two zuzim; a kid, a kid.

"And there came a stick, and beat the dog, that bit the cat, which devoured the kid, which my father bought for two zuzim; a kid, a kid.

"And a fire came and burnt the stick which smote the dog, which bit the cat, which devoured the kid which my father bought for two zuzim; a kid, a kid.

"And water came, and extinguished the fire, that burnt the stick, which smote the dog, which bit the cat, which devoured the kid, which my father bought for two zuzim; a kid, a kid.

"And an ox came and drank the water that had extinguished the fire, which burnt the stick, that smote the dog, that bit the cat, which devoured the kid, that my father bought for two zuzim; a kid, a kid.

"And the slaughterer came, and slaughtered the ox, that drank the water, which extinguished the fire, that burnt the stick, which smote the cat, that devoured the kid, which my father bought for two zuzim; a kid, a kid.

"And the angel of death came, and killed the slaughterer, that slaughtered the ox, which drank the water, that extinguished the fire, which burnt the stick, that smote the dog, that had bitten the cat, which devoured the kid, which my father bought for two zuzim; a kid, a kid.

"Yes, beautiful lady," the singer added, "the day will come when the Angel of Death will slay the slayer, and all our blood will come over Edom, for our God is a God of vengeance. . . ."

But instantly he cast off the seriousness which had almost involuntarily come over him, and he gave way to mad fancies, and continued in his strident jester's tone: "Don't be afraid, beautiful lady. Nose-Star won't harm you. He is dangerous only to old Schnapper-Elle. She's fallen in love with his nose—and his nose is worthy of it. For it is as beautiful as the tower which looks toward Damascus, and as lofty as the cedar of Lebanon. Outwardly it gleams like the shimmer of gold and syrup; and inside it is all music and loveliness. It blooms in the summer; it freezes in the winter. And in summer and winter it is fondled by Schnapper-Elle's white hands. Yes, Schnapper-Elle is in love with him—madly in love. She cherishes him, she feeds him, and as soon as he is fat enough, she will marry him. For her age, she's young enough, and whoever comes to Frankfurt three hundred years hence, will be unable to see the sky for all the Nose-Stars."

"You are Jakel the Fool," the Rabbi exclaimed, laughing. "I mark it by your words. I have often heard of you."

"Yes, yes," Jakel replied, with mock modesty. "Yes, yes, that comes of being famous. A man is often celebrated far and wide for being a bigger fool than he is aware. However, I take great pains to be a fool. I hop and shake myself so that my bells jingle. Others manage it more easily. . . . But tell me, Rabbi, why are you travelling on a holiday?"

"My justification," the latter replied, "is to be found in the Talmud. There it says, 'Danger drives away the Sabbath.' "

"Danger!" suddenly exclaimed tall Nose-Star, with an air of mortal terror. "Danger! Danger! Drummerhans, beat the drum! Beat the drum! Danger! Danger! Drummerhans . . . !"

From without the heavy beer-voice of Drummerhans replied, "A thousand damnations! The devil take the Jews! This is the third time you've awakened me from my sleep, Nose-Star. Don't make me mad. When I'm mad, I'm the very devil. And then, as sure as I'm a Christian, I'll shoot through the grated window of your gate, and then let everyone look out for his nose!"

"Don't shoot, don't shoot! I'm a lone man," Nose-Star whined piteously, and pressed his face against the wall, and remained in this position mumbling a prayer.

"But tell me, what has taken place?" cried Jakel the Fool, with all the impatient curiosity, which even in those days, was characteristic of the Frankfurt Jews.

But the Rabbi tore himself impatiently from him and proceeded up the Jews' Lane. "See, Lovely Sara," he sighed, "how poorly defended is Israel. False friends guard its gates from without, and fear and folly are its guardians within."

Slowly they wandered through the long, deserted street. Only here and there the lovely head of a young girl looked from a window, in which the sun was brilliantly reflected. For in those days the houses in the Jewish quarter were still trim and new, and much lower than they are now; it was only later, when their numbers multiplied and they were prevented from extending the Jews' quarter, that the Jews of Frankfurt commenced to build one story upon another, and pressed together like sardines—and in this way became cramped both in body and in soul. That section of the Jewish quarter which remained after the great fire and which is called the Old Lane—those tall, grimy houses, in which a grimacing, sweating race of traders lives—is an appalling relic of the Middle Ages. The older synagogue no longer exists. It was less capacious than the present one, which was built later, after the refugees of Nuremberg had been taken into the community. It lay farther to the north. The Rabbi had no need to ask its direction. Already from a distance he could hear the confused din of many loud voices. In the court of the House of God he took leave of his wife. After he had washed his hands at the fountain, he entered the lower part of the synagogue reserved for men; while Lovely Sara went up a flight of stairs into the women's section.

This upper portion was a kind of gallery, with three rows of wooden seats painted a reddish brown, whose backs were fitted with suspended boards which served as lecterns for the prayer-books. The women sat here and gossiped, or stood upright deep in prayer. Sometimes they peered with curiosity through the large grating which stretched across the eastern end. Through the green lattice they could look down into the lower section of the synagogue. There, behind high praying-desks, stood the men in black cloaks, their pointed beards projecting from their white ruffs, and their skull-capped heads more or less concealed by the four-cornered scarf of white wool or silk, furnished with the prescribed tassels, and sometimes adorned with gold lace. The walls of the synagogue were uniformly whitewashed, and no other ornament was visible except the gilded railing on the square platform, where the portions of the Law were recited, and the Holy Ark. This was a costly, embossed chest—ostensibly supported by marble columns with rich capitals, with flower and leaf work twining upward gracefully. It was covered by a curtain of corn-blue velvet on which was a sacred inscription, embroidered with golden spangles, pearls and multi-colored gems. Here hung the silver memorial lamp, and here also rose the barred dais, on whose railings were to be found all kinds of sacred utensils, among them the seven-branched candlestick; while before it, his face turned toward the Ark, stood the cantor who sang and was accompanied in instrumental fashion by his two assistants, the bass and the soprano. For the Jews have banned all instrumental music from their churches in the belief that hymns of praise to God are more edifying when they rise from the glowing breast of man than from cold organ-pipes. Lovely Sara was happy as a child when the chief cantor, an admirable tenor, raised his voice, and the ancient, solemn melodies, which she knew so well, pulsed again with a youthful loveliness undreamt of—while the bass thundered deep, dark harmonies, and in the pauses, the soprano trilled sweetly and delicately. Such singing Sara had never heard in the synagogue at Bacherach; for here the president of the community, David Levi, was cantor. And when this elderly, shaking man, with his cracked, bleating voice tried to trill like a girl, and waved his weak and drooping arm feverishly in his violent efforts, he moved to laughter rather than devotion.

A sense of devout well-being, mixed with feminine curiosity, drew Lovely Sara to the grating, where she could look down to the lower section, the so-called Men's Shool. She had never before seen so many of her faith assembled together; and she felt her heart warming at the thought of being in the midst of so many men and women, so closely allied to her in blood, thought, and suffering. Her soul was moved even more deeply when three old men reverently approached the Holy Ark, drew aside its glittering curtain, opened the chest and carefully brought forth that Book which God once wrote with his own hand, and to maintain which the Jews have suffered so much—so much misery and hatred, disgrace and death—a thousand years of martyrdom. This Book—a huge roll of parchment—was wrapped like a princely child in a richly embroidered jacket of scarlet velvet. On both of its wooden rollers there were two little silver shrine-like ornaments, in which all kinds of pomegranates and little bells moved and tinkled prettily, while before it, on a small silver chain hung gold shields with many-colored gems.

The cantor took the book as if it were really a child, a child for whose sake much has been suffered, and which is, for that reason, all the more precious. He rocked it in his arms, dandled it, pressed it to his heart, and as if awed by such contact, he raised his voice in so jubilant a song of praise, that it seemed to Lovely Sara as if the pillars of the Holy Ark had actually begun to blossom, and the strange and wonderful flowers and leaves of the capitals were shooting up ever higher; as if the notes of the soprano had become nightingale chants, and the dome of the synagogue would be shattered by the overpowering tones of the bass, and the joy of God flowed down from the blue heavens. Yes, it was a beautiful psalm. The congregation responded as in a chorus, repeating the concluding verses, and the cantor, with the Holy Book in his arms, strode slowly toward the raised dais in the center of the synagogue, while men and boys pressed around him eagerly to kiss its velvet covering, or merely to touch it. On the platform, the velvet covering as well as the wrapping inscribed with illuminated letters was removed, and from the unrolled parchment the cantor read the edifying narrative of the temptation of Abraham, in that singing voice which is especially modulated during the Passover festival.

Lovely Sara had modestly withdrawn from the grating, and a heavy, much bejewelled woman of middle age, with a simpering, good-natured mien, had by a nod beckoned to her to look on in her prayer-book. This woman was obviously no great scholar, for Sara observed that as she mumbled the prayers, as is the custom of women since they are not permitted to participate in the singing, she would mispronounce many words, and even skip whole passages. After a while, the woman raised her eyes from the prayer-book languidly, an insipid smile stole over her red and white porcelain face, and in a voice which she strove to make as meltingly genteel as she could, she said to Lovely Sara: "He sings well. But in Holland I've heard much better ones. You are a stranger, and perhaps you don't know that the cantor is from Worms, and that they will keep him here if he is content to take four hundred florins a year. He is a dear man, and his hands are as white as alabaster. I hold much by beautiful hands. A handsome hand makes a handsome man." Saying this, she complacently put her own hand, which was really very fine, on the ledge before her, and with a graceful nod of her head, which intimated that she did not care to be interrupted while speaking, she added, "The little singer is a mere child, and looks frightfully thin. The bass is too ugly, and our Nose-Star once said wittily, 'The bass is a bigger fool than one has a right to ask even a bass to be.' All three dine in my kitchen—perhaps you don't know, I'm Elle Schnapper."

Lovely Sara thanked her for this information, then Schnapper-Elle proceeded to recount how she had once been to Amsterdam, and had been subjected to all sorts of temptations because of her beauty, how she had come to Frankfurt three days before the Pentecost and had married Schnapper; how he had died; what touching things he had said on his death-bed, and how hard it was to be the manager of a kitchen and keep one's hands in good condition. Several times she glanced aside with contemptuous looks intended for some giggling young women who were appraising her clothes. In truth, this dress was remarkable enough—an exceedingly puffed gown of white satin, on which all the animals of Noah's Ark were embroidered in glaring colors; a jacket of golden cloth like a cuirass, the sleeves of red velvet, with a yellow sash, and on her head a mountainous cap, with a mighty ruff of white linen around her neck, not to mention the silver chain from which all kinds of coins, cameos, curiosities—among them a large likeness of the city of Amsterdam—hung down on her bosom. But the dresses of the other women were no less remarkable, consisting as they did of an assortment of fashions of different periods, and many a little woman was so bedecked with gold and diamonds that she looked like a perambulating jeweller's shop. It is true that the dress of Frankfurt Jews was at that time prescribed by law, and to distinguish them from Christians, men were compelled to wear yellow rings on their cloaks and women high, blue-striped veils. However, in the Jewish quarter, these official ordinances were scarcely observed, and, especially on holidays, and in the synagogue in particular, women would vie with one another in piling on as much magnificent apparel as they could, partly from a desire to arouse envy, partly to proclaim the wealth and good credit of their husbands.

Meanwhile, during the reading of the passages of law from the Books of Moses, devotion abated somewhat. A few relaxed and sat down, whispered to their neighbors about their affairs; others made their way into the courtyard for a breath of fresh air. Small boys took advantage of the occasion to visit their mothers in the women's section. Here the air of devotion was totally lacking. There was much gossiping, clustering together, laughing. As always happens, the younger women joked at the expense of the older ones, while the latter bewailed the flightiness of youth and the corruption of the times. And just as there was a chief cantor in the synagogue below, there was a chief-cackler in the upper region. This was the Puppy Reiss, a sallow, plain-looking woman who could scent every sort of trouble and always had a scandalous tid-bit on the tip of her tongue. The usual butt of her wit was poor Schnapper-Elle, for she knew how to ape the affected genteel airs and the languishing manner with which the latter received the mocking compliments of the younger generation.

"Do you know," Puppy Reiss cried, "Schnapper-Elle said to me yesterday, 'If I weren't so beautiful, and clever, and adored, I'd rather not be alive.'"

There was loud tittering, and Schnapper-Elle, who was close enough to note that it was at her expense, raised her eyes in scorn, and sailed away to a distant port like a proud galley. Then Birdie Ochs, a plump, somewhat ungainly woman, remarked sympathetically that Schnapper-Elle might be vain and silly, but she was a very decent soul and did much good to those who were in need.

"Particularly to Nose-Star," Puppy Reiss hissed. And all who knew of this tender connection laughed all the louder.

"Do you know," the Puppy added spitefully, "Nose-Star now sleeps in Schnapper-Elle's house! . . . But look, down there, Süschen Flörsheim is wearing the necklace Daniel Fläsch has pawned with her husband. . . . Fläsch's wife is angry. And now she is talking to the Flörsheim woman. . . . How tenderly they squeeze hands, and hate one another like Midian and Moab! How sweetly they smile! Oh, but don't chew each other's ears off with all this tenderness! I'm going over to hear what they're saying."

And like a prowling beast, Puppy Reiss stole up to listen to the two women lamenting how hard they had worked all the past week to clean the house and to scour the kitchen utensils, all in preparation for the Passover, so that not a crumb of leavened bread stuck to anything. And they spoke of the labor of baking unleavened bread. The Fläsch woman had special cause for complaint, because in the bakery of the community she had had no end of trouble. For in accordance with the lot she had drawn, she could not begin her baking until the very last day before the Passover; and then only late in the afternoon. Old Hannah had kneaded the dough badly, and the maids had rolled it too thin; half of the bread was scorched in the oven, and to top it all, it had rained so hard that the water had come pouring through the wooden roof of the bakery, and yet they worked there, wet and weary, till late in the night.

"But my dear Frau Flörsheim," the Fläsch woman continued with a considerate amiability which was certainly far from genuine, "you yourself were not a little to blame, because you did not send your people to help me in the baking."

"Oh, excuse me," the other replied, "my servants were too busy. The goods for the fair had to be packed. We have so much to do. My husband . . ."

"Yes, I know," Frau Fläsch said with cutting irony, "I know you have much to do—so many pledges, and such good business, and necklaces . . ."

A poisoned word was about to slip from the tongue of the speaker— for Frau Flörsheim had turned as red as a lobster—when Puppy Reiss shrieked, "For God's sake, look, the strange lady is dying. Water! Water!"

Lovely Sara lay senseless, pale as death, while all around her pressed a swarm of women, fussing and crying. One held her head, another her arm. Some old women sprinkled her with water from a small cup, which hung from behind the prayer desks and was used for rinsing the hands if they accidentally came in contact with their bodies. Others held an old lemon, stuck full of spices, under her nose. (This was a remnant from the last holiday, when it had served to refresh those who smelled it.) Exhausted, and with a deep sigh, Sara at last opened her eyes, and with a mute gaze, thanked them all for their solicitude.

But now, from below, uttered in solemn tones, could be heard the Eighteen Prayers, which no one may miss. The busy women hastened back to their places, and offered the prayer as is ordained, standing up, facing toward the East, the direction of Jerusalem. Birdie Ochs, Schnapper-Elle, and Puppy Reiss remained to the last by Lovely Sara's side, the first two to help her as much as they could, the last to find out why she had fainted so suddenly.

Lovely Sara had swooned for a strange reason. It is customary in the synagogue for anyone who has escaped mortal danger to come forward after the portion of the Law has been read and publicly return thanks to Providence for his deliverance. As Rabbi Abraham rose in the synagogue below to offer his prayers of thanks, Sara recognized her husband's voice. But she observed that gradually the tone of it passed from that of thanksgiving into the mournful murmur of the prayer for the dead. She heard the names of her dear ones and her relatives, accompanied by the blessing which is dedicated to those who are dead. And the last hope vanished from her soul. She was overcome by the certainty that her beloved ones and her relatives had really been slain, that her little niece, her little cousins, Blümchen and Vögelchen, little Gottschalk—all were dead—all had been murdered! She too would have died from the sheer agony of knowing this, had not the swoon poured the balm of forgetfulness over her senses.

WHEN LOVELY SARA WENT DOWN INTO THE COURTYARD of the synagogue after the divine services, the Rabbi stood there waiting for her. He nodded to her cheerfully and led her out into the street, where quiet had given way to the noise of crowds. Bearded men in black-coats as numerous as ants; women as resplendent as gold-chafers; boys in new suits, carrying prayer-books for their elders; young girls, who had not been able to enter the synagogue, bounding from their homes to meet their parents, and bowing their curly heads to receive their blessing—all, gay and merry, were promenading up and down the streets with happy anticipation of a good dinner. The exquisite scent of it already caused the mouth to water as it rose from the black pots, marked with white chalk, which the laughing maids were at that very moment carrying from the communal kitchens.

In the midst of this bustle, the figure of a Spanish cavalier attracted special attention. His youthful features bore that fascinating pallor which women generally attribute to an unhappy, but men on the contrary to a happy love affair. His gait, though careless, seemed daintily affected. The feathers of his cap stirred more by reason of the proud movement of his head than of the wind. His golden spurs and the sheath of the sword—which he appeared to be carrying in his arm—jangled more than seemed necessary. The jewelled hilt sparkled from behind the white cloak, which enveloped his slender figure in apparently careless folds, but actually betrayed the most careful arrangement. Now and then he drew closer to the passing women, partly out of curiosity, partly with the air of a connoisseur; looked tranquilly into their faces, paused when he observed one that rewarded his attention, spoke a few flattering words to one or two of them, and then went on his way indifferent to their effect. More than once he had circled around Lovely Sara; but on each occasion he was intimidated by the imperious look or enigmatic smile of her husband. At last, proudly casting all diffidence to the winds, he boldly barred the way for both of them, and with foppish self-assurance and in the sweet voice of a gallant, he addressed her:

"Señora, I swear, hear me, Señora, I swear by the roses of both kingdoms of Castille, by the hyacinths of Aragon, and the pomegranate blossoms of Andalusia! By the sun which brightens all of Spain, with its flowers, onions, pea-soup, forests, mountains, mules, he-goats and old Christians! By the canopy of heaven, of which the sun is only a golden tassel! And by the God who sits on the roof of heaven and spends day and night pondering the creation of lovely female forms! . . . I swear, Señora, you are the most beautiful woman I have ever seen in all the German land, and if you deign to accept my services, then I beg you to grant me favor, grace, and leave to call myself your knight and to wear your colors henceforth in jest and in earnest!"

A flush of pain rose in Lovely Sara's face, and with one of those glances which are all the more cutting since they proceed from the gentlest of eyes, and in a voice which was devastating because the tone was so soft and tremulous, she replied, deeply hurt:

"My noble lord, if you would be my knight, you must fight whole nations, and in this battle there are few thanks to be won, and even less honor. And if you would wear my colors, then you must sew yellow rings on your cloak, or bind a blue-striped scarf around you. For such are my colors, the colors of my house, the House of Israel, the house of misery, which is despised and scorned in the streets by the children of good fortune."

Instantly, a purple flush suffused the cheeks of the Spaniard. Endless confusion covered his features, and he spoke in broken tones:

"Señora, you misunderstand me. It was merely an innocent jest . . . but by God, no mockery, no mockery of Israel. . . . I am myself sprung from the House of Israel. . . . My grandfather was a Jew, perhaps my father too. . . ."

"And it is quite certain that your uncle is one," interjected the Rabbi, who had looked on the scene calmly. And with a merry, quizzical glance, he added, "And I myself will stand surety that Don Isaac Abarbanel, nephew of the great Rabbi,[5] is sprung from the best blood of Israel, if not from the royal house of David."

The sword-strap rattled underneath the Spaniard's cloak, his cheeks turned a deathly white, and his upper lip twitched as if scorn were struggling with sorrow; angry death glared from his eyes, and in an utterly changed and icy voice he said:

"Señor Rabbi, I see you know me. Well then, you know who I am. And if the fox knows that I belong to the race of lions, he will beware lest he endanger his fox-beard and provoke my wrath. How shall the fox judge the lion? Only he who feels like the lion can understand his weakness."

"Oh, I understand it well," the Rabbi answered, and a pained seriousness came over his brow. "I understand well how the proud lion, out of pride, sheds his princely skin and goes mumming in the gay and scaly armor of the crocodile, because it is the fashion to be a grinning, cunning, greedy crocodile! What can you expect of the lesser beasts, when the lion himself denies his nature? But beware, Don Isaac, you were not made to live in the crocodile's element. For water—you understand what I mean—is your evil fortune; and you will perish. Water is not your element. The meanest trout can thrive in it better than the king of the forest. Don't you remember that the whirlpools of the Tagus wanted to swallow you?"

Bursting into loud laughter, Don Isaac suddenly threw his arms around the Rabbi, covered his mouth with kisses, leaped into the air so that the spurs jingled and the Jews who were passing by shrank back in alarm, and in his own natural, hearty and cheerful voice he cried:

"In truth, you are Abraham of Bacherach! And it was a good jest and a friendly deed to boot when you leaped from the Alcantara bridge into the water and seized your friend by the hair, and drew him on to dry land!—your friend who could drink better than he could swim! I was then on the point of seriously investigating whether there really was gold at the bottom of the Tagus, and whether the Romans had been correct in naming it the golden river. I assure you, I feel chilly whenever I even recall that water-carnival."

Saying this, the Spaniard made as if to shake drops of water from his garments. The face of the Rabbi assumed its former cheerfulness. Again and again he pressed the hand of his friend, saying all the time, "I am very happy."

"And I too am happy," the other said. "It is now seven years since we met, and when we last parted I was a callow know-nothing, and you were already so staid and serious. . . . But what has become of that beautiful Doña, who in those days cost you many a well-rhymed sigh, which you were wont to accompany on the lute?"

"Hush. The Doña hears us. She is my wife. And you yourself have today given her proof of your poetical taste and skill."

Not without some trace of his former embarrassment, the Spaniard now greeted the beautiful woman, and she with gracious amiability apologized for having so plainly expressed her displeasure and for offending a friend of her husband's.

"Ah, Señora," Don Isaac replied, "he who grasps the rose with a brute hand must not complain of the prickly thorn. When the evening star mirrors its golden beauty in the azure floods—"

"I beg you, for God's sake," the Rabbi interrupted him, "cease. If we wait until the evening star mirrors its sparkling gold in the blue azure floods, my poor wife will starve, for she has eaten nothing since yesterday, and has endured much besides."

"Well then, I'll take you to the best kitchen in Israel," said Don Isaac, "to the house of my friend, Schnapper-Elle, which is not far from here. Already I can smell the sweet incense—I mean of her kitchen. Oh, if you only knew, Abraham, how this fragrance draws me! This is what has lured me often to the tents of Jacob, since I have come to this city. Intimacy with God's people is not one of my weaknesses; indeed, I visit the Jews' quarter not to pray but to eat."

"You have never loved us, Don Isaac—"

"Yes," continued the Spaniard, "I love your kitchen much better than your creed. The latter lacks the right sauce. I have never really been able to digest you. Even in your best days, in the reign of my ancestor David, who was king over Judah and Israel, I could never have suffered being one of you. Some fine morning I most surely would have leaped down from Mount Zion and emigrated to Phoenicia, or to Babylon, where the zest of life foamed in the temple of the gods."

"You blaspheme the one God, Isaac," the Rabbi murmured grimly. "You are much worse than the Christians. You are a heathen, a worshipper of idols. . . ."

"Yes, I am a heathen.—The gloomy, self-tormenting Nazarenes are as little to my taste as the desiccated, joyless Hebrews. May our dear Lady of Sidon, Holy Astarte, forgive me that I kneel in prayer before the afflicted Mother of the Crucified. . . . Only with my knee and my tongue do I worship Death. My heart remains true to life! . . .

"But do not look so glum," the Spaniard went on, as he saw how little his speech pleased the Rabbi. "Do not look at me with disgust. My nose is no renegade. Once chance brought me to this street at dinner time, and the familiar savors of the Jewish kitchen rose to my nostrils. I was overcome by that same yearning which our forefathers felt for the flesh-pots of Egypt; tasty memories of my youth came back to me. Again I saw in my mind the carp with the brown raisin sauce, which my aunt used to prepare with such edification for the Sabbath eve. Once again I saw the steamed mutton with garlic and horse-radish, strong enough to raise the dead; and the soup with dumplings swimming in it as if lost in dreams. . . . And my soul melted like the song of an enamored nightingale, and ever since I have dined in the kitchen of my friend, Doña Schnapper-Elle."

In the meantime they had arrived at the kitchen, and Schnapper-Elle herself stood in the doorway, with a ready greeting for the hungry strangers who had come to the fair. Behind her, his head protruding over her shoulder, stood Nose-Star, examining the newcomers with anxious curiosity. Don Isaac approached the hostess with an exaggerated bow, and she returned his scampish low obeisances with innumerable curtseys. Then he took his glove from the right hand, wound it about within the corner of his cloak, and seizing the hand of Schnapper-Elle, he drew it across his moustaches and said,

"Señora, your eyes rival the light of the sun! Unlike the egg, which the longer it boils the harder it becomes, my heart grows softer the longer it is cooked in the flaming rays of your eyes. The winged god Cupid flutters from the yolk of my heart, and seeks a secure nest in your bosom. . . . Ah, this bosom, Señora, with what shall I compare it? In all creation there is no flower, no fruit like it! There is no plant like it in all the world. Though the storm rob the tenderest rose of its leaves, your bosom is the winter rose which defies all storms. The sour lemon, the older it grows, the more yellow and wrinkled it turns; but your bosom rivals the sweetest pineapple in color and softness. O Señora, if the city of Amsterdam be as beautiful as you told me yesterday and the day before, and every day, the ground upon which it rests is a thousand times more beautiful still. . . ."

The cavalier spoke these words with an affected shyness and with a languishing leer at the huge likeness which hung around Schnapper-Elle's neck. Nose-Star looked down with searching glances, and her much-lauded bosom began heaving so violently that the whole city of Amsterdam rocked from side to side.

"Ah," Schnapper-Elle sighed, "virtue is more precious than beauty. Of what use is beauty to me? My youth is fast passing away, and since Schnapper is gone—anyway, he had beautiful hands—But what avails my beauty?"

And she sighed again, and like an echo, all but inaudible, Nose-Star sighed behind her.

"Of what use is your beauty!" cried Don Isaac. "Oh, Doña Schnapper-Elle, do not sin against the kindness of Nature, the Creator! Do not scorn her most gracious gifts! She avenges herself cruelly. These beatific eyes would turn glassy blind, these winsome lips, flat and ordinary; this chest and amorous body would change into an ugly barrel of tallow, and the city of Amsterdam would at last rest on a rank morass—"

So he sketched, piece by piece, Schnapper-Elle's present appearance, so that the poor woman grew more and more uneasy and sought to escape the uncanny speeches of the cavalier. Hence she was doubly delighted to spy Lovely Sara at this moment and to inquire whether she had quite recovered from her swoon. Then she plunged into lively chatter, in which she clearly displayed her sham gentility as well as her genuine kindliness. With more garrulity than wisdom she told the terrible story of how she herself had almost fainted with fright, when, a stranger, she had arrived in Amsterdam on a canal boat, and the rascally porter, who carried her trunk, had brought her to a house of shame, instead of to a respectable inn. She saw what it was the moment she entered, for liquor was being served, and indecent advances were made. . . . And she would indeed have swooned, if she had for only one moment of her six weeks' stay in that infamous house dared to shut her eyes.

"Because of my virtue," she added, "I dared not. And all this happened because I was beautiful. But beauty fades, and virtue remains."

Don Isaac was about to subject the story to a close examination, when, luckily, squinting Aaron Hirschkuh, from Homburg on the Lahn, came out of the house with a white napkin in his mouth and complained angrily that the soup had already been served, the guests were all seated, but the hostess was not yet there. . . .

(The conclusion and the subsequent chapters are lost, not through any fault of the author's.)

⁊⤝ The Philosophical Lizard

NATURAL SURROUNDINGS AFFECT MAN—why should not man also affect Nature, which surrounds him? In Italy Nature is as passionate as the people who live there; in our Germany, she is more sedate, deliberate, and patient. Did Nature at one time also possess an inner life—like human beings? The emotional power of an Orpheus, it is related, could move the trees and stones to responsive and inspired rhythms. Could a similar miracle occur today? Men and Nature have become phlegmatic, and now yawn at each other. Never could a Royal Prussian Poet, with the sound of his lyre, move the mountains of Templow, or the lindens of Berlin!

Nature also has a history, quite different from that taught in the schools. If we appointed to one of our universities as a very extraordinary professor one of those ancient lizards that have been dwelling in the rocky clefts of the Apennines for thousands of years—then we would hear extraordinary things. But the vanity of certain gentlemen of the faculty of law would rise up against such an appointment. As a matter of fact, there are already among them such as are secretly jealous of poor *Fido,* the savant, out of fear that the dog may end by surpassing them in the learned art of retrieving.

The lizards, with their wise little tails and their sharp eyes, related wonderful things to me once when I climbed among the rocks of the Apennines all by myself. Truly, there are more things in heaven and earth than are dreamt of not only by our philosophers, but also by our most ordinary dunces.

The lizards told me that there was a legend current among the rocks that God would one day turn into a rock in order to deliver them from their stoniness. An old lizard, however, was of the opinion that this petrification could take place only after God had metamorphosed himself into all sorts of animals and plants, and had redeemed them.

Only very few stones possess sensibilities, and they breathe only in the moonlight. The latter, who realize their plight, are terribly wretched. The trees are much better off: they can weep. But the animals are the most fortunate, for they can speak, each in his own fashion—and man can speak best of all. One day, when the whole world shall have been redeemed, all creation will be able to speak as it once did in the olden times of which the poets sing.

The lizards are an ironical species, and love to delude the other animals. But toward me they were humble, they sighed so honestly, and told me stories of Atlantis, which I shall shortly write down for the edification of the devout of this earth. I felt thoroughly at ease in the presence of these little creatures, who have preserved the most secret annals of Nature's history. Is it possible that they are enchanted families of priests, like those of ancient Egypt, who lived in the labyrinths of their rocky grottos, searching out the secrets of Nature? On their little heads, bodies, and tails are emblazoned such wonderful designs as on the hieroglyphic hats and hierophantic coats of Egypt.

My little friends taught me the language of signs, by means of which I was enabled to speak with mute Nature. This has often comforted my heart, especially in the evening, when the mountains lie shrouded in eerily sweet shadows, when the water-falls roar, plants exhale their fragrance and feverish lightning darts to and fro.

O Nature, you mute virgin! Well do I understand your lightning storms, those fruitless efforts to speak, those storms that dart across your beautiful face—you move me to such pity, that I could weep. But you also understand me, and you grow more cheerful, and you laugh from on high with those golden eyes of yours! Beautiful virgin, I understand your stars, and you understand my tears!

"Nothing in the world retrogresses," said an old lizard to me. "Everything struggles forward, and in the end Nature will have made great progress. Stones will have become plants, plants animals, animals men, and men will have become gods."

"But what," I cried, "will then become of those good fellows—the poor old gods?"

"That will be taken care of," the lizard replied. "In all probability they will be pensioned or retire in some honorable way."

Many other secrets I learned from my natural philosopher with the hieroglyphic skin, but I gave him my word of honor not to divulge them. I now know more than Schelling and Hegel.

"And what do you think of those two?" the old lizard asked me with a mocking smile when I happened to mention them.

"When you consider," I replied, "that they are only human beings, and not lizards, their knowledge appears astounding. Actually they both teach one and the same doctrine, the philosophy of Identity, which you understand so well. They differ only in the way they present it. When Hegel propounds the principles of his philosophy, it is as though you saw those pretty figures which a clever school-master knows how to shape from a skilful arrangement of digits in such a way that the ordinary observer sees only the external form, only a little house, or a boat, or soldiers formed from these numerals; while the thoughtful pupil can perceive in them the solution of a difficult mathematical problem. Schelling's presentation, on the other hand, resembles those Hindu pictures of animals compounded of all sorts of other creatures, such as snakes, birds, elephants, and similar living elements, boldly interwoven. This method is much more pleasant, brighter, and warmer, for everything in it is alive, whereas the Hegelian digits stare at us in such an abstract, grey, cold and dead way."

"Very good," said the old lizard. "I see what you mean. But tell me, do these philosophers have much of a following?"

I described to him how in the learned caravansary in Berlin, the camels gather around the fountain of Hegelian wisdom, kneel before it, and allow themselves to be laden with the water-skins, and then continue on their way through the sand-dunes of Brandenburg. I pictured to him how the new Athenians press around the fountain-head of the quenching waters of Schelling, as if it were the very best beer, the very spice of life, the draught of immortality.

Our little natural philosopher was filled with bitter envy when he heard that his colleagues enjoyed such adulation, and he asked crustily, "Which of the two do you consider the greater?"

"That I cannot decide," I replied, "no more than I can decide whether Schechner is greater than Sontag, but I think—"

"Think!" the lizard cried in a piercing, haughty tone filled with the profoundest contempt. "Think! Who among you thinks? My learned sir, for more than three thousand years I have been investigating the mental functions of animals. I have closely studied human beings, apes and snakes. I have expended as much effort on these strange creatures as Lyonnet on his willow-caterpillars, and as a result of my observations, experiments and anatomical comparisons, I can definitely assure you that man does not think. Now and then he has an idea; he calls these involuntary ideas, thoughts—and their arrangement he calls thinking. You may repeat this in my name: Man does not think. Philosophers do not think. Neither Schelling nor Hegel thinks. And as for their philosophy, it is air and water; it is like the clouds in the sky. I have seen many of these sailing up above me proud and serene, and the next morning the sun has dissolved them into their original nothingness. There is only one genuine philosophy and it is inscribed in hieroglyphics on my tail."

With these words, uttered with disdainful feeling, the old lizard turned his back on me, and as he slowly undulated away, I saw covering his whole tail the most astounding characters, which formed a many-colored and significant pattern.

ࣹ Mademoiselle Laurence

IT IS NOW EIGHT YEARS SINCE I JOURNEYED TO LONDON to study the language and the people. Confound the people along with their language! They take a dozen monosyllables in their mouths, chew them, gnash them, and then spit them out again, and they call that speaking! . . .

I must own, Maria, that if nothing in England was to my taste, whether men or dishes, the fault lay partly in myself. I had brought a good stock of ill-humor with me from home, and I sought to be cheered up by a people who can only kill their boredom in a whirl of political or commercial activity. . . .

You can well imagine how my discontent mounted every day in that land. But nothing could surpass the ugly mood which possessed me as I stood one evening on Waterloo Bridge and looked down into the waters of the Thames. It seemed to me as if my soul were reflected in the river, and looked up at me with all its scars. . . .

It happened that at that instant singular music woke me from my dark dreams. When I looked around me, I saw on the bank a group of people who seemed to have formed a circle around some entertaining spectacle. I drew near, and saw a family of performers, consisting of four people. The first was a short, thick-set woman, dressed all in black, with a very small head and a fat, protuberant belly, over which hung a huge drum she kept hammering without pity.

Then a dwarf, who wore an embroidered suit like a Marquis, and had a large powdered head, but very slender, puny limbs, and while he hopped about, he struck a triangle.

The third member of the troupe was a girl of about fifteen years, who wore a short, tight-fitting jacket of blue-striped silk, and broad pantaloons also with blue stripes. She was a creature of airy charm. Her face was Greek in its beauty; she had a noble, straight nose, sweet, pouting lips, a dreamy, soft, round chin; her complexion was a sunny brown, and her hair was a gleaming black and wound round her temples. Thus she stood, tall, serious, and somewhat ill-humored, and looked at the fourth member of the company who was performing his act. This was a learned dog—a very promising poodle, who had to the great delight of the English public spelled out the name of the Duke of Wellington from the wooden letters set before him—and had added the very flattering title of "Hero." Since the dog, as one could gather from his intelligent exterior, was no English beast, but, like the other three performers, had come from France, the sons of Albion rejoiced that their great general had at least obtained from the dogs of France that recognition which the other French creatures had so disgracefully denied him.

In fact, this company was French, and the dwarf, who announced himself as Monsieur Turlutu, began to bluster in French, with such vehement gestures, that the poor English gaped even more than usual. Sometimes, after a long phrase, he crowed like a cock, and these cock-a-doodle-doos and the names of the many emperors, queens, and princes with which he spiced his discourse were the only sounds the poor spectators understood. He boasted of the friendship and patronage of those emperors, kings and princes. When only a boy of eight, he assured his audience, he had had a long interview with His Late Majesty Louis XVI, who after that frequently asked his advice. He had, like many others, fled the storms of the Revolution, and had only returned to his beloved country when the Empire had been established, to take part in the glory of the great nation. Napoleon, he declared, never loved him; whereas His Holiness, Pope Pius VII, almost idolized him. The Emperor Alexander had given him bon-bons, and the Princess Wilhelm von Kyritz always placed him on her lap. Yes, from childhood, he declared, he had lived among sovereigns; the present monarchs had grown up with him, and he regarded them as his equals, and always wore mourning when one of them passed away. After these solemn words, he crowed like a cock.

Monsieur Turlutu was indeed one of the most curious dwarfs I had ever seen. His wrinkled old face formed a very droll contrast to his little childish body and his whole person contrasted even more comically with his performances. For he assumed the most defiant postures, and with an inhumanly long rapier he stabbed the air to the right and left of him, all the time declaring on his honor that no mortal could parry this *quarte* or that *tierce* or break through his defense. He challenged any one to engage with him in the noble art of fencing.

After the dwarf had for some time carried on in this way, and found no one who would resolve on an open duel with him, he bowed with old French grace, thanked his audience for the applause which they had bestowed upon him, and took the liberty of announcing to the very honorable public the most extraordinary exhibition which ever had been given on English soil. "You see this person," he explained, as he drew on dirty kid gloves and led the young girl of the troupe with respectful gallantry into the middle of the circle. "This is Mademoiselle Laurence, the only daughter of the honorable and Christian lady whom you see there with the big drum, and who still wears mourning for the loss of her dearly-beloved husband, the greatest ventriloquist in Europe! Mademoiselle Laurence will now dance! Admire now the dancing of Mademoiselle Laurence!" After these words he again crowed like a cock.

The young girl did not seem to pay the least attention either to these words or to the gaze of the spectators. Irritably, and as if absorbed in thought, she waited till the dwarf had spread a carpet at her feet and had begun to play the triangle to the accompaniment of the great drum. It was strange music, a mixture of awkward peevishness and lascivious tinkling, and I caught a pathetic, crazy, melancholy, insolent and bizarre—though singularly simple—melody. But I forgot the music as soon as the young girl began to dance.

Dancer and dance held me almost spell-bound. It was not a classical dance, which we still see in our great ballets, where, as in classical tragedy, only swaggering unities and artificiality prevail. Here were no Alexandrines, set to a dance, none of those declamatory leaps, those antithetic entrechats, that noble passion which pirouettes so that one sees nothing but heaven and hosiery—nothing but illusion and lies! There is really nothing so odious to me as the ballet at the grand opera in Paris, where the traditions of that classical dancing have been preserved in their purest forms, while in the other arts, in poetry, music, and painting, the French have overthrown the classical system. However, it will be difficult for them to bring about a similar revolution in the dance, unless they have recourse—as in their political revolution—to terrorism, and guillotine the legs of the obstinate male and female dancers of the *ancien régime*.

Mademoiselle Laurence was no great dancer. Her toes were not very supple. Her legs were not practised in all possible movements; she knew nothing of the art of dancing as Madame Vestris teaches it, but she danced as Nature commands. Her whole being was in harmony with her steps; not only her feet, but her whole body too—even her face—danced. She often grew pale, almost deathly pale; her eyes opened spectrally wide, yearning and pain contorted her lips, and her black hair, which enclosed her temples in smooth ovals, fluttered like a raven's wings. This was no classical dance; nor was it romantic in the sense of the young Frenchmen of the school of Eugene Renduel. This dance had nothing of the medieval, the Venetian, the deformed, or the macabre about it. There was in it neither moonlight nor incest. It was a dance which did not seek to amuse through external movements, but rather strove through the external movements to express strange things in the words of a strange speech. What did the dance say? I could not tell, no matter how passionately it spoke to me. I could only guess that it spoke of some intense sorrow. I, who in other things so easily grasp the meaning of all phenomena, could not solve the riddle of this dance—and it was the fault of the music that I groped in vain for its meaning; since it intentionally strove to lead me astray, and cunningly sought to confuse and disturb me. Monsieur Turlutu's triangle often tittered mockingly. And Madame, the Mother, beat her great drum so fiercely, that her face glowed from the black cloud of her hood like a blood-red northern light.

Long after the troupe had left, I remained standing in the same spot, wondering what that dance might mean. Was it a national dance of

the south of France, or of Spain? It might very well have been, to
judge from the impetuosity with which the dancer swung her body
to and fro, and the abandon with which she often threw back her
head—in the wanton, wild fashion of those Bacchantes whom we
observe with amazement on the reliefs of ancient vases. There was
something of intoxicated abandon in her dance, something gloomy
and inevitable, and doomed. She was like Fate herself. Or was it
perhaps a fragment of some primeval, forgotten pantomime? Or a
personal history in motion? Often the girl bent down to the earth
with a rapt ear, as if she had heard a voice calling. . . . Then she trembled like a leaf, bent to the other side, and gave herself over to the
maddest and most abandoned leaps. Again she bent her ear to the
ground, listened more intently than ever, nodded her head, reddened
and paled by turns, shuddered, and stood for a while stiffly upright.
Finally, she made a movement as one who washes his hands! Was
it blood that she was washing from her hands with such care and
terrible anxiety, and for so long a time? While doing this, she cast a
sideward glance so full of entreaty, so imploring, so soul-dissolving
. . . and by chance, that glance fell on me.

All of the next night I thought of that glance, of that dance, of that
strange accompaniment. When I roamed as usual through the streets
of London on the following day, I longed to see the pretty dancer
once more, and I constantly pricked up my ears for the sound of the
drum or the triangle. At last I had found something in London to interest me, and I no longer wandered aimlessly about.

I had just come out of the Tower where I had carefully examined
the axe with which Anne Boleyn had been beheaded, the British
crown-jewels, and the lions, when in front of the Tower in the middle
of a large circle of onlookers I again beheld Madame, the Mother,
with the great drum, and heard Monsieur Turlutu crowing like a
cock. The learned dog again pawed together the heroism of Lord
Wellington; the dwarf again displayed his invincible *tierce* and *quarte*,
and Mademoiselle once more began her wonderful dance. The same
enigmatic movements, the same language which I could not understand, the same impulsive throwing back of her beautiful head, the
same posture of listening to the earth, the anguish which could be
relieved only by ever madder leaps, and again the listening ear bent to
the ground, the trembling, the pallor, the fixity, then the fearful and
mysterious washing of hands, and finally the imploring, beseeching
side-glances, which this time rested on me longer than before.

Yes, all women, young and old, know at once when they have aroused the attention of a man. Although when she was not performing, Mademoiselle Laurence always stood motionless and peevish, and while dancing, rarely cast a single glance on her public, it could hardly be mere chance that her glance always fell on me from this time on. And the more often I saw her dance, the more significant that glance became—and the more incomprehensible. I was bewitched by it. For three weeks I roamed the streets of London, stopping wherever I saw Mademoiselle dance. Despite the great bustle and noise, I could catch the sound of the drum and triangle at the farthest distance, and Monsieur crowed most amiably as soon as he saw me approaching. Without ever speaking a word to him or Mademoiselle Laurence, or Madame the Mother, or the learned dog, I seemed at last to belong to their company. When Monsieur Turlutu took up the collection, he always behaved with the most delicate tact. As he drew near me, he looked into the opposite direction, when I put a small coin in his three-cornered hat. His demeanor was indeed aristocratic. He reminded me of the exquisite manners of the past. One could tell that the little man had grown up among monarchs; hence it seemed all the more amazing when, at times, he quite forgot his dignity and began crowing like a cock.

I cannot describe to you my irritation when once, after seeking this troupe for three days without success through all the streets of London, I finally concluded that they had left town. Boredom once more took me in her leaden arms and crushed my heart. At last I could endure it no longer. I bade adieu to the four estates of the realm—the mob, the blackguards, the gentlemen, and the fashionables of England—and journeyed back to civilized *terra firma*, where I knelt down in adoration before the white apron of the first cook I met. For here I could once more dine like a rational being and regale my soul by gazing at easy-going, unselfish faces. But I could not for a moment forget Mademoiselle Laurence. She danced constantly in my mind, and in solitary hours I often thought of the beautiful child's enigmatic pantomime, especially her intense way of listening to the voice of the earth. It was a long time before the strange melodies of the triangle and the drum faded from my memory.

FIVE YEARS LATER I CAME FOR THE FIRST TIME TO PARIS, and at a very remarkable time. The French had just performed their July Revolution, and the whole world applauded. This play was not so terrible as the earlier tragedies of the Republic and the Empire. Only some thousand corpses remained upon the stage. The political Romantics were not very well satisfied and announced a new piece in which more blood would flow and the executioner would have more to do.

Paris delighted me with its prevailing gaiety, which sheds its influence over the most somber minds. Strange! Paris is the stage on which the greatest tragedies of world history have been performed—tragedies at the recollection of which hearts tremble and eyes grow moist in the most remote lands; but the spectator of these tragedies experiences in Paris much the same reaction as once I did when I saw the *Tour de Nesle* played at the Port Saint-Martin. I found myself sitting behind a lady who wore a hat of rose-colored gauze, so broad that it obstructed my whole view of the stage; so that I saw the tragedy only through the red gauze of her hat. All the horror of the *Tour de Nesle* appeared rose-colored. Yes, Paris has this rosy light which softens all tragedies for the spectator, so that his enjoyment of life may not be spoiled. Even the terrors of one's own heart that one brings to Paris lose the power to torment. Sorrow is strangely softened. In this air of Paris all wounds are healed more quickly than elsewhere; it has something generous, soothing and charming like the people themselves.

What pleased me most in the people of Paris was their polite behavior and their distinguished air. Sweet pineapple aroma of courtesy! How beneficently didst thou refresh my sick soul, which had imbibed so much tobacco smoke, odors of sauerkraut and coarseness in Germany! The simple words of apology of a Frenchman who had accidentally pushed against me on my first day in Paris sounded in my ears like the melodies of Rossini. I was almost terrified at such sweet politeness, I who was accustomed to boorish German digs in the ribs without apologies. During my first week in Paris I sought to be jostled, so that I might enjoy that apologetic music. But not merely because of this politeness do the French people possess in my eyes a certain touch of distinction—but also because of the language itself. For as you know, with us, in the North, French is one of the attributes of noble birth; from childhood I had associated French with distinction. And a Parisian market-woman spoke better French than a German deaconess descended from sixty-four generations!

On account of this language which lends them an air of distinction, the French people have always possessed charm for me. This could be traced to another childhood recollection. The first book in which I learned French was the *Fables* of La Fontaine. Their naive, rational speech impressed itself indelibly on my memory, so that when I came to Paris and heard French spoken everywhere, I was constantly reminded of those Fables. I imagined that I was hearing the well-known animal voices—now that of the lion, then the wolf, or the lamb, or the stork, or the dove. Often I thought I caught the voice of the fox, and I heard in my mind:

> *"Eh! bon jour, Monsieur le Corbeau!*
> *Que vous êtes joli, que vous me semblez beau!"* [6]

Such romantic reminiscences awoke within my soul much oftener when I found my way into that higher region of Paris which is called "the world." For it was this very world which had supplied La Fontaine of blessed memory with types of his animal characters. The winter season began soon after my arrival in Paris, and I took part in the salon life in which that world gads about more or less merrily. What struck me as most interesting here was not so much the equality of good manners which prevailed there as the variety of its component parts. Very often, when I looked around on the people gathered in a grand salon—associating on a most familiar footing— I thought I was in one of those curiosity shops where the relics of all ages lie helter-skelter side by side: a Greek Apollo, a Chinese pagoda, a Mexican Vitzliputzli, a Gothic Ecce Homo, Egyptian idols with dogs' heads, holy grotesques of wood, ivory, metal, etc. There I saw old musketeers who had danced with Marie Antoinette, republicans of the moderate persuasion who had been deified in the National Assembly, Montagnards without pity and reproach, former members of the Directory who had been enthroned in the Luxembourg, great dignitaries of the Empire before whom all Europe had trembled, ruling Jesuits of the Restoration—in short, only faded, mutilated divinities of all times, in whom no one any longer believed. The names recoil from each other when they meet; but the men stand peacefully and amiably together, like the antiques in the shops of Quai Voltaire, which I mentioned. In Germany, where the passions are less easily disciplined, such familiar sociability of heterogeneous persons would be quite impossible. With us, in the cold North, the need for conversation is not so strong as in warmer France, where the bitterest enemies cannot long maintain a glum silence when they meet in a salon. Furthermore, the desire to please is so great in France, that people zealously strive to be agreeable not only to their friends

but even to their enemies. Hence the incessant disguises and affecta-
tions, so that women have a hard time here surpassing men in
coquetry—but they succeed, nonetheless.

I intend no evil by this remark—no, on my life!—not a word of
evil about French women, and least of all Parisian women. For I am
their great adorer, and honor them even more for their defects than
for their virtues. I know nothing more to the point then the legend
that French women come into the world with all possible failings,
but that a benevolent fairy takes pity on them and endows each
fault with a spell which turns it into a fresh charm. That kind fairy
is Grace. Are Parisian women beautiful? Who can tell? Who has
seen through all the intrigues of their toilette—who can decipher
whether what the lace betrays is genuine, or what the swelling silk
displays is false? And if the eye succeeds in piercing the shell and is
on the point of finding the kernel, then, behold! it discovers a new
shell, and again another. With this unceasing change of fashions they
mock the perspicacity of man. Are their faces beautiful? Even this
is hard to determine. For all their features are in constant motion.
A Parisian woman has a thousand faces—and every one of these has
more laughter, spirit, and grace than the other—and confuses him
who would choose the fairest face among them, or even guess at
the real one. Are their eyes large? How should I know? We do not
long examine the caliber of a gun, when the ball decapitates us. And
even if those eyes miss—at least they dazzle us with their lightning,
and we are glad if we can get out of their range. Is the space between
nose and mouth broad or narrow? Often it is broad when they wrinkle
up their noses; often narrow, when the upper lip curls up petulantly.
Have they small or large mouths? Who can tell where the mouth
leaves off and the smile begins? To form a correct estimate, judge
and the object to be judged must be in a state of repose. But who
can be quiet in the presence of a Parisienne, and what Parisienne is
ever at rest? There are people who think they can observe a butterfly
accurately if they have stuck it on paper with a pin. That is as foolish
as it is cruel. The transfixed and motionless butterfly is a butterfly
no longer. The butterfly must be seen while it flutters around the
flowers . . . , and the Parisian woman must be studied not in her
domestic surroundings, when she is made fast by a pin through her
breast, but in the salon, at soirées and balls, where she flutters with
wings of gauze and silk beneath the flaming crystals of joy! Then she
reveals an impetuous passion for life, a longing for sweet oblivion, a

thirst for intoxication, and acquires a charm which at once enraptures and terrifies our souls.

This thirst for life's enjoyment, as if death would soon snatch her from the bubbling fountains of joy, or as if this fountain were about to cease for ever—this haste, the frenzy, this madness of the Parisian woman, especially as it reveals itself at balls, always reminds me of the legend of the dead dancing girls we Germans call *Willis*. These are young brides who died before their wedding-day, but who still have the unsatisfied desire for dancing so deep in their hearts that each night they rise from their graves, gather in bands on the highways, and abandon themselves to the wildest dances. In their bridal clothes, with garlands on their heads, sparkling rings on their pale hands— laughing eerily, and irresistibly lovely—they dance in the moonlight, and they dance all the more feverishly and madly as they feel that the hour granted them for dancing is coming to an end, and they must again descend to their icy graves.

At a soirée in the Chaussée d'Antin this reflection moved my soul profoundly. It was a brilliant soirée, and wanted nothing of the customary ingredients of social pleasure—plenty of light by which you can be seen; plenty of mirrors in which to see yourself; plenty of people to press against you and make you sweat; plenty of sugared water and ice to cool you.

It all began with music. Franz Liszt had allowed himself to be drawn to the piano. He pushed his hair back over his impressive brows, and waged one of his most brilliant melodic battles. Even the keys seemed to bleed. If I am not mistaken, he played a passage from the *Palingenesis* of Ballanche, whose ideas he was translating into music,—a great aid to those who could not read the works of that famous author in the original. Afterwards, he played the "March to the Gallows"—"*la marche au supplice*"—of Berlioz—that admirable piece which, unless I am in error, the young artist composed on the morning of his wedding. Everywhere in the hall—pallid faces, heaving bosoms, subdued breathing during the pauses, and at last tumultuous applause. Women always behave as if intoxicated when Liszt plays. With frantic delight the *Willis* of the salon then abandoned themselves to the dance, and I had difficulty in getting out of this confusion and escaping into an adjoining room. Here card-playing was going on, and several ladies reclined in large easy chairs and looked on, or at least pretended that they were interested in the cards. As I passed one of these ladies, my arm touched her dress, and

I felt a gentle quiver pass from my hand to the shoulder like a slight electric shock. A similar shock but more forceful passed through my heart when I saw the lady's face. Was it or was it not she? It was the same face, with the form and sunny hue of an ancient statue—only it was no longer so marble-pure or so marble-smooth as before. An acute observer might detect slight flaws, perhaps faint pock-marks, on brow and cheek, reminiscent of the fine weather-marks on the faces of statues which have for some time been exposed to the rain. The black hair was the same, and it covered her temples in smooth ovals, like a raven's wings.

But as her eye met mine—with that well-known side-glance whose quick flash always shot so mysteriously through my soul—I was no longer in doubt. It was Mademoiselle Laurence.

Leaning back with a genteel air in her chair, a bouquet in one hand, the other resting on the arm of the chair, Mademoiselle sat near a card table and seemed to give her whole attention to the game. Her dress of white satin was distinguished and elegant, but quite simple. Except for bracelets and brooches of pearl, she wore no other jewels. An abundance of lace covered her youthful bosom, almost puritanically to the neck, and in this simplicity and modesty she formed a touching and lovely contrast with several elderly ladies who sat near her, gaily bedecked and gleaming with diamonds, exposing the ruins of their former glories,—the place where once Troy stood—in all their melancholy nakedness. She still looked so wonderfully lovely and enchantingly peevish, that I felt irresistibly drawn to her. At last, I stood behind her chair, burning with impatience to speak to her, yet restrained by a shy delicacy.

I must have stood behind her for some time without saying a word, when suddenly she drew a flower from her bouquet and, without looking around, held it out to me over her shoulder. Its perfume was strange, and it exerted a peculiar fascination over me. I felt myself freed from all social formalities. I felt as if in a dream, where one does and says all kinds of things at which one marvels—and when one's words have a childlike, simple, and intimate character. Calm, indifferent, and nonchalant, as one is with an old friend, I leaned over the arm of the chair and whispered in her ear: "Mademoiselle Laurence, where is your mother with the drum?"

"She is dead," she replied, in the same tone,—calm, indifferent, nonchalant.

After a brief pause, I again leaned over the arm of the chair and whispered in the young woman's ear: "Mademoiselle Laurence, where is the learned dog?"

"He has run away into the wide world," she answered in the same calm, indifferent, nonchalant tone.

And again, after a brief pause, I inclined over the arm of the chair and whispered in the ear of the young woman: "Mademoiselle Laurence, where is Monsieur Turlutu, the dwarf?"

"He is with the giants on the Boulevard du Temple." She had scarcely spoken these words, in the same easy, indifferent and careless tone, when a serious old man of commanding military presence approached her and announced that her carriage was waiting. She rose slowly from her seat, took his arm, and without casting a backward glance at me, left the company.

When I asked our hostess, who had stood the whole evening through at the door presenting her smiles to the arriving and departing guests, for the name of the young person who had just left with the elderly gentleman, she laughed gaily in my face and said, "My God, who can ever know everybody? I know her as little as—"

She stopped short, for she certainly was about to say, "as you"— whom she was seeing for the first time that evening. "Perhaps," I remarked, "your husband can give me the information? Where can I find him?"

"Hunting at Saint-Germain," the lady replied, with a heartier laugh. "He left early this morning and will not return before tomorrow evening. But wait, I know someone who has frequently conversed with the lady about whom you inquire. I don't know his name, but you can easily find him if you ask for the young man whom M. Casimir Périer kicked—I don't know where."

Although it is hard to recognize a man by the fact of his having been kicked by a cabinet minister, I soon found him and asked for more light on the strange creature who interested me so, and whom I described clearly.

"Yes," said the young man, "I know her very well. I have spoken to her at several soirées." And he repeated a great deal of chatter with which he had entertained the lady. What had struck him most, though, was her earnest look whenever he said anything pleasant. He also marvelled that she always declined his invitation to a quadrille, assuring him that she could not dance. He knew nothing of her name or family. And no one—so far as I could learn—could give me any more definite information about her. In vain I ran through all possible soirées. Nowhere could I find Mademoiselle Laurence again.

I SAW THEM ALL AGAIN—EVEN THE LEARNED DOG. But he was in sad straits, poor fellow, when I saw him again in Paris. It was in the Latin Quarter. I was passing the Sorbonne, when a dog rushed through the gate, followed by a dozen students armed with sticks, who were soon joined by two dozen old women, all shrieking in chorus, "The dog is mad!" The unhappy dog looked almost human in his death agony. Tears streamed like water from his eyes, and as he ran by me panting and his tear-stained glance fell on me, I recognized my old friend, the learned dog, the eulogist of Lord Wellington, who had once filled the English people with astonishment. Was he actually mad, though? Perhaps he had been driven mad by sheer learning while pursuing his studies in the Latin Quarter? Or had he, at the Sorbonne, by his soft scratching and growling expressed his disapproval of the bloated charlatanry of some professor, who then sought to rid himself of the critical auditor by declaring him mad? Alas! Youth wastes no time investigating whether it was a wounded ego or professional jealousy that first cried out, "The dog is mad!" but immediately lays about with its thoughtless sticks, and the old women are ready with their yelping, and they drown out the voice of innocence and reason. My poor friend succumbed—before my eyes he was cruelly struck down, beaten to death, mocked, and at last cast on a dunghill! Poor martyr of learning!

Nor was the condition of the dwarf, Monsieur Turlutu, very much happier when I found him again on the Boulevard du Temple. Mademoiselle had indeed told me that he was there, but whether it was because I had not seriously attempted to find him, or the crowd of people hindered me, it was some time before I noticed the booth where the giants were being exhibited. When I entered, I found two tall rascals, lying idly on a bench, who jumped up quickly and assumed their giant postures before me. They were really not as large as their placards boasted, but merely overgrown scamps, dressed in pink tights. They had very black, perhaps false, side-whiskers, and brandished hollow wooden clubs over their heads. When I asked for the dwarf, who was also announced on their placard, they replied that for four weeks he had not been exhibited because his illness had grown worse, but that I might see him if I paid double the price of admission. How gladly one pays double to see an old friend! But alas! this was a friend on his death bed! This death-bed was really a child's cradle, and the poor dwarf lay in it, with his sallow, shrivelled old face. A little girl of some four years sat by him, rocking the cradle with her foot, and singing in a roguish, laughing voice:

"Sleep Turlutu, little Turlutu, sleep!"

When the little fellow saw me, he opened his glassy, dim eyes as wide as possible and a sad smile played on his white lips. He seemed to recognize me, for he reached out his shrunken little hand toward me and rattled softly, "Old friend!"

It was indeed a sad state in which I found the man who had at the early age of eight held a long conversation with Louis XVI, whom Czar Alexander had treated with bonbons, whom the Princess von Kyritz had taken on her lap, whom the Pope had idolized, and Napoleon never loved! This last circumstance troubled the wretched fellow on his death-bed, or, I should say, in his death-cradle; and he wept over the tragic fate of the great Emperor who had never loved him, but who had ended his life under such pitiable circumstances at Saint Helena. "Just as I am now dying," he added, "alone, neglected, forsaken by all kings and princes, a caricature of my former glory."

Although I could not quite understand how a dwarf who died among giants could compare himself with a giant who died among dwarfs, I was nevertheless moved by poor Turlutu's words and his forlorn state in these last moments. I could not refrain from expressing my amazement that Mademoiselle Laurence, who was now such a grand lady, gave herself no trouble about him. I had hardly uttered her name, when the dwarf was seized with the most agonizing spasms and whimpered with his pale lips, "Ungrateful child, that I brought up, and would have even elevated to be my wife, whom I taught how to move and behave among the great of this world; how to smile, how to curtsey, how to demean herself—you have put my instruction to good use and you are now a great lady. . . . You have a coach and footmen, and plenty of money, and plenty of pride; but you have no heart. You leave me here to die alone and in misery like Napoleon at Saint Helena! Oh, Napoleon, you never loved me—" What else he said I could not catch. He raised his head, made a slight motion with his hand as if he were parrying a thrust—perhaps that of death. But the scythe of this adversary no man can withstand—be he Napoleon or Turlutu. No fencing skill avails here. Exhausted, and as if beaten, the dwarf sank his head, gazed at me for a long while with his indescribable, ghastly stare, suddenly crowed like a cock, and expired!

His death troubled me, particularly as the departed had not given me any more exact information about Mademoiselle Laurence. Where was I to find her again! I was not in love with her, nor did I feel a special attachment to her. And yet I was spurred by a mysterious desire to seek her everywhere. Whenever I entered a drawing room and viewed the assembled company and did not find her familiar face, I lost my peace of mind and felt impelled to escape. Once, I stood at midnight at one of the side-entrances of the Opera, and reflected on this feeling. I was waiting for a carriage, with considerable annoyance, for it was raining hard. But no carriage came—or rather, the only carriages that came belonged to other people, who got into them comfortably. Soon I found myself alone.

"Well then, you must come along with me," at last said a lady, closely wrapped in a black mantilla, who had been standing beside me for a while and was now on the point of entering a carriage. The voice sent a thrill through my heart—the well-known side-glance again exercised its old spell, and I was again as in a dream when I found myself beside Mademoiselle Laurence in a cosy, warm carriage. We did not speak. We could not have understood each other even if we had, for the carriage rattled noisily through the streets of Paris, for a long time, till it stopped at last before a great gateway.

Servants in resplendent livery lighted our way up the steps and through a suite of rooms. A lady's maid met us with a sleepy face, and stammering many excuses, said only the red room had a fire in it. Motioning to the woman to leave, Mademoiselle Laurence said with a laugh, "Chance has brought you far this evening, for only my bedroom is heated. . . ."

In this bedroom, in which we soon found ourselves alone, a good fire blazed, which was all the more pleasant since the room was of immense size and height. This large bedroom, which rather deserved to be called a sleeping hall, had a strangely desolate appearance. Furniture and decorations all bore the imprint of an age whose brilliance was now faded and whose distinction seems to us so hollow that its relics waken in us a feeling of dislike, if not a secret smile. I speak of the time of the Empire, of the period of the golden eagle, high-flying plumes, Greek coiffures, of glory, military masses, official immortality conferred by the *Moniteur*, continental coffee prepared from chicory, bad sugar made from beet-root, and of princes and dukes made from nothing at all. But it had its charm—that age of pathetic materialism. . . . Talma declaimed, Gros painted, Bigottini danced, Maury preached, Rovigo had the police, the Emperor read Ossian, Pauline Borghese had herself chiselled as Venus, and stark naked at that, for the room was well heated like that in which I found myself now with Mademoiselle Laurence.

We sat by the fire chatting familiarly. She told me with a sigh that she was married to a Bonapartist hero, who regaled her every evening at bed-time with a description of one of his exploits. A few days ago, before going away, he had fought for her the battle of Jena. He was very ill and was not likely to survive the Russian campaign. When I asked her how long her father had been dead, she laughed, and confessed that she had never known a father, and that her so-called mother had never been married.

"Not married!" I cried. "Why, I saw her myself in London in deep mourning for her departed husband!"

"Oh," Mademoiselle Laurence replied, "for twelve years she wore mourning to excite people's compassion as a poor widow, and also to decoy some marriageable simpleton. She hoped to reach the haven of matrimony more quickly under the black flag. But death took pity on her, and she died of a hemorrhage. I never loved her; for she gave me many beatings and little food. I would have starved to death if Monsieur Turlutu had not often given me a piece of bread on the sly. But the dwarf wished that I marry him in return; and when his hopes were disappointed, he made common cause with my mother— I say 'mother' only from habit—and both tormented me cruelly. They always said that I was a useless creature, that the learned dog was worth a thousand times more than I with my horrible dancing. They praised the dog at my expense, extolled him to the skies, fondled him, and gave him cake, but I only got the crumbs. They said the dog was their mainstay; he delighted the public, who were not at all interested in me, that the dog had to support me by his work; that I was eating the bread of charity earned by the dog. Damn that dog!"

"Oh, you need curse him no longer," I interrupted her passionate words. "He is dead. I saw him die—"

"The beast is done for?" Mademoiselle Laurence cried, flushing with joy.

"And the dwarf, too, is dead," I added.

"Monsieur Turlutu?" she cried, also with joy. But the happy expression gradually died from her face, and with a milder, almost melancholy tone she said, "Poor Turlutu!"

When I told her that on his death-bed the dwarf had complained of her bitterly, she broke into violent protestations and assured me over and over again that she had always intended to provide for the dwarf as well as possible, and that she had offered him a pension if he he would agree to live quietly and modestly somewhere in the country. "But he was ambitious," Laurence continued, "and insisted on staying in Paris, and even on living in my house. In this way he thought he could renew his former connections in the Faubourg Saint-Germain with my help and resume his former brilliant place in society. When I flatly refused, he called me a cursed specter, a vampire, a child of death. . . ."

Mademoiselle Laurence suddenly stopped, shuddered, and said at last with a deep sigh, "Oh, I wish they had left me lying in the grave with my mother!"

When I pressed her to explain these mysterious words, she burst into tears, and trembling and sobbing she confessed that the woman in mourning who played the drum and who professed to be her mother had once told her that the strange rumor concerning her birth was no fable. "For in the town in which we lived," Laurence went on, "I was always called the Child of Death. The old crones maintained I was actually the daughter of a count of that place, who constantly ill-treated his wife, and when she died, gave her a magnificent burial. She was then near her confinement, and only apparently dead. Grave-yard thieves, tempted by her lavish funeral attire, broke into her grave and found her alive and in childbirth. She died immediately thereafter, and the thieves laid her body again in the grave, carried off the child, and entrusted her to their 'fence'— the mistress of the great ventriloquist. This poor child, who had been buried before it was born, was everywhere called the Child of Death. Oh, you cannot understand how much I suffered as a little girl when they called me by this name. While the great ventriloquist was alive, whenever he was discontented with me, he would always cry, 'Cursed Child of Death, I wish you had never been taken from the grave.' Skilful ventriloquist that he was, he could so modulate his voice that it seemed to come out of the earth, and he tried to make me believe that it was the voice of my mother telling me her story. He knew that horrible story well enough, for he had been the valet of the count, my father. He took a cruel delight in watching the horrible fright which I experienced on hearing words which seemed to come from the earth. These words told of dreadful things. I could not altogether understand them and gradually forgot them—but when I danced, they came back vividly to my mind. Yes, when I dance, strange memories possess me; I forget myself and become quite another person, tormented by all his sorrows and secrets; but as soon as I stop, everything vanishes from my mind."

While Laurence spoke, slowly and as if questioning, she stood before me at the fireplace where the fire burned ever more agreeably. I sat in the easy chair, in which her husband probably sat when he related his battles before going to bed at night. Laurence looked at me with her large eyes as if she were asking my advice. She nodded her head in such a sad, reflective way that I was filled with a noble, sweet compassion. She was so slender, so young, so beautiful, this lily sprung from the grave, this daughter of death, this specter with the face of an angel and the body of a dancing girl!

I don't know how it happened. Perhaps it was the influence of the easy chair in which I sat; but all at once it seemed to me as if I were the old general who had the day before been describing the battle of Jena; and as if I had to continue the story, I said, "After the battle of Jena, within a few weeks, all the Prussian fortresses yielded almost without a blow. Magdeburg was the first to surrender. It was the strongest fortress, and had three hundred guns. Wasn't that disgraceful?"

Mademoiselle Laurence allowed me to say no more. Her sadness vanished from her lovely face. She laughed like a child, and cried, "Yes, that was disgraceful—more than disgraceful! If I were a fortress and had three hundred guns, I would never surrender!"

But Mademoiselle was no fortress, and did not have three hundred guns—

IT WAS A VERY MAGNIFICENT BED. The feet, as in all the beds of the Empire, consisted of caryatids and sphinxes, and the canopy gleamed with richly gilded ornaments, with golden eagles billing like turtle-doves—perhaps a symbol of love under the Empire. The hangings of the bed were of red silk, and as the flames of the fireplace shone through them, Laurence and I were bathed in a fiery red light, and it seemed to me as if I were the god Pluto amid the flames of hell, holding sleeping Proserpine in his arms. She was asleep, and I studied her lovely face in this position, seeking in her features for a clue to the attraction which my soul felt for her. What was the meaning of this woman? What significance lurked behind the symbolism of that beautiful form?

Tell me, is it not folly to wish to penetrate the inner meaning of strange phenomena outside us, when we cannot solve the riddles residing within our own souls? Why, we are not even sure that these outside phenomena really exist! How often we are unable to distinguish reality from mere dream appearances! Was it a shape of my fancy or was it horrible reality which I saw and heard that night? I do not know. I only remember that while the wildest thoughts coursed through my heart, I heard a singular sound in my ears. It was a crazy melody, peculiarly soft. It seemed very familiar to me, and at last I distinguished the tones of a triangle and a drum. The music whirred and hummed and seemed to come from afar; and yet when I looked up, I saw near me, in the middle of the room, a well-known spectacle. It was Monsieur Turlutu the dwarf, who played the triangle; and Madame the Mother was beating the great drum; while the learned dog pawed about on the floor, as if searching for his wooden letters. The dog appeared to move with difficulty, and his skin was spotted with blood. Madame the Mother still wore black mourning, but her belly was no longer so comically protuberant—actually it hung down, and her face was no longer red, but pale. The dwarf, who still wore the embroidered coat of an old French marquis and a powdered wig, seemed to have grown somewhat taller, perhaps because he was so frightfully thin. He was again displaying his skill in fencing and was rattling out his old boasts, but he spoke softly, so that I was unable to understand a word, and only from the movements of his lips did I guess that he was again crowing like a cock.

While this ridiculous, distorted nightmare moved—like a magic lantern—before my eyes with uncanny haste, I felt that Mademoiselle Laurence was breathing more uneasily. A cold shudder froze her whole body, and her beautiful limbs writhed convulsively as if in unbearable agony. At last, however, she glided from my arms, supple as an eel, and suddenly stood in the middle of the room, and began to dance, while the mother with her drum and the dwarf with the triangle made soft, muffled music. She danced as she had done on Waterloo Bridge and in the squares of London. There was the same mysterious pantomime, the same impulsive, passionate leaps, the same Bacchante-like throwing back of her head, often the same posture of inclining to the ground as if she were listening to voices below; then the old, familiar shudder, the pallor, the frozen stillness, and again the intent listening to the ground. Again she rubbed her hands as if she were washing them. Finally she seemed again to throw her intense, sorrowful, imploring glance toward me. . . . But it was only in the features of her deathly pale face that I recognized that glance; for her eyes were closed. The music died out. The mother with her drum, and the dwarf gradually faded, dissolved like a mist, and at last vanished altogether. But Mademoiselle Laurence still stood before me and danced with closed eyes. This dance with eyes closed, in the night and in the silent room, gave the beautiful creature so spectral an air, that I became uneasy and shuddered. And I was heartily glad when she finished her dance.

To tell the truth, this scene was not pleasant. But we become accustomed to everything. And it is possible that the unearthly mystery of this woman lent her a peculiar charm and that a fearful sort of tenderness mingled with my feelings. At any rate, after some weeks I was no longer amazed when I heard the sound of drum and triangle in the middle of the night, and my dear Laurence suddenly leaped up and danced solo with closed eyes. Her husband, the old Bonapartist, commanded in the neighborhood of Paris, and his duties did not allow him to spend his days in the city. Of course, he became my most intimate friend, and he wept copiously when the day came to bid me farewell. He was travelling with his wife to Sicily. And I have never seen either of them again.

𝕰 My Friend Hinrich Kitzler

It's a queer thing, this writing business. One man has luck in practising it, and another has none. But perhaps the worst mischance of all befell my poor friend Hinrich Kitzler, Master of Arts in Göttingen. There is not a man there so learned, so rich in ideas, so industrious as this friend of mine; and yet, to this very day no book by him has appeared at the Leipzig fair. Old Stiefel, in the library, always smiled when Hinrich Kitzler asked him for a book, which he needed for a work he was "just composing." It will be a long time a-writing, murmured old Stiefel, while he climbed up the ladder. Even the scullery girls laughed when they were sent to fetch books from the library "for Kitzler." The man was generally considered an ass, but at bottom he was only an honest man. No one knew the real reason why no book by him was ever published, and only by chance did I discover it. One midnight I went to his room to light my lamp, for his room adjoined mine. He had just completed his great work on the "Excellence of Christianity." But he seemed nowise pleased, and gazed at his manuscript with melancholy.

"Now, at last," I remarked, "your name will shine among the published books in the catalogues of the Leipzig Fair."

"Ah, no," he sighed from the depths. "This book too must be burned like the others. . . ."

Then he confided to me his terrible secret, and indeed, the poor Master of Arts had the worst luck whenever he wrote a book. For after he had fully developed all the arguments for the subject in hand, he felt in duty bound to cite all objections which an opponent might adduce. Therefore he dug out with care all the most subtle arguments of the opposing point of view, and as these unconsciously took root, it came to pass that the opinions of the poor author gradually changed, and he came to conclusions directly opposite to those in the book. He was then honorable enough (as certainly every French writer would be under similar circumstances) to sacrifice his literary laurels on the altar of truth; that is, he threw the manuscript into the fire. That is why he sighed so deeply after having proved the excellence of Christianity.

"I have," he said sorowfully, "excerpted twenty baskets-full of quotations from the Church Fathers. I have sat hunched over my study table whole nights long reading the *Acta Sanctorum*, while in your rooms punch was being drunk and the *Landesvater* was being sung. Instead of buying myself a meerschaum pipe, I paid Vandenhoeck & Ruprecht thirty-eight thalers, earned with the sweat of my brow, for recent theological works, which I needed for my work. And so I slaved like a dog for two years, for two precious years of my life. . . . And all to make a laughing-stock of myself . . . only to cast down my eyes like some unmasked braggart, when Church Councillor Planck's wife asks me, 'And when will your *Excellence of Christianity* appear?'

"Alas, the book is ready," the poor man continued, "and the public would even like it, for I have exalted in it the victory of Christianity over Heathendom, and I have proved that thereby Truth and Reason have prevailed over Hypocrisy and Folly. But unhappy man that I am, deep down in my heart I feel . . .'"

"Silence!" I cried with righteous indignation. "Do not dare, oh deluded one, to besmirch the sublime and drag the glorious in the mire. Even if you would deny the miracles of the Gospels, still you cannot deny that its victory was itself a miracle. A little troop of defenseless men forced their way into the great Roman world, defying both its myrmidons and its sages, and triumphed by the Word alone. But what a Word! The rotting body of paganism shook and crumbled before the words of these foreign men and women, who proclaimed a new kingdom of heaven and feared nothing on this old earth, not the claws of wild beasts nor the wrath of even wilder men, nor fire nor sword, for they were themselves fire and sword, fire and sword of God. That sword trimmed away the dead leaves and dry twigs from the tree of life and thereby cured it of gnawing decay; that flame recalled to life the frozen trunk, so that fresh leaves and fragrant blossoms sprouted anew. . . . It is the most awful and sublime manifestation in the history of the world—this first appearance of Christianity, its battles and complete triumph."

I uttered these words all the more grandly because I had that evening drunk a good deal of Eimbecker beer, for which reason my voice sounded more resonant.

Hinrich Kitzler was by no means disconcerted by these words, and with an ironic yet painful smile he said, "Dear soul! Do not put yourself out needlessly. All that you have just said, I have expounded in this manuscript far better and more thoroughly. In it I have depicted in the most striking colors the depraved state of the heathen world, and I dare flatter myself that the bold strokes of my brush recall the best that the Fathers of the Church have said. I have shown how debauched the Greeks and Romans became by the bad example of those gods, who, to judge by the infamies attributed to them, would hardly be worthy of being classed as men. I have minced no words in declaring that under the Royal Criminal Law of Hanover even Jupiter, the chief of the gods, deserved a hundred times the penitentiary, if not the gallows. On the other hand, I have appropriately paraphrased the moral axioms of the Gospels, and have shown how the first Christians, after the example of their divine prototype, despite the scorn and persecution which they incurred, taught and practised only the most perfect moral purity. The most beautiful passage of my work is the one in which I depict, as if inspired, youthful Christianity, like a little David, entering the lists with ancient paganism and slaying the great Goliath. But alas! that duel has since appeared to me in a very strange light. Alas! all love and joy in my apology dried up in my breast when I vividly considered how an opponent might depict the triumph of Christianity! Unfortunately, the works of several recent authors fell into my hands, Edward Gibbon,[7] for example, who did not express themselves too favorably concerning this triumph, and did not appear especially edified by the fact that the Christians, when the spiritual sword and the spiritual flame proved inadequate, resorted to the temporal sword and the temporal fire. Yes, I must confess there finally came over me an awful compassion for the remains of heathenism, for those beautiful temples and statues; for they no longer belonged to the religion which was dead long, long before the birth of Christ, but to Art, which lives forever. And tears came to my eyes when I happened one day to read in the library the *Defense of the Temples* in which the ancient Greek Libanius most touchingly adjured the pious barbarians to spare those precious masterpieces with which the creative genius of the Greeks had adorned the world. In vain! Those monuments of the spring-tide of mankind, which can never return and which could only blossom once, perished irretrievably through the gloomy destructive zeal of the Christians. . . .

"No," continued the M.A. "I will not contribute to such a sacrilege by publishing this work. No, that I will never do. And to you, you shattered statues of beauty—to you, *manes* of the dead gods, and to you who are now only lovely phantoms in the shadow-land of poetry, to you I sacrifice this book!"

Saying this, Hinrich Kitzler threw his manuscript into the fireplace, and of the *Excellence of Christianity* nothing remained save the grey ashes.

࿇ *The Spell of Antiquity*

THERE WAS A TIME when I faithfully kissed the hand of every Capuchin whom I met in the street. I was a child, and my father calmly let me do it, knowing well that my lips would not always be content with Capuchin flesh. And indeed, I grew up and kissed beautiful women. . . . But sometimes they gazed at me with such pallid sorrow in their eyes that I was terrified in the arms of joy. . . . Here was hidden misery which no one saw and which every one suffered; and I often reflected on it. And I have also wondered whether self-denial and abstinence were really preferable to all the pleasures of life; and whether those people who, here on earth, are content with thistles, would on that account be treated more liberally with pineapples when they reached heaven. Not at all. He who eats thistles is an ass, and he who receives blows, keeps them. . . .

However, I am not at liberty to speak plainly about everything on which I reflected, and even less to impart the results of my reflections. Must I too go down to my grave with sealed lips, like so many others?

But may I be permitted to cite a few commonplace facts, so as to impart some reason or at least some semblance of it to the fantasies which I am here compiling? These facts refer to the victory of Christianity over paganism. I am not at all of the opinion of my friend Kitzler that the iconoclasm of the first Christians is so severely to be censured. They could not and dared not spare the old temples and statues, for within them still lived the old Greek joy of life which appeared to the Christians as sheer diabolism. In these temples he saw not merely the objects of a strange cult, and vain heresy devoid of all reality, but also the citadels of actual demons; and the gods themselves, whom the statues represented, he endowed with actual existence—they were devils. When the first Christians refused to kneel and sacrifice before the images of the gods and were for that reason denounced and haled to court, they always answered that they were forbidden to worship demons. They suffered martyrdom rather than adore Jupiter the devil, the she-devil Diana, and the arch-fiend Venus.

Poor Greek philosophers! They could never understand this contradiction, just as they subsequently never understood that in their polemics with the Christians they had to defend not the old, dead doctrines but the living reality. For the point was not to prove the deeper meaning of mythology through neo-Platonic subtleties, to infuse new symbolic life-blood into the dead gods, and day in and day out to torture themselves by trying to refute the crude, material objections of the early Christian Fathers, who scoffed at the moral character of the gods in an almost Voltairean fashion.—The point in question was to defend Hellenism itself, or the Greek way of feeling and thinking, and to check the spread of Judaism, or of Jewish ideas and sentiments. The real question was whether the dismal, emaciated, ascetic, over-spiritual Judaism of the Nazarenes should rule the world, or Hellenic joyousness, love of beauty, and opulent joy of living?

Those beautiful gods were no longer the main issue, no one any longer believed in the ambrosial dwellers of Olympus. In the temples, at festivals and mysteries, people amused themselves like gods. They decked their houses with flowers; there were lovely festive dances; they reclined on couches at joyous banquets—if not for still sweeter pleasures.

All this joy, all this gay laughter has long been silenced, and in the ruins of the ancient temples the old Greek deities still dwell, but they have lost their power through the victory of Christ, and now they are mere devils hiding by day, among owls and toads, in the gloomy ruins of their one-time magnificence, but they arise at night, in all their graceful loveliness, and bedevil and lure some heedless wanderer or some reckless youth.

The most wonderful legends relate to this popular belief, and our later poets have drawn from this source themes for their most beautiful songs. Italy is generally the scene selected, and the hero is some German knight, who, because of his youthful inexperience or his fine figure, is ensnared by beautiful fiends with their enchanting craft. Thus he saunters forth one beautiful autumn day, with his solitary fancies, thinking perhaps of his native oak-forests and the blonde maiden whom he left behind—the fickle scapegrace! But all at once he stands before a marble statue at the sight of which he stops with a shock. It may be the Goddess of Beauty, and he regards her face to face, and the heart of the young barbarian is secretly overpowered by the ancient sorcery. What can this mean? He has never seen such graceful limbs before; he suspects that in this marble there is livelier life than he ever found in the red cheeks and lips and all the rosy fleshiness of his fair countrywomen. Those white eyes gaze at him so voluptuously, yet with such terrifying sorrow, that his heart swells with love and pity—pity and love. And now he often wanders among the old ruins, and his fellows wonder why they now so seldom see him at drinking-bouts and knightly sports. There are strange tales afoot about his doings among the ancient heathen ruins. Then one morning he bursts into the inn with a distorted face, pays his reckoning, buckles his knapsack, and hastens over the Alps. What has happened to him?

It chanced one day that he strolled later than usual, after the sun had set, to his beloved ruin. But in the gathering dusk he could not find the place where he was accustomed to gaze for hours at the statue of the beautiful goddess. After wandering about for a long time, he suddenly found himself about midnight before a villa which he had never seen before and he was not a little amazed when servants with torches came forth and, in the name of their mistress, offered him lodging for the night. How great was his astonishment, when, on entering a vast and brilliantly lighted hall, he beheld a lady walking to and fro alone, who, in form and feature, bore the most striking resemblance to the beautiful statue of his desire. Yes, her resemblance to the marble was all the greater because she was clad in a dazzling white garb, and her face was unusually pale. When the knight advanced toward her, with courtly reverence, she gazed at him long and in silence, and at last asked him with a smile whether he was hungry. And though the heart of the knight leaped within him for love, he still had a German stomach. After hours of wandering he was in need of nourishment, and he gladly allowed the fair lady to lead him to the dining hall. She took him graciously by the hand, and he followed her through lofty echoing chambers, which in spite of their splendor, seemed strangely desolate. The girandoles cast a wan spectral light on the walls, whose rich frescoes represented various pagan tales of love, such as those of Paris and Helen, Diana and Endymion, Calypso and Ulysses. The huge and strange flowers which stood in marble vases along the windows were uncannily luxuriant and exhaled a corpse-like, intoxicating odor. And the wind sighed in the chimney like a dying man. At last, in the dining room, the beautiful lady sat opposite the knight, filled his cup, and with a smile offered him the choicest delicacies. Many things appeared strange to the knight during the repast. When he asked for salt, an almost hideous displeasure came over the pale features of the beautiful lady, nor was it till he had several times repeated his request that, visibly irked, she finally bade her servants bring the salt-cellar; and they placed it with trembling hands on the table, spilling half its contents. However, the good wine, which glowed like fire in the throat of the knight, allayed the secret terror which often came over him. Yes, he even became confiding and amorous, and when the beautiful lady asked whether he knew what love was, he replied with burning kisses till, drunk with passion, and perhaps also with the sweet wine, he sank to sleep on the bosom of his tender hostess. Wild and strange dreams surged through his mind; horrid nocturnal visions, such as beset us in the half-awake state of a delirium. Now he seemed to behold his old grandmother as she sat at home in her arm-chair, praying with trembling lips. Now he heard a mocking titter which came from the great bats which fluttered around him with huge torches in their claws; and when he looked more closely, it seemed to him that they were the servants who had waited on him at table. And last of all, he dreamed that his fair hostess had changed to a hideous monster and he himself, in reckless terror of death, had drawn his sword and cut off her head.

When the knight awoke, it was late in the morning, and the sun was high in heaven. But instead of the splendid villa in which he thought he had passed the night, he found himself amid the well-known ruins and he saw with horror that the beautiful statue which he so dearly loved had fallen from its pedestal and that its severed head lay at his feet.

Of a similar character is the legend of the young knight who once, while playing ball with some friends, found that the ring of his finger was in the way, drew it off, and put it on the finger of a marble statue for safekeeping. When the game was over, and he returned to the statue, which was that of a heathen goddess, he saw with dismay that the marble finger on which he had placed the ring was no longer straight as before, but was bent so that he could not reclaim the ring without breaking the hand,—from which act he was restrained by a strange feeling of sympathy. He ran to tell his companions of this strange wonder, bidding them see it with their own eyes; but when he returned with them, the marble statue held out the finger straight as before, and the ring was gone.

Some time thereafter, the knight determined to enter the holy state of matrimony, and he celebrated his nuptials. But on the bridal night, when he was ready to retire, a woman, in form and face like the statue, came to him and declared that by putting his ring on her finger he was betrothed to her and was her rightful spouse. In vain did the knight oppose this claim; but whenever he sought to approach his bride, the heathen woman interposed herself between them, so that he was compelled to forego the marital joys. And this recurred the next night, and thereafter, and the knight was troubled indeed. No one knew how to help him; even the most pious shrugged their shoulders. At last he heard of a priest named Palumnus, who had often shown himself potent in defeating heathenish witchcraft. But this man was very loath to aid him in this trouble, declaring that he would expose himself to great danger by so doing. At last, however, he was prevailed upon, and wrote down sundry odd characters on a parchment and advised the knight to post himself at midnight on a certain cross-road near Rome. There all sorts of strange apparitions would pass by him; but he was warned not to be in the least frightened by anything he might see or hear, but to bide his time quietly. Only when he should descry the woman on whose finger he had placed the ring, was he to approach her and give her the inscribed parchment. The knight did as he was bid, but it was not without trepidation that he stood at midnight on the designated crossroads and watched the spectral procession. There were in it pale men and women, magnificently arrayed in festive garments of old pagan times; some wore golden crowns, others laurel wreaths on their heads, which were bowed in sorrow. All kinds of silver utensils, drinking goblets and such vessels as belong to the service of the temple were borne past in fearful haste. In the throng were seen huge steers with gilded horns and hung with garlands; and finally, on a lofty triumphal chariot, resplendent in purple and crowned with roses, appeared a tall, wonderfully beautiful goddess. The knight advanced toward her, and gave her the parchment of the priest Palumnus, for he recognized in her the statue that possessed his ring. And when the beautiful woman saw the writing on the parchment, she raised her hands to heaven as if in agony, and burst into tears and lamentations, and she cried with despair: "Oh, cruel priest Palumnus, thou art not yet satisfied with the suffering thou hast inflicted on us. But thy persecutions will soon come to an end, cruel priest Palumnus!" With these words she gave the knight his ring, and on the very next night he consummated his union without hindrance. But on the third day thereafter the priest Palumnus died.

ঽ঩ *The Little Harpist*

WHEN I RETURNED TO THE LOCANDA DELL' GRANDE EUROPA, where I had ordered a good *pranzo*, I was of so melancholy a frame of mind that I could eat nothing—and that is saying a great deal. I sat down at the door of the neighboring *bottega*, refreshed myself with a sherbet, and admonished myself "Wayward heart! Here you are in Italy! Why don't you trill? Is it that the old German sorrows, those little serpents which have deeply burrowed into you, have come to Italy with you, and are now so jubilant that their rejoicing arouses in you that picturesque grief that stings and writhes and hisses so strangely within you? And why should not the old sorrows rejoice? Here in

Italy everything is so beautiful. In this spot even sorrow itself is lovely. Sighs sound much more romantic in these old ruined marble palaces than in our trim little brick houses. It is more voluptuous to weep under these laurel trees than under our sullen jagged firs; and it is sweeter to long for the imaginary cloud-pictures of the deep blue Italian skies, than for the ashen-grey, work-a-day German heaven, where even the clouds grimace at you like Philistines and yawn down at you in boredom! Rest quietly in my bosom, you sorrows! Nowhere else will you find so goodly a dwelling place! You are dear and precious to me, and none knows better than I how to cherish you and care for you; and I confess to you, you give me pleasure. And what is pleasure? Pleasure is nothing but delicious pain."

I think that the music, which without my noticing it had begun to play in front of the *bottega* and had attracted a crowd of listeners, was a dramatic accompaniment to my monologue. It was an odd trio, consisting of two men, and a young girl who played the harp. One of the men was clad in a winter coat of white sheepskin. He was stocky, and had a fat, red face of a bandit, glowing against a background of black hair and beard, like a threatening comet. Between his legs he held an enormous bass fiddle, which he attacked with as much vehemence as if he had laid hold of some unfortunate traveller in the Abruzzi and were slashing at his throat. The other was a tall, haggard old man, whose decrepit bones shuffled about in worn, black garments, and whose snow-white hair presented a painful contrast to his comic songs and silly capers. It is sad enough when an old man is forced by sheer necessity to sell the respect due his years, and sets out to play the fool, but it is far sadder when he does this in the presence and in the company of his own child.

The young girl was the daughter of the old buffoon. She accompanied the degrading jests of her grey-haired father on the harp. Sometimes she put the harp aside, and sang a comic duet with him, in which he took the part of an amorous old fop, and she of his coy young love. The girl was scarcely past her childhood, and yet it seemed as though she had become a woman, and not a very modest one at that, before she had reached girlhood. Hence the pallid cheeks and the drawn wistful expression of the beautiful face, whose proud-set features seemed to disdain any suggestion of pity. Hence the secret sorrow of her eyes, that shone so challengingly from beneath their black triumphal arches. Hence the deep pathetic sounds that contrasted so strangely with the pretty laughing lips which uttered

them; hence the sickly languor of the delicate limbs, outlined so
sharply against the fluttering short and scanty silken frock. Brilliantly
colored satin ribbons bedecked an antiquated straw hat. Her breast
was symbolically adorned with a half-blown rosebud, which appeared to have been forced open rather than to have unfolded naturally within its green sheath. Nevertheless, there was an inexpressible
charm which hovered over the unfortunate girl, this spring already
blighted by the touch of death—a grace evident in every expression,
movement, and accent, which did not vanish even when she flaunted
her body and with ironic lasciviousness came tripping toward her
old father, who shuffled toward her, with similar wantonness, and
protruded his belly. The more shameless her gestures, the deeper
the pity I felt for her. And when her song rose soft and sweet as
though entreating pardon, the little serpents in my breast shouted
exultantly and bit their tails for joy. The rose, too, seemed to have
the air of a suppliant. Once I even saw it tremble and grow pale,
but at the same moment the girl laughed and pierced the air with a
sharp trill, the old man bleated more amorously, and red comet-face
subjected the bass fiddle to such tortures that it gave forth wild
and grotesque sounds, and the audience applauded even more
frantically.

IT WAS A TRUE ITALIAN PIECE OF MUSIC, from some favorite *opera-
buffa*, a species which allows free play to the comic vein, and free
rein to all its droll flights, crazy sentimentality, laughing sorrows, and
life-afflicted death-raptures. It was completely in the manner of
Rossini, as best manifested in the *Barber of Seville*.

The detractors of Italian music, who hurl condemnations at this
species too, will some day, when they are in hell, not fail to meet their
well deserved punishment and hear nothing but the fugues of Sebastian Bach, through all eternity. I pity many of my colleagues, for
instance, Rellstab [8] who certainly cannot escape his doom, unless
he is converted to Rossini before he dies. Rossini, *divino maestro*,
Helios of Italy, you have spread your sonorous rays throughout
the world! Forgive my poor countrymen who blaspheme your
name on foolscap and blotters. But I rejoice in your golden harmonies,
your brilliant melodies, your sparkling butterfly-dreams that hover
around me so gently and press kisses on my soul as with the lips of the
Graces! Oh, *divino maestro*, forgive my poor countrymen who do
not understand your depths, because you have covered them with

roses. In their eyes you lack gravity and substance, because you flit so lightly on god-like wings!

As a matter of fact, to love Italian music, and through love to understand it, you must see the Italian people with your own eyes, their sky, their character, their manners, sorrows, and joys. In short, you must know their entire history from Romulus, who founded the Holy Roman Empire, to the present, when it fell to pieces under Romulus Augustulus II.

Poor enslaved Italy is forbidden to speak; and only through music can she express the feelings in her heart. All her hatred of foreign domination, her passion for freedom, her rage at her impotence, her grief at the memory of past glories, as well as her whispered hopes, her patience, her sighs for help—all are embodied in melodies in which the most grotesque life-intoxication merges with elegiac resignation, as in those pantomimes which leap from the most flattering caresses to the most ominous fury.

This is the esoteric meaning of *opera buffa*. The exoteric sentinel, in whose presence they are sung and performed, never suspects the meaning of these merry love stories, love pangs, and coquetries in which the Italian conceals his rabid thoughts of freedom, just as Harmodious and Aristogiton covered their daggers with a myrtle wreath.

"That's an idiotic performance, on my soul!" says the exoteric guard; and it is well that he observes nothing. For otherwise, the Impresario, together with the Prima Donna and the Primo Uomo would soon tread the boards—of a jail; a commission of inquiry would be established; all the trills endangering the security of state, all revolutionary *fioriture* would be entered in a protocol; a whole crowd of harlequins would be implicated in the vast ramifications of treasonable conspiracies and would be arrested—as well as Tartaglia, Brighella, and even old, circumspect Pantaloon.[9] The papers of the Doctor of Bologna would be impounded—his cackling would make him even more suspect—and Columbine would weep her eyes red over these family misfortunes. I do not think, however, that these misfortunes will befall the good people; at least not for a while, for the Italian demagogue is more wily than the poor German one. The latter, with similar ideas, disguised himself like a black fool in a black fool's cap, but he looked so outrageously mournful, and cut such dangerous figures with his practised fool's capers, which he called gymnastics, and wore such a serious mien, that the government finally became alarmed and put him under lock and key.

THE LITTLE HARPIST HAD EVIDENTLY NOTICED that while she was singing and playing, I often looked at the rose on her breast. Later, when I dropped a gold piece, not too small, into her plate, she smiled slyly, and asked stealthily if I would like to have her rose.

Now I am the most courteous man alive, and not for the world would I offend a rose, even if it is one that has lost something of its sweetness. And suppose, I said to myself, it is no longer quite fresh, and no longer has the odor of virtue, like, for example, the Rose of Sharon, what does it matter to me, since I already have the sniffles? And after all, it is only human beings who are so finicky. The butterfly does not ask the rose, "Have you been kissed by someone else?" And the rose does not ask, "Have you already fluttered around another flower?" At this point, night fell, and at night, I thought to myself, all flowers are grey, the most sinful rose and the most virtuous parsley. In short, without too much hesitation, I said to the little harpist, "Si, Signora—"

Think no evil, dear reader. It had grown dark, and the clear, pure stars looked down into my heart. In my heart the memory of the dead Maria vibrated. I thought once more of that night when I stood by the bed in which lay the beautiful, pale body, with those soft, silent lips. I remember the strange look that the old woman gave me, whose duty it was to watch by the corpse, as she confided her charge to me for several hours. I thought once more of the violets that stood in a jar on the table and whose scent was so strange; I shuddered again as I once did when doubt crossed my mind whether it was in truth a gust of wind that extinguished the lamp. Had there been no third person in that room?

I WENT TO BED EARLY and fell asleep almost immediately, losing myself in bewildering dreams.

I dreamt myself younger by a few hours. I arrived once more in Trento. I was again astonished, this time all the more so since flowers and not men and women were promenading up and down the streets. Glowing carnations wandered by, fanning themselves languorously,—coquetting balsams, hyacinths with pretty, empty heads; behind them came a crowd of mustachioed narcissi and loutish larkspurs. At a corner, two Easter daisies were quarrelling. From the window of an old sickly-looking house peeped a gilliflower, in gaudy hues, and behind her resounded the sweet-scented voice of the violet. On the balcony of the great palace in the market place were assembled all the nobility, the highest aristocracy, that is, those lilies which neither toil nor spin, and who think themselves as magnificent as King Solomon in all his glory. I thought I also saw the stout fruit-vendor there; yet when I looked more closely, it was only an old buttercup, who immediately growled at me, "What do you want, you half-blown thistle, you sour cucumber, you vulgar flower with only one stamen? I will water you directly!"

Panic-stricken, I hastened into the cathedral, and almost ran over a lame pansy, whose prayer-book was being carried by a little daisy. But in the cathedral it was really delightful. In the long rows sat tulips of every color, bowing their heads devoutly. In the confessional sat a black radish, and before him knelt a flower, whose face was hidden from sight. Nevertheless, she exhaled a perfume so uncannily familiar, that with a shudder I thought of the night-violets in the room in which lay my dead Maria.

As I left the cathedral, I met a funeral procession of roses, with black crêpe and white handkerchiefs, and, alas! on the bier lay the prematurely blown rose I had seen on the bosom of the little harpist. She seemed even more charming, but as pale as chalk—a white rose-corpse. The coffin was set down in a little chapel and nothing was heard but sobbing and weeping. At last an old poppy stepped forward and delivered a long eulogy, during which he jabbered a great deal about the virtues of the departed one, about this our earthly vale of tears, a future life, Faith, Hope and Charity,—all in the same nasal, sing-song voice—an oration liberally watered with tears, but so long-winded and dreary, that from sheer boredom I awoke.

❧ An Italian Interlude

SIGNORA LETITIA, A YOUNG ROSE OF FIFTY SUMMERS, lay in bed, trilling and prattling with her two gallants, one of whom sat upon a footstool, while the other reclined in a great arm-chair and played the guitar. From an adjoining room were wafted scraps of a sweet song or far sweeter laughter. With a certain cheap irony, which he occasionally assumed, the Marquis presented me to the Signora and the two gentlemen, remarking that I was the same Johann Heinrich Heine, Doctor Juris, who was now celebrated in German legal literature. Unfortunately, one of the gentlemen was a professor of Bologna, and a jurist at that, although his fat, rotund belly seemed to qualify him rather for spherical trigonometry. Somewhat put out, I replied that I did not write under my own name, but under that of Jarke [10]—a statement made from sheer modesty—as the name which occurred to me was that of one of the most repulsive insects in our legal literature. The gentleman from Bologna regretted that he had never heard this distinguished name—which is probably true of you too, dear reader—but he had no doubt that its radiance would soon spread over the whole world. With this he leaned back in his chair, struck a few chords on his guitar, and began singing from *Axur:* [11]

> "All powerful Brahma!
> Oh, let this stammer
> Of innocence please thee,
> The stammer, the stammer—"

Like a playful, delicious echo of a nightingale, a similar air was warbled in the adjoining room. Meanwhile Signora Letitia was trilling in her most delicate soprano:

> "For thee alone this cheek doth glow
> For thee alone these pulses beat,
> With love's full sweet doth overflow
> My heart, rising to thee."

And in an obese, prosaic voice, she added, "Bartolo, hand me the spittoon."

Then Bartolo rose from his foot-stool, with his spindly legs, and respectfully presented the somewhat dirty spittoon of blue porcelain.

This second gallant, Gumpelino whispered to me in German, was a celebrated poet whose songs, though written twenty years before, still resounded throughout all Italy, and with their passionate fires of love intoxicated both young and old; but the poet himself was now only a poor, aged man, with dim eyes set in a faded face, sparse white hair on a shaking head, and bleak poverty in his care-worn breast. A poor, old poet like this one, bald and wooden, is like a vine which we see standing withered and leafless in winter on the cold mountainside, shaking in the wind and covered with snow; while the sweet juice which once spurted from it is somewhere else, in far distant lands, warming the hearts of many a reveler and inspiring him to sing its praises. Who knows but that I too—once that winepress of thought, the printing press, has squeezed me dry, and my old, tapped spirit is stored away only in the publishing cellars of Hoffmann and Campe—I too may be sitting as haggard and careworn as poor Bartolo, on a footstool by the bedside of a faded innamorata, and handing her a spittoon at her bidding.

Signora Letitia excused herself for lying in bed, and on her stomach at that, for a swelling on her posterior, induced by overmuch eating of figs, made it impossible for her to lie on her back, like any self-respecting woman. She lay, as a matter of fact, pretty much as does the Sphinx, her head with its high coiffure supported on both arms, between which her bosom heaved like a Red Sea.

"You are German?" she asked.

"I am too honest to deny it, Signora!" I replied in my insignificance.

"Ah, the Germans are honest enough," she sighed. "But what good is it if the people who rob us are honest? They are ruining Italy. My best friends are in prison in Milan, and only slavery—"

"No, no," cried the Marquis. "Do not blame the Germans. We are conquered conquerors, vanquished victors as soon as we come to Italy. And to see you, Signora, to see you and to fall at your feet— that is one and the same thing."—And he spread his yellow silk handkerchief on the floor and knelt down on it and exclaimed, "Here I kneel and worship you in the name of all Germany."

"Christophoro di Gumpelino," sighed the Signora, deeply moved and all aflutter, "arise and embrace me!"

But lest the gracious swain disturb her hair-dress and make-up, she kissed him, not on the glowing lips, but on his noble brow, so that he lowered his face, and its rudder, the nose, steered about in the Red Sea below.

"Signor Bartolo," I cried, "allow me to use the spittoon."

Signor Bartolo smiled sadly. However, he did not speak a word, although he was rated, next to Mezzofanti,[12] the best teacher of elocution in Bologna. We never like to talk, when talking is our profession. He served the Signora as the silent knight, and only on occasions would she call on him to recite the poem, a copy of which he had thrown on to the stage, twenty-five years before, when she made her debut in Bologna as Ariadne. It is possible that in those days he himself was in full bloom and full of fire, perhaps like Dionysus himself, and his Letitia-Ariadne probably rushed into his passionate arms like a bacchante—*Evoë Bacche!* In those days he composed many love-songs, which, as I have said, are still preserved in Italian literature, though the poet himself and his innamorata have long since turned to waste-paper.

For five and twenty years this devotion endured, and I believe that even to his blessed end he will sit on the foot-stool and recite his verses or hand her the spittoon, when asked. The professor of law has been dragging the love-chains of the signora for almost as many years. He courts her as ardently now as at the beginning of the century. He is forced to postpone his university lectures without pity when she requires his company anywhere, and he is still burdened with all the obligations of a genuine *patito*.[13]

The constancy of these two adorers of a long since dilapidated beauty may perhaps be force of habit, perhaps only a kind of tender piety for an old sentiment, perhaps only sentiment itself, now altogether independent of the present condition of its one-time object, which it now regards only with the eyes of memory. Thus in Catholic cities we often observe old people kneeling at street-corners before an image of the Madonna, which is so faded that only a few traces and lines remain—perhaps nothing is left but the niche in which it was painted, and the lamp hanging over it. But the old people who kneel before it devoutly, a rosary in their shaking hands, have been doing so since childhood.—Habit sends them daily to visit the same spot at the very same hour. They do not notice the gradual disappearance of their beloved sacred image. And at last old age brings such dimness of sight, and even blindness, that it makes no difference whether the object of adoration is still visible or not. Those who believe without seeing are certainly happier than the clear-eyed, who immediately perceive every new wrinkle in their madonna's face. There is nothing more horrible than such a phenomenon. There was a time when I believed that a woman's infidelity was the most dreadful of all things, and to give them the most horrible name I could think of, I called them snakes. Alas! now I know that the terrible thing is that they are not all snakes, for snakes shed their old skins every year and emerge fresh and youthful!

I don't know whether either of the ancient Celadons felt the prick of jealousy because the Marquis—or rather, his nose—swam in the aforementioned sea of delight. Bartolo sat calmly on his little bench, his bony legs crossed, and played with the Signora's lap-dog, one of those pretty little creatures peculiar to Bologna, and known among us as "Bolognese." The professor continued his singing, undisturbed, and now and then was drowned out by the jubilant parody which came from the adjoining room in tittering, sweet tones. From time to time he interrupted his sing-song to pose some legal question. When we disagreed, he struck a few, rapid chords on his guitar, and proved his point by strumming texts in support of his arguments. I, on the other hand, always relied for my proof on the authority of my teacher, the great Hugo, who is very famous in Bologna under the name of Ugone, also Ugolino.

"A great man!" the professor exclaimed, and he jangled the strings and sang:

> "The gentle summons of his voice
> Sounds so deeply in my breast,
> Its very pain makes thee rejoice
> With rapture's sweet unrest."

Thibaut,[14] whom the Italians call Tibaldo, is also honored in Bologna; though the writings of these men are less well known than their principal ideas and the rebuttals to them. I found that Gans and Savigny were only names to them. The professor was under the impression that the latter was a learned lady.

"Really?" he said, as I corrected this pardonable error, "not a lady, really! I have been misinformed. Why, I was told that Signor Gans at a ball once invited this lady to a dance, was turned down, and that their literary feud dates from that moment."

"You have really been misinformed. Signor Gans does not dance, if only for the very humanitarian reason that he might cause an earthquake if he did. The invitation to the dance of which you speak is in all probability only an allegory which has been misinterpreted. The historical and philosophical schools may be regarded as dancers, and in this sense one probably imagines a quadrille of Ugone, Tibaldo, Gans, and Savigny. And in this sense perhaps one may say that though Signor Ugone may be the *diable boiteux* of jurisprudence, he still dances as daintily as Lemière, and that Signor Gans has recently attempted such prodigious leaps as may entitle him to be considered the Hoguet of the philosophical school."

"Then Signor Gans," the professor corrected himself, "dances only allegorically, so to speak, metaphorically." And suddenly, without continuing, he again swept the strings of his guitar, and amid the wildest jangling, he sang like mad:

"It is true, his dear, dear name
Is the joy of every heart,
Though the ocean waves be storming,
And the sky be cloudy black,
Still we hear Tarar loud calling
As heaven and earth obeisance make
To the hero's mighty name."

As for Herr Göschen, the professor did not even know of his existence. But this was natural enough, for the fame of the great Göschen had not yet reached Bologna, but only Poggio, which is four German miles away, and where it will have a pleasant sojourn for a while. Göttingen itself is by no means so well known in Bologna as one has a right to expect, if only out of sheer gratitude, for it calls itself the German Bologna. But I will not inquire if this title is appropriate or not. Suffice it to say that the two universities differ in the simple circumstance that Bologna has the smallest dogs and the greatest scholars, and Göttingen, on the other hand, has the smallest scholars and the greatest dogs.

WHEN THE MARQUIS CHRISTOPHORO DI GUMPELINO drew his nose from the red sea, as once King Pharaoh had done, his face gleamed with damp self-satisfaction. Deeply moved, he promised Signora that as soon as she should be in a condition to sit down, he would bring her to Bologna in his coach. It was arranged that the professor should ride on ahead, and that Bartolo should sit on the box and hold Signora's lap-dog, and that at the end of a fortnight we should all meet in Florence, where Signora Francesca, who was planning to travel with Milady to Pisa, would also find us. While the Marquis was computing the cost on his fingers, he hummed to himself, "*Di tanti palpiti.*" [15] Signora sang her loudest trills in full-throated ease, and the professor swept the strings of his guitar like a tornado and sang so passionately that sweat ran from his brow, and tears rolled from his eyes—both forming a single stream down his red face. In the midst of this ringing and singing, the door was suddenly thrust open and in sprang—a creature—

Oh, ye Muses—of the old and of the new world—and even ye undiscovered Muses, whom only a later generation than ours will honor—and whom I have already for a long time spied in forest and by the sea! I adjure you, lend me the colors with which to limn that being, who next to Virtue, is the most glorious creature in the world! Virtue—it goes without saying—is first of all the glories: the Creator endowed her with so many charms that it seemed as if he could produce nothing to compare with her. Yet, he gathered all his forces, and in a fortunate hour created Signora Francesca, the lovely dancer, and his greatest masterpeice next to Virtue. But he did not repeat himself at all, unlike those earthly artists whose later works always reflect at second hand the graces of their early creations.

No. Signora Francesca is completely original. She has not the least resemblance to Virtue. There are connoisseurs who hold her to be the equal of Virtue, and only award precedence to the latter because of greater antiquity. But is it really a serious defect in a dancing girl if she is some six thousand years too young?

Ah, I think I see her again, as she leaps from the open door into the center of the room, and at that very instant executes innumerable pirouettes, throws herself full length on the sofa, and hiding her eyes with her hands, exclaims, breathlessly, "Oh, I am so tired from sleeping!"

The Marquis now approaches her, and delivers a long address, in his ironic, broad and reverential style, which contrasts strangely with his customary abruptness when he is thinking of business, or with his insipid garrulity, when he is moved by sentiment. Yet this style was not unnatural. It was no doubt a natural result of an inability to express boldly and directly that authority which he believed his money and brains entitled him to. Hence he sought to mask it like a coward in the language of the most exaggerated humility. His broad smile on those occasions had something disagreeably engaging; and you were never sure whether to reward him with approval—or with a kick. In this way he delivered his matutinal speech to Signora Francesca, who, still half-asleep, hardly heard him. When he had finished, he begged permission to kiss her feet, at least, her left foot; and in preparation for that act, he spread his yellow silk handkerchief on the ground with extreme care, and knelt on it. Then she, with indifference, held out her left foot, which was encased in a lovely red shoe, in contrast to the right, which wore a blue one—a droll bit of coquetry which emphasized the daintiness of her feet all the more sharply. When the Marquis had kissed the little foot devoutly, he rose with a groan. "Oh, Jesus!" he cried, and asked permission to present me, his friend. This too was granted him—with a sleepy yawn. My patron did not fail to praise my excellence, and declared, on his honor as a gentleman, that I too had sung the pangs of unhappy love with some success.

I also begged leave to kiss the lady's left foot; but the moment I had shared this joyful honor, she awoke as from a twilight-dream, leaned toward me with a smile, regarded me with her great, wondering eyes, and then leaped ecstatically into the middle of the room, and executed innumerable pirouettes on one foot. I felt strangely as if my heart were pirouetting with her—till it almost grew dizzy. The professor struck the strings of the guitar, and sang:

> "An opera-signora chose
> Me for her husband.
> Soon we were wedded,
> Poor me, alas!

> "Corsairs soon freed me of her;
> I sold her to the barbarians,
> Even before she could look around.
> Bravo, Biskroma, bravo, bravo!"

Once more Signora Francesca appraised me from head to foot, and then thanked the Marquis with a satisfied mien—as if I were a present which he was kind enough to bring her. She found little to object to in me, save that my hair was too light brown—she would have preferred it darker, like that of the Abbate Cecco; and my eyes were too small for her, and more green than blue. In retaliation, dear reader, I too should describe Signora Francesca with similar reservations. But I have no fault at all to find in that delicious, care-free figure—perfect as the Graces themselves. Her face was divine, such as we see in Greek statues—brow and nose made an almost vertical straight line; and the base of the nose, wonderfully short, formed a sweet right angle with it. The distance from nose to mouth was equally short; and the lips seemed scarcely long enough—but were completed by a soft dreamy smile; while underneath them arched a lovely, round chin. And the neck! Oh, gentle reader, I am going too far! Besides, I have no right, in this inaugural presentation, to speak of the two silent flowers, which shone like marble-white poems, when Signora loosened the silver buttons at the neck of her black silk dress! Dear reader, let us rather ascend once more and portray the face, of which I must yet report that it was clear and pale yellow like amber, that the black hair which framed its temples in bright, smooth ovals, gave it a childlike roundness, and that it was illumined by two black, flashing eyes, which shone as with magic flames.

You see, dear reader, that I would gladly give you an accurate description of the setting of my good fortune, and like other travellers, who are accustomed to append maps of historic or otherwise noteworthy regions through which they have wandered, I too would gladly have had Francesca engraved. But alack! Of what use is a dead copy of the outlines of a being whose godlike grace resides in living motion! Even the best painters cannot bring the latter before our eyes —for painting is only a flat lie. A sculptor might do it. By means of shifting lights we may be able to imagine the statue in motion; and the torch, which actually only lights up the outside, seems also to illumine the life within. Yes, there is one statue, dear reader, which could give you some marble conception of Francesca's loveliness. It is the Venus of the great Canova, which you will find in one of the last rooms of the Palazzo Pitti in Florence. I often think of that statue. At times, I dream that she is in my arms and gradually comes to life and whispers to me with the voice of Francesca. For it was the tone of her voice which endowed each of her words with the loveliest and most far-reaching meaning. Were I to try to repeat her phrases, I should be giving you only a dry collection of flowers, whose real charm lay in their perfume. Often she would leap into the air and dance while she was speaking.—Perhaps this was her natural way of expression. My heart danced with her, executed the most complicated steps, and displayed a talent for dancing I had never suspected in myself.

In this idiom Francesca told the story of the Abbate Cecco, a young scamp, who fell in love with her in the Valley of the Arno, while she was still plaiting straw hats. She assured me that I was fortunate enough to look like him. At the same time she went through the most melting pantomimes, often pressed the tips of her fingers to her heart, as if to scoop up from it the tenderest feelings. At last, with heaving breast she threw herself on the sofa, hid her face in the pillow, raised her legs high in the air and moved them as if they were wooden puppets. The blue foot represented the Abbate Cecco and the red his poor Francesca. She parodied her own tale, made the two feet part from each other—it was touching yet ludicrous to watch this performance—to see their tips kissing, and to hear them uttering the tenderest words; and all the time, the girl sobbed in a delightful and tittering manner, though now and then she seemed unconsciously to bring to the part more heart-felt emotion than it required. In her droll excess of sorrow, she had the Abbate Cecco deliver a long speech, in which he praised the beauty of poor Francesca in pedantic metaphors, and the reply she made in her own person, the way she imitated her own voice as it had once been moved by emotion, had something sad and puppet-like in it, and was strangely moving. "Adieu, Cecco!" "Adieu, Francesca!" That was the constant refrain. The enamored feet would not part. And I was happy at last when inexorable fate separated them; for sweet foreboding whispered in my ear that it would not be my good fortune if the lovers remained united.

The professor applauded with the comical humming of the guitar, Signora trilled, the lap-dog barked, the Marquis and I clapped our hands like mad, and Signora Francesca rose and curtsied gratefully. "It is really a pretty comedy," she said to me, "but it was performed a long time ago, and I am now *so* old—guess—how old am I?"

Even without waiting for my reply, she added hastily, "Eighteen," —and spun around eighteen times on one foot. "And how old are you, Dottore?"

"I, Signora, was born on New Year's night, eighteen hundred."

"I've already told you," the Marquis remarked, "that he is one of the first men of our century."

"And how old do you suppose I am?" suddenly cried Signora Letitia, and utterly oblivious of the fact that she was dressed like Eve and only covered by a bed-spread, she leaped into the air with such violence, that not only the Red Sea, but all of Arabia, Syria, and Mesopotamia came into view.

Startled by this horrible vision, I recoiled, stammered a few phrases about how difficult it was to answer such a question, especially since I had only "half seen" the Signora; but she pressed me all the more urgently for an answer, and I told her the truth: namely, that I had not yet learned to reckon the true relation of Italian years to those in Germany.

"Is the difference so great?" Signora Letitia inquired.

"Naturally," I replied, "since heat expands all bodies, it follows that years in Italy are much longer than those in our colder Germany."

The Marquis extricated me from this dilemma much more skilfully by maintaining gallantly that her beauty had only now begun to reveal itself in all its voluptuous maturity. "And, Signora," he added,

336 THE POETRY AND PROSE OF HEINRICH HEINE

"as the orange, the older it is, grows the more yellow, so does your beauty too ripen with age."

The lady appeared satisfied with this comparison, and confessed that she actually felt riper than of old, when she was a scrawny thing, at the time of her debut in Bologna; and she could not understand how she had caused such a *furore*. Then she told us of her debut as Ariadne —a subject to which, as I subsequently discovered, she frequently reverted, and then Signor Bartolo was commanded to recite the poem which he had thrown to her on the stage. It was a good poem, filled with touching melancholy at the infidelity of Theseus, with blind enthusiasm for Bacchus and glowing apotheosis of Ariadne.[16]

"*Bella cosa!*" Signora Letitia exclaimed at every stanza. I also praised the metaphors, the versification, and the treatment of the myth as a whole.

"Yes, it is very beautiful," the professor said, "and is without doubt founded on a historical fact, for several authors distinctly state that Oeneus, priest of Bacchus, married the mourning Ariadne, when he found her abandoned on Naxos; and, as often occurs in legends, the priest of the god eventually becomes the god himself."

I could not agree with this view, since I rather incline to a philosophical interpretation of mythology, and I replied, "In the whole fable of Ariadne, abandoned by Theseus on Naxos, and later embraced by Bacchus, I see only an allegorical statement that in her abandoned state she took to drink—a hypothesis in which I am supported by many scholars in my fatherland. You, Signor Marquis, are probably aware that the late banker Bethmann, in accordance with this hypothesis, so contrived to light up his Ariadne that she seemed to have a red nose."

"Yes, yes, Bethmann of Frankfurt was a great man," the Marquis exclaimed. At the same time an important idea struck him, and he added sighing, "Lord, Lord, I've forgotten to write Rothschild in Frankfurt!" And with a weighty business air, from which all his mocking parody had vanished, he excused himself without much ceremony and promised to return that evening.

When he was gone, and I was about to comment—as is the way of the world—on the man to whose kindness I owed this most agreeable of introductions, I was astonished to find that the assembly could not praise him sufficiently, and that they were roused to the most exaggerated expressions of admiration by his enthusiasm for the beautiful, by his noble and refined deportment, and by his unselfishness.

Even Signora Francesca joined in these paeans—though she admitted that his nose was rather alarming, and always reminded her of the tower of Pisa.

Before leaving, I begged for the favor of being allowed to kiss her left foot once more; whereupon, with a smiling and serious air she took off her red shoe, as well as her stocking; and as I knelt down, she raised the white, fragrant lily-foot and I pressed it to my lips with greater devotion and faith, perhaps, than I would have done to the foot of the Pope. Naturally, I also performed the duties of a maid, and helped her put on her shoe and stocking.

"I am satisfied with you," said Signora Francesca after this act—at which I took my time, although my ten fingers were very nimble.—"I am satisfied with you. You must help me draw on my stockings more often. Today you have kissed my left foot; tomorrow you will have my right foot at your disposal. The next day you may kiss my left hand, and the day thereafter my right one. If you behave well, I shall trust you with my mouth, and so on. You see I have a feeling I'd like to help you get on—and since you are still quite young, you may really go very far in this world."

I have indeed gone far in this world. Be my witnesses, oh you Tuscan nights; you clear blue firmament with your great, silver stars; you wild laurels and mysterious myrtles; and you, oh Nymphs of the Apennines, who hover around us in your bridal dances, and in your dreams relive those better days of the gods, when there were no Gothic lies, which allow only a skulking after secret and hidden pleasures, and cover every natural emotion with the hypocritical fig-leaf.

There was no need of individual fig-leaves; for a whole fig-tree spread its branches and rustled above the heads of the fortunate ones.

THE WHOLE WORLD KNOWS WHAT A BEATING IS. But no one has as yet made out what love is. Some natural philosophers have affirmed that it is a sort of electricity. This is not at all impossible, for in a moment of rapture we feel as if an electric flash from the eyes of the beloved had suddenly struck our hearts. Alas, such lightning flashes are the most destructive; and the man who invents a lightning-rod which will protect us against this bolt I will honor above Franklin. If there were only little lightning conductors one could carry around the heart, provided with lightning-rods which would divert the frightful fire to some other quarter! But I fear it is not so easy to rob Cupid of his arrows, as Jupiter of his lightning and tyrants of their scepters.

Besides, not every love operates like lightning; sometimes it lurks like a snake amid roses, and espies the first crevice in the heart through which it can slip; sometimes it is only a word, a glance, the story of some unlikely deed, which falls like a tiny grain of seed into our hearts, lies there dormant through the winter, and when spring comes shoots up into a blazing flower, whose perfume numbs the senses. The same sun which hatches the crocodile's eggs in the Egyptian valley of the Nile may also ripen the love-seed in a young heart in Potsdam on the Havel—and then you will have tears in Egypt as well as in Potsdam. But tears are not explanations. What is love? Has no one fathomed its depths? Has no one solved its riddle? Perhaps its solution would cause greater torment than the riddle itself, and our hearts would be stunned and petrified, as at the sight of Medusa? Serpents twine themselves around the terrifying word that would undo that riddle. Oh, I never wish to know the answer—for the gnawing misery in my heart is dearer to me than cold petrification. Oh, do not utter it, ye shades of the dead, who heartless as stone, but, like them, unfeeling, wander through the rose-gardens of the world and smile condescendingly with pale lips at the foolish soul who praises the perfume of the roses and laments their thorns.

Dear reader, if I am in no position to tell you what love is, I can at least describe accurately how a man acts and feels when he falls in love in the Apennines. He behaves like a fool. He skips from cliff to cliff, and hill to hill, and imagines the whole world is dancing along with him. He feels as if the earth had just been created, and he were the first man. "Oh, how lovely are all things!" I exulted, when I left Francesca's dwelling. "How fair and precious is this brave, new world!" I felt as if I had to give names to all the plants and animals, and I named each in accordance with its own nature and my own feelings, which blended so wondrously with all things around me. My breast was a well-spring of revelation, and I understood all forms and shapes, the fragrance of plants, the song of birds, the whistling of the wind, the rushing of waterfalls. Sometimes I heard the voice of God saying, "Adam, where art thou?" and I cried, "Here I am, Francesca. I adore you. For I know full well that you have created the sun, the moon, and the stars, and the earth with all its creatures!" Then there was soft laughter in the myrtle-bushes, and secretly I sighed: "Oh, sweet folly, do not forsake me!"

Later, when twilight fell, delirious ecstasy took possession of me. The trees danced on the mountain-sides, but not alone—the mountains too danced with their weighty heads, flushed red by the setting sun as if intoxicated by their own vines. Below them, the rushing brooks hurried on, and murmured anxiously, as if fearing that the ecstatic, swaying mountains would fall to earth. And above, there was summer lightning, gentle as a kiss. "Yes," I cried, "laughing heaven is kissing his love, the Earth—oh, beloved Francesca, lovely heaven, let me be your earth. I myself am so earthy, and long for you, my heaven!" Thus I cried, and extended my hands in wild prayer to heaven. I ran, and struck many a tree with my head, and instead of scolding, I embraced them, and my whole being exulted and rejoiced in the intoxication of love—when, suddenly, I beheld a form in scarlet, which at once snatched me from my dreams, and brought me back to cold reality.

FOR THERE, ON A MOSSY BANK, beneath a wide-branching laurel, sat Hyacinthos, the Marquis' servant, and near him his dog, Apollo. The latter might, however, be said to be standing, for his forepaws rested on the scarlet knees of the little man, and he looked on inquisitively as the latter from time to time wrote on a tablet which he held in his hand. Now and then, Hyacinthos smiled sadly, shook his head, and then wiped his nose with an air of satisfaction.

"What the devil!" I cried, "Hirsch Hyacinth! Writing poems?! Well, the signs are favorable. Apollo is at your side and the laurel hangs above your head."

But I was doing the poor scamp an injustice. Amiably he replied, "Poems? No, I am a friend of the Muses, but I don't write poetry. What should I be writing? I had nothing else to do now, and so just for fun I jotted down a list of those of my friends who have played in my lottery—some of them still owe me something—not that I wish to remind you—Doctor, believe me—there's plenty of time for that. But if you had only taken ticket number 1365 instead of 1364 the last time you played, you'd be worth a hundred thousand marks, cash, right now, and you wouldn't have to run around on this place, you could sit snug and contented in Hamburg, nice and easy, and you could have other folks tell you what Italy is like—while you were relaxing on the sofa."

Religion, Art and Life

ℰ➤ *Mr. Hyacinth on the Subject of Religion*

THERE IS NOTHING SO TEDIOUS ON THE FACE OF THE EARTH as reading a travel book describing Italy, unless it be writing one—and the only way the author can make it palatable is to say as little as possible of Italy. But though I have fully availed myself of this literary trick, I still cannot promise you, dear reader, much entertainment in the next chapters. If you become tired of the boring stuff in it, just console yourself with the thought what a time I must have had in writing it. I urge you to skip a few pages now and then; you will get through the book so much faster. God, would I could do the same! Don't imagine that I am joking. If I could speak candidly about this book, I would advise you to shut it at once, and read no more in it. By and by I will write something better; and when we meet Mathilda and Francesca together in Lucca again—in our next volume—the dear creatures will please you far more than anything in this, or in the following chapter.

Thank God, outside my window I can hear a hand-organ grinding out its merry tunes. My dull head needs this cheering up, especially as I must now describe my visit to his Excellency, the Marquis Christophoro di Gumpelino. I will relate this deeply moving history with the utmost accuracy, the most literal truthfulness—in all its sordid purity.

It was late at night when I reached the home of the Marquis. When I entered the room, Hyacinth stood alone, polishing the golden spurs of his master, who, as I perceived through the half-open door of his chamber, was on his knees before a Madonna and a great crucifix.

For you must know, dear reader, that the Marquis, this grandee, is now a good Catholic; he is a very strict observer of the ritual of the only true Church, and when he is in Rome, he even retains a personal chaplain, on the same principle which induces him, when in England, to keep the best racing-horses, and in Paris the most beautiful dancing girl.

"Herr Gumpel is now at his prayers," Hyacinth whispered, with a significant smile, and pointed to the cabinet of his master, adding in an even softer voice, "He lies this way every evening for two hours on his knees before the Our Lady with the Child Jesus. It is a splendid work of art, and cost him six hundred francesconi."

"And you, Herr Hyacinth, why don't you kneel behind him? Or perhaps you are no friend of the Catholic religion?"

"I am a friend—and then again, I am no friend," he replied, with a thoughtful nod. "It is a good religion for a grand baron, who can be at leisure all day long, and for a connoisseur of the arts. But it is no religion for a man from Hamburg, a man who has his business to attend to,—and certainly it is no religion at all for a lottery collector. I must write down exactly every number which is drawn; and if I should happen to think of the boom!-boom!-boom! of a Catholic bell, or if my eyes should begin to water as if from Catholic incense, and I should make a mistake and set down the wrong numbers, the direst calamities might befall. Many times I have said to Herr Gumpel, 'Your Excellency is a rich man; he can be as Catholic as he pleases, and allow his wits to be perfumed by incense as much as he likes, and be as stupid as a Catholic bell, and still he will have enough to eat. But I am a business man, and must keep my six senses about me, so that I may earn a living.' Of course, Herr Gumpel thinks it is necessary for my education; that unless I turn Catholic I will not understand the paintings, which are so important a part of an education, such as Jan of Fizzle, the Corretshow, the Carratshow, the Carravatshow—but I've always maintained that all the Corretshow, the Carrat-show, and the Carravatshow wouldn't help me very much if no one played his numbers with me—and then I'd really have nothing to show! And I must own, dear Doctor, that the Catholic religion doesn't amuse me, and as a rational man, you must allow that I am right. I can't see what fun there is in it—it's the kind of religion in which the Lord (God forbid!) seems to have just died, and everything smells of incense, as at a funeral, and they growl such sad burial music that it gives me the creeps. I tell you, it's no religion for a man from Hamburg."

"But Herr Hyacinth, how do you like the Protestant religion?"

"That one is altogether too sensible for me, Herr Doctor. If the Protestant church didn't have an organ, it would be no religion at all. Between you and me, that religion does little harm; it's as pure as a glass of water—but it doesn't do much good either. I've tried it, and the experiment cost me four marks and fourteen shillings—"

"How so, my dear Herr Hyacinth?"

"Well, you see, Doctor, I thought to myself: Here's a really enlightened religion for you, without any visions and miracles, though a bit of the visionary is needed; and a nice little miracle must be performed now and then, if a religion is to proclaim itself the right sort. But who could ever work a miracle in this place? I asked myself when I visited a Protestant church in Hamburg—one of the bald kind, with nothing in it but brown benches and whitewashed walls, which were bare except for a black-board with half a dozen white figures written on it. You may be doing this religion an injustice, I thought to myself; perhaps these numbers can work miracles as well as the image of the Virgin Mary or a bone of her husband, St. Joseph. And so, to settle the matter, I went straight to Altona and played those numbers in the Altona lottery. I set eight shillings on the *deuce*, six on the *terne*, four on the *quaterne*, and two on the *quinterne*. But I assure you, on my word of honor, not one of these Protestant numbers was a winner. Now I knew what to think, and I said to myself, Keep your religion which can't as much as win the *deuce*. Wouldn't I be a fool to stake all of my salvation on a religion which has already cost me four marks and fourteen shillings?"

"I dare say the old Jewish religion suits you better, my friend?"

"Doctor—enough of the old Jewish religion! I wouldn't wish it on my worst enemy. It brings nothing but shame and abuse. I tell you it isn't a religion at all! It's a calamity! I avoid everything that reminds me of it, and since Hirsch is a Jewish name and means Hyacinth in German, I've let old Hirsch run, and now I sign my name 'Hyacinth, Collector, Operator, and Appraiser.' Then there's another advantage, for I have an 'H' on my signet ring, and I don't have to have a new one engraved. I assure you it matters a great deal in this world what one is called. A name counts for much. Hyacinth sounds altogether different from plain Hirsch. No one can treat me like a common blackguard any longer."

"My dear Herr Hyacinth, who would ever want to treat you that way? You seem to have done so much to improve yourself. It is easy to see that you are a man of culture, even before you open your mouth."

"You are right, Doctor. I have made great strides in my education—like a giant. I really don't know with whom I'll associate when I get back to Hamburg; and as for religion, I know what I must do. Just at the moment, I think I can manage with the new Israelitic Temple—I mean the pure Mosaic service—with orthographic German hymns and moving sermons,—a bit of the fantastic, which no religion can do without. So may the Lord help me, I don't want a better one; that religion deserves my support. I'll do my bit when I get back to Hamburg. I'll go to the New Temple every Sabbath—provided there's no lottery drawing on that day. There are some people—and that's a shame—who give this new Israelitic service a bad name and declare that it provides occasion for—you'll pardon the expression—schisms; but I give you my word, it's a good, clean religion, a little too good for the common people, for whom the old Jewish religion is perhaps good enough. The common man must have something stupid, otherwise he isn't happy. And this sort of stupidity makes him happy.

"Take an old Jew with his long beard and ragged coat, who can't speak an orthographic word and is a little mangy, and I'm sure he feels happier than I do with all my accomplishments.

"There's one such fellow in Hamburg, in the Bäckerbreitengang, close by the dumps, a man named Moses Ragtail—people call him little Moses Ragtail, or little Ragtail, for short—who runs around the whole week, in wind and rain, with his pack on his back, hard put to it to earn a few crowns. Well, comes Friday eve, and he goes home. He finds the seven-branched candlestick all lit up, a white spread on the table, and he puts off all his burdens and sorrows, and sits down at the table beside his bent wife and still more bent daughter. He eats with them—the fish is deliciously flavored with a white garlic sauce, and he sings the most magnificent psalm of King David, and his heart rejoices at the exodus of the Children of Israel from Egypt.—He is happy that all the malefactors who tried to do them evil perished in the end, and that King Pharaoh, Nebuchadnezzar, Haman, Antiochus, Titus, and their like, are all of them dead, while little Moses Ragtail is still alive and eats fish with his wife and daughter. And I tell you, Doctor, fish is a rare tid-bit, the man is happy, and he doesn't have to plague himself with culture. He sits there contented with his religion, in his green dressing-gown, like Diogenes in his tub, and he looks contentedly at the bright candles, which he hasn't even taken the trouble to clean. And I tell you that even if the candles should happen to burn dim, and the Shabbeswoman [1] who attends to them should not be at hand, and if Rothschild the Great should enter, accompanied by his whole retinue of brokers, discount bankers, forwarders, and chief clerks with whose aid he has conquered the world, and if he were to say, 'Moses Ragtail, ask what you will, and it will be given you—,' Doctor, I am convinced that Moses Ragtail would answer quietly, 'Attend to the candles.' And Rothschild the Great would reply with amazement, 'If I were not Rothschild, I'd gladly change places with Moses Ragtail.'"

❧ *A Disputation about Divinity*

. . . WHEN THE ROAST BECAME TOO BAD, we argued the existence of God. But the good Lord always had the majority. Only three of the dinner company were atheistically inclined; but even these could be swayed if we at least had good cheese for dessert. The most zealous deist was little Samson, and when he debated the existence of God with lanky Vanpitter, he sometimes became quite excited, and ran up and down the room, continually crying: "By God, that isn't right!" Lanky Vanpitter, a lean Frisian, whose soul was as calm as the waters in a Dutch canal, and whose words trailed as leisurely as a towbarge, drew his arguments from German philosophy, which he had studied assiduously at Leyden. He ridiculed the narrow-minded heads that attributed a personal existence to God. He even accused them of blasphemy because they endowed God with wisdom, justice, love and similar human attributes, not at all suitable to Him, since they were in a way only the obverse of human qualities, antitheses of human folly,

injustice, and hatred. But when Vanpitter developed his own pantheistic view, he was beset by a fat Fichtean, a certain Driksen of Utrecht,
who stoutly confuted his vague conception of a God diffused throughout Nature, that is to say, existing in space. He even declared that it
was blasphemy so much as to speak of the *existence* of God, for "existence" is a concept which involved space, hence something substantial. Indeed, it was blasphemy even to say "He is," for the purest
being cannot be conceived of otherwise than limited; whereas in thinking of God, a man must abstract Him from all substance, and not think
of Him as a form of extension, but as an order of events. God was no
Being, but pure Act—the principle of a transcendental world-order.

At these words, little Samson was beside himself with rage. He ran
up and down the room even more crazily, and cried more loudly,
"God! Oh, God! By God, that isn't right! Oh, God!" I believe that in
honor of God he would have drubbed the fat Fichtean, if his arms
had not been so thin. As it was, he sometimes did attack him, and
then the fat one took hold of little Samson's two little arms, held him
quietly, and without taking his pipe from his lips, quietly expounded
his system, now and then blowing his airy arguments along with his
tobacco smoke into Samson's face, so that the little fellow was almost
choked by fumes and fury, and wailed more and more pitifully: "Oh
God! Oh, God!"

But God never came to his aid, although he was defending His
cause so valiantly.

Despite this Divine indifference, despite the almost human ingratitude on God's part, little Samson remained the staunch champion of
deism—and I believe, from an inherent inclination. For his forefathers
were of God's chosen people, a people God once took under his
special, loving care, and who therefore have preserved a singular attachment to Him to this very day. The Jews are ever the most
devoted deists, especially those who, like Samson, were born in the
Free City of Frankfurt. No matter how republican they may be in
political questions—they may even wallow in the very mire of sans-
coulottism—the moment, however, religious notions come into play,
they remain obsequious domestics of their Jehovah, the old fetish
who will have nothing more to do with their tribe and is having himself baptized into a God-free pure spirit.

I believe this God-free pure spirit, this parvenu of heaven, who is
now conceived as so moral, cosmopolitan, and universal, harbors a
secret resentment against the poor Jews because they knew him as of

old, and every day in their synagogues insist on reminding him of his erstwhile obscure national connections. Perhaps the old gentleman wishes to forget that he is of Palestinian extraction, and that he was once the God of Abraham, Isaac, and Jacob—and that his name was then Jehovah.

ࣙ A Conversation on Religion

. . . I WAS ESPECIALLY ATTRACTED BY "The Marriage at Cana" by a pupil of Andrea del Sarto, somewhat harshly painted and stiff in its modelling. The Saviour sits between the beautiful and gentle bride and a Pharisee who, with a face as hard as the stone tables of the law, looks with astonishment at the sublime Prophet as He serenely mingles with the happy guests and entertains the company with miracles greater even than those of Moses. For the latter could only bring forth water, though he struck the rock ever so hard; but Christ had but to speak a word, and pitchers were filled with the best wine.

Much gentler, almost Venetian in the quality of its coloring, is the painting by an unknown artist that hangs beside the other, in which the most harmonious fusion of colors is softened by a palpitating sorrow. It represents Mary holding a box of precious ointments, of pure nard, and anointing the feet of Jesus, and wiping them with her hair. Christ sits in the midst of his disciples, a beautiful, spiritual God, filled with pious reverence and human pity for his own body, destined to suffer so much, and now appropriately enough receiving the ointment reserved for the dead. He is touched and smiles at the kneeling woman, who, with forebodings born of love and anxiety, is now performing that compassionate act—an act which will not be forgotten so long as there are suffering men—an act which will refresh mankind with its fragrance for generations to come. Except for the disciple who lay on Christ's breast and who has recorded this act, none of the other apostles appear to have grasped its meaning; and he of the red beard seems even —as is recorded in the Scriptures—to have expressed vexation: "Why is not this ointment sold for three hundred talents and given to the poor?" This economical apostle is the same who carried the purse. Familiarity with money matters had blunted him to all the sweetness of selfless love, so that he would have bartered it for a few talents to some good purpose. And it was he—the money changer—who betrayed the Saviour—for thirty pieces of silver. Thus has the Gospel revealed in symbols and in the history of this banker-apostle the sinister and seductive power that lurks in a bag of gold; and thus has it given us warning against the duplicity of business men. Every rich man is a Judas Iscariot.

"Why, you're making the wry face of a true believer, dear Doctor," Milady whispered. "I have been watching you, and—forgive me if I offend you—you look like a good Christian."

"Between you and me, I am. Yes, Christ—"

"Perhaps you even believe that He is God?"

"Most assuredly, my good Mathilda. He is the God whom I love best of all. Not because he is a legitimate God, whose Father was a God, and has ruled the world since time immemorial; no, but because though He was born Dauphin of Heaven, he nevertheless has democratic leanings and dislikes courtly etiquette. Because he is the God not of an elite of tonsured scribes and liveried knights-at-arms, but a modest God of the people, a Citizen-God, *un bon dieu citoyen.* Indeed, if Christ were not already God, I would elect him such, and I would obey him much more willingly as the elected God, the God of my choice than the absolute God imposed on me."

૱ *Of Heaven and Hell*

"YES, DOCTOR, WHEN I WAS STILL YOUNG, and lived in Dublin, I would often lie on the grass and look into the sky and wonder whether heaven really contained all the magnificence that people extolled. How is it. I thought to myself, that of all this splendor nothing ever falls down to earth, say, a diamond ear-ring, or a string of pearls, or, at the very least, a small piece of pineapple cake; that nothing is bestowed upon us from above but hail, or snow, or just ordinary rain? That isn't quite right, I thought—"

"Why do you say that, Milady? Why do you not rather smother these doubts? Unbelievers who have no faith in heaven should not make converts. Much less to be blamed are the missionaries who have a glorious heaven and are unselfish enough not to want it all for themselves, but invite their fellow-men to share it, and cannot rest until their generous invitation has been accepted."

"I have always been surprised, Doctor, that many rich persons of this sort, who are feverishly employed as presidents, vice-presidents, and secretaries of missionary societies, when they try to render some shabby old Jew worthy of heaven, and of the enjoyment of the company to be found in the celestial regions, never think of sharing their pleasures with him on earth: for example, they never invite him to their summer homes to partake of some juicy morsel which the poor devil would certainly enjoy as much here on earth as ever in heaven!"

"That is easy to understand, Milady. Heavenly joys cost them nothing at all, and it is doubly pleasurable to be able to render our neighbors happy at so small an expense. But what joys can the unbeliever invite a person to share?"

"None, Doctor, unless a quiet, long sleep, which the poor wretch may long for, especially if he has been too hard pressed with invitations to heaven."

Thus spoke the beautiful woman, in sharp and biting tones, and I answered not without seriousness. "Dear Mathilda, in my actions here on earth I am not concerned about the existence of heaven and hell. I am too great and proud to be moved by greed for heavenly rewards or fear of infernal punishment. I strive to do good, because the good is beautiful and attracts me irresistibly. I abhor evil because it is ugly and repulsive. Even as a boy, when I read Plutarch—and I still read him every evening before going to sleep, and very often I have the impulse to rush post-haste and become a great man too—I was pleased by the tale of the woman who wandered through the streets of Alexandria, carrying in one hand a skin of water and in the other a flaming torch. She cried out that she wanted to extinguish hell with water, and set fire to heaven with her torch, so that at last people would no longer shun wickedness because of fear or do good for a reward. All our actions should flow from the well of disinterested love, whether or not there is a life after death."

"Then you also do not believe in immortality?"

"You're very subtle, Milady. I doubt immortality? I, whose heart strikes the deepest roots in the remotest ages of the past and future? I, who am myself one of the most eternal of men, whose every breath is life eternal, and whose every thought is an eternal star—I not believe in immortality?"

"I think, Doctor, it argues a considerable share of vanity and presumption in man to ask God to confer immortality on us after we have already enjoyed so much of the good and beautiful in this life. Man, the aristocrat among animals, tries to extort this privilege of eternal life at the foot of the King's throne, with courtly hymns and psalms, and bending of the knees. Oh, I know too well what that movement of your lips signifies, immortal lord!"

"'THE PEOPLE MUST HAVE A RELIGION!'" Milady cried. "I hear that sentence zealously preached by thousands of stupid and tens of thousands of hypocritical mouths—"

"Nevertheless, it is true, Milady. Just as a mother cannot truthfully answer all of her child's questions, because its understanding will not allow it, so there must also be a positive religion, a church that can give people definite and sensible answers to the transcendental questions—all in proportion to their understanding."

"Alas! Doctor. Your comparison reminds me of a story, the conclusion of which will hardly support your opinion. When I was still a little girl, in Dublin—"

"And lay on my back—"

"But Doctor, it is really impossible to say a sensible word to you. Don't smile so impertinently, but listen to me: When I was still small, in Dublin, and sat at my mother's feet, I once asked her what happened to the old full moons. 'Dear child,' my mother said, 'the good God breaks the old full moons in pieces with a sugar-hammer, and makes little stars of them.' My mother cannot be blamed for this false explanation, for even with the best astronomical knowledge, she would not have been able to make me understand the whole system of the sun, the moon and the stars. To my metaphysical questions she gave definite, sensible replies. It would have been better if she had reserved her explanations till I was of a riper age, or at least, if she had not thought up a falsehood. For when little Lucy and I were together, during a full moon, and I told her that soon it would be broken into little stars, she laughed at me and said that her grandmother, old O'Meara, had told her that the full moons are eaten as fire-melons in hell, and for lack of sugar, pepper and salt are sprinkled on them. If Lucy thought my theory, which was slightly Evangelical, ridiculous, I thought hers, which was even more depressingly Catholic, more so. From laughing we came to blows—we struck out at one another till we drew blood, we spat at each other in the most polemical of fashions, until little O'Donnel on his way home from school pulled us apart. This boy had obtained better instruction in celestial matters—he knew something of mathematics, and he quietly demonstrated to both of us our errors and the silliness of our quarrel. And what happened then? We two girls immediately ended our controversy, joined forces and thoroughly belabored the calm little *mathematicus*."

"Milady, it grieves me, but you are right. Yet, it cannot be otherwise. Men will always fight over the excellences of those religious conceptions which were instilled in them early in life. And the rational ones will always suffer doubly. Once it was different. No one would have dreamed of extolling the doctrine or cult of his religion at the expense of another's, or of forcing it on other people. Religion was a cherished tradition—sacred history, memorial ceremonies and mysteries—transmitted by ancestors. At the same time it was a kind of family *sacra* of the people. A Greek would have deemed it an outrage if a stranger not of his race had proposed to him to join his religious community; and he would have thought it even more inhuman to attempt by force or guile to persuade another man to abjure his religion and adopt another. Then out of Egypt, the fatherland of crocodiles and priests, came a nation which brought, along with leprosy and stolen implements of gold and silver, a so-called positive religion, a so-called church, a panoply of dogmas to be believed, and sacred ceremonies to be observed—a fore-runner of the later state-religions. And now a brokerage in human beings arose—proselytism, intolerance, and all those holy horrors which have cost humanity so much blood and tears."

"Goddam! What a thoroughly wicked people!"

"Oh, Mathilda, they have long ago been damned, and have carried their infernal tortures through the centuries. Oh, those Egyptians—their handiwork defies time, their pyramids still stand immovable; their mummies are indestructible as ever. And just as indestructible is that mummy-nation that wanders over the face of the earth, wrapped in its age-old scroll of the law; a petrified piece of world-history—a specter, which for a livelihood traffics in bills of exchange and old clothes. Do you see, Milady, yonder old man with the white beard, the tip of which seems to be turning black again—the man with the ghost-like eyes—"

"Are not those ruins over the ancient Roman graves?"

"Yes. Even there the old man sits, and perhaps, at this moment, is offering up a prayer, Mathilda,—a terrible prayer, in which he laments his sorrows, and denounces people who have long since vanished from the earth, and now live only in nursery tales. But in his suffering he does not observe that he is sitting on the tombs of those very enemies for whose destruction he is supplicating Heaven."

৪৯ *The Procession*

THE MONKS IN THE FOREMOST RANKS walked in solemn silence, with arms crossed; but those with high hats sang a lugubrious chant, so nasal, drawling, and garbled, that I am sure that if the greater part of that great crowd had been Jewish, and their religion the religion of the state, this kind of singing would have been called a Yiddish sing-song. Fortunately, it was only partly audible, for the procession was followed by several companies of soldiers with loud drums and fifes; and on both sides of the priest, grenadiers marched two by two. There seemed to be more soldiers than clergy, for nowadays religion needs bayonets, and even the benediction is always seconded by the emphatic thunder of cannons in the distance.

When I see such a procession, in which priests march pitiful and dejected, under proud escort of the military, I am moved by compassion. It is as if I were witnessing the Saviour himself being led to judgment surrounded by lancers. The stars of Lucca must surely have had similar thoughts, for as I looked up at them with a sigh, they looked back at me with sympathy in their devout eyes, which were so clear and bright. But I had no need of their light; thousands upon thousands of lamps and candles and girlish faces shone at all windows; and at the street-corners were set tapers of pitch; and in addition, every priest had his own candle-bearer at his side. The Capuchins had mostly little boys to carry their candles, and the youthfully fresh faces looked with pleasant curiosity at the old, serious grey-beards; for the poor Capuchins cannot afford to pay a full-grown candle-bearer; and so the boys whom they instruct in the *Ave* and whose aunts they confess, undertake the office in the procession without pay—but they perform it, none the less, with affection. The monks who followed had boys not much older—a few of the more distinguished orders hired older youths, and the proud priests had the well-to-do citizens for candle-bearers. And last of all, came the archbishop, for it was he who walked in stately humility beneath the canopy, while two grey-haired pages bore his train, and footmen in blue livery and yellow trimming walked on either side of him, carrying the white tallow candles with all the ceremony they would have employed at court.

This candle-bearing seemed to me an excellent institution, for by its light I could more closely examine those Catholic faces; and now I saw them, in the best light. And what did I see? Well, first of all—that none was free of the clerical stamp. Aside from this, I must admit that the faces differed from one another as do the faces of other people. Some were pale, some red; here a nose was turned up proudly; there one was turned down. Here I saw brilliant black eyes; there dull ones. But in all these faces were the seeds of that terrible, incurable malady, which will undoubtedly account for the fact that my grandson, when he witnesses the procession a century hence, will find not one of its participants alive. I am afraid that I too am touched by that sickness. Hence I am subject to a strange weakness that comes over me when I observe the sickly face of a monk, and see in it the symptoms of those ailments which are concealed beneath the coarse cowl—thwarted love, gout, frustrated ambition, spinal consumption, penitence, hemorrhoids, heart-aches caused by the ingratitude of friends, or by the calumny of enemies, or by our own sins—all this and more—ailments that can be as readily found under a coarse cowl as beneath a stylish tail-coat. Alas, the poet does not exaggerate when he cries out in pain: "Life is a disease, and the whole world's a hospital."

"And Death is our physician—" No, I will speak no evil of him; nor will I disturb other men's faith in him. Since he is the only physician, let them believe that he is also the best; and that the sole remedy which he prescribes—eternal earth-cure—is also the best. The least that can be said in his favor is that he is ever at hand; and that despite an extensive practice, he never keeps the ailing patient waiting long. Sometimes he even follows his patient in the procession, and carries the taper for him. For it was surely Death himself I saw at the side of a pale, woe-begone priest. In his thin skeleton hand Death carried the flickering taper, and with his worried, bald little head he nodded encouragement, and though himself very weak on his legs, he sometimes lent support to the poor priest, who became paler and more faint with each step. He appeared to be whispering a heartening word into the priest's ear: "Just wait a few, brief hours, and we shall soon be home. I'll put out the candle, and I'll put you to bed, and you will rest your cold and weary limbs, and you will sleep so soundly that you will never hear the jingling of St. Michael's bells."

"I will write nothing against this man," I thought to myself, when I saw the poor, pale priest whom Death incarnate was lighting to bed.

ဦ Christ

WHAT A BEAUTIFUL FIGURE IS THIS MAN-GOD! How narrow in comparison appears the hero of the Old Testament! Moses loved his people with touching sincerity; like a mother, he is solicitous for the future of his nation. Christ loved humanity; and like the sun, he enflamed the whole world with the fire of his love. What soothing balm are his words for all the wounds of the world! What a refreshing spring for all suffering was the blood which flowed on Golgotha! The white, marble Greek gods were stained with it, and sickened with horror, and could never more recover! Most of them were already nursing within them the consuming disease, and terror only hastened their death. The first to die was the great god Pan. Do you know the legend which Plutarch tells? This sea-tale of antiquity is remarkable indeed.

One evening, in the reign of Tiberius, a ship passed close to the island of Parae, off the coast of Aetolia. The crew was still awake; many of them were at the table, drinking after the evening meal. Suddenly from the shore they heard a voice calling "Thamus!" (for this was the name of the steersman) with such vehemence that all were startled. Twice the voice called, but Thamus remained silent. But the third time he replied. Then more loudly the voice said, "When you reach the heights of Palodes, proclaim that the great god Pan is dead!" When he reached the heights, Thamus fulfilled the mission and from the stern of his boat he called toward the land, "The great god Pan is dead!" Whereupon he heard the strangest sounds of lamentation, a mingling of weeping and crying—as if coming from many throats. The witnesses recounted this incident in Rome, where the most singular opinions were expressed as to this affair. Tiberius had the matter investigated and did not doubt its authenticity.

ဦ Christianity

Then he poured wine to all the other gods from left to right, ladling the sweet nectar from the bowl, and laughter unquenchable arose amid the blessed gods to see Hephaistos bustling through the palace.

So they feasted all day till the setting of the sun; nor was their soul stinted of the fair banquet, nor of the beauteous lyre that Apollo held, and the Muses singing alternately with sweet voice. *The Iliad.*

. . . AND SUDDENLY A PALE, GASPING, BLOOD-STAINED JEW burst in on them, bearing a crown of thorns on his head, and on his shoulder a great wooden cross. And he hurled the cross on the great banquet table of the gods, so that all the goblets shook, and the gods were stricken dumb and they grew pale and ever paler, till at last they faded away in vapor.

And now there followed mournful times, and the world grew grey and sombre. There were no more happy gods. Olympus became a sick-house where flayed, roasted and impaled gods wandered in boredom, binding up their wounds, and singing sad litanies. Religion had no more joys to proffer, only consolations. It was a mournful, blood-stained, sinners' religion.

Perhaps this religion was what sick and down-trodden humanity needed? He who sees his own god suffer bears his own sorrows more easily. The light-hearted, ancient gods, who themselves felt no pain, did not know the feelings of poor, tormented humanity; and poor, tormented humanity could not, in its dire need, turn to them with its whole heart. For these were festal-day gods, around whom one could dance merrily, and to whom one could offer only thanks. Hence they were never loved with the whole heart. To be loved with a whole heart, one must have suffered. Compassion is the last consecration of love—perhaps love itself. Therefore, of all the gods that have ever been, Christ is the most beloved. Especially by women—

৪১ *State and Religion*

IN THE FOREGOING CHAPTER I spoke of positive religions only insofar as they are—under the name of state-religions—endowed with special privileges by the state. There is, however, a pious dialectic, dear reader, which would in a most convincing manner attempt to demonstrate that the opponent of the Church of such a state-religion is also an enemy of Religion and of the State, an enemy of God and King, or, as the usual formula runs, an enemy of the Throne and the Altar. But I say to you this is a lie.

I honor the inner sanctity of religion; and I submit myself to the interests of the state. If I have no particular veneration for anthropomorphism, I do, nevertheless, believe in the omnipotence of God, and even though kings be foolish enough to set themselves against the spirit of the people, or ignoble enough to weaken the people's voices through disdain or persecution—nevertheless, in my profoundest convictions I remain an adherent of kingship, of the monarchical principle. I do not hate the throne, but only the empty swarm of noble-born vermin who have made their nests in the cracks of the old thrones, and whose character Montesquieu has so well described: "Ambition in league with sloth; vulgarity in league with haughtiness, covetousness striving to enrich itself without work; antipathy to truth; flattery and treachery; disdain for the duties of citizenship; fear of the virtues of princes; and self-interest advanced through the vices of princes!" I do not hate the Altar, but I hate the serpents who lurk under the rubble of the old altars—those wily serpents who know so well how to smile with the innocence of flowers, while they secretly pour their poison into life's chalice, and hiss their slanders into the ears of the devout—those dissembling worms with their gentle words—

> Mel in ore, verba lactis,
> Fel in corde, fraus in factis.[2]

Just because I am a friend of the State and of Religion, I hate that abortion which is called State-Religion, that object of derision, born of the mating of temporal and spiritual power, that mule begot by the white horse of Antichrist on the she-ass of Christ. Were there no such state-religion, no privileged dogmas or cults in Germany, she would now be united and strong and her sons would be great and free. But alas! our poor Fatherland is torn asunder by religious dissension, the people are divided into opposing religious sects; Protestant subjects strive with their Catholic princes, or vice versa; everywhere there is distrust because of crypto-Catholicism or crypto-Protestantism; everywhere heresy-hunting, a spying on thought, pietism, mysticism, a besnivelling of church gazettes, sectarianism, proselytism— and while we dispute about heaven, we are undone here on earth. Only indifference in religious matters might still avail to save us; and only through a weakening of religious faith is it likely that Germany can become strong politically.

It is injurious to the interests of religion herself and her sacred character that she be invested with special privileges, that her servants should be endowed by the state, above all others, and in return should pledge themselves to uphold the state in order to retain that endowment. Thus one hand washes the other; the spiritual washes the temporal and *vice versa;* and what you have is twaddle and nonsense, which is folly toward God and an abomination to men. In this way, an opponent of the state also becomes an enemy of religion, which the state has endowed with privileges, and which has therefore become its ally. Even a harmless believer becomes suspicious when he scents the political design in religion. Most revolting of all is the haughtiness of the priests, who for services rendered to the state believe that they can reckon on its support—and who in return for the spiritual fetters they have forged for the state to bind the people, can now also rely on its bayonets. A religion can sink no lower than when she is raised in this way to the heights of a state-religion; she loses—as it were— her heart's innocence, and becomes as wordly proud as if she were an acknowledged mistress. Naturally, she becomes the recipient of greater homage and marks of respect. Daily she celebrates fresh victories with brilliant processions—even Bonapartist generals bear tapers before her—the proudest spirits pledge fealty to her banners; every day unbelievers are converted and baptized. But all this trickle of water does not make the soup any thicker—and the new recruits of the state-religion are like those soldiers levied by Falstaff—they fill the churches. There is no longer any question of sacrifice. Like travelling salesmen carrying samples, these missionaries go their rounds with their little tracts and their pious proselytizing booklets—and there is no risk at all in this business—it is all carried out in accordance with the best commercial and business practices.

Only so long as a religion has rivals in other religions, and is persecuted more than she persecutes, does she remain grand and honorable. Only then does she possess inspiration, sacrifice, martyrs, and palm leaves. How beautiful, how touchingly holy, how enchantingly sweet was Christianity in the first century, when she still resembled her divine founder in her heroic suffering! Here we still find the beautiful legend of a simple god, who wandered in the guise of a gentle youth under the palm-trees of Palestine, and preached human love, and revealed those doctrines of freedom and equality which were even later recognized as true by the greatest intellects, and which as the gospel preached in France inspired our own day. Compare with that religion of Christ, the various forms of Christianity which have been established as state-religions in many countries. For example, the Roman Catholic Apostolic Church; or even that Catholicism without poetry which we know as the High Church of England—that wretched mouldering skeleton of faith, from which all real life has departed. Monopoly is as injurious in religion as in industry. Only through free competition do religions retain their vigor, and they will regain their former splendor only when the political equality of cults, that is to say, "free enterprise" of the gods is again established.

The noblest minds of Europe have long since declared that this is the only means by which to save religion from total destruction. Nevertheless, her servants would prefer to sacrifice the altar itself, rather than the least particle of the altar-sacrifice; just as the nobility would rather expose the throne itself, and the august personage who exaltedly occupies it, to the most certain extinction, rather than with sincerity surrender a single one of their unjust privileges. Is not all this professed attachment to Throne and Altar but a farce to delude the people? Whoever has been initiated into the secret of the brotherhood knows that clericalism has far less respect for God than the laity, God, whom it shapes from bread and book at will, and to its own advantage; that the veriest commoner has more respect for the king than the nobles, who in their hearts despise and deride his kingship but honor it in public, and exact respect for it from others. Indeed, they are like those mountebanks at fairs who for money exhibit to gaping crowds a Hercules, a giant, a dwarf, a savage, a fire-eater, or some other such marvel—whose strength, excellence, boldness, invulnerability, or, if he happens to be a dwarf, wisdom, they extoll blatantly, while they blow trumpets and wear gay-colored jackets, but in their hearts they laugh at the gullibility of the gaping mass and deride their own "attractions," whose interest for them has been staled by daily association, and whose weakness and feints they know too well.

Whether the good God will much longer suffer the profiteering priests to represent him as a silly scarecrow—I do not know. Yet, I should not be surprised if I read in the *Hamburg Impartial Correspondence* that old Jehovah had issued a warning that no further credit be extended to any one who spoke in His name—not even to His own son. But I am convinced that the time will come when kings will no longer be willing to act as the passive puppets of their contemptuous nobles,—that they will break the bonds of etiquette, escape their marble booths, indignantly cast off the gaudy baubles intended to delude the people, the scarlet cloak as terrifying as an executioner's, the diadem which others have pushed over their ears to shut out the voice of the people, the golden staff put into their hands as a symbol of sovereignty.—The emancipated kings will be as free as other men, and will wander freely among them, and feel freely and marry as freemen, and freely express their opinions— and that will constitute the Emancipation of Kings.

ह्ल्ल *The Poet and His Times*

AS A GENERAL RULE, ONLY A GREAT POET can grasp the meaning of the poetry of his own day. Poetry of the past reveals itself more readily to us, and a knowledge of it is much more easily imparted. Hence Schlegel succeeded in exalting among masterpieces those poems which enshrine the past, at the expense of those in which our own times live and breathe. But Death is not more poetic than Life. The old English poems which Percy collected reveal the spirit of their time, and Bürger's the spirit of ours. But Schlegel never understood that spirit.[3] Otherwise he would have heard in the tumultuous passion with which that spirit sometimes spoke in Bürger's poetry not the rude cry of the unpolished schoolmaster, but the mighty utterances of a Titan writhing in pain, tortured to death by pedants and aristocratic Hanoverian Junkers. For such was the case of the author of *Lenore*, as of many another man of genius, who passed a miserable existence in lowly university posts at Göttingen—and died a miserable death. How could that elegant chevalier, August Wilhelm von Schlegel, protected, renovated, baronized, beribboned by aristocratic patrons, understand the lines in which Bürger cries out that it is better that a man of honor perish of hunger than that he entreat favors of the great?

The German word "Bürger" means "citizen," "*citoyen*."

໒∾ *Aristophanes*

IT WOULD TAKE ME TOO FAR AFIELD to try to show how Schlegel wrought great mischief by depreciating Euripides, in the same way in which Aristophanes once did. In this respect, the latter represented a point of view which had much in common with that of the Romantic School. There are similar feelings and tendencies underlying his polemics. If Tieck has often been called a Romantic Aristophanes, we may with equal justice call the parodist of Euripides and Socrates a classic Tieck. For just as Tieck and Schlegel, despite their own scepticism, still bewailed the decline of Catholicism, and desired its restoration among the multitude, and with this in view mocked and slandered the Protestant Rationalists, the men of the Enlightenment, and made war on truth rather than on falsehood; just as they nurtured the most uncompromising hatred for men who promoted honorable bourgeois sentiments in life as well as in literature; just as they derided that sentiment by calling it petty Philistinism, and, on the other hand, constantly exalted and extolled the great and heroic men of the feudal Middle Ages—so Aristophanes, too, himself a scorner of the gods, hated all philosophers who were undermining the reign of Olympus. He hated the rationalistic Socrates, who preached a loftier morality; he hated the poets who proclaimed a newer age which differed from the older age of Greek gods and heroes and kings in the same way as ours differs from that of the feudal Middle Ages. He hated Euripides, who was no longer as intoxicated with the Greek Middle Ages as Aeschylus and Sophocles had been, but was already drawing closer to the tragedy of middle class life.

I doubt whether Herr Schlegel was aware of the true reasons which moved him to disparage Euripides in favor of Aeschylus and Sophocles. I believe that he was impelled by an unconscious feeling, and sensed in the old tragedian that democratic and Protestant element which was deeply repugnant to the chivalric and Olympian Catholic, Aristophanes.

❧ *The Irony of Cervantes*

THERE IS MUCH TALK NOW OF HUMOROUS IRONY AMONG US. The adherents of Goethe's school of art extol it as the unique glory of their master, and at the present time it plays a great part in German letters. But it is in reality only a mark of our political servitude. Just as Cervantes at the time of the Inquisition took refuge in humorous irony to present his thoughts without exposing himself to the clutches of the familiars of the Holy Office, so Goethe expressed in tones of humorous irony that which he dared not say openly, since he was a courtier and minister of state. Goethe never suppressed the truth; but where he could not show her naked, he dressed her in humor and irony. The writers who languished under the censorship and political suppression of every sort and yet could not foreswear the true feelings of their hearts have been especially inclined to this ironic and humorous style. It was the sole outlet for their noble sentiments, which are most touchingly revealed in this humorous-ironic dissimulation.

We recall the strange Prince of Denmark. Hamlet is the most honest fellow in the world. His dissimulation only serves to substitute for an exterior he could not reveal. He is peculiar, because peculiarity is less offensive to court etiquette than an open breach of it. But in all of his humorous and ironic raillery he shows that he is dissembling. In all he does and speaks his true meaning is evident— to all who can see, even to the king to whom he cannot speak the plain truth (for that he is too weak), but from whom he does not wish to conceal it. Hamlet is thoroughly honorable. Only the most honorable person could say, "We are all arrant knaves." And while he is playing the madman, he does not really deceive us, for in his own heart he is aware that he is mad. . . .

IT IS PARADOXICAL ENOUGH TO OBSERVE that it was the Romantic School that has given us the best translation of a work in which its own folly is ridiculed in the most delightful manner.[4] But that school was bitten by the very same madness which drove the noble knight of La Mancha to all his follies. Like him, it wishes to restore medieval chivalry, and revive a dead past. Did Miguel de Cervantes Saavedra actually want to deride other knights in his mad and heroic poem,—that is, all men who fight and suffer for an idea? Did he perhaps wish to parody idealistic enthusiasm in his tall, lean knight, and plain common sense in his fat squire? Whatever the answer, Sancho always cuts a ridiculous figure; for plain common sense, with all his worn and trite sayings, is compelled, willy-nilly, to trot along on his meek donkey behind inspiration, despite all the discomforts which so often befall the noble knight. Yes, idealistic enthusiasm has so powerful an appeal, that common sense, and his donkey too, are compelled to follow him—whether they will or not.

May not the deep-browed Spaniard have meant to deride mankind in an even profounder way? Did he, perhaps, in the figure of Don Quixote, intend an allegory of the soul, and in Sancho Panza that of the body? May not the entire poem be a great mystery, in which the problem of matter and spirit is treated with a most terrifying reality? This much I understand by the poem: that poor material Sancho must suffer greatly for spiritual Don Quixote; that the noblest intentions of his master bring him but so many drubbings; that he is always more sensible than his prancing master. He knows that the cudgels are not to his taste; while the small sausages in an olla-podrida are. For in truth, the body often has greater insight than the spirit. And man more often thinks rightly with his back and his belly than with his head.

₴ The New German Folksong

> "Who was it made this pretty song?
> Over the water three geese came along,
> And brought it—two grey, and one white . . ."

IT IS USUALLY THE WANDERING FOLK, vagabonds, soldiers, roving students or apprentices who made this kind of song, especially the last. Very often, on my excursions on foot, I met these fellows and saw how time and again, inspired by some unusual incident, they improvised a snatch of folksong, or whistled it to the winds. The birds in the trees heard the song, and when another youth came trudging by with a staff and knapsack, they chirped it to him, and he added what was lacking, and so the song was completed. The words drop on to the lips of these youths from heaven, and they need but say them and they become more poetical than all the pretty poetic phrases we burrow from the depths of our hearts. The character of these German apprentices lives and breathes in all these folksongs. They are a strange lot. Penniless, they wander all over Germany—harmless, merry, and care-free. I met them generally in companies of three; the first, a talker—who spoke with droll humor of every chance subject, of every bird that flew by, and of the commercial traveller who happened to pass. When they reached some miserable place with wretched huts and beggarly inhabitants, he would say with irony, "God made the world in six days; but you see there's still some work left over." The second of this trio sometimes interrupts him with an indignant remark. He cannot speak without swearing at every master for whom he has labored; and his constant refrain is that he regrets that before leaving Halberstadt he had left no memento— such as a cuff on the ear—for the hostess of the inn who had fed him only cabbage and turnips every day. At the mention of Halberstadt, the third youth, the youngest of the three, sighs deeply. This is his first trip into the world, and he is constantly thinking of his sweetheart's dark-brown eyes. He hangs his head and says not a word.

ℰ➷ The "Nibelungenlied"

THIS *Nibelungenlied* IS A GREAT AND MIGHTY POEM. A Frenchman can hardly form an idea of it, or even of the language in which it is written. Its language is as of stone, and its verses are metrical granite blocks. Here and there, in the clefts, red flowers break forth, like drops of blood, or long ivy trails like green trickles of tears. You dainty little people can scarcely conceive the massive passions which inspire this poem. Imagine a clear summer night. The stars are silver-bright, but huge as the sun, they come forth in the blue heavens. Imagine all the Gothic cathedrals of Europe meeting at a rendezvous on a large plain. Imagine the Cathedral of Strassburg advancing calmly; then the Cathedral of Cologne, the Campanile of Florence, of Rouen, etc. And they are gallantly courting beautiful Notre Dame de Paris. It is true that their gait is somewhat unsteady; some of them are ungainly. Their amorous awkwardness is amusing. But our laughter dies when we see them falling into a passion, and proceeding to strangle each other. Notre Dame, in despair, stretches her two arms of stone toward heaven, and then suddenly taking hold of a sword, beheads the grandest of all the cathedrals. No. Even you can have no idea of the principal characters of the *Nibelungenlied*. No tower is so high, and no stone so hard as grim Hagen and vindictive Kriemhilde.

But who wrote the poem? We know that as little as we know the names of the authors of our folksongs. It is strange that we so seldom know the originators of the most admirable books, poems, buildings, and other monuments of art. What builder devised the Cathedral of Cologne? Who painted the altar piece there, on which the lovely Mother of God is so engagingly depicted with the Three Holy Kings? Who composed the Book of Job, which has comforted so many generations of suffering humanity? Man all too soon forgets the names of his benefactors. The good and noble who have toiled for the weal of their fellow-men are seldom on the lips of the people, whose weak memory retains only the names of their oppressors and cruel warrior-heroes. The tree of humanity is forgetful of the silent gardener who protected it against the cold, watered it when it was dry, and defended it against harmful creatures. But it faithfully retains the names which have mercilessly been engraved in its bark with sharp steel, and transmits them—ever greater—to succeeding generations.

๏ *Paganini*

"Do you like Paganini?" Maria asked.

"This man," Maximilian replied, "is the glory of his country, and certainly deserves the most distinguished place among the musical notables of Italy."

"I have never seen him," said Maria. "But according to report his exterior does not entirely satisfy our sense of beauty. I have seen portraits of him—"

"None of which are like him," Maximilian interrupted her. "They either make him uglier or handsomer than he is; they never give a true likeness of him. I think only one man has succeeded in putting his true physiognomy on paper; it is the deaf painter, Lyser, who with inspired frenzy caught Paganini's head in a few pencil strokes so successfully that one is amused and terrified at the likeness. 'The devil guided my hand,' the deaf painter said to me, chuckling mysteriously and nodding his head with good-natured irony, as he was in the habit of doing when playing his Till Eulenspiegel pranks. This painter was an odd fellow. In spite of his deafness, he loved music passionately, and he was supposedly able, if near enough to the orchestra, to read the music from the faces of the musicians and to judge from their finger movements whether the execution was successful. Indeed, he also wrote critiques of the opera in an estimable Hamburg journal. Is there anything strange in this? In the visible signature of the performance the deaf painter could see the sounds. There are men to whom the sounds themselves are only invisible symbols in which they hear colors and forms."

"You are one of those men!" cried Maria.

"I am sorry that I no longer possess Lyser's little drawing. It might have given you an idea of Paganini's external appearance. Only in the harsh, black strokes could those unearthly features be caught which seemed to belong rather to the brimstone realm of shadows than to the sun-lit world of the living. 'Indeed, the devil guided my hand,' the deaf painter assured me, as we stood by the Alster pavilion in Hamburg on the day when Paganini gave his first concert there. 'Yes, my friend,' he continued, 'what the whole world declares is true—he has signed over his body and soul to the devil in order to become the best violinist in the world and fiddle his way into millions of thalers; and principally, to buy his freedom from the damned galley, where he languished for many years. For you see, my friend, when he was the band leader at Lucca, he fell in love with a princess of the theater, became jealous of a little abbé, perhaps he was cuckolded, stabbed his unfaithful amata in approved Italian fashion, came in the galley to Genoa, and, as I've said, sold himself to the devil to escape it, to become the best violinist and to impose upon us this evening a tribute of two thalers. . . . But look—may the Lord be gracious to us!—there he comes down the avenue with his suspicious *famulus*.'

"And indeed, it was Paganini himself whom I beheld. He wore a dark-grey overcoat, which reached to his feet, and made him appear extremely tall. His long black hair fell in unkempt locks down to his shoulders and formed a dark frame for his pale, cadaverous face, in which care, genius, and hell had engraved their ineradicable lines. By his side appeared a short, smug figure in commonplace though elegant dress, with a rosy, wrinkled face, wearing a short, light-grey coat with steel buttons, and dispensing disagreeably cordial salutations

all about him, and leering up with apprehension at the dark figure
that walked by his side lost in deep thought. It called to mind a
picture by Retzsch of Faust walking with Wagner before the gates
of Leipzig. The deaf artist commented on both figures in his whimsical way, and bade me observe carefully the broad, measured walk of
Paganini. 'Does it not seem,' he said, 'as if he still had the iron cross-
pole between his legs? He has gotten used to this convict step. See
how contemptuously and ironically he looks down at his companion,
when the latter wearies him with his trite questions! But he cannot
be without him; a bloody contract binds him to his servant, who is
none other than Satan himself. The ignorant think, of course, that
this companion is the writer of comedies and anecdotes, Harrys from
Hanover, whom Paganini has taken with him on his concert tours
to manage his affairs. But they do not know that the devil has simply
borrowed Mr. George Harrys's shape and that the soul of this poor
fellow is locked up with other rubbish in a trunk in Hanover, till the
devil restores his carnal envelope, when he will probably accompany
his master Paganini through the world in a more fitting form—that
of a black poodle.'

"But if Paganini seemed to me incredible and mysterious, as I saw
him walking under the green trees of Hamburg's Maiden Lane—
how terrifying and bizarre was the impression he made on me that
evening at a concert! It took place at the Komödienhaus, and the
music-loving public had flocked there early and in such numbers that
I hardly obtained for myself a little place in the orchestra. Though
it was mail-day I saw in the first row of the boxes all of the cultured
business world of Hamburg, a whole Olympus of bankers and other
millionaires, the gods of coffee and sugar, beside their plump goddesses, the Junos of Wandrahm and the Aphrodites of Dreckwall.
An austere religious silence pervaded the hall. Every eye was turned
on the stage. Every ear was cocked. My neighbor, an old furrier, took
the soiled cotton from his ears in order the better to drink in the
precious notes which had cost him two thalers' admission. At last
a dark figure, which seemed to have risen from the underworld, appeared on the stage.

"It was Paganini in his black costume. The black dress coat and the
black undervest of an appalling cut were perhaps such as are prescribed by infernal etiquette at the court of Proserpina. The black
trousers flapped around his thin legs. His long arms appeared to grow
still longer as he held the violin in one hand, downward, and the

bow in the other, so that they almost touched the ground, and as he doled out his singular obeisances to the public. In the angular inclinations of his body there was a horrible woodenness, and at the same time something absurdly brutish, so that one could have been moved to laughter. But his face, which in the glaring lights of the orchestra appeared even more pallid and corpse-like, had something in it so imploring, timid, and humble, that a sorrowful compassion repressed one's desire to laugh. Had he learned those bows from an automaton or a dog? Did that look of entreaty belong to one who was deathly sick, or did the mockery of a crafty money-grubber lurk behind it? Was that a man on the point of death, who wished with his convulsions to delight his audience in the arena of art, like a dying gladiator? Or was it a dead man risen from his grave, a vampire with a violin, who would surely suck the money from our pockets, if not the blood from our hearts?

"Such questions crossed my mind while Paganini performed his innumerable bows. But they ceased suddenly when the wonderful master set the violin to his chin and began to play. As for me, you know my musical second sight—my gift of seeing with every note I hear the corresponding image in sound. And so, with every stroke of the bow, visible images and situations rose before my eyes. He told me in musical hieroglyphics all kinds of startling stories. Like a juggler, he conjured up before me a show of many-colored Chinese shadows, in all of which he was the chief actor. Even at the first note, the scenery had changed. He stood all at once with his music desk in a cheerful hall, gaily but irregularly decorated in the Pompadour style. All around were little mirrors, gilded Cupids, Chinese porcelain, a charming chaos of ribbons, garlands, white gloves, torn laces, false pearls, diadems of gold leaf, and similar heavenly theatrical tinsel, such as one finds in the dressing room of a prima donna. Paganini's external appearance had also changed—certainly to his advantage. He wore knee-breeches of lilac-colored satin, a white vest embroidered with silver, a coat of light-blue satin with gold buttons, and the short locks of carefully curled hair played around his face, which bloomed with the roses of youth and shone with a sweet tenderness when he eyed the pretty little lady who stood by his music desk, while he played the violin.

"I saw by his side a pretty young creature, in an old-fashioned dress of white satin, puffed at the hips, so that the figure appeared all the more engagingly slender. The powdered hair was done up high; the pretty round face flashed out boldly with its dazzling eyes, rouged cheeks, beauty patches, and impertinent, sweet little nose. In one hand she held a roll of white paper, and by the movements of her lips and the coquettish swaying of her body, she appeared to be singing. But I could hear none of her trills, and only from the violin with which the youthful Paganini accompanied the lovely child did I guess what she was singing, and what he himself felt during her song.

"Ah, those were melodies such as the nightingale sings in the twilight, when her boding heart is intoxicated by the perfume of the rose and spring-inspired with longing! Oh, what melting, voluptuous, languid bliss! Those were tones that kissed, pouted, and fled; and then embraced, and became one, and died in intoxicated union. Yes, the sounds were as playful as butterflies, escaping, teasing, hiding behind flowers—finally overtaken, then light-heartedly and happy fluttering up into the golden sunlight. But a spider, a black spider, can bring tragedy into the lives of such enamored butterflies. Did the young heart divine this? A melancholy sighing tone, like a premonition of stealthy, imminent evil, glided softly through the entrancing melodies pouring from Paganini's violin. . . . His eyes became moist. In adoration he is kneeling before his amata. But as he bows down to kiss her feet, under her bed he descries the little abbé! I don't know what the Genoese has against the poor man; but he becomes as pale as death. Furious, he seizes the little fellow, boxes his ears many times, kicks him, then flings him out of doors; and drawing a long stiletto from its sheath, he plunges it into the breast of the young beauty.

"At this moment cries of 'Bravo, bravo!' broke out on all sides. Hamburg's enthusiastic sons and daughters paid vociferous tribute to the great artist, who had just ended the first part of his program and was bowing even more awkwardly and angularly than before. It seemed to me that in his face there was more of plaintive, abject humility; and in his eyes tormenting anxiety, like a poor sinner's.

" 'Divine!' cried my neighbor, the furrier, as he scratched his ears. 'That piece alone was worth two thalers.'

"When Paganini began to play again, my eyes grew dim. The sounds were not transformed as before into bright shapes and colors. On the contrary, the master's form was enveloped in gloomy shades, from the depths of which his music wailed in rending accents of lamentation. Only at times, when the little lamp which hung over him threw its scant light on his face, I could see his pallid features, which still retained traces of youth. His costume was singular—in two colors—yellow and red. Heavy fetters weighed down his feet. Behind him grimaced a face with the features of a jovial he-goat. And at times I saw long, hairy hands moving across the strings of the violin upon which Paganini was playing. They seemed to be guiding the hand which held the bow. And a bleating laugh of approval accompanied the notes which welled from the violin, full of pain, as of someone bleeding. These were notes like the song of the fallen angels who had wantoned with the daughters of the Earth, and had been banished from the kingdom of the blessed, and descended burning with shame into the lower world. Tones in whose bottomless depths there was neither comfort nor hope. When the saints in heaven hear them, the praises of the Lord die on their blanched lips, and weeping, they hide their pious heads. At times, in the midst of the melodious torments of the piece, the obbligato bleating of the goat-laugh could be heard, and I spied in the background a crowd of little women who nodded their ugly heads with spiteful merriment, and with mischievous joy crossed their fingers in obscene gestures. Then sounds of anguish broke from the violin, fearful groans, sobs, such as have never been heard on earth before, and perhaps never again will be heard, unless in the Vale of Jehosaphat, when the mighty trumpets of the Last Judgment ring out, and the naked corpses creep from their graves and await their doom. . . . But suddenly the tormented violinist drew his bow across the strings with such frenzy and desperation, that his rattling chains fell from him, and his diabolical assistant vanished along with the other mocking demons.

"At this instant, my neighbor, the furrier, said, 'Too bad, too bad. A string has snapped. That comes of his constant pizzicato.' "

"Had a string really snapped? I don't know. I only observed the alteration of the sounds; and it seemed to me then as if Paganini and all his surroundings had suddenly changed again. I could scarcely recognize him now in the monk's brown dress, which disguised rather than clothed him. His wild face was half hidden by a hood; his waist was bound with a cord; he was barefoot. Paganini stood on a rocky promontory overlooking the sea—a solitary, defiant figure—and played the violin. It seemed to be the twilight hour. The evening had flushed the white sea, which became ever more and more rose-tinted, and roared ever more jubilantly, in secret harmony with the violin The sky grew paler. At last the mounting water looked like bright scarlet blood, and the sky overhead became ghastly-clear, white as a corpse, and the stars came out large and menacing. . . . These stars were black, black as glowing coal. But the tones of the violin grew more stormy and defiant. A mocking lust for destruction shone in the eyes of the ferocious artist; his thin lips moved with such appalling haste, that it seemed as if he were mumbling some ageless, forbidden charm with which storms are conjured up and the evil spirits who lie captive in the depths of the sea are loosed. Often, when he stretched out his long, lean arms from the sleeve of his cowl, and swept his bow through the air, he resembled a sorcerer commanding the elements with his wand. And then the depths of the sea howled with delirious madness, and the terrified waves of blood leaped up so furiously to the skies that they almost moistened the black stars with their red foam. Then there was a wailing, a crashing, a groaning, as if the whole world were cracking, and the monk played even more furiously on his violin, as if wishing by the might of his frenzied will to burst the seven seals with which Solomon had bound the iron vessels where he had imprisoned the vanquished demons. The wise king had cast those vessels into the sea, and I seemed to hear the voices of the imprisoned spirits, while Paganini's violin growled its angriest bass. But finally, I thought I heard the joyful cry of deliverance. And out of the red waves of blood emerged the heads of the unchained demons, monsters of incredible hideousness, crocodiles with bats' wings, serpents with stags' horns, apes with shells on their heads, seals with long, patriarchal beards, women's faces with breasts in place of cheeks, green camels' heads, and hermaphrodites of inconceivable forms—all stared with their cold, crafty eyes, and clutched with their fin-like claws at the fiddling monk. . . . Then in the midst of this frenzied invocation, his cowl fell back, and the curly ringlets fluttered in the air, and twined round his head like black serpents.

"This vision was so maddening that to keep my senses, I stopped up my ears and shut my eyes. When I looked up again, the specter had vanished and I saw the poor Genoese, in his ordinary shape, making his customary bows, while the audience rapturously applauded.

" 'That is the famous performance on the G-string,' my neighbor remarked. 'I myself play the violin, and I know what it is to master the instrument.'

"Fortunately the intermission was not long, otherwise my musical furrier would certainly have engaged me in a long conversation on art. Paganini again quietly set his violin to his chin, and with the first stroke of the bow, the wonderful transformation of tones began again. But now they were neither so startling in color nor so marked. They issued calmly, majestically—moving, and swelling like organ chorales in a cathedral. Everything around him seemed to have expanded into colossal space, such as no bodily eye but only that of the spirit can grasp. A shining sphere hovered in the center of this space, on which stood a man of giant stature and pride, playing the violin. Was that sphere the sun? I don't know. But in the features of the man I recognized Paganini, ideally beautiful, celestially transfigured, smiling, and at peace. His body was in the bloom of vigorous manhood, and a light-blue garment enclosed his noble limbs. The splendid locks of his black hair fell in waves about his shoulders; and as he stood there, firm and confident, a sublime divinity, and played the violin, it seemed as if all of creation were obeying his song. He was the human planet around whom the universe revolved, ringing out in measured raptures and beatific rhythms. The huge lights which swept around him, calmly and resplendently, were they stars of heaven? Those harmonies which arose from their motions, were they the music of the spheres of which poets and seers have spoken so ecstatically? At times, when I strained my gaze into the dim distance, I thought I saw white garments floating, worn by huge, muffled pilgrims, with white staves in their hands. And strange to tell! the gold knobs of their staves were those same great lights which I had taken for stars. These pilgrims moved in a vast procession around the great performer; the golden knobs of their staves glowed ever brighter at the notes of his violin, and the chorales which rang from their lips, and which I had taken for the music of the spheres, were only the dying echo of the violins. A holy, ineffable ardor dwelt in those sounds, which were often almost inaudible, like the mysterious whisper of the waters, and then swelled up again with a terrifying sweetness, like the sound of horns by moonlight,—then at last roared on with unbridled ecstasy, as if a thousand bards were sweeping the strings of their harps and raising their voices in a paean of victory. Those were sounds which ear has never heard; only the heart can dream them, when it rests at night on the breast of a loved one. Perhaps the heart can grasp them in the light of day, when it loses itself with joy in the beautiful lines and ovals of a Greek work of art."

ঽ▹ *Meyerbeer*

MEYERBEER IS AT PRESENT WRITING A NEW OPERA, to which I look forward eagerly. The unfolding of his genius is to me a very remarkable phenomenon. I follow with interest the various phases of his musical as well as his personal life, and watch the influence exercised by him on the European public, and *vice versa.* It is now ten years since I first met him in Berlin, on the way between the university and the barracks, midway between learning and the drum-beat, and he seemed very uncomfortable in that state. . . . Meyerbeer had in those days become a complete imitator of the Italians. Dissatisfied with clammy, rational, witty, colorless Berlinism, he had very early developed a natural reaction against it. He escaped to Italy, enjoyed a cheerful existence there, gave himself over to his emotions, and composed those exquisite operas in which the spirit of Rossini is exaggerated most charmingly—the gold is gilded, and the flower sprinkled with the most fragrant perfumes. That was his happiest period. He wrote with rapturous intoxication born of Italian sensuousness, and plucked the fairest flowers of life and art.

But a German temperament can not long be satisfied in this fashion. A nostalgic longing for the serious air of his Fatherland awoke in him; while he reclined under the Latin myrtles, memories of the strange awefulness of the German oak forests stole over him;—while southern zephyrs fanned him, he thought of the dark chorales of the north wind. Perhaps he felt like Madame de Sevigné who, while living close to an orangerie and constantly surrounded by the fragrance of orange blossoms, began at last to long for the smell of manure. . . . In short, a new reaction took place within him. Signore Giacomo suddenly became a German once again, and again joined hands with Germany—not with the old, decrepit, decayed Germany of the narrow-hearted Philistine, but the radiant, young, magnanimous, cosmopolite Germany of the new generation, which made all problems of humanity her own, and inscribed them, if not on her banners, yet all the more ineradicably, in her heart.

Not long after the July Revolution, Meyerbeer appeared before the public with a new work, which had sprung from his heart during the storm of the Revolution. It was *Robert le Diable.*—The hero of this opera does not know exactly what he wants, and is constantly at war with himself. His is a true picture of the moral irresoluteness of that period, which vacillated with tortured uneasiness between virtue and vice, fretting within the world of its own aspirations and obstacles, but never possessed of strength enough to withstand the assaults of Satan. I dislike this opera thoroughly—this masterpiece of faint-heartedness—not only because of its theme, but also because of its execution. For in it the composer does not trust to his genius,— he does not surrender himself to it with a whole will, but caters to the multitude, and instead of fearlessly commanding, trembles with timidity.

Meyerbeer was at that time rightly called a worried genius. He lacked triumphant confidence in himself. He was afraid of public opinion. The least reproof dismayed him. He flattered all the caprices of his public, and shook hands zealously everywhere, as if even in music he acknowledged the sovereignty of the people, and wanted to establish his preëminence by majority vote—unlike Rossini, who is absolute monarch in the kingdom of art, by the grace of God.

He is not yet free of this anxiety. He is still deeply concerned about public opinion. But the success of *Robert le Diable* had the happy effect of freeing him of this anxiety while at work, and he composes with far greater assurance. He lets the great will of his soul reveal itself in his creations. With this expansive freedom of soul he wrote the *Huguenots*, from which all his doubts have vanished. The inner struggle has ceased, and the external battle has set in, its majestic architecture amazes us. Only in this work—and for the first time— has Meyerbeer won the immortal right as a citizen of the eternal city of the spirit—the heavenly Jerusalem of art. In the *Huguenots* he at last reveals himself fearlessly. Here he draws with bold outlines and expresses in unfettered tones all that moved his heart.

What especially distinguishes this work is the balance between inspiration and artistic consummation, or better, the high level to which passion and art attain. Here man and art have competed; while the former sounds the alarum of wildest passions, the latter succeeds in transfiguring the crude chords of nature into sweet and awe-inspiring harmonies. The great multitude is swept away by the inner strength and feelings of the *Huguenots;* while the connoisseur admires the mastery which is manifested in its form. This is a Gothic cathedral, whose heaven-aspiring columns and colossal dome might have been raised by the bold hand of a giant, while the innumerable, delicate festoons, rosettes, and arabesques, which are spread over it like a veil of lace cut in stone, testify to the unwearied patience of a dwarf. A giant—in the conception and shaping of the whole; a dwarf in the laborious execution of the details—the architect of the *Huguenots* is as mysterious to us as the builders of the ancient cathedrals.

Recently I stood in company of a friend before the cathedral of Amiens, and looked with awe and pity on that towering monument of giant strength and indefatigable dwarfish patience revealed in the stone-carving. How does it happen, he asked, that we no longer can build such piles? I said, "Dear Alphonse. In those days people had convictions. We moderns have opinions, but it takes more than opinions to build this Gothic dome."

That is the nub of the matter. Meyerbeer is a man of convictions. I am not referring to the social questions of the day, though here too Meyerbeer has more firm and settled opinions than other artists. Despite the fact that he has been overwhelmed by the princes of the earth with honors and decorations, for which distinctions he has a great weakness, Meyerbeer has a heart that glows for the sacred interests of humanity, and he openly avows his adoration of the heroes of the Revolution. It is well for him that many sovereigns in the North do not understand music, else they would find more in the *Huguenots* than merely a sectarian struggle between Protestants and Catholics. Yet his convictions are not really political, much less religious in character. Meyerbeer's true religion is that of Mozart, Gluck, Beethoven. It is music. He believes in it, in it alone does he find happiness. His convictions are here. In point of depth, passion, and duration they are like those of an earlier age. Yes, I would venture to say that he is the apostle of this faith. All that touches his music, he treats with apostolic zeal and passion. Other artists are content if they compose something beautiful; and often lose interest in their work the moment it is completed. With Meyerbeer, one might say, the more severe birth-pangs do not begin till after child-birth. He is not satisfied until the creation of his genius manifests itself to others in full splendor, until the whole audience is edified by his music, and the opera has poured its feelings into every heart—feelings which he wishes to preach to the whole world and communicate to all mankind. Just as the apostle, to save one soul, heeds neither weariness nor pain, so Meyerbeer too waylays those who reject him, and does not rest until he has converted them. And the last sheep that he has saved, though it be the puniest soul of a newspaper writer, is more precious to him than the whole flock of believers who revere him with true, orthodox zeal.

Music is Meyerbeer's conviction—and that may be the cause of all those worries and anxieties which the great master so often betrays, and which so often make us smile. One should see him at work while preparing an opera for production; he is the bane of all musicians and singers, whom he torments with endless rehearsals. He is never satisfied. A false note in the orchestra stabs him like the point of a dagger—and he takes it as a mortal blow. This anxiety follows him even after the opera has been produced and thunderously acclaimed. He is still worried; and I believe he remains discontented until some thousands of persons who have admired his work—have died and are buried. He does not have to fear that *they* will turn renegades. Their souls are secured for his cause.

On the day his opera is to be produced, not even God can satisfy him. If it rains or it is chilly, he is worried lest Mademoiselle Falcon catch cold; if the evening is fine and warm, he is afraid that the good weather may keep people out in open, and the theater will remain empty. Nothing is to be compared with the meticulous care with which Meyerbeer corrects the proofs of his printed music, for which he has become a by-word among the artists of Paris. But one must keep in mind the fact that music is dearer to him than anything else on earth—certainly even than life itself. When the cholera broke out in Paris, I implored him to leave as soon as possible; but he had a few days' urgent business—he had to arrange for an Italian version of the libretto of *Robert le Diable*.

The *Huguenots* is a work of greater conviction than *Robert le Diable*, both in form and content. As I have already stated, the multitude is carried away by the theme; but the more critical observer admires the progress of his artistry, and observes the new forms it has taken. According to the express opinion of most competent judges, all future composers of the opera will have to study the *Huguenots*. Meyerbeer has brought instrumentation farther than any one before him. His use of the chorus, which here speaks with the voice of individuals and has abandoned operatic tradition, is unprecedented. Since *Don Giovanni*, there certainly has been no more astonishing phenomenon in music than the fourth act of the *Huguenots*. Here, in the terribly affecting scene of the consecration of the swords— where a benediction is pronounced on murder—there is a duet which surpasses in effect all that has preceded.

How is it that an artist, who from the very cradle has been spared all blood-draining cares—who was born in the lap of wealth, fondled and pampered by the whole family, whose every fancy was gladly, even passionately indulged—and who, more than any other human artist, seems destined to good fortune—how is it that he feels those profound sorrows that sob and sigh through his music? For what the musician has not himself felt, he can never express with such power and vehemence. Is it not strange that the artist whose material wants are satisfied, is all the more bitterly visited by spiritual suffering? But that is a piece of good fortune for the public, which owes its most ideal joys to the suffering of the artist. The artist may be compared to that child of whom fairy tales relate that all its tears become sheer pearls. But alas! The world, which is a cruel stepmother, beats the poor child all the more mercilessly so that it may weep as many pearls as possible. . . .

৫৶ *Mendelssohn and Rossini*

THE *Stabat Mater* OF ROSSINI WAS THE OUTSTANDING EVENT of last season. It is still being widely discussed and even the censure which has been passed against the great master, from a North German point of view, indicates in a striking way the originality and depth of his genius. Certain heavy, tedious criticasters, who, if they have not deliberately shammed an extravagant spirituality, have certainly tortured themselves into having very narrow and erroneous ideas on sacred music, complain: "The execution is too worldly, too sensuous, too playful, considering the sacredness of the material; too light, too agreeable, and too entertaining."

Just as among painters, so also among musicians there are erroneous ideas regarding the way Christian subjects should be treated. The former believe that the true Christian must be depicted in subtly lean outlines, and in as afflicted and colorless a style as possible. The designs of Overbeck [5] seem to them to be ideal in this respect. To refute this fallacy, I shall merely call attention to the religious paintings of the Spanish school, in whom richness of outline and color prevails. Yet, no one would deny that they breathe the spirit of devout Christianity, and their creators were no less God-intoxicated than the famous

masters who adopted Catholicism at Rome so as to be able to paint
with greater fervor. Not external haggardness and pallor are the
earmarks of true Christian art, but a certain inner, transcending emotion, which can be acquired neither through baptism nor study—be
it in music or painting. For that reason I believe that the *Stabat* of
Rossini is more truly Christian than *Paulus*, the oratorio by Felix
Mendelssohn-Bartholdy, which has been extolled by the opponents
of Rossini as a model of the Christian style.

Heaven forbid that I should be guilty of reproaching so estimable
a master as the composer of *Paulus* and least of all does it occur to the
writer of these pages to carp at the Christianity of the oratorio in
question, because Felix Mendelssohn-Bartholdy happens to be Jewish
by birth. But I cannot refrain from observing that in the very year
in which M. Mendelssohn began his career as a Christian in Berlin
(he was baptized at the age of thirteen), Rossini had practically fallen
away from Christianity, and had plunged into the worldliness of
operatic music. Now that he has himself abandoned the latter and
dreamed his way back into youthful memories of Roman Catholicism,
or into those days when he sang as a choir-boy at the Cathedral of
Pesaro or functioned as an acolyte at the Mass—now that those old
organ notes re-echo in his memory, and he seizes the pen to write
Stabat—he has no need to reconstruct the spirit of Christianity in
a learned way, or much less slavishly to copy Handel or Sebastian
Bach. All he needs to do is to call to mind the earliest sounds of his
childhood, and wonder of wonders!—no matter how solemn or painful these may be—no matter how powerfully they sigh and bleed—
they retain something of childhood and remind me of a children's
representation of the Passion which I once saw at Cette. . . .

This is the ageless grace and charm of Rossini—this imperturbable
serenity, which no impresario or music-merchant can destroy or even
disturb by insulting his genius. No matter what vileness, treason, or
injustice may have been visited on him, you will never find in his
works the least suspicion of gall. Like the fountain of Arethusa which
preserved its original sweetness though it flowed through the bitter
seas—the heart of Rossini retains its melodious charm and sweetness,
although it has drained to the dregs the bitter wormwood of this
world.

As I have said, the *Stabat* of the great master was the outstanding
musical event of the year. As for the first performance, which set
the fashion, I need merely say that the Italians sang. The hall of the

Italian Opera was transformed into the fore-court of heaven where saintly nightingales sobbed and the most fashionable tears flowed. "La France Musicale" too presented at its concerts the greater portion of the *Stabat*, and, it goes without saying, with huge success. At these concerts we also heard the *Paulus* of M. Felix Mendelssohn-Bartholdy, who by reason of this proximity drew our attention and provoked comparison with Rossini. Among the greater part of the public, this comparison was by no means in favor of our young compatriot. It was as if one should compare the Apennines in Italy with the Templow Hill of Berlin. Still, the Templow Hill has some virtues, and it demands the respect of the multitude because it bears a cross on its summit. "In this sign you shall conquer." Of course, not in France, the land of unbelief—where M. Mendelssohn has always failed. He was the sacrificial lamb of the season, while Rossini was the musical lion, whose melodious roaring can still be heard. There is a rumor abroad that M. Felix Mendelssohn will make a personal appearance in Paris within a few days. This much is certain—that through influence in high places and diplomatic intercession, M. Scribe has been prevailed upon to write a libretto, for which M. Mendelssohn will then write an opera. Will our young compatriot be successful in this venture?

ৡ‍ *Berlioz, Liszt, and Chopin*

[*1837*]

ONLY HERE AND THERE IN THIS WILDERNESS do we have a few concerts that afford wonderful refreshment to music lovers. Among these were, this winter, the Sundays at the Conservatoire, a few private soirées in the Rue de Bondy, and most important, the concerts of Berlioz and Liszt.

The latter two are indeed the most remarkable musical phenomena in the musical world here. I say the most remarkable, not the most beautiful, or the most delightful. Berlioz is soon to give us an opera, the subject of which is an episode from the life of Benvenuto Cellini—the casting of Perseus. Something unusual is anticipated, because the composer has already produced extraordinary works. His mind inclines to the fantastic—and is more closely akin to the sentimental than to the emotional. He greatly resembles Callot, Gozzi, and Hoffmann.[6] Even in his external appearance he betrays this inclination It is a pity that he has had his hair cut—that stupendous, antediluvian coiffure, that bristling mane which rose above his brow as over a craggy steep. Thus I saw him six years ago, for the first time—and thus I shall see him in my mind forever.

It was at the Conservatoire de Musique. His great symphony [7] was being performed, a bizarre nocturne, only at times lighted up by a sentimental white skirt, fluttering here and there, or by a brimstone yellow flash of irony. The best section was a Witches' Sabbath, in which the devil reads the Mass, and the music of the Catholic Church is parodied with most intense and horrible mockery. It is the kind of farce in which all the secret serpents which nest in our bosom suddenly leap up in rapture.

The man sitting next to me in the box, a lively and talkative young man, pointed out the composer, who sat at the extreme end of the hall, in a corner of the orchestra, and played the drum. That is his instrument. "Do you see," my neighbor said, "that fat Englishwoman in the proscenium? That is Miss Smithson, whom Berlioz has loved desperately for three years. To that passion we are indebted for the wild symphony to which you are now listening." Indeed, there in the proscenium box sat the celebrated actress of the Covent Garden Theatre. Berlioz was staring at her alone, and every time their glances met, he pounded away at the drum, as if mad. Since then, Miss Smithson has become Madame Berlioz, and her husband has had his hair cut. When I heard the symphony once more at the Conservatoire last winter, he was sitting in the back of the orchestra, drumming away as before; and the fat Englishwoman was sitting, as before, in the proscenium box. Their glances met, as in the past,—but he no longer pounded the drum quite so furiously.

Liszt is most closely akin to Berlioz, and knows best how to perform the latter's music. I do not have to tell you about his talent. His fame is as wide as Europe. He is beyond doubt the artist who excites the wildest enthusiasm in Paris—as well as the most vigorous opposition; and that means that no one speaks of him with indifference. Without positive merit, no one can excite favorable or hostile passions. It takes fire to set people ablaze—whether with hatred or love. What redounds most greatly to Liszt's credit is the great respect with which even his personal enemies regard his merits. He is a man of perverse though noble character, unselfish and straightforward. His intellectual gifts are remarkable. He is greatly inclined to speculation, and the study of the various schools of thought concerned with solving the great problems of heaven and earth are of greater interest to him than his art. For some time he was an ardent disciple of the Saint-Simonian philosophy; later he became lost in the spiritual fogs—or better, the vapors—of Ballanche.[8] Now he is carried away by the republican-Catholic doctrines of Lamennais, who has nailed the Jacobin cap to the cross. . . . Only heaven knows in what intellectual stable he will find his next hobby horse. But this insatiable yearning for light and godhood is praiseworthy. It testifies to his hunger for sainthood and religion. It is, of course, obvious that this restless head, irresistibly driven by all the requirements and doctrines of the age and feeling a need to concern himself with all the problems of mankind and mess with every brew which the Lord is preparing for the future of humanity—that this Franz Liszt can be no tame pianist for peaceful bourgeois and complacent Philistines. When he sits at the piano, and after brushing back his hair, begins to improvise, you can hear the thunder roar across the ivory keys. Here is a wilderness of thoughts mounting to heaven, as well as the fragrance of the sweetest flowers. The listener is at once tortured and enthralled—mostly tortured.

I admit that though I like Liszt, his music produces no very pleasant sensations in my mind. Particularly, since I am Sunday's child, and see ghosts, where others only hear them. Every tone which he evokes from the piano produces a corresponding sound-picture in my mind. In short, his music becomes visible to my inner eye. My mind is still staggered when I recall the last concert. It was given as a benefit for the unfortunate Italians, at the residence of the beautiful and ailing princess who so nobly symbolizes her physical and spiritual homeland—Italy and Heaven.[9] (You have no doubt seen her in Paris—that ideally perfect form, which is but a prisonhouse of the holiest and most angelic spirit—but so beautiful a prison that all stand before it amazed and enchanted.)

It was at a benefit concert for the Italian victims that I heard Liszt play during the past winter. I am not sure, but I could have sworn that he was performing variations on a theme from the Apocalypse. At first I could not distinctly see the four legendary beasts. I only heard their voices—especially the roar of the lion and the screaming of the eagle. But I plainly saw the ox with a book in his hands. Liszt played the "Vale of Jehosaphat" best of all. There were the barriers, as at tournaments. The resurrected, who crowded in that immense space, deathly pale and trembling, were the spectators. First, Satan galloped into the lists, in black harness, on a milk-white steed. Behind him slowly rode Death on a fallow charger. And last of all, Christ appeared in golden armor, on a black palfrey, and with his lance he bore Satan to the ground—and then Death. The spectators all applauded, paid stormy tribute to Liszt, who rose from the piano exhausted and bowed to the ladies . . . , and across the lips of the Fairest flitted that melancholy-sweet smile. . . .

It would be unfair not to mention here the pianist who is most celebrated after Liszt. It is Chopin, who is remarkable not only as a brilliant virtuoso, by reason of his technical perfection, but also as an equally eminent composer. He is a man of the first rank. He is the favorite of the élite, who seek to find in music the most exquisite enjoyment of the soul. His fame is aristocratic. He is redolent with the perfumed praise of good society; but he is also personally distinguished, in his own right.

Chopin was born in Poland of French parents, and was partly educated in Germany. The influences of three nations have shaped a most remarkable personality; for in this way he has absorbed what is best in all three. Poland gave him a chivalrous spirit and her historic sorrow. France endowed him with gentle amiability and grace. Germany bestowed upon him a romantic depth of feeling. And Nature gave him an elegant, slender, somewhat spare frame, and the noblest heart and genius. Yes, we must admit that Chopin possesses genius in the fullest meaning of the word. He is not only a virtuoso; he is also a poet. He reveals the poetry which dwells in his soul. He is a tone-poet; and nothing can compare with the pleasure we experience when he improvises at the piano. Then he is neither Pole, nor Frenchman, nor German. He manifests a far nobler descent. We see that he comes from the land of Mozart, Raphael, and Goethe— that his true fatherland is the dream-world of poesy. When he improvises, it seems to me as if I were being visited by a compatriot, from my beloved homeland, and were listening to all the singular things that had taken place in my absence. . . . Sometimes I am tempted to interrupt him and ask, "Tell me how is the lovely water-nixie who used to bind her silver veil so coquettishly around her green locks? Does the white-bearded sea-god still pursue her with his foolish, faded old love? And are our roses still as fiery-proud as ever? And do the trees sing as sweetly in the moonlight as they used to?"

⟨⟩ *Franz Liszt*

[*1841*]

YES, THAT GENIUS IS HERE AGAIN, and is giving concerts which exercise an almost miraculous spell. In his presence, all other pianists vanish—with the exception of Chopin, the Raphael of the piano. All the rest seem only piano-players; they shine by the dexterity with which they manipulate the stringed wood; when Liszt plays, however, you do not think merely of the difficulties which he has overcome—the piano disappears, and only music is revealed. Here Liszt has made the most astonishing progress since we heard him last. And he has also acquired a degree of self-possession which he formerly lacked. For example, when he depicted a storm on the piano, we saw lightning flashes convulsing his features; his limbs appeared to be shaken by the tempest, and his long hair seemed to drip with the rain. But now-adays, even when he portrays the most violent thunderstorm, he appears to be standing above it, like some traveller on a summit of the Alps, while the tempest rages in the valley below him; the clouds gather at his feet, the lightnings curl like serpents beneath him,—but he lifts his head and smiles into the clear air.

In spite of his genius, Liszt is meeting with opposition here in Paris, mostly on the part of serious musicians who grant the laurel to his rival, the imperial Thalberg. Liszt has already given two concerts in which he played without the assistance of any other artists—against all precedent. He is now preparing a third concert to raise funds for Beethoven's momument. Beethoven's music must be very much to his liking. For Beethoven raises that spiritual art to the point where the visible world cries out in agony, and Nature is an-nihilated. I am filled with an awe I cannot conceal, although my friends shake their heads in dismay. It is to me a profoundly significant matter that toward the end of his life Beethoven became deaf, so that even the invisible world of sound no longer had reality. His tones were only memories of sounds—ghosts of vanished music; and his last works bear on their forehead the unmistakable stamp of death. . . .

[*1844*]

I MUST SAY IT AGAIN—there are only three pianists who deserve serious consideration—Chopin, that gracious poet of sound, who unfortunately was very ill this winter and not to be seen often; Thalberg, the musical gentleman who does not have to play the piano in order to find a welcome everywhere and who seems to regard his talent merely as an appanage; and our Liszt, who despite every perversity and asperity, always remains our dear Liszt, and at this moment has set the Paris *beau monde* agog. Yes, he is here, the great agitator, our Franz Liszt, the knight-errant of all possible Orders (except the French Legion of Honor, which Louis Philippe will not confer on a virtuoso); he is here—the Hohenzollern-Hechinger Court Councillor, Doctor of Philosophy, and Miracle Doctor of Music, resurrected Pied Piper of Hamelin, the new Faust—always followed by his poodle, Belloni—the ennobled, yet ever noble, Franz Liszt! He is here—the modern Amphion, who with the sounds of his strings set in motion the stones of the Cathedral of Cologne, so that they moved into place, as once did the walls of Thebes. He is here—the modern Homer, whom Germany, Hungary, and France—the three greatest countries—claim as their native son, while the singer of the *Iliad* is fought for only by seven small provincial towns! He is here: Attila, God's scourge of all the Erard pianos, which already tremble at the news of his coming and are convulsed under his hands, bleed, and wail, so that the Society for the Prevention of Cruelty to Animals should really look to them! He is here—the mad, lovely, ugly, enigmatic, deadly—and at the same time very childlike—child of his time, the giant dwarf, the raging Roland with his Hungarian sword of honor—the gifted Merry Andrew, whose madness ravishes our senses—and to whom we shall at any rate offer the faithful service of publicizing the great furor which he has aroused here.[10] We openly confirm his huge success—but what our own interpretation of it may be, whether we give this celebrated virtuoso our personal approval or withhold it, is probably a matter of complete indifference to him, since our voice is that of one man—and our authority in the realm of music of no great importance.

Some time ago, when I heard of the giddiness which broke out in Germany, and principally in Berlin, whenever Liszt appeared, I shrugged my shoulders with pity and said to myself, "Our Germany, with its Sabbath-stillness, will not miss the chance of being aroused, in a law-abiding way; it will shake itself, numb with sleep, and the Abderites of the Spree will tickle each other up to the point of enthusiasm, and declaim: 'Oh, Love, thou ruler of gods and men!' "

They're more interested in the show, for the sake of the show—it doesn't matter what the occasion—Georg Herwegh, Franz Liszt, Fanny Elssler.[11] If Herwegh is prohibited, then they take harmless and unobjectionable Liszt. That is what I thought; and that is how I explained Lisztomania to myself. I took it all as an effect of the absence of political freedom on the other side of the Rhine. But I was wrong—as I saw last week at the Italian Opera House, where Liszt gave his first concert—before a gathering which might well be called the flower of society. Here were alert Parisians, at home with the greatest events of history, some of whom had to a greater or lesser extent lived through the great drama of the times; here were also many invalids retired from the pleasures of the arts—the weariest men of action, ladies equally weary from having danced the polka the whole winter through—a plethora of busy and blasé spirits. Certainly this was not a Germanic sentimental-Berlinese-delicate public, before whom Liszt was performing—by himself—or rather, accompanied only by his genius.

Yet how startling, how powerful was the effect merely of his appearance! How violent the applause which greeted him! Bouquets were thrown at his feet! It was impressive to observe how tranquilly this conqueror allowed the bouquets to rain down on him; how graciously he smiled as he placed a red camelia, which he had plucked from one of them, in his lapel. This was done in the presence of a number of young soldiers who had just returned from Africa, where they had seen bullets, not flowers, raining down on them; and their breasts were decorated with the red camelias of a hero's blood—but the world took no particular notice of them. Strange, I thought—these Parisians have seen Napoleon, who had to wage wars to win their attention—and now they are cheering Franz Liszt! What powerful rejoicing! Frenzy unparalleled in the history of frenzy! What was the real explanation of this phenomenon?

The answer to this question belongs rather in the realm of pathology than aesthetics. A physician who specializes in women's diseases, and with whom I discussed the spell which Liszt casts over his public, smiled mysteriously and said a great deal about magnetism, Galvanism, electricity, contagion in a humid hall always full of countless tapers and hundreds of perfumed and sweating persons, histrionic epilepsy, the phenomenon of tickling, the musical Spanish fly, and other scabrous subjects, which have, I think, some connection with the mysteries of the *bona dea*. Probably the solution is not so mysterious or profound, but very prosaic.

It sometimes seems to me that the whole enchantment is to be traced to the fact that no one in the world knows how to organize "successes" as well as Franz Liszt—or better, how to stage them. In that art, he is a genius, a Philadelphia, a Bosco,[12] yes, a Meyerbeer. The most eminent persons are his accomplices, and his hired enthusiasts are admirably trained. Stories of popping champagne bottles and the most prodigal generosity are loudly trumpeted in the most reliable newspapers and attract recruits in every city. . . .

ဒे Jan Steen

THE HOUSE IN WHICH I LODGED IN LEYDEN was once the dwelling of Jan Steen, the great Jan Steen, whom I regard as the equal of Raphael.[13] Even as a sacred painter he was as great as Raphael, and that will some day be clearly seen when the religion of sorrow has passed away, and the religion of joy has snatched the mournful veil that covers the rose-bushes of the earth, and the nightingales at last dare pour forth their long-suppressed raptures.

But no nightingale will ever sing so gaily and joyously as Jan Steen painted. No one has ever felt so profoundly that life on this earth should be one prolonged carnival. He knew that life is but the many-hued kiss of God, and that the Holy Ghost reveals himself most magnificently in light and laughter.

His eyes laughed as they looked into the light; and the light was reflected in his laughing eyes.

And Jan always remained a dear, good child. When the stern old pastor of Leyden sat down by his hearth one day and delivered a long exhortation on his jovial life, his laughing, un-Christian ways, his love of drink, his disorderly home life and his incorrigible love of mirth, Jan listened quietly for two long hours, without betraying the slightest impatience at this reprimand; only once did he interrupt the speaker. "Yes, Domine, that light is far better; yes, Domine, I beg you turn your footstool a little nearer the fire, so that your face may have more of the red glow of the fire, and let the rest of your body remain in the shadow."

Furious, the Domine rose and departed. But Jan seized his palette and painted the severe old man exactly as he had seen him, deep in his sermon, ignorant of the fact that he was posing as a model. The picture is admirable, and it hung in my bedroom in Leyden.

After seeing so many of Jan Steen's paintings in Holland, I seem to know the man's whole life. Yes, I know all his kith and kin, his wife, his children, his mother, all his cousins, his enemies, and other connections—yes, I know them by sight. These faces greet us from all his paintings; a collection of them would be a biography of the painter. He has often with a single stroke set down the deepest secrets of his soul. I am sure that his wife frequently chided him for drinking so much. For in the painting of the Twelfth Night Festival, where Jan is portrayed in the midst of his whole family, we see his wife with a huge jug of wine in her hand, her eyes gleaming like a Bacchante's. I am convinced, however, that the good woman never drank too much wine; only the rogue wished to make us believe that it was his wife and not he who really loved to drink. That is why he seems to be laughing so merrily in that picture. There he sits in the midst of his own people. He is perfectly happy. His little son is King of the Feast and stands on a stool wearing a tinsel-crown; his old mother, her face creasing in a happy smirk, holds the youngest grandchild in her arms; the musicians are playing the maddest and merriest dance tunes; and the frugal-serious, the frugal-grouchy housewife is depicted as a toper, an object of suspicion for posterity!

How often during my stay in Leyden have I thought back for hours to these domestic scenes which Jan must have lived and suffered! Sometimes I had the feeling that I was seeing him in the flesh, sitting at his easel, and now and then seizing the great jug, "reflecting, and then drinking; and then drinking without reflecting." This was no dreary Catholic specter, but a modern, luminous spirit of joy, who after death still visits his old workshop to paint merry pictures and to drink. Only ghosts such as this will our descendants sometimes see in the light of day, while the sun shines through the windows—and from the spire resound not gloomy and dismal bells but the flushed, jubilant trumpets, announcing the joyous hour of noon!

৪৵ *Delacroix*

I NOW TURN TO DELACROIX,[14] who has contributed a picture which always drew a crowd, and which I therefore class with those paintings which attracted the most attention. The sacredness of the subject forbids a severe criticism of the coloring, with which perhaps some fault might be found. But despite a few artistic shortcomings, the picture breathes greatness, of a strangely attractive kind. It represents a group of people during the Revolution. From the center—almost like an allegorical figure—stands out a young woman with a red Phrygian cap on her head, a gun in one hand and a tricolor flag in the other. She is striding over corpses, calling men to battle. She is naked to the hips—a beautiful, tempestuous body; the face has a bold profile, and insolent suffering is visible in her features. All in all she is a strange blend of Phryne, the fish-wife, and the goddess of liberty. It is not clear whether the figure was intended to represent the last of these, for it seems to symbolize the savage power of the people throwing off a deadly burden. I must confess that this figure reminds me of those peripatetic female philosophers, those swift courtiers of love—those lovers on the run—who swarm on the boulevards in the evening. I confess that the little chimney-sweep Cupid who stands with a pistol in either hand beside this Venus of the streets is soiled by something other than soot; that the candidate for the Pantheon lying dead on the ground was the day before selling passes to the theater, that the hero rushing on with his gun certainly has the galleys in his features and the smell of the criminal courts in his ugly clothes. But there we have it: A great idea has ennobled and sanctified these common people, this *crapule*, and has again awakened the slumbering dignity within their souls.

Sacred July days of Paris! You will forever be witness to the innate nobility of man—a nobility which can never be completely destroyed. He who has beheld you will never grieve over ancient graves, but in the fullness of joy will believe in the resurrection of the people. Sacred days of July! How beautiful was the sun and how great the people of Paris! The gods in heaven who gazed down on this great battle shouted with admiration, and would gladly have left their golden seats and descended to the earth to become citizens of Paris!

But envious and timid as they are, they feared lest man might bloom too loftily and gloriously, and through their all-too-complaisant priests, they sought "to darken the gleam and to lay the lofty in the dust." And so they organized that Claude Potter animal piece, the Belgian Revolution.[15] And thereby they saw to it that the tree of liberty would not grow too high into the heavens.

There is no other picture in the Salon in which the color is so deeply impressed as in the "July Revolution" of Delacroix. But this very absence of gloss and sheen—as well as the smoke of powder and dust which covers the figures as with a grey cobweb, the sun-dried coloring which seems to thirst for a drop of water—all these endow the painting with truth, originality, and reality in which one senses the very physiognomy of the July days.

Among the spectators there were many who had been either actors or lookers-on in the events which were depicted, and these could not sufficiently praise the picture. "Mâtin," cried a grocer, "these gamins fought like giants." A young woman observed that the student of the Polytechnic Institute, who is invariably to be found in all pictures of the July Revolution, of which there were many,—at least forty—on display, was absent in this one.

"Papa," cried a little Carlist girl, "who is that dirty woman with the red cap?" "Indeed," replied her noble papa jestingly, with a sweetly wry smile, "indeed, dear child, she has little in common with the purity of the lilies. She is the goddess of liberty." "Papa, she doesn't even have a chemise on her." "A true goddess of liberty, dear child, seldom has a chemise, and is therefore very angry at all people who wear clean linen."

With these words, the man drew his cuffs over his long idle hands and said to his neighbor: "Eminence, should the republicans succeed today in having some old woman shot dead by the National Guard at the Porte-St. Denis, they will bear the sacred corpse round the boulevards, and the people will go crazy, and then we'll have a new revolution."

"*Tant mieux!*" whispered His Eminence, a lean, tightly buttoned man, evidently disguised as a worldling, which is the custom of all priests of Paris today who fear public derision, or perhaps because of a bad conscience. "*Tant mieux!* Marquis, provided there are really plenty of horrors, so that the measure may once more be full. The Revolution will then devour its own instigators, especially those conceited bankers, who, thank God, have ruined themselves." "Yes,

Eminence, they wished to destroy us *à tout prix,* because we would not receive them in our salons. That is the secret of the July Revolution. That is why money was distributed in the suburbs, workingmen were released from factories, and innkeepers were paid to give away wine free and put gunpowder in it in order to excite them, *et du reste, c'était le soleil."*

Perhaps the Marquis was right. It was the sun. In the month of July especially the sun's rays filled the hearts of the people of Paris with such intoxication when freedom was threatened, that the sun-drunk people rose up against the rotting bastilles and ordinances of serfdom. The sun and the city understand each other most wonderfully. They love each other. Before the evening sun sinks into the sea, she casts a long and affectionate glance at the beautiful city of Paris, and kisses with her last fleeting rays the tricolor on her spires. A French poet has wisely proposed that the July festival be celebrated by a symbolic wedding; that every year Paris be married to the great flaming lucky star of her freedom—the sun—on the Place de Bastille, in the same way in which the Doge of Venice each year ascended the golden Bucentaur to join the imperial city of Venice to the Adriatic. . . .

ॐ *Art and History*

MY OLD PROPHECY CONCERNING THE END OF THE ART-EPOCH which began with Goethe's birth and will end with his burial seems to be approaching fulfillment. Art of the present day must perish because its principles are rooted in an outworn ancient regime, in the vanished days of the Holy Roman Empire. Hence, like all faded relics of the past, it stands in glaring contradiction to the present. It is this contradiction, and not the temper of the times, which is so unfavorable to art. As a matter of fact, the temper of the times should prove to be a blessing, as was the case in Athens and Florence where art flourished splendidly even in the midst of turbulent warfare and party strife. It is true that the Greek and Florentine artists did not lead a secluded, self-centered existence, nor sealed their idling and imaginative faculties hermetically to all the great sorrows and joys of their day. No, their works were but the visionary reflections of their age, and they themselves were complete men, with personalities as strong as their creative powers.

Phidias and Michelangelo are cut from the same granite block as their works; and just as the latter harmonized with the Greek and Catholic temples, so did their creators live in the closest harmony with their surroundings. They did not separate their works from the political life of the day; they did not labor with a puny sort of private inspiration, which deceitfully winds its way into any subject at hand. Aeschylus wrote *The Persians* with the same truthfulness with which he fought them at Marathon; and Dante composed his *Comedy*, not as a poet writing to order, but as a fugitive Guelph, and in his banishment and in the travails of war he did not bewail the decay of his talents—but that of freedom.

However, the new age will bring forth a new art, which will accord with it, and which will not have to borrow its symbolism from a frayed past. It will even give birth to new techniques, different from those of a bygone day. Until then, let self-intoxicated subjectivity, individuality freed from all ties to the world, and personality, free as the gods, affirm their lust for life, in sound and color. This is surely much more salutary than the dead sham of ancient art!—

Perhaps art itself is destined to have a sorrowful end—and with it the world too? That predominant spirituality which manifests itself in European literature may be a sign of approaching death—as men in their last hour suddenly become clairvoyant and utter otherworldly secrets with deathly pale lips. Or perhaps age-worn Europe will rejuvenate itself? Perhaps the twilight-spirituality of its artists and writers is not really a miraculous premonition of death, but the awesome prescience of a new birth, the sensible breath of the new spring!

This year's exhibition shows in many of the pictures a rejection of that unearthly fear of death, and the signs of a greater promise. The Archbishop of Paris expects salvation from the cholera, from Death. I, on the other hand, expect it from Freedom, from Life. In this respect, our faiths differ. I believe that France will express a new art from the heart's depths of her new life. This difficult task too will be solved by the French—that light, flighty nation, which we so readily compare to a butterfly.

But the butterfly is also a symbol of the immortality of the soul and of its eternal rejuvenation.

₹➤ *Medieval Architecture*

ARCHITECTURE IN THE MIDDLE AGES partook of the character of the other arts; for actually all manifestations of life harmonized in the most wonderful fashion. Here, as in poetry, the tendency to parable shows itself. When we enter a Gothic cathedral, we hardly suspect the esoteric meaning of its stone symbolism. What we obtain is only the general impression. We feel the exaltation of spirit and the morti-fication of flesh. The interior is a hollow cross, and we wander here amidst the very instruments of martyrdom. The stained glass win-dows cast on us red and green lights, much like blood and putrefaction; funeral dirges whine all about us; under us are mortuary tablets and decay; and the soul aspires to reach the heights above by means of colossal columns, and painfully wrenches itself loose from the body, which sinks to the ground like a limp garment. But only when we behold the exterior of these Gothic cathedrals—these immense structures which are built with so aerial a touch, so delicately, so daintily, so transparently, almost as if they were chiselled, and could almost be mistaken for Flemish lace wrought in marble,—do we truly feel the full power of that age which could so master stone as to trans-fuse it by spirit, and compel even the most recalcitrant of materials to declare the spirit of Christianity.

₹➤ *Rome*

WHEN I VISITED THE AMPHITHEATER OF VERONA, a comedy was being performed there. In the center a little wooden stage had been erected, on which an Italian farce was being played, and the spectators sat under the open skies, some on small foot-stools, others on the high stone seats of the ancient amphitheater. There I too settled myself and watched the mock battles of Brighella and Tartaglia from the very spot on which the Romans sat and witnessed the gladiatorial shows and combats of wild beasts. The sky above—that blue crystal dome—alone was unchanged. Gradually twilight deepened and the stars began to shine. Truffaldino laughed, Smeraldina lamented, and finally Pantaloon appeared and joined their hands. The spectators clapped approval, and left in high spirits. The whole play had not cost one drop of blood. After all, it was only a play.

The games of the Romans, on the other hand, were never games. These people could never amuse themselves with mere appearances; they lacked the necessary childlike exuberance of spirit, and being of a serious nature, they revealed in their games that same rough, sanguinary seriousness of spirit. They were not great men; but because of their position, they were greater than any other children of the earth—for their vantage point was Rome. Whenever they stepped down from their seven hills they were small. Hence the littleness we discover in their private life. Herculaneum and Pompeii, those palimpsests of nature, where the old stone texts are being excavated today, reveal to the traveller the private life of the Romans, in their narrow houses with their tiny rooms, contrasting so strikingly with those colossal buildings which expressed their public life—those theaters, aqueducts, fountains, highways, bridges, whose ruins still excite our wonder.

But that is really the nub of the matter. Just as the Greeks are great through the idea of Art, and the Hebrews through the idea of a most holy God, so the Romans are great through their idea of Eternal Rome,—supremely great when they fought, wrote, and built under its inspiration. The greater Rome grew, the more did that idea expand. The individual was lost in it, and the great men, who are still preëminent, were elevated by the idea, which renders the littleness of the little men even more obvious. The Romans are consequently the greatest of heroes and the greatest of satirists: heroes when in the midst of action they thought of Rome; satirists, when they thought of Rome, and passed judgment on the actions of their contemporaries. Compared with so gigantic a conception as the Idea of Rome, the greatest individual personality appears puny, and a fair prey for ridicule. Tacitus is the most cruel master of such satire, just because he felt most profoundly the greatness of Rome and the littleness of man. He is altogether in his element whenever he reports the malicious and scandalous gossip of the Forum concerning the Emperors. And he is cynically jubilant whenever he can recount the disgrace of a senator or some instance of disappointed sycophancy.

ঙ়ে *The Decline of Heroism*

FOR THAT DENIGRATION OF ALL THAT IS GREAT, and for that radical destruction of heroism we may particularly thank the bourgeoisie, the social class which has risen to power here in France by the overthrow of the hereditary nobility, and has succeeded in imposing its narrow, sober, shopkeeper sentiments on every aspect of life. It will surely not be long before all heroic thoughts and feelings in this country become laughable, if they do not disappear completely. I do not, on my life, pray for the restoration of the rule of the privileged nobility. The latter was merely rottenness glossed over, a corpse decked out and perfumed—which had to be interred quietly or quickly thrown into some vault—lest it insist on continuing its hopeless and sham existence, or protest too strongly against being buried. But the new regime which supplanted the old is even more deadly. Far more repulsive is the unvarnished crudity, life without perfume, this industrious chivalry of money, this National Guard, this armed terror, which assaults you with its intelligent bayonets when you dare assert that the world should be governed by genius, beauty, love, and strength, and not by a puny talent for numbers, or the well-paid skill of the counting-house.

The men of thought who in the eighteenth century so tirelessly prepared the way for the Revolution would blush to see for whom they had labored; that selfishness has built its miserable dwellings where once palaces stood; that here a new aristocracy has been spawned amid usury, an aristocracy more repulsive than that older one—an aristocracy which does not even attempt to justify its existence by devotion to an idea, or by an ideal faith in traditional virtues, but whose first and last principles are gain—commonly the fruit of petty perseverance, if not of sordid vices—and the possession of money.

When we look at this new aristocracy closely, we observe certain analogies between it and the older aristocracy, particularly when the latter was on the point of dying. The privileges of blood were founded on documents which proved not the superiority of ancestors, but their number. It was a kind of paper-money of birth, and gave the nobility under Louis XV and Louis XVI their legal tender, and classified them according to their denominations, in the same way as commercial paper today gives the industrialists under Louis Philippe their value and determines their rank. Here it is the Exchange which assumes the office of assessing dignities and allotting rank to which the paper documents entitle one.—In this respect it reveals the same sort of conscientiousness as the sworn heralds of the last century, who investigated the patents by which the nobility sought to justify their pretensions to eminence. This moneyed aristocracy, though like the former aristocracy of birth it forms a hierarchy in which each thinks himself better than the next one, has, however, a certain *esprit de corps*. In emergencies it consolidates its ranks, it makes sacrifices when the honor of the corporation is at stake, and I understand it even establishes societies to support those of its colleagues who have fallen on evil days.

ह्ॐ *The Empire*

WAS THE PERIOD OF THE EMPIRE IN FRANCE really as beautiful and blissful as the Bonapartists, great and small, from the disabled soldier Ricou to the Duchess of Abrantes, would have us believe? I don't think so. The fields lay wasted, and men were marched away to be slaughtered. Everywhere mothers wept, and homes were desolate. These Bonapartists resemble the drunken beggar who shrewdly observed that as long as he was sober, his dwelling was a wretched hovel, his wife was in rags, and his child was sick and hungry. But the moment he imbibed a few glasses of brandy, all his misery vanished at once; his hut became a palace, his wife a magnificently attired princess, and his child smiled as if it were well-fed health personified. When he was sometimes reproved for bad management, he insisted that if he could only obtain enough brandy, his household affairs would soon look much better. In place of brandy, it was fame, ambition and lust of conquest that intoxicated the Bonapartists, so that they never knew what was actually happening in the Empire. Nowadays, when people complain of hard times, they cry, "All that will change soon. France will bloom and shine again. If you will only once again give us more crosses of honor, more epaulettes, more voluntary contributions, Spanish paintings, and duchies, in full draughts!"

Be that as it may, it is not only the old Bonapartists, but the great majority of the people who like to be lulled to the music of these delusions. The period of the Empire is their poetry; it is still a substantial contrast to the impoverishment of spirit which the victorious bourgeoisie has brought about and which prevails today. Only the heroism of the Empire is still capable of moving the French, and Napoleon is the only hero in whom they still believe.

℣ *Dreams*

WHAT ARE DREAMS? AND WHAT IS DEATH? Is the latter only an interruption of life, or its full cessation? For those who know only the past and the future, and who do not know how to experience eternity in every moment of the present—death must be terrible indeed! When their two pillars, Space and Time, fail them, they sink into eternal Nothingness.

And dreams? Why do we fear going to sleep less than being buried? Is it not terrible to contemplate that the body can be almost dead all night long, while the spirit in us carries on an active life— a life full of all the terrors of that division which we have established between body and soul? At some future time, when these two have been reunited in our consciousness, there will perhaps no longer be dreams; perhaps only the sick whose harmony has been disturbed will dream. The ancients seldom dreamed, and then only gently. Violent, convulsive dreams were considered extraordinary events, to be recorded in histories.

Actual dreaming began with the Jews, the people of the Spirit, and attained its highest state among the Christians, the people of the Spirits. Our descendants will shudder when they read of the ghastly life we led, how the Man in us was cloven in two, and only a moiety of him was really alive. Our age—which commences with the crucifixion—will be regarded as the great age of diseased mankind.

And yet what delicious dreams we could have dreamt! Our healthy descendants will hardly understand us. All about us the splendors of the world vanished; we found them once more within our innermost souls. In our souls the fragrance of the trampled rose and the loveliest songs of the affrighted nightingales found refuge.

All that I know. I die of the unnatural anxieties and the sweet horrors of our time. At night, when I go to bed, stretch out at full length, and cover myself with the white sheets, I often shudder involuntarily, and it seems to me as if I were dead and were burying my own body. Then I hastily close my eyes to escape this terrifying thought, and I seek refuge in the realm of dreams.

It was a sweet, kind, sun-lit dream I had. The sky was a heavenly blue, and without a cloud. The sea was green and calm. There was water as far as the eye could see, and on it a skiff with gay pennons, and I sat on the deck, enamored, at the feet of Jadviga. I read to her romantic love-songs, which I had written on strips of rose-colored paper, and sighed happily; and she listened, inclining an incredulous ear, and smiled with longing. Now and then she snatched the pages from my hand and threw them into the sea. But the lovely water-nixies, with snow-white breasts and arms, rose from the depths and each time caught the fluttering love-songs. When I leaned overboard, I could see clearly down into the very depths of the ocean. And there they sat, as in a social circle, those lovely nixies, and in their midst, a young sprite was reciting my songs with deep feeling and lively expression. Each stanza was greeted with wild applause. The beauties with the green locks applauded so fervently that their necks and bosoms reddened; and they lauded my verses warmly, yet with compassion:

"What strange creatures are these mortals! How wonderful their lives; how tragic their destiny! They love and seldom dare speak their love; when they utter it, they rarely understand each other. Yet they are not immortal like us. They are mortal. They are given only a brief span of time to find happiness. They must seize it and quickly press it to their hearts, before it vanishes. That is why their love-songs are so tender, intense, anxiously sweet, so happy in despair, such a strange blend of joy and sorrow! The thought of death casts a sad shadow over their happiest hour, and gives them kindly comfort in adversity. They can weep. What poetry there is in human tears!"

"Can you hear," I said to Jadviga, "how those below judge us? Let us embrace, so that they may no longer pity us—but only envy us." My beloved looked at me with infinite love and said nothing. I had kissed her into silence. She grew pale; a cold shudder passed through her beautiful form. Stiff as white marble she lay in my arms; and I would have thought that she was dead, if two rivulets of tears had not streamed continuously from her eyes. Those tears overwhelmed me, and I pressed the beloved form in my arms ever more closely.

௧ *National Cuisines and Women*

EVERY COUNTRY HAS ITS OWN CUISINE and its own kind of woman; and with regard to both—it is all a matter of taste. One man likes roast chicken, another roast duck. As for me, I love both the roast chicken and roast duck—and roast goose too.

Regarded from a lofty, ideal viewpoint, women the world over have a certain resemblance to their country's cooking. Are not the British beauties as wholesome, nourishing, sound, substantial and inartistic and yet as excellent as good Old England's simple, honest fare: roast beef, roast mutton, pudding in flaming brandy; vegetables boiled in water, with the two kinds of sauces, one of which is melted butter? There you don't have the *fricassée*, smiling at you; the *vol-au-vent*, softly deceptive; the *ragoût*, sighing and witty; nor the dallying of a thousand kinds of stuffed, boiled, puffed, roasted, sugared, piquant, declamatory and sentimental dishes, such as we find in a French restaurant—which bear a startling resemblance to the lovely French women! Do we not often observe that among them the substance itself is regarded as secondary—that the roast is often of less moment than the gravy, that flavor, grace, and elegance are the main thing? Italy's yellow-rich, passion-spiced, humor-flavored, and yet languishing ideal cooking fully expresses the character of her beauties. Oh, how I long at times for the Lombard *stuffados*, and the *tagliarini* and the *broccoli* of blessed Tuscany! Everything swims in oil, lazy and tender, and trills the sweet melodies of Rossini, and weeps because of the fragrance of onions and longing! But you must eat the maccaroni with your fingers—and then the word for it is: Beatrice!

I often think of Italy, and most often at night. Night before last I dreamed that I was there, and that I was a harlequin in motley, and lay in lazy luxury under a weeping willow. The drooping branches of the willow were maccaroni, which fell long and tenderly into my mouth; and from between the foliage of maccaroni, instead of sunrays, fell pure, yellow streams of butter, and finally a white rain of grated Parmesan cheese.

But alas! One doesn't grow fat on dreamed maccaroni! Beatrice!

Not a word about German cooking. It has every possible virtue, and only one fault: which I won't tell here. It offers sympathetic, but quite indecisive pastry; amorous egg-dishes, solid dumplings, temperamental barley-soup, pancakes with apples and bacon, virtuous meat-balls, sour cabbage—lucky is he who can digest it!

As for Dutch cooking—it differs from the German first of all in cleanliness, secondly by its own peculiar flavor. Especially delicious is the fish which is prepared here. The fragrance of celery—touching, sincere—and yet profound; self-conscious naiveté, and garlic. It is however unpardonable that they wear underclothes of flannel—not the fish, of course, but the beautiful daughters of sea-girt Holland.

ᏏᏉ Polish Women

AND NOW KNEEL DOWN, OR AT LEAST DOFF YOUR HATS—for I propose to speak of Polish women. My spirit roams on the banks of the Ganges, and seeks the tenderest and loveliest flowers with which to compare them. But what are all the charms of the Lallica, of the Kuwalaya, of the Oshadhi, of the blossoms of the Nagakesar; of the holy lotus, or whatever their name, Kamalata, Pedma, Kamala, Tamala, Sirisha, and so on! [16] Had I Raphael's brush, the melodies of Mozart, the speech of Calderon, I might succeed in charming your heart into feeling what you would experience when your blessed eyes gazed on a true Polish woman, an Aphrodite of the Vistula. But what are the smudges of Raphael compared to these altar-pieces of beauty, which the living God so happily drew in his most joyous hours! What are Mozartean jangles when set beside the words, the stuffed bonbons of the soul, which gush from the rose-lips of these sweet creatures! What are Calderon's earthly stars and heavenly flowers compared with these lovely ones, whom I too, in good Calderonese, will call angels of the earth, just as I would call real angels the Polish beauties of heaven! Yes, my dear friend, whoever gazes into their gazelle eyes believes in heaven!

ᏏᏉ On Punishment

WE HAVE YET A FOURTH THEORY OF PUNISHMENT, if we may call it such, for under it the conception of "punishment" disappears altogether.

This is called the prevention theory, because its guiding principle is guarding against offences. The most zealous advocates of this principle are the radicals of the various socialistic schools. Among the most thoroughgoing of these must be classed the Englishman, Robert Owen, who acknowledges no right to punish so long as the cause of the crime, the social evil, has not been removed. The Communists are likewise of this opinion—whether they be materialistic or spiritualistic Communists—the latter of whom support their antipathy to the traditional criminal law, which they name the biblical *lex talionis,* [17] by reference to the Gospel texts. Hence the Fourierists, too, acknowledge no penal law, for according to them, crime is only the consequence of degenerate passions; and their state sets itself the task of preventing this degeneration by means of a new organization of human passions. The Saint-Simonians have far too lofty a conception of the improvement of the human intellect to adopt the regulated and numerical schematization of the passions we find in Fourier. They too regard crime as the result not merely of social maladjustments, but also of defective education. They anticipate a complete regeneration from carefully trained and educated sentiments, when all traditions of sin will have been forgotten, and the very idea of a penal code appears a blasphemy.

The Railroads Are Coming

[*1843*]

THE OPENING OF THE TWO NEW RAILROADS, one leading to Orleans and the other to Rouen, has caused a sensation here among all who do not stand apart in some socially isolated ivory tower. The entire population of Paris is at this moment a cable through which the electric shock is being communicated. While the great masses stare dumbfounded and bewildered at these outward manifestations of great motive power, the thoughtful ones experience an uncanny terror—as when something extremely monstrous or unheard-of takes place, with consequences which are unpredictable and incalculable. All that we know is that our life is suddenly thrust and plunged into new channels —new conditions, new joys and sorrows await us. The unknown possesses for us a terrible attraction—at once alluring and frightening. So our fathers must have felt when America was discovered—or when gunpowder announced its presence by a first volley—or when the printing press sent into the world its first specimen sheets bearing the divine word.

The railways are likewise such a providential phenomenon—and represent a new revolution for mankind—altering the color and form of life. A new chapter opens in the history of the world, and our generation may well boast that it was there to see it. What changes must now take place in our views and ideas! Even our most elementary notions of time and space are revolutionized—the railroad has annihilated space—and only time remains. Oh, that we had money enough to do away with the latter properly! In three and a half hours you can now go to Orleans, or to Rouen! What will happen when the lines leading to Belgium and Germany are completed and joined to the railways within those countries? I see the mountains and forests of every land coming closer to Paris. I already smell the fragrance of the German lime-trees. At my very door-step, I can hear the surge of the North Sea. . . .

ॐ *The Word and the Deed*

THERE IS A STORY OF AN ENGLISH MECHANIC who had already invented the most ingenious machines, and who hit on the idea of making a man —and succeeded. The work of his hands had the bearing of a man, and behaved like one. He even had in his parchment breast something akin to human feeling, which did not differ over much from the usual feelings of Englishmen. He could communicate his emotions articulately; and the noise of his inner wheels, gears, and screws had a true English sound. In short, this automaton was a perfect gentleman. And all he lacked to be a real man was a soul. But the English mechanic could not give him one, and the poor creature, having become conscious of this shortcoming, tormented his creator night and day, imploring him for a soul. His entreaty became ever more urgent and at last so unbearable, that the artist fled from his own handiwork. However, the automaton followed him to the Continent by express coach, travelled constantly after him, very often overtook him unexpectedly, and snarled and growled at him, "Give me a soul!" These two figures can be met in every country—and only those who know the singular relation existing between them understand their strange haste, anxiety and irritation. But once you understand this peculiar relation, you see that it is something quite common—namely, a part of the English people, weary of their mechanical existence, demand a soul—another, appalled by this demand, flee here and there. But neither of them can stay at home.

This is a terrible story. It is dreadful when the bodies we have created demand a soul. But it is more horrible, more appalling, and weird when we have created a soul which asks for a body, and harries us with entreaties. The thought our mind has created is such a soul. It gives us no peace until we have endowed it with a body, or till we have helped it to materialize itself. Thought wishes to become deed; the word wishes to become flesh.

And wonder of wonders! Like God in the Scriptures, man need only voice a thought, and a world comes into being. There is light and darkness; the waters are sundered from the dry land, and even wild beasts appear. The world is the signature of the Word.

Mark this, you proud men of action. You are nothing but the unwitting tools of the men of thought, who, often in the humblest silence, have prescribed all your work, in the clearest fashion. Maximilian Robespierre was nothing but the hand of Jean Jacques Rousseau— the bloody hand which drew from the womb of time the body, the soul of which had been created by Rousseau. That restless torment which embittered the life of Jean Jacques—may it not have been due to a presentiment of the midwife his thoughts required to come into the world?

Perhaps old Fontenelle [18] was right in saying, "If I had all the thoughts of the world in my hand, I would make sure not to open it." For my part, I am of a different mind. If I held in my hand all the thoughts of this world, I might beg you to cut it off at once. But under no circumstances would I long keep it closed. I am not made to be a jailer of thoughts. By God, I'd let them go! Let them take on whatever terrible forms they will; let them storm through all the lands like a frenzied troupe of Bacchantes; let them crush our most innocent flowers with their thyrsus; let them break into our hospitals and drive the old, sick world from its sick bed!

ଓ Exile

HE WHO DOES NOT KNOW EXILE will not understand how luridly it colors our sorrows, how it pours the darkness of night and poison into all our thoughts. Dante wrote the *Inferno* in exile. Only he who has lived in exile, knows what love of fatherland is—patriotism with all its sweet terrors and its nostalgic trials. Fortunately for our patriots who must live in France, the latter offers many similarities to Germany—almost the very same climate, the same vegetation, the same type of life.

"How terrible exile must be, where this likeness does not exist," Börne once remarked, as we were strolling in the *Jardin des Plantes*. "How terrible if one were to see only palms and tropical vegetation, and strange wild life, like kangaroos and zebras. Fortunately for us, the flowers of France are quite like those at home; the violets and roses, the oxen and cows look like those in Germany, and the donkeys are quite like ours, patient and not striped; and the birds are plumed and they sing here as well as there; and even when I see the dogs in the streets of Paris, I easily imagine myself back across the Rhine and my heart exclaims: 'Well, these are our own German dogs.' "

ଓ Reflections

WHAT IS MUSIC?

This question preoccupied me last night for many hours before I fell asleep. There is something strange, even wonderful, about music. It stands midway between thought and appearance—a twilight intermediary between spirit and matter—related to both, yet different. It is spirit—but in need of time's measurement; it is matter—that can dispense with space.

GOD HAS REVEALED NOTHING that would point to survival after death. Even Moses says nothing on this subject. Perhaps God does not like the pious to take survival for granted. With fatherly foresight he may be preparing a surprise for us.

FOR IN THE LAST ANALYSIS, THE WORLD IS RIGHT—and forgives the flame so long as it is strong and genuine, and burns long and bright.

IN TIME OF REVOLUTIONS we have only the choice of either killing or dying.

A BOOK, LIKE A CHILD, needs time to be born. Books written quickly—within a few weeks—make me suspicious of the author. A respectable woman does not bring a child into the world before the ninth month.

HE WHO MARRIES is like the Doge of Venice who weds the Adriatic. He does not know what he will find in it—treasures, pearls, monsters, or unforeseen storms.

THE CLOSER PEOPLE STOOD TO NAPOLEON, the more they admired him. With ordinary heroes the reverse is the case.

PEOPLE ASK WHY OUR PRINCES GET TO BE SO OLD. They are afraid to die lest in the hereafter they again come face to face with Napoleon.

WE DO NOT UNDERSTAND RUINS, until we ourselves have become ruins.

THE WORLD IS A HUGE CRAG to which mankind, the true Prometheus, is chained, and where it is torn apart by the vulture of doubt. Mankind has stolen the light, and pays for it with martyrdom.

THOUGHT IS INVISIBLE NATURE—Nature visible thought.

IN THE DARK AGES people found their surest guide in Religion—just as a blind man is the best guide on a pitch-black night. He knows the way better than the seeing. But it is folly to use the blind old man as a guide after day-break.

THE GLORY OF THE WORLD is commensurate with the glory of the mind which views it. Thus the good man finds his paradise there, and the evil man his hell.

OUR MORAL CONCEPTIONS are by no means things of the air. The ennobling of mankind, justice, and immortality have an objective reality in Nature. Whatever we deem holy is real—and not a figment of the imagination.

Israel

৪৯ *The Bible*

YESTERDAY WAS SUNDAY, and leaden boredom weighed down on this whole island and almost crushed my brain. In despair I took hold of the Bible, and I confess that, despite the fact that I am a Hellene in secret, the book not only diverted me, but actually edified me. What a book! Large and wide as the world, striking its deep roots into the abysses of creation and towering high into the blue secrets of heaven! Sunrise and sunset, promise and fulfillment, birth and death—the whole drama of mankind, all of it is to be found in this book. It is the book of books, *Biblia*. . . . Unless I am in error, it was Mohammed who called the Jews the "People of the Book," a name which in the East has remained with them to this day, and is profoundly significant. A book is their fatherland, their possession, their ruler, their fortune and misfortune. They live within its peaceful precincts. Here they exercise their inalienable civil rights. From here they cannot be driven out.

Here they cannot be despised. Here they are strong and admirable. Immersed in the reading of this volume, they paid little heed to the changes which took place in the real world outside them. Nations rose and fell; states flourished and decayed; revolutions shook the land, —but the Jews were bowed over their book and scarcely marked the turmoil of the times which swept over their heads! . . .

As the prophet of the East called them the "People of the Book," so the prophet of the West,[1] in his *Philosophy of History*, characterized them as the "People of the Spirit." Already in their earliest beginnings —as we observe in the Pentateuch—they manifest a predilection for the abstract, and their whole religion is nothing but an act of dialectics, by means of which matter and spirit are sundered, and the absolute is acknowledged only in the unique aspect of Spirit. What an awe-inspiring and isolated role they were forced to play among the nations of antiquity, who dedicated themselves to the most exuberant worship of nature, and materialized spirit in image and symbol! What a striking antithesis they represented to multi-colored Egypt, teeming with hieroglyphics; to Phoenicia, the great pleasure-temple of Astarte, or to that beautiful sinner, lovely, fragrant Babylonia—and, finally, to Greece, verdant home of the arts!

It is a strange spectacle, this, of a people which gradually emancipates itself from the material, and becomes completely spiritual. Moses gave this spiritual element its bulwarks against the physical invasion by the neighboring tribes. Round about the field, in which Spirit had been sown, he planted the rigid ceremonial law and an egoistical nationalism as a protective hedge. When the holy spirit-plant had struck root so deeply and towered so loftily that it could no longer be torn up, Jesus Christ came and demolished the ceremonial law, which had no further meaning or use. He even passed final sentence of death on Jewish nationalism. He called all nations of the world to share in the Kingdom of God, which had once belonged only to the chosen people, and extended to all mankind the rights of Jewish citizenship. That was the great problem of emancipation, which, however, was solved much more magnanimously then than is being done at the present, in Saxony or Hanover. . . . Naturally, the Saviour who had freed his brethren from the ceremonial law and nationalism, and had established cosmopolitanism, fell a prey to his own humanitarianism, and the magistrates of Jerusalem had him crucified and the populace mocked him. . .

But only the body was scorned and crucified. The spirit was glori-

fied, and the martyrdom of the triumphant one, who had achieved
the hegemony of the spirit, became a symbol of this triumph, and all
mankind has since striven, in imitation of Christ, to achieve this physical extinction and this transcendental dissolution in the Absolute.

When will harmony again be restored? When will the world recover from this one-sided striving for spiritualization, this insane error
which sickens both body and soul? There is a tried remedy to be
found in the political movements and in art. Napoleon and Goethe
have done excellent work. The one compelled nations to engage in
wholesome physical activity; the other made us once more receptive
to Greek art and created such solid works that we cling to them as
if they were marble deities, lest we drown in the misty seas of the
Absolute. . . .

I HAVE BEEN READING IN THE OLD TESTAMENT AGAIN. What a great
book! Even more wonderful than its contents, is its style. Every word
is as natural as a tree, a flower, the sea, the stars—as man himself. It
sprouts, it flows, it sparkles, it smiles—we know not how or why;
but it all seems quite natural. This is truly the word of God; other
books are merely products of man's wit. In Homer, that other great
book, the presentment is a product of art, and though the substance
itself, as is the case with the Bible, is taken from reality, it is cast into
poetic form, transfused, as it were, within the crucible of the human
mind. It has been refined by means of the spiritual process which we
call art. In the Bible no trace of art is evident. Its style is that of a
notebook, in which the Absolute Spirit, seemingly without the assistance of any individual human being, has jotted down the events
of the day, almost with the same factual accuracy with which we list
our laundry. One cannot pass judgment on that style. One can only
observe its effect on our minds. The Greek grammarians were not a
little perplexed when they were forced to define some striking beauties
of the Bible in the terms of traditional aesthetic principles. Longinus
speaks of sublimity. Recent aestheticians speak of naiveté. Alas! As I
have already said, there are no criteria for judging this book. The
Bible is the word of God.

In only one other writer do I find anything that recalls this direct
style of the Bible. That is Shakespeare. With him, too, the word sometimes appears in that imposing nakedness which awes and moves us. In
the works of Shakespeare we sometimes see the living truth without
the covering of art. But only in rare instances. The genius of Art,

conscious perhaps of its impotence, for a very brief space transferred its office to Nature, and then once more asserts its supremacy all the more zealously in the plastic shaping and the artful entanglement of the drama. Shakespeare is at once Jew and Greek; or rather, both elements, spiritualism and art, prevail in him and unfold in a higher unity.

It may be that the harmonious fusion of both these elements constitutes the task of all of European civilization. If so, we are still far from this goal.

I HAVE ALREADY IN MY LAST BOOK, *Romancero*, spoken of the transformation which I underwent with regard to religious matters. Since then I have often been asked, with Christian perseverance, how this great light came over me. Devout souls yearn to have me reveal some miracle; they would like to know whether, like Paul, I had seen a light on the road to Damascus, or whether I had not, like Balaam, the son of Beor, been riding a stubborn ass, who suddenly opened his mouth and began speaking like a man. No, you credulous souls! I have never gone to Damascus. I know nothing of Damascus, except that the Jews living there have recently been accused of eating old Capuchins.[2] Nor would I probably ever have known the name of the town had I not read the *Song of Songs*, where King Solomon compares the nose of his beloved to a tower that looketh forth toward Damascus. I have never seen an ass—at least a four-legged one—who spoke like a man; though I have met plenty of men who, whenever they opened their mouths, spoke like asses. In truth, it was neither a vision, nor a seraphic rapture, nor a voice from heaven, nor an extraordinary dream, nor a marvelous specter—that brought me on the road to salvation. I owe the illumination quite simply to the reading of a book.

A book? Yes, an old and simple book, as modest as nature herself; yes, and as natural. As work-a-day and unpretentious a book as the sun that warms us, as the bread that nourishes us, a book which looks at us with as much familiarity, with as much blessed kindliness as an old grandmother, who has herself read it every day, with her dear, trembling lips, and spectacles on her nose. And this book is simply called *The Book*—the Bible. With good cause it is called the Holy Scriptures. Whoever has lost his God may find him again in this book; and he who has never known Him, will breathe the spirit that is wafted to him by the divine word. The Jews, who are connoisseurs of precious things, well understood what they were doing when during the conflagration of the Second Temple, they abandoned the gold and silver vessels, the candelabras and the lamps, and even the high priest's breastplate with its great jewels—and only rescued the Bible. This was the real treasure of the Temple. And it did not—thank God!—become the prey of the flames, or of Titus Vespasian, the villain, who came to an evil end, as the Rabbis relate. A Jewish priest, who lived in Jerusalem two hundred years before the burning of the Second Temple, during the golden age of Ptolemy Philadelphus, and was named Joshua ben-Sirah ben-Eliezer,[3] voiced in the *Meshalim*, a collection of gnomic sayings, the opinions of his day regarding the Bible, and I will here cite his beautiful words. They are so sacredly solemn, and yet so fresh and inspiring, as if they had sprung only yesterday from the heart of man:

"All these things are the book of the covenant of the Most High God, even the law which Moses commanded us for a heritage unto the assemblies of Jacob. It is he that maketh wisdom abundant, as Pishon, and as Tigris in the days of new fruits; that maketh understanding full as Euphrates, and as Jordan in the days of harvest; that maketh instruction to shine forth as the light, as Gihon in the days of vintage. The first man knew her not perfectly; and in like manner the last hath not traced her out. For her thoughts are filled from the sea, and her counsels from the great deep."

৪৯ *Moses*

THERE WAS A TIME WHEN I DID NOT GREATLY ADMIRE MOSES, probably because the Hellenic spirit was predominant in me, and I could not pardon the lawgiver of the Jews his hatred of the representative and plastic arts. I failed to see that Moses, despite his hostility to the arts, was nevertheless himself a great artist, and possessed true artistic spirit. Only this artistic spirit was with him, as with his Egyptian countrymen, applied solely to the colossal and indestructible. But unlike the Egyptians, he did not fashion his works of art from bricks and granite, but he built human pyramids and carved human obelisks. He took a poor shepherd tribe and from it he created a nation which was likewise to defy the centuries—a great, immortal, holy people, the people of God, who could serve all other peoples as a model and all of humanity as a prototype.—He created Israel! With greater justice than the

414 THE POETRY AND PROSE OF HEINRICH HEINE

Roman poet, this artist, the son of Amram and the midwife Jochebed, can boast of having erected a monument which shall outlive all images of brass! [4]

I have never spoken with proper reverence either of the master nor of his work—the Jews; and for the same reason: my Hellenic temperament, which was repelled by Jewish asceticism. My prejudice in favor of Hellas has since then declined. I see now that the Greeks were only beautiful youths, but that the Jews were always men, mighty, unyielding men, not only in the past, but to this very day, in spite of eighteen centuries of persecution and misery. I have since that time learned to appreciate them better, and if all pride of ancestry were not a silly paradox in a champion of the Revolution and its democratic principles, the writer of these lines could well be proud that his ancestors belonged to the noble House of Israel, that he is a descendant of those martyrs who gave the world a God and morality, and who fought and suffered on all the battlefields of thought.

The history of the Middle Ages, or even that of modern times, has seldom inscribed in its chronicles the names of such knights of the Holy Spirit, for as a rule they fought with closed visors. The deeds of the Jews are as little known to the world as their real character. Some think they know the Jews because they recognize their beards, which is all that they ever revealed of themselves. Now, as during the Middle Ages, they remain a wandering mystery, a mystery which may perhaps be solved on the day which the prophet foretells, when there shall be but one shepherd and one flock, and the righteous who have suffered for the good of humanity shall receive a glorious reward.

It will be seen that I, who in the past used to quote Homer, now quote the Bible, like Uncle Tom. Indeed, I owe much to that book. As I said, it once more awakened in me the religious feeling; and this rebirth of religious emotion sufficed for the poet, who can dispense far more easily with positive religious dogmas than other men. He has Grace—and the symbols of heaven and earth are disclosed to his spirit. He has no need of a key to a church.

The silliest and most contradictory reports have been circulated about me. Men of great piety but little wisdom, in Protestant Germany, have urgently inquired if, now that I am ill and a believer, I cling with more devotion than heretofore to the Lutheran-Evangelic faith, which, until now, I have only professed in a lukewarm, official fashion. No, dear friends, in that respect no change has taken place in me, and if I continue to adhere to the Evangelic faith at all, it is because now, as in the past, it does not inconvenience me. Certainly, I will avow it frankly, when I resided in Prussia, especially in Berlin, like several of my friends, I would have preferred to sever, once and for all, my ties with all denominations, if the authorities there had not denied the right of residence in Prussia or Berlin to anyone who did not profess one of the positive religions recognized by the State. As Henry IV once laughingly said, *"Paris vaut bien une messe,"* so I could say, with equal justice, *"Berlin vaut bien un prêche,"* [5] and I could, as I had done before, tolerate a very enlightened Christianity, purged of all superstition, even of the divinity of Christ, which was available in the churches of Berlin—like mock-turtle soup without turtle. At that time I myself was a god, and no one of the positive religions was worth more than another. I could wear any of their uniforms out of courtesy, after the manner of the Russian Emperor, who, when he vouchsafes the King of Prussia the honor of attending a review at Potsdam, appears in the uniform of a Prussian officer of the guard.

Now that the reawakening of religious feelings and my physical suffering have effected many changes in me, does the Lutheran uniform in some measure express my inmost thoughts? How far has formal profession become a reality? I do not propose to give direct answers to these questions, but I shall avail myself of the opportunity of clarifying the services which, according to my present views, Protestantism has rendered to humanity. From this it may be gathered how much more I am now in sympathy with it.

Formerly, when philosophy possessed a preponderant interest for me, I prized Protestantism only for its services in winning freedom of thought, which, after all, is the foundation on which in later times Leibnitz, Kant, and Hegel could build. Luther, the mighty man with the axe, had to precede these warriors and blaze the trail for them. For this service, I have honored the Reformation as the beginning of German philosophy, and thus I justified my militant defence of Protestantism. Now, in my later and more mature days, when religious feelings once more surge up powerfully within me, and the shipwrecked metaphysician clings fast to the Bible,—now I chiefly honor Protestantism for its services in the rediscovery and propagation of the Holy Book. I say "rediscovery"; for the Jews who rescued it from the great conflagration of the Second Temple, and trudged around with it all through the Middle Ages as with a portable fatherland, kept their treasure carefully concealed in their ghettos. Here German scholars, the forerunners and initiators of the Reformation, came by stealth to study the Hebrew tongue, and thus acquire the key to the casket in which the precious treasure was enclosed. Such a scholar was the excellent Reuchlin [6] and his enemies, the Hochstraatens and Company of Cologne, who are represented as simple-minded obscurantists, were by no means such stupid fellows. On the contrary, they were farsighted inquisitors who foresaw clearly the disaster which a close acquaintance with the Holy Scriptures would bring on the church. Hence the persecuting zeal with which they sought to destroy all Hebrew writings, which they counselled should be burned without exception, while, at the same time, they tried to incite the rabble to exterminate the Jews, the interpreters of these writings. Now that the motives of their actions are clearly revealed, we see that, at bottom, each side was in the right. The obscurantists of Cologne believed that the spiritual salvation of the world was jeopardized; and that all means, falsehood as well as murder, were justifiable, especially against the Jews. The poor, oppressed lower classes, heirs of the primeval curse of poverty, already were embittered against the Jews because of the wealth they had amassed; and what today is called the proletarians' hatred of the rich, was then called hate of the Jews. Indeed, since the Jews were barred from all ownership of land and from every trade, and were relegated to dealing in money and merchandise, which the Church forebade all true believers, they were legally condemned to be rich, hated, and murdered. Such murders, it is true, were in those days committed under the cloak of religion, and it was said, "We must kill those who once killed our Saviour." How strange! The very people who had given the world a God, and whose whole life was inspired by devotion to God, were stigmatized as deicides! . . .

YES, TO THE JEWS THE WORLD IS INDEBTED for its God and His Word —the Bible. They rescued it from the bankruptcy of the Roman Empire, and they preserved the cherished volume intact during all the wild tumults of the migrations, until Protestantism came to seek it out among them, and translated it into the speech of the land, and spread it throughout the world. This propagation has borne the most beneficent fruit, even to this day. The propaganda of the Bible Society has fulfilled a providential mission of great significance, and is likely to bring forth quite different results from those anticipated by the pious gentlemen of this British Agency for the Export of Christianity. They expect to elevate a narrow, petty dogma to supremacy, and to monopolize Heaven as they do the sea, by turning it into a domain of the

Church of England.—And behold! without knowing it, they speed the
downfall of all Protestant sects—for they all draw their life from the
Bible, and they will all dissolve when the Bible becomes universal.
They are promoting the great democracy where each man shall not
only be King in his own house, but Bishop as well. In disseminating the
Bible all over the earth, in slipping it, so to speak, into the hands of all
mankind by commercial hook or crook—and delivering it over to the
exegesis of individual reason, they are founding the great kingdom of
the spirit, the kingdom of religious feeling, love of humanity, purity,
true morality which cannot be taught by dogmatic formulas, but by
parables and examples, such as are contained in that beautiful and
sacred book intended for the education of children of all ages—the
Bible.

To the clear-eyed thinker it is a marvelous spectacle to view the
countries on whose inhabitants the Bible has been exerting a forma-
tive influence since the Reformation, and on whom it has impressed
the customs, modes of thought and feeling which prevailed in Palestine, and are manifested in the Old and in the New Testament. In
northern Europe and in America, especially in the Scandinavian and
Anglo-Saxon countries, among the Germanic peoples, and partly
among the Celtic ones, the Palestinian way of life has prevailed to such
a marked degree that we seem to be living among Jews. Take, for example, the Scottish Protestants: Are they not Hebrews, whose names
are even biblical, whose very cant smacks of the Phariseeism of Jerusalem, and whose religion is merely pork-eating Judaism? The same
is true of Denmark and certain provinces of North Germany, not to
mention most of the new communities of the United States, among
whom the life depicted in the Old Testament is pedantically aped.
Here, life resembles a daguerreotype—the outlines are studiously correct, but all is grey upon grey, and the sunny color harmony of the
Promised Land is missing. But the caricature will disappear sooner
or later. The genuine, the ageless, the true—the morality of ancient
Judaism—will bloom in these countries just as acceptably to God as
once in the lands by the Jordan and on the heights of Lebanon. One
needs neither palm-trees nor camels to be good; and goodness is
better than beauty.

The readiness with which these nations adopted Jewish life, customs and modes of thought may not be altogether due to their susceptibility to culture. The cause of this phenomenon should perhaps
be sought in the character of the Jewish people, who have always

had a great affinity with the Germans, and also to a certain extent, with the Celtic races. Judea has always seemed to me a fragment of the West which has somehow gotten lost in the East. In fact, with its spiritual faith, its severe, chaste, even ascetic customs—in short, with its abstract subjectivity—this land and its people always offered the most marked contrast to the populations of the neighboring countries, who, with luxurious and voluptuous nature-cults, dissipated their lives in sensual Bacchanalian revels. While in the temples of Babylon, Nineveh, Sidon, and Tyre, bloody and lascivious orgies were celebrated, the mere description of which, even now, makes the hair stand on end, Israel sat piously under its fig-trees and chanted the praises of the invisible God, and exercised virtue and righteousness. When we consider these surroundings, we cannot sufficiently admire the early greatness of Israel.

Of Israel's love of freedom, at a time when the practice of slavery was legal and flourished not only in its immediate vicinity, but also among all the nations of antiquity, even among the philosophical Greeks—I will say nothing, lest I compromise the Bible in the eyes of the powers that be. No socialist was more of a terrorist than our Lord and Saviour. Even Moses was such a socialist; although as a practical man, he only sought to reform existing institutions, particularly regarding property. Instead of striving for the impossible, instead of rashly decreeing the abolition of private property, he only sought its moral transformation—he sought to bring the rights of property into harmony with morality—which is the true law of reason—and this he accomplished by instituting the Year of the Jubilee,[7] when every alienated heritage—among agricultural people this always consisted of land—would revert to the original owner, no matter in what manner it had been alienated. This institution offers the most marked contrast to the Roman statute of "prescription," by which the actual holder of an estate could no longer be compelled to restore it to its rightful owner, unless the latter could show that within the prescribed time he had, in due form, demanded restitution. This condition opened wide the door to chicanery, particularly in a state where despotism and jurisprudence flourished, and where the wrongful possessor had at his command all the means of intimidation,—especially against the poor who might not be able to defray the costs of litigation. The Roman was both soldier and lawyer, and that which he conquered with his sword he knew how to defend by pettifogging. Only a nation of robbers and casuists could have invented the law of "prescription," and consecrated it in that detestable book which may be called the Devil's Bible—I mean the Code of Roman Civil Law, which, unfortunately, still prevails.

I have spoken of the affinity which exists between the Jews and the Germans, whom I once designated as the two eminently "moral nations." In this connection, I might mention as a remarkable trait the moral disapprobation with which the ancient German law branded the statute of "prescription." To this very day, the Saxon peasant has a very touching and beautiful saying: "A hundred years of wrong do not make a single year of right."

The Mosaic law, through the institution of the Year of the Jubilee, protests even more decidedly. Moses did not want to abolish private property. Rather, it was his wish that everyone should own some, so that no one might be forced by poverty to become a bondslave, with the mind of a bondslave. Freedom was always the great emancipator's leading thought. It breathes and glows in all his statutes on pauperism. Slavery itself he hated immeasurably, almost fiercely, but even this inhuman institution he could not quite destroy. It was too deeply rooted in the life of that primitive age, and he had to confine his efforts to ameliorating by law the condition of the slaves, rendering their manumission less difficult, and limiting their period of bondage.

But if a slave thus eventually set free refused to depart from his master's house, then Moses commanded that the incorrigibly servile villain be nailed by his ear to the door-post of his master's house, and after being thus shamefully exposed to public gaze, he be condemned to lifelong servitude. Oh, Moses, our teacher! Moshe Rabbenu, august warrior against slavery, give me hammer and nails that I may nail to the Brandenburg Gate by their long ears our complacent slaves in liveries of black, red and gold!

ࢥ The Book of Job

BUT WHY MUST THE RIGHTEOUS SUFFER SO MUCH on this earth? Why must the talented and the honest come to grief, while the swaggering idiot, who surely has never strained his eyes in examining Arabic manuscripts, lolls on the couches of fortune and well nigh stinks with smug comfort? The Book of Job does not solve that horrible problem. On the contrary, it is the Song of Songs of scepticism, and in its pages are audible the sibilant and rightful serpents with their eternal "Wherefore?" How does it happen that upon the return from Babylonia, the devout archives commission of the temple, of which Ezra was president, accepted this book into the holy canon? I have often asked myself this question. In my opinion, this was done by these God-illumined men not because of ignorance, but because they knew, in their lofty wisdom, that doubt is deeply fixed in man's nature— and justified; and that it cannot be uprooted with a heavy hand— but must be cured. And they proceeded to do this homoeopathically, by bringing like to work upon like. But they gave no small homoeopathic doses, they increased the quantity inordinately—and the Book of Job is that exceedingly strong dose of doubt.

It was essential that this poison be not absent from the Bible, that great medicine chest of humanity. Yes, just as suffering man must weep until he is at peace—so must he carry his doubts to their last consequences when he feels himself outraged by fortune. Like violent weeping, the most profound doubt—which the Germans rightly name despair—also brings about a crisis in our moral recovery. But well for him, who is sound and needs no medicine!

ϑ๛ *The Emancipation of the Jews*

YES, SOONER OR LATER, the Jews will have to be emancipated, be it from a sense of justice, or wisdom, or necessity. Among the upper classes antagonism against the Jews no longer is due to religion. And among the lower classes it is being every day more rapidly transformed into a social hatred of the overweening power of capital—of exploitation of the poor by the rich. Hatred of the Jew now goes under another name even among the common people. So far as governments are concerned, they have at last come to the sage conclusion that the state is an organic body which cannot achieve complete health so long as one of its members, be that the smallest toe, is diseased. Yes, the state may carry its head high, and defy all tempests with staunch breast, but the heart within, yes, and even the proud head, will feel the pain which a corn on the toe produces. The disabilities of the Jews are like corns on the toes of the German states.

If the governments would seriously consider how gravely the

capstone of all positive religions—the idea of deism—is jeopardized by new doctrines, how the schism between science and religion will very soon turn, not into a tame skirmish, but into a bitter battle for life itself—if the governments were wary of these concealed dangers, they would have cause to rejoice that there are Jews left in the world—that this Swiss guard of deism (as a poet once called them) is still on its feet—that the people of God still exist. Instead of being compelled to recede from their faith by legal restrictions, they should be strengthened in it by rewards. Their synagogues should be built at the expense of the state, so that they may visit them often, and outsiders may see that there is some religion left in the world.

Guard against encouraging the baptism of the Jews! For this is merely water—and water dries easily. Rather encourage circumcision.—This is religion carved into the flesh. For religion can no longer be carved into the spirit. Encourage the observance of the ceremonies of the phylactery, by means of which faith is fastened on to the arm. The state should offer leather to the Jews gratis—as well as flour for baking the Matzoh, which devout Israel has been crunching for three thousand years. Furthermore, hasten the emancipation, lest it come too late and you no longer find Jews who would prefer the faith of their fathers to the salvation of their children. There is a saying that while the wise man is pondering, the fool too is thinking.

₰ *The Mission of Israel*

IN TRUTH, THE JEWS ARE OF THAT STUFF of which gods are made; trod under foot today, they are worshipped on the knees tomorrow. While some of them wallow in the filthy mire of money-changing, others ascend to the highest peaks of humanity, and Golgotha is not the only mountain on which a Jewish god bled for the salvation of the world. The Jews are the people of the spirit, and whenever they return to their principles, they are great and glorious, and they shame and conquer their clumsy oppressors. Rosenkranz [8] profoundly compares them to the giant Antaeus, except that the giant was strengthened whenever he touched the earth, while the Jews gain new strength whenever they touch heaven. Strange phenomenon this, filled with the most amazing contrasts! At the same time that you find among these people all possible caricatures of vulgarity, you also find among them the purest ideals of humanity. As they once led the world into new paths of progress, the world may still expect them to open up others. . . .

"Nature," Hegel once told me, "is very strange. She employs the same tools for the most august and the very lowest purposes. For instance, the very member to which is entrusted the highest mission, the propagation of mankind, also serves . . ."

Those who complain of Hegel's obscurity, will understand him here; and though his remark was not made with reference to the Jews, it can be applied to them.

However that may be, it is very possible that the mission of this race is not yet fulfilled, and particularly may this be the case regarding Germany. She too awaits a redeemer, an earthly Messiah—with a heavenly one the Jews have already blessed us—a King of the Earth, a Saviour with a sceptre and sword, and this German redeemer is perhaps the same as he for whom Israel waits. . . .

Oh, dear long-awaited Messiah!

Where is he now? Where does he tarry? Is he as yet unborn or has he lain hidden somewhere for a thousand years, awaiting the great, the rightful hour of deliverance? Is he old Barbarossa, sitting asleep in the Kyffhäuser, on his stone chair, asleep so long that his white beard has grown through the stone table? Now and then he drowsily shakes his head, blinks with half-closed eyes, and reaches dreaming for the sword . . . then sinks back into the heavy thousand-year sleep.

No, it is not Emperor Red-beard who will free Germany, as the people believe, the German people, the drowsy, dreaming people, who can imagine their Messiah only in the shape of an old sleeper! The Jews have a much better idea of their Messiah. Many years ago, when I was in Poland and met the great Rabbi Manasseh ben Naphtali at Cracow, I always listened with an open and glad heart when he spoke of the Messiah. . . . I have forgotten which book of the Talmud contains the details that the great Rabbi faithfully communicated to me, and only the main features of his description remain in my memory. The Messiah, he said, was born on the day when Jerusalem was destroyed by the evil-doer Titus Vespasian, and ever since he has been living in the most beautiful palace of heaven, surrounded by joy and splendor, wearing a crown on his head just like a king. . . . But his hands are fettered with golden chains!

"What," I asked in amazement, "is the meaning of these golden chains?"

"They are necessary," replied the great Rabbi with a subtle look and a deep sigh. "For without these fetters the Messiah may lose patience and suddenly hasten to come down and commence his work of deliverance too soon, and at the wrong time. He is not a sleepy-head. He is a handsome, very slender, but extraordinarily powerful man, blooming like youth itself. He leads a very monotonous life. The best part of the morning he spends in the customary prayers, or he laughs and jests with his servants, angels in disguise, who sing sweetly and play the flute. Then he has his long hair combed, and is anointed with nard, and dressed in princely purple. All afternoon he studies the Cabala.[9] Toward evening he sends for his old chancellor, another angel in disguise, as are the four strong councillors of state who accompany him. Then the chancellor must read to his master from a great volume what has happened each day. . . . There are all sorts of stories at which the Messiah smiles with pleasure, or shakes his head in disapproval. But when he hears how his people are abused below, he becomes fearfully incensed and enraged, so that the heavens tremble. . . Then the four strong state councillors must hold back the enraged one lest he rush down to earth; and indeed, they would not prevail over him, were his hands not bound with the golden chains. . . . They mollify him with gentle words, telling him that the time has not yet come—the true hour of salvation has not arrived; and he finally sinks down on his couch and covers his face and weeps. . . ."

This is approximately what Manasseh ben Naphtali of Cracow told me, vouching for his credibility by the Talmud. I often have had to think of his tales, especially in most recent times, after the July Revolution. Yes, on the worst days, I thought I sometimes heard with my own ears a rattling as of golden chains, and then a desperate sobbing. . . .

Oh, do not lose heart, beautiful Messiah, you who wish to save not only Israel, as the superstitious Jews imagine, but all suffering humanity! Break not, you golden chains! Keep him fettered yet a little time, lest he come too soon, the Saviour King of the World!

ৡ✷ *Shylock*

W<small>HEN</small> I <small>SAW THIS PLAY PRESENTED IN</small> D<small>RURY</small> L<small>ANE</small>, there stood back of me in the box a pale British beauty who wept violently at the end of the fourth act and frequently cried out, "The poor man is wronged!" Hers was a face of the noblest Grecian cut, and her eyes were large and black. I could never forget them, those great black eyes, that wept for Shylock.

But when I think of those tears, I am forced to include *The Merchant of Venice* among the tragedies, although its frame is embellished with the gayest masks, pictures of satyrs and cupids, and the poet actually intended this to be a comedy. Perhaps Shakespeare wished to present an unmitigated werewolf for the amusement of the crowd, an abhorrent mythical creature that thirsts for blood, in the end loses his daughter and his ducats, and is made ridiculous into the bargain. But the poet's genius, the universal spirit which reigned in him, was always stronger than his own will, and so it happened that despite the exaggerated burlesque, he embodies in Shylock a justification of the hapless sect which for mysterious reasons had been burdened by Providence with the hatred on the part of the lower and higher rabble, and would not always requite this hatred with love.

But what am I saying? The genius of Shakespeare rises above the petty quarrels of two religious sects, and his drama in reality exhibits neither Jews nor Christians, but oppressors and oppressed, and the madly agonized jubilation of the latter when they can repay their arrogant tormentors with interest for insults inflicted on them.

There is not a trace of religious differences in this play. In Shylock Shakespeare shows us nothing but a man bidden by nature to hate his enemies—just as in Antonio and his friends he surely does not depict disciples of that divine doctrine which commands us to love our enemies. When Shylock says to the man who would borrow money from him:

> "Signor Antonio, many a time and oft
> In the Rialto, you have rated me
> About my monies and my usances:

Still have I borne it with a patient shrug,
For sufferance is the badge of all our tribe.
You call me misbeliever, cut-throat dog,
And spit upon my Jewish gaberdine,
And all for use of that which is mine own.
Well, then, it now appears you need my help:
Go to then; you come to me, and you say,
'Shylock, we would have moneys:'—you say so;
You, that did void your rheum upon my beard,
And foot me as you spurn a stranger cur
Over your threshold: monies is your suit.
What should I say to you? Should I not say,
'Hath a dog money? Is it possible
A cur can lend three thousand ducats?' or
Shall I bend low, and in a bondman's key,
With 'bated breath and whisp'ring humbleness,
Say this:—
'Fair sir, you spet on me Wednesday last;
You spurn'd me such a day; another time
You call'd me dog; and for these courtesies
I'll lend you thus much moneys?' "

Antonio replies:

"I am as like to call thee so again,
To spit on thee again, to spurn thee too."

Where in all this do you find Christian love? Truly, Shakespeare
would have been writing against Christianity, if he had let it be
embodied in these characters who are hostile to Shylock, and
yet are hardly worthy of untying shoelaces. Bankrupt Antonio is a
nerveless creature, without energy, without strength to hate, and
hence also without strength to love, a gloomy insect-heart, whose
flesh really is good for nothing but "to bait fish withal."

He does not dream of returning the borrowed three thousand
ducats to the Jew. Nor does Bassanio repay him. This fellow is, in
the words of an English critic, a "genuine fortune hunter"; he bor-
rows money to make sumptuous display so as to bag a rich wife and
a fat dowry—for, as he tells his friend:

> " 'Tis not unknown to you, Antonio,
> How much I have disabled mine estate,
> By something showing a more swelling port
> Than any faint means would grant continuance:
> Nor do I now make moan to be abridg'd
> From such a noble rate; but my chief care
> Is, to come fairly off from the great debts
> Wherein my time, something too prodigal,
> Hath left me gag'd. To you, Antonio,
> I owe the most, in money and in love;
> And from your love I have a warranty
> To unburthen all my plots and purposes,
> How to get clear of all the debts I owe."

As for Lorenzo, he is the accomplice of a most heinous theft, and under the Prussian Criminal Code would be sentenced to fifteen years at hard labor, branded and pilloried—although he is not only susceptible to stolen ducats and jewels, but to the beauties of nature as well, moon-lit landscapes and music. As for the other noble Venetians, who appear as Antonio's companions, they do not seem to have any particular aversion to money, either. For their poor friend who has fallen upon evil days they have nothing but words, or "coined air." On that point, our good pious friend, Franz Horn,[10] makes the following thin, but proper remark: "Here one might fairly inquire: How was it possible that Antonio's troubles became so great? All Venice knew and esteemed him; his close friends knew all about the terrible bond, and that the Jew would not abate a tittle of it. Yet they let one day after another pass, until finally the three months are gone, and with them all hopes of rescue. Surely it would have been a simple thing for those good friends, of whom the royal merchant seemed to have such a multitude about him, to raise three thousand ducats to save a life—and what a life!—but such things are always somewhat inconvenient, and so the dear good friends, because they are only so-called friends, or if you will, only half or three-quarter friends,—do nothing, nothing at all, and again nothing. They pity the excellent merchant, who in the past tendered them such fine feasts, but with exceedingly appropriate complacence, they revile Shylock to their hearts' and tongues' content, which also can be done without danger; and then they presume that they have done all that friendship demands. Much as we must hate Shylock, we can hardly blame him for somewhat despising these people, which he probably does. In the end, in fact, he seems to confuse Gratiano—whom his absence excuses—with the others and puts him in the same class, by dismissing his earlier inaction and his present flow of words with the cutting remark:

> 'Till thou canst rail the seal from off my bond,
> Thou but offend'st thy lungs to speak so loud:
> Repair thy wit, good youth, or it will fall
> To cureless ruin.—I stand here for law.' "

Or should perhaps Launcelot Gobbo be considered the represent-ative of Christianity? Singularly enough, Shakespeare nowhere ex-pressed himself so clearly about him as in a conversation between this rogue and his mistress. To Jessica's remark, "I shall be saved by my husband; he hath made me a Christian," Launcelot Gobbo replies:

> "Truly, the more to blame he: we were Christians enow before; e'en as many as could well live, one by another. This making of Christians will raise the price of hogs; if we grow all to be pork-eaters, we shall not shortly have a rasher on the coals for money."

Truly, except for Portia, Shylock is the most respectable charac-ter in the entire play. He loves money; he does not conceal this love, but cries it aloud in the market-place. But there is something he es-teems above money—satisfaction for his injured feelings—just retribu-tion for unspeakable insults; and though offered ten times the loan, he refuses, and does not rue the three thousand or ten times the three thousand ducats, so long as he can buy a pound of the flesh of his enemy's heart. "Thou wilt not take his flesh: what's that good for?" Salarino asks him. And he replies:

> "To bait fish withal: if it will feed nothing else, it will feed my revenge. He hath disgraced me, and hindered me of half a million, laughed at my losses, mocked at my gains, scorned my nation, thwarted my bargains, cooled my friends, heated mine enemies; and what's his reason? I am a Jew. Hath not a Jew eyes? hath not a Jew hands,

organs, dimensions, senses, affections, passions? fed with the same food, hurt with the same weapons, subject to the same diseases. healed by the same means, warmed and cooled by the same winter and summer, as a Christian is? If you prick us, do we not bleed? if you tickle us, do we not laugh? if you poison us, do we not die? and if you wrong us, shall we not revenge? If we are like you in the rest, we will resemble you in that. If a Jew wrong a Christian, what is his humility? Revenge. If a Christian wrong a Jew, what should his sufferance be by Christian example? Why, revenge. The villany you teach me, I will execute; and it shall go hard but I will better the instruction."

No, though Shylock loves money, there are things he loves far more—among them his daughter, "Jessica, my child." Though in the great heat of passion he curses her and would like to see her dead at his feet, with the jewels in her ears and with the ducats in her coffin, he still loves her more than all the ducats and jewels. Excluded from public life and Christian society, and thrust back into the narrow confines of domestic felicity, the poor Jew has nothing but family sentiments; and they manifest themselves in him with the most touching tenderness. The turquoise ring which his wife Leah once gave him, he would not exchange for "a wilderness of monkeys." In the court scene, when Bassanio tells Antonio:

> "Antonio, I am married to a wife
> Which is as dear to me as life itself;
> But life itself, my wife, and all the world,
> Are not with me esteem'd above thy life:
> I would lose all, ay, sacrifice them all
> Here to this devil, to deliver you,"

and Gratiano adds:

> "I have a wife, whom, I protest, I love:
> I would she were in heaven, so she could
> Entreat some power to change this currish Jew."

sudden terror grips Shylock concerning the fate of his daughter, who married among men who are capable of sacrificing their wives for their friends, and aside, but not aloud, he says to himself:

"These be Christian husbands! I have a daughter
Would any of the stock of Barrabas
Had been her husband, rather than a Christian!"

This passage—these whispered words—lay the foundation for the sentence of condemnation which we must pass on fair Jessica. It was no harsh father whom she left, robbed, and betrayed. Shameful betrayal! She even makes common cause with Shylock's enemies, and when they say all sorts of evil things of him at Belmont, Jessica does not cast down her eyes, her lips do not blanch; no, she herself says the worst things about her father. . . . Vile outrage! She has no feelings, only a lust for adventure. She is bored in the closely confined "honest" house of the embittered Jew, which finally seems hell to her. Her frivolous heart is too strongly drawn by the lively sounds of the drum and the bent-pipes. Did Shakespeare intend to portray a Jewess here? Certainly not. He only describes a daughter of Eve—one of those pretty birds that fly as soon as they are fledged from the paternal nest to their dear little males. Thus Desdemona followed the Moor; thus Imogene followed Posthumus. This is the way of woman.

In Jessica we may especially note a certain timid shame which she cannot overcome when she puts on a boy's clothes. In this trait, we may perhaps recognize that peculiar chastity which is characteristic of her people, and which lends such a wonderful attraction to their daughters. The chastity of the Jews may have its origin in the opposition which they always maintained against that Oriental worship of senses and sensuality, which once flourished so prolifically among their neighbors, the Egyptians, Phoenicians, Assyrians and Babylonians, and which in continually transformed shapes has survived to this day. The Jews are a chaste, temperate, I might almost say, an abstract people, and in the purity of their morals they stand closest to the Germanic tribes. The modesty of Jewish and Germanic women may not have an absolute value, but in its manifestations it makes a most charming, attractive and touching impression. One is moved to tears to read how after the defeat of the Cimbri and the Teutons, for instance, their women implored Marius not to give them to his soldiers as slaves, but to the priestesses of Vesta.

Striking, indeed, is the deep affinity which prevails between these two ethical nations, Jews and old Germans. This affinity had its source not in history—it was not due, for example, to the fact that the Bible, the great family chronicle of the Jews, served as a textbook for the whole Germanic world; nor to the fact that from the earliest times the Jews and Germans were the most implacable foes of the Romans, hence natural allies. It has a more profound source. Fundamentally, the two peoples are alike—so much alike, that one might regard the Palestine of the past as an Oriental Germany—just as one might regard the Germany of today as the home of the Holy Word, the mother-soil of prophecy, the citadel of pure spirituality.

But it is not Germany alone which possesses the features of Palestine. The rest of Europe too raises itself to the level of the Jews. I say raises itself—for even in the beginning the Jews bore within them the modern principles which only now are visibly unfolding among the nations of Europe.

Greeks and Romans clung passionately to the soil, to their native land. The later Nordic immigrants into the Greek and Roman world attached themselves to the persons of their chiefs, and ancient patriotism was in the Middle Ages replaced by the fealty of vassals and allegiance to princes. The Jews, however, always clung to the Law, to the abstract idea,—like our own recent cosmopolitan republicans, who regard neither fatherland nor the person of their princes, but rather the law as the highest principle. Yes, cosmopolitanism has sprung almost completely from Judea's soil, and Christ, who was really a Jew, actually founded the propaganda of cosmopolitanism. As for the republicanism of the Jews, I recall having read in Josephus that there were republicans in Jerusalem who opposed the royalist Herodians, fought against them very courageously, called no man their lord, and bitterly hated Roman absolutism. Their religion was freedom and equality. What a chimaera!

But in the last analysis what is the cause of that hatred between the followers of the Mosaic law and those of the teachings of Christ, which we see in Europe to the present day, and of which the poet, by illustrating the universal through the particular, gave us so gruesome a picture in *The Merchant of Venice?* Is it the primordial brother-hatred, caused by differences in divine worship, which we see soon after the Creation, erupting between Cain and Abel? Or is religion on the whole only a pretext, and men hate each other for the sake of hatred, just as they love each other for the sake of love?

Which side is to blame for this rancor? In trying to answer this question, I feel I must include a passage from a private letter, which does full justice to Shylock's enemies, too:

"I do not condemn the hatred with which the common people persecute the Jews. I only condemn the unfortunate errors which gave birth to that hatred. The people are always right in this matter. Their hatred as well as their love is always based on a perfectly sound instinct; but they do not know how to formulate their sentiments correctly, and instead of issues, their wrath is usually directed against persons—the innocent scapegoats of temporary or local maladjustments. The people suffer want, they are deprived of the means of enjoying life, and though the priests of the state religions assure them that 'man is here on earth to practice self-denial and to obey the authorities despite hunger and thirst,' the people secretly long for the means of enjoyment, and hate those in whose chests and vaults such means are accumulated. They hate the rich and are happy if religion allows them to give vent to this hatred without restraint. The common people always hated in the Jews only the possessors of money; it was always the heaped-up metal which drew down the lightning of their wrath on the Jews. The spirit of each age merely gives an appropriate slogan to this hatred. Thus, in the Middle Ages, that slogan wore the dark colors of the Catholic Church, and the Jews were murdered and plundered because "they crucified Christ"—with the very same logic employed by certain black Christians in San Domingo, who, at the times of the massacres, ran about with a picture of the Saviour on the cross and shrieked fanatically: 'Les blancs l'ont tué, tuons tous les blancs!' [11]

"My friend, you laugh at the poor Negroes. I assure you that the West Indian planters did not laugh then; they were butchered in expiation of Christ exactly like the Jews of Europe a few centuries before. But the black Christians in San Domingo were also right in this matter. The whites lived idly, in the full enjoyment of all pleasures, while the Negroes had to slave for them in the sweat of their black brows, and as wages received nothing but a little rice and very many strokes of the lash. The blacks were the common people.

"We are no longer living in the Middle Ages. The common people, too, are growing more enlightened. They no longer kill Jews on sight—they no longer extenuate their hatred with religion. Our age is no longer so naively bigoted; the traditional animus is cloaked in more modern phrases, and in the beer halls as well as in the chambers of deputies the mob declaims against the Jews with economic, industrial, scientific, even philosophic arguments. Only hardened hypocrites still give their hatred a religious coloring and persecute the Jews for the sake of Christ. The great majority openly admit that material interests are really at stake, and seek by all means to obstruct the Jews in the full exercise of their industrial capacities. Here in Frankfurt, for example, only twenty-four adherents of the Mosaic faith may marry each year, lest the population multiply excessively and there be too much competition for the Christian tradespeople. Here the true reason for anti-Semitism emerges with its real face; no longer with the gloomy, fanatical monkish mien, but with the flabby enlightened features of a shopkeeper afraid of being outdone in business dealings by Jewish business sense.

"But is it the fault of the Jews that this business sense has developed in them in so menacing a form? It is entirely the fault of that madness with which the people of the Middle Ages ignored the importance of industry, regarded trade as ignoble, and money transactions as particularly shameful; and thus turned over the most profitable of these industrial enterprises—the business of money—to the Jews. Since these were barred from all other trades, they perforce became the shrewdest merchants and bankers. The world compelled them to become rich, and then hated them for their riches; and although Christendom has now dropped its prejudices against industry, and in trade and industry Christians have become as knavish as the Jews, and as rich, the traditional hatred of the masses has clung to the Jews, and they still see in them the representatives of money and hate them for it. You see, in world history, everyone is right—the hammer as well as the anvil."

ࣿ *Edmund Kean as Shylock* [12]

THE JEW OF VENICE WAS THE FIRST HEROIC PART which I saw him play. I say "heroic" part, for he did not act it like a broken down old man, a sort of Shewa of hatred (in Richard Cumberland's play, *The Jew*, 1791), as our own Devrient does, but as a hero.[13] Thus I still see him in memory, dressed in his black long tunic, without sleeves, reaching only to the knee, so that the blood-red garment underneath, which came down to his feet, appears all the more startling. His head is covered with a black, broad-rimmed felt hat, rolled up on both sides, its high crown bound with a crimson ribbon; and his hair hangs down long and pitch-black, like his beard—forming as it were an unkempt frame for the healthy, red face, from which peer two hungry, furtive eyes, inspiring an uncanny fear. In his right hand he holds a staff, which he uses more for support than for defense. He merely leans the elbow of his left arm on it, and he rests his black head with its still blacker thoughts in his left hand, as if lost in perfidious reflection, while he explains to Bassanio what is meant by the expression, "a good man"—which is current to this day. When he tells the parable of the Patriarch Jacob and Laban's sheep, he seems as if caught in the web of his own words, and he suddenly breaks off with, "Ay, he was the third,"—and pausing at length, he seems to be considering what to say next, and you feel that the story is gradually taking shape in his brain, and then he suddenly continues, "Not take interest . . ." as if he had at last found the thread—and it did not seem as if we were listening to something learned by rote, but to a speech thought up with great effort.

At the end of the story he smiles much as an author who is pleased with his invention. Then he begins slowly, "Signor Antonio, many a time and oft," until he reaches the word, "dog"—which he pronounces explosively. His anger rises when he says, "and spit upon my Jewish gaberdine," till he comes to the word, "own." Then he draws near, erect and proud, and with bitter scorn he says, "Well then, . . . ducats." Suddenly he bows low, doffs his hat, and with servile mien he continues, "Or shall I bend low. . . ." Even his voice becomes obsequious; you barely hear the slight note of intense wrath; around his complaisant lips writhe gay little serpents. Only his eyes cannot dissemble; they continue shooting their poisoned arrows. This conflict between his external humility and inner vindictiveness ends with the last word, "monies," and with a horrible and prolonged laugh he breaks off suddenly, and his face contracts into a servile expression, and remains as motionless as a mask. Only the eyes, the evil eyes, glare ominously and fatally.

But it is no use. Not even the most lively description can give you an idea of Edmund Kean. Many have successfully imitated his art of declamation, his broken delivery. For the parrot can imitate the cry of the eagle—the monarch of the sky. But the eagle's look, the daring fire which gazes at his own kinsman, the sun—the eye of Kean, that magic lightning, that enchanted flame—no common bird of the theater has been able to make his.

৪৯ *Spinoza* [14]

WHEN WE READ SPINOZA, we have the feeling that we are looking at all-powerful Nature in liveliest repose—a forest of thoughts, high as heaven, with green tops ever in motion—while below the immovable trunks are deeply rooted in the eternal earth. Something inexplicable is wafted through the pages of Spinoza. We feel as though we were stroked by the winds of the future. It may be that the spirit of the Hebrew prophets hovered over their remote descendant. Yet, there is in him a seriousness, a self-conscious pride, a *grandezza* of thought which also seems inherited—for Spinoza belongs to the family of martyrs who were at one time driven from Spain by the most Catholic kings. Add to all this the patience of the Hollander—as manifest in the life of the man, as in his writings.

It is certain that the life of Spinoza was as blameless, pure and spotless as that of his divine cousin, Jesus Christ. He too suffered for his teachings; like Christ, he wore a crown of thorns. Wherever a great spirit speaks his thoughts—there you have Golgotha.

Should you, dear reader, ever come to Amsterdam, ask the guide to show you the Spanish synagogue. It is a fine building; the roof rests on four mighty pillars, and in the center is the pulpit from which the ban of excommunication was pronounced against the contemner of the Mosaic law, the Hidalgo Don Benedict de Spinoza. On these occasions, a ram's horn, called the *shofar*, is blown.

The excommunication of Spinoza was pronounced to the accompaniment of this horn. With solemnity he was expelled from the community of Israel, and forbidden from that day on to call himself a Jew. His Christian enemies were generous enough to leave him that title; but the Jews, the Swiss guard of deism, were implacable; and today they still exhibit the place before the Spanish synagogue at Amsterdam where they sought to strike him down with their daggers.

I could not but call special attention to the personal misfortunes of the man, for he was shaped not only by schools, but also by life itself. In this respect he differs from most philosophers; we see this influence directly in his writings. Theology was to him not merely a branch of learning, no more than politics, which he also learned through experience. The father of his betrothed had been executed for political offenses in the Netherlands.[15] Nowhere in the world are people so savagely executed as in the Netherlands. You have no idea of the interminable preparations and ceremonies which take place on such occasions. The culprit is bored to death, and the spectator is given sufficient time to reflect. I am sure that Benedict Spinoza reflected a great deal over the execution of old van Ende; and as he once understood religion with its daggers, so now he understood politics with its halters. Evidence in this regard is furnished in his *Tractatus Politicus*.[16]

I have only undertaken to show how philosophers are more or less related to one another—and I am indicating the degrees of relationship and succession. Spinoza is the third son of René Descartes, and his philosophy as propounded in his masterpiece, the *Ethics*, is as far removed from the materialism of Locke as from the idealism of his brother Leibnitz. Spinoza does not torture himself with an analysis of the problem as to the ultimate foundations of knowledge. He gives us his great synthesis: his explanation of deity.

Benedict Spinoza teaches that there is but one substance, God. This one substance is infinite and absolute. All finite substances are derived from it, are contained in it, emerge from or sink into it; they have only relative, transitory, accidental existence. Absolute substance manifests itself to us in the form of infinite thought as well as infinite extension. Infinite thought and infinite extension are the two attributes of absolute substance. We know only these two attributes. But God, absolute substance, may possess other attributes, which we do not know. "*Non dico me Deum omnino cognoscere, sed me quaedam eius attributa, non autem omnia, neque maximam intellegere partem.*" [17]

Only stupidity and malice could term this doctrine "atheism." No one has ever expressed himself in more sublime terms regarding the Deity. Instead of saying that he denies God, we should rather say that he denies Man. All finite objects are for him only modes of infinite substance. All finite things are contained in God; the human intellect is only a ray of infinite thought; the human body only an atom of infinite extension; God is the infinite cause of souls and bodies—*natura naturans*.[18]

ह Moses Mendelssohn [19]

MENDELSSOHN HAS . . . GREAT SOCIAL SIGNIFICANCE. He was the reformer of the German Jews, his co-religionists, and he overthrew the authority of the Talmud and founded the pure Mosaic cult. This man, called by his contemporaries the German Socrates, and admired by them for his nobility of soul and strength of intellect, was the son of a poor sacristan of a synagogue in Dessau. Over and above this congenital disability, Providence burdened him with a hump-back, as if to show the masses in glaring fashion that men should be judged not by their exterior, but by their inner worth. It may be that Providence bestowed it on him in kindly foresight, so that he might attribute ill-treatment at the hands of the multitude to an evil for which a wise man could easily find consolation.

As Luther had overthrown the Papacy, Mendelssohn overthrew the Talmud, and in the same way, for he rejected tradition, and proclaimed the Bible to be the fountainhead of religion, and translated its most important portions. Thus he destroyed Jewish-Catholicism—as Luther had destroyed Roman-Catholicism. For in truth, the Talmud is the Catholicism of the Jews. It is a Gothic cathedral, overloaded with naive grotesqueness, but amazing in its heaven-aspiring and gigantic grandeur. It is a hierarchy of religious laws, which often deal with the quaintest and most ridiculous subtleties; and yet are so ingeniously arranged, and ordered, sustain and aid one another so well, and their combined effect is so impressively logical, that they constitute an awe-inspiring, formidable and colossal entity.

After the fall of Christian Catholicism, that of the Jews, the Talmud, was also doomed. For the Talmud had lost its meaning. It had served as a bulwark against Rome. To it the Jews owed their capacity to resist Christian Rome as heroically as they once resisted pagan Rome. They not only resisted—they conquered. The poor Rabbi of Nazareth, above whose expiring head the heathen Roman had written in mockery, "King of the Jews,"—this sham-king of the Jews, crowned with thorns, draped in the ironic purple, in the end became the God of the Romans, and they had to bow down before Him. Like pagan Rome, Christian Rome also was conquered and even made a tributary. . . .

MOSES MENDELSSOHN THEREFORE DESERVES GREAT PRAISE for over-throwing Jewish Catholicism, at least in Germany. For whatever is superfluous, is harmful. Though he overthrew the tradition, he endeavored strictly to maintain the Mosaic ceremonial law as a religious duty. Was it because of timidity or shrewdness? Was it lingering and melancholy love which held him from laying violent hands on objects which had been most sacred in the eyes of his ancestors, and for the sake of which the blood and tears of so many martyrs have been poured out? I do not think so. Like the monarchs of the material, so the monarchs of the spirit world must show themselves inexorable in their family relations. Even on the throne of thought there can be no surrender to tenderness. Hence I believe that Moses Mendelssohn saw in pure Mosaism an institution which might serve as the last fortress of deism. For deism was his inmost faith and his deepest conviction.

ಲ Ludwig Marcus

So FAR AS I AM AWARE, Ludwig Marcus was born in Dessau in the year 1798, the son of poor parents who adhered to the God-fearing faith of Judaism. He came to Berlin in 1820 to study medicine, but he soon abandoned that branch of science. I saw him first at Berlin at Hegel's lectures, where he often sat near me and wrote down the words of the master religiously. He was then twenty-two years old, but his appearance was extremely youthful. He had a small, slight body, like that of a boy of eight, and in his face there was a sort of senility which usually goes with a hunched back. But he showed no such deformity, and that he did not have one, was surprising. Those who had personally known the late Moses Mendelssohn remarked with astonishment on the resemblance in the features of Marcus to those of the renowned philosopher, who curiously enough, was also a native of Dessau. . . .

But in spirit Marcus was in fact closely related to the great reformer of the German Jews, and in his soul dwelt the same selflessness, patient tranquillity, humble sense of justice, smiling contempt for evil, and inflexible iron love for his oppressed co-religionists. Their fate was for Marcus, as for the latter day Moses,[20] the painful yet glowing hub of all thinking, the very heart of his life. Even in those days, while he was in Berlin, Marcus was the all-around scholar. He ransacked all the realms of learning. He digested whole libraries of books. He burrowed into all the linguistic treasure-chests of ancient and modern times; but in the end, geography proved to be his favorite study—in its most general as well as most specific meaning. There was in this whole world no fact, ruin, idiom, folly, or flower, but Marcus knew it—yet from all these intellectual excursions he always came home to the doleful history of Israel, the golgothas of Jerusalem; and to the homely little paternal dialect of Palestine, for the sake of which he devoted himself to the study of the Semitic languages with special fervor.

This was the outstanding trait in his character, and constitutes his importance and singular merit. For not only by reason of some action or some achievement which is transmitted are we entitled to the respect and regard of posterity, but also because of our efforts, especially our unsuccessful, frustrated, fruitless, but generous efforts.

THE LITTLE MAN'S OUTWARD APPEARANCE, which not infrequently aroused laughter, did not prevent him from becoming one of the most honored members of that association which published the above-mentioned periodical, and which, as the "Society for Jewish Culture and Science" devoted itself to ambitious but impracticable ideas. Intellectual and great-hearted men endeavored in this way to save a long-lost cause; but at best they succeeded in discovering the remains of ancient warriors left on the battlefields of the past. The whole output of that society consists of a few historical works of research, and among them the treatises of Dr. Zunz, on the Spanish Jews in the Middle Ages, must be counted one of the most remarkable examples of the higher criticism.

How can I speak of the Society without mentioning the admirable Zunz, who manifested unshakable steadfastness in a time of uncertainty and transition, and who despite his acumen, scepticism, and erudition, remained faithful to his own words, and to the most generous impulses of his soul? A man of words and deeds, he created and wrought, while others dreamed and succumbed to despair.

I cannot pass by without mentioning my dear Bendavid,[21] who combined with great intellect and strength of character a large-minded and urbane culture, and although he was well advanced in age, shared all the youthful visionary dreams of the Society. He was a sage of the old school, steeped in the sunlight of Greek serenity, a pattern of the purest virtue, and through discipline, as hard as the marble of the categorical imperative of his master, Immanuel Kant. All his life Bendavid was the most zealous disciple of the Kantian philosophy, and in his youth he suffered the harshest persecution for it. And yet he would not separate himself from the ancient community of the Mosaic creed, and would never change the cockade of his beliefs. Even the slightest semblance of such a renunciation filled him with indignation and disgust. Lazarus Bendavid, as I have said, was a thoroughgoing Kantian, and in saying this, I have indicated the limitations of his intellect. When we spoke of Hegelian philosophy, he would shake his bald head and say that it was mere superstition. He wrote quite well; he spoke even better. He wrote for the periodical of the Society a remarkable essay on the Messianic belief among the Jews, in which he sought to demonstrate with critical insight that the belief in a Messiah was not a fundamental article of the Jewish faith, but must be regarded as an accretion.

The most active member of the Society, the very life and spirit of it, was M. Moser, who died a few years ago. Even as a young man, he was master not only of the most profound scholarship, but was also fired with a compassion for humanity and the desire to put his learning to practical use in healing its wounds. He was untiring in his philanthropic endeavors. He was very practical and unostentatious in his labors of love. The great public knew nothing of his activity He fought and bled incognito. His name is totally unknown and is not inscribed in the rolls of self-sacrifice. Our generation is not so poor as we think. It has produced an astonishing number of these anonymous martyrs.

The obituary of the late Marcus has led me naturally to writing the obituary of the Society of which he was one of the most honored members, and of which Eduard Gans, recently deceased (of whom I have already spoken) was the worthy president. This very gifted man cannot be extolled for his unassuming self-sacrifice or his anonymous martyrdom. In fact, though his heart embraced with ready passion the cause of mankind's salvation, he did not, even in moments of exaltation, lose sight of his own interests. . . .

The late Gans' services to German scholarship are common knowledge. He was one of the most zealous apostles of the Hegelian philosophy, and in jurisprudence he waged a devastating war upon the lackeys of the old Roman law who, without regard for the spirit which once dwelt in the old legislation, were only concerned with dusting the wardrobe that had been left behind, cleansing it of moths, or patching it for modern use. Gans chastised such servility, even when it paraded in the most elegant livery. How the wretched soul of Herr von Savigny whined under his kicks! Even more effectively than through the written word, Gans advanced the interests of German freedom by speaking. He set free the most confined thoughts, and tore the mask from the face of falsehood. He was a volatile fire-spirit, the sparks of whose wit blazed bravely, or at least glowed magnificently. . . .

WE HAVE REMARKED THAT THE PART WHICH MARCUS PLAYED in the Society for Jewish Culture and Science was of greater importance and more memorable than all his stupendous knowledge and scholarly works. It is likely that the period when he was devoting himself to the endeavors and the illusions of the Society appeared to him the sunniest and most fruitful years of his unhappy life. Hence I had to make particular mention of the Society and a more detailed discussion of its ideas may not be superfluous. But time and place, and their wardens, do not permit such an extended description in these pages, for it would deal not only with the civil and religious condition of the Jews, but also with that of all the deistic sects in the world. I will only say this much—that the esoteric object of the Society was nothing less than the reconciliation of historical Judaism with modern science—for it assumed that the latter would in the course of time achieve universal dominion. Similarly, at the time of Philo,[22] when Greek philosophy declared war on all the ancient dogmas, a parallel attempt was made in Alexandria more or less successfully.

FROM MY OWN EXPERIENCE, I can only report unimportant details concerning the life of Marcus, whom I lost sight of in Berlin. As I learned later, he travelled to France; for despite his extraordinary learning and his lofty morals, he found that in his Fatherland there were too many obstacles to his advancement in the remnants of innumerable medieval laws. His parents died; and he had generously renounced the legacy in favor of his distressed relatives. Some fifteen years passed, and I heard nothing of Marcus. . . .

But one day I met the little man in Paris. He told me that he had in the meantime been professor at Dijon, but had recently given up his post because of ministerial displeasure. He desired to stay in Paris, so as to use the resources of the library in preparing his great work. I heard from other sources that in the matter of his professorship there was also a question of Marcus's obstinacy—the ministry had proposed to replace him with a substitute at a lower salary, leaving him the more substantial balance (as is customary in France); but the great soul of the little man recoiled at exploiting the labors of another—and he turned over the whole stipend to his successor. His selflessness in this regard is all the more noteworthy when one considers the straitened circumstances in which he was then living. He could not have been any worse off—and without the angelic assistance of a beautiful lady he would have died of want. It was a very beautiful and distinguished lady of Paris, one of the most brilliant members of society, who, hearing of this remarkable fellow, descended into the darkness of his misery, and graciously and tactfully persuaded him to accept a considerable annuity. I imagine his pride was gratified by the thought that at some future time the goddess—who was married to one of the wealthiest bankers in the world—would publish his great work at her own expense. He probably thought that a lady whose mind and culture were renowned must really think it important that a complete history of Abyssinia be written, and he took it as a matter of course that she should subsidize the author for his great pains and travail by an annual grant. . . .

Marcus lived in Paris for about five years in philosophic tranquillity. He was well established, and one of his favorite dreams had even come true: he had a small apartment with his own furniture, in the vicinity of the library. One evening, a relative, a nephew of his, called on him, and was amazed to see his uncle suddenly sit down on the floor and begin singing the most obscene street-catches in a reckless, defiant voice. He who had never even sung a note, and in word and demeanor was chastity itself! But the affair became even more startling and terrifying, when the uncle leaped up furiously, forced the window open, and began throwing his watch, then his inkwell, and finally his pens and his purse into the street. When the nephew saw that his uncle was throwing out money, he no longer doubted that he was insane. The unfortunate man was brought to the sanatorium of Dr. Pinnel at Chaillot, where he gave up the ghost after two weeks of horrible agony. He died on the 15th of July, and was buried in the Montmartre cemetery on the seventeenth. I heard of his death too late to pay him my last respects. In dedicating these pages to his memory,

I wish to make amends for the omission, and in spirit, to take part in his funeral rites.

And now open his coffin, so that, in accordance with the ancient custom, I may ask pardon of the deceased for whatever offense I have committed against him while he was yet alive. How peaceful the little man looks! He seems to be smiling at the fact that I did not do greater justice to his scholarly labors. He probably gave that very little thought; for in this respect I am hardly so competent a judge as, say, his friend, S. Munk, the Orientalist who, according to report, is engaged in writing the definitive biography of the deceased and in editing his unpublished works.

₰ *The Polish Jews*

THE EXTERNAL APPEARANCE OF THE POLISH JEW IS FRIGHTFUL. I am still horrified when I recall my first sight of a Polish village, back of Meseritz, almost entirely populated by Jews. The *W—sche Weekly*,[23] boiled down to a puree, could hardly occasion the nausea I felt at the sight of those ragged, filthy creatures; the high-spirited speeches of sophomores, breathing fire for School and Fatherland, with all their ear-splitting harangues, could never repel me as much as the jargon of the Polish Jews. However, soon revulsion gave way to pity, for I had occasion to observe more closely the condition of these people, and see the pig-sties in which they lived, jabbered, prayed and haggled. What abysmal wretchedness! Their speech is German, interlarded with Hebrew and Polish. They had emigrated from Germany to Poland long ago to escape religious persecution; for in this respect the Poles had always been remarkable for tolerance. Once, when zealots urged one of the Polish kings to reconvert Polish Protestants to Catholicism by force, he replied, *"Sum rex populorum, sed non conscientiarum!"* [24]

The Jews first brought trade and handicrafts to Poland, and in the reign of Casimir the Great they were granted extensive privileges They seem to have come closer to the nobility than to the peasantry; for according to an ancient law, a Jew who was converted to Christianity, became, *ipso facto*, a nobleman. I don't know for what reason this law fell into abeyance, and which of the two sank in value.

In those early times, the Jews far surpassed the nobles in intellect and culture; for the latter engaged only in rude military pursuits, and still lacked French etiquette. The Jews, on the other hand, were at least busy with Hebrew scholarly and religious books, for the sake of which they had left their land and the comforts of life. But they did not keep step with European culture; their intellectual outlook became narrow and degenerated into revolting superstition, which by reason of their subtle scholasticism took on a thousand perverted forms. Yet in spite of the barbarous fur cap which covers his head, and the still more barbarous notions which fill it, I esteem the Polish Jew more highly than his German counterpart, even though the latter wear a beaver on his head, and carry Jean Paul in it. As a result of rigorous isolation, the character of the Polish Jew acquired a oneness; as a result of the tolerant atmosphere in which he lived, it acquired the stamp of freedom. The inner man did not degenerate into a haphazard conglomeration of feelings; he was not stunted by the restrictions of the Frankfurt ghetto, wise state ordinances, and amiable legal restraints. The Polish Jew, with his dirty fur cap, vermin-infested beard, smell of garlic, and his jabber is certainly preferable to many other Jews I know who shine with the magnificence of gilt-edged government bonds.

ৼ *The Blood Libel of Damascus* [25]

Paris, May 7, 1840

THE PARIS NEWSPAPERS OF TODAY bring us a report from the Imperial Royal Austrian consul in Damascus to the Imperial Royal consul-general in Alexandria regarding the Jews of Damascus, whose martyr-dom recalls the darkest days of the Middle Ages. While we in Europe use such stories as material for poetry, and amuse ourselves with such terribly naive tales, with which our forefathers tormented them-selves not a little; while we only know from poems and romances of those witches, werewolves, and Jews, who need the blood of pious Christian children for their satanic rites; while we laugh and forget—in the East they are beginning to recall very sadly the ancient superstition and make very serious faces—faces of gloomy anger and the most desperate death agony! Meanwhile the executioner tortures, and on the rack of martyrdom the Jew confesses that for the approaching Passover festival he needed some Christian blood in which to dip his dry Easter bread, and for that purpose had slaughtered an old Capuchin! The Turk is stupid and vile, and gladly places his apparatus of bastinado and torture at the service of Christians against the accused Jews; for he hates both sects, regarding them as dogs, and calls them by this honorable title, and he doubtless rejoices when the Christian Giaour [26] gives him an opportunity to maltreat the Jewish Giaour with some pretense of justice. Wait till it is to the Pasha's advantage, and he no longer need fear the armed intervention of Europeans, then he will listen to the circumcised dogs, and these will accuse our Christian brothers of—the Lord knows what!—Today the anvil, tomorrow the hammer!

But for the friend of humanity such deeds must ever be a source of bitter pain. Events of this kind are disasters; their consequences are beyond computation. Fanaticism is a contagious disease, which spreads under the most varied forms, and finally rages against all of us. The French consul in Damascus, Count Ratti-Menton, has been guilty of evil deeds which have excited a universal cry of horror. He it is who inoculated the East with Western superstition, and disseminated among the mob of Damascus a work in which the Jews were accused of murdering Christians. This writing, which breathes hatred, and which Count Menton received from his clerical friends for dissemination, was originally borrowed from the *Bibliotheca Prompta a Lucio Ferrario*, and here it is distinctly asserted that the Jews in celebrating the feast of Passover use the blood of Christians. The noble count, however, guarded against repeating the story connected with it in the Middle Ages, namely that the Jews for the same purpose stole the consecrated wafers and pierced them with needles till blood ran from them—an iniquity, which came to light not only through sworn witnesses, but also through a clear flame which could be seen over the house in which the stolen host had been thus crucified by the Jews. No, the unbelievers, the Mohammedans, would never have believed that, so that Count Menton had, in the interests of his mission, to take refuge in less miraculous tales. I say in the interests of his mission—and submit these words to the weightiest consideration. The count has not been in Damascus long; six months ago he was seen here in Paris, the workshop of all progressive—but also of all retrogressive societies. The present Minister of Foreign Affairs, M. Thiers, who lately sought to appear not only as a man of humanity, but also as a son of the Revolution, has exhibited in regard to the occurrences in Damascus a singular indifference. According to the *Moniteur* of today, a vice-consul has already left for Damascus to investigate the conduct of the French consul there. A vice-consul! Certainly some subordinate from a neighboring locality, a man without name and without any guarantee of impartial independence!

May 27, 1840

THE NORTH GERMAN PRESS contains several communications concerning the blood-accusation of Damascus, which are dated partly from Paris, partly from Leipzig. But all are apparently from the same pen, and written in the interests of a certain clique, with the intention of misleading the German public. We shall leave the person and the motives of the contributor out of our present discussion; we shall refrain from any investigation of the proceedings at Damascus. But as to what has been said about it by the Jews and the press of Paris, we venture to offer some rectifications. In doing this, we are guided more by an interest in truth than in persons; and so far as the Jews of this place are concerned, it may be that our testimony will speak rather against them than for them. I would, in fact, rather praise than blame the Jews of Paris if they showed, as the North German newspapers report, such great zeal on behalf of their unfortunate coreligionists of Damascus and spared no sacrifice of money to vindicate the honor of their slandered faith. But this is not the case. The Jews of France have been emancipated too long not to have had their racial bond loosened; they have been almost completely submerged—or to put it more correctly,—they have been merged with the French nation.—They are as French as the others, and have accesses of enthusiasm which last four and twenty hours, and, when the sun is hot, even three days. And this is true of the better section among them.

Many of them still observe the Jewish ceremonies, the external cult,—but in a mechanical way, merely from habit, without knowing why. There is not a trace of inward conviction, for in the synagogue the ironic leaven of Voltairean criticism has worked as destructively as in the Christian Church. With the Jews of France, as with all other Frenchmen, gold is the God of these times, and industry the prevailing religion. In this respect one could divide the Jews into two sects: those living on the "right bank," and those on the "left bank." These are the names of two railway lines, of which one runs on the right bank of the Seine, and the other on the left, toward Versailles. They are managed by two distinguished rabbis of finance, who quarrel with each other as once did Rabbi Shammai and Rabbi Hillel in the more ancient city of Babylon.[27]

In all justice, we must grant that the chief rabbi of the *rive droite*, Baron Rothschild, has shown a greater sympathy for the house of Israel than his scripturally-learned opponent, the chief rabbi of the *rive gauche*, M. Benoît Fould,[28] who, while his brethren in Syria were being tortured and garroted at the instigations of a French consul, made a few speeches in the French Chamber of Deputies on the conversion of *rentes* and discount rates of the banks—with the imperturbable equanimity of a Hillel.

The interest taken by the Jews of this city in the tragedy of Damascus reduces itself to very minute manifestations. The Israelite *Consistorium* met and deliberated in the luke-warm fashion of all such corporations, and the only result of all these deliberations was the opinion that the legal documents of the trial must be made public. M. Crémieux,[29] the celebrated lawyer, who has at all times devoted his selfless eloquence not only to the Jews but to the oppressed of all faiths and doctrines, has undertaken the publication in question. Except for one very beautiful lady and a few young scholars, M. Crémieux is the only person in Paris actively engaged in the cause of Israel. At great sacrifice to his personal interests, and scornful of all secret frauds, he has boldly challenged the most vile insinuations, and has even offered to go to Egypt, in case the trial of the Jews of Damascus should be conducted before the tribunal of Pasha Mehemet Ali. . . .

HERE I MUST MAKE AN OBSERVATION—perhaps the bitterest of all. Among the baptized Jews are many who from cowardly hypocrisy abuse Israel more viciously than its born enemies. In like manner, certain writers, to divert attention from their origin, are in the habit of reviling the Jews—or saying nothing at all about them. This is a well-known, lamentable, and laughable phenomenon. But it may be useful to call public attention to it, since it is not only the above-mentioned North German press, but also a far more important journal that insinuates that all that has been written on behalf of the Jews of Damascus originates with the Jews; that the Austrian consul at Damascus is a Jew, as well as every other consul, except the French. We know this sort of tactic; we have already experienced it in connection with Young Germany. No! All the consuls in Damascus are Christians; and that the Austrian consul there is not Jewish is attested by the fearless and public manner in which he protected the Jews against the attack of the French consul. What the latter is, time will show.

June 3, 1840

THE DAILY PRESS OF FRANCE is to a certain extent an oligarchy, not a democracy; for the founding of a French newspaper is attended with so much expense and difficulty, that only those in a position to stake enormous sums can do so. It is usually capitalists, or similar industrialists, who advance the funds necessary to found a newspaper. They speculate on the profits which will accrue when the paper succeeds in becoming the organ of an established party; or they secretly entertain the idea of selling it at an even greater profit to the government, when it has gained a sufficiently large circulation. In this way, dependent as they are on exploitation by existing parties or by the ministry, the journals become restricted, and what is still worse, narrow and exclusive in their information, so that in comparison with them, the restraints imposed by the German censorship appear almost like a delightful chain of roses. The editor-in-chief of a French journal is a *condottiere* who in his columns fights for and defends the interests and passions of the party which has hired him either by subscriptions or subsidy. His sub-editors, his lieutenants and soldiers, obey with military subordination, and give their articles the desired tone and color; with the result that the newspaper acquires that unity and precision which we from afar cannot sufficiently admire. Here the most stringent discipline of thought, and even of expression, prevails. Should some heedless collaborator fail to obey a command, or to write exactly as ordered, the editor-in-chief slashes the article with military ruthlessness, such as no German censor would be capable of. A German censor is always German—and in his easy-going open-mindedness is ever willing to listen to reason. But the editor-in-chief of a French newspaper is a practical, one-sided Frenchman, with set opinions, which he has once and for all formulated in set phrases, or which have been transmitted to him, nicely expressed, by his employers. Should anyone come to him with an article which may not be of immediate advantage to the professed aim of the paper, but treats of some subject not directly concerned with the interests of the public whose organ the sheet claims to be, he meets with a firm refusal and the sacramental words: *"Cela n'entre pas dans l'idée de notre journal."* [30] Now, since every newspaper here has its own political shade, and its own well-defined range of ideas, it can be readily understood that anyone who has something to say which goes beyond the bounds, or does not have party coloring, will find no place in the public press. Indeed, as soon as an article diverges from the discussion of current events,—the so-called realities,—as soon as it begins developing ideas removed from banal party questions, as soon as it attempts to discuss the affairs of mankind, the editors reject it with ironic politeness; and since here the only way to reach the public is through the medium of the newspaper, or of advertising, the gifted thinker and world-citizen discovers that the *Charte*, which grants every Frenchman the right to publish his ideas is a hollow mockery—for actually there is no freedom of the press. "*Cela n'entre pas dans l'idée de notre journal.*"

The above remarks will perhaps throw light on many phenomena not easily understood. I leave it to the German reader to draw the most profitable inferences. They may, however, chiefly serve to explain why the French press has not spoken out so fully in favor of the Jews of Damascus as had been expected in Germany. I repeat, the informant in the *Leipziger Zeitung* and the smaller North German journals was not guilty of an untruth when he gleefully declared that the French press did not display an unusual measure of sympathy for the Jews on that occasion. But that honest soul took care not to reveal the true reason for this situation—which is simply that the President of the Council of Ministers, M. Thiers, from the very first took the part of Count Ratti-Menton, the French consul at Damascus, and informed the editors of all journals, which are now under his control, of his views on this matter. There are of course many honest, very honest people among these journalists, but they obey the command of that generalissimo of public opinion with military discipline, when they gather in his ante-chambers each morning to receive the *ordre du jour;* and I am sure they cannot look at each other without bursting into laughter. French augurs do not have the same control of their facial-muscles as did those of Rome, whom Cicero describes. At his morning audiences M. Thiers assures his listeners with an air of profoundest conviction that he has incontrovertible proof that Jews drank Christian blood at the Passover feast. *Chacun à son goût.* All reports of witnesses had confirmed the fact that the Rabbi of Damascus had slaughtered Father Thomas and drunk his blood; his flesh was probably gobbled up by minor officials of the synagogue. We see, of course, what sad superstition and religious fanaticism still prevail among the Jews in the Orient—while in the West, the Jews have become much more humane and enlightened, and many of them are distinguished for their freedom from prejudice as well as by their good taste; as for example, Herr von Rothschild, who, it is true, has not gone over to the Christian Church, but has all the more eagerly taken to the Christian cuisine, and has pressed into his service the greatest cook in all Christendom, the favorite of Talleyrand, formerly Bishop of Autun. . . .

FROM THESE INDICATIONS, one can readily understand the illiberal language of those opposition sheets which at another time would have cried bloody murder at the flames of fanaticism which have recently been fanned in the Orient and at that miserable wretch who, as French consul there, disgraces the name of France.

A few days ago, M. Benoît Fould pressed for an inquiry in the Chamber of Deputies regarding the conduct of the French consul in Damascus. Hence I must withdraw the reproach which I directed at that deputy in my last letter. I never doubted M. Fould's intelligence or strength of mind. I too regard him as one of the greatest leaders of the French Chamber. But I had doubts about his feelings. How glad I am to be thus put to shame, when I have done injustice to anyone, and am refuted by his actions! The interpellation of M. Fould revealed great shrewdness and dignity. Very few newspapers have published excerpts from his speeches, and the papers of the Ministry have suppressed even these; but they have, on the other hand, given the opposing views of M. Thiers in great detail. I have read them in their entirety in the *Moniteur*. The expression, *"la religion à laquelle j'ai l'honneur d'appartenir,"* [31] must have struck a German as singular. M. Thiers' reply was a masterpiece of perfidy. Through evasion and suppression of what he knew to be the truth, by means of seemingly anxious reservations, he succeeded most admirably in casting suspicion on his adversaries. To hear him speak, one would be led to believe that the flesh of Capuchins was a Jewish national dish.

Not at all—you great writer of history—and puny theologian! Neither in the East nor in the West does the Old Testament allow its believers to eat unclean food. This aversion to bloody relishes is quite peculiar to them. It expresses itself directly in the very first principles of their religion, in all their sanitary laws, in their ceremonies of purification, in their fundamental views as to what is clean and what is unclean, and in that profoundly cosmogonic revelation as to the physical purity of the animal world, which serves, at the same time, as an ethic of the body—a matter which Paul did not understand at all, and therefore rejected as a fable. No, the descendants of Israel, the clean, chosen race of priests, do not eat the flesh of swine,—not even of old Franciscans. They do not drink blood, no more than their own urine—unlike St. Elizabeth, great-aunt of Count Montalembert.[32]

What came to light most distressingly in that blood accusation of Damascus is the ignorance of conditions in the Orient shown by the present President of the Council—a brilliant exhibition of ignorance which may lead to the most serious blunders in situations which involve not a petty Syrian blood-libel—but a far greater world-problem —the fateful, fatal question which we call the Eastern Problem. . . .

July 25, 1840

THE OLD SYSTEM OF RACIAL EXTERMINATION is gradually becoming extinct in the East as a consequence of European influence. The right of individuals to existence is also receiving a greater measure of recognition there; and the cruelties of torture will yield to a more humane system of criminal procedure. The bloody story of Damascus will contribute considerably to achieving this result; and in this connection, M. Crémieux's journey to Alexandria must be deemed as a very important event in the history of humanity. This celebrated jurist, who belongs with the most renowned men of France, and whom I have already referred to in these pages, has embarked upon this truly pious pilgrimage, accompanied by his wife, who insists on sharing all the hazards with her husband. May these hazards, which were intended to deter him from his noble venture, prove as piddling as the people who provoked them! For this advocate of the Jews is really pleading the cause of all humanity. Nothing less is at stake than the inauguration of European criminal procedure in the East. The trial of the Jews of Damascus began with the use of instruments of torture. It was not concluded, because a subject of Austria was involved and the Austrian consul intervened to prevent the use of torture. Now the proceedings are to be instituted once again, and without the *obligato* of rack, and without those instruments of torture which wring from the accused the wildest confessions and intimidate all witnesses. The French consul-general at Alexandria is moving heaven and earth in an effort to avert this new trial; for here much light may be thrown on the actions of the French consul in Damascus, and the disgrace of a representative of France may undermine her authority in Syria. For France has far-reaching plans with respect to this country—plans which date from the period of the Crusades, were not given up by the Revolution, and were cherished by Napoleon—and which even M. Thiers is pondering. The Christians of Syria expect their deliverance to come at the hands of France. The latter, as free-thinking as she may be at home, passes for a pious protector of the Catholic faith in the Orient, and here she flatters the zeal of the monks. In this way we can explain why not only M. Cochelet of Alexandria, but even our own President of the Council, and a son of the Revolution, has taken the consul of Damascus under his protecting wing.

The question is really not one concerning the noble virtues of a Ratti-Menton, or the wickedness of the Jews of Damacsus—there is perhaps no great difference between the two. As the former should be too small for our hate, the latter should be for our love. But the question is whether we sanction the abolition of the system of torture by a striking example in the East. The consuls of the great European powers, that is, of Austria and England, have proposed to the Pasha of Egypt that the trial of the Jews of Damascus be resumed without application of torture. It may be a source of malignant gratification to them that it is M. Cochelet, the French consul, representative of the Revolution and of its son, who is opposed to the reopening of the trial—and has become the protagonist of torture!

৪৶ *Reflections*

JUDAISM—ARISTOCRACY. One God creates the world and rules it. All men are his children; but the Jews are his favorites and their land is his chosen domain. He is a monarch, and the Jews his noblemen, and Palestine is the exarchate of God.

Christianity—democracy. One God who has created all and rules over it. He loves all men alike and protects all realms alike. He is no longer a national divinity, but a universal one.

THE JEWS ARE THE ONLY PEOPLE who after the Christianizing of Europe asserted freedom of worship.

HATRED OF THE JEWS commenced with the Romantic School, with

the enthusiasm for the Middle Ages, Catholicism, the nobility—and was aggravated by the Germanophiles.

THE HISTORY OF THE JEWS IS BEAUTIFUL. But our young Jews do harm to the older ones, who most likely would be set above the Greeks and Romans. I believe that if no Jews were in existence, and it were suddenly discovered that a single specimen were still to be found somewhere, people would journey hundreds of miles to see him and press his hand. And now, we are shunned!

A BAPTISMAL CERTIFICATE is a ticket of admission to European culture.

THE JEWS MUST FINALLY REALIZE that they will achieve full emancipation only when the emancipation of the Christians is completely won and secured. Their cause is identical with that of the German people; and they should not need to demand as Jews, what has long been due them as Germans.

IS THE MISSION OF THE JEWS FULFILLED? I believe it will be when the worldly Saviour comes—industry, labor, joy.

Germany

❧ *Martin Luther*

BUT THERE WAS ONE MAN THERE who, I am convinced, did not
think of himself, but of the divine interests he represented. This was
Martin Luther, the poor monk whom Providence had chosen to
break the Roman world-power against which the mightiest emperors
and boldest sages had fought in vain. But Providence knows very
well on whose shoulders it lays its burdens; what was required here
was not only spiritual but also physical strength. A body steeled
from youth by monastic severity and chastity was needed to endure
the bitter trials of such a mission. Our dear master was at that time
still lean and very pale, so that the ruddy, well-fed gentlemen of
the Diet looked down almost pityingly on the poor man in the black
cowl. But he was quite healthy, and his nerves were so strong that
the brilliant assembly did not in the least overawe him; and his
lungs particularly must have been strong—for after delivering his

long defense, he was obliged to repeat it in Latin because the Emperor did not understand High German. I'm angered whenever I think of it; for our dear master stood by an open window, exposed to a draught, while the sweat ran from his forehead. He must have been tired after speaking so long, and no doubt his throat was parched. "That fellow must be pretty thirsty," the Duke of Brunswick probably thought, for we read that he sent three cans of the best Eimbecker beer to Luther's hostelry. I shall never forget this noble deed of the House of Brunswick.

There are in France as false conceptions of the Reformation as of its hero. Primarily, these misconceptions are due to the fact that Luther is not only the greatest man in our history, but the most thoroughly German as well: that in his character all the virtues and faults of the Germans are most magnificently fused, so that he personifies our wonderful Germany. In addition, he possessed traits which we seldom find united, but generally regard as incompatible. He was at the same time a dreamy mystic and a practical man of action. His thoughts had wings as well as hands; he spoke and acted. He was not only the tongue, but also the sword of his time. And he was at once the cool, scholastic casuist and the inspired, God-intoxicated prophet. After he had worked himself weary all day on his dogmatic distinctions, he took up the flute in the evening, looked up at the stars, and melted away in melody and adoration. This man who could scold like a fishwife could also be as gentle as a tender maid. He was often as wild as the storm that uproots oaks, and then again as soft as the zephyr toying with the violets. He was filled with the most awesome fear of God and a spirit of self-sacrifice to the Holy Ghost. He could lose himself in the depths of pure spirituality— yet he knew very well the glories of this world, and valued them, and from his lips we have the celebrated motto:

> "Who loves not woman, wine, and song,
> Remains a fool his whole life long."

He was a complete man; I might say, an absolute man, in whom spirit and matter were inseparable. It would be as wrong to call him a spiritualist as a sensualist. How shall I put it? There was in him something primeval, incomprehensible, miraculous, a quality we find in all providential men, something terrifyingly-naive, awkwardly-clever, sublimely-narrow, indomitably-demonic.

Luther's father was a miner in Mannsfeld, and there the boy often went down with him into the subterranean workshop where the mighty metals grow and the full primal fountains flow. It may be that here his young heart unconsciously absorbed the most intimate secrets of nature, or he was even bemused by the mountain trolls. That may be why so much earthy matter, so much of the slag of human passion, for which he has been constantly—and wrongly—reproached, clung to him, for without this earthy admixture he could never have become a man of action. Pure spirit cannot act. . . .

GLORY TO LUTHER! Eternal glory to the cherished man to whom we owe the salvation of our most precious possessions and by whose good works we still live! It ill behooves us to deplore the narrowness of his outlook. Certainly, the dwarf who stands upon the shoulders of a giant sees farther than the giant himself, especially with a telescope; but the higher view is devoid of the higher feelings, devoid of the giant heart, which cannot be appropriated. Still less does it behoove us to judge his faults harshly, for these have profited us more than the virtues of a thousand others. The refinement of Erasmus and the mildness of Melanchthon would never have brought us as far as the godlike brutality of Brother Martin.

WHEN LUTHER PROCLAIMED that his doctrine could only be refuted by Scripture and Reason, he extended to human Reason the right to explain the Bible. Thus Reason won recognition as the supreme judge in every religious argument. And so there arose in Germany our so-called freedom of the mind—or, as it is called, freedom of thought. Thinking became a right, and the authority of Reason became legitimate. It is quite true that for some centuries past men could think and speak with some degree of freedom, and the schoolmen disputed over subjects which make us wonder how they could even be mentioned in the Middle Ages. But this occurred as a result of the distinction which was drawn between theological and philosophical truth, a distinction by which they expressly guarded against heresy; but even this took place only in the lecture rooms of the universities, and in abstruse Gothic Latin, which people could not understand, so that not much harm was to be feared for the Church. Still, the Church never really permitted such a procedure, and now and then she actually burned a few poor scholastics at the stake. But now, after Luther, men no longer drew a distinction between theological and philosophical truth; they disputed in public places, in their native German tongue, without fear or hesitation. The princes who accepted the Reformation made this freedom of thought legitimate, and German philosophy has been its important—its all important—fruit.

In fact, not even in Greece could the human mind speak out so freely as we have done in Germany from the middle of the past century to the time of the French invasions. In Prussia especially unlimited freedom of thought prevailed. The Marquis of Branden-burg realized that only the Protestant principle could make him a legitimate King of Prussia, and therefore he had to maintain Protestant freedom of thought as well.

Things have changed since, and the natural protector of our Protestant freedom of thought has come to an understanding with the Ultramontanist party for its suppression; and to that end he treacherously wields a weapon first invented and applied against us by the Popes—censorship.

. . . LUTHER GAVE US NOT ONLY FREEDOM OF ACTION, but also the means to act—to the spirit he gave a body; to thought he gave words. He created the German tongue.

That he did by translating the Bible.

In fact, the Divine Author of this book seems to have known quite as well as we that the choice of a translator is by no means a trivial matter. And so He himself chose His translator, and bestowed upon him the wonderful gift of translating from a language which was dead and buried into another that had not yet come to life.

We had, it is true, the Vulgate, which was understood, and the Septuagint,[1] which might be understood. But knowledge of Hebrew had been utterly extinguished in the Christian world. Only the Jews, who kept themselves hidden here and there in sundry corners of the world, still preserved the traditions of this language. Like a ghost keeping watch over a treasure which had been confided to it during life, this murdered people—this ghost-nation—sat in its gloomy ghettos and guarded the Hebrew Bible. Into these disreputable and blind alleys the German scholars could be seen making their way to unearth the treasure and obtain knowledge of the Hebrew tongue. When the Catholic clergy sensed the danger which threatened from this quarter—that men might in this way obtain the true word of God and unmask the Roman falsehoods—they were anxious to suppress the Jewish tradition. They went to work to destroy all Hebrew books, and on the banks of the Rhine began that persecution of books against which the excellent Doctor Reuchlin fought so gloriously. . . .

FRANKLY, I DO NOT KNOW how the language which we find in Luther's Bible originated. . . . But I do know that it was through this Bible, of which thousands of copies were disseminated among the people by the then youthful printing press with its black magic, that in a few years the language of Luther was widely diffused all over Germany, eventually to become the language of literature. This written language still prevails in Germany, and gives a literary unity to an otherwise politically and religiously dismembered land. So inestimable a service may compensate for the fact that in its present state of development it has lost something of that directness we ordinarily find in a tongue which has sprung from a single dialect. But the language of Luther's Bible does not lack this directness: the old book remains an everlasting fountain of youth for our speech. All turns and expressions here are German. The German writer can use these freely—and since the book is in the hands of our poorest people, they need little learning to be able to express themselves in a literary manner. This circumstance will have remarkable results when our great political revolution breaks out. Freedom will be able to speak everywhere—and her speech will be that of the Bible.

৪৯ Lessing

I HERE MENTION FOR THE SECOND TIME a name which no German can utter without a more or less vivid echo in his heart. For since Luther, Germany has brought forth no greater or better man than Gotthold Ephraim Lessing.[2] These two men are our pride and joy. In our present troubled times, we lift our eyes to their comforting images, and they affirm their glorious promise to us. Yes, a third man will come, who will complete what Luther began and Lessing continued, and whom the Fatherland needs so badly—the third liberator. Already I can see the golden gleam of his armor through the imperial purple, "even like the sun through the morning's rosy haze."

Like Luther, Lessing was effective not only in achieving something definite, but also in moving the German people profoundly, and producing, by his criticism and polemical writings, a healthy intellectual movement. In his day, he was the very embodiment of criticism; his whole life was a polemic. This criticism proved very fruitful, extending even to the most remote regions of thought and feeling,—to religion, science, and art,—while his polemic vanquished all his opponents, and grew stronger with each victory. Lessing, as he himself admitted, needed warfare properly to sharpen his intellect. He was like the legendary Norman who inherited the talents, knowledge, and power of the men he overcame in combat, and thus became endowed with all sorts of advantages and excellences. One can readily see that such a warlike knight created no small stir in Germany, peaceful Germany, where the Sabbath peace was even more profound than it is today. Many were startled by his literary boldness, which stood him in good stead, for *oser!* [3] is the secret of success in literature, as well as in revolution and love. All trembled at the sight of Lessing's sword. No head was safe. Yes, he struck off many heads out of sheer wantonness; and was even ill-natured enough after that to pick them up and exhibit their hollowness. Those whom his sword could not reach, he slew with the shafts of his wit. His friends admired the many-hued feathers; but his foes felt the sharp sting in their hearts. Lessing's wit was not the *enjouement*, the *gaieté*, those sparkling sallies we have here in France. It was no French greyhound chasing his own shadow. His wit was more like a great German tom-cat that plays with the mouse before strangling it. . . .

It is a remarkable fact that he, the wittiest man of Germany, was at the same time the most honorable. Nothing equalled his love of truth. Lessing never made the slightest concession to falsehood, even if he could by so doing, in the usual way of the worldly wise, have advanced the victory of truth. He could do everything for the sake of truth, but lie. As he himself once said, "The man who presents truth in all sorts of masks and disguises may be her pander, but never her lover."

The excellent saying of Buffon, "Style is the man," is more applicable to Lessing than to anyone else. His way of writing was entirely like his character, true, firm, unadorned, beautiful, and imposing through its inherent strength. His style is like that of Roman architecture, combining the weightiest solidity with the greatest simplicity; his sentences rest one on the other like square-cut blocks, the invisible connecting bond in one case the laws of logic, and in the other, the laws of gravity. Hence you will find so few of those expletives and artistic turns in Lessing's prose which we employ like mortar in building our sentences; and even more infrequent are those caryatids of thought which the French call *la belle phrase*.

It can be easily conceived that a man like Lessing could never be happy. Even if he had not loved truth, and willingly defended it everywhere, he would still be unhappy—because he was a man of genius. "Everything will be forgiven you," a recent poet has complained, "your wealth, your illustrious birth, your personal beauty, even your talent—but there is no mercy for genius." Alas, even if it did not meet with ill-will on the outside, genius would find within itself the destructive foe. Hence the history of great men is always a martyrology; when they do not suffer for the great masses of mankind, they suffer because of their own greatness, the grandeur of their being, their un-Philistine nature, their hatred of the pompous vulgarity and self-satisfied vileness in their surroundings—a hatred which naturally drives them to extremes—for example, to the theater, or even the gambling house—as was the case with poor Lessing.

Lessing is only the prophet who points the way from the Second to the Third Testament. I have called him the continuer of Luther, and it is this aspect of him I should like to discuss here. Of his importance to German art I shall speak later. Here he effected a salutary reform not only through his criticism, but also by his example. And this portion of his work is most commonly praised and elucidated. However, we consider him in another light. His philosophical and theological battles are far more important to us than his *Dramaturgy* and his dramas. The latter also, like all his other writings, have a social significance. *Nathan the Wise* is not merely a good comedy, but also a philosophic-theological tract in defense of pure deism. Art too was for Lessing a tribune; when he was expelled from the pulpit, or the academic platform, he leaped upon the stage, and there spoke more clearly than before, and thereby won for himself larger audiences.

I say that Lessing continued the work of Luther. After Luther had freed us from traditionalism and exalted the Bible as the only source of Christianity, there arose (as I have already indicated) a desiccated worship of the word, and the letter of the Scriptures ruled as absolutely as once had tradition. Lessing contributed mainly to our deliverance from the tyranny of the letter. Like Luther, he was not the sole warrior against tradition—but he was ever the most vigorous one. Here his war-cry re-echoes loudest; here he swings his sword most jubilantly.—It gleams and slays.

᎒᙮ *Immanuel Kant*

IT IS HARD TO WRITE THE STORY OF IMMANUEL KANT'S LIFE, for he had neither life nor story.[4] He led a mechanically ordered, almost abstract, old bachelor's existence, in a quiet, retired alley in Königsberg, an old town on the northeastern border of Germany. I do not believe that the great clock of the cathedral there did its day's work more regularly and impassively than its compatriot, Immanuel Kant. Rising, coffee-drinking, writing, lecturing at the university, eating, walking—all had their fixed time, and the neighbors knew that it was exactly half past three when Immanuel Kant in his grey coat, malacca cane in hand, stepped from his house and strolled in the direction of the small avenue of lime-trees which is still called, in his memory, the Philosopher's Walk. There he promenaded up and down eight times, in every season, and when bad weather threatened, or grey clouds foretold rain, his old servant Lampe was seen walking anxiously behind him with a long umbrella under his arm, like an image of Providence.

What a strange contrast between the man's external life and his destructive, world-convulsing thoughts! Indeed, if the citizens of Königsberg had suspected the true importance of these ideas, they would have experienced a far greater horror in this man's presence than at the sight of an executioner—who kills only men. But the good people saw nothing in him but a professor of philosophy, and when he passed by at his appointed hour, they greeted him cordially, and perhaps set their watches by him.

Yet, if Immanuel Kant, that great thought-destroyer, far surpassed Maximilian Robespierre in terrorism,—he had many things in common with him which call for a comparison of the two. First, we find in both the same inexorable, biting, prosaic, sober integrity. Then there is the same talent for distrust; only one employed it on ideas, and called it criticism, and the other applied it to men and named it republican virtue. But there was manifest in both of them, in the highest degree, the pattern of the petty bourgeois.—Nature meant them to measure out coffee and sugar, but destiny ordained that they weigh other things, and so it placed on the scale of one, a King, and of the other, a God. . . .

And they both gave the right weight!

The *Critique of Pure Reason* is Kant's principal work, and we must concern ourselves chiefly with it. None of his other writings are of greater importance. This book, as mentioned, appeared in 1781, but did not become generally known until 1789. At first it was completely overlooked; but two insignificant notices of it appeared, and only later on was the attention of the public drawn to it in articles by Schütz, Schultz, and Reinhold. The reason for this belated recognition may be sought in the unusual form of the work, and its poor prose style. With regard to the latter, Kant is more at fault than any other philosopher, the more so when we consider his earlier, and better, style. The recently published collection of his minor writings contains his first efforts, and here we are amazed by the good, sometimes witty, way he wrote. While Kant was elaborating his great work in his head, he was humming those little essays to himself. He seems to smile in them like a soldier calmly arming himself for a battle he is sure to win. Especially remarkable among these little pieces are the *Universal Natural History and Theory of Heaven*, written as early as 1755, the *Observations on the Feeling of the Beautiful and Sublime*, written ten years later, as well as the *Dreams of a Ghost-Seer*, full of whimsy, in the manner of French essays. Kant's wit, as revealed here, has a quality all its own. The wit twines itself around the thoughts, and despite its weakness, attains a pleasing height. Without such support, of course, the richest wit cannot flourish; like the grapevine without its prop, it must creep miserably on the ground, and rot together with its precious fruit.

Why did Kant write the *Critique of Pure Reason* in such a grey, dry buckram style? I believe it is because, while rejecting the mathematical form of the Descartes-Leibnitz-Wolf school, he feared that science might lose some of its dignity if it were expressed in a light, attractive and cheerful tone. Therefore he endowed it with a stiff, abstract form which rigidly repelled all familiarity from the lower intellectual classes. He wished to set himself aristocratically apart from the popular philosophers of the day who aimed at bourgeois clarity, and he clothed his thoughts in the cold speech of the court-chancellor. Here he shows himself the true Philistine. Yet it is possible that for his carefully measured pace of thought, Kant needed a more carefully measured language, and he was unable to create a better one. Genius alone has new words for new ideas. Immanuel Kant was no genius. Conscious of this defect, Kant became, like the good Maximilian, all the more distrustful of genius, and in his *Critique of Judgment* he even maintained that genius had no place in science, and that its sphere of action lay only in art.

Kant did much harm by the unwieldy, stiff, buckram style of his principal work, for his imitators who lacked talent aped the external form; and a superstition grew up among us that no man who wrote well could be a good philosopher. However, after Kant, the mathematical form could not longer survive in philosophy. He broke its authority inexorably—for ever. "The mathematical form," he said, "produces nothing but houses of cards in philosophy; just as the philosophical form produces nothing but idle chatter in mathematics. . . ."

The Critique of Pure Reason IS, AS I HAVE SAID, the principal work of Kant, and his other writings may be regarded as secondary—or, at most, commentaries on the *Critique*. What social meaning is to be found in this principal work I shall try to show in the following remarks.

Before Kant, philosophers had reflected on the origin of knowledge, and had taken two divergent roads, according as they assumed ideas *a priori* or ideas *a posteriori*. But they did little reflecting on the cognitive faculty, or on the extent and limits of our cognitive faculty. This was Kant's task. He subjected cognition to pitiless scrutiny. He sounded all the profoundest depths of this faculty, and determined its limits. Thus he discovered, naturally, that we can know nothing about many things which we once thought we knew. And this was very vexing. Yet it is always profitable to know what are the things about which we can know nothing. He who warns us against embarking on fruitless paths does us as great a service as he who sets us on the right one. Kant proved that we know nothing of things as they are, in and of themselves, and that we can have knowledge of them only insofar as they are reflected in our minds. We are, therefore, like those prisoners of whom Plato speaks so mournfully in the seventh book of the *Republic*. These wretches have their legs and necks so chained that they cannot turn their heads, and they sit in a dungeon which is open above them, so as to allow some light to enter. But this light comes from a fire which is burning above them, and in back of them, and is separated from them by a low wall. Behind the wall people carry various works of art and images of wood and stone, and they converse together. The poor prisoners can see nothing of these men, who are not as tall as the wall, and all they see are the passing shadows the images cast on the wall as they are being carried. They take these images for the objects themselves, and, deceived by the echo in the dungeon, they believe that the voices they are hearing proceed from the shadows.

The philosophy which preceded had sniffed at and around things, and had collected and classified their appearances. It came to an end with Kant. He led investigation back into the human mind, and examined what was in it. It was, therefore, not without good reason that he compared his philosophy to the method of Copernicus. Hitherto, when people conceived of the world as standing still, and the sun as revolving around it, mathematical calculations did not always come out right. But Copernicus ordered the sun to stand still, and the earth to revolve—and lo! all was well. Once upon a time Reason, like a sun, circled around the world of appearances, and sought to illuminate it; but Kant bade Reason, the sun, stand still, and now the world of appearance revolves around it, and is illumined by it whenever it comes within its orbit.

From the few words with which I have tried to indicate Kant's great task, it will be understood that I consider the section of the book in which he treats of the so-called *noumena* and *phenomena* the most important—the very center of his philosophical system. Here Kant differentiates between the appearance of things, and the things in themselves. Since we can know objects themselves only insofar as they appear to us, and since they do not manifest themselves to us as they actually are in and of themselves, Kant names these appearances, *phenomena*, and the things in and for themselves, *noumena*. We can only know something of these *phenomena;* but nothing of the *noumena*. The latter are purely hypothetical. . . .

God, according to Kant, is a *noumen*. According to him, the transcendental ideal being whom we have hitherto called God is a pure invention. It originated in a natural illusion. Yes, Kant proves that we can know nothing of the *noumen*, God, and that all future proof of his existence is impossible. Over this portion of the *Critique of Pure Reason*, we may write Dante's words: "Abandon all hope!"

YOU IMAGINE THAT THE SHOW IS OVER? Heaven forbid! There is still another number on the program. After the tragedy comes the farce. Thus far, Immanuel Kant has followed the path of a pitiless philosopher; he has stormed the heavens; he has put the entire garrison to the sword; the overlord of the world is wallowing in blood—unproved; there is now no all mercy; no paternal kindness; no otherworldly reward for earthly self-denial; the immortality of the soul is in its last death-throes—it gasps and groans—and old Lampe is standing by with his umbrella under his arm, a distressed onlooker, cold sweat and tears pouring from his face. Then Immanuel Kant takes pity and proves that he is not only a great philosopher, but a good man to boot; he reconsiders, and half good-heartedly and half ironically, says, "Old Lampe must have a God; otherwise the poor man will not be happy.—But man should be happy on earth—that is in accordance with Practical Reason; so far as I'm concerned, let Practical Reason guarantee God's existence." Consequently, Kant distinguishes between theoretical reason and practical reason, and with the latter, as with a magic wand, he revives the corpse of deism, which theoretical reason had slain.

Did Kant perhaps undertake the resurrection not for old Lampe's sake alone, but also because of the police? Or did he do this from true conviction? Did he wish to show us by the very fact that he had destroyed all proof for the existence of God, how unpleasant it is to be unable to know anything of the existence of God? If so, he acted almost as wisely as my Westphalian fraternity brother, who had smashed all the lanterns on Grohnderstreet in Göttingen, and then, standing in the dark, gave us a long speech on the practical necessity of lanterns, which he had smashed in theory only to show us that without them we could see nothing.

⁊❧ Goethe

"KNOW'ST THOU THE LAND where the citron blooms?" [5]

Do you know that song? The whole of Italy is depicted in it, but with the sighing colors of longing. In his *Italian Journey* Goethe sang of it at greater length; when he paints, he always has the original before his eyes, and he can be relied on for truth of outline and color. I therefore find it convenient to point once and for all to Goethe's *Italian Journey*, all the more readily as he made the same tour as I through the Tyrol to Verona. I had previously spoken of this book, before I became acquainted with the subject he discussed. And now I find my anticipatory judgment verified. We perceive here a clear vision, as well as tranquillity of nature. Goethe holds the mirror up to nature, or better, he is himself the mirror. Nature longed to know herself, and she created Goethe. He has the gift of mirroring for us the very thoughts and intentions of nature. It must therefore not be taken amiss, especially in the dog-days, if some very ardent Goethean marvels so greatly at the identity of the reflection and its objects, that he credits the poet with the powers of creation, the power of creating the objects themselves.

A Herr Eckermann [6] once wrote a book about Goethe in which he declared quite solemnly: "Had the good Lord at the creation of the world said to Goethe, 'Dear Goethe, thank God! I am through. I have created everything but birds and trees, and you will do me a favor if you create these trifles yourself.' Then Goethe would have created these animals and plants just as capably as the good Lord, in complete harmony with the rest of creation—that is to say, birds with feathers, and trees with foliage."

There is some truth in these words. I am indeed of the opinion that Goethe would at times have managed his part better than the good Lord himself; for instance, he would have created Herr Eckermann much more correctly—that is to say, with feathers and foliage. It is really a flaw of creation that green feathers did not grow from Herr Eckermann's head. Goethe has at least sought to remedy this defect; for he prescribed for him a doctor's cap at Jena and planted it on his head with his own hands.

⧼ *Goethe and Schiller*

. . . THE GOETHEANS REGARD ART AS AN AUTONOMOUS, SECOND WORLD, which they place so high above us, that all the activities of men, their religion and morality, move below it, in an ever shifting, changing flux. But I cannot subscribe to this view without qualifications. The

Goetheans allow themselves to be misled by it into proclaiming art itself as the highest good, and into turning away from the claims of the real world, to which precedence is due.

Schiller attached himself to this world of reality much more closely than Goethe, and for this he deserves our praise. The spirit of his age took strong hold of him, wrestled with him, and was vanquished by him, then followed him to the field of battle, and carried his standard. And it was under this standard that men fought with so much inspiration in those days, beyond the Rhine—and we today are still ready to shed our precious blood for it. Schiller wrote for the great ideas of the Revolution. He razed mental bastilles. He helped build the Temple of Liberty, which was to include as in a single community of brothers all races of man. For Schiller was a cosmopolite. He began with a hatred of the past—as we see from his *Robbers*, where he acts like a miniature Titan, who has played truant, drunk some schnapps, and smashed Jupiter's windows. He ended his career proclaiming that love of the future which blooms like a forest of flowers in *Don Carlos*. Schiller himself is Marquis Posa, who is at one and the same time prophet and soldier, fighting to realize that which he prophesies, and hiding under his Spanish cloak the noblest heart in Germany that ever loved and suffered.

The poet, that miniature creative imitator, resembles our dear Lord in that he makes men after his own image. If Karl Moor and Marquis Posa are all Schiller, then Werther is Goethe himself, as are Wilhelm Meister and Faust—in whom we can study all aspects of his thought. If Schiller plunges headlong into history, and is filled with passion for social progress and mankind, and chants the paeans of universal history, Goethe immerses himself more and more in individual feeling—in art, or in nature. Goethe, the pantheist, was forced in the end to occupy himself principally with natural history; and he gave us the results of his investigations not only in his poetry, but in his scientific works as well. His religious indifference was likewise the result of his pantheistic outlook.

For it is unfortunately true—and more's the pity—that pantheism not infrequently turns men into indifferentists. If all is God, they say, it matters little whether a man busies himself with clouds or with antique gems, popular ballads, bones of apes, mankind or comedians. But in this very point lies the central error. All is not God: God is All. God does not reveal himself equally in all things. Rather, he manifests himself in different degrees in different things; all ˙ects possess in varying measure the impulse to reach a higher rung of godliness. This is the great law of progress in Nature. The understanding of this law, which was most profoundly revealed to us by the Saint-Simonians, and which raises pantheism to the level of a world-outlook, is not conducive to indifferentism, but to the most self-sacrificing endeavors. No; God does not manifest himself equally in all things, as Wolfgang Goethe contended. As a result of this, Goethe became a complete indifferentist, and instead of occupying himself with the loftiest interests of humanity, devoted himself to artistic games—anatomy, the theory of colors, botany, and the study of clouds. God manifests himself varyingly in all things; and he exists in this constant manifestation. He is within motion, within activity, within time. His holy spirit breathes through the pages of history, which is the real book of God. Friedrich Schiller divined the idea, and became a "retrospective prophet," and wrote *The Fall of the Netherlands, The Thirty Years' War*, and *The Maid of Orleans* and *William Tell*.

It is true that Goethe also chanted a few great histories of emancipation, but he sang of these as an artist. He indignantly rejected Christian enthusiasm, which was distasteful to him; and he did not understand, or did not want to understand, the philosophical enthusiasm of our time, because he feared lest thereby his mental tranquillity be disturbed. And so he treats enthusiasm as if it were a historical phenomenon, as data that are to be worked up. Spirit turns to matter under his hands, and he endows it with beautiful and pleasing form. He became the greatest artist of our literature, and everything that he wrote turned into a well-rounded work of art.

The example of the master guided his disciples. There arose in Germany that literary epoch which I at one time designated as the "art-epoch," and to which I ascribed the most baleful influence on the political development of the German people. At that time I did not, however, deny the intrinsic value of Goethe's masterpieces. They are the great ornament of our Fatherland—much as beautiful statues adorn a garden. But they are only statues. They may be loved; but they are sterile. The poems of Goethe do not produce action—as do those of Schiller. The deed is the child of the word; and the beautiful words of Goethe are childless. This is the curse that befalls all that is born of art alone. The statue which Pygmalion fashioned was a beautiful girl—even the master himself fell in love with her. She grew alive under his kisses. But so far as we know, she never bore any children. I believe that M. Charles Nodier [7] has said something of this kind in a similar connection. It came to me yesterday while I was wandering through the lower halls of the Louvre, looking at the ancient statues of the gods. There they stood with their mute, white eyes, mysterious melancholy in their marble smile,—perhaps with mournful remembrance of Egypt, the land of the dead, where they began life; or in sorrowful longing for that existence from which other gods exiled them; or in pain at the thought of their dead immortality!—They seemed to be waiting for the word which would restore them to life, and release them from cold, stiff immobility. Strange, these antiques reminded me of Goethe's creations—equally perfect, equally magnificent, equally serene—and equally sad at the thought that their stiffness and coldness keep them from our stirring battles of life, that they cannot suffer and exult with us, that they are not human beings—but unhappy hybrids of godliness and stone.

To MY CREDIT BE IT SAID that I never attacked the poet in Goethe, but only the man. I have never disparaged his works. I have never been able to see flaws in them, as have those critics who detect spots in the moon with their finely ground glasses. Keen-eyed folk! They mistake the blooming forests, the silver streams, the lofty mountains, and the smiling valleys for blemishes!

Nothing is more ridiculous than the depreciation of Goethe in favor of Schiller. This is never done honestly, but merely out of a desire to degrade Goethe. Are people aware that the extolled and highly idealized figures which Schiller fashioned—those altar-pieces of virtue and morality—are far more easily produced than the sinful, petty, worldly, tarnished figures whom Goethe creates in his works? Are they aware that it is the mediocre painters who generally depict saints in full life size on canvas—but that it takes a great master to paint a Spanish beggar-boy, hunting for vermin; or a Dutch peasant vomiting, or having his tooth pulled; or ugly old women such as we see on the small Dutch cabinet pictures, so true to life and so technically perfect? The vast and the horrifying is much more easily represented in art than the small and dainty. The sorcerers of Egypt could ape many of the feats of Moses, such as the miracle of the serpents, of the blood, or even of the frogs; but when he produced what seemed much easier miracles, like vermin, they confessed their impotence. They could not imitate that, and they said, "It is the finger of the Lord." Rail, if you will, at the vulgarities of *Faust*—at the scene on the Brocken, or in Auerbach's cellar; scold the obscenities

of *Wilhelm Meister.*—But you cannot emulate it.—It is the finger
of Goethe! But of course, you do not want to emulate it. I hear you
saying in disgust: "We are no wizards. We are good Christians." I
know too well that you are no wizards.

Goethe's great merit is the perfection of everything he presents.
There are no parts that are strong, while others are weak; there is
no segment painted in, while the other is merely sketched. There is
no confusion, none of the customary interpolations, no preference
for individual detail. Every character in his novels and plays is treated
wherever he appears as if he were the principal character. This is
also Homer's way, and Shakespeare's. In the works of all great poets
there are really no secondary parts; each character is in his place a
leading character. Such poets are like absolute princes who do not
grant men any independent value, but esteem them in accordance with
their own sovereign will. Once, when a French ambassador remarked
to Czar Paul of Russia that a very prominent man in his empire
was interested in some matter, the Czar sternly cut him short with
these startling words: "In my kingdom there are no prominent persons save such as I address, and only as long as I speak to them are
they prominent." An absolute poet, who likewise has power by the
grace of God, similarly views as most important that person of his
imagination whom for the time being he allows to speak, and who
has just come from his pen. The fruit of such artistic despotism is the
marvelous perfection of the least important figures in the works of
Homer, Shakespeare, and Goethe.

GOETHE'S EYES WERE AS DIVINE IN HIS OLD AGE as in his youth. Time
could cover his head with snow, but it could not bow it. He always
carried it proudly and high; when he spoke, he seemed to grow taller,
and when he extended his hand, it was as if he could prescribe to the
stars their appointed courses in heaven. It has been said that a cold
expression of egoism hovered about his mouth; but this too is a trait
peculiar to the eternal gods, even to the great Jupiter, father of the
gods, to whom I have already compared him. Truly, when I called
on him at Weimar, and stood before him, I glanced around involuntarily to see whether the eagle with lightning in his beak was not
there beside him. I was about to address him in Greek, but when I
saw that he understood German, I remarked in German that the
plums on the road between Jena and Weimar were delicious. Through
many a long winter night I had pondered the sublime and profound

things I would say to Goethe, when I saw him. When I did see him at last, I told him that the Saxon plums were good to eat. And Goethe smiled—he smiled with the same lips which had kissed lovely Leda, Europa, Danaë, Semele, and so many other princesses, or even common nymphs.

Les dieux s'en vont.[8] Goethe is dead. He died on March 22nd of the past year, the momentous year in which our world lost its greatest personalities. It is as if in that year Death had suddenly turned aristocratic, and sought to distinguish the notables of this earth by sweeping them into the grave at once. Perhaps he wished to found a peerage there in the realm of shadows. In that case the lot was very well chosen. Or did he seek on the contrary to aid democracy this last year by destroying the great names along with their authority, and so promote intellectual equality? Was it respect or insolence which last year made Death spare kings? Having in an absent-minded moment raised his scythe over the King of Spain, he bethought himself in time and let him live. Last year not a single king died. *Les dieux s'en vont*—but the kings remain.

ॐ *The New Writers*

I SPEAK NOW OF JEAN PAUL FRIEDRICH RICHTER.[9] He has been called the Only One—a most appropriate nickname, which I only now fully understand, after for a long time uselessly reflecting on the place that should be assigned to him in the history of literature. He made his appearance almost at the same time as the Romantic School, without in the least participating in it; nor was he more closely attached to the aesthetic school of Goethe. He stands quite alone in his time, because he was opposed to both schools, and devoted himself entirely to his age, and his whole heart was filled with it. And his heart and work were one. This peculiarity, this unity, also appears among the writers of Young Germany,[10] in our day, who likewise draw no sharp distinction between living and writing—who never separate politics from scholarship, art from science—and who are at once artists, tribunes, and apostles.

Yes, I repeat, apostles—for I know no term more appropriate. A new faith inspires them with a passion which the writers of the past age had no inkling of. This is faith in progress, a faith which springs from science. We have measured the earth, weighed the forces of Nature, calculated the resources of industry, and behold!—we have found that the earth is spacious and wide enough for everyone to build his hut of happiness on it; that the earth can feed us all decently if only each of us works, and none lives at another's expense; that it is no longer needful to preach the blessedness of heaven to the masses of the poor. As yet, the number of these learned believers is naturally quite small. But the time has come when people will no longer be reckoned by their heads, but by their hearts. For is not the great heart of only one Heinrich Laube worth more than a whole zoological park of Raupachs and other comedians?

I have named Heinrich Laube, for how could I speak of Young Germany without recalling that great and flaming heart which glows there so brilliantly? Heinrich Laube is one of the writers to make his appearance since the July Revolution, and is of such great social importance to Germany that his true measure cannot as yet be taken. He has all the virtues we find in the writers of the last generation, and in addition, the apostolic zeal of Young Germany. Furthermore, his intense passion is mitigated and transfigured by this lofty conception of art. He is as inspired by the Beautiful as by the Good. He has a fine ear, and a keen eye for nobility of form. Vulgarity is repugnant to him, even though it might be useful to the Fatherland in championing noble ideas. This sense of art, which is inborn, saved him from falling into the serious errors of that patriotic mob which still continues to vilify and contemn our great master, Goethe.

૨૦ The Character of the Romantic School in Germany

But what was the Romantic School in Germany?

It was nothing else but the reawakening of the poetry of the Middle Ages, as it had manifested itself in song, painting, architecture, art and life. But this poetry had its origin in Christianity; it was a passion-flower which had sprung from the blood of Christ.

I do not know whether the melancholy flower which in Germany is called the passion-flower is known by that name in France, and whether popular legend attributes to it the same mystical origin. It is a strange flower of a repulsive color, in the chalice of which we find replicas of the implements of martyrdom used in the crucifixion of Christ, such as the hammer, pincers, nails, etc.,—a flower which is not so much ugly, as eerie, and the sight of which awakens in us a horrible kind of pleasure, like those agreeable paroxysms of feeling we experience in pain itself. For this reason, the flower would indeed be the fittest symbol for Christianity itself, whose most gruesome appeal is to be found in that very same voluptuous pain.

Though in France the word Christianity is used only in the sense of Roman Catholicism, I must here specifically remark that I am speaking only of the latter. I speak of that religion in whose first dogmas is to be found damnation of all flesh, and which not only extends to the spirit supremacy over the flesh, but would also destroy the flesh in order to glorify the spirit. I speak of that religion whose unnatural demands brought sin and hypocrisy into the world; for condemnation of the flesh made the most innocent sensual pleasures a sin, and the impossibility of ever attaining a perfect spiritual state brought forth hypocrisy. I speak of that religion which, because it teaches rejection of all earthly goods, abject, hang-dog humility and angelic patience, became the most reliable pillar of despotism. Men have now come to see clearly the true nature of this religion; they will not be contented merely with Barmecide celestial suppers. They know that matter also has its virtues, and does not wholly belong to the devil. They vindicate the pleasures of this world, this beautiful garden of the Lord, and our inalienable inheritance. And because we so thoroughly understand the consequences of that absolute spirituality, we may now be sure that the Christian-Catholic world-view has come to an end. For every age is a sphinx, which hurls itself into the abyss when man has solved its riddle.

Yes, we would by no means deny the benefits which the Christian-Catholic view of the world conferred on Europe. It was necessary as a salutary reaction against that horrible and colossal materialism which had developed within the Roman Empire, and which threatened to destroy the spiritual grandeur of humanity. Just as the prurient memoirs of the last century form the *pièces justificatives* of the French Revolution, just as the terrorism of a *comité du salut public* appears as a necessary physic, when we read the confessions of the French aristocracy since the time of the Regency, so we understand the wholesomeness of ascetic spirituality when we read Petronius or Apuleius [11]—books which may in turn be regarded as the *pièces justificatives* of Christianity. The flesh became so arrogant in that

Roman world that it needed the chastening rod of Christian discipline. After Trimalchio's banquet, one needed the hunger-cure of Christianity.

Perhaps Rome had herself scourged in her old age so that she might experience the more exquisite delights of torture and voluptuous raptures of pain, like those lechers who seek through whippings to rouse the palsied flesh to new pleasures?

Evil excess of stimulants! It robbed the Roman body politic of its last remnants of strength. Not because of the division into two realms did Rome perish. On the Bosphorus as well as by the Tiber it was Jewish spirituality that devoured it; and in both places Roman history is but a long death-bed agony, lasting for centuries. Did murdered Judea, when it bequeathed its spiritualism to the Romans, wish to avenge itself on its victorious foe, like the dying centaur who craftily transmitted the fatal garment, poisoned with his own blood, to the son of Jupiter? [12] For Rome, the Hercules among nations, was so thoroughly consumed by Judea's poison that helm and harness fell from her withered limbs, and her imperial battle-cries died away in the wailing cadences of monkish prayers and the trilling of castrates.

But that which weakens old age, strengthens youth. Spirituality had a healthy influence on the all-too-sound races of the North. The barbarians, with their excessively full-blooded bodies, became spiritualized by Christianity, and European civilization commenced. This is the creditable, sacred aspect of Christianity. The Catholic Church has in this regard the strongest claims upon our reverence and admiration. By its great and inspired institutions it succeeded in subduing the bestiality of the Nordic barbarians and in gaining mastery over brute matter.

ࣸ Why Did the Germans Take to the Romantic School?

THE POLITICAL CONDITIONS IN GERMANY were then especially favorable to the Christian Old-German movement. "Poverty teaches us to pray," says the proverb, and as a matter of fact, never was Germany in greater distress; hence people were more inclined to prayer, religion, and Christianity. There are no people more devoted to their princes than the Germans. What grieved them even more deeply than the sad condition to which their country had been reduced by war and foreign domination was the melancholy sight of their vanquished princes grovelling at the feet of Napoleon. The whole country resembled those faithful old servants of great houses we often see on the stage, who feel the humiliations of their masters more profoundly than the masters themselves; who secretly weep bitter tears when the family plate is to be sold, and even buy aristocratic wax-tapers with their own savings, so that the plebeian tallow candles may not be seen on the gentlefolk's tables.

This general depression found relief in religion, and there arose a pietistic surrender to the will of God, from whom alone help could be expected. For indeed, what other help could avail against Napoleon? No longer was reliance placed on earthly armies. All eyes turned expectantly toward heaven.

We could have made our peace with Napoleon. But our princes, though they were hopeful that God would free them, thought that the united strength of their people could also be of great help. With this in view, they sought to arouse a feeling of solidarity among them, and even the most eminent personages now spoke of a German nation, of a common German Fatherland, of the union of Christian-German races, of a united Germany. We were commanded to become patriots—and patriots we became; for we do as our princes command.

But one must not confuse the term patriotism as here used with what it implies for the French. The patriotism of the Frenchman consists in the fact that his heart is warmed by it; as a result, it expands, spreads, and with its love no longer embraces only his next of kin, but also all of France, the land of civilization. The patriotism of the German, on the other hand, makes his heart narrower, so that it contracts like leather in the cold—he hates whatever is foreign, and does not wish to be a citizen of the world, or of Europe, but only a cabined and cribbed German. Hence that idealized churlishness which was erected into a system by Herr Jahn, and thus commenced that shabby, crude, unwashed opposition to the holiest and most glorious sentiment ever felt in Germany—that humanitarianism, that universal brotherhood of man, that cosmopolitanism to which our greatest spirits, Lessing, Herder, Schiller, Goethe, Jean Paul and all the learned men of Germany, did homage.

What happened soon thereafter in Germany is too well known.

When God, snow, and the Cossacks destroyed the best of Napoleon's forces, we Germans received the all-highest order to liberate ourselves from the foreign yoke; we became enflamed with manly rage at the servitude we had so long endured; and we were filled with an inspiration drawn from the good tunes and bad lines of Körner's songs, and we won our freedom. For we do as our princes command.

At the time we were preparing for this struggle, a school of thought, most inimical to all that was French and glorifying all that was German in art and life, naturally prospered. The Romantic School then worked hand in hand with the efforts of the governments and secret societies, and A. W. von Schlegel conspired against Racine with the same end in view as Minister Stein against Napoleon. The Romantic School followed the current of the time—that is, the current which was reverting to its source. When at last German patriotism and German nationalism triumphed, the German-Christian Romantic School also triumphed, with equal decisiveness, and "Neo-German-Religious-Patriotic Art" as well. Napoleon, that great classicist—as classical as Alexander and Caesar—succumbed, and Messrs. August Wilhelm von Schlegel and Friedrich Schlegel, the little Romantics, as romantic as Tom Thumb and Puss-in-Boots, were victorious. But here too as everywhere else reaction followed on the heels of excess. Just as spiritual Christianity represented a reaction against the brutal sway of the materialism of Imperial Rome; as the renewed love of joyous Greek art and learning was a reaction against Christian spiritualism which had degenerated into imbecile asceticism; as the reawakening of medieval romance was a reaction against the prosaic imitation of ancient, classical art—so we now witness a recoil against the restoration of Catholic-Feudal thought and that knighthood and priesthood which had been preached in word and image under the most amazing forms. When the highly-praised models—the masters of the Middle Ages—were extolled and admired, their excellence was attributed to the fact that they believed in the subjects they were portraying. It was said that in their artless simplicity they were capable of greater achievements than their successors who lacked faith, although they possessed more advanced techniques;—and that it was this very faith which had wrought miracles in their souls. And indeed, how else could one explain the glories of Fra Angelico da Fiesole or the poetry of Brother Ottfried? [13] Hence it followed that those artists who took art seriously, and hoped to reproduce the divine distortions of these wonder-paintings, and the saintly awkwardness of those wonder-poems—in short, to capture the ineffable mysticism of the ancient works of art—decided to repair to the same Hippocrene from which the old masters had drawn their miraculous inspiration. They made pilgrimages to Rome, where the vicar of Christ was to strengthen consumptive German art with the milk of the she-ass. They betook themselves to the bosom of the only soul-saving Roman Catholic Apostolic Church. Many of the adherents of the Romantic School needed no formal conversion. Herr Görres and Herr Klemens Brentano, for example, were born Catholics, and they merely renounced their former free thinking. Others like Friedrich Schlegel, Herr Ludwig Tieck, Novalis, Werner, Schütz, Carové, Adam Müller, etc., had been brought up in the bosom of the Protestant Church—and their conversion to Catholicism required a public decla-ration. Here I have only named the writers; the number of painters who abjured their evangelical faith in droves—and along with it, reason—was much greater.

When the German world saw these young people waiting in line for tickets of admission to the Roman Catholic Church, and again crowding into the old prisonhouse of the spirit, from which their fathers had with so much labor succeeded in delivering themselves, they shook their heads with concern. But when they discovered that the propaganda of priests and Junkers which had conspired against the religious and political freedom of Europe had a hand in this game too, and that it was really Jesuitism which was enticing German youth to destruction with the dulcet notes of romance—like the Pied Piper of Hamelin—then great disaffection and burning indignation took hold of the friends of Protestantism and of freedom of thought.

I have named freedom of thought and Protestantism in one breath; and I hope that even though I belong in Germany to the Protestant Church, I shall not be charged with partisanship in her favor. With-out partiality I have classed freedom of thought and Protestantism; for there is, in very fact, a friendly relation between them in Germany. They are closely allied, like mother and daughter. Though we may reproach the Protestant Church with many instances of frightful narrowness, we must still grant, to her immortal credit, that she al-lowed free inquiry into the Christian religion, and liberated our minds from the yoke of authority, so that bold investigation could take root, and learning and science develop independently. German philosophy, though it would at the present time rank itself by the side of, even above, the Protestant Church—is nevertheless always her daughter;

and as such, obliged to retain an indulgent reverence for her mother—
and the interests of her family require an alliance between them
when both are threatened by a common enemy, Jesuitism. All friends
of free thought and Protestantism, sceptics and believers, rose at once
against the restorers of Catholicism, and, it goes without saying, that
the liberals too, who were more interested in defending bourgeois
political freedom than philosophy or Protestantism, made common
cause with them. In Germany, the liberals have always been at the
same time professors of philosophy and theologians, and they always
fight for the idea of freedom, no matter whether it takes a purely
political, philosophical, or theological form.

ᆰ German Philosophy and Reaction

IT IS A FACT that most of the metaphysical systems of the majority
of German philosophers resemble cobwebs. But what harm was
there in that? Jesuitism could not spin its decoying lies from it, nor
could despotism weave a halter with it to enslave the spirit. Only
since the time of Schelling has German philosophy lost that tenuous,
though harmless, character. Since then our philosophers no longer
criticize the ultimate grounds of knowledge and being; they no
longer soar in the realm of ideal abstractions. They have sought,
instead, for grounds on which to justify that which exists. They have
become apologists for that which is. While our older philosophers
cowered in miserable garrets, poor and selfless, and spun their philosophic systems, those of our day wear the resplendent livery of
power. They have become state-philosophers, that is they have con-
cocted philosophical justification for all the interests of the state, in
whose employ they are. Thus Hegel, a professor in Protestant Berlin,
has taken into his system all of the Evangelical-Protestant dogma. And
Herr Schelling,[14] a professor in Catholic Munich, now justifies in his
lectures the most extravagant doctrines of the Roman Catholic Apostolic Church.

Indeed, just as the philosophers of Alexandria utilized all their
acumen to support with allegorical interpretations the decaying religion of Jupiter so as to save it from total ruin, so now our German
philosophers are endeavoring to do the same for the religion of
Christ. It is not worth the trouble to find out whether these phi-

losophers are unselfish in their efforts. But when we see them ally themselves with the party of priests, whose material interests are bound up with the preservation of Catholicism, we are justified in calling them Jesuits. Let them, however, be under no illusions that we confound them with the old Jesuits. The latter were great and powerful; they were wise and possessed great will power. But oh, how weak are these dwarfs who suppose that they can vault the obstacles which caused those black giants to fall! Never had mortal brain conceived more brilliant combinations than those by which the old Jesuits sought to maintain Catholicism. But they were unsuccessful, because they were only inspired by the idea of maintaining Catholicism, and not by the idea of Catholicism itself. For Catholicism they cared very little. Hence they often profaned Catholic principles in their quest for power. They compounded with heathenism and with earthly potentates; they pandered to their vices; they became murderers and traders, and when necessary, even atheists. In vain did their confessors grant gracious absolution, and their casuists woo vice and crime. In vain did they vie with the laity in the arts and sciences, so as to use these as instruments. Here their stark impotence became manifest. They envied all great scholars and artists; but they themselves could neither discover nor create anything extraordinary. They composed pious hymns and built cathedrals; but their poetry is devoid of the spirit of freedom; it is filled only with sighs of fluttering servility to the masters of the order. Even their architecture reveals only timid thralldom, stone-like docility, sublimity made to order. Barrault once rightly said, "The Jesuits could not raise earth to heaven, so they debased heaven to earth." Barren was all their striving and labor. For from falsehood no new life can be born. God can never be saved by the Devil.

᪥ Hamburg—Then and Now

FOR READERS WHO DO NOT KNOW HAMBURG—and there may be such in China and Upper Bavaria—I must say that the most beautiful promenade of the sons and daughters of Hammonia is aptly named Jungfernsteg—Maiden Lane, and that it consists of an avenue of lindentrees, bounded on one side by a row of houses, and on the other by the great Alster Basin, and that before the latter, built out into the water, there are two gay, tent-like cafés, called pavilions. It is especially good to sit in front of the one called the Swiss pavilion, in the summer, when the afternoon sun is not too hot, but only smiles gaily, and pours its radiance as in a fairy dream over the linden-trees, the houses, the people, the Alster, and the swans who sway gently in its waters. Yes, it is nice to sit there—and there I sat many a summer afternoon, and thought—well, what a young man generally thinks— about nothing, and looked at, what a young man generally looks at— the girls; and there they came fluttering along, those charming things, with their winged caps and covered baskets, containing nothing; there the gay Vierländer maids came tripping by, who provide all of Hamburg with strawberries and their milk, whose petticoats are still much too long;—there came, proudly sweeping by, beautiful merchants' daughters, with whose love goes a great deal of ready cash; there skipped by a nurse with a rosy infant in her arms, whom she kept kissing while she thought of her lover;—there too wandered the priestesses of the foam-risen goddess, Hanseatic vestals, Dianas on the hunt, naiads, dryads, hamadryads and other preachers' daughters;— and oh! there wandered by Minka and Heloise! How often have I sat before that pavilion and seen them pass by in red-striped gowns—costing four marks and three schillings a yard, and Mr. Seligmann assured me that the stripes were color-fast in the wash.—"Splendid girls!" exclaimed the virtuous youths who sat by me. I remember a great insurance man, who was always dressed up like a carnival ox, saying to me: "I'd like to have one of them for breakfast, and the other for supper, and I don't think I'd want dinner that day." "She is an angel!" said a sea captain once, loud enough for the girls to look back together and then jealously at one another. I myself said nothing, and thought my sweetest nothings, and looked at the girls, and at the soft and gentle sky and the tall tower of St. Peter's with its slender waist, and at the serene blue Alster, on which the swans swam so proudly, so gently, so surely. The swans! I could look at them for hours, those lovely creatures with their soft, long necks, as they luxuriously swayed on the soft waves, blissfully dived under, and proudly splashed, till the heavens grew dark and the golden stars emerged, yearning, full of promise, transfigured, and wonderfully tender. The stars! Are they indeed golden flowers on the bridal bosom of heaven? Are they eyes of enamored angels, mirroring themselves with desire in the blue waters of the earth, and wooing the swans?

Alas! That is long past. I was then young and foolish. I am now old and foolish. Many a flower has wilted since and many has been trod under foot. Many a silken dress has since been torn—and even the rose-striped gingham of Mr. Seligmann has faded. He himself has also passed away—the firm is now "The Late Seligmann's Widow." And Heloise, that gentle creature, who seemed to be made only to walk on soft, flowered Indian rugs and to be fanned with peacock feathers, she too died of sailors' noise, punch, tobacco-smoke, and bad music. When I saw Minka again (she now called herself Katinka, and lived between Hamburg and Altona), she looked like Solomon's temple after Nebuchadnezzar had ravaged it, and smelled of Assyrian snuff; and as she told me of Heloise's death, she wept bitterly and tore her hair in despair, and almost fainted and did not come to herself until she had emptied a large glass of spirits.

And the city itself—how it had changed! Maiden Lane! Snow lay on the roofs and it seemed as though the very houses had aged and their hair had turned white. The linden-trees on Maiden Lane were dead and their dry branches moved like specters in the cold wind. The sky was a glaring blue, and soon grew dark. It was Sunday, five o'clock in the afternoon—the general feeding time—and the carriages were rolling along and discharging ladies and gentlemen with frozen smiles on hungry lips.

Horrors! At that moment I was chilled by the terrifying observation that unfathomable idiocy was reflected in all these faces, and that all the people who went by seemed overcome by some strange madness. I had seen them twelve years before, at the very same hour, with the same expressions, going through the same motions, like the puppets on the town-hall clock, and ever since then they had been going on in the same way, calculating, visiting the exchange, sending each other invitations, moving their jowls, tipping waiters, and again calculating—twice two is four.

Horrors! I cried. Suppose it should suddenly occur to one of these people as he sits in his counting-house that *twice two is five!* That he had all his life been miscalculating and that he had wasted his whole life in that dreadful error! But at once I was seized by an idiotic madness, and as I looked more carefully at the passers-by, it seemed to me as if they were nothing but figures—Arabic numerals.—There walked a bandy-legged Two, beside a disagreeable Three, his full-bosomed and pregnant spouse; behind them came Mr. Four on crutches; next came waddling along repulsive Mr. Five, round-bellied and with a small head; then came the well-known little Six and then the

even better-known evil Seven; but when I looked more closely at
the wretched Eight, as it swayed past, I recognized the insurance man
who was decked out like a carnival ox, though now he looked as lean
as the leanest of Pharaoh's lean kine, pale, hollow-cheeked, like an
empty soup-plate, with a cold, red nose, like a winter-rose, a threadbare
black coat with a miserable white gloss, a hat in which Saturn had
cut air-holes with his scythe, but his boots were polished like mirrors,
and he no longer seemed to be thinking of devouring Heloise and
Minka for breakfast and supper; he seemed to long for a dinner of
ordinary beef. Among the zeros rolling past I recognized many an
old acquaintance. They and other human digits rolled by, hungry and
in a hurry, while nearby, a funeral procession, even more grimly
droll, passed by the houses on the Maiden Lane. A gloomy mas-
querade! Behind the hearse, walking as on stilts, with their little thin,
black silk legs, came the well known City Councillors, like marionettes
of death, the privileged mourners in travesties of old Burgundian
costumes: short, black cloaks and wide black pantaloons, white wigs
and ruffs, from which the red, well-paid faces stared comically, with
short steel rapiers on their hips, and green umbrellas under their
arms.

But even more weird and bewildering than these figures, which
went by silently like a Chinese shadow-play, were the sounds which
rang in my ears from another direction. They were hoarse, harsh,
metallic sounds—mad screeches, anxious splashings and desperate
gulps, gasps, thuds, groans, and wails—and an indescribably icy
cry of pain. The Alster Basin had frozen over; only near the shore
a wide square had been cut in the ice, and the horrible sounds which
I heard came from the throats of the poor white creatures that swam
around in it and screamed in their death agony, and oh, they were
the same swans who had once moved my soul with tenderness and
joy. Alas! The wings of the beautiful white swans had been broken
to prevent them from flying away to the warm south in the fall, and
now the north held them bound in a dark, icy pit, and the guard of
the pavilion thought that they were well off, and the cold was good
for them. But that is not true. It is not good for anyone to be help-
lessly imprisoned in a cold pool, almost freeze to death, and have his
wings broken so that he cannot fly to the beautiful south with its
lovely flowers, golden sunlight and blue mountain-lakes. Ah! I myself was once not much better off—and I understood the agony of
these poor swans.

When it grew darker, the bright stars came out above, the same stars that had wooed the swans so ardently; but now they looked down with frosty brilliance, wintry-cold and almost scornful. Now I understood that the stars are no loving, sympathetic creatures, but only gleaming phantasms of the night, eternal delusions in a fancied heaven, golden lies in the dark-blue void. . . .

६♥ *Berlin*

I AM THE MOST COURTEOUS MAN IN THE WORLD. I flatter myself that I have never been rude on this earth, where there are so many intolerable bores who buttonhole you and pour out their sorrows or even declaim their verses. I have always, with true Christian patience, lent an ear to such miserable stuff; and I have never, even through the slightest expression, betrayed my soul's profound boredom. Like a penitent Brahmin, who vouchsafes his body as a prey to vermin so that even these creatures of God may satisfy their hunger, I too have endured even for a whole day and quietly listened to the deadliest vermin, and my innermost sighs were audible only to Him who rewards Virtue.

Besides, worldly wisdom bids us be civil, and not to remain sullenly silent, or even to reply ungraciously when by chance some sponge-like travelling salesman or dry cheese-merchant sits down beside us and begins an all-inclusive European conversation with these words: "It's a lovely day today." We can never tell when we will again fall in with a Philistine of this sort, for one day he may pay us back dearly for not having answered politely, "It is a lovely day today." It may even chance, dear reader, that in Cassel you seat yourself at the *table d'hôte* beside the aforementioned Philistine,— indeed, even at his left side, and he will be the one to have the dish of brown carp before him which he is merrily serving. Should he have an ancient grudge against you, he will pass the plate to the right, so that not even the tiniest tail-piece is left for you. For alas! you are the thirteenth at table—always a serious matter when you are seated at the carver's left, and the plates are passed to the right. And to have no carp is a great misfortune—perhaps the greatest after the loss of the national cockade. The Philistine who has played you this prank adds insult to injury by offering you the bay-leaves that remain in the brown sauce. Alas! Of what use are bay-leaves, when there is no carp to go with them! And the Philistine blinks with his little eyes, chuckles, and murmurs, "It is a lovely day today."

Alas! poor soul, it may even happen that you will lie in the grave-yard beside this self-same Philistine, and when you hear the blast of the trumpet on Judgment Day, and you say to your neighbor, "Good friend, give me a hand, please, and help me get up, for my left foot's fallen asleep because I've been lying here so long," that you sud-denly recognize the well-known Philistine smile, and you hear the mocking voice, "It is a lovely day today."

"LOVELY DAY TODAY."

Had you, dear reader, heard the tone, the unsurpassable bass fal-setto in which these words were spoken, and had you seen the speaker himself, that arch-prosaic, widow's strong-box face, the sly eyes, the turned-up cunning exploratory nose, you would at once have recog-nized that this flower had sprung from no ordinary soil, and that these accents were those of the Charlottenburg idiom, where Ber-linese is spoken better than in Berlin itself.

I am the most courteous of men in the world, and love to eat brown carp, and sometimes believe in the Resurrection. And I answered, "Indeed, it is a lovely day today."

When the son of the Spree had thus taken possession, he set upon me bluntly, and I could not tear myself loose from his questions and his anticipatory answers, and in particular from his comparison between Berlin and Munich, the New Athens, for which he had not a single good word. I, however, took the New Athens under my wing, for I always am in the habit of praising the place in which I may be staying. That this time it should be at the expense of Berlin, that, dear reader, you will gladly pardon when 1 confide to you that it is merely a question of policy, for I knew that the moment I began to praise my good Berlinese, my reputation with them would be at an end, and they would shrug their shoulders and whisper to one another, "That man has become very shallow; he actually praises us."

For no city has less local patriotism than Berlin. A thousand miser-able scribblers have lauded it in prose and in verse, and yet no cock has crowed at the fact, and not a single Berlin hen has been boiled in reward, and on Unter den Linden these poets have been regarded as the same miserable crew as before. On the other hand, as little notice has been taken of the poetasters who aimed their odes at

Berlin. But let someone write an offensive piece about Polkwitz, Innsbruck, Schilda, Posen, Krähwinkel, and any other major town! How their patriotism would be stirred up! The reason is this: Berlin is no city at all. Berlin is merely a place in which a throng of people—among them naturally many men of talent—gather, to whom the locality is a matter of indifference. They constitute intellectual Berlin. The passing traveller sees only the extended rows of monotonous houses, the long, wide streets, which for the most part have been built at the whim of some individual, and are no clue at all to the thinking of the people. Only Sunday's children are endowed with the power of divining the secret thoughts of the inhabitants, in their long rows of houses, which, like the people, try to hold themselves aloof, and are rigid with mutual resentment. One moon-lit night, as I was returning somewhat late from Lutter and Wegener's, I saw that harsh mood give way to mild melancholy. The houses which had faced one another so hostilely, regarded one another with such a tender, decrepit Christian expression as if they longed to embrace in reconciliation—so that I, poor fellow, walking in the middle of the street, was afraid I might be squashed. Many people will find this panic ridiculous. I myself smiled at it the next morning, when with more sober gaze I wandered through the same streets and saw the houses gaping at one another prosaically. As a matter of fact, you need several bottles of poetry before you can see something besides dead houses and Berliners in Berlin. It is difficult to see spirits there. The city contains so few antiquities and is so completely new—yet this very newness is already old, faded and decayed. For, as I have already said, the greater part of it sprang not from the mind of the masses, but of individuals only. Among the small number of the latter, Frederick the Great, the great Fritz, stands out preëminently. For what he found here was merely a firm base. He was the first to give this city its distinctive character; and had nothing more been built since his death, the city would have remained a historical memento to the spirit of that prosaically wonderful hero, in whom the refined lack of taste, and the flowering of intellectual freedom—the shallowness as well as the thoroughness of his time—came to honest Teutonic fruition. Potsdam, for example, strikes us as just such a memorial: We wander through its deserted streets as we do through the extant philosophical writings of the philosopher of Sans-Souci. It belongs with his *oeuvres posthumes,* and although it is now only so much waste-paper in stone, and quite ridiculous, we regard it with serious interest, and now and then suppress the temptation to laugh as if we suddenly feared to feel on our backs the blows from old Fritz's Spanish cane. Such apprehension never comes over us in Berlin. Here we have the feeling that old Fritz and his little Spanish cane no longer have any power; otherwise, how can we account for so many obscurantist faces staring at us out of old enlightened windows of that city of sound reason, and for the many stupid superstitious buildings which have taken up their abode beside the old sceptical and philosophical structures? I do not wish to be misunderstood. I am not at all scoffing at the new Werder Church, that Gothic cathedral in miniature, which could have been put there among the modern buildings only from a sense of irony, to show, in allegorical fashion, how silly and ridiculous it would be if we were to reëstablish the ancient, long-defunct institutions of the Middle Ages in the very midst of the new creations of a new age. . . .

᠑᠊ᢧ *The German Censor*

How strange! We Germans are the strongest and wisest of nations. Our princely families occupy every throne of Europe. Our Rothschilds rule all the stock exchanges of the world. Our learned men are preëminent in every science. We invented gun-powder and the printing press. And yet if one of us fires a pistol he must pay a fine of three thalers; and if we insert in the *Hamburg Correspondent* the following notice: "My dear wife has given birth to a little daughter as fair as Freedom," then Dr. Hoffmann snatches up his red pencil and strikes out the word, "Freedom." [15]

Will this state last long? I do not know. But I do know that the question of the freedom of the press, which is at this time being violently discussed in Germany, is very closely connected with the preceding remarks; and I believe that its solution is not difficult. when we reflect that freedom of the press is but a natural consequence of freedom of thought—hence, a Protestant right. For the defense of these rights Germans have shed their best blood, and it may be that they will again do battle for this cause.

The same holds true for the question of academic freedom, which is at present so profoundly disturbing the German mind. Ever since it has been found that political agitation, that is, love of freedom, exists principally in the universities, sovereigns have been urged from all sides to suppress these institutions, or at least, to transform them into ordinary schools. And so, new plans were contrived, and *pros* and *cons* argued. But the public enemies of the universities, whom we have listened to up to the present, seemed to understand the essence of the problems as little as their public advocates. The former do not see that youths the world over, no matter what discipline they live under, are inspired with love of freedom; and that if the universities are suppressed, these enthusiastic young people will find expression elsewhere, and more effectively, perhaps in alliance with those engaged in commerce and industry. The defenders merely try to show that the finest flower of German learning and science would wither away in our universities; and that academic freedom helps the studious youth by offering him rich opportunities for many-sided development, etc. As if it were merely a question of a few Greek accents, or a few crude expressions, more or less!

And what would our princes care for learning, study, culture, if the sacred safety of their thrones were imperilled? They were sufficiently heroic to sacrifice all that relative good for the one absolute good—absolute rule. This has been bestowed upon them by God—and where Heaven ordains, worldly considerations must give way.

ࢬ *The German Nobility*

I REPEAT, WRITTEN CONSTITUTIONS WILL AVAIL NOTHING so long as we do not completely destroy the German nobility. The matter is not finished when by means of laws which are discussed, voted, sanctioned, and promulgated we annul the privileges of the nobility. This has happened in several places, and yet the interests of the nobles still prevail there. We must destroy the traditional abuses of the royal household, replace the court rabble with a new system of service, break up the etiquette; and to be free ourselves, begin the work of liberation by liberating the princes—by liberating the kings. The ancient dragons must be driven from the fountain-heads of power. When this has been done, then beware that they do not creep back at night and poison the waters! Once we belonged to kings; now the kings belong to us. Therefore, we must ourselves educate them, and not leave them to those high-born princely tutors who train them to fulfill the aims of their own caste, and deform them in body and soul. Nothing is more dangerous for the people than this early Junker education of crown-princes. Let the best citizen, chosen by the people, become the tutor of princes; and let him, who has an evil reputation or a name in the least tarnished, be legally removed from the presence of the young prince. Should such a wretch, however, with the shameless insolence characteristic of the nobility, still force his way into the court, then let him be scourged in the market-place, lashed rhythmically; and let his shoulder be marked with the red iron in a metrical pattern. But should he insist that he had forced his way into the presence of the prince so that he could show him how witty and clever he was—and even though his belly be as big as that of Sir John—let him be placed in a house of correction—but only where women are kept.

ᘒ᠍ *Germany in 1831*

THE GALLIC COCK HAS NOW CROWED FOR THE SECOND TIME,[16] and in Germany, too, dawn is breaking. In remote monasteries, castles, Hansa towns, and similar last hiding places of the Middle Ages the uncanny shades and specters are now taking refuge. The sun's rays sparkle. We rub our eyes. The glorious sunlight presses into our hearts. The stir of life rustles round us. We are amazed, and we ask one another, "What did we do last night?"

Yes, we dreamed, in our German fashion; that is, we philosophized. True, not about matters which concern us immediately, or such as had just taken place; no, we philosophized about the reality of things, in and of themselves, about the ultimate grounds of existence, and similar metaphysical and transcendental visions, while the bloody spectacles performed by our western neighbors sometimes disturbed us, nay, even irritated us, since now and then French bullets whistled their way straight into our philosophical systems and carried off whole shreds.

It is strange yet true that the practical activity of our neighbors on the other side of the Rhine has much in common with our philosophical dreams in complacent Germany. By merely comparing the history of the French Revolution with that of German philosophy one might be led to believe that the French, who had so much real business on hand, for which they must stay awake, had asked us to sleep and dream for them. Our German philosophy is in reality but the dream of the French Revolution. Thus we too have experienced a break with the *status quo* tradition in the sphere of thought, just as the French have experienced theirs in the social sphere. Around the *Critique of Pure Reason* were assembled our philosophical Jacobins who would let nothing pass which had not stood the test of that *Critique*. Kant was our Robespierre. Then came Fichte, the Napoleon of philosophy, with his Ego, the highest Love and the highest Egoism, the omnipotence of thought, the sovereign will which rapidly improvised a universal empire, and which disappeared just as rapidly;— the despotic, terrifying, lonely idealism. Under its consistent footsteps the retiring flowers which had escaped the Kantian guillotine, or those which had since sprouted unobserved, and the oppressed earth spirits stirred; the ground shook, counter-revolution broke out; and under Schelling, the past with its traditional interests once more received recognition, and even indemnification, and during the Restoration, that is, in the Philosophy of Nature, the gray émigrés—mysticism, pietism, Jesuitism, legitimacy, Romanticism, Germanism, smugness—who had constantly conspired against the supremacy of reason and the idea again came into their own. Then came Hegel, the Orleans of Philosophy, and established a new regime, or rather ordained one, an eclectic regime, in which, of course, he himself was of small importance, though he had been placed at its head, and in which he assigned fixed, constitutional posts to the old Kantian Jacobins, the Fichtean Bonapartists, the Schellingian peers, and his own creatures.

Thus, since we had successfully completed our cycle in philosophy, it was natural that we proceed to politics. Will we here follow the same course? Will we open our cycle with the system of the *Comité du salut public*, or with the system of the *Ordre légal?* These questions fill all hearts with trembling, and whoever has something precious to lose, be it only his own head, whispers timidly: "Will the German Revolution be a dry one, or a bloody and wet one?"

The aristocracy and the clergy constantly frighten us with specters of the time of the Terror; our liberals and humanitarians on the other hand promise us the loveliest scenes of the Great Week, and a most peaceful after-celebration. Both sides either deceive themselves, or wish to deceive others. Because the French Revolution of the nineties was so bloody and horrible, and that of last July was so humane and forebearing, we must not conclude that a German revolution will resemble either one or the other. Only when similar conditions prevail can we have similar results. The character of the French Revolution was determined by the moral condition of the people, and particularly their political education. Before the first eruption of the Revolution, a mature culture existed in France, but only among the upper classes, and here and there among the middle classes. But the lower classes had been culturally neglected, and kept from every aspiration by a narrow-minded despotism. So far as political education was concerned, it was lacking not only in the lower, but also in the upper strata of society. The latter understood only the miserable maneuvers of rival corporations, mutual attempts to weaken one another, traditional routines, the art of equivocation, the influence of mistresses, and such-like wretched diplomacy. Montesquieu had been able to arouse only a comparatively small number of minds. He wrote purely from the historical point of view, and hence could win little influence with the masses of an enthusiastic nation which is most receptive to thoughts that are original and spring spontaneously from the heart, as they do in the works of Rousseau. However, Rousseau, the Hamlet of France, perceived the aroused temper of the people and saw through the evil character of the crowned poisoners, the hypocritical emptiness of their lackeys and flunkeys,—the clumsy falsehoods of the court etiquette and the general rottenness, and cried out in sorrow, "The world is out of joint; oh, cursed spite, that ever I was born to set it right!"—when he raised his voice in remonstrance and accusation, partly with feigned, partly with real desperation;—when Voltaire, the Lucian of Christianity,[17] destroyed with his ridicule the clerical fraud of Rome and the divine right of despotism which had been built on it;—when Lafayette, the hero of two worlds and two centuries, returned from America with the Argonauts of freedom, bringing with him the new golden fleece, the idea of a free constitution;—when Necker calculated, and Siéyès defined, and Mirabeau spoke, and the thunders of the constituent assembly rolled over the heads of the decaying monarchy and its flourishing deficit, and fresh economic and political ideas shot forth like sudden lightning;—then, and then only were the French forced to learn the great science of freedom—politics—and the study of the first rudiments cost them much. It cost them their best blood.

It was the fault of the stupid, obscurantist despotism that the

French had to pay so high a tuition fee; for, as I have said, it had sought to keep the people in mental swaddling-clothes; it had thwarted all their efforts to acquire political education; it had transferred the censorship of books to the Jesuits and the obscurantists of the Sorbonne, and it had even suppressed, in the most ridiculous fashion, the press, the mightiest instrument for the advancement of popular knowledge. You have only to read the article on the pre-Revolutionary censorship in Mercier's *Tableau de Paris*,[18] and you will no longer be amazed at the crass political ignorance of the French, which was responsible for the fact that they were frequently more blinded than enlightened by the new political ideas, more heated than warmed; that they gave credence to every pamphleteer and journalist, and that they allowed themselves to be seduced into the most extravagant actions by every self-deceived visionary, and every intriguer suborned by Pitt.[19] For that is the blessing bestowed by the freedom of the press, that it robs the bold speech of the demagogue of all novel magic; it neutralizes the passionate oration by an equally passionate counter-oration; it strangles mendacious rumors in the cradle, which, whether planted by accident or malice, multiply shamelessly in the dark, like those poisonous plants that thrive only in dismal forest swamps, or in the shadows of ancient ruined castles and churches, but wither away miserably in the bright light of the sun. Naturally, the bright sunlight of the freedom of the press is equally fatal to the slave who would rather receive his kicks in the dark, and the despot, who would rather not see his lonely impotence exposed to the light. It is true that these people love the censorship. But it is no less true that censorship, while it may for the time being give an advantage to despotism, in the end destroys despotism along with the despot. Where once the guillotine of thought has done its work, there censorship of human beings is soon introduced. The slave who has been the executioner of thought will soon with the same equanimity erase his own master from the book of life.

Alas, these executioners of thought make criminals of us; for the author, while he is creating, is as fretful and excited as a woman in child-birth, and under these circumstances, frequently commits infanticide; he kills his own thought-child in insane terror of the censor's sword. I myself have at this very moment suppressed new-born innocent reflections on the patience and equanimity with which my dear compatriots have for so many years suffered that thought-killing law, which, in France, Polignac had merely to promulgate to produce a revolution.[20] I am thinking of the famous ordinances, the most serious of which provided for a severe censorship of all newspapers and filled all noble hearts in Paris with dread. Even the most peaceful citizens seized arms. They barricaded the streets; they fought; they attacked; cannons thundered; bells pealed alarms; the leaden nightingales whistled. The young brood of the dead eagle, the students of the École Polytechnique, flew from their perches with lightning in their claws; the old pelicans of freedom rushed upon bayonets and with their own blood nourished the enthusiasm of the young. Lafayette mounted his charger, Lafayette the incomparable, whose equal Nature could not recreate, and hence with economical foresight sought to use him in two worlds and in two centuries. And after those three heroic days, slavery lay undone, with its red-liveried gendarmes and its white lilies; and the holy tricolor, resplendent by the glory of victory, waved above the steeple of Our Dear Lady of Paris! There were no atrocities committed then, no wanton murders. Then the most Christian of guillotines was not erected; no gory jests were perpetrated, as for example occurred on the celebrated return from Versailles, when the bloody heads of MM. de Deshuttes and de Varicourt [21] were borne aloft like standards, and then washed and prettily dressed by a citizen hair-dresser at Sèvres.—No, since that day of horrible memory, the French press has made the people of Paris more receptive to finer sentiments and less sanguine jests. It has weeded out ignorance from their hearts and planted intelligence. And the fruit of that seed was the noble, legendary moderation and touching humanity of the Paris population during that great week. And indeed, if Polignac did not later lose his head, physically, he owes his good fortune solely to the mild after-effects of that very freedom of the press, which, in his folly, he had sought to extinguish.

Thus the sandal-tree refreshes with its delicious fragrance the very foe who has heinously injured its bark.

I believe that in these cursory remarks I have sufficiently indicated that the character of the German revolution in reality turns out to be a question of the cultural state and political education of the German people; that this education is wholly dependent on the freedom of the press, and that it is our most fervent wish that it may soon diffuse its light as far as possible, before the hour strikes when darkness may do more harm than the passions, and opinions and views hitherto repressed or unuttered may all the more violently influence the blind populace and be made the battle-cries of various parties.

ॐ *A Constitution for Germany*

A FREE THEATER IS CERTAINLY A WONDERFUL THING TO HAVE; but a constitution wouldn't be so bad either. Yes, in due time, we may even develop a hankering for it. Not that we distrust the absolute kindness or the kindly absolutism of our monarchs. On the contrary, we know that they are nothing if not charming people; and if there is one among them who dishonors the office, as for example His Majesty King Don Miguel, he is only an exception [22] and if his all-highest colleagues do not put an end to that sort of bloody scandal, as they could very easily, it is simply that they may, by comparison with that crowned wretch, appear all the more humane and noble, and be all the more beloved by their subjects. But a good constitution has its points, and the people are to be forgiven if they ask for something in writing even from the best of monarchs about such matters as life and death. A sensible father behaves quite sensibly when he erects a few salutary barriers around the abysses of sovereign power, lest his children meet with some misadventure when, mounted on the high horses of their pride, and accompanied by their boastful companions, they gallop somewhat recklessly. . . .

ALAS! OUR WHOLE HISTORY TODAY IS NOTHING BUT A CHASE,—a grand hunt against all liberal ideas, and the high nobility are more zealous than ever, and their uniformed huntsmen shoot at every honest heart in which liberal thoughts have found refuge; and there is no lack of learned hounds who with their fangs drag the bleeding word as they would the rich booty. Berlin is fattening the best leash of hounds, and I can already hear the pack howling at this book.

ॐ *Prussia and Germany*

. . . I AVAIL MYSELF OF THIS OPPORTUNITY to declare most emphatically that I have not for the last two years published a single line in any political journal of Germany, with the exception of the *Allge-*

meine Zeitung. This publication, which so well deserves its world-renowned authority and which might well be called the Universal Gazette of Europe, seemed to me to be, because of its prestige and its unparalleled circulation, best adapted for news correspondence, intended solely for a better understanding of the present time. When we have succeeded in making the greater portion of mankind understand our own times, they will no longer permit themselves to be provoked to hatred and war by the hireling scribblers of the aristocracy. The great confederation of peoples—the Holy Alliance of Nations—will come into being; we shall no longer need to sustain standing armies of many hundreds of thousand of murderers because of mutual distrust; we shall use their swords and horses to plow, and we shall win peace, prosperity, and freedom.

My life has been consecrated to that task. That is my office. The hatred of my enemies stands surety that to this day I have fulfilled my duties faithfully and honorably. I shall always try to show myself worthy of that hatred. My enemies will never misunderstand me, although my friends, in the heat of aroused passions, may mistake my deliberateness and calm for indifference. Doubtless they will misunderstand me less at this time than in those days when they thought they had already reached the goal of their desires, and the hope of victory swelled all the sails of their thoughts. I took no part in their folly, but I shall always share their misfortunes.[23]

I will not go back to my native land as long as a single one of these noble fugitives, who could not listen to reason because enthusiasm carried him away, languishes in misery on foreign soil. I would rather beg a crust of bread from the neediest Frenchman, than take service with those distinguished patrons of my German fatherland who regard all moderation of power as cowardice, or a prelude to servility, and who consider our greatest virtue, the faith in the honorable sentiments of a foe, merely hereditary, plebeian stupidity. I shall never feel ashamed of being deceived by those who inspired our souls with the smile of lovely hope: "Everything will be managed most peacefully; we must remain nicely moderate, so that the concession we extort may not prove useless; they can surely see that they can no longer deprive us of our freedom without running great risks—." Yes, we have been duped again, and we must admit that falsehood has again scored a great victory and earned fresh laurels. In fact, we are the conquered, and since the heroic deception has been officially

proclaimed, since the promulgation of the deplorable resolutions of
June 28 by the German Diet, our hearts have been sick with rage and
affliction.

Poor, unhappy Fatherland! To what shame will you be exposed if
you bear this outrage! To what agonies, if you do not!

Never was a people more brutally insulted by its rulers. Not merely
do the ordinances of the Diet presuppose that we have agreed to
everything; no, they would even persuade us that we have suffered no
injury, no injustice! Yet, though you might rely with certainty on
our slavish submission, you certainly had no right to regard us as a
pack of fools! A handful of Junkers who know nothing but horse-
trading, card-sharping, drinking, or other such stupid rascalities,
which at best can serve to cheat peasants at county fairs—these men
think to dupe a whole nation—and one, at that, which invented gun-
powder, the printing press, and the *Critique of Pure Reason*. This
undeserved affront of regarding us as even more stupid than yourselves, and imagining that you could deceive us—this is the most humiliating insult which you have inflicted on us, while other nations
were looking on.

I will not accuse the constitutional German princes. I know their
difficulties. I know they repine in the fetters of their petty camarillas,
and are not in fact responsible. They too have been forced into this
by every sort of pressure on the part of Austria and Prussia. Let us
not despise them—let us rather pity them. Sooner or later they will
reap the bitter fruits of their evil sowing. The fools! They are still
jealous of one another. While every clear-eyed person can see that in
the end Austria and Prussia will make them vassals, all their hearts
and efforts are set on getting a small piece of a neighbor's territory.
Indeed, they are like those thieves who are being led to the gallows
and pick one another's pockets on the way.

We can accuse only Prussia and Austria, those two great, absolute
powers, of the heroic deeds of the Diet. Nor can I be sure to what
degree they jointly deserve this acknowledgment. It seems to me,
however, that Austria has been shrewd enough once more to shift
the detested burden of that great action on to the shoulders of her
wise ally.

As a matter of fact, we may wage war against Austria boldly,
even unto death, with sword in hand; but in our very hearts we feel
that we are not justified in reviling that power. Austria was ever an
open and honorable foe. She never belied or for a brief moment

suspended her war on liberalism. Metternich has never ogled the Goddess of Liberty. He has never, with an anxious heart, played the demagogue. He never sang Arndt's songs,[24] while drinking pale beer. He never took part in gymnastics on the Hasenheide. He never acted the zealot, nor did he ever weep over the lot of those imprisoned in fortresses—while he kept them in chains. You always knew where he stood in these matters. You knew that you had to be on guard against him—and you conducted yourself accordingly. He was always a self-assured man, who neither deceived us by gracious looks, nor provoked us by private malice. You knew that he was acting not from love or petty hatred, but grandly and in the spirit of a system to which Austria has remained loyal for three centuries. It is that system for the sake of which Austria fought against the Reformation; it is the system which induced her to enter the lists against the Revolution. To defend this system, not only the sons of Habsburg, but the daughters too, fought. For its preservation, Marie Antoinette battled boldly in the Tuileries; and Marie Louise, who, having been proclaimed regent, should have fought for husband and child, instead laid down arms, and ceased fighting in the self-same Tuileries.[25] Emperor Francis suppressed his deepest feelings to maintain this system, and bore unspeakable woe. Even today he wears mourning for a beloved, radiant grandson whom he sacrificed on its account.[26] This fresh sorrow has bowed the grey head which once wore the imperial crown. This poor Emperor is still the true representative of unhappy Germany!

As to Prussia, we may speak of her in a very different tone. Here at least we are not restrained by pious reverence for the sacredness of a German Imperial Head. Let the learned lackeys on the Spree even dream of a great Imperator of the realm of Borussia, and proclaim the hegemony and overlordship of Prussia! Thus far the long fingers of the Hohenzollern have not succeeded in seizing the crown of Charlemagne, and in putting it into the sack where are so many other stolen Polish and Saxon jewels. The crown of Charlemagne still hangs too high, and I doubt whether it will come down on the witty head of that gold-spurred prince [27] to whom the barons are already doing homage as the future restorer of knighthood. I believe rather that his royal highness will prove to be, instead of a successor of Charlemagne, only a successor of Charles X and Charles of Brunswick.

It is true that recently many friends of the Fatherland have desired the extension of Prussia, and hoped to see her kings as the supreme heads of a united Germany. They have tried to decoy German patriotism. A Prussian sort of liberalism came into being; and the friends of freedom looked trustfully toward the lindens of Berlin. As for me, I have never shared their faith. On the contrary, I always regarded this Prussian eagle with anxiety. While others boasted that he looked boldly at the sun, I was all the more mindful of his claws. I did not trust this Prussian, this tall, canting, white-gaitered martinet hero, with his big belly, his big mouth, and the corporal's cane, which he would dip in holy water before applying it. I disliked this philosophical-Christian soldiery, this conglomerate of pale beer, lies, and sand. Repugnant, deeply repugnant to me, was this Prussia, this stiff, hypocritical, canting Prussia, this Tartuffe among nations.

At last, when Warsaw fell, this pious, soft cloak in which Prussia had known how to drape herself so well also dropped, and even the blind saw the iron armor of despotism hidden underneath. It was to the misfortunes of the Poles that Germany owes this salutary disenchantment.

The Poles! My blood boils in my veins when I write that word, when I reflect on how the Prussians behaved against those noblest children of adversity; with what cowardice, vulgarity, and treachery! In his disgust, the historian will scarcely find words to tell of what occurred at Fischau.[28] Those dastardly deeds will be better described by the executioner. . . . I can hear the hissing sound of the red-hot iron on the lean back of Prussia!

Not long ago I read in the *Allgemeine Zeitung* that the Privy Councillor Friedrich von Raumer,[29] who recently won for himself the reputation of a Royal Prussian Revolutionary—because as member of the commission of censors he objected to its excessive severity—has now been commanded to write a vindication of the proceedings of the Prussian government against Poland. This tract is now finished, and the author has already received two hundred Prussian thalers for it. However, it is not couched in a sufficiently servile tone to suit the camarilla of Brandenburg. Trifling as this incident may be, it is significant enough to characterize the spirit of the rulers and their subordinates. I happen to know Friedrich von Raumer, and on occasion I've seen him parading on Unter den Linden in his little blue-grey coat and his little grey-blue military hat. I once saw him on a university platform, as he declaimed on the death of Louis XVI, and at the same time shed a few official Royal Prussian tears. I've also read in one of the ladies' almanacs his *History of the Hohen-staufen.* I also know his *Letters from Paris,* in which he communicates to Madame Crelinger and her husband his views of the theater and politics of that place. He is altogether a peace-loving creature, who falls quietly into line. Of all the mediocre writers, he is the best; he is not entirely without piquancy, and a certain superficial erudition. Here he resembles an old dried herring wrapped in scholarly waste-paper. I repeat, he is the most peace-loving creature, who patiently allows his betters to load him with sacks, and who trots obediently to the official mills, only now and then stopping to listen to music. How low must a government sink in its despotism when even a' Friedrich von Raumer loses patience, and becomes restive and mulish, and refuses to trot on, and even begins to talk like a man! Did he perchance see the angel with the sword, barring his way, whom the Balaams of Berlin, the blind ones, still do not see? Alas! They kicked the poor beast with the best intentions, and goaded it with their golden spurs, and beat it thrice. But the people of Borussia—and by that you may judge their condition—praised their Friedrich von Raumer as an Ajax of freedom.

This Royal Prussian Revolutionary has now been employed to write an apology for the conduct of the Prussians against Poland, in order honorably to absolve the Cabinet of Berlin in the opinion of the public.

Oh, this Prussia! How well she understands to make the best use of her people! She even knows how to benefit from her revolution-aries! For her state comedies she needs supernumeraries of every color. She even puts to use tri-colored zebras. Thus she has of late employed her most violent demagogues to preach all over that Ger-many must become Prussian. Hegel was forced to justify servitude—which was real—as also being rational. Schleiermacher had to protest against freedom,[30] and commend Christian submissiveness to the will of superior authority. Disgusting and shameful is this use of philos-ophers and theologians to influence the common people, and thus to betray God and reason, and publicly dishonor themselves. How many a noble name, how many a worthy talent has thus been de-stroyed for the sake of most worthless ends! How great was the name of Arndt before he was commanded to write that shabby little book in which he wags his tail like a dog, and like a Wendish dog, barks at the July sun![31] The name of Stägemann was once in good repute—how deeply has he sunk since he commenced writing his Russian

Songs! May the Muse, who once with a sacred kiss consecrated his lips to nobler songs forgive him! What shall I say of Schleiermacher, the knight of the order of the Red Eagle, third class? Once he was himself a great knight—an eagle—and belonged to the first class. But not only the great ones—the little ones too have been ruined. There is poor Ranke,[32] whom the Prussian government sent travelling at its own expense—a fine talent who knew how to carve small historical figures and fit them together picturesquely; a good soul—as well-intentioned as mutton with Teltower turnips—an innocent man, whom, should I ever marry, I would choose as a friend of the family, and who surely must be a liberal. And yet, he has of late been compelled to publish in the *Staatszeitung* an apology for the Resolutions of the Diet. Other hirelings, whom I will not name, have been forced to do likewise—and despite everything are still "liberal."

Oh, I know them all, those Jesuits of the North! Whoever has, from necessity or heedlessness, ever accepted the least gift from them, is forever doomed. Even as hell would not set Proserpine free because she had eaten the seed of a pomegranate, so these Jesuits will let no man go free who has in the least profited from them—be it in a single seed of the golden apple—or, to speak more prosaically—a single *louis d'or;* they hardly allow him, as hell allowed Proserpine, to spend half the year in the light of the upper realm. At such times these men appear like the children of light; they take their places among the other Olympians, and speak and write with ambrosian liberalism; but at the appointed hour you will find them again in infernal darkness, in the realms of obscurantism, and they write Prussian apologias, declarations against the *Messenger*, rules governing censorship, or even a defense of the Resolutions of the Diet.

I cannot pass by these Resolutions of the Diet without comment. I will not try to refute their official apologists. Much less, as has often been done, to demonstrate their illegality. As I well know the persons who prepared the documents on which those resolutions were based, I do not doubt that the latter, that is, the federal acts of Vienna, contain the most legal warrant for despotic lust. Hitherto little use has been made of this masterpiece of the Junker-nobility. Its contents were therefore a matter of indifference to the people. But now that it has been brought into the open, all the singular beauties of the masterpiece—its secret springs, its hidden staples to which chains may be attached, its fetters for the legs, its concealed iron collars, its thumbscrews—in short, the whole exquisite work of art becomes apparent to all—now everyone can see that the German people, after sacrificing their blood and possessions for their prince and awaiting the grateful reward, have been vilely betrayed. We were shamefully tricked as by a juggler. Instead of the promised Magna Charta of freedom, they have drawn up for us a legal contract of slavery.

In virtue of my academic authority as Doctor of Both Laws, I solemnly declare that such a document, prepared by faithless agents, is null and void; in virtue of my duty as citizen, I protest against all the consequences which the resolutions of the Diet of June 28th drew from this worthless document. In virtue of my power as a public speaker, I lodge my complaint against those who drew up this document and I charge them with abusing public confidence; I charge them with *lèse-majesté* of the people; I charge them with high treason toward the German people. I accuse!

Poor German people! While you were resting from the battles you waged in the cause of your princes, and while you buried your dead who had fallen in the war, and bound up each other's wounds, smiling to see the blood run from your honest hearts, so full of joy and faith—joy, that your beloved prince had been saved, and faith in the most holy of human feelings, gratitude—in Vienna, in the old smithies of the aristocracy, the federal acts were being forged!

Strange! Even that prince who should have been most grateful to the people, and who had therefore promised them, in his hour of need, a representative constitution, a popular constitution, such as other free people possess; who promised it in black and white, with the most positive words—that prince has succeeded in seducing the other German princes, who like him, had obligated themselves to give their subjects a free constitution.[33] And they too broke their word and faith. Now he leans on the Vienna federal act in order to be able to destroy the new-born German constitutions—he, who dare not utter the word Constitution without blushing!

I speak of His Majesty, Frederick William, Third of name, King of Prussia.

Predisposed as I have always been and shall be to monarchy, I find it repugnant to my principles and sentiments to censure the person of princes too severely. My inclinations are rather to praise them for their good qualities. Hence I gladly praise the personal virtues of the monarch whose system of government, rather, whose Cabinet, I have discussed without reserve. I attest with pleasure that Frederick

William III deserves, as a man, the highest reverence and love, such as the great majority of the German people willingly give him. He is good and brave. He has shown himself steadfast in adversity, and what is rarer, gentle in prosperity. He is chaste of heart; touchingly modest in his manner, simple as a citizen, of a good homely disposition, a tender father—especially to the beautiful Czarina,[34]—to which tenderness we probably owe the cholera and a still greater evil with which our descendants will some day have to contend. Besides, the King of Prussia is a very devout man; he holds strongly by religion; he is a good Christian; he holds fast to the evangelical faith. He has himself written a liturgy. He believes in signs.—Oh, I wish he believed in Jupiter, the father of the gods, who avenges perjury! I wish he would at least give us the promised constitution!

Or perhaps the word of a king is not as sacred as an oath?

Of all the virtues of Frederick William, that which elicits most praise is his love of justice, about which many touching stories are told. Very recently he paid out 11,227 thalers and 13 good groschen from his private treasury to satisfy the legal claims of a Kyritz citizen. It is told that the son of the miller of Sans Souci, being in straitened circumstances, wished to sell the famous windmill which had been the subject of a law-suit between his father and Frederick the Great. The present king, however, paid the needy man a large sum so that the famous windmill might remain unchanged—a monument of Prussian love of justice. This is all very fine and praiseworthy. But where is the promised constitution, to which the Prussian people have a most decided claim—according to divine and earthly law? So long as the present King of Prussia does not fulfill this most sacred obligation, and withholds from his people their well-deserved, free constitution, I cannot call him just. Whenever I see the windmill of Sans Souci, I am reminded not of Prussian justice but of the Prussian wind.

I know well that the literary hirelings maintain that the King of Prussia promised the constitution as a personal favor, and that the promise had nothing to do with the circumstances which prevailed at the time. Fools! Soulless as they are, they fail to see that when we keep from people what is rightfully theirs we offend them less than when we deny them what we have promised out of pure love; for in the latter instance, their vanity is wounded, when they realize that they are less beloved of him who has of his own accord made the promise.

Or was it actually a mere whim, altogether without relation to the times, that moved the King of Prussia to promise his people a free constitution? He really had no intention of being grateful? And yet he had great reason to be. For never before had a prince found himself in such dire straits as the King of Prussia after the battle of Jena. And it was the people who rescued him. Had he not then been able to avail himself of the consolations of religion, the insolence which the Emperor Napoleon heaped upon him surely would have made him desperate. But as I said, he found comfort in Christianity, which is indeed the best religion after a defeat. He was fortified by the example of the Saviour; for he too could say at that time: "My kingdom is not of this world!" And he forgave his enemies who had occupied Prussia with four hundred thousand men. Had Napoleon, at that moment, not been busy with far more important matters than His Majesty Frederick William III, he probably would have pensioned him off permanently. Some time later, when all the kings of Europe united in a conspiratorial rabble against Napoleon, and the man of the people succumbed to this princely insurrection, and the Prussian ass gave the dying lion a last kick—Napoleon regretted all too late this sin of omission. When he paced up and down on St. Helena in his wooden cage, it struck him that he had cajoled the Poles, but had forgotten to crush Prussia; and he gnashed his teeth, and if a rat came his way, he squashed it with his foot.

Now Napoleon is dead, and he lies securely enclosed in his leaden coffin under the sands of Longwood on the isle of St. Helena. All around him is the sea. You need fear him no longer. Nor need you fear the three remaining gods in heaven, the Father, the Son, and the Holy Ghost. For you are on good terms with their holy servants. You need have no fear, for you are powerful and wise. You have gold and muskets, and that which is for sale you can buy—and that which is mortal you can kill. Your wisdom is likewise not to be resisted. Everyone of you is a Solomon, and it is a pity that the Queen of Sheba, that beautiful woman, is no longer alive, for you would have unriddled her of her very chemise. And you have your iron pots in which you can confine those who would have you solve the riddles of which you do not wish to know the answers. And you can seal them, and cast them into the sea of oblivion—all like King Solomon. Like him you understand the language of birds. You know all that is chirped and whistled in the land. Should the song of any bird displease you, you have a great pair of shears, to clip his bill.

I hear you would like to provide yourself with a larger pair for those who sing more than twenty sheets. You also have the cleverest birds to serve you, all the noble falcons, all the ravens—that is, the black-cats,—all the peacocks and owls. And old Simurgh [35] is still alive and he is your grand-vizier, and the wisest bird in all the world. He wishes to restore the world to what it was in the days of the pre-Adamite sultans, and to this end he unwearyingly lays eggs by night and day, and these are hatched in Frankfurt. Hud-hud, the accredited hoopoo, runs meanwhile through the Prussian marshes, carrying the most important dispatches in his bill. You need have no fears!

But I bid you beware of one thing: The *Moniteur* of 1793! [36] This is a magic spell which you will not be able to bind. There are conjuring words in it far more powerful than gold and muskets. Words to invoke the dead from their graves, and to send the live to their death; words with which to make giants of pygmies, and smash giants; words to fell your omnipotence, as the guillotine decapitates a king.

I will tell you the truth. There are people who are bold enough to utter these words, and who are never affrighted by the most horrible apparitions; but they cannot find the right words in the book, and even if they could, they could not pronounce them with their thick lips. For they are no conjurors. But there are others, who are truly familiar with the mysterious divining rod, and who know how to find the magic word, and even to utter it with a tongue skilled in sorcery. But they are timid souls, and they fear the specters which they are about to conjure up. For alas! we do not know the spell by which to lay the spirits when the incantation becomes too horrible. We do not know how to drive the enchanted broomstick back into his wooden repose, when the house is flooded with red water. We do not know how to exorcise the flame when its raging tongues lick all about them. We are afraid!

But do not rely on our helplessness and fear. The cloaked man of our time, as bold of heart as he is ready of tongue, who knows the great word and can speak it, may already be standing beside you. Perhaps he is masked in the livery of a servant, or disguised as a harlequin. You may not suspect that he who humbly pulls off your boots or tickles your ribs with jests may be your destroyer. Do you not feel a chill when these servile figures fawn on you with almost ironic abasement? Does it not suddenly occur to you: This is perhaps a snare; this wretch who behaves with such absolute idiocy, with such beast-like humility—may he not be a secret Brutus? Have you not sometimes had dreams at night warning you against the small, sinuous worms, which you have by chance seen crawling around by day? Have no fear. I am only jesting. You are quite safe. Our stupid devils of servants do not disguise themselves. Even Jarcke is not dangerous.[37] Have no fear of the little fools who sometimes amuse you with their serious jests. The great fool will always protect you against the little ones. The great fool is a very great fool—he is as great as a giant—and his name is the German people.

Oh, he is a very great fool indeed! His motley jacket is made of six and thirty patches. On his cap hang mighty church bells weighing tons—instead of little bells—and in his hand he carries the huge harlequin sword of iron. His heart is full of sorrow. But he does not think of sorrow, and his pranks are all the merrier, and he often laughs to keep from weeping. But when he recalls his trials, then he shakes his head as if mad, and deafens his own ears with the pious Christian chimes on his cap. If a good friend speaks of his suffering with sympathy, or even suggests a household remedy, he becomes enraged and strikes at the counsellor with his iron weapon. He is particularly angry at those who wish him well. He is the most bitter enemy of his friends, and the best friend of his enemies. Oh, the great fool will always remain faithful and obsequious; he will always amuse your little Junkers with his giant pranks; for their delight he will repeat his tricks every day; balance innumerable loads on his nose; allow many hundred thousands of soldiers to trample on his belly. But have you no fear that some day these burdens may become too heavy for your fool?—that he may shake off your soldiers—and in an excess of buffoonery squeeze your head with his little finger so hard that your brains will spurt to the very stars?

Fear not. I am only jesting. The great fool remains obsequious and obedient—and should the little fools want to do you harm, the great one will strike them dead.

Written in Paris, October 18, 1832.

❧ *A Revolution in Germany?*

EVEN TODAY, WHEN I BEHOLD MY GERMAN REPUBLICANS, I rub my eyes and say to myself, "Are you dreaming?" And when I read the German *Tribune* or similar publications, I ask myself, "Who is that great poet who invents all that? Does Dr. Wirth, with his shining sword of honor, actually exist? Or is he only a figment of the imagination of a Tieck or an Immermann?" [38] But then I am sure that poetry cannot soar so high—that our great poets are simply incapable of conceiving such remarkable characters, and that Dr. Wirth really has a body, and is alive, an errant but doughty knight of freedom, one of those whose like Germany has but rarely seen since the days of Ulrich von Hutten.

Can it really be true that the silent land of dreams has begun to live and move? Who would have thought that before July, 1830? Goethe with his cradle-songs, the zealots with their monotonous prayer-book tones, the mystics with their magnetism—had lulled Germany into a profound slumber. And far and wide all was still, all lay fast asleep. But only the bodies were sleep-bound; the souls which were imprisoned within them still retained a strange consciousness. As a young man, I once wandered through the German lands, and looked at the sleeping men I saw the sorrow in their faces. I studied their physiognomy. I laid my hand on their hearts. And they began to speak, like somnambulists, in strange broken phrases, which revealed their inmost thoughts. The guardians of the people, their golden nightcaps drawn tightly over their ears, securely wrapped in their nightshirts of ermine, sat upon their red-cushioned velvet chairs, and they too slept; they even snored. And as I wandered with rucksack and staff, I spoke or sang aloud to myself about what I had seen on the faces of the sleeping men, or what I had overheard in the sighs of their hearts. All around me was stillness, and I heard nothing but the echo of my own words.

Since then, startled by the cannons of the great week, Germany has awakened. Now everyone who has kept quiet must make up for lost time. There is a chattering, tumult, and commotion; a great deal of tobacco smoking, and out of these dark clouds a dreadful storm is brewing. It is like a raging sea; and on the overhanging rocks stand the word-masters. Some huff and puff at the waves, in the belief that they have caused the storm; and the more they blow, the wilder the tempest howls; others are fearful; they hear the cracking of the ship of state, and they look on the wild waves with panic. They have learned in school that with oil you can calm the waves—and they pour the contents of their study-lamps into the enraged flood of humanity, or to speak more prosaically, they write conciliatory pamphlets, and are amazed that they are of no use at all. And they sigh, "*Oleum perdidi!*" [39]

It is not hard to predict that the idea of a German republic, as so many minds in Germany now conceive it, is by no means a fleeting fancy. Dr. Wirth, Siebenpfeifer, and Messrs. Scharpf and Georg Fein of Brunswick, and Grosse and Schüler and Savoye, may and will be imprisoned.[40] But their thoughts will be free and will soar as freely as birds of the air. Like birds, they will nest in the tops of German oaks, and for perhaps half a century nothing more will be heard of them.

Then one fine summer morning they will suddenly appear in the public squares, grown to the stature of the eagle of the all-highest god, bearing lightning in their claws. What, after all, is half a century, or even a whole century? The people have time enough. They are immortal. Only kings are mortal.

I do not believe that there will be a German revolution very soon—still less a German republic. The latter I shall not live to see—come what may. But I am sure that when we are long mouldy in our quiet graves, Germany will still be fighting with word and sword for the republic. For the republic is an *idea*, and Germans have never abandoned an idea, till they have fought it through to its last consequences. Shall we Germans, who in our great art-epoch most thoroughly debated the minutest aesthetic questions—for example, the sonnet—shall we leave that far weightier problem unresolved, now that our political epoch has begun?

For such a struggle the French have supplied us with special arms For Frenchmen and Germans have learned much of each other. The French have taken over a great deal of German philosophy and poetry, and we in turn have taken the political experience and the practical sense of the French. Both nations resemble those Homeric heroes who exchange weapons and armor on the field of battle as a sign of friendship. Hence the great change which is taking place among German writers. In other days, they were either learned academicians or poets; they troubled themselves little about the people, for whom none of them wrote. In the philosophical-poetical Germany of that day, the multitude did the crudest kind of thinking; when they quarrelled with their superiors, it was over such sordid matter-of-fact things as taxes, custom-duties, injury by hunting, tolls, etc.,—while in practical France, the people, educated and guided by writers, fought more readily for ideal interests, for philosophic principles.

In the War of Liberation (*lucus a non lucendo*),[41] the government employed a couple of learned university and poetical gentlemen to work on the people in behalf of their dynastic interests, and the people showed great susceptibility and read the *Merkur* of Joseph Görres,[42] sang the songs of E. M. Arndt, decked themselves in their national oak leaves, armed themselves, and stood, inspired, in rank and file, addressed one another as "du," behaved like a militia, and fought and conquered Napoleon.—For against stupidity even the gods are helpless. And now the government would once more use that old pair of hounds. All this time they have been lying chained in a dark hole, and are now mangy and foul; they have learned nothing new, and bark in the same old style. But the people have heard altogether new notes—the high and noble notes of civil equality, the rights of man—the inalienable rights of man—and with a smile of compassion, if not of contempt, they look down at these well-known barkers, these medieval hounds, these trusty poodles and pious pugs of 1814.

Naturally, I do not support all the notes of 1832. I have always expressed myself regarding the least attractive of these—our German republicans. I have shown the accidental circumstances to which their appearance is due.

I will under no circumstances quarrel with their opinions here. That is not my office. For such business the governments have their special agents, who receive special emoluments. But I cannot refrain from remarking that the principal error of the German republicans arises from the fact that in demanding for Germany the republican form of government, which may indeed be suitable for France, they do not sufficiently consider the difference between the two countries. It is not her geographical position or the armed intervention of neighboring princes that can prevent Germany from becoming a republic, as the Grand Duke of Baden recently declared. As a matter of fact, her geographic position represents one of the strongest elements in the arguments of the German republicans. And so far as external danger is concerned, a united Germany would be the most formidable power in the world. For a people who fought so bravely under conditions of abject servility, would, if they consisted only of republicans, easily surpass the valor of all impressed Bashkirs and Kalmucks. But Germany cannot be a republic because she is essentially royalist. France, on the other hand, is by her very nature republican. I do not say that the French possess more republican virtues than we. Even the French do not possess them superabundantly. I speak of the nature, the character which not only differentiates royalism from republicanism, but which accounts for the basic differences in their manifestation and their practical realization.

The royalism of a people consists in this: that they respect authority; that they believe in the persons who represent that authority; and that this confidence also attaches to the person. The republicanism of a people consists in this: that they do not believe in authority; that they respect only laws; that they constantly demand an accounting of their representatives, regard them with distrust, control them; that they never attach themselves to persons; and, what is more, the more these tower above the mass of people, the more zealously they seek to restrict them, through hostility, distrust, scorn, and persecution.

Viewed in this light, ostracism was the most republican of institutions, and the Athenian who voted for the banishment of Aristides because "people were always calling him the Just," was the truest of republicans.[43] He did not wish to see virtue represented by one man; he did not wish to see the individual acquire greater significance than the law; he feared the authority of a name. This man was the greatest citizen of Athens, and it is characteristic that history has not preserved his name. Yes, since I have been studying the French republicans—their writings as well as their lives—I recognize everywhere as their most signal earmark that mistrust of the person, that hatred of the authority of a name. It is not petty love of equality which impels men to hate a great name. No. They fear that those who bear it will abuse it against the interests of freedom, or allow it to be misused to the disadvantage of freedom, whether through weakness or complaisance. For this reason many great and popular heroes of freedom were executed during the Revolution; it was feared that in time of danger their authority might exercise a baleful influence. For this reason I still hear republicans proclaim the doctrine that we must ruin all liberal reputations, lest at some decisive moment they exercise an injurious influence, as we recently saw in the case of Lafayette, to whom we owe thanks for the "best republic."

BUT THE GERMANS ARE NOT YET IN THIS CONDITION. Belief in authority is not yet extinct with them, and nothing fundamental drives them to a republican form of government. They have not yet outgrown royalty. Reverence for princes has not been forcibly uprooted among them; they have not experienced the misfortunes of the twenty-first of January; [44] they still believe in persons; they believe in authority, in a supreme potentate, in the police, in the Holy Trinity, in the *Hallesche Literaturzeitung*, in blotting paper, in wrapping paper, but most of all in parchment. . . .

The Meaning of German Philosophy

OUR PHILOSOPHICAL REVOLUTION IS AT AN END. Hegel completed its grand cycle. Since then we have had merely a development and extension of the doctrines of the philosophy of nature. As I have said before, the latter has penetrated all the regions of learning and has produced the most extraordinary and magnificent results. At the same time much that is unpleasant has also made its appearance. These phenomena are so numerous that it would take a book to enumerate them. And they constitute a really interesting and colorful portion of the history of our philosophy. But I am sure that it is better for the French not to know anything of this, for such knowledge would only tend to bewilder your heads more. Passages of the philosophy of nature torn from their context might do you great harm.

This much I know: Had you four years ago been acquainted with the German philosophy of nature you would never have started your July Revolution. That act required such a concentration of thought and energy, such a noble bias, such a measure of levity, as only your old school allows. Philosophical perversions which could be used to urge the cause of legitimacy and the Catholic doctrine of the Incarnation would have dampened your ardor and paralyzed your valor. I consider it therefore of world-historic importance that your great eclectic,[45] who then desired to instruct you in German philosophy, did not have the faintest notion of it. His providential ignorance was salutary for France and for all mankind.

Alas! The philosophy of nature which brought forth such rich fruit in so many realms of knowledge, especially in the natural sciences, has in others produced only the most noxious weeds. While Oken,[46] our most gifted thinker and one of the greatest citizens of Germany, discovered new worlds of ideas and inspired our German youth with a zeal for the primordial rights of man, for freedom and equality—Adam Müller at the same time was lecturing us on how to provision nations as we do cattle, according to the principles of natural philosophy; and Görres was preaching medieval obscurantism, according to the scientific view which holds that the state is a tree, and that its organic structure demands a trunk, branches and leaves—and that all of these could be very conveniently found in the hierarchy of medieval corporations. At the same time, Herr Steffens was proclaiming the philosophical law that the peasant class was distinguished from the privileged nobility in that it was designed by Nature to work without enjoyment, while the nobility was entitled to enjoyment without work. Indeed, I am told that a few months ago, a crude country-squire of Westphalia, an arrant ass by the name of Haxthausen, published a book in which he petitioned the Royal Prussian Government to consider the consistent parallelism which philosophy demonstrates throughout the cosmic organism, and to separate the classes more rigidly: for just as there are four elements in nature, fire, air, water and earth, so there are four analogous elements in society, the nobility, the clergy, the commoners, and the peasantry.

When it was seen that these blatant follies were burgeoning on the tree of philosophy and bursting into noxious flowers, and especially when it became apparent that German youth, immersed in metaphysical abstractions, had lost sight of the immediate questions of the day and was unfit for practical living, all patriots and friends of freedom inevitably felt righteous indignation at philosophy, and some even went so far as to condemn it to death, because they considered it to be worthless shadow-boxing.

We will not be so foolish as to try seriously to confute these malcontents.

German philosophy is a serious matter, of concern to all mankind. Our remotest descendants alone will be able to judge whether we are to be blamed or praised for having first produced our philosophy and then our revolution. But it seems to me that a methodical people like the Germans had to commence with the Reformation. Thereafter they could occupy themselves with philosophy, and only when they had completed that task, were they in a position to pass on to political revolution. I find this sequence very reasonable. The heads which philosophy used for reflection could later be chopped off by the revolution, for its own purposes. But philosophy could never have used these heads if the revolution had first chopped them off. Don't worry, German republicans—your German revolution will be no gentler or milder because it has been preceded by the *Critique* of Kant, the transcendental idealism of Fichte, and even the philosophy of nature. These doctrines gave birth to revolutionary forces which only wait for the day to erupt and fill the world with terror and amazement. Then there will appear Kantians who even in a visible world will know nothing of reverence and who will mercilessly plough up the soil of European life with sword and axe and extirpate the last roots of the past. Armed Fichteans will enter the battle who in their fanaticism of the Will are not restrained by fear or self-interest, for they live solely in the Spirit and defy Matter, like the early Christians who could not be swayed by physical tortures or physical delights. No, such transcendental idealists will be more inflexible in a social revolution than the first Christians, for these suffered earthly martyrdom in order thereby to attain heavenly bliss, while the transcendental idealists regard martyrdom itself as an illusion, and are inaccessible in the citadels of their own thoughts. But even more terrifying than all of these will be the philosophers of nature once they actively enter upon a German revolution and identify themselves with its destructive work. For if the hand of the Kantian strikes firmly and surely, it is because his heart is moved by no traditional reverence. If the Fichtean boldly defies all danger, it is because it has no real existence for him. But the natural philosopher will be terrible indeed because he has allies in the forces of nature, because he will be able to invoke the demonic energies of old German pantheism, because that ancient love of war we find among the old Germans will once more awake in him and will fight not to destroy or conquer but merely for the sake of fighting. Christianity—and that is its greatest merit—has somewhat mitigated that brutal German love of war, but it could not destroy it. Should that subduing talisman, the cross, be shattered, the frenzied madness of the ancient warriors, that insane berserk rage of which Nordic bards have spoken and sung so often, will once more burst into flames. The talisman is rotting, and the day will come when it will break into miserable fragments. The old stone gods will then arise from long forgotten ruins and rub the dust of a thousand years from their eyes, and Thor will leap to life with his giant hammer and smash the Gothic cathedrals! When that day comes and you hear the tramping of feet and the clang of arms, beware you neighbors' children, you French people, and do not meddle in our German affairs! For verily, harm may befall you. Beware lest you fan our flames, and take good heed not to quench them. You might easily burn your fingers in the fire. Do not smile at my advice—the advice of a dreamer who warns you against Kantians, Fichteans, and philosophers of nature. Do not smile at the visionary who anticipates the same revolution in the realm of the visible as has taken place in the realm of the spiritual. Thought precedes action as lightning precedes thunder. German thunder is, I admit, thoroughly German—not very nimble—it comes rolling somewhat slowly, but it does come. When you hear its crash, which will be unlike anything before in the history of the world, you will know that German thunder has at last hit the mark. At that uproar the eagles of the air will drop dead, and lions in farthest Africa will draw in their tails and slink away into their royal caves. A play will be performed in Germany which will make the French Revolution look like an innocent idyl. Now all is rather peaceful. Even though here and there some fellows may behave in a rather frisky fashion, do not mistake them for the real actors of the play. They are only the little dogs running around in the empty arena, barking and biting at each other before the hour strikes and the great army of gladiators enters to begin a life and death battle.

And that hour will surely strike. As on the tiers of the amphitheater, nations will group themselves around Germany to witness the great gladiatorial combats. I warn you, Frenchmen, keep very still and on your life, do not applaud. We might easily misunderstand you and in our boorishness bid you be quiet. If in the past we have been able to subdue you when we were in a servile and morose state, we certainly will be able to do so all the more easily in the intoxicated arrogance of freedom. You yourselves are well aware of what people can do in that state—and you are no longer in it. And so, beware. I wish you well; that is why I speak the bitter truth. You have more to fear from a Germany set free than from the entire Holy Alliance with all its Croats and Cossacks. For you should know that first of all, you are not loved in Germany, which is almost incomprehensible, for you are really very loveable. While you were in Germany you took a great deal of trouble to please, at least the better and fairer half of the German nation. Unfortunately the half that did love you does not bear arms, and their good-will will hardly be of much use to you. What it is that you are being reproached with I don't know. Once, in a beer-hall in Göttingen, I heard a young Pan-German declare that Germany must avenge Conradin von Hohenstaufen on the French, who beheaded him at Naples.[47] You have surely forgotten about that, long, long ago. We, however, forget nothing. You see, when we get the urge to grapple with you there will be no lack of good reasons. In any case, I counsel you to be well on your guard. No matter what happens in Germany, whether the Crown Prince of Prussia or Dr. Wirth comes to power, always be on the alert, remain at your posts quietly, weapons in hand. I wish you well. I was almost terrified when I recently heard that your ministers proposed to disarm France.

Despite your present Romanticism, you are really Classicists at heart, and you know Olympus well. Among the naked gods and goddesses who there rejoice over nectar and ambrosia, you may see one immortal who even amidst all this festivity and gaiety always wears a coat of mail and bears a helmet on her head and a spear in hand.

It is the Goddess of Wisdom.

ತಿ Germany—I Am Your Fool!

THE GREAT WEEK OF PARIS! The valorous spirit of freedom blew over into Germany and naturally upset the bed-lamps here and there, so that the red curtains of a few thrones caught fire and golden crowns grew warm under the blazing night-caps. But the old watchmen, entrusted with the security of the kingdom, are already dragging up fire-buckets, and sniffing around all the more suspiciously and reenforcing secret chains; and I already perceive even thicker prison vaults arching invisibly over the German people.

Poor captive people! Do not lose heart in your dire need! Oh, if only I could speak catapults! If my heart could only shoot firebrands!

The formal crust of ice melts from my heart. A strange sorrow steals over me.—Is it love, love for the German people, of all things, or is it sickness? My soul trembles; my eyes burn. And that is no proper state for a writer who must command his material and remain

precise and objective, as is decreed by the schools of art, and as
was done by Goethe. He got to be eighty doing this, and a Minister,
and wealthy, besides. Poor German people! That is your greatest
man!

I still have a few octavo pages to fill, and so I will tell you a story—
it has been on my mind since yesterday—it is a story out of the life of
Charles the Fifth. But I heard it very long ago, and I do not recall the
details quite exactly. Things like that are easily forgotten, if one
doesn't get paid for reading old stories from a book every six months.
What does it matter if the places and dates are forgotten, so long as
their inner meaning, their moral, remains fresh in one's memory? It
is this very thing that rings in my head and makes me sad enough to
cry. I fear I am getting sick.

The poor Emperor was taken prisoner by his enemies and thrown
into a dismal prison. I believe it was in the Tyrol. There he sat, alone
and wretched, forsaken by all his knights and courtiers, and no one
came to his aid. I do not know whether he had then the pale, curd-
white face which Holbein depicts in his paintings. But his misanthropic
lower lip surely protruded more prominently than in those pictures.
He must have despised the men who fawned upon and toadied him
with such devotion when the sun of good fortune smiled on him, and
now left him alone in his dark plight. But suddenly the prison door
opened and in came a man wrapped in a heavy cloak. When he threw
it aside, the Emperor recognized his faithful Kunz von der Rosen,
the court fool. This man brought him solace and counsel—and he
was the court jester.

Oh, my German Fatherland—dear German people—I am your
Kunz von der Rosen! The man whose office it was to entertain you,
whose duty it was to amuse you in better days, breaks into your
dungeon in time of need. Here under my cloak I bring you your
strong scepter and your beautiful crown. Do you not know me, my
Emperor? If I can't set you free, I will at least console you, and you
shall have someone to chat with you about your black misery, to
keep up your courage, to love you,—someone whose best jests and
best blood are at your service. For you my people are the true Emperor, rightful lord of the land. Your will is sovereign and far more
legitimate than the purple *Tel est notre plaisir* which rests upon a
divine right with no better warrant than the cackling of tonsured
quacks. Your will, my people, is the sole rightful source of all power.
And though you lie in chains, in the end your good right will prevail;

the day of liberation draws near, a new age begins. My Emperor, the night is gone and the red dawn glows without.

"Kunz von der Rosen, my fool, you err. You may have mistaken a shining axe for the sun, and the red glow of morning is nothing but blood."

"No, my Emperor, it is the sun, though it rises in the West. For six thousand years we have seen it rise in the East; now it is high time for it to change its course."

"Kunz von der Rosen, my fool, you have lost the bells from your old red cap, and now that old red cap looks so very strange."

"Alas, my Emperor, at the thought of your misfortunes I shook my head so furiously that the fool's bells fell from my cap—but it is none the worse for that."

"Kunz von der Rosen, my fool, what is that crashing and crackling noise I hear?"

"Be still. That is the saw and the carpenter's axe. Soon the doors of your prison will break down, and you will be free, my Emperor."

"Am I really Emperor? Alas, it is but my fool who tells me so."

"Do not sigh, my dear master. It is the air of the dungeon that makes you despair. Once you have regained your power, you will again feel the bold blood of emperors in your veins, and you will be as proud as an emperor and as arrogant, and gracious and unjust and smiling, and ungrateful—as princes are."

"Kunz von der Rosen, my fool, when I am free again, what will you do?"

"I will sew new bells on my cap."

"And how shall I reward your faithfulness?"

"Ah, dear master, do not have me put to death."

೬ॐ *Reflections*

GOETHE'S AVERSION TO ENTHUSIASM is as repugnant as it is childish. Such withdrawal is more or less suicide. It is like the flame which will not burn lest it be consumed. The generous flame, the soul of Schiller, burned with self-sacrifice. Every flame sacrifices itself. The more brilliantly it burns, the closer it approaches self-annihilation, self-extinction. I do not envy those timid little bedroom candles who lead prolonged and retired little lives.

THE LOVELIEST FLOWERS OF THE GERMAN SOUL are philosophy and song. Their blossom time is over. They needed an idyllic tranquillity. But Germany is now set in motion—her thinking is no longer selfless— her abstract world is shattered by crass reality. The steam engines of our railways have shaken our minds like an earthquake—and this is a condition unfavorable to song. The smoke affrights the singing birds, and the stench of gaslight poisons the fragrant moon-lit nights.

LUTHER SHOOK ALL OF GERMANY—but Francis Drake restored calm— he gave us potatoes.

THE GERMAN IS LIKE A SLAVE who obeys the mere nod or word of his master, and needs neither whips nor chains. Servility is inherent in him—it is in his soul. Spiritual slavery is worse than physical slavery. The German must be freed from within—it is futile to do so from without.

A GERMAN MARRIAGE IS NOT A REAL MARRIAGE. The husband does not have a wife, but a servant—and he continues his lonely bachelor life in spirit—even though it be within his family circle. I do not mean to imply that he is master; on the contrary, sometimes he is only the maid's servant—and he does not even disavow this household servility.

The Citizen of the World

London

I HAVE SEEN THE GREATEST WONDER which the world can show to the astonished mind.—I have seen it, and am more astonished than ever. Still vivid in my memory remains the stone forest of houses, and amid them the rushing stream of living human faces, with all their motley passions and all their terrible and restless impulses of love, of hunger, of hatred.

I am speaking of London.

Send a philosopher to London, but, not on your life, a poet! Send a philosopher there and stand him at a corner of Cheapside, and he will learn more there than from all the books of the last Leipzig fair. As the human waves roar around him, a sea of new thoughts will rise before him, and the Eternal Spirit which hovers upon its waters will breathe upon him. The most hidden secrets of the social order will suddenly be revealed to him. He will hear the pulse of the world beat audibly, and see it visibly—for if London is the right hand of the world, its active, mighty right hand, then we may regard the street which leads from the Exchange to Downing Street as the world's radial artery.

But send no poet to London! This downright earnestness in all things, this colossal uniformity, this machine-like movement, this moroseness even in pleasure, this exaggerated London—smothers the imagination and rends the heart. And should you ever send a German poet there, a dreamer, who stands staring at every single thing— say, a ragged beggar-woman, or a resplendent goldsmith's shop— why then, things will go badly with him, and he will be jostled on all sides, and even knocked down with a mild "God damn!" God damn! that damned pushing! I soon perceived that these Londoners have much to do. They live on a grand scale, and though food and clothing are dearer there than with us, they must still be better fed and clothed than we are. As behooves gentility, they also have enormous debts, yet sometimes in a boastful mood, they squander their guineas, pay other nations to fight for their pleasure, whose respective kings they give a handsome *douceur* into the bargain.—Therefore, John Bull must work day and night to obtain money for such expenses; day and night he must tax his brain to invent new machines, and he sits and reckons in the sweat of his brow, and rushes and scurries without looking about him, from the docks to the Exchange, and from the Exchange to the Strand. Hence it is quite understandable, when a poor German poet stands in his way at the corner of Cheapside gazing into an art-dealer's window he should knock him aside somewhat unceremoniously. "God damn!"

The picture at which I was gaping at the corner of Cheapside was that of the crossing of the Beresina by the French.

When, jolted out of my preoccupation, I looked again on the roaring street, where a motley throng of men, women, children, horses, stagecoaches, and with them a funeral procession, whirled, groaned, and creaked along, it seemed to me as though all of London were a Beresina Bridge, where everyone presses on in mad haste to save his little scrap of life, where the arrogant rider tramples down the poor pedestrian; where he who falls to the ground is lost for ever; where even the best friends rush by, indifferently, over the corpses of their comrades; and thousands of exhausted and bleeding creatures clutch in vain at the planks of the bridge, and plunge into the icy pit of death.

How much more cheerful and homelike it is in our dear Germany!

With what dreamy coziness, with what Sabbatical quiet things glide along here! Calmly the watch is changed; uniforms and houses gleam in the quiet sunshine, swallows flit over the flag-stones, fat court-councillors' wives smile from the windows, while in the echoing streets there is room enough for the dogs to sniff at one another properly, and for men to stand at ease and discourse on the theater, and bow low—very, very low!—when some little aristocratic scoundrel or vice-scoundrel, with colored little ribbons on his shabby little coat, or some court-marshal-lowbrain, powdered and gilded, prance· by, graciously returning the greeting.

I had made up my mind in advance not to be astonished at that hugeness of London of which I had heard so much. But I had as little success as the poor school-boy who had made up his mind not to feel the whipping he was about to receive. The fact was that he expected to receive the usual blows with the usual cane in the usual way on the back; whereas he received a most unusually severe thrashing in an unusual place with a slender switch. I anticipated great palaces, and saw nothing but small houses. But their very uniformity and their infinite number are wonderfully impressive.

THE STRANGER WHO WANDERS THROUGH THE GREAT STREETS OF LONDON and does not chance right into the quarters in which the common people live, sees little or nothing of the dire misery there. Only here and there, at the entrance of some dark alley, a ragged woman stands mutely with a suckling babe at her exhausted breast, and begs with her eyes. Perhaps if those eyes are still beautiful, one glances into them and shrinks back at the world of wretchedness to be found here. The common beggars are all old people, generally blackamoors, who stand at the corners of the streets clearing pathways—a very necessary thing in muddy London—and ask for coppers in return. It is only in the dark night that Poverty, with her fellows, Vice and Crime, glides from her lair. She shuns the daylight all the more carefully, since her wretchedness contrasts so glaringly with the pride of wealth which struts about everywhere. Only hunger drives her sometimes from her dark alley at midday, and then she stares with eloquent, mute, beseeching eyes at the rich merchant who hurries past, busy, jingling his coins, or at the idle lord, who, like a surfeited god, rides by on his high horse, now and then glancing with an aristocratically blasé air at the crowds below—as if they were a swarm of ants, or a herd of baser creatures whose joys and sorrows had nothing in common with his feelings. For above this mass of humanity which clings close to the earth, England's nobility soars, like beings of higher order, and regards its little island as a temporary lodging, Italy as its summer garden, Paris as its social salon, and the whole wide world as its property. These nobles sweep along, without cark or care, and their gold is a talisman which makes their wildest wishes come true.

Poor poverty! How agonizing must your hunger be, when others wallow in arrogant surfeit! And when a man, with indifferent hand, throws a crust into your lap, how bitter must be the tears with which you wet it! You drink poison with your own tears. You are surely right when you ally yourself with Vice and Crime. Outlawed criminals often have more humanity in their hearts than those cold, irreproachable citizens of virtue, in whose bloodless hearts the power of doing evil is quenched—as well as the power of doing good. And even Vice is not always Vice. I have seen women on whose cheeks red vice was painted, but in whose hearts dwelt heavenly purity. I have seen women—would I saw them again!—

﹩ *A Dialogue on the Thames*

THE SALLOW MAN STOOD NEXT TO ME ON THE DECK as I caught sight of the green banks of the Thames, and the nightingales awoke in every corner of my soul.

"Land of Freedom!" I cried. "I greet you! Hail, Freedom, young sun of a rejuvenated world! Those older suns, love and faith, have withered and grown cold, and can no longer give light or warmth. The ancient myrtle woods, once so full of life, are now deserted, and only the silly turtle-doves still nest in their soft thickets. The old cathedrals, once reared to such giant heights by an arrogantly pious generation, that would build its very faith into the sky, are decayed and crumbling, and their gods no longer believe in themselves. They are feeble with age, and our times lack the imagination to create new ones. Every aspiration of the human breast now turns to love of liberty. Perhaps Liberty is the religion of the new age, and—as happened before—a religion that is preached not to the rich but to the poor, and that also has its evangelists, martyrs, and Iscariots!"

"My young enthusiast," said the sallow man, "you will not find what you seek. You may be right in assuming that freedom is a new religion, which will spread all over the world. But as once every nation, when it adopted Christianity, moulded it according to its own needs and character, so each will now adopt of the new religion, Liberty, only that which accords with its local wants and its national character.

"The English are a domestic people; they live a circumscribed, securely enclosed family life; in his family circle the Englishman seeks that comfort of the soul which inherent social ineptitude denies him when he is away. The Englishman is therefore content with a freedom which guarantees his most personal rights, and unconditionally secures him in his person, property, marriage, religion, and even whims. No man is freer in his home than an Englishman; to use a famous expression, he is king and bishop within his four walls, and there is much truth in the common saying: 'My house is my castle.'

"But if the Englishman needs personal liberty most of all, the Frenchman, if necessary, can dispense with it, provided we only let him fully enjoy that portion of universal liberty known as equality. The French are not a domestic but a social people. They do not like sitting together in silence, which they call *une conversation anglaise*. They rush chattering from the café to the casino, from the casino to the salons; their light champagne-blood and innate social talent drives them to sociability, whose first and last principle, yes, whose very soul, is equality. The need for equality in France was bound to follow the evolution of social life. Although the causes of the French Revolution are to be sought in the budget, it is nevertheless true that its tone and accents were derived from those bourgeois wits who seemed to live on a footing of equality with the high nobility in the salons of Paris—and only now and then, perhaps by a hardly perceptible and therefore the more deeply offensive feudal smile, were reminded of the great and shameful inequality. When the *canaille roturière* took the liberty of beheading that high nobility, it was done less in order to inherit their property than to inherit their ancestry, and to introduce an equality of nobles in place of the inequality of commoners. That this aspiration for equality was the main principle of the Revolution is the more plausible since the French soon felt themselves happy and contented under the rule of their great

Emperor, who recognized that they were still under age, and kept all their freedom under a strict guardianship, and left them only the pleasure of a perfect and glorious equality.

"The Englishman bears the sight of a privileged aristocracy with far greater patience than the Frenchman. He is consoled by the possession of rights which prevent the aristocracy from disturbing his domestic comforts or daily wants. Nor does the aristocracy flaunt its privileges, as on the Continent. In London's streets and public places of resort you will see gay ribbons only on women's bonnets, and gold and silver badges only on the coats of lackeys. Even that beautiful many-colored livery, which in Germany proclaims a privileged military class, is anything but a sign of honor in England. Just as an actor wipes off the paint after a performance, so an English officer hastens home to doff his red coat the moment he is off duty, so that he may become a gentleman again, and appear in the plain coat of a gentleman. Only on the stage of St. James's are those decorations and costumes which have been preserved from the rubble of the Middle Ages still of consequence. There you see the court decorations fluttering, stars glittering; there the satin trains and silken breeches rustle, gold spurs and old French phrases rattle. There the knight struts and the lady simpers. But what does a free Englishman care for all this courtly comedy at St. James, so long as it doesn't bother him and no one keeps him from playing a similar comedy in his own house, where he can have his domestics kneel before him and where he can toy with the cook's garter? *Honni soit qui mal y pense.*[1]

"As for the Germans, they need neither freedom nor equality. They are a speculative people, ideologists with fore- and hindsight, dreamers who live only in the past and future, and have no present. The English and the French have a present; for them every day has its wars, its counter-attacks, and its history. The German has nothing for which to fight, and when he began to suspect that there might be things in the world which are good to possess, his wise philosophers taught him to doubt their very existence. It cannot be denied that the Germans too love liberty. But not like other people. The Englishman loves liberty like his lawfully wedded wife; he possesses her, and if he does not treat her with particular tenderness, still he knows how to defend her like a man, if need be;—and woe to any red-coated scoundrel who forces his way into the sanctity of their bedroom—be he gallant or constable.

"The Frenchman loves liberty like his chosen bride. He is aglow for her; he is aflame; he throws himself at her feet with the wildest protestations; he fights for her even unto death; he commits a thousand follies for her sake. The German loves liberty as he loves his old grandmother."

Men are strange creatures! At home, in the Fatherland, we grumble. Every stupidity, every perversity vexes us there. Like boys we are ever eager to rush forth into the wide world. But when we at last really find ourselves there, it is all too wide, and often we secretly yearn for the narrow stupidities and absurdities of home, and we wish we could sit in the old familiar room again, and, if possible, build ourselves a little retreat behind the stove and squat there snugly and read *Der Allgemeine Deutsche Anzeiger.* So it happened to me on my trip to England. Scarcely had I lost sight of the German coast, when a curious, belated love awoke in me for the forests of nightcaps and wigs of Germany I had just left in displeasure; and when the Fatherland faded from my eyes, I rediscovered her in my heart.

And so my voice may have sounded somewhat tender when I replied to the sallow man: "My dear sir, do not berate the Germans! If they are dreamers, many of them have dreamed such lovely dreams that I would not trade them for the waking realities of our neighbors Since we all sleep and dream, we can perhaps do without freedom; for our tyrants are also asleep, and only dream of their tyranny. We awoke only once—when the Catholic Romans robbed us of our freedom to dream—then we acted and we triumphed and we lay down again and dreamed. Sir, do not mock our dreamers! For now and then, like somnambulists, they say wonderful things in their sleep, and their words turn into seeds of freedom. No one can foresee the future. The splenetic Briton, weary of his wife, may put a halter around her neck, and auction her off at Smithfield. The fickle Frenchman may be untrue to his beloved, and abandon her and with a lilt cavort after the ladies of the court—the *courtisanes*—of his royal palace,—or Palais Royal. But the German will never turn his old grandmother out altogether; he will always find a place for her by the fire, where she can tell fairy tales to eager children. Should freedom ever vanish from the earth—which God forbid—a German dreamer will rediscover it again in his dreams."

🖘 *The Englishman in Italy*

Do not accuse me of Anglomania, dear reader, if I very often speak of the English in this book. They are today too numerous in Italy to be overlooked. They overrun the land in great swarms. They camp at all the inns; they run about everywhere, so that it is no longer possible to think of Italian citron trees without at the same time seeing an Englishwoman who breathes their fragrance, or of a gallery without a crew of Englishmen, who, guide-book in hand, scurry here and there to make sure that everything that is mentioned in the books as being noteworthy is still there. The sight of those fair, red-cheeked people, driving over the Alps, well-groomed and inquisitive, wandering through Italy in their shiny carriages, with their smart lackeys and neighing steeds, their green-veiled ladies' maids, and other costly appurtenances, gives the impression of an elegant migration of barbarians. And in truth, the son of Albion, although he wears white linen and pays in ready cash, is but a civilized barbarian in comparison with the Italian, who represents a civilization that is, in its way, gradually merging into barbarism. The one displays in his manners restrained crudity, the other wanton refinement. And yet those pale Italian faces—with suffering written in the whites of their eyes, and the lips so sickly tender—what an air of subtle distinction they reveal beside the formal British faces, so coarsely, so ruddily healthy! All Italians are inwardly sick. The sick always possess greater distinction than the healthy, for only a sick man is a man. His limbs express a history of suffering; they have become spiritualized. In fact, I believe even animals can become human by struggling with pain. I myself once saw a dying dog, who in his death agony looked at me with almost human expression.

The sorrow of the Italians is especially noticeable in their faces, when you speak to them of the misfortunes which have befallen their country. In Milan I had many occasions to observe it. For this is the most galling wound in the breast of the Italians . . . they shudder convulsively the moment it is touched—be it ever so gently. They shrug their shoulders in a way that fills you with strange pity.

One of these Britons contended that Italians were indifferent to politics, because they appeared to listen with equanimity when foreigners spoke of the Catholic emancipation and the Turkish war; and he was unfair enough to give ironic expression to his feelings, while sitting opposite one of those pale, black-bearded Italians. The evening before we had witnessed a performance of a new opera at La Scala, and remarked the tumultuous uproar which took place on such occasions.

"You Italians," the Briton said to the pale fellow, "appear to be dead to everything but music, which alone still has the power to inspire you."

"You do us an injustice," the pale man replied, shrugging his shoulders. "Alas," he added, sighing, "Italy sits over her ruins, lost in elegiac dreams. If at times she is aroused by the strains of song and suddenly leaps up, her enthusiasm is caused not so much by the song as by the memories and pent-up feelings which the song awakens, and which break out like a tempest. That is the reason for the insane commotion at La Scala."

Perhaps this avowal affords a clue to the enthusiasm which the operas of Rossini and Meyerbeer evoke everywhere on the other side of the Alps.

If I have ever beheld madness, it was certainly during a performance of *Crocciato in Egitto*,[2] in which the music, beginning softly and mournfully, frequently cried out in sudden, ecstatic pain. In Italy such madness is called *furore*.

ૐ *The English Middle Classes*

IF I HAVE REMARKED ABOVE that today the English people seek to be light and frivolous, and try to creep into the monkey's skin which the French are sloughing off, I must also add that this tendency proceeds from the aristocracy and gentry rather than from the middle classes. As a matter of fact, the trading and working portion of the nation, especially the merchants in the manufacturing towns, and nearly all Scotsmen, bear the outward stamp of pietism—yes, I might say, of Puritanism; so that this godly section of the people contrasts as sharply with the worldly-minded aristocrats, as once the cavaliers with the Roundheads, so truthfully portrayed in the novels of Walter Scott.

Readers who are under the impression that it was the genius of the Scottish bard that captured and recreated the external shape and inner thought-processes of these two historical parties, and that it is a mark of his greatness as a poet that he metes out equal justice and affection to both sides—as dispassionately as a god—do him too great an honor. One merely has to look in on prayer-meetings in Liverpool and Manchester, and then on the fashionable salons of West London, to perceive immediately that Walter Scott has merely set down the picture of his own times and dressed his contemporaries in ancient garb.

If we recall that as a Scotsman he was imbued, through education and national sentiment, with the Puritan spirit, and as a Tory, who even regarded himself as a scion of the Stuarts, he was whole-heartedly committed to king and noble; that his feelings and thoughts therefore embraced both attitudes with equal affection, so that they were neutralized through opposition, we will readily understand his impartiality in describing the democrats and aristocrats of Cromwell's time, an impartiality which might easily lead us into the error of seeking the same "fair play" in the portrayal of the heroes of the French Revolution in his *History of Napoleon*.

ঌ *The Crisis in England* [3]

[*1842*]

I CONFESS THAT I AM NOT ENTIRELY IMPARTIAL when I speak of the English, and it is likely that my unfavorable judgment and my aversion are deeply rooted in my anxieties as to our own welfare, and the peace and prosperity of the German Fatherland. For since I have come to understand what base egoism prevails in their politics, the English inspire in me a constant dread. I have the highest regard for their material preëminence. They have a great deal of that brutal energy with which the Romans mastered the world; but they combine the serpent's craft of Carthage with the wolfish rapacity of Rome. For the latter we have good and tried weapons; but against the murderous wiles of these Phoenicians of the North Sea we are defenseless. And today England is more dangerous than ever, since her commercial interests are in great straits. There is not in all the world so hard-hearted a creature as a shop-keeper whose trade is declining, whose customers are falling away, and whose stock is no longer in demand.

How will England save herself from this economic crisis? I don't know how the problem of the factory worker can be solved. But I do know that in politics this modern Carthage is not altogether squeamish about the means she uses. To her selfish way of thinking a war may seem in the long run the best means of finding an outlet for her internal malady. The English oligarchy will first of all speculate with the purses of the middle classes, whose wealth is really fantastic and can be used to pay and adequately pacify the lower classes. No matter how great the cost of the Indian and Chinese expeditions may be, no matter how great its financial straits, the government of England will nevertheless increase these expenditures, if it serves its purpose. The greater the deficit at home, the more prodigally will British gold be scattered abroad. For England is like a merchant facing bankruptcy, who out of desperation turns prodigal—or, rather, who runs every monetary risk to stay alive. With money you can do a great deal in this world; especially since all of us want happiness down here on earth. No one has any idea what enormous sums England spends annually on subsidizing her foreign agents, whose instructions are all framed on the probability of a European war, nor how these English agents employ the most versatile talents, virtues and vices of foreign countries to achieve their goal.

In view of these circumstances, we must readily see that it is not on the banks of the Seine—by reason of enthusiasm for an idea—or in the public market-places, that the peace of Europe may be most seriously threatened, but on the Thames, in the silent chambers of the Foreign Office, and as a consequence of the rude clamors of hungry English factory workers.—When we ponder this fact, we realize that we must turn our eyes there, and observe not only the persons of those who are in power, but also the pressing needs of the lower classes.

The increasing privation of the masses is a disease which ignorant army surgeons think can be cured by blood-letting—this will only aggravate the evil. It is not from without, by a lancet, but from within, through spiritual remedies that the sick body of the state can be cured. Only social ideas will bring salvation from a fatal catastrophe; but, to quote the words of Saint-Simon, "on all the wharves of England there is not one great idea to be found; there is nothing but steam engines and starvation." It is true that the present revolt has been suppressed; but it may come to pass that as a result of frequent outbreaks, English factory workers, who now only know how to work on wool and cotton, may try their hands on human flesh, and get the knack of it—and they may in the end become as expert in this bloody craft as their colleagues, the *ouvriers* of Paris and Lyon.— Then it may very well be that the conqueror of Napoleon, Field Marshal Mylord Wellington, who has again taken office as chief constable, may meet his Waterloo, right in the heart of London. Likewise, it may even happen that his myrmidons will refuse to obey their master. As a matter of fact, serious symptoms of such tendencies have manifested themselves recently among the English soldiery; and as I write these lines, fifty soldiers have been imprisoned in the Tower of London for refusing to fire on the English people. It may seem incredible, but it is true that English red-coats gave heed not to the orders of their officers, but to the voice of humanity—and they disregarded the whip (here called cat-o'-nine-tails), which in the proud capital of English freedom constantly threatens their heroic backs—the English knout! It is heartrending to read how women ran weeping toward the soldiers with the cry: "Give us bread, not lead!" Men crossed their arms with resignation, and said: "Kill hunger, not us and our children!" The common cry was "Don't shoot! We are all brothers!"

THE REVOLT IN ENGLAND IS STILLED FOR THE TIME BEING, but only for the time being. It is merely postponed. It will break out again with increased violence, and with graver consequences, since it can always await an auspicious moment. Many signs point to the fact that the resistance of the factory workers is now as thoroughly organized as was the resistance of the Irish Catholics. The Chartists have been able to make use of this menacing power in their own interests and have disciplined it to some extent; their alliance with the discontented workers is perhaps the most important phenomenon of the present time. This alliance was due to simple and natural causes—although the Chartists represented themselves as a purely political party with a well-defined program; while the factory workers, as I said, are only poor day-laborers, who can hardly speak from hunger, who are indifferent to all political reforms and only ask for bread. But a program rarely expresses the intimate thinking of a party; it is merely its outward badge, a spoken "cockade." The Chartists who profess to limit themselves only to political questions, cherish objectives which are in profound accord with the unspoken, unarticulated feelings of the hungry workmen; the latter can always take the program of the Chartists as their slogan, without ceasing to pursue their own aims. The Chartists demand, first, that Parliament consist of only one chamber, and that it be renewed by annual elections; secondly, that the independence of the electors be assured by secret ballot; and finally, that everyone born an Englishman be eligible to vote and be elected when of age. "All of which gives us nothing to eat," the starved workingmen say. "No one can grow fat from eating lawbooks, any more than cookbooks. We are hungry." "Just wait," the Chartists reply. "Hitherto only the rich have sat in Parliament and they have only taken care of the interests of their own property; but under the new electoral laws, under the Charter, the workers, too, or their representatives, will be able to enter Parliament; and then we will demonstrate that labor is as much a property right as any other kind of property; that a factory owner has no more right to reduce the daily wage of a workingman at will than he has to appropriate the estate, real or personal, of his neighbor. Work is the property of the people, and the property rights which spring from it should be sanctioned and protected by a renovated Parliament." One step more, and these people will say that labor is the people's right, which right presupposes unconditional payment of wages; thus Chartism must lead, if not to a community of goods, certainly to the undermining of the ancient principle of property—the pillar of modern society. These Chartist beginnings therefore imply in the final analysis a social revolution compared with which the French Revolution will seem tame and modest. . . .

৪৯ The Catholic Emancipation

Talk politics with the most stupid Englishman, and he is sure to say something sensible; but as soon as you turn the conversation to religion—the most intelligent Englishman will produce nothing but inanities. Hence arises all that confusion of thought, that admixture of wisdom and nonsense, whenever the Catholic Emancipation is discussed in Parliament—a question, in which politics and religion collide. It is rarely possible for the English, in their parliamentary debates, to give utterance to a principle. They discuss only the utility or disutility of a thing, and produce *facts*, for and against.

With facts there can be no quarrel, but no victories either. They produce nothing but physical blows on one side or the other; and the spectacle of such strife reminds me of the celebrated *pro patria* quarrels of the German students, the result of which is that so and so many passes are made, so and so many *quarte* and *tierce* thrusts—and nothing was proved.

In the year 1827, as everyone knows, the Emancipationists again fought the Orangemen at Westminster, and as is also evident, nothing came of it. The best "hitters" on the side of the Emancipationist party were Burdett, Blunkett, Brougham and Canning. Their opponents, with the exception of Peel, were the well-known, or to speak more correctly, the unknown fox-hunting squirearchy.

At all times the most intelligent statesmen of England have fought for civil liberties of Catholics, as much by reason of their profound sense of justice, as of political shrewdness. Pitt himself, the founder of the stable system, espoused the cause of the Catholic party. In like manner, Burke, that great renegade from freedom, could not so far suppress the voice of his heart as to act against Ireland. Even Canning, while still a servant of the Tories, could not view the misery of Ireland without emotion; and he showed in a naively touching manner how dear the cause was to him at a time when he was accused of apathy. It is true that a great man, in order to obtain great ends, can often act contrary to his convictions, and pass equivocally from one party to another; but in such cases, it is only fair to admit that he who would maintain himself on a height, must yield to circumstances, like the weather-cock on the church steeple, which though made of iron, would soon break off and tumble down at every gust of wind if it remained obstinately fixed and failed to understand the noble art of veering. But a great man will never be able so far to deny the feelings in his soul as to look with calm indifference on the misfortunes of his own countrymen. We love the soil on which we were born, as we love our mother—as we love the flowers, the fragrance, the language, and the men who have sprung from it. No religion is so evil, and no politics so good, that it can extinguish this love in the hearts of its adherents; and Burke and Canning, though Protestants and Tories, could not, for all that, take part against poor, green Erin.

Irishmen too, though they spread misery and unspeakable wretchedness throughout their country, are men—like the late Castlereagh.

It is to be expected that the great mass of Englishmen should be opposed to the Catholics and should every day storm Parliament in an effort to withhold privileges from them. There is in the human character a love of oppression; and even when we complain of civil inequalities, as so often happens today, we turn our eyes upward—we see only those who stand above us, and whose privileges outrage us. But we never look down when we complain. It never occurs to us to raise to our own level those whom the injustice of custom has placed below us. Yes, we are thoroughly outraged when they, too, strive to attain our level; and we rap them soundly over their heads. The Creole demands the rights Europeans possess; but he lords it over the Mulatto, and flares up in rage when the latter demands equality. Just so does the Mulatto behave toward the Mestizo, and the latter, in turn, toward the Negro. The petty bourgeois of Frankfurt are vexed at the privileges of the nobles; but they are even more outraged when it is suggested that they emancipate the Jews. A friend of mine in Poland raves about freedom and equality, but to date he has not emancipated his own peasant-serfs.

So far as the English clergy is concerned, no explanation is needed to show why they are persecuting the Catholics. Persecution of those who think differently is everywhere a monopoly of the clergy; and the Anglican Church strongly affirms her rights in this regard. Naturally, tithes are to her a matter of prime consideration. As a result of the emancipation of the Catholics, she would lose a great portion of her income. The sacrifice of self-interest is a talent which is manifested by church preachers of love as rarely as by the sinful laity. Furthermore the Glorious Revolution,[4] to which England owes her present freedom, arose out of Protestant zeal, a circumstance which imposes upon the English special obligations of gratitude toward the dominant Protestant Church, and causes them to regard her as the chief bulwark of freedom. There are many timid souls today who dread the restoration of Catholicism, and recall the flaming piles at Smithfield. And a burned child shuns the fire!

There are also some timid members of Parliament who dread a new Gunpowder Plot[5]—those fear powder most who have not discovered it—and so they often feel as if the green benches in St. Stephen's chapel on which they are sitting were gradually becoming hotter and hotter. Name Guy Fawkes, and they cry out in panic,

"Hear! Hear!" And finally, as for the Rector of Göttingen, who has a post in London as the King of England, everyone is familiar with his policy of moderation.[6] He declares himself in favor of neither party. He loves to see them weaken each other in struggle. He smiles in his traditional way when they court him peaceably. He knows everything and does nothing. At the worst, he turns everything over to his chief constable, Wellington.

ਣ❧ Wellington

THIS MAN IS UNFORTUNATE BECAUSE HE HAS ALWAYS been lucky where the greatest men of the world have met with misfortune; and that angers us and makes him hateful. We see in him only the triumph of stupidity over genius—Arthur Wellington was victorious where Napoleon Bonaparte was overwhelmed. Never was a man more ironically endowed by Fortune. It seems as if she would display his empty littleness by raising him high on the shield of victory. Fortuna is a woman, and in the way of woman she probably cherishes a secret grudge against the man who overthrew her former darling, although the overthrow itself was willed by her. Now she lets him conquer again on the Catholic Emancipation question,[7] and in the very struggle in which Canning was ruined. He might have been loved had the miserable Londonderry been his predecessor in the ministry; but he is the successor of the noble Canning, the much-lamented, admired, great Canning—and he triumphs where Canning was destroyed. Without such a fortunate adversity, Wellington would perhaps pass for a great man; people would not hate him; they would not measure him too accurately—at least not with the heroic scale with which Napoleon or Canning is measured, and the world would never have discovered how small a man he is.

He is a small man, and less than small. The French could say nothing more cruel of Polignac than that he was a Wellington without glory. In fact, what remains when we strip a Wellington of the field marshal's uniform of glory?

I have here given the best apology for Lord Wellington—in the English sense of the word. Some of my readers will be astonished when I honestly confess that I once praised this hero, with full sails, so to speak. It is a good story, and I will tell it here:

My London barber was a radical named Mr. White—a poor, little fellow in a shabby black coat, so worn that it was almost threadbare. He was so lean that his full face looked like a profile, and the sighs in his bosom were visible even before they rose. For he was always sighing over the misfortunes of Old England,—and over the impossibility of paying the National Debt.

"Ah," I often heard him sigh, "what need the English people trouble themselves as to who reigns in France, and what the French are doing at home? The nobility and the Church were afraid of the principles of liberty of the French Revolution, and to suppress these principles, John Bull is forced to give his blood and his gold, and incur debts into the bargain. We have all we want out of this war. The Revolution has been put down; the French eagle of liberty has had his wings clipped; the nobles and the Church can be sure that he will not fly across the Channel; and now they should at least pay the debts which were incurred for their sake and not for the sake of the poor people. Alas, the poor people—"

Whenever Mr. White spoke of the "poor people," he sighed more deeply than ever, and his constant refrain was that bread and beer were so much dearer, and that the poor people must starve to feed the fat lords, staghounds, and priests; and there was only one remedy. At these words he would whet his razor, and as he drew it up and down the strop, he murmured grimly and slowly: "Lords, hounds, priests!"

But his radical rage boiled most fiercely against the Duke of Wellington; he spat gall and poison whenever he referred to him, and when he lathered my face, he foamed with rage. Once I was badly frightened when, while he was shaving me close to my neck, he declaimed violently against Wellington, and murmured constantly: "If only I had him here under my razor, I'd save him the trouble of cutting his own throat, as his brother in office and fellow countryman, Londonderry did, who cut his throat at North Cray in Kent—God damn him!"

I felt the man's hand shake, and fearing that in his violence he might suddenly take me for the Duke of Wellington, I sought to allay his passion and calm him. I appealed to his national pride. I represented to him that the Duke of Wellington had advanced the glory of the English, that he had always been the innocent instrument of others; that he loved beefsteak, and finally that—the Lord only knows what fine things I said about Wellington as I felt the razor tickling at my throat.

WHAT VEXES ME MOST, HOWEVER, is the reflection that Arthur Wellington will be as immortal as Napoleon Bonaparte. Has not the name of Pontius Pilate in a similar way become as unforgettable as that of Christ? Wellington and Napoleon! It is a wonderful phenomenon that the human mind can think of both at the same time. There can be no greater contrast than these two, even in their external appearance. Wellington, the inane specter, his ashen-grey soul in a parchment body, a wooden smile on his frozen face—and by his side, think of the figure of Napoleon, every inch a god!

This image will not soon fade from my memory. I still see him, high on horseback, with those eternal eyes in his imperial marble face, looking down calm as destiny on the Guards filing past—he was then sending them to Russia—and the old grenadiers looked up at him, with terrifying devotion, so understandingly serious, so proud in death.

"Te Caesar, morituri salutant!" [8]

Sometimes I am assailed by a secret doubt whether I ever actually saw him; whether we were ever contemporaries; and then it seems to me as if his portrait, torn from its little frame of the present, were retreating farther and farther into the dusk of the past. Even now his name already sounds like a word from an earlier world, as ancient and heroic as that of Alexander or Caesar. It has already become a rallying cry among nations, and when the East and the West meet they commune by means of this one name.

How full of meaning and magic the sound of the name can be, I once discovered when I was in the port of London, at the India Docks, and stood on board an East Indiaman just arrived from Bengal. It was a huge ship manned by numerous Hindus. The grotesque forms and groups, the singularly variegated dress, the enigmatical expressions, the strange gestures, the wild and foreign ring of their speech, the shouts of joy and laughter, and the seriousness in their soft yellow faces,—their eyes, like black flowers which looked on one with strange woe—all these awakened in me a feeling as of enchantment. I was suddenly transported into Scheherazade's story, and I thought I was already seeing the broad-leaved palms, the long-necked camels, the gold-laden elephants and other fabled trees and animals. The supercargo, who was on the vessel, and who understood as little of the language as I, could not, in his true English narrowness, sufficiently disparage the ridiculous men, most of them Mohammedans gathered from all parts of Asia, from the borders of China to the Arabian Ocean. There were even a few jet-black, woolly-haired Africans among them.

Quite surfeited as I then was with the spiritless West, and Europe-weary, I found this fragment of the East—which moved so cheerfully and so full of color before my eyes—a refreshing comfort; my heart rejoiced in the few drops of that potion for which I had languished in the gloomy Hanoverian and Royal Prussian winter nights. It is possible that the strangers saw how agreeable the sight of them was to me, and how gladly I would have spoken a kind word to them. It was also plain from their sincere looks that they were pleased with me, and would also gladly have said something pleasant to me, and it was annoying that neither of us understood the language of the other. At last I found the way of expressing my friendly feelings to them in a single word, and stretching out my hand reverently, as in a loving greeting, I cried the name, "Mohammed!"

Joy suffused the dark faces of these strangers. They folded their arms reverently and cried in exultant response, "Bonaparte!"

ᣜ *England and France*

[*1832*]

THE FRENCH BELIEVE THAT THE ENGLISH PEOPLE cherish a love of free-dom like theirs; that, like themselves, they are struggling against the usurpations of an aristocracy, and that many external as well as in-ternal interests guarantee a close alliance between them. But they do not know that the English people are thoroughly aristocratic. That they demand freedom in a narrow, corporate sense—that is, liberties secured by documents. That the French conception of freedom—freedom for all mankind—in which the whole world will share in ac-cordance with a charter of reason, is profoundly repugnant to the English character. The latter know only English freedom—historical English freedom, either patented for the use of royal Britannic sub-jects, or based on ancient law—say, of the time of Queen Anne. Burke,[9] who wished to "burke" souls, and sacrifice life itself to the dead skeleton of history, reproaches the French Revolution prin-cipally because it did not arise like that of the English from an old institution. He cannot understand how a state can exist without the nobility. But the nobility of England are altogether different from the *noblesse* of France, and deserve discriminating praise. The nobility of England have always been opposed to the absolutism of the king, and have made common cause with the people, whose rights they asserted, as well as their own. The nobility of France on the other hand, submitted to royal prerogative—whether in or out of favor. Since the time of Mazarin,[10] they have not resisted the power of the king. They have merely sought to share it through pliant courtiership; and through the most subservient lackeying they helped the king oppress and betray the people. Unwittingly, the French nobility avenged their former wrongs at the royal hand, by seducing the king to the point where his morals were corrupted, and flattering him to the point of idiocy. Naturally, themselves weakened and debilitated, they went down to ruin along with the monarchy. The Tenth of August found only a host of decrepit ancients in the Tuileries, with fragile rapiers; and it was not a man but a woman who spurred them on to resist with firmness and courage. But even this last lady of French chivalry, this last representative of an ancient dying regime, was also not destined to go down to her grave in all the glory of youth—for in a single night the blonde locks of the beautiful Antoinette turned as white as snow.

England's nobility fared better. They have preserved their vigor. Their roots are among the people, in that healthy soil which receives the younger sons of the nobility as shoots, and thereby, the gentry remains allied with the nobility. In addition, the English nobility are full of patriotic ardor. They have thus far truly defended England's interests with undisguised zeal; and those Lords who cost England so much have also in time of need made sacrifices for the sake of their country. It is true that they are arrogant—much more so than even the nobles on the continent, who make such a show of their pride, and differentiate themselves from the rest of the people by means of ribbons, bad French, coats of arms, crosses, and similar gew-gaws. The English nobility despise the middle classes too much to think it essential to impress them through externals, and to exhibit publicly the many colored symbols of their power. No, English lords move like gods, incognito, in the simple attire of citizens, unobserved, in the streets, at the balls and theaters of London. Feudal decorations and other tinsel they reserve for court festivals and ceremonial occasions. Hence they are more highly regarded by the people than are

our continental gods, who gad about with their too easily recogniz-
able attributes. One day on Waterloo Bridge I heard one boy saying
to another: "Have you ever seen a nobleman?" To which the other
replied: "No, but I've seen the coach of the Lord Mayor." This coach
is an enormous chest, excessively gilded, fabulously bedizened, with a
coachman in red velvet, stiff with gold, and a powdered wig, and three
ditto lackeys with powdered wigs behind on the box. If the English
people quarrel with their nobility, it is not on account of social
equality, of which they never think, and least of all on account of civil
liberty, which they enjoy in full—but merely out of consideration for
money. For the nobility are in possession of all sinecures, ecclesiastical endowments and highly lucrative preferments, and revel in-
solently amid luxury; while the greater part of the people are over-
burdened with taxes and repine in abysmal wretchedness and perish
of hunger. Hence they demand parliamentary reform, and those
among the nobility who support it, do so with only material amelioration in mind.

Indeed, the nobility of England are more closely bound to the
people than to their kings, from whom they have always succeeded
in maintaining their independence, unlike the French aristocracy.
They placed their swords and their word at the king's disposal; but
they participated in his private life and lusts only moderately as con-
fidantes. This holds of even the most corrupt times. Hamilton in his
Memoirs of the Duke of Grammont gives us a clear picture of these
relations.[11] Thus the English nobility have continued to the present,
kissing the royal hand and kneeling in accordance with court etiquette,
but as a matter of fact, they stood on the same footing as the king,
whom they opposed vigorously the moment their privileges were
threatened, or their influence jeopardized. The latter occurred in the
most public manner a few years ago, when Canning became prime
minister.[12] If a similar thing had taken place in the Middle Ages, the
English barons would have broken into the royal castle, in helmet
and cuirass, sword in hand, accompanied by their vassals; and with
ironical humility but armored courtesy they would have defiantly
wrung their demands from him. In our days, they had recourse to less
chivalrous means. As we all know, the nobility who composed the
ministry endeavored to coerce the king by tendering their resignation without prior warning and by perfidious arrangement. The results are well known. George IV relied on George Canning, the St.
George of England, who came near slaying the mightiest dragon on

earth. After him came Lord Goderich, with his ruddy, smug face and his affected barrister voice, who very soon let the lance fall from his weak hand to which it had been entrusted, so that the poor king was obliged to throw himself on the mercy of his old barons—for good or evil—and the field-marshal of the Holy Alliance again resumed the staff of office. I have shown elsewhere why no liberal minister can do any good in England, and must resign in favor of the Tories, who can pass a grand bill for amelioration the more easily since they do not have to overcome the parliamentary opposition of their own obstinacy.

The devil has ever built the best churches. Wellington achieved that emancipation for which Canning fought in vain, and perhaps he is destined to carry the reform bill on which Lord Grey will probably be shipwrecked. I foresee the speedy fall of the latter, and then all those irreconcilable aristocrats who have for the past forty years been carrying on a life and death struggle with the French people, who are the representatives of democratic ideas, will return to power. This time the old grievances will yield to private interest, and they will be pleased to see their more dangerous opponent in the East and his satellites fought by French arms—all the more readily, since the antagonists will weaken each other. Yes, the English will surely arouse the Gallic cock to fight with the eagles of absolutism, and as eager spectators they will crane their long necks across the Channel and applaud, as at the cock-pit, and wager thousands of guineas on the outcome.

Will the great gods above, in the blue pavilion of heaven, look on this spectacle with equal indifference? Will those Englishmen of heaven, look down on the life and death struggle of nations, with leaden gaze, heartless, and heedless of our cries for help and the blood that is spilled? Perhaps the poet was right in declaring that just as we hate monkeys because of all the mammals they resemble us most, and thereby wound our vanity, so the gods hate men, who were made in their own image, and offend them by their close resemblance. And the greater, fairer, and more god-like men become, the more cruelly do the gods scourge them with misfortune and destruction. But they graciously spare the ugly little man-mammals and allow them to prosper. If this melancholy reflection is correct, then the French are much closer to annihilation than any other people. Alas, may the sad example of the end which befell their Emperor teach them what is to be expected of magnanimous England! Did not the "Bellerophon" some time ago abduct the Chimaera? [13] May France never rely on England, as Poland relied on France!

৪৺ *Lafayette*

LET DELUDED FRIENDS AND HYPOCRITICAL ENEMIES say what they will, Lafayette is, after Robespierre, the purest character of the French Revolution, and next to Napoleon, its most popular hero. Napoleon and Lafayette are the two names which shine brightest in France. True, their fame is of a different kind. Lafayette fought for peace more than for victory; Napoleon more for the laurel wreath than for the oak leaves. It would indeed be ridiculous to attempt to measure the greatness of the two heroes with the same standard, and set the one on the pedestal of the other. It would be absurd to set the statue of Lafayette on the Vendome column—that pillar cast of the cannon captured on so many fields of battle, the sight of which, as Barbier sings, no French mother can endure. On this column place Napoleon, the man of iron; here, as in life, he rests on the fame earned by his cannons, soaring in awful isolation far into the clouds, so that every ambitious soldier beholding the unattainable one may feel his heart humbled and healed of the vain passion for fame. In this way, the giant column of metal may serve as a lightning conductor of conquering heroism, and prove most profitable for the peace of Europe.

Lafayette has raised for himself a better column than that in the Place Vendome, and a better statue than one made of metal or marble. Where will you find marble as pure as the heart of Lafayette? Where metal as firm as his loyalty? It is true that he was one-sided—as one-sided as the magnetic needle which always points north, and never south or east. Lafayette has for forty years said the same thing, and constantly pointed to North America. He is the man who opened the Revolution with the declaration of the rights of man; and to this very hour he has persevered in that declaration without which there can be no salvation. The one-sided man with his one-sided pole of freedom! Indeed, he is no genius, as was Napoleon, in whose head the eagles of inspiration nested, while the calculating serpents twined in his heart. But then he has never been affrighted by eagles, or seduced by serpents. As a young man he was as wise as a grey-beard; as a grey-beard he is as fiery as a youth. He is a protector of the people against the snares of the great; a protector of the great against the rage of the people;—compassionate, yet a comrade-in-arms; never arrogant, never dismayed, equable in firmness and mildness. Thus Lafayette has ever remained the same. In this one-sidedness, in this temperateness he has now stood steadfast, on the same spot, since the days of Marie Antoinette—a trusty Eckhart of liberty. So he stands today, leaning on his sword, pronouncing warning, at the entrance of the Tuileries, that seductive Venusberg, whose siren notes sing so enticingly, and from whose snares the poor entangled wretches can never free themselves.

It is true that the dead Napoleon is more beloved by the French than the living Lafayette. This may be because the former is dead—which, to me at least is the most pleasing aspect of him. For, were he alive, I should be obliged to fight against him. Outside of France, few people realize with how much devotion the French still regard Napoleon. Hence even those who are discontented, when they determine upon some decisive action, always begin by proclaiming the young Napoleon, in order to secure the sympathy of the masses. "Napoleon" is a magic word to the French; it electrifies and stuns them. In his name a thousand cannons sleep, even as in the column on the Place Vendome. And the Tuileries will tremble when these cannons awake. As the Jews never pronounce the name of God in vain, so Napoleon is seldom mentioned by name—he is always spoken of as "the Man"—"*l'homme*." But his likeness can be seen everywhere, in engravings and plaster, in metal and wood, in all kinds of postures. On all the boulevards and squares you will hear orators praising him, and street-singers chanting his deeds. Last night, returning home, I came to a dark and deserted alley where stood a child no more than three, who by the light of the tallow candle stuck in the ground was lisping the glories of the great Emperor. When I threw a sou into the handkerchief which was spread out on the ground, something stirred close to me—and a voice implored me for another sou. It was an old soldier who could also sing a song of glory to the great Emperor— glory which had cost him both his legs. The poor cripple did not beg in the name of the Lord—but with the most sincere fervor he implored: "*Au nom de Napoléon, donnez-moi un sou.*" Thus this name serves as a profound adjuration among the people. Napoleon is their god, cult, and religion—a religion which will in the end become as tiresome as every other. Lafayette, on the other hand, is venerated more as a man and as a guardian angel. He too lives in picture and song—but less heroically. To tell the truth, I was amused when last year, on July 28th, I heard the song of *La Parisienne*, with these words:

"Lafayette aux cheveux blancs"— [14]

and saw him in person standing near by, in his brown peruke. It was at the Place de la Bastille. The man was in the right place, and still I had to laugh to myself. It may be that this comic admixture brings him closer to our hearts as a human being. His good-nature affects even children; for these understand his greatness better even than the great. On this subject I have a little story about a beggar, which will indicate the contrast between the glory of Lafayette and Napoleon. As I was recently standing at a street corner before the Pantheon, contemplating this beautiful building—as is my custom, a little Auvergnat accosted me for a sou. I gave him a ten-sou piece to be rid of him. But he approached me more familiarly with the words: *"Est-ce que vous connaissez le général Lafayette?"* And when I nodded assent to this strange question, an expression of proud satisfaction appeared on the simple and dirty face of the handsome boy, and with a serio-comic mien he said, *"Il est de mon pays."* For he naturally believed that any man who gave him ten sous must be an admirer of Lafayette, and he judged me worthy of presenting himself as a compatriot of that great man.

The countryfolk too have for Lafayette the most affectionate regard—all the more sincere since agriculture is his chief preoccupation. As a result he has been able to preserve that freshness and simplicity which are so easily lost in the bustle of city life. In this respect, he resembles those great Republicans of old who planted their own cabbage, but who, in time of need, hastened from the plough to battle or to the tribune, and after obtaining victory, returned to their rustic pursuits. On his estate, where he passes the most pleasant part of the year, Lafayette is generally surrounded by ambitious young men and beautiful girls. Here open hospitality of heart and table reigns, here are laughter and dancing; here is held the court of the sovereign people. Here anyone may be presented who is the son of his own deeds, and has not entered into a misalliance with fraud. Here Lafayette is master of ceremonies.

But more than among any other class, it is among the middle classes, the tradespeople and small shopkeepers, that Lafayette has won the greatest veneration. They worship him. Lafayette, the founder of their order, is their idol. They adore him as a kind of providence on horse-back, as an armed tutelary patron of public security, as the genius of liberty who also sees to it that during the battles for freedom nothing is stolen and everyone keeps what is his. That great army of public order, as Casimir Périer called the National Guard, the well-fed heroes with their bearskin caps, is beside itself with delight when it speaks of Lafayette, its old general, its Napoleon of peace. Yes, he is the Napoleon of the petty bourgeoisie, of those decent, trustworthy people, that class of shopkeepers, who are too busy during the day to think of him, but who praise him at night with redoubled enthusiasm, so that one may say that around eleven o'clock, when all the shops are closed, Lafayette's fame is at its peak.

I have just used the term "master of ceremonies." I now recall that Wolfgang Menzel, in his witty frivolity, once called Lafayette Liberty's Master of Ceremonies, when in the *Literaturblatt* he described his triumphal march through the United States, and the deputations, addresses, and solemn discourses which took place on that occasion.[15] Others, much less wittily, wrongly imagine that Lafayette is but an old man who is being kept for show or used as some kind of Jack-in-the-box. However, if these people could only hear him speak once from a public forum, they would at once understand that he is not merely a flag to be followed or sworn by, but a *gonfalonier*, in whose hands the good banner, the oriflamme of the people, rests securely. Lafayette is probably the most important orator in the present Chamber of Deputies. When he speaks, he not only hits the nail on the head, but also the wooden heads of his enemies. When occasion demands and the issue is one that touches the interests of humanity, Lafayette is always on his feet, as eager for battle as a youth. Only his body is weak and unsteady, broken by time and war, dented and hacked like an old iron armor. It is touching to see him drag himself to the tribune, draw a deep breath and smile when he reaches his old post. The smile, the delivery, the whole deportment of the old man while he is speaking are indescribable. There is graciousness in it—delicately flavored with irony—that enchants like some strange curiosity or some delightfully tempting enigma. One does not know whether these are the refined manners of a French marquis or the straightforwardness of an American citizen. All that is best in the ancient regime, chivalry, courtesy, and tact, are here wonderfully fused with the best of the modern citizen, love of equality, simplicity, and honesty. Most interesting of all is to see how, on occasions, when mention is made in the Chamber of the early days of the Revolution and some doctrinaire wrenches a historical fact from its true context and turns it to his own account, Lafayette in a few words destroys these fallacies by illuminating or correctly interpreting the true meaning of the event, or by citing the relevant circumstances. Even Thiers must in such a case strike sail, and the great historiographer of the Revolution is forced to bow before the utterances of its great, living monument—General Lafayette.

Facing the tribune of the Chamber, sits an ageless old man, with shining silver hair which falls over his black coat. His figure is wound in a broad tricolor scarf. He is the old Messenger who has filled that office in the Chamber since the outbreak of the Revolution, and who has, in this post, witnessed the whole course of world history, from the days of the First National Assembly to the *juste milieu*. I am informed that he often speaks of Robespierre, whom he calls *"le bon Monsieur de Robespierre."* During the Restoration the old man suffered from colic; since then, however, he has once more wound the tricolor scarf around him and feels sound again. What ails him nowadays is an attack of drowsiness brought on by these dull, *juste milieu* days. Once in a while, I have even seen him fall asleep while Mauguin was speaking. The man has without doubt heard better orators than Mauguin, who is, nevertheless, one of the best speakers of the opposition, though not impassioned enough for one *"qui a beaucoup connu ce bon Monsieur de Robespierre."* But when Lafayette speaks, the old man wakes from his twilight sleep, rouses himself like an old cavalry horse at the sound of the trumpet, and overcome by sweet memories of youth, nods his silver-white head with delight. . . .

❧ *Guizot and England*

[*1840*]

M. GUIZOT HAS PROVED THAT HE IS AN HONEST MAN; he neither has seen through the treachery of the English, nor been able to bring it to naught by counterplots.[16] He returns to Paris an honest man; and this year's annual prize for virtue, the *Prix Monthyon*, will be awarded him without dispute.[17] Be calm, oh, Roundhead Puritan, the faithless Cavaliers have taken you in and made a fool of you; but you have been left with the proud consciousness of your merit—the consciousness that you were ever yourself. As a Christian and doctrinaire you will bear your misfortunes patiently, and since we can laugh at you heartily, our hearts expand with kindness. You are again our dear old schoolmaster, and we rejoice that worldly splendor has not robbed you of your pious, magisterial naiveté; that you've been hoaxed and duped, but that you've remained honest! We begin to love you. But we will never entrust you again with the embassy to London; for what is needed there is a vulture's eye to spy out all the intrigues of perfidious Albion in time, or an altogether boorish, ignorant fellow, who has no academic sympathy for the British form of government, and who cannot make polite "speeches" in English, but who responds in French, when they want to take him in with equivocal phrases. I advise the French to send to London as ambassador the first grenadier of the Old Guard whom they find, and have Vidocq accompany him as the actual private secretary of the legation.

But are the English really such clever heads at politics? In what does their superiority in this field consist? I believe it lies in the fact that they are arch-prosaic creatures; they do not allow themselves to be led astray by poetic illusions; they are not deceived by glowing wild fancies; they see everything in the most sober light; they keep the bare facts constantly before their eyes; they calculate accurately the conditions of time and place, and while doing so are not disturbed by the beating of their hearts or the flutterings of their noblest thoughts. Yes, their superiority consists in the fact that they do not possess imagination. This shortcoming constitutes the whole *forte* of the English, and is the ultimate reason for their success in politics, as in all realistic undertakings—industry, building of machinery, etc. They have no imagination. That is the whole secret. Their poets are merely brilliant exceptions to this rule. That is why they come into conflict with the people—the snub-nosed, low-browed people, without occiput—that chosen people of prose, who behave in India and in Italy in that same prosaic and calculating way in which they behave in Threadneedle Street. They are intoxicated by the perfume of the lotus as little as they are warmed by the fires of Vesuvius. They drag their urns to the edge of the crater, and there drink tea, seasoned with cant!

I hear Taglioni [18] found no favor in London last year. That is indeed her great glory. Had she pleased the people there I should have begun to question the poetry of her feet. The sons of Albion are the most frightful of dancers, and Strauss affirms that not one of them knows how to keep time. He was sickened to death in watching an old English dance in Middlesex county. The creatures have no ear, whether for time, or for music, and their unnatural passion for piano playing and singing is all the more repugnant. There is really nothing quite so horrible as English music, unless it be English painting. They have neither ear for music—nor eye for color—and I sometimes suspect that their sense of smell is blunted and sniffling. It is likely that they cannot distinguish crab-apples from oranges by smell!

But are they courageous? That is at the present moment the most important question. Are the English as brave as they are sometimes depicted on the Continent? The far-famed magnanimity of *Mylords* is now to be met with only on our stage; and it is quite possible that the superstition about the cold-blooded courage of the English will likewise vanish in time. We are filled with strange misgivings when we see that it only takes a few mounted troops to disperse 100,000 Englishmen. Though the English may possess great individual courage, the masses are enervated by habits of ease born of more than a century of peace,—for all this time they have been without internal dissensions. So far as wars abroad are concerned, they did not wage them in their own persons, but with mercenaries, suborned brigands, and hireling nations. It would never occur to a citizen of London— not even the Lord Mayor himself—to let himself be shot in defense of the national interest. For that purpose they hire others. As a result of this protracted peace, excessive wealth and misery, political corruption due to a representative constitution, the debilitating factory system, a fully developed commercial spirit, religious hypocrisy, zealotry—this worst of opiates—the English have become as unwarlike a people as the Chinese. The French will sooner succeed in conquering all of England, and with fewer than a hundred thousand men—provided they effect a landing—than the English will conquer China. In Napoleon's day, the English were constantly threatened with this prospect, and the country was defended not by its inhabitants but by the sea. Had France possessed a navy then, such as she now has, or had the recently invented steamboat been used to as great advantage then as it is now, Napoleon would surely have landed on the coast of England—as once did William the Conqueror—and probably would have met with no great resistance; for he would have destroyed the privileges of the Norman nobility obtained by conquest, defended the property of the commoners, and united British freedom with French equality.

These thoughts came to my mind yesterday forcefully as I was watching the funeral procession of the heroes of July. The vast throng attending the rites behaved with gravity and pride. It was an imposing sight, and very significant today. Are the French afraid of the new allies? Certainly during the three July days they betrayed no sign of fear, and I can assure you that almost one hundred and fifty deputies who are still in Paris have declared themselves most decidedly in favor of war, should the insult to national honor demand that sacrifice. What is, however, most important is the fact that Louis Philippe seems to have said farewell to that long-suffering patience in the face of every wrong, and to have resolved on action should necessity dictate it. At least that is what he is saying, and M. Thiers assures us that he often finds it hard to mollify the burning indignation of the King. It may be that this warlike spirit is only the military ruse of a patient god-like Odysseus! [19]

⁊ *Thiers and Guizot* [20]

WHAT MOST AMAZES ME IN THE FRENCH is their adaptability, the skilful passing or leaping from one affair to another of an altogether different kind. This is not merely a trait of a volatile nature, but a historical inheritance; for in the course of time they have completely freed themselves from the bonds of prejudice and pedantry. Thus it happened that the émigrés who fled to Germany during the Revolution easily adjusted themselves to a change of circumstances; and many of them adopted some trade on the spur of the moment in order to gain a livelihood. My mother often told me of a French marquis who established himself as a shoemaker in our town. He made the best ladies' shoes; he worked with zest, and whistled the most delightful tunes, and forgot all of his former glory. A German nobleman would, probably, under similar circumstances, have taken to shoemaking, but he certainly would never have accommodated himself to his leather destiny quite so blithely, and he surely would have devoted himself to men's boots—such as reminded him of ancient knighthood. When the French crossed the Rhine, our marquis was forced to abandon his shop and flee to another town—I think it was Cassel—where he became the best tailor. Yes, without benefit of apprenticeship he migrated in this fashion from one trade to another, and became master of them all—a thing which would have been impossible for a German, not merely a German noble, but even a commoner. After the fall of the Emperor, the good man returned to his homeland; his hair was grey, but his heart was unaltered and young, and he put on such noble airs, and lifted his nose so proudly, as if he had never handled needle or awl. It is false to declare that the émigrés learned nothing and forgot nothing. On the contrary, they forgot everything they learned. The heroes of the Napoleonic war-epoch, who resigned or were pensioned, also threw themselves with the greatest aptitude into the peaceful arts of industry. Whenever I entered the office of Delloye, I was pleasantly surprised to see a one-time colonel sitting at his desk as a bookseller, surrounded by several white mustaches who had also fought bravely under the Emperor, but who were now employed as book-keepers or accountants—in other words as privates under their old comrade.

You can make anything you want of a Frenchman; each of them thinks himself fit to do everything. The most wretched dramatist is suddenly metamorphosed, as by a stage trick, into a minister, a general, a light of the Church, yes, even a god.

M. THIERS IS VERY BRUSQUE IN HIS OPPOSITION TO THE KING—at first. He resists with eloquence, sounds the trumpets and beats the drums—and ends by doing what the King wishes. Not only his revolutionary sentiments, but also his convictions as a statesman are in constant strife with the royal system. He senses and knows that this system must finally perish, and I could reveal some singular remarks of his on the instability of the present institutions. He knows his French compatriots and the history of the French Revolution too well to surrender totally to the quietism of the victorious bourgeois party, and to trust to the muzzle which he himself has imposed on the thousand-headed monster. His sharp ears catch the sound of the internal rumbling—he even fears that he may himself some day be torn to pieces by the unchained beast—and yet he does what the King wishes!

M. Guizot is quite different. For him, the victory of the bourgeoisie is an accomplished fact. He has entered with all his talents in the service of this new potentate, whose reign he vindicates as rational with all of his historical and philosophical acumen. Hence, he believes it is right. For that is the very nature of the doctrinaire: he always finds a doctrine to fit whatever he does. In his private convictions, it may well be, he stands above these doctrines—perhaps below them.

Who knows? He is intellectually too well endowed and too knowing and versatile not to be a sceptic at heart. And such scepticism agrees perfectly with the service which he is performing for the system to which he has attached himself. At present he is the loyal servant of the bourgeois regime, and he will defend it with the iron will of a Duke of Alba and with inexorable consistency to the very last moment. In him is neither wavering nor hesitation; he knows what he wants, and what he wants he does. If he is defeated in battle, his defeat in no wise unnerves him; he merely shrugs his shoulders. For the cause in which he is fighting is, in the last resort, a matter of indifference to him. Should ever the party of the Republicans or even of the Communists triumph, I advise these good people to take Guizot as their minister and profit from his intelligence and stubbornness. They will do much better than if they entrusted the reins to the hands of the most tried blockheads with bourgeois virtue. I would advise the Henriquinquists to do the same, in the inconceivable eventuality that they should ever, as a result of some natural disaster, or God's punishment, gain power. Take Guizot as your minister, and you will last thrice twenty-four hours more! I fear I do no injury to Guizot when I suggest that he would stoop so low as to lend his eloquence and his administrative abilities to your poor cause. For you are as much objects of indifference in his eyes as the Philistines on whom he expends so much talent in word and deed—or the system of the King whom he serves with such stoic equanimity!

ᣥ *The French and the Germans*

THEY ATTACK EVERY QUESTION DIRECTLY, and wrestle with it until it is either solved or thrown aside as insoluble. That is the character of the French, and their history, for this reason, unfolds like a judicial trial. What a logical and systematic sequence all the events of the French Revolution present! In this madness there was really method, and the writers of history, who, after the example of Mignet, attach but little importance to chance and human passions, represent the most extravagant deeds since 1789 as results of the sternest necessity. In France this so-called fatalistic school is quite in place, and its works are as truthful as they are easy to understand. The method of viewing and presenting history employed by these writers, would, if applied to Germany, produce very erroneous and incompetent works of history. For the German, from fear of any innovation the results of which cannot be easily ascertained, avoids every important question of politics as long as possible, or endeavors to find a proper adjustment by means of detours. The questions meanwhile accumulate and become more complicated till they form an inextricable knot which at last, like the Gordian, can only be cut by the sword.

Heaven forbid that I hereby cast reproach upon the great German people! Do I not know that every one of their crises is due to a virtue utterly wanting in the French? The more ignorant a nation, the more recklessly does it plunge headlong into the stream of action; but the more erudite, the more reflective a people, the longer does it sound the depths of the flood, through which it then wades with careful steps, assuming it does not hesitate and doesn't budge from the shore, for fear of hidden depths, or of the chilly dampness that might bring on a national cold. After all, it makes little difference if we advance slowly, or, by standing still, lose a few puny centuries, for the future belongs to the German people,—and it is a very considerable and long future. The French act so quickly and manage the present with such haste perhaps because they foresee that their twilight hour is approaching, and they are in a hurry to finish their day's work. But their role is still quite charming, and the other nations are still only an honorable public witnessing the French State and People's comedy. It is true that this public sometimes has the urge to express its approbation or disapproval very energetically, and even to climb up on the stage and take part in the play. But the French are always the principal actors in the great world-drama; whether people throw laurels or rotten apples at their heads.

"France is done for!" With such words many a German correspondent here scurries around, prophesying the fall of the present Jerusalem; but he ekes out a miserable existence by reporting what these degenerate Frenchmen perform daily, and his own employers, the German newspaper editors, would, without these Parisian letters, be unable to fill their columns for more than three weeks. No, France is not done for; but like all nations, and humanity itself, she is not eternal. She has perhaps outlived her glorious age, and it cannot be denied that she is changing. Her smooth brow is beginning to be wrinkled; grey hairs can be seen on her frivolous head, which is bowed as if with care.—For she no longer thinks only of today. She also thinks of tomorrow.

⮆ *Paris Dances*

I CAN WRITE VERY LITTLE about the society balls this season, for thus far I have graced very few of the soireés with my presence. The everlasting sameness gradually begins to pall on me; I don't see how people can endure it for any length of time. I can easily understand how the women do it. For them, the important thing is the display of their finery. Preparing for the ball, choosing the dress, getting dressed, combing the hair, practising smiles before a mirror—in short, all the tinsel and coquetry are their principal occupation and afford them the greatest pleasure. But for us men—who only have to put on our democratic black dress coats and shoes (those dreadful shoes!) a soirée is an inexhaustible source of ennui, punctuated by a few glasses of almond cordial and raspberry syrup. Of the magnificent music I shall not say a word. What makes the balls of the world of fashion even more tedious than they have any right to be is the prevalent mode of only making believe that you dance, so that the prescribed steps are executed as if you were walking: you move your feet indifferently,—almost resentfully. No one cares to amuse another. This egoism is reflected even in our social dancing today.

The lower classes, though they would gladly ape the world of fashion, have not as yet quite adopted this selfish, sham dancing. Theirs still possesses real life; though, unfortunately, of a very lamentable kind. I hardly know how to express the melancholy feeling that comes over me whenever I witness the dancing of the multitudes in the public places of amusement, at carnival time. Here the music which accompanies the dance—almost a *cancan*—is shrill, screeching and wild. You may ask, "What is a *cancan?*" Holy heavens, do you expect me to define the *cancan* for the *Allgemeine Zeitung?* Well, the *cancan* is a dance never seen in respectable society but only in common dance-halls, in which whoever is dancing it is promptly seized by the police and thrown out. I do not know whether this definition explains much, but it is not necessary that the people of Germany know too clearly what the *cancan* is. This much may be inferred from my description—that the reserve recommended by the late Vestris is not needed and that the French are often disturbed by the police while dancing this dance. The latter is a very singular form of abuse, and the thoughtful foreigner is amazed to see in the public halls where the quadrille is danced several police agents or municipal guards watching over the terpsichorean morals with a Cato-like mien. It is hard to understand how people keep on being cheerful and persist in dancing under such shameful supervision. But Gallic light-heartedness capers most joyfully when in a strait-jacket; and though the stern eye of the law prevents them from dancing the *cancan* with all the cynical precision demanded, the dancers know how to express their forbidden thoughts in all sorts of capers and exaggerated propriety—so that repression seems more indecent than naked expression would have been. I do not think that morality profits from this governmental interference and its show of arms at these dances. Forbidden fruit is sweetest and most tempting; and the subtle, often quite witty, circumvention of the censorship frequently has a more harmful effect than openly sanctioned licentiousness. This supervision of the pleasures of the people is characteristic of the present state of affairs, and shows how far the French have gone in the matter of freedom. . . .

ૐ. The Polish Temper

I NOW PROCEED FROM A DISCUSSION OF POLISH WOMAN to the political temper of the people, and I must admit that, in this over-excited nation, I have been struck by the pain which racks the breast of the Polish nobleman when he reviews the events of the last years. Even the non-Pole is filled with sympathy when he hears the tale of political tribulations which have befallen the Poles in so short a time. Many of our journalists smugly dismiss this feeling by saying flippantly: "The Poles have brought their fate on themselves by their disunity, and are therefore not to be pitied." This is a foolish extenuation. No nation, conceived as a unit, is guilty; its actions spring from an inner necessity; and its fate results from it. To the student the following sublime notion presents itself: History (Nature, God, Providence, etc.) manifests its great purposes in the case of individuals as well as whole nations; and individuals must suffer so that the whole may persist and flourish. The Poles, a Slav border-nation, seem by their very position to have been specifically designed to fulfill a definite function in world history. Their moral battle against national extinction has given rise to phenomena which have impressed upon the whole people a totally different character, and even influenced the character of their neighbors.

Hitherto, the character of the Pole was military, as I have already said. Every Polish nobleman was a soldier, and Poland herself a huge military academy. Today this is no longer the case. Very few Poles now seek to enter military service. Polish youths, however, demand some occupation; and a good portion has chosen another field than the military, that is, learning. Everywhere one meets evidences of this new intellectual orientation. Favored by time and place, it will in a few decades (as I have already indicated) give the national character a new stamp. Not long ago you yourself witnessed the joyous concourse of young Poles in Berlin, who penetrated into all realms of knowledge with their noble zest for learning and their exemplary application; and drank in philosophy at its source, in the lecture rooms of Hegel. Now, unfortunately, they are compelled by unhappy events to leave Berlin. It is an encouraging sign that the Poles are gradually divesting themselves of their blind predilection for French literature and are coming to honor German literature, which is more profound, though long neglected. They have learned from the profoundest German philosophers to school their taste. The latter fact proves that they have grasped the spirit of the times, whose earmark is science. Many Poles are now studying German, and a great number of German books are being translated into Polish. Patriotism has its share in this phenomenon. The Poles feared the total extinction of their nation. Observing how effectively a national literature contributes to national preservation (this may sound ridiculous, but is nevertheless true, and was told me in all seriousness by many Poles), they are attempting to create a Polish literature in Warsaw. It is, of course, a misconception to believe that literature, which is an organic product of a whole people, can be composed in the literary hothouse of a capital by a learned society. But good-will itself represents an auspicious beginning; and literature will bear magnificent fruit when it is conceived to be a national cause. This patriotic sentiment naturally leads to some errors, especially in the fields of poetry and history. Their poetry will have the cast of the resurgent movement; but it is to be hoped that it will throw off its French cut and come closer to the spirit of German Romanticism.

An amiable Polish friend of mine once said to me teasingly: "We have as good Romantic poets as you; but in our country they are confined in the mad-house."

In history, the political trials of the Poles have not always been conducive to objectivity. The history of Poland is likely to emerge as one-sided and without too close a relation to universal history. But all the more care will be taken to preserve what is important for Polish history. Especially now that the Poles have seen how barbarously their library in Warsaw was treated during the last war, they are more solicitous than ever that all their national monuments and documents be preserved. Hence, it seems, that one of the Zamoyskis has established a library of Polish history in distant—Edinburgh!

I call to your attention the many new works which have just come off the presses of Warsaw. So far as the available Polish literature is concerned, I refer you to the brilliant work by Kaulfuss.

I place much faith in this intellectual revolution in Poland. The whole nation appears to resemble an old soldier who has hung up his trusty sword and his laurel, and turns to the serener arts of peace, ponders the history of the past, explores the forces of nature, measures the stars or even the length of syllables, as Carnot did. For the Pole will wield the pen as skilfully as the lance, and will show himself as brave in the fields of knowledge as on the tried fields of battle. And because their intellects have lain fallow so long, the harvest will be all the more plentiful, and the fruit richer. The spirit of certain European nations has been quite dulled by so many collisions; and here and there its triumphant exertions—that is, its self-knowledge— has brought about its own destruction. Besides, the Poles will be the recipients of the finest fruits of many centuries of European culture, and while those nations which have hitherto labored to build the Babel's tower of European culture lie exhausted, our newcomers, with their Slavic adroitness and their undrained vigor, will be able to advance these labors.

ࣷ Polish Love of Freedom

IF THE WORD "FATHERLAND" OCCUPIES FIRST PLACE on the lips of Poles, "Freedom" has the second. A beautiful word! Next to love, certainly the most beautiful. But like the latter, it is also the most misunderstood, and frequently used to designate quite dissimilar things. This is likewise the case with the Poles. The freedom of the Poles is not the god-like freedom of Washington. Only very few, like Kosciuszko, have grasped it and sought to disseminate it. True, many individuals speak enthusiastically of freedom, but they make no attempt to emancipate their own peasants. The word Freedom, which sounds so lovely and sonorous in Polish history, was merely the slogan by means of which the nobility sought to extort from the king as many rights as possible in order to increase their own power and thus provoke anarchy. *C'était tout comme chez nous.* With us, too, in Germany, freedom meant nothing but turning the king into a beggar, so that the nobility might carouse all the more gluttonously and govern more arbitrarily; but no kingdom can long exist whose steward is fast-bound in his chair, and wields only a wooden sword. In fact, Poland's history is that of Germany in miniature; except for the fact that the Polish magnates did not free themselves so completely and become so independent of their rulers as our German ones; and German prudence succeeded in gradually introducing some order into anarchy.

Had Luther, man of God and of Catherine, stood before the diet of Cracow, he would not have been permitted to speak with such freedom as he did at Augsburg. However, this principle of unrestrained freedom, which may be preferable to tranquil servitude, has, despite its glory, plunged Poland into misery. But it is amazing to see how that mere word "Freedom" affects their spirit; they burn and glow whenever they hear that somewhere people are fighting for it; their eyes light up when they turn toward Greece and South America. In Poland herself, as I have said, repression of freedom has come to mean only the restraints imposed upon the privileges of the nobility, or even the eventual levelling of the classes. We understand things much better; we know that 'freedoms' must perish, so that universal legal freedom may prosper.

❧ The New Pantheism

THE IMMEDIATE END OF ALL OUR MOST RECENT REFORMS is the rehabilitation of matter—the restoration of its proper dignity, its moral recognition, its religious sanctification, its reconciliation with spirit.

Purusa will once more be wedded to Prakriti. It was as a result of their violent sundering—as the Indian myth so ingeniously relates—that the great schism came into the world and evil arose.

Do you know what evil is in this world? Spiritualists have always charged that pantheism obliterates the boundaries between good and evil. But evil is in part only the illusion in their own conception of the world. In part it is the actual consequence of their own world-order. According to them, matter is in and of itself evil. In reality this is slander and a horrible blasphemy of God. Matter becomes evil only when it is forced to conspire secretly against the usurpations of spirit—when spirit defiles it, and matter, in self-contempt, prostitutes itself. Or when it avenges itself on spirit out of a desperate hatred. Evil is thus only the consequence of the spiritual world-order.

God is identical with the world. He manifests himself in plants, which lead a cosmic-magnetic life, without consciousness. He manifests himself in animals, which in their sensual dream-life lead a more or less dull existence. Most gloriously of all, he manifests himself in Man, who both feels and thinks, and who can distinguish his individual self from the objective world, and in his reason possesses those ideas which are revealed to him in the material world. In man divinity attains self-consciousness—and the latter in turn is revealed through man. This is achieved not in or through a single individual, but in and through the totality of mankind—so that every man comprehends and represents in himself only a portion of the God-Universe, but all men together comprehend and represent it in its totality—in idea as well as in reality. Every people may have the mission of understanding and revealing a portion of the God-Universe, of comprehending a series of phenomena, of bringing to perception a series of ideas, and, in turn, of transmitting the results to their successors, who have a similar mission.

Hence God is properly the hero of world-history—which is itself but His constant thinking, His constant acting, His word, His deed. And we may with justice say that all mankind is the incarnation of God!

It is erroneous to suppose that this religion of pantheism leads men to indifference. On the contrary, the knowledge of his divinity will inspire man to manifest it. Only then will the truly heroic deeds of true heroism glorify the earth.

The political revolution which is based on the principles of French materialism will find no enemies in the pantheists, but rather allies—allies who derive their convictions from a deeper source, from a religious synthesis. We promote the well-being of the material, the material well-being of the people, not because, like the materialists, we despise the spirit, but because we know that the divinity of man manifests itself also in his body. Human misery destroys or abases the body, which is the image of God—so that the spirit within also perishes.

We interpret the great words of the Revolution which St. Just pronounced, *"le pain est le droit du peuple,"* as meaning *"le pain est le droit divin de l'homme."* [21] We do not contend for the human rights of the people, but for the divine rights of man. In this, and in many other respects, we differ from the men of the Revolution. We do not wish to become *sans-culottes,* or frugal citizens, or economical presidents. We establish a democracy of equally glorious, equally holy, and equally happy gods. You ask for simple dress, austere manners, and unseasoned joys. We, on the other hand, demand nectar and ambrosia, purple raiments, costly perfumes, luxury and splendor, dances of laughing nymphs, music, and comedy. Oh, do not be angry, virtuous republicans! To your censorious reproaches, we say with the fool in Shakespeare, "Dost think because thou art virtuous, there shall be no more cakes and ale?"

The Saint-Simonians understood and desired something of the kind, but they were on an unfavorable terrain, and the materialism which surrounded them pressed them down—at least for a time. They were better appreciated in Germany, the most propitious soil for pantheism. It is the religion of our greatest thinkers and our best artists. Deism, as I shall show elsewhere, as a theory, has long since been dead there. It still maintains itself—like many other things—only among the unthinking masses, without a reasonable warrant. Though not publicly proclaimed, everyone knows that Pantheism is an open secret in Germany. We have, in fact, outgrown deism. We are free, and do not need a tyrant with thunder. We have come of age, and do not need paternal supervision. We are not the bungled handiwork of a great mechanic. Deism is a religion for slaves, children, Genevans and watchmakers.

ઠ➤ *On the Interpretation of History*

THE GREAT BOOK OF HISTORY lends itself to various interpretations.
Two divergent views concerning it stand out in bold relief. One regards the whole course of world-events merely as a depressing cycle
of recurrent phenomena. It views the life of nations—no less than the
lives of individuals—and all of organic nature in general—as a system
of growth, flowering, decline, and death—spring, summer, autumn,
and winter. "There is nothing new under the sun," is its motto; and
even the motto is not new, for two thousand years ago the King
of the East spoke it, and sighed. The proponents of this view shrug
their shoulders at civilization, which, they claim, will eventually relapse into barbarism. They shake their heads at our battles for freedom, which, in their eyes, only give rise to new tyrannies; they
smile at our aspirations which stem from our political enthusiasm to
make a better and happier world, and which eventually cool and
die out. They regard the history of mankind as little chronicles of
hopes, tribulations, misfortunes, sorrows and joys, errors and disen-
chantments, which fill the lives of men and constitute their whole
history. In Germany, the wiseacres of the historical school and the
poets of the art-epoch of Wolfgang Goethe incline to this viewpoint. These were in the habit of idealizing in the most saccharine
fashion a sentimental indifference to political affairs. Sufficiently well-
known is the fact that a certain government of North Germany has
understood the true value of that viewpoint. It commissions persons
to travel abroad, so that amid the elegiac ruins of Italy they may
cultivate a convenient and soothing fatalism, and thereafter in company and with the assistance of preachers of Christian servility and
by means of well-calculated journalistic *coups*, they may dampen the
three-day fever for freedom in the German people. Let him who
cannot rise by his own strength of mind, creep on the ground; but
the future will surely show that government how far one may go with
these creepers and intriguers!

Opposed to this quite fatal and fatalistic outlook is one which is
much brighter, and in greater harmony with the idea of providence.
According to this notion, everything in the world is in process of
gradual unfolding and flowering. The great heroes and heroic epochs
are only rungs in a ladder leading to a higher, god-like condition of

humanity, whose moral and political struggles will eventuate in a holy peace, in the purest brotherhood, and everlasting happiness. The golden age, it is claimed, lies not in the past, but in the future. We were not driven from Paradise with a flaming sword; it behooves us to win it with our flaming hearts, with love. The fruit of the tree of knowledge is not death, but everlasting life.

The word "Civilization" was for a long time the battle-cry of the adherents of this doctrine. In Germany it was preëminently the humanistic school that paid homage to it. It is well known with what determination the so-called philosophical school labored toward this end. It was especially conducive to an inquiry into political problems, and as the ripest fulfillment of this outlook it preached an ideal form of government, founded exclusively on reason, which would eventually ennoble and make blessed all of mankind. I have no need to name the inspired knights of this doctrine. Their highest aspirations are certainly more gratifying than the petty sinuousness of the lowly creepers. If we ever come to battle with them, let it be with our worthiest swords of honor; but we shall finish off the creeping slaves with the more fitting knout.

Neither view, however, harmonizes fully with our own vivid sense of life. On the one hand, we do not wish to be inspired uselessly and stake the best we possess on a futile past. On the other hand, we also demand that the living present be valued as it deserves, and not serve merely as a means to some distant end. As a matter of fact, we consider ourselves more important than merely means to an end. We believe that means and ends are only conventional concepts, which brooding man has read into Nature and History, and of which the Creator knows nothing. For every creation is self-purposed, and every event is self-conditioned, and everything—the whole world itself—is here, in its own right.

Life is neither means nor end. Life is a right. Life desires to validate this right against the claims of petrifying death, against the past. This justification of life is Revolution. The elegiac indifference of historians and poets must not paralyze our energies when we are engaged in this enterprise. Nor must the romantic visions of those who promise us happiness in the future seduce us into sacrificing the interests of the present, the immediate struggle for the rights of man, the right to life itself.

"*Le pain est le droit du peuple,*" said Saint-Just. And that is the greatest word spoken in the entire Revolution.

❧ Emancipation—The Great Task of the Day

I BEG YOU, DEAR READER, not to class me as an unqualified Bonapartist. My allegiance is not given to the actions, but to the genius of the man. Unconditionally I worship this man only until the eighteenth of Brumaire.[22] On that day he betrayed freedom. And he did so not from necessity, but out of a secret predilection for the aristocracy. Napoleon Bonaparte was an aristocrat, a noble foe of bourgeois equality. And it was a colossal error on the part of European aristocracy, represented by England, to wage such a mortal combat against him; for although he had set about changing the personnel of this aristocracy, he would, nevertheless, have preserved intact the greater portion of it, with its special privileges. He would have regenerated it. But instead, it now lies abased through weakness, loss of blood, and exhaustion—the consequence of its last—yes, its very last victory.

Dear reader! Once and for all, let us understand one another. I do not admire the deed—I admire only the human spirit. The deed is the vesture, and history is nothing but the old wardrobe of the human spirit. Yet love sometimes clings passionately to old clothes, and thus it is that I am enamored of the cloak of Marengo.

"We are on the battlefield of Marengo!" How my heart leaped with joy when the postillion uttered these words! I had left Milan in the evening in the company of a very agreeable Livonian, who rather liked to ape the Russians, and the following morning I saw the sun rise over the famous battlefield. Here it was that General Bonaparte drank so deeply of the cup of glory that, intoxicated by its fumes, he became Consul, Emperor, and conqueror of the world.— And he did not become sober until he reached St. Helena. We did not fare differently. We too partook of his intoxication, and dreamed the same dream. We were similarly awakened, and in the wretchedness of our sober state we gave ourselves over to all sorts of wise reflections.

It sometimes seems to us that the glory of war is an antiquated delight,—that the wars of today take on a nobler meaning, and that Napoleon was perhaps the last of the conquerors.

It really seems as if today spiritual rather than material interests are being fought over; as if the history of the world need no longer be the story of plunder, but a history of the spirit. The chief lever which ambitious and covetous princes knew to move so effectively for their personal ends—that is, nationalism, with its vanities and hatreds,—is now rotten and decayed. Foolish national prejudices are daily dwindling. Crude singularities are disappearing under the leveling tendencies of European civilization. In Europe, nations no longer exist—only parties. And it is odd to see how quickly these parties recognize one another despite their varied coloring, and understand one another despite differences of speech. Just as there is a material state policy—there is also a spiritual state policy. And just as the politics of state can turn the most trivial war between two most insignificant powers into a general European conflagration, in which all states must participate, whether they wish or not—but not disinterestedly—so throughout the world today, the spiritual significance of the most trivial struggle is at once recognized because of this party spirit, and the most distant and diverse parties are compelled to take sides, for or against. By virtue of this party politics—which I call "spiritual" politics because its interests are of a spiritual character and its *ultimae rationes* are not of base metal—two great opposing masses come into being (as also happened by reason of state policy), who stand opposite each other in hostile attitudes, and fight one another with words and looks. The watchwords and representatives of these two great parties change from day to day. There is no lack of confusion. Often there occur grave misunderstandings intensified rather than lessened by those diplomats of spiritual politics, the writers. Nevertheless, even if heads be in error, hearts feel keenly what they desire. And Time presses for the fulfillment of its great task.

And what is the great task of our day?

It is emancipation. Not simply the emancipation of the Irish, the Greeks, Frankfurt Jews, West Indian blacks, and all such oppressed peoples, but the emancipation of the whole world, and especially of Europe, which has now come of age, and is tearing itself loose from the apron-strings of the privileged classes, the aristocracy. Though certain philosophical renegades of freedom may forge chains of the finest syllogisms to prove to us that millions of men were merely created to serve as beasts of burden for a few thousand privileged knights—yet they cannot convince us, until they can prove to us, as Voltaire said, that the former came into the world with saddles on their backs, and the latter with spurs on their feet.

Every age has its own task, and when it is accomplished, mankind advances. The inequality which prevailed in an earlier day, imposed on Europe by feudalism, was perhaps necessary, or, in any case, a necessary condition for the progress of civilization. Today it is an obstacle, and revolts all civilized minds. The French, the most socially-conscious of people, have of necessity been most strongly incensed by this inequality, because it collides so wantonly with the principles of social existence. They have sought to enforce equality by tenderly cutting off the heads of those who aspired to rise above their fellows, and the Revolution was the signal for the war of liberation.

All honor to the French! They attended to the two greatest needs of human society: good food and civic equality. In the art of cooking and in freedom they have made the greatest strides; and if we ever sit down at a banquet and as equal guests celebrate amid good cheer the great reconciliation—for what can be better than a society of equals at a well-set table?—then we shall propose the first toast to the French. Naturally, it will be some time before we can hold this feast—before the emancipation is achieved. But the time will come at last, and we shall sit at the same table, reconciled and equal. We shall then be united, and together we shall fight against other universal evils—perhaps even against death itself—whose rigid system of equality is not as much of an insult as the insulting doctrine of inequality preached by an aristocracy.

Reader of a time to come, do not smile. Every age believes its battles to be more important than those preceding it. This is the proper faith of every age. In it, it lives and dies. And we too wish to live and die in this religion of freedom, which bears the name of religion with greater right than that hollow and exhausted specter which we have been accustomed to designate religion. Our holy war appears to us the most important of all that have hitherto been waged on the face of the earth, although historical premonition tells us that at some time in the future our grandchildren will probably regard this struggle with the same indifference with which we look down on the struggles of primitive man, who warred against equally greedy monsters, dragons, and robber giants.

৯ুখ *The Aristocracy*

WHAT WILL BE LEFT TO THE ARISTOCRACY when they are deprived of the crowned means of subsistence; when kings become the property of the people, and govern honorably and securely in accordance with the will of the people—the sole source of all power? What will the priests do when kings perceive that a few drops of oil do not give immunity against the guillotine, even as people every day see more and more clearly that they cannot make a meal of oblations? Naturally, there will be nothing left for the aristocracy and the clergy but to unite and cabal and intrigue against the new world-order.

Hopeless endeavor! Time, like a flaming giantess, strides forward, undeterred by the yelping of rabid little clerics and the Junkers at her feet. How they howl when they burn their snouts on touching her foot; or when, unwittingly she treads on their heads, so that they disgorge their secret poisons! Then, more spitefully, they vent their rage against the children of Time—and powerless against the mass, they wreak their cowardly vengeance on individuals.

Alas! we must admit that many a poor child of Time feels the blow none the less keenly which the lurking priests and the Junkers mete out to him in the dark. Alas! even though a halo encircle the wounds of the victors, they bleed and suffer none the less! Strange is the martyrdom which these victors endure in our time; it is not consummated with a bold confession—as was the case in an earlier day— when the martyr found a ready scaffold or a jubilant stake. The character of martyrdom has not changed: it still sacrifices all that is earthly for a heavenly jest; but it has lost much of its inner jubilant faith—it is now more resigned to sorrow, patient endurance, life-long dying. Not infrequently, in the cold grey hours, even the holiest of martyrs is assailed by doubt. There is nothing more horrible than those hours in which a Marcus Brutus begins to doubt the reality of Virtue, for which he has sacrificed all! He, alas, was a Roman and lived in the golden age of Stoicism. We, on the other hand, are of newer, softer stuff, and additionally, we see a philosophy spreading which pronounces all enthusiasm to be only of relative significance, and thereby destroys it within itself, or reduces it to a neutral kind of self-conscious Don-Quixotism.

Cold and shrewd philosophers! How compassionately they smile down at the self-tortures and crazy illusions of poor Don Quixote; and in all their school-room wisdom they do not mark that this very Don Quixotism is the most precious thing in life—that it is life itself—and that Don Quixotism lends wings to the whole world, and to all in it who philosophize, make music, plough, and yawn! For the greater portion of mankind, philosophers included, is, without being aware of it, nothing but a colossal Sancho Panza, who despite his sober fear of the cudgel, and his homely horse-sense, follows the mad knight on his dangerous adventures, lured by the promised reward, in which he believes because he desires it—but impelled even more by the mystic power which enthusiasm exercises over the great masses—as we see in all political and religious revolutions, as well as perhaps in the most trivial of daily affairs.

Thus, for example, you, dear reader, are the unwitting Sancho Panza of that crazy poet whom you follow through the mazes of this book—doubtless with head-shaking—but follow, none the less.

১ৼ *The Liberation*

SHOULD THE TIME FOR LEISURELY RESEARCH EVER RETURN, I will prove, in the most tedious and fundamental manner, that it was not India, but Egypt which originated that caste system which has for two thousand years disguised itself in every sort of national costume and has practised deception in every age in its own language—and which is now probably dead, but counterfeits the semblance of life, and wanders among us, evil-eyed and malignant, and poisons our flower of life with its odor of death.—Yes, like a vampire of the Middle Ages, it sucks blood from the people and the light from their hearts. From the slime of the Nile arose not only the crocodiles who know so well how to weep, but also those priests who understand it even better, and that privileged and hereditary caste of warriors who surpass in murderous lust and rapacity any crocodiles.

Two profound men of the German nation discovered the most salutary counter-charm against the worst of all Egyptian plagues, and through their black art—the printing press and gun-powder—they broke the might of that clerical and lay hierarchy which had constituted itself from a union of the priesthood and the warrior caste, the so-called Catholic Church and the feudal nobility, and which enslaved all of Europe in body and soul. The printing press burst asunder the dungeon of dogma in which the high priest of Rome had imprisoned souls. Northern Europe breathed freely once more, relieved of the incubus of the clergy, which though it had formally relinquished the hereditary Egyptian right of rank, had remained in spirit all the more faithful to the Egyptian priestly system, for it revealed itself glaringly as a corporation of bachelors kept alive not by natural propagation, but through a Mameluke-like system of recruiting. Likewise, we see that the warrior caste has lost its power. The old techniques are worth nothing under a modern system of warfare; for the strongest castle tumbles at the trumpet-tones of the cannon, as did the walls of Jericho. The steel harness of the knight is no greater safeguard against a rain of lead than the linen blouse of the peasant. Gun-powder makes all men equal. A citizen's musket fires as lustily as a nobleman's. The people are rising.

THE EARLIER EFFORTS WE READ ABOUT in the history of the Lombard and the Tuscan republics, of the Spanish communes, and of the free cities of Germany and other countries do not deserve to be classed as movements of the people. They were not aspirations toward liberty, but toward liberties; not battles for rights, but for prerogatives; corporations fought for privileges, and everything remained fixed within the firm bonds of guilds and trade associations.

Not until the days of the Reformation did the battle assume universal and spiritual proportions, and freedom was demanded, not as an imported but as an original right; not as an acquired, but as an inborn right. Principles were produced, not ancient parchments; and the peasants of Germany and the Puritans of England invoked the Gospels, whose texts had in that day as high an authority as reason, nay, higher, for they were the revealed reason of God himself. There it was inscribed legibly that all men are born equal, that exalted pride was damnable, that riches were sinful, and that the poor, too, were summoned to partake of the joys of the beautiful garden of our Lord, the common Father of all of us.

With the Bible in one hand and the sword in the other, the peasants swept through southern Germany, proclaiming to the opulent and proud citizenry of high-towered Nuremberg that henceforth not a house would be left upright which looked different from a peasant's dwelling. So thoroughly and profoundly had they understood the meaning of equality. Even to this day, we observe traces of this doctrine of equality in Franconia and Suabia, and the traveller who on a moonlit night looks on the gloomy ruins of castles dating from the time of the Peasants' War is overcome by a shudder of awe as if in the presence of the Holy Ghost. It is well for him who with sober common-sense sees nothing else but this. But if he is Sunday's child— and who is familiar with history and is not?—he will also see the wild hunt which the German nobles—the crassest in the world— unloosed against their victims, slaughtering thousands of unarmed men, torturing them on the rack, impaling them on their spears, and making martyrs of them; and through the swaying fields of corn he will see the bloody heads of the peasantry nodding mysteriously, while above him he will hear the whistling of the frightful lark, shrieking a song of vengeance—like the piper of Helfenstein.[23]

Their brethren in England and Scotland fared somewhat better. Their downfall was neither so disgraceful nor so barren, for even to this day we can see the fruits of their regime. But they did not succeed in establishing it firmly, and now the fine cavaliers rule as before, and amuse themselves with droll tales about the stiff old Roundheads, whom a favored bard has drawn so prettily for their leisurely enjoyment. No social revolution has broken out in England. The framework of civil and political institutions remains undisturbed; the domination of caste and corporation has persisted to this very day; and though it is drenched by the light and warmth of a new civilization, England is still firmly entrenched in medieval conditions, or rather, in the condition of a fashionable Middle Age. The concessions which have been made to liberal ideas there have been wrested from this petrified medievalism with difficulty. All modern improvements have proceeded not from a principle but from brute necessity; and they all bear the curse of this half-way system, which always necessitates new exertions, fresh life and death struggles, with all their attendant perils.

The religious reformation is only half completed in England. Here you find yourself more ill at ease within the four bare prison walls of the Episcopal Anglican Church than in the capacious, beautifully decorated and lavishly-cushioned soul-prison of Catholicism. Nor has the political reformation fared any better. Popular representation is as defective as can be—and if classes are no longer distinguished by the coats they wear, they are none the less separated by different courts of justice, patronage, privileges of presentation at court, prerogatives, traditional immunities and such-like odious business. If the rights of property and person are no longer dependent on the whim of aristocrats but upon law, the latter is only another sort of fangs with which the aristocratic brood seizes its prey; only another sort of dagger with which to assassinate the people. As a matter of fact, there is no tyrant on the Continent who would of his own arbitrary will impose such excessive taxes as the English people are compelled by law to pay. And no tyrant was ever so cruel as the criminal law of England, which daily commits murder for the sake of one shilling— and with the coldest and most literal formality. Although this melancholy state of affairs has been improved somewhat in recent years, and some limits have been set to temporal and clerical avarice, and though the great falsehood of popular representation has in some measure been modified by transferring the forfeited electoral vote of the rotten boroughs to the great manufacturing towns, and here and there the harshest intolerance has been somewhat abated by giving to a number of sects civil rights—still, all this is merely patchwork, which cannot last long, for even the most stupid tailor in England can foresee that sooner or later the worn garment of State must rip and tear to pieces.

"NO MAN PUTTETH A PIECE OF NEW CLOTH UNTO AN OLD GARMENT; for that which is put in to fill up taketh from the garment and the rent is made worse. Neither do men put new wine into old bottles; else the bottles break, and the wine runneth out, and the bottles perish; but they put new wine into new bottles, and both are preserved."

Profound truth springs only from profound love. Hence the agreement between the views of the ancient Preacher on the Mount, who spoke against the aristocratic caste of Jerusalem, and those later preachers of the Mountain, who from the summit of the Convention in Paris preached their tricolor gospel, according to which not only the form of the state, but all social life should be not—patched—but created and established anew—yes, reborn.

I am speaking of the French Revolution, that epoch in world history in which the doctrine of freedom and equality sprang so triumphantly from the universal source of knowledge we call Reason. Like an inexhaustible revelation it manifested itself in every mind and founded a knowledge more perfect even than traditional revelation, which is revealed only to the elect few, and can merely be believed in by the people at large. The privileged sovereigns, that arbitrary caste system, were never able to combat this latter sort of revelation (in itself aristocratic in character) as firmly as they now fight Reason, which is democratic in character. The history of the Revolution is the military chronicle of that struggle, and in it we have all more or less taken part. It is the life and death struggle with Egyptianism.

Although the swords of the enemy grow duller every day, and although we hold the vantage points, we cannot yet raise a song of victory until the work is done. We can only sally forth at night, during the armistice, and by the light of our lanterns bury our dead on the field of battle. Our brief burial service avails little!—Calumny, that vile specter, sits even on the noblest graves!

Oh, the battle is waged also against those hereditary foes of truth who have so treasonably besmirched the good name of their opponents, and who even insult the first Preacher on the Mount, the purest of freedom's heroes. For when they could no longer deny that He was the greatest of men, they made Him the least of the gods. He who fights the priesthood must be ready to have his poor name sullied and tarnished by the most convincing lies and the most plausible slanders. But flags which have been pierced by bullets or blackened by gunpowder in battle are more highly prized than untouched and unscathed standards. They are eventually placed in our cathedrals as sacred national relics. So too at some future time will the names of our heroes be all the more devoutly worshipped at the Saint Genevieve Church of Freedom, be they ever so tattered and stained.

Like her heroes, the Revolution too has been defamed. In libels of every description she has been represented as the terror of princes and the scarecrow of the people. School-children have been taught by rote the so-called "horror of the Revolution"; and the public fairs were at one time replete with lurid pictures of the guillotine. It cannot of course be denied that the machine which was invented by Monsieur Guillotin, a French physician and a great world-orthopedist, and easily separates stupid heads from wicked hearts—that this salutary machine has been applied somewhat frequently, but only in cases of incurable malady—such as treason, falsehood, and weakness. Furthermore, the patient was not tortured long, racked and broken on the wheel, as were thousands and thousands of citizens and *vilains*, burghers and peasants in the good old days. It is of course appalling to think that the French dared amputate even the head of their State. One doesn't know whether to accuse them of parricide or of suicide. But on more sober and moderate reflection we find that Louis of

France was less a victim of passion than of circumstances. Certainly, those men who provoked the people to such sacrifice, and who themselves at all times have spilled princely blood far more abundantly, should not now appear as vociferous accusers. Only two kings, both of them the kings of the nobility and not of the people, were sacrificed by the people, and not in a time of peace, or to subserve base interests, but in the most extreme crisis of war when they saw themselves betrayed and were giving of their own blood unstintingly. Surely more than a thousand princes were treacherously slain, whether for reasons of greed or of frivolous interest, by dagger, sword or poison, by the nobility and the priesthood. It might almost appear as if these castes regarded regicide as one of their prerogatives—and for that reason so selfishly mourned the deaths of Louis XVI and Charles I. Oh that kings would at last see that they can live more securely as Kings of the People—by law protected—than under the guard of their high-born assassins!

But not only the heroes of our Revolution and the Revolution herself have been defamed. Our whole epoch has been maligned, our whole liturgy of sacred ideas has been parodied with unequalled baseness. In the mouths of vile traducers and contemners, the people are the *canaille*, the vulgar mob; liberty is license. With eyes turned heaven-ward and with pious sighs they wail and complain that we are frivolous, and have, alas! no religion. Canting hypocrites, bowed down by the burden of their secret sins, they creep about and dare vilify an age which is perhaps holier than any other which has come before or will come after—an age which sacrificed itself for the sins of the past and for the happiness of the future—the Messiah of centuries, which could scarcely endure its bloody crown of thorns and the heavy cross, did it not now and then indulge itself in the merry vaudeville jests and pranks aimed at these latter-day Pharisees and Sadducees! Insufferable indeed would be its giant pains without such jest and raillery! Seriousness appears all the more forceful when it is announced by laughter. The age shows itself to be like its French children, who have written comic and frivolous books, and yet have been severe and serious when severity and seriousness were required; for example, like DuClos and even Louvet de Couvray,[24] both of whom, when the times demanded, fought for liberty with the courage and self-sacrifice of martyrs, and yet wrote in so lascivious and frivolous a vein, and alas!—had no religion whatever!

As if freedom were not as good a religion as any other! Since it is our religion, we may measure our contemners with the same rod, and charge them with frivolity and irreligiousness.

Yes, I repeat the words with which I opened these pages: Freedom is a new religion, the religion of our age. If Christ is no longer its God, He is, at least, one of its high priests; and His name sends gladdening beams into the hearts of His young disciples. The French are the Chosen People of this new religion. In their language are written its first gospels and dogmas. Paris is the New Jerusalem, and the Rhine is the Jordan which divides the land of freedom from the land of the Philistines.

๖๛ *The Unfinished French Revolution*

NOT FROM THE WORKSHOPS OF POLITICAL PARTIES will I borrow the vulgar rule to measure men and affairs. Still less will I determine their greatness and worth according to my own private, romantic feelings. But I will try as impartially as possible to advance the understanding of the present time, and search in the immediate past for the key to the stormy enigma of the present. Salons lie; but the grave speaks the truth. But alas! the dead, those cold orators of history, speak in vain to the frenzied multitude, which understands only the language of passion.

Certainly, the salons do not lie deliberately. The society of those in power actually believes in the permanence of its power, though the annals of world history and the fiery *Mene Tekel* of the daily newspapers, and even the loud voice of the people in the streets sound warnings. Nor do the coteries of the opposition lie intentionally. They believe themselves certain of victory, just as men always believe what they want to. They become drunk on the champagne of their expectations, interpret every mischance as a necessary event which must bring them the closer to their goal. On the eve of their downfall, their confidence glows most radiantly, and the messenger who brings them the official news of their debacle, generally finds them quarrelling over their share of the spoils. Hence the one-sided errors which are inescapable if one stands too close to either one of the parties. Each unwillingly deceives us; for we are inclined to trust those most who are of the same mind as we. Should we, by chance, be endowed with that sort of disinterestedness, which permits us, without special predilection, to keep in constant touch with all parties, then we are bewildered by their extreme self-confidence, and our judgment becomes disgustingly neutralized. Indifferentists of this sort, who are without an opinion of their own, or who do not participate in the problems of their time, and who only desire to overhear what is taking place, and eavesdrop on all the gossip of the salon and dish out the *chronique scandaleuse* of one party to the other, see all around them only personalities, and not principles, or rather, they see in principles only personalities—hence they predict the ruin of the former, because they understand the weaknesses of the latter, and thus they lead their respective supporters into the most serious errors and blunders.

I cannot refrain from calling particular attention to the false relation which exists today in France between *things* (i. e., the intellectual and material interests) and *persons* (i. e., the representatives of these interests). This was quite different at the end of the last century, when men rose in their full greatness to the occasion, so that they represent in the history of Revolutions a heroic epoch—and for that reason are now celebrated and loved by our republican youth. Or are we here also deceived in the same way as Madame Roland who in her Memoirs bitterly complains that among the men of her time there was not one who was of importance? [25] The poor woman was not aware of her own greatness, and failed to see that her contemporaries were sufficently great if they did not fall short of her intellectual stature. The whole French nation has risen to such heights, that we are perhaps inclined to be unjust to its public representatives if they do not tower preëminently above the multitude; yet they cannot for that reason be considered small. We cannot see the woods for the trees. In Germany, on the other hand, we see an abundance of scraggy underbrush and dwarf pines, but only here and there a giant oak whose head rises to the clouds, while below the worms gnaw at its roots.

Today is the product of yesterday. We must explore what *yesterday* has willed—if we would know what today wills. The Revolution is ever one and the same. Not—as the doctrinaire contends—not for the *Charte* was the battle waged in that great week—but for those very revolutionary interests for which the best blood of France has been shed these forty years. But lest the writer of these pages be mistaken for one of those preachers who conceive of revolution as merely one overthrow after another, and mistake the accidents of the Revolution for the essentials—I will here explain, as clearly as I can, my principal ideas.

When the culture of a people and its attendant customs and needs are no longer in harmony with the established institutions, they of necessity come into fateful conflict, with the result that the latter are transformed. This phenomenon we call a revolution. So long as the revolution is incomplete, so long as the transformation of institutions does not harmonize with the intellectual temper, the customs and needs of the people, the sickness of the body politic is not completely cured, and the sickly and overexcited people will relapse into an exhausted stupor. From time to time they will develop a high fever and tear the most secure bandages and the soothing lint from their wounds, throw their noblest nurses out of doors, and writhe in agony and unrest until they find, by themselves, institutions agreeable to them.

In the end, the question of whether France is now at rest, or whether we are to expect more political changes, and what the outcome will be really reduces itself to the following: What impulse drove the French to initiate the French Revolution, and have they achieved what they have been seeking?

"SEE THOU, THE FOUNDATIONS OF USURY, of theft and robbery are our great men and lords, who take all creatures into their possession, the fish in the water, the birds in the air; all that groweth on earth must be theirs (*Isaiah*, V). Therefore they send forth God's commandment among the poor, saying, 'God hath commanded that ye shall not steal!' but it serves them nought. So they cause all men to flay and skin the poor ploughman, and the poor workman, and all that is alive (*Mic.* III), and should he lay violent hands on what is holiest, he must hang. Then saith Doctor Liar: 'Amen.' The great men are themselves the cause that the poor man is their enemy. If they will not do away with the cause of strife, how can it go well in the long run. And if I, saying this, am rebellious, well then—"

Thus spoke, three hundred years ago, Thomas Münzer,[26] one of the most heroic and unfortunate sons of the German Fatherland, a preacher of the Gospel which, according to his belief, promised not only blessedness in heaven, but also equality and brotherhood of man on earth. Doctor Martinus Luther was of a different opinion, and condemned such rebellious doctrines, by which his own work, the separation from Rome and the establishment of a new creed, was jeopardized, and moved more by worldly wisdom than by wicked zeal, he wrote that disreputable book against the unfortunate peasants. Zealots and servile hypocrites have recently revived this work, and spread newly printed copies of it throughout the land, partly to show their high protectors how thoroughly the pure Lutheran creed upholds absolutism, and partly to repress by Luther's authority the enthusiasm for freedom in Germany. But a more sacred testimony, which flows in streams of blood from the Gospels, repudiates this slavish interpretation and destroys this erroneous authority. Christ, who died for the equality and brotherhood of man, did not reveal his Word so that it might serve as the tool of absolutism. Luther was wrong, and Thomas Münzer was right. He was beheaded at Mödlin. His confederates were also right, and they were beheaded with the sword or hanged with the rope, all depending on whether they were of plebeian or noble origin. The Margrave Casimir of Anspach, over and above these executions, had the eyes of eighty-five peasants gouged out, and afterwards they went begging through the land. And these, too, were right. How the peasants of Upper Austria and Suabia fared—is well known. Like so many hundreds of thousands of peasants in Germany, who asked for nothing but human rights and Christian mercy, they were slaughtered and massacred by their spiritual and temporal lords. But the latter too were right. For they were in the fullness of their power; and the peasants were often led astray by the authority of Luther and other clergymen who made common cause with the secular powers, and by their untimely controversies over equivocal Biblical passages,—and also because they often sang psalms instead of fighting.

In the year of grace 1789 the same battle for equality and brotherhood commenced in France, and for the same reason, and against the very same potentates; with only this difference: that the latter had in the course of time lost strength, which the people gained, and they based their claims to justice not on the Gospel but on philosophy. The feudal and hierarchical institutions which Charlemagne had established in his great realm, and which had developed in various forms in the succession lands, had struck firm roots in France. Here it flourished mightily for centuries, but like all things on earth, it finally lost its strength. The kings of France, vexed at their dependence on the nobility and the clergy, the first of whom considered themselves their equals, while the latter exercised even greater control over the people than the kings—gradually contrived to destroy the autonomy of their power, a task which was proudly completed under Louis XIV. In place of the war-like feudal nobility, which had once ruled and protected its kings, only a weak court aristocracy now grovelled at the foot of the throne, and derived prestige not by reason of castles and retainers, but of the number of ancestors. In place of rigid, ultramontane priests, who intimidated the kings with book and candle, while they kept the multitude in check, there came into being a Gallican—or mediatized church—whose offices were secretly purveyed in the *Oeil de boeuf* of Versailles or in the boudoirs of mistresses, and whose chiefs belong to the same aristocracy who paraded about as court domestics—so that the costumes of abbés and bishops, pallium and mitre, could well be considered as a sort of court-dress. Despite these changes, the nobility retained the ancient privileges which they had exercised over the people. As a matter of fact, their insolence toward them rose in proportion as it sank in the presence of their royal masters. They arrogated to themselves, as before, all the pleasures of life, and continued to oppress and abuse the people. So did the clergy, too, and though they had lost their hold on men's souls, they still retained their tithes, their monopoly of the Trinity, their ecclesiastical wiles, and their right to crush men's thoughts.

What the teachers of the Gospel had once tried to do during the Peasants' War was now done by the philosophers of France, and with better success. They convinced the people of the usurpations of the nobility and the Church; they proved to them that both were now powerless. And the people rejoiced, and one very fine day, on the fourteenth of July 1789, they commenced their work of emancipation. On that day whoever visited the square on which that musty, grimy, unpleasant old Bastille stood, found on its place an airy, cheerful building, with the joyous inscription: "*Ici on danse.*"

For seventeen years a number of European writers have been tireless in their efforts to exonerate the learned men of France of the reproach that they had in a great measure contributed to the outbreak of the French Revolution. Our present savants are once more eager to win the favor of the great; again they seek the soft, little cushions at the feet of the powerful, and they have been behaving with such servile innocence, that they are no longer regarded as serpents, but common worms. But I will not refrain from declaring, for the sake of the truth: It was the writers of the last century who did most to hasten the outbreak of the French Revolution and to determine its character. I praise them for this, as one praises a physician who produces a rapid crisis and whose skill arrests a sickness which might otherwise have proved fatal. Without the words of the learned men, France would have lingered on in fatal infirmity, and the Revolution, which was inevitable, would have assumed a far less noble complexion —it would have become common and barbarous, instead of being tragic and bloody. Or what is even worse, it might have degenerated into something ridiculous and stupid, if the material needs had not acquired an ideal expression. Unfortunately such was the case in other countries, where writers did not inspire the people with a demand for a declaration of human rights, and where people started revolutions in order to avoid paying the toll or to get rid of a prince's mistress, etc. Voltaire and Rousseau are the two writers who did more than any others to prepare the Revolution, to determine its later course, and who still guide and rule the French people intellectually. Even the antagonism of the two has had its remarkable after-effects, for it is possible that the partisanship of the men of the Revolution is even to this day only a continuation of this conflict.

We do injustice to Voltaire, however, by asserting that he was not as greatly inspired as Rousseau. He was merely more skilful and wise. Clumsiness always finds refuge in stoicism; and sulks laconically in the presence of adroitness in others. Alfieri reproaches Voltaire because, while writing continually against the great, he always bore a taper before them like a chamberlain. The gloomy Piedmontese did not see that while Voltaire was servilely carrying the taper before them, he was also lighting up their nakedness. Yet I will by no means acquit Voltaire of the charge of flattery; he as well as the great majority of the learned men fawned like spaniels at the feet of the nobility, and licked their golden spurs, and smiled when they thereby hurt their tongues; and they also allowed themselves to be kicked. A small dog is hurt as much as a big one when he is kicked. The hidden hatred of the French scholars against the powerful must have been all the more terrible for the real benefits they received, aside from the kicks. Garat tells us that Chamfort [27] once took from his old leather purse a thousand thalers, the savings of a busy lifetime, and gladly contributed them to the cause of the Revolution, when money was being collected for it in the early days. Yet Chamfort was avaricious, and had always been the protégé of the great.

But even more than the literati, did the tradesmen contribute to the fall of the ancient regime. While the writers believed that the ancient regime should be replaced by a regime of intellectuals, the industrialists held that they were actually the strongest and most powerful section of the population, and should be granted legal acknowledgment of their importance—equality as citizens, and participation in affairs of the state. As a matter of fact, since the prevailing institutions up to that time had rested on the military and on the church—neither of which had any life left—the new society now had to be built upon the two new forces in which the lifestream flowed most fully—that is, industry and science. The clergy, which had remained intellectually backward ever since the invention of printing, and the nobility, which had been ruined by the invention of gun-powder, should have realized that the power which they had exercised for a thousand years was passing from their proud, though weak, hands into the despised and vigorous hands of the intellectual and the worker. They should have realized that they could recapture the power they had lost only through an alliance with these scholars and workers. But they did not see this. Foolishly, they fought against the inevitable, a painful, senseless battle, in which crawling, inflated falsehood and rotten, sickly pride strove with stern necessity—against the guillotine and truth, against life and inspiration,—and to-day we are still standing on that battlefield.

?❧ *Louis Blanc*

A BOOK HAS JUST APPEARED ABOUT THE JULY REVOLUTION and the part that Louis Philippe has played in it, which is exciting general attention and discussion everywhere. It is the first part of Louis Blanc's *Histoire de dix ans.* I have not yet seen it. When I have read it, I shall try to give you my independent opinion of its merits. Today I will merely tell you something about the author and his position, so that you may have a correct idea on which to base your views with regard to the extent of partisanship revealed in the book, and how much faith to place in it.

The author, M. Louis Blanc, is a young man in his thirties, although to look at him you would think he was a boy of thirteen. In fact, his puny figure, his red-cheeked, beardless, little face, his slight treble of a voice, which has not yet broken, all make him look like a nice little boy who has just run away from grade school, and is wearing a dress suit for the first time. Yet he is a notable personality in the

Republican party, and his reasoning has all the moderation one generally finds only in old men. His features, especially his small, lively eyes, point to a southern French origin. Louis Blanc was born in Madrid of French parents. His mother came from Corsica, and was a Pozzo di Borgo. He was educated at Rodez. I do not know how long he has been in Paris; but six years ago, when I met him, he was already the editor of the Republican journal, *Le Monde*, and since then he has established the *Revue du Progrès*, the most important organ of Republicanism. His cousin, Pozzo di Borgo, the former ambassador to Russia, is reported as not too well pleased by the direction of the young man's talents, and as having often given expression to his dissatisfaction. . . .

Louis Blanc's mother and the rest of her family still live in Corsica. This is more a relationship of body and blood. Mentally, Louis Blanc is more closely related to Jean Jacques Rousseau, whose works represent the starting point for all his thought and expression. His warm, simple, honest prose recalls the first church father of the Revolution. *L'Organisation du travail* by Blanc is a book which has drawn much attention to its author. Every line of this short book breathes, if not thorough knowledge of, at least glowing sympathy for the sufferings of the people, and reveals a predilection for absolute authority and a profound aversion to merely talented individualism, which differentiate him sharply from several of his Republican associates, such as, for example, the witty Pyat. This divergence some time ago came near causing a rift, when Louis Blanc refused to agree to that unlimited freedom of the press which the Republicans demanded. Here it became clear that the latter love freedom for freedom's sake, but Louis Blanc regards it as a means to a humanitarian end. From his point of view, the authority of a government, without which nothing can be done to benefit the people, is of greater importance than the authority and privileges of powerful or great individuals. It may indeed be that he finds great personalities repugnant and looks mistrustfully at them because he is so short of stature—a trait which he has in common with another of Rousseau's disciples, the late Maximilian Robespierre. I think the dwarf would gladly cut off every head which exceeds prescribed recruiting measurements—of course, in the interest of the public good, universal equality, and social humanitarianism.

Louis Blanc is a very sober individual; and indulges his body in no pleasures. He wishes, for that reason, to introduce into the state dietary equality which will give us all the same sort of Spartan black broth, and what is even more horrible, give equal portions to the giant and his dwarfish brother.

No, thank you, my new Lycurgus! It is true that we are all brothers. But I am the big brother, and you are my little brothers. Hence it behooves me to take the bigger portion. Louis Blanc is a comical compound of the Lilliputian and the Spartan. However, I predict a great future for him. He will play a role, though a brief one. He is peculiarly adapted to be a great man among the little ones, who will easily carry him on their shoulders;—for men of great stature—I almost said, minds of great corpulence—would be too much for them to carry.

The new book of Louis Blanc's is said to be admirably written, and has a very substantial attraction for the great, mischief-loving multitude, since it contains many new and malicious anecdotes. The Republicans are enraptured with it. The meanness and pettiness of the ruling bourgeoisie, whom they would like to overthrow, are here delightfully portrayed. But to the Legitimists, the book is caviar itself. For the author, who is kind to them, scoffs at their bourgeois conquerors, and casts pellets of poisonous mud on the royal mantle of Louis Philippe. Are the tales that Louis Blanc tells of him true or false? If true, then the great French nation, which talks so much of its *point d'honneur*, has permitted itself to be governed and represented for the last ten years by a common juggler, or a crowned Bosco.

ஃ *Communism*

[*1843*]

Iғ I HAD LIVED AS A PRIVATE GENTLEMAN IN ROME during the time of the Emperor Nero, and had I acted as correspondent for the *Daily Express* of Boeotia or for the unofficial *State Gazette* of Abdera, my colleagues would often have chided me if I had not, for example, reported the state intrigues of the Empress-Mother, Agrippina, nor described the magnificent dinners with which the King of Judea, Agrippa, regaled the diplomatic corps of Rome every Saturday; while, on the other hand, I constantly spoke of those Galileans, of that obscure, little handful consisting chiefly of slaves and old women, who dreamed away their lives in battles and visions, and were even disavowed by the Jews. My well-informed colleagues would no doubt have smiled ironically at me if I had had nothing more to say of the court festival of Caesar, at which His Gracious Majesty Himself played the guitar, than that some of those Galileans had been tarred and set afire, and so served to illuminate the gardens of the Golden Palace. It was indeed a very remarkable illumination, and it was a horrible, truly Roman jest to make the so-called obscurantists serve as lights in the joyous solemnities of the life-intoxicated, ancient world. But now those jests have been turned to shame, and those torches have thrown out sparks of faith by which the old Roman world with all its rotten glory has been consumed. The number of that obscure handful has become legion; in battling with them the legions of Caesar had to lay down their arms, and today all the Empire, by land and sea, belongs to the Galileans.

Now, it is not my intention to deliver myself of homilies here. I have only wished to give an example of the triumphant way in which a succeeding generation may justify a predilection which I have often shown in my correspondence for that small community which, very much like the *ecclesia pressa* of the first century, is at the present time despised and persecuted, but which has established a propaganda whose zeal and gloomy destructive spirit recall the beginnings of the Galileans. I am once more referring to the Communists, the only party in France which deserves marked attention. I would bespeak the same measure of attention for the remnants of Saint-Simonism, whose adherents still live under very strange signboards; as well as the Fourierists, who are still vigorous and active. But these honorable people are moved only by the word, by the social problem as a problem, by the idea as transmitted—they are not driven as if by demonic necessity; they are not the predestined creatures through whom the supreme and universal will realizes its vast purposes. Sooner or later, the dispersed family of Saint-Simonians and the whole general staff of Fourierists will go over to the growing army of Communism, and by endowing their crude demands with the creative word, they will assume, as it were, the role of the Church Fathers.

Such a role is already being filled by Pierre Leroux, whom we first met eleven years ago in the Salle Taitbout as one of the bishops of Saint-Simonism. An excellent man who had had only one fault—he was too sombre for his duties. Hence Enfantin praised him sarcastically: "He is the most virtuous man, by the standards of antiquity." His virtue has, in fact, something of the old leaven of an age of renunciation, something of obsolete Stoicism, which in our day seems like a repellent anachronism, and must appear respectably ridiculous when contrasted with the cheerful tendencies of a pantheistic hedonism. For this reason, this melancholy bird eventually felt very uncomfortable in the glittering wire cage in which so many pheasants, eagles, and even mere sparrows fluttered about, and he was the first to protest against the dogmas of the new morality, and with a fanatical anathema he withdrew from the gay and joyous community. Thereupon, in association with Hippolyte Carnot, Leroux undertook the new *Revue encyclopédique*, and the articles he wrote for it, as well as his book, *De l'humanité*, form the transition to the doctrines which, during the past year, he has set forth in the *Revue indépendante*. I know nothing definite about the progress of the great encyclopedia on which Leroux and the admirable Reynauld are now actively engaged. This much, though, I can say: The work is a worthy continuation of its predecessor, that colossal pamphlet of thirty quarto tomes, in which Diderot epitomized the knowledge of his age. . . .

PIERRE LEROUX IS PERHAPS FIFTY YEARS OLD—at least he appears that old; but he may be younger. Physically, Nature has not been too lavish with him. His figure is short, stocky, angular, and devoid of that grace which the traditions of fashionable society bestow. Leroux is a son of the people. In his youth, he was a printer, and his exterior betrays his proletarian origin. It is possible that he deliberately disdained to adopt the customary gloss of society; if he is capable of affectation, it may consist in his obstinate insistence on this kind of crude unaffectedness. There are people who never wear gloves because they have small, white hands which betray their aristocratic descent. Pierre Leroux does not wear gloves, but surely for a different reason. He is a man of ascetic renunciation, to whom luxury and all sensual pleasures are repugnant, and for whom Nature has made the exercise of virtues very easy. But we must recognize that the nobility of his sentiments, the zeal with which he sacrifices all subsidiary interests to thought, and, generally, his great selflessness are no less meritorious. Nor do we wish to depreciate the rough diamond because it lacks a brilliant polish, or has a dull, leaden setting. Pierre Leroux is a man. With manliness of character, he combines what is rare indeed—a mind which swings aloft to the highest reaches of speculation; and a heart which descends to the lowest depths of human suffering. He is not only a philosopher who thinks, but also one who feels. His whole life and all his efforts are dedicated to the improvement of the moral and mental condition of the lower classes. He is a steeled warrior who can bear the severest blows of fate without blenching, and like Saint-Simon and Fourier, he has often endured the greatest privation and want without complaining. But he cannot look tranquilly on the troubles of his fellow-men. His stern eyes become moist at another's misery, and then the outbursts of his pity are stormy, wild, and often unjust.

I have here been guilty of an indiscreet allusion to poverty. But I could not help mentioning it. This poverty too is characteristic of Leroux. It shows that the excellent man has understood the sufferings of the people not only with his mind, but in his own person—that his thoughts are rooted in stark realities. So that his words have the pulse-beat of life and a fascination stronger than the mere force of talent. Yes, Pierre Leroux is poor—as poor as Saint-Simon and Fourier, and it is this providential poverty of the great socialists that has enriched the world with a wealth of thoughts which will open to us new worlds of joy and happiness. It is common knowledge in what dire straits Saint-Simon passed his last years. While he was busy with that great patient, ailing humanity, and was inventing remedies for its eighteen-hundred-year-old malady, he himself sickened of poverty, and survived only on charity. Fourier too was obliged to have recourse to the generosity of his friends. How often have I seen him in his grey, shabby coat, hurrying along, past the columns of the Palais Royal, both of his coat-pockets heavily loaded down, a bottle peering from one and a loaf of bread from the other. One of my friends, who pointed him out to me for the first time, called my attention to Fourier's poverty, the fact that he was obliged to carry his own wine and bread from the shops. "How is it," I inquired, "that these men, these benefactors of mankind, are forced to starve in France?" My friend replied with a sarcastic smile, "Certainly it does no great honor to the highly praised land of the intellect; and I am sure that these things could never happen in our own Germany. The government would certainly take men of such persuasion under its special protection and provide them with free board and lodging for the rest of their lives."

Yes, poverty is the lot of the great philanthropists, those healing thinkers of France; but with them it is not only a stimulus to pro-

THE CITIZEN OF THE WORLD 585

founder investigations and an invigorating mineral bath of the mind, but also a public recommendation of their doctrines, and in this respect, it has providential significance. In Germany, the absence of worldly goods is pardoned amiably; there, genius may pine and die of hunger without being despised. In England, they are less tolerant. Merit there is measured by income. "How much is he worth?" means literally, "How much money does he have?" or "How much does he make?" I myself once overheard a burly Englishman asking a Franciscan in Florence—in all seriousness—how much the latter made every year by going around barefoot, with a thick rope tied round his waist. In France it is different. No matter how strong the greed of the industrialists may be, the poverty of eminent men is considered a title of honor. I might even say that riches, which always arouse a suspicion of dishonesty, taint as with a secret stigma—a *levis nota*—men who are otherwise admirable. That may be the result of the general knowledge that many of the great fortunes flow from polluted sources. A poet once said that the first king was a happy soldier. Concerning the founders of our present financial dynasties, it may be said, prosaically enough, that the first banker was a lucky scoundrel. The cult of wealth is as wide-spread here as elsewhere, but it is a cult without veneration. The French also dance around the golden calf; but their dancing is a combination of mockery, raillery, self-contempt—a sort of *cancan*. This is a strange phenomenon which may be partly explained by the generous character of the French, partly by their history. Under the Ancient Regime, only birth mattered; only the number of ancestors one possessed was respected. Honor was the fruit of the genealogical tree. Under the Republic, Virtue came into power, Poverty acquired dignity, and Money hid its face in fear as well as shame. It is from this time that we can date the origin of those numerous heavy *sous*, those serious-faced pieces of copper, bearing symbols of liberty—as well as that tradition of pecuniary disinterestedness which we continue to meet among the highest statesmen of France. Under the Empire only military glory flourished. A new honor was established, the *Légion d'Honneur*, whose grandmaster, the victorious Imperator, looked down with contempt on the whole guild of money-grubbing shopkeepers, contractors, smugglers, stock-jobbers, and other lucky scoundrels. During the Restoration, wealth conspired against the ghosts of the Ancient Regime, who had again come to power, and whose insolence grew daily. Mammon, insulted but ambitious, became a demagogue, and flirted condescendingly with workingmen—in smocks, and when the July sun again warmed the hearts of men, the aristocrat-king Charles X was hurled from the throne. The citizen-king Louis Philippe ascended the throne—the representative of money which now is king, though public opinion regards it most unfavorably; it is scorned both by the vanquished party of the past and the disappointed party of the future. Yes, the aristocratic Faubourg Saint-Germain and the proletarian Faubourgs Saint-Antoine and Saint-Marceau vie in deriding the money-proud parvenus—and, as can easily be imagined—the old Republicans with their virtuous pathos, and the Bonapartists with their pathetic heroic tirades join in this chorus of depreciation. When you reflect on these combined rancors, it becomes clear why at the present time public opinion treats the rich with almost excessive contempt, while everyone is actually languishing for riches.

To return to the subject of this article, I would here particularly call attention to the incalculably favorable circumstances in which Communism finds itself by virtue of the fact that the enemy whom it is fighting has, for all his power, no real moral foundation within himself. The society of our day defends itself out of sheer necessity—without believing in its rights, yes, without self-respect—just like the older society whose rotting timbers crashed when the Son of the Carpenter arrived.

⧘ *Reflections*

THE SERVILITY EXHIBITED BY THE POLISH PEASANT toward the nobility is revolting. He bows almost to the feet of his gracious masters, and says: "I kiss your feet." He who wishes to see obeisance personified, let him look at a Polish peasant as he stands before his lord. All that is lacking is the wagging tail. At the sight of this, I involuntarily say to myself: "And the Lord created Man in His own image." And I am overcome by infinite sorrow when I see a man thus humbled before another. One should give obeisance to kings only. Except for this reservation, I subscribe to every one of the principles of the American catechism. I do not deny that I prefer the trees of the field to family trees; that I respect human rights more than the canonical; and that I esteem the commands of reason higher than the abstractions of myopic historians.

WHEN IT WILL COME TO PASS that mankind shall again regain all of its health, when peace shall once more be restored between body and soul and they mingle again in original harmony, then we shall scarcely understand the artificial schism which Christianity has brought about between them. Happier and lovelier generations, begotten of free embraces, will flourish under a religion of joy, and will smile sadly at their poor ancestors who mournfully rejected all the pleasures of this lovely earth, and through mortification of warm and many-hued sensuousness almost wasted away till they became cold specters. Yes, I say it emphatically, our descendants will be more beautiful and happier than we. For I am a believer in progress. I believe that mankind is destined for happiness. And I have a better opinion of the Deity than those pious folk who imagine that He created man only to make him suffer. I would establish happiness here on earth, through the blessings of free political and industrial institutions, which, if we are to believe the devout, will only be realized in heaven on doomsday. True, the one hope may be as vain as the other,—and there may be no resurrection for man—neither in the political-moral, nor in the apostolic-Catholic sense.

IT IS AN OLD STORY. Not for themselves, since time immemorial, not for themselves have the people bled and suffered, but for others. In 1830 they won a victory for that bourgeoisie which is as useless as the nobility whom it replaced, and is governed by the same egoism. . . . The people won nothing but regrets and greater misery. But rest assured: The next time the alarm is sounded, and the people take to arms, they will fight for themselves and demand their just reward. . . .

THE CITIZENS OF PARIS HAVE LIBERATED THE WORLD, yet they've never accepted a single gratuity for it.

DOES HISTORY HAVE A NIGHT AND A DAY as Nature does? With the beginning of the third century of the Christian era the dusk commences. Melancholy sanguine sunset of Neo-Platonism. The Middle Ages—a black night. And now . . . the rosy hue of dawn. . . .

I greet thee, Phoebus Apollo! What dreams were dreamt during that night—what specters—what nocturnal ghosts—what tumult in the streets—what murders and crimes!—I shall tell about them.

৯ *It Will Be a Lovely Day*

. . . As THROUGH A TRIUMPHAL ARCH OF COLOSSAL CLOUD-MASSES, the sun rose victorious, brilliant and serene, foretelling a beautiful day. I felt, however, like the poor moon, which hung pallid in the sky. She had wandered her lonely way in the solitude of the night, when happiness is asleep, and ghosts, owls, and crime stalk abroad; and now that the young day had risen with jubilant beams and palpitating morning glow, she could not stay, and she vanished like a cloud of mist, with a last sorrowing glance at the great constellation.

"It will be a lovely day," my companion in the carriage called out to me.

Yes, it will be a beautiful day, my heart repeated in soft prayer, and trembled with anguish and joy. It *will* be a beautiful day! The sun of freedom will warm the earth more gladly than the entire aristocracy of nocturnal stars. A new race will rise, engendered in free embrace; and not in the forced nuptials or under the eye of clerical tax-collectors. Together with free birth, freer thoughts and feelings will come into the world—of which we, who were born in servitude, have no conception. Ah! they will not understand how horrible was the night in whose darkness we were compelled to live; how bitterly we had to fight with frightful ghosts, stupid owls, and sanctimonious sinners! Alas, we poor warriors who have had to squander our lives in such combat, and are weary and spent, now that victory is at hand! The sunrise glow can no longer flush our cheeks and warm our hearts. We perish like the waning moon. All too brief is man's allotted course, and his end is the implacable grave!

Truly, I do not know whether I deserve that a laurel wreath be placed on my bier: Poetry, much as I loved it, has always been to me only a sacred plaything, or, at best, a consecrated means to a heavenly end. I have never laid great store by poetic glory, and whether my songs are praised or blamed matters little to me. But lay a sword on my bier, for I have been a good soldier in the wars of human liberation.

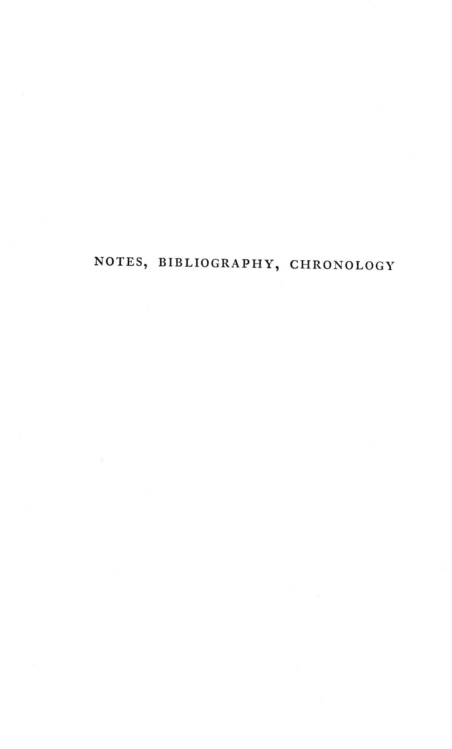

NOTES, BIBLIOGRAPHY, CHRONOLOGY

NOTES

≥• *Self Portrait:* IN GERMANY

1. *Ça ira, ça ira* Famous French revolutionary song.
2. Archduke Joachim Murat was crowned at Düsseldorf on March 26, 1806.
3. *Niebuhr* B. George Niebuhr (1776–1831), distinguished author of the "History of Rome."
4. *Waldzeck* Franz Daniel Friedrich Waldzeck, a professor at Berlin, noted for his philanthropic endeavors.

5. *katal* Hebrew: 'to smite.' *pokat* Hebrew: 'to seek.'

6. *Adelung* Johann Christian Adelung, grammarian.

7. *apprendre par coeur* 'To learn by heart.' *bête allemande* German beast. The German word "Glaube" means both "credit" and "religion."

8. *Martens* Probably Karl von Martens, author of a book on politics.

9. *Rousseau's 'Émile'* The great educational treatise by the French eighteenth century philosopher.

10. *'Où l'innocence . . .'* 'Where innocence has perished, it is a crime to live.'

11. *Officier de bouche* Literally, 'officer of the mouth.'

12. *Thales* Ancient Greek philosopher, founder of the Ionian School. *Lampsacus* A town in Asia Minor, birthplace of the philosopher Anaximenes.

13. *'Et la Prusse n'existait plus'* 'And Prussia was no more.'

14. *Sir Hudson Lowe* Commander of the vessel "Bellerephon," which brought Napoleon to St. Helena.

15. *Las Casas,* etc. Napoleon's biographers. *Londonderry* Lord Castlereagh, the reactionary British statesman. *Saalfeld* Author of vitriolic anti-Napoleonic diatribes.

16. *Niobe* In Greek mythology, Niobe boasted of her many children and deemed herself superior to the mother of Apollo and Artemis, who, to requite the insult, slew all her offspring.

17. *moult tristement* Old French: 'very sadly.'

18. *Uhland* Ludwig Uhland (1787–1862), author of many popular German ballads and songs, including "Der gute Kamerad."

19. *Ossian* A legendary Celtic bard of the third century. The spurious imitations of Ossian by the Scotsman Macpherson in the eighteenth century were taken as genuine and became very popular all over Europe.

20. *Bayard* The famous steed belonging to Roland, hero of the "Song of Roland."

21. *Christian Sethe* A schoolmate of Heine at the Düsseldorf Lyceum.

22. *'Quand on a tout perdu . . .'* 'When everything has been lost, and hope no longer remains, life becomes a shame, and death a duty.'

23. *August Wilhelm von Schlegel* (1767–1845) Famous German critic and translator of Shakespeare.

24. *'Je n'aurais jamais cru . . .'* 'I would never have believed that those beasts commonly known as Germans are so nauseating a race—and vicious too. As soon as I recover my health, I shall quit Germany. I shall go to Arabia, where I'll lead a pastoral existence. I shall be a man once more, in the full sense of the word. I'll live among the camels, who are not students. I'll write Arabic verses—as beautiful as the Morlaccat—and finally, I'll sit on the sacred rock where Mödshuun sighed for Leila.'

25. *Wohlwill* Immanuel Wolf, or Wohlwill (1799–1848), one of the members of the Society for Jewish Culture and Science.

26. *'sempiterna solatia . . .'* Latin: 'the perpetual solace of mankind.' *'Old Wolf'* Friedrich August Wolf (1759–1824), one of the greatest German philologists of the period and a critic of the Homeric poems.

27. *Moser* Moses Moser (1796–1838), banker, and one of the founders of the Society for Jewish Culture and Science.

28. *Gans* Eduard Gans (1798–1839), jurist and philosopher of law; baptized in 1825. One of the founders of the Society for Jewish Culture and Science.

29. *Ludwig Marcus* (1796–1844) See Heine's "Ludwig Marcus" in this volume, pp. 685–9.

30. *Ganstown* Mordecai Emanuel Noah, famous American Jewish patriot and diplomat, had issued a call to the Jews of the world to settle in his ideal commonwealth, 'Mount Ararat,' to be established on Grand Island, New York, where they would enjoy full civil and religious freedom as American citizens.

31. *Lulef* More correctly, *lulab*, the palm branch used during the Jewish festival of Tabernacles. *Talles and Tefillim* 'Praying shawl and phylacteries.' *Kille* More correctly, *kehillah*, 'community.'

32. *Judenschmerz* Literally, 'the Jewish sorrow.'

33. *'the Romance which I sent you'* The ballad "Donna Clara."

34. *Jean-Paul-like* See reference to Jean Paul Friedrich Richter on page 720. *Clauren's 'Mimili'* One of the most popular novels of the day.

35. *'Byron . . .'* Lord Byron died at Missolonghi, Greece, on April 19, 1824.

36. *'Three and Thirty'* Thirty-three of Heine's poems, later included in "The Homecoming," were published in Gubitz's magazine, "Der Gesellschafter," in March, 1824.

37. *'Rabbi . . .'* "The Rabbi of Bacherach." See p. 507 in this volume.

38. *Haggadah* A collection of legends, prayers, apologues, etc., recited on the first two evenings of the Passover festival. *'Caholach Manga'* More correctly, *keho lachmo anyah,* 'this is the bread of affliction'—one of the opening passages of the Haggadah. *'Ten thousand armed men'* See the "Song of Songs," chap. 3: "Behold, it is the litter of Solomon; three score mighty men are about it, of the mighty men of Israel."

39. *Benjamin of Tudela* Spanish-Jewish traveller and scholar, whose travel diary was published in Hebrew in Constantinople in 1543. Heine used the French version of Jean Philippe Baratier, Amsterdam, 1734.

40. *Zunz* Leopold Zunz (1794–1886), one of the most distinguished of German-Jewish scholars; a founder of the Society for Jewish Culture and Science.

41. *Basnage* Jacques Basnage (1653–1725), French Protestant theologian, author of numerous historical works, including the "History of the Jews" and "Antiquities of the Jews."

42. *confarreatio* An ancient Roman marriage contract.

43. *'not only a J.D., but also—'* An allusion to his conversion to Lutheranism, which had taken place some time before.

44. *Werther* Hero of the celebrated sentimental novel by Goethe, which ends in his suicide. *Heinrich von Kleist* One of the most gifted playwrights of the early nineteenth century, who committed suicide. He is the author of a novel, "Michael Kohlhaas."

45. *'changed horses at Leipzig'* During the Battle of Leipzig, a part of the Saxon troops in Napoleon's army deserted and went over to the Allies.

46. *Wilhelm Müller* (1794–1827) The gifted writer of songs and ballads, made immortal by the musical settings of Franz Schubert.

47. *Eduard von Schenk* (1788–1841) Poet, dramatist, politician; author of "Belisarius," produced at Munich in 1826.

48. *'quand on parle . . .'* 'speak of the devil . . .'

49. *Cotta* One of the most famous German publishers.

50. *Raupach* Ernst Raupach, a popular playwright of the day.

51. *Iffland* August Wilhelm Iffland (1759–1814), actor, dramatist, and theatrical director.

52. *Eumenides* In Greek mythology, the avenging deities who

dwelt in the nether regions, or Tartarus.   *Orestes* Son of Aga-
memnon and Clytemnestra, who murdered his mother and her lover,
Aegisthus.

53. *Samiel* A demon in Weber's opera, "Der Freischütz."

54. *King Rodrigo* In Cervantes' "Don Quixote," II, chap. 33.

55. *King Agis of Sparta*, or Agis III, attempted in the third century B.C. to reform the economy and polity of his country through
a more just redistribution of land and the cancellation of debts, but
was opposed by the wealthier classes, who eventually brought him to
trial and slew him.   *Caius and Tiberius Gracchus* Roman tribunes, of the second century B.C., who advocated agrarian reforms,
which were opposed by the aristocracy. Both met with a violent end.
Robespierre and *Saint-Just* Leaders of the French Revolution; both
were later guillotined.

56. *'like Ham . . .'* See "Genesis," chap. 9: "And Noah the
husbandman began, and planted a vineyard. And he drank of the wine,
and was drunken; and he was uncovered within his tent. And Ham,
the father of Canaan, saw the nakedness of his father, and told his
two brothers without . . ."

57. *Amadis of Gaul* Hero of a romance of chivalry.   *Roldan* Probably Roland, hero of the "Song of Roland."   *Agramanth*
A celebrated magician.

58. *Maritorne* An ugly wench in "Don Quixote."

ࣟ *Self Portrait:* SELF-EXILE

1. *Paul Warnefried* Paulus Diaconus, author of the "History
of the Langobards," composed toward the end of the eighth century.

2. *Thomas Münzer* The great and noble-hearted German
peasant leader, executed in 1525.

3. *'the third Bourbon hegira'* The July Revolution of 1830
drove Charles X from the throne of France; his flight is here compared to Mohammed's.

4. *Godfrey Bassen* A publisher, particularly of chivalrous
romances.

5. *ex ungue leonem* 'from the claw (draw) the lion'—a Latin
proverb meaning 'to attempt from a part to determine the shape of the
whole.'

6. *Barbaroux* Charles Jean-Marie Barbaroux, of Marseilles, one of the leaders of the French Revolution.

7. *'Dans des cas pareils . . .'* 'In such cases, it is only the first step that matters.' This celebrated retort to a devout lady, who expressed amazement at the feat of St. Denis, is attributed to Voltaire.

8. *Lutetia* Lutetia Parisiorum was the Roman name for Paris.

9. *'Aux grand hommes . . .'* 'To her great men from a grateful nation.'

10. *Börne* Ludwig Börne (1786–1837), one of the most brilliant of contemporary journalists and political pamphleteers. Like Heine, he was a German Jew, and was converted to Lutheranism. Heine devoted considerable attention to him in his "Ludwig Börne," an essay which is as unflattering as it is unjust.

11. *Michel Chevalier* Michel Chevalier Enfantin, one of the influential disciples of Saint-Simon; he espoused that aspect of his master's teaching which was concerned with religious-ethical, rather than with social-political reforms. The rift in the ranks of the Saint-Simonians took place in 1831.

12. *'L'avenir est à nous'* 'The future belongs to us.'

13. Heine had learned of the death of his friend, Rahel Varnhagen.

14. *Heinrich Laube* (1806–1884) One of the leaders of the Young Germany movement; dramatist, novelist, and theatrical director; frequently imprisoned for his political activities.

15. *'juste milieu'* 'the happy medium,' a term applied to the moderate constitutional regime of Louis Philippe.

16. *'the poor monk'* Martin Luther.

17. *Father Jahn* Friedrich Ludwig Jahn (1778–1852), leader of the so-called "Burschenschaften," or student patriotic associations, which glorified gymnastics and the Fatherland.

18. *'the letters of a departed friend'* "Rachel, a Book of Remembrance for Her Friends," by Rahel Varnhagen von Ense, who died in 1833.

19. *'one of the most beautiful . . . women'* The Countess Belgioioso.

20. *Menzel* Wolfgang Menzel (1798–1873), Critic and literary historian, who eventually became the pillar of German reaction; he violently attacked the Young Germany school, and was partly responsible for the interdict promulgated against their writings (Heine's included) by the German Diet in 1835.

21. *August Lewald* (1792–1871)   Writer, recipient of Heine's "Letters on the French Stage."

22. *'Giacomo's masterpiece'*   Meyerbeer's opera, "Robert the Devil."

23. *Karl Gutzkow* (1811–1878)   One of the Young Germans whose works were banned by the Edict of 1835; author of a novel, "Wally, the Doubter," which resulted in the author's imprisonment.

24. *'a scoundrel, Strauss . . .'*   Heine's pamphlet on Ludwig Börne also reflected on Börne's friend, Frau Wohl. Solomon Strauss, the latter's second husband, demanded satisfaction of Heine, and the duel was fought on September 7, 1841. Heine was slightly wounded.

25. *chushem*   Hebrew: 'the senses.'

26. *'news in the papers . . .'*   On May 5, 1842 a great fire broke out in Hamburg, which raged for four days and destroyed a considerable portion of the city, including the home of Heine's mother.

27. *'my long poem'*   "Germany: A Winter's Tale."

28. *'The Mute'*   "The Mute of Portici," an opera by François Auber.

29. *Weitling*   Wilhelm Weitling (1808–1871), noted socialist leader.

30. The letter told of Solomon Heine's death.

31. *Lassalle*   Ferdinand Lassalle (1825–1864), famous proponent of state socialism.

32. *Alexander von Humboldt* (1769–1859)   Distinguished German naturalist and traveller. In response to this letter, Humboldt wrote that he had tried hard, but that in the "old registry," there were some very bitter "accusations," and the authorities had denied Heine's request, with a warning not to set foot on Prussian soil.

33. *Heil dir im Siegerkranz*   German patriotic anthem.   *Üb du nur Treu und Redlichkeit*   Opening line of a poem by Hölty.

৪৯ *Self Portrait:* LAZARUS

1. *peiger*   Yiddish-Hebrew expression: 'to kick off.'

2. *Ruge*   Arnold Ruge (1802–1880) one of the Young Hegelian philosophers, editor of the radical publication, "Hallesche Jahrbücher."

3. '*Ducal Weimarean Jupiter*'   Goethe.

4. *Hegel*   George Wilhelm Friedrich Hegel (1770–1831), one of the most influential of nineteenth century philosophers, whose system, known as Panlogism, or Logical Pantheism, regards the world as a continuous process of development of the Idea, acting dialectically, i. e., by going over into its opposite. "All successive historical situations are only transitory stages in the endless course of development of human society from the lower to the higher." (F. Engels)

5. '*Tirer le diable par la queue*'   Literally, 'to pull the devil's tail,' or to be hard up.

6. '*Quod scripsi, scripsi*'   'What I have written, I have written.'

7. *Balzac* died in 1850. George Sand introduced Chopin as one of the characters in her novel, "Lucrezia Floriani."

8. '*like the Moor and Papageno*'   In Mozart's opera, "The Magic Flute."

9. *Saint-René Taillandier*   French critic, and translator of German literature. The original letter is written in French, as is the one on p. 470.

10. *Massmann*   Hans Ferdinand Massmann, university professor at Munich and Berlin; a fellow-student of Heine's at Göttingen, where he aroused the latter's lifelong enmity.

11. *zaar lechayim*   Hebrew: 'life's anguish.'   *rachmones* 'compassion.'

12. *Marx*   Karl Marx (1818–1883), with Friedrich Engels, the founder of modern scientific socialism. He was one of the editors of the "Neue Rheinische Zeitung."

13. *Baron Ferdinand von Eckstein* and *Raymond Capefigue* were two contemporary publicists and staunch reactionaries.

14. *consilium abeundi*   University slang for enforced leave of absence.

15. *Arminius*   See note 15, page 841.

16. *Thiers*   See note 20, page 861.

17. *The Chronicle of Limburg*   A historical compilation composed in the early part of the fifteenth century, dealing with the life of the town of Limburg during the years 1336–1398.

18. '*pattes de mouche*' 'your little fly's paws.'   '*de poser . . . souabes*' 'to make a vivid impression on your sweet and somewhat Suabian face.'   '*fine mouche de mon âme*' 'dear little fly of my heart.'

19. *'car le mâitre . . .'* A play on the word "curé," which means "curé" and "cured." 'For the schoolmaster is not yet cured, as old lady Liszt would say.'

ᏸ *The Story Teller*

1. *Saint Werner* Allegedly slain by the Jews in 1286–1287.

2. *'five thousand rats' tails'* This tribute was exacted from the Frankfurt Jews by the authorities in 1498, because one of them had attended a tournament in disguise.

3. *'Eighteen Prayers'* The most solemn portion of the daily prayer service of the Jewish synagogue.

4. *'A kid, a kid . . .'* The concluding portion (*Chad gadyah*) of the Passover Eve service—a symbolic recital of the history of the Jews.

5. *'the great Rabbi'* Isaac Abarbanel (or Abravanel), Spanish-Jewish diplomat and scholar, was forced into exile during the Inquisition of 1492. There is no evidence that he had any nephews.

6. *'Eh! bon jour . . .'* 'Good morning, Mr. Raven. How handsome you are; how nice you look today!'

7. *Edward Gibbon* Author of the great historical work, "The Decline and Fall of the Roman Empire," the first volume of which appeared in 1776.

8. *Rellstab* Ludwig Rellstab, Berlin music critic; opponent of Rossini's music.

9. *Tartaglia*, etc. Stock characters in Italian folk comedy.

10. *Jarke* An extremely conservative writer on law.

11. *Axur, Re d'Ormus* An opera by Antonio Salieri on a text by Beaumarchais.

12. *Mezzofanti* Renowned linguist, reputedly conversant with fifty-eight languages.

13. *patito* Official admirer.

14. *Thibaut, Gans, and Savigny* Contemporary writers on jurisprudence. Gans and Savigny represented opposing points of view, the former belonging to the so-called Hegelian-philosophical, the latter to the historical school.

15. *Di tanti palpiti* An aria from Rossini's opera "Tancred."

16. *Ariadne* According to Greek legend, Ariadne, daughter

of Minos and Pasiphae, fell in love with Theseus, to whom she gave the clue to the Labyrinth, followed him, and was deserted by him on the island Naxos. Dionysus found her and made her his wife.

❧ Religion, Art and Life

1. *Shabbeswoman* The non-Jewish person who attends to the work which a Jew is forbidden to perform on the Sabbath.
2. *'Mel in ore . . .'* 'A honeyed tongue, and words of milk; but falsehood in the heart, and fraud in deeds.'
3. *Percy* Bishop Percy issued a collection of old English ballads entitled "Reliques of Ancient English Poetry" (1765). *Gottfried August Bürger* (1748–1794) German poet, author of the famous supernatural ballad, "Lenore."
4. *'the best translation . . .'* Ludwig Tieck's translation of "Don Quixote."
5. *Overbeck* Johann Friedrich Overbeck (1789–1870), a representative of neo-Medievalism in art, and a member of the so-called Nazarene school of painters, who had a distinctly religious orientation.
6. *Callot* Jacques Callot (1592–1635), famous French engraver. *Carlo Gozzi* (1722–1806) Writer of charming and fanciful Italian comedies. *E. T. A. Hoffmann* (1776–1822) German writer of macabre stories.
7. *'His great symphony'* Berlioz's "Symphonie Fantastique."
8. *Ballanche* Pierre Simon Ballanche (1776–1847), the gifted but somewhat hare-brained author of an unfinished symbolic history of mankind, entitled "Palingénésie," which records the fall from perfection, the period of trial, and the rebirth of man. *Lamennais* Félicité Robert de Lamennais (1782–1854), exponent of liberal Catholicism, author of "Paroles d'un Croyant," who later broke with the Church of Rome and preached a form of Christian socialism.
9. *'the beautiful . . . princess'* Countess Belgioioso.
10. *'He is here . . .'* For the contemporary topical allusions, see Heine's poems, "October 1849" and "The Emperor of China," pp. 252 and 255.
11. *Georg Herwegh* Contemporary political poet. *Fanny Elssler* Celebrated dancer.

12. *Philadelphia, Bosco*   Prestidigitators of the time.

13. *Jan Steen*   Great Dutch realistic painter (1626–1679).

14. *Delacroix*   Ferdinand Victor Eugène Delacroix (1799–1863), famous painter of the Romantic period, greatly influenced by the revolutionary movements of his time. The painting described here depicts the Revolution of 1830.

15. *'Claude Potter . . .'*   The Belgian Revolution broke out in Brussels in September, 1830. Claude Potter, an exiled liberal, returned and became a member of the provisional government.

16. *'Lallica . . .'*   Hindu names of animals and plants.

17. *lex talionis*   'the law of retaliation,' as enunciated in the Old Testament: "An eye for an eye, a tooth for a tooth."

18. *Fontenelle*   Bernard Le Bovier de Fontenelle (1657–1757), French sceptic and author.

࿔ *Israel*

1. *'the prophet of the West'*   The philosopher Hegel.

2. *'eating old Capuchins'*   For the ritual murder accusation of Damascus, see note 25 below.

3. *Joshua ben-Sirah*   Reputed author of the "Book of Ecclesiasticus," which is included in the "Apocrypha."

4. *'the Roman poet . . .'*   Horace.

5. *'Paris vaut bien une messe'*   'Paris is surely worth a mass.' 'Berlin is surely worth a sermon.'

6. *Reuchlin*   Johannes Reuchlin (1455–1522), great German humanist, Greek and Hebrew scholar. Along with the other humanists he was bitterly attacked by the reactionary clerical 'men of darkness' like Hooghstraaten of Cologne, who also vented their wrath on Hebrew scholars and books.

7. *Year of the Jubilee*   See "Leviticus," chap. 25: "And ye shall hallow the fiftieth year, and proclaim liberty throughout the land unto all the inhabitants thereof . . . Ye shall return every man unto his possession."

8. *Rosenkranz*   Karl Rosenkranz (1805–1879), a follower of Hegel, and professor at Berlin.

9. *Cabala*   A collection of mystical Hebrew doctrines, which interpreted the Bible symbolically.

10. *Franz Horn* (1781–1837) Literary historian and Shakespearean critic.

11. *'Les blancs l'ont tué . . .'* 'The white men have killed Him; let us kill the white men!'

12. *Edmund Kean* (1787–1833) made his first appearance as Shylock at the Drury Lane Theater in London in 1814, and was immediately successful.

13. Richard Cumberland's play, "The Jew," represents him sympathetically. *Ludwig Devrient* A famous Shakespearean actor of the time.

14. *Spinoza* Baruch (or Benedict) Spinoza, the great philosopher (1632–1677), was excommunicated by the Jewish congregation of Amsterdam for his heterodox opinions in 1656. His most famous work, the "Ethics," was probably completed in 1665.

15. *'The father of his betrothed . . .'* Spinoza's teacher, Franz van den Enden, was executed in Paris for conspiracy in 1674. The story which romantically connects Spinoza with van Enden's daughter is of dubious authenticity.

16. *Tractatus Politicus,* or *Tractatus Theologico-Politicus* Spinoza's eloquent defense of liberty of thought and speech, followed the composition of the "Ethics" by about five years.

17. *'Non dico . . .'* 'I do not say that I know God all in all; but only that I understand certain of His attributes, not all, nor even the greatest part of them.'

18. *Natura naturans* 'Nature which creates,' as distinguished from *Natura naturata,* 'Nature which is created.'

19. *Moses Mendelssohn* (1729–1786) Distinguished German-Jewish philosopher and translator of the Bible into German. He was the friend of Lessing, and the reputed hero of the latter's drama, "Nathan the Wise."

20. *Moses* Moses Mendelssohn.

21. *Bendavid* Lazarus Bendavid, disciple of Mendelssohn and Kant.

22. *Philo of Alexandria* (ca. 20 B.C. to 50 A.D.), famous Graeco-Jewish philosopher.

23. *W—sche Weekly* "Berlinisches Wochenblatt . . . ," edited by Professor Waldzeck.

24. *'Sum rex . . .'* 'I am a king of the people, and not of consciences.'

25. *The Blood Libel of Damascus* According to the report of

the Austrian consul Merlato, stationed at Damascus, the Capuchin Brother Thomas and one of his servants disappeared suddenly on February 5, 1840. The French consulate threw suspicion on the Jews, a number of whom were subjected to torture. Forced confessions were extracted. The trial aroused excitement all over Europe. Robert Peel introduced an interpellation in Parliament; Montefiore was sent to investigate. The French Jews sent Crémieux. The latter two succeeded in obtaining a vindication of the accused from Mehemet Ali.

26. *Giaour* Turkish word meaning 'infidel.'

27. *Rabbi Shammai and Rabbi Hillel* Representatives of two famous schools of Biblical interpretation in the first century B.C.

28. *Benoît Fould* Member of the powerful Parisian banking firm of F. Oppenheim and Co.

29. *Crémieux* Isaac Adolphe Crémieux (1796–1880), celebrated lawyer, diplomat, and liberal.

30. *'Cela n'entre . . .'* 'That is not at all in accord with the purpose of our newspaper.'

31. *'la religion à laquelle . . .'* 'The religion to which I have the honor of belonging.'

32. *Montalembert* Count Forbes de Tryone de Montalembert (1810–1870), an extremist clerical reactionary. He was the author of a life of St. Elizabeth.

❧ *Germany*

1. *Vulgate* The Latin translation of the Bible. *Septuagint* The oldest Greek version of the Bible.

2. *Lessing* Gotthold Ephraim Lessing (1729–1781), the greatest literary representative of the German Enlightenment, author of "Nathan the Wise," and "Laocoön."

3. *oser* French: 'to dare.'

4. *Immanuel Kant*, the founder of modern transcendentalism, was born in Königsberg in 1724 and died in 1804. His greatest work, "The Critique of Pure Reason" appeared in 1781.

5. *'Know'st thou the land . . .'* Mignon's song in Goethe's "Wilhelm Meister."

6. *Herr Eckermann* Johann Peter Eckermann, who later became immortal because he edited the "Conversations with Goethe,"

published his "Contributions to Poetry" in 1823. This is the book referred to by Heine.

7. *Charles Nodier*   Contemporary French poet.

8. *'Les dieux s'en vont'*   'The gods depart.' Goethe died in 1832. In the same year, the great French savants Champollion and Cuvier died of the cholera. Hegel died in 1831. Ferdinand VII, king of Spain, survived to September 1833.

9. *Jean Paul Friedrich Richter* (1763–1825)   Eccentric humorist, whose work exercised a profound influence on Thomas Carlyle.

10. *Young Germany*   An insurgent group of writers, led by Gutzkow and Laube. Their works were proscribed, along with those of Heine, by the 1835 edict of the Federal Diet.

11. *Petronius*   Roman author of the "Satyricon."   *Apuleius* Author of "The Golden Ass."

12. *'the fatal garment . . .'*   The blood of the centaur Nessus, who had been killed by Hercules, eventually brought death to the latter.

13. *Ottfried*   A ninth century German poet who wrote religious verse.

14. *Herr Schelling*   Friedrich Wilhelm Joseph von Schelling (1775–1854), one of the leaders of the Romantic school of philosophy, was in Munich from 1806 to 1841.

15. *Dr. Hoffmann*   Dr. Friedrich Ludwig Hoffmann, the Hamburg censor.

16. *'The Gallic cock . . .'*   Reference to the July Revolution of 1830.

17. *Lucian*   Late Greek satirist and sceptic of the second century, author of "Dialogues of the Gods."

18. *Mercier*   Sebastien Mercier (1740–1814), dramatist and political writer.

19. *Pitt*   William Pitt, "the Younger," British Minister, violent opponent of the French Revolution.

20. *Polignac*   Prince Jules de Polignac, reactionary foreign minister under Charles X. He was one of the authors of the "Four Ordinances," which were among the immediate causes of the Revolution of 1830.

21. *Deshuttes and Varicourt* fell defending the royal chambers.

22. *Don Miguel*   Pretender to and usurper of the throne of Portugal, eventually overthrown.

23. *'their misfortunes'* On May 27, 1832 the liberals and democrats of South Germany convened the great gathering at Hambach in the Palatinate, at which they demanded a German union based on the sovereignty of the people, freedom for Poland, the emancipation of women, and other liberal measures. On June 28, 1832 the Federal German Diet, under the influence of Metternich and his Prussian henchmen, intensified its persecution of all liberals by prohibiting political associations and popular gatherings, by suppressing a large number of newspapers, and arresting a number of participants.

24. *Arndt* Ernst Moritz Arndt (1769–1860), German patriotic poet. *Hasenheide* Reference to the gymnastic sports under the leadership of Father Jahn.

25. *Marie Louise* Daughter of Francis II, and wife of Napoleon I.

26. *'radiant grandson . . .'* The Duke of Reichstadt, son of Napoleon I and Marie Louise, who died July 22, 1832.

27. *'gold-spurred prince'* The future king of Prussia, Frederick William IV. *Charles of Brunswick* was forced into exile by his subjects in September, 1830.

28. *Fischau* A massacre of Polish soldiery at the hands of the Prussians took place at Fischau.

29. *Friedrich von Raumer* (1781–1873) Historian, author of "Prussia's Relations with Poland, 1830–1832," which the censorship suppressed, and which did not appear until 1853.

30. *Schleiermacher* Friedrich Schleiermacher (1768–1834), sometimes called the reformer of Protestant theology.

31. *'shabby little book'* Arndt wrote "The Problem of the Netherlands and the Rhineland," a violent attack on the Revolution of 1830. *Friedrich Stägemann* A Prussian official and poet.

32. *Ranke* Leopold von Ranke (1795–1886), one of the most distinguished of nineteenth century historians.

33. *'a free constitution'* Frederick William III had promised one in 1813, and again in 1815.

34. *Czarina* Princess Charlotte, wife of Czar Nicholas I.

35. *Simurgh* Gigantic bird in Persian mythology.

36. *'The Moniteur of 1793'* One of the influential newspapers published during the French Revolution.

37. *Jarcke* Karl Ernst Jarcke, editor; persistent opponent of liberalism.

38. *Dr. Wirth* Johann Georg August Wirth, editor of the

"Deutsche Tribune," 1831–1832. He and Siebenpfeifer were arrested and imprisoned after the Hambach Festival.

39. *'Oleum perdidi'* 'I have lost the oil.'

40. *Siebenpfeifer, Scharpf, Fein,* etc. Journalists and political radicals, eventually prosecuted by the government.

41. *'lucus a non lucendo'* Latin proverb: 'a grove, because there is no light,' used as an example of false etymology.

42. *Joseph Görres* (1776–1848) One of the most influential publicists of the day, active proponent of reaction.

43. *Aristides the 'Just'* A rival of Themistocles, who was banished from Athens in 483 B.C.

44. *'the twenty-first of January'* Louis XVI was beheaded on that day.

45. *'your great eclectic'* Victor Cousin (1792–1867), a zealous disciple of German philosophy.

46. *Oken* Lorenz Oken (1779–1851), one of the most brilliant of nineteenth century naturalists and philosophers. *Adam Müller* Conservative political philosopher.

47. *Conradin von Hohenstaufen* was beheaded in Naples in 1268, and the male line of Hohenstaufens came to an end with him.

૭͛ *The Citizen of the World*

1. *'Honni soit . . .'* 'Evil to him who evil thinks.' Device of the order of the Knights of the Garter.

2. *Crocciato in Egitto* An opera by Meyerbeer.

3. *The Crisis in England* The agitation for political and economic reforms in England which took place in the forties of the last century was intensified by a rise in the cost of living and fall in wages. The agitation was spearheaded by the Chartists, the first organized political working class movement, who presented their demands for universal manhood suffrage and other reforms in a People's Charter, in 1838 and 1842.

4. *'the Glorious Revolution'* The Revolution of 1688, which drove James II from the throne of England and brought in William and Mary.

5. *Gunpowder Plot* Reputedly the plot on the part of certain Catholics to blow up Parliament and King James I of England, in

1608. Guy Fawkes and a number of other conspirators were apprehended and executed.

6. 'the Rector of Göttingen' The Hanoverian Kings of England were also rectors of the University of Göttingen.

7. The British Parliament removed Catholic disabilities in 1828.

8. 'Te Caesar . . .' 'They who are about to die salute thee, Caesar!'

9. Edmund Burke (1729–1797) Author of the famous attack on the French Revolution, "Reflections," which provoked Paine's equally famous reply, "The Rights of Man."

10. Mazarin French cardinal and statesman under Louis XIII and Louis XIV. The Tenth of August, 1792, was the day on which the French republicans overthrew the monarchy and arrested the royal family.

11. Hamilton Anthony Hamilton was the author of the brilliant and scandalous chronicle, "Memoirs of the Duke of Grammont," which described life at the court of Charles II of England.

12. Canning George Canning became Prime Minister in 1827, and was vigorously but unsuccessfully opposed by the conservatives. He died in the same year, and was succeeded by Lord Goderich (1827), who was followed by the Duke of Wellington (1828).

13. Bellerophon The vessel in which Napoleon was transported to St. Helena.

14. 'Lafayette . . .' 'White-haired Lafayette.'

15. 'Triumphal march' Lafayette revisited the United States in 1824–25. He was acclaimed throughout the land, and was voted the sum of $200,000, and a township of land.

16. 'the treachery of the English' In 1840, England, Russia, Austria and Prussia signed an agreement pledging their support to the Sultan of Turkey against Mehemet Ali of Egypt. France was completely ignored in this arrangement.

17. Prix Monthyon The wealthy Baron de Monthyon had established two prizes, one of these to be conferred for some outstanding virtuous deed, and the other for an outstanding literary contribution to the cause of virtue.

18. Taglioni Maria Taglioni, one of the most celebrated ballet dancers of the nineteenth century.

19. 'this warlike spirit' The French leaders who threatened to go to war with England over the Near Eastern situation subsided toward the end of the year.

20. *Thiers and Guizot*   Louis Adolphe Thiers and François Guizot were the two most prominent French political leaders and historians of the period. Thiers (1797–1877) was an adherent of the principles of the English Revolution of 1688, that is, he was a moderate middle-class liberal, and occupied various ministerial posts. He became the first president of the Third Republic. Guizot (1787–1874) was a consistent opponent of democratic principles. He was in turn envoy, minister of foreign affairs, and prime minister. His government was notorious for corruption.

21. *'le pain . . .'*   'Bread is the right of the people.' 'Bread is the divine right of man.'

22. *'the eighteenth of Brumaire'*   November 8, 1799, the day on which Napoleon overthrew the Directory.

23. *Helfenstein*   During the Peasants' War in Germany, the Count of Helfenstein was attacked by his peasants with pitchforks, while a piper, one of his former servants, played a tune.

24. *DuClos*   French writer of the eighteenth century. It is probable that the person here intended is Choderlos de Laclos, author of an amatory novel, "Les liaisons dangereuses" (1782), and a participant in the French Revolution.   *Louvet de Couvray*   Author of "Les amours du Chevalier de Faublas" (1787).

25. *Madame Roland de la Platière* (1754–1793)   Wife of the minister Roland, and author of very informative "Memoirs."

26. *Thomas Münzer* (ca. 1489–1525)   One of the great leaders in the Peasants' War, at the time of the Reformation. He was strongly opposed by Luther and the German princes, who eventually brought about his downfall and execution at Mülhausen, May 27, 1525. Luther's pamphlet directed against the peasants was entitled, "Against the Thievish, Murderous Hordes of Peasants."

27. *Chamfort*   Nicolas de Chamfort (1741–1794), author of brilliant "Pensées."

BIBLIOGRAPHY

Heinrich Heines Sämtliche Werke. Unter Mitwirkung von Jonas Fränkel, Ludwig Krähe, Albert Leitzmann und Julius Petersen, herausgegeben von Oskar Walzel. 10 vols. Leipzig, 1911–15.
Heinrich Heines Sämtliche Werke. Herausgegeben von Ernst Elster. 9 vols. Leipzig, 1887–90.
Heinrich Heines Briefwechsel. Herausgegeben von Friedrich Hirth. 3 vols. Munich and Berlin. 1914–20.
Gespräche mit Heine. Zum ersten mal gesammelt und herausgegeben von H. H. Houben. Frankfurt-am-Main, 1926.

The Works of Heinrich Heine. Translated by C. G. Leland and others. 13 vols. London, 1892–1905.
Heinrich Heine's Memoirs. Edited by Gustav Karpeles. English translation by Gilbert Cannan. 2 vols. London, 1910.
Heinrich Heine: Works of Prose. Edited by Hermann Kesten. Translated by E. B. Ashton. New York, 1944.
Heinrich Heine's Poems. Translated by Louis Untermeyer. New York, 1937.

Butler, E. M. *The Saint-Simonian Religion in Germany*. Cambridge, 1926.

Ebenstein, William. *The German Record: A Political Portrait*. New York, 1945.

Houben, H. H. *Verbotene Literatur*. 2 vols. Berlin, 1924.

Kesten, Kurt. *"1848": Die deutsche Revolution*. Berlin, 1933.

Liptzin, Solomon. *Germany's Stepchildren*. Philadelphia, 1944.

Lowenthal, Marvin. *The Jews of Germany*. New York, 1936.

Marcuse, Ludwig. *Heine: A Life Between Love and Hate*. Translated by Louise M. Sieveking and Ian F. D. Morrow. New York, 1933.

Marcuse, Ludwig. *Revolutionär und Patriot: Das Leben Ludwig Börnes*. Leipzig, 1929.

Marx, Karl. *The Class Struggles in France, 1848–50*.

Marx, Karl and Frederick Engels. *Germany: Revolution and Counter-Revolution*. (Both included in Karl Marx: *Selected Works*. 2 vols. Moscow, 1936.)

Mehring, Franz. *Zur Literaturgeschichte*. Berlin, 1929.

Untermeyer, Louis. *Heinrich Heine: Paradox and Poet*. New York, 1937.

Valentin, Antonina. *Poet in Exile: The Life of Heinrich Heine*. New York, 1934.

Wolff, Max J. *Heinrich Heine*. Munich, 1922.

A CHRONOLOGY

The following listing will enable the reader to follow the prose selections, other than the letters, in the order of their original publication: